HIGHER ALGEBRA

HALL & KNIGHT

CLASSIC TEXTS SERIES

HIGHER ALGEBRA

HALL & KNIGHT

Henry Sinclair Hall
MA
Formerly Scholar of Christs College, Cambridge

Samuel Ratcliff Knight
BA
Formerly Scholar of Trinity College, Cambridge

 Arihant Prakashan, Meerut

Arihant Prakashan, Meerut

ॐ **Administrative & Production Offices**

Corporate Office
'Ramchhaya' 4577/15, Agarwal Road, Darya Ganj, New Delhi -110002
Tele: 011- 47630600, 43518550; Fax: 011- 2 3280316

Head Office
Kalindi, TP Nagar, Meerut (UP) - 250002
Tele: 0121-2401479, 2512970, 4004199; Fax: 0121-2401648

ॐ **Sales & Support Offices**
Agra, Ahmedabad, Bengaluru, Bhubaneswar, Bareilly, Chennai, Delhi, Guwahati, Haldwani, Hyderabad, Jaipur, Jhansi, Kolkata, Kota, Lucknow, Meerut, Nagpur & Pune

ॐ **ISBN** : 978-93-5176-253-9

ॐ **Price** : ₹195

Typeset by Arihant DTP Unit at Meerut

Printed & Bound By
Arihant Publications (I) Ltd. (Press Unit)

For further information about the products from Arihant,
log on to www.arihantbooks.com *or email to* info@arihantbooks.com

PREFACE

The present work is intended as a sequel to our Elementary Algebra for Schools. The first few chapters are devoted to a fuller discussion of Ratio, Proportions, Variation, and the Progressions, which in the former work treated in an elementary manner, and we have here introduced theorems and examples which are unsuitable for a first course of reading.

From this point the work covers ground for the most part new to the student, and enters upon subjects of special importance : these we have endeavoured to treat minutely and thoroughly, discussing both bookwork and examples with that fulness which we have always found necessary in our experience as teachers.

It has been our aim to discuss all the essential parts as completely as possible within the limits of a single Volume, but in a few of the later chapters it has been impossible to find room for more than an introductory sketch; in all such cases our object has been to map out a suitable first course of reading, referring the student to special treatises for fuller information.

In the chapter on Permutations and Combinations we are much indebted to the Rev. W.A. Whitworth for permission to make use of some of the proofs given in his Choice and Chance. For many years we have used these proofs in our own teaching, and we are convinced that this part of Algebra is made far more intelligible to the beginner by a system of common sense reasoning from first principles than by the proofs usually found in algebraical text-books.

The discussion of Convergency and Divergency of Series always present great difficulty to the student on his first reading. The inherent difficulties of the subject are no doubt considerable and these are increased by the place it has ordinarily occupied and by the some what inadequate treatment it has hitherto received. According we have placed this section somewhat later than is usual, much through has been bestowed on its general arrangement, and on the selection of suitable examples to illustrate the text; and we have endeavoured to make it more interesting and intelligible by previously introducing a short chapter on Limiting Values and Vanishing Fractions.

In the chapter on Summation of Series we have laid much stress on the "Method of Differences" and its wide and important applications. The basis of this method is a wellknown formula in the calculus of Finite Differences, which in the absence of a purely algebraical proof can hardly be considered admissible in a treatise on algebra. The proof of the Finite Difference formula which we have given Arts. 395, 396, we believe to be new and original, and the development of the Difference Method from this formula has enabled us to introduce many interesting types of series which have hitherto been relegated to a much later stage in the student's reading.

We have received able and material assistance in the chapter on Probability from the Rev. T.C. Simmons of Christ's College, Brecon and our warmest thanks are due to him, both for his aid in criticising and improving the text, and for placing at our disposal several interesting and original problems.

It is hardly possible to read any modern treatise on Aualytical Conics or Solid Geometry without some knowledge of Determinants and their applications. We have therefore given a brief elementary discussion of Determinants in Chapter 33., in the hope that it may provide the Student with a useful introductory course, and prepare him for a more complete study of the subject.

The last chapter contains all the most useful propositions in the Theory of Equations suitable for a first reading. The Theory of Equation follows so naturally on the study of Algebra that no apology is needed for here introducing propositions which usually and find place in a separate treatise. In fact, a considerable part of Chapter 35., may be read with advantage at a much earlier stage, and may conveniently be studied before some of the harder sections of previous chapters.

It will be found that each chapter is as nearly as possible complete in itself, so that the order of their succession can be varied at the discretion of the teacher; but it is recommended that all sections marked with an asterisk should be reserved for a second reading.

In enumerating the sources from which we have derived assistance in the preparation of this work, there is one book to which it is difficult to say how far we are indebted. Todhunter's Algebra for schools and Colleges has been the recognised English text-book for so long that it is hardly possible that any one writting a text-book on Algebra at the present day should not be largely influenced by it. At the same time, though for many years Todhunter's Algebra has been in constant use among our pupils, we have rarely adopted the order and arrangement to make frequent use of alternative proofs; and we have always largely supplemented the text by manuscript notes, These notes, which now appear scattered throughout the present work, have been collected at different, times during the last twenty years, so that it is impossible to make definite acknowledgment in every case where assistance has been obtained from other writers. But speaking generally, our acknowledgments are chiefly due to the treatises of Schlomilch, Serret, and Laurent; and among English writers, besides Todhunter's Algebra, we have occasionally consulted the works of De Morgan, Colenso, Gross and Chrystal.

To the Rev. J. Wolstonholme, D.Sc. Professor of Mathematics at the Royal Indian Engineering College, our thanks are due for his kindness in allowing us to select questions from his unique collection of problems; and the consequent gain to our later chapters we gratefully acknowledge

It remains for us to express our thanks to our colleagues and friends who have so largely assisted us in reading and correcting the proof sheets; in particular we are indebted to the Rev. H.C. Watson of Clifton College for his kindness in revising the whole work, and for many valuable suggestions in every part of it.

May, 1887

H.S. Hall

S.R. Knight

Some minor changes were made in this well-known text-book by Mr. L.Crosland a few years ago. Further corrections have now been incorporated and on p. 405, Mr. J.D. Hodson has provided a new proof for an example on probability which will help the student.

The Publishers

CONTENTS

Chapter 1 Ratio

Chapter 2 Proportion

Chapter 3 Variation

Chapter 4 Arithmetical Progression

Chapter 5 Geometrical Progression

Chapter 6 Harmonical Progression Theorems Connected with The Progression

Chapter 7 Scales of Notation

Chapter 8   Surds and Imaginary Quantities

Chapter 9   The Theory of Quadratic Equations

Chapter 10   Miscellaneous Equations

Chapter 11   Permutations and Combinations

Chapter 12   Mathematical Induction

Chapter 13 Binomial Theorem Positive Integral Index

Chapter 14 Binomial Theorem. Any Index

Chapter 15 Multinomial Theorem

Chapter 16   Logarithms

Chapter 17   Exponential and Logarithmic Series

Chapter 18   Interest and Annuities

Chapter 19 Inequalities

Chapter 20 Limiting Values and Vanishing Fractions

Chapter 21   Convergency and Divergency of Series

Chapter 22   Undetermined Coefficients

Chapter 27   Recurring Continued Fractions

Chapter 28   Indeterminate Equations of the Second Degree

Chapter 29   Summation of Series

Chapter 30 Theory of Numbers

Chapter 31 The General Theory of Continued Fractions

Chapter 32   Probability

Chapter 33   Determinants

Chapter 34   Miscellaneous Theorems and Examples

Chapter 35   Theory of Equations

Attachment

Chapter 1

RATIO

1. Definition : Ratio is the relation which one quantity bears to another of the *same* kind, the comparison being made by considering what multiple, part, or parts, one quantity is of the other.

The ratio of A to B is usually written $A : B$. The quantities A and B are called the *terms* of the ratio. The first term is called the antecedent, the second term the consequent.

2. To find what multiple or part A is of B, we divide A by B, hence the ratio $A : B$ may be measured by the fraction $\dfrac{A}{B}$, and we shall usually find it convenient to adopt this notation.

In order to compare two quantities they must be expressed in terms of the same unit. Thus the ratio of Rs. 2 to 15 nP is measured by the fraction $\dfrac{2 \times 100}{15}$ or $\dfrac{40}{3}$.

Note : A ratio expresses the *number* of times that one quantity contains another, and therefore *every ratio is an abstract quantity*.

3. Since by the laws of fractions,

$$\frac{a}{b} = \frac{ma}{mb},$$

it follows that the ratio $a : b$ is equal to the ratio $ma : mb$; that is, *the value of a ratio remains unaltered if the antecedent and the consequent are multiplied or divided by the same quantity.*

4. Two or more ratios may be compared by reducing their equivalent fractions to a common denominator. Thus suppose $a : b$ and $x : y$ are two ratios. Now $\dfrac{a}{b} = \dfrac{ay}{by}$, and $\dfrac{x}{y} = \dfrac{bx}{by}$; hence the ratio $a : b$ is greater than, equal to, or less than the ratio $x : y$ according as ay is greater than equal to, or less than bx.

5. The ratio of two fractions can be expressed as a ratio of two integers. Thus the ratio $\dfrac{a}{b} : \dfrac{c}{d}$ is measured by the fraction $\dfrac{\dfrac{a}{b}}{\dfrac{c}{d}}$, or $\dfrac{ad}{bc}$ and is therefore equivalent to the ratio $ad : bc$.

6. If either, or both, of the terms of a ratio be a surd quantity, then no two integers can be found which will *exactly* measure their ratio. Thus the ratio $\sqrt{2} : 1$ cannot be exactly expressed by any two integers.

7. Definition : If the ratio of any two quantities can be expressed exactly by the ratio of two integers, the quantities are said to be commensurable; otherwise, they are said to be incommensurable.

Although we cannot find two integers which will exactly measure the ratio of two incommensurable quantities, we can always find two integers whose ratio differs from that required by as small a quantity as we please.

Thus $\qquad \dfrac{\sqrt{5}}{4} = \dfrac{2.236067\ldots}{4} = 0.559016\ldots$

and therefore $\qquad \dfrac{\sqrt{5}}{4} > \dfrac{559016}{1000000}$ and $< \dfrac{559017}{1000000}$;

so that the difference between the ratios $559016 : 1000000$ and $\sqrt{5} : 4$ is less than .000001. By carrying the decimals further, a closer approximation may be arrived at.

8. Definition : Ratios are *compounded* by multiplying together the fractions which denote them; or by multiplying together the antecedents for a new antecedent, and the consequents for a new consequent.

Example : Find the ratio compounded of the three ratios

$$2a : 3b, \ 6ab : 5c^2, \ c : a$$

The required ratio $= \dfrac{2a}{3b} \times \dfrac{6ab}{5c^2} \times \dfrac{c}{a}$

$$= \dfrac{4a}{5c} .$$

9. Definition : When the ratio $a : b$ is compounded with itself the resulting ratio is $a^2 : b^2$, and is called the duplicate ratio of $a : b$. Similarly $a^3 : b^3$ is called the triplicate ratio of $a : b$. Also $a^{1/2} : b^{1/2}$ is called the subduplicate ratio of $a : b$.

Examples :   (1) The duplicate ratio of $2a : 3b$ is $4a^2 : 9b^2$.

            (2) The subduplicate ratio of $49 : 25$ is $7 : 5$.

            (3) The triplicate ratio of $2x : 1$ is $8x^3 : 1$.

10. Definition : A ratio is said to be a ratio of *greater inequality,* of *less inequality,* or of *equality,* according as the antecedent is *greater than, less than,* or *equal to* the consequent.

11. *A ratio of greater inequality is diminished, and a ratio of less inequality is increased, by adding the same quantity to both its terms.*

Let $\dfrac{a}{b}$ be the ratio, and let $\dfrac{a+x}{b+x}$ be the new ratio formed by adding x to both its terms.

Now $\qquad \dfrac{a}{b} - \dfrac{a+x}{b+x} = \dfrac{ax - bx}{b(b+x)} = \dfrac{x}{b}\dfrac{(a-b)}{(b+x)}$;

and $a - b$ is positive or negative according as a is greater or less than b.

Hence if $a > b$, $\qquad \dfrac{a}{b} > \dfrac{a+x}{b+x}$;

and if $a < b$, $\qquad \dfrac{a}{b} < \dfrac{a+x}{b+x}$;

which proves the proposition.

Similarly it can be proved that *a ratio of greater inequality is increased, and a ratio of less inequality is diminished, by taking the same quantity from both its terms.*

12. When two or more ratios are equal many useful propositions may be proved by introducing a single symbol to denote each of the equal ratios.

The proof of the following important theorem will illustrate the method of procedure.

If $\qquad \dfrac{a}{b} = \dfrac{c}{d} = \dfrac{e}{f} = \ldots,$

each of these ratios $= \left(\dfrac{pa^n + qc^n + re^n + \ldots}{pb^n + qd^n + rf^n + \ldots} \right)^{\frac{1}{n}},$

where p, q, r, n are any quantities whatever.

Let $\qquad \dfrac{a}{b} = \dfrac{c}{d} = \dfrac{e}{f} = \ldots = k;$

then $\qquad a = bk, \ c = dk, \ e = fk, \ldots;$

whence $\qquad pa^n = pb^n k^n, \ qc^n = qd^n k^n, \ re^n = rf^n k^n, \ldots;$

$\therefore \quad \dfrac{pa^n + qc^n + re^n + \ldots}{pb^n + qd^n + rf^n + \ldots} = \dfrac{pb^n k^n + qd^n k^n + rf^n k^n + \ldots}{pb^n + qd^n + rf^n + \ldots} = k^n;$

$\therefore \quad \left(\dfrac{pa^n + qc^n + re^n + \ldots}{pb^n + qd^n + rf^n + \ldots} \right)^{\frac{1}{n}} = k = \dfrac{a}{b} = \dfrac{c}{d} = \ldots$

By giving different values to p, q, r, n many particular cases of this general proposition may be deduced; or they may be proved independently by using the same method. For instance,

if
$$\frac{a}{b} = \frac{c}{d} = \frac{e}{f} = \dots,$$

each of these ratios $= \dfrac{a + c + e + \dots}{b + d + f + \dots}$;

a result of such frequent utility that the following verbal equivalent should be noticed : *When a series of fractions are equal, each of them is equal to the sum of all the numerators divided by the sum of all the denominators.*

Example 1. If $\dfrac{a}{b} = \dfrac{c}{d} = \dfrac{e}{f}$, shew that

$$\frac{a^3 b + 2c^2 e - 3ae^2 f}{b^4 + 2d^2 f - 3bf^3} = \frac{ace}{bdf}.$$

Let
$$\frac{a}{b} = \frac{c}{d} = \frac{e}{f} = k;$$

then
$$a = bk, \ c = dk, \ e = fk;$$

$$\therefore \frac{a^3 b + 2c^2 e - 3ae^2 f}{b^4 + 2d^2 f - 3bf^3} = \frac{b^4 k^3 + 2d^2 f k^3 - 3bf^3 k^3}{b^4 + 2d^2 f - 3bf^3}$$

$$= k^3 = \frac{a}{b} \times \frac{c}{d} \times \frac{e}{f} = \frac{ace}{bdf}.$$

Example 2. If $\dfrac{x}{a} = \dfrac{y}{b} = \dfrac{z}{c}$; prove that

$$\frac{x^2 + a^2}{x + a} + \frac{y^2 + b^2}{y + b} + \frac{z^2 + c^2}{z + c} = \frac{(x + y + z)^2 + (a + b + c)^2}{x + y + z + a + b + c}.$$

Let $\dfrac{x}{a} = \dfrac{y}{b} = \dfrac{z}{c} = k$, so that $x = ak, \ y = bk, \ z = ck;$

then
$$\frac{x^2 + a^2}{x + a} = \frac{a^2 k^2 + a^2}{ak + a} = \frac{(k^2 + 1) a}{k + 1};$$

$$\therefore \ \frac{x^2 + a^2}{x + a} + \frac{y^2 + b^2}{y + b} + \frac{z^2 + c^2}{z + c} = \frac{(k^2 + 1) a}{k + 1} + \frac{(k^2 + 1) b}{k + 1} + \frac{(k^2 + 1) c}{k + 1}$$

$$= \frac{(k^2 + 1)(a + b + c)}{k + 1}$$

$$= \frac{k^2 (a + b + c)^2 + (a + b + c)^2}{k (a + b + c) + a + b + c}$$

$$= \frac{(ka + kb + kc)^2 + (a + b + c)^2}{(ka + kb + kc) + a + b + c}$$

$$= \frac{(x + y + z)^2 + (a + b + c)^2}{x + y + z + a + b + c}.$$

13. If an equation is homogeneous with respect to certain quantities, we may for these quantities substitute in the equation any others proportional to them. For instance, the equation

$$lx^3y + mxy^2z + ny^2z^2 = 0$$

is homogeneous in x, y, z. Let α, β, γ be three quantities proportional to x, y, z respectively.

Put $\quad k = \dfrac{x}{\alpha} = \dfrac{y}{\beta} = \dfrac{z}{\gamma}$, so that $x = \alpha k$, $y = \beta k$, $z = \gamma k$;

then $\qquad\qquad l\alpha^3\beta k^4 + m\alpha\beta^2\gamma k^4 + n\beta^2\gamma^2 k^4 = 0$,

that is, $\qquad\qquad l\alpha^3\beta + m\alpha\beta^2\gamma + n\beta^2\gamma^2 = 0$;

an equation of the same form as the original one, but with α, β, γ in the places of x, y, z respectively.

14. The following theorem is important.

If $\dfrac{a_1}{b_1}$, $\dfrac{a_2}{b_2}$, $\dfrac{a_3}{b_3}$, ... $\dfrac{a_n}{b_n}$ *be unequal fractions, of which the denominators are all of the same sign, then the fraction*

$$\frac{a_1 + a_2 + a_3 + \ldots + a_n}{b_1 + b_2 + b_3 + \ldots + b_n}$$

lies in magnitude between the greatest and least of them.

Suppose that all the denominators are positive. Let $\dfrac{a_r}{b_r}$ be the least fraction, and denote it by k; then

$$\frac{a_r}{b_r} = k; \quad \therefore a_r = kb_r;$$

$$\frac{a_1}{b_1} > k; \quad \therefore a_1 > kb_1;$$

$$\frac{a_2}{b_2} > k; \quad \therefore a_2 > kb_2;$$

and so on;

$\quad \therefore$ by addition,

$$a_1 + a_2 + a_3 + \ldots + a_n > (b_1 + b_2 + b_3 + \ldots + b_n)\, k;$$

$$\therefore \frac{a_1 + a_2 + a_3 + \ldots + a_n}{b_1 + b_2 + b_3 + \ldots + b_n} > k; \text{ that is, } > \frac{a_r}{b_r}.$$

Similarly we may prove that

$$\frac{a_1 + a_2 + a_3 + \ldots + a_n}{b_1 + b_2 + b_3 + \ldots + b_n} < \frac{a_s}{b_s},$$

where $\dfrac{a_s}{b_s}$ is the greatest of the given fractions.

In like manner the theorem may be proved when all the denominators are negative.

15. The ready application of the *general principle* involved in Art. 12 is of such great value in all branches of mathematics, that the student should be able to use it with some freedom in any particular case that may arise, without necessarily introducing an auxiliary symbol.

Example 1. If $\dfrac{x}{b+c-a}=\dfrac{y}{c+a-b}=\dfrac{z}{a+b-c}$,

prove that $\dfrac{x+y+z}{a+b+c}=\dfrac{x(y+z)+y(z+x)+z(x+y)}{2(ax+by+cz)}$.

Each of the given fractions $=\dfrac{\text{sum of numerators}}{\text{sum of denominators}}$

$$=\frac{x+y+z}{a+b+c} \qquad \ldots(1)$$

Again, if we multiply both numerator and denominator of the three given fractions by $y+z$, $z+x$, $x+y$ respectively,

each fraction

$$=\frac{x(y+z)}{(y+z)(b+c-a)}=\frac{y(z+x)}{(z+x)(c+a-b)}=\frac{z(x+y)}{(x+y)(a+b-c)}$$

$$=\frac{\text{sum of numerators}}{\text{sum of denominators}}$$

$$=\frac{x(y+z)+y(z+x)+z(x+y)}{2ax+2by+2cz} \qquad \ldots(2)$$

$\therefore$ from (1) and (2),

$$\frac{x+y+z}{a+b+c}=\frac{x(y+z)+y(z+x)+z(x+y)}{2(ax+by+cz)}.$$

Example 2. If $\dfrac{x}{l(mb+nc-la)}=\dfrac{y}{m(nc+la-mb)}=\dfrac{z}{n(la+mb-nc)}$,

prove that $\dfrac{l}{x(by+cz-ax)}=\dfrac{m}{y(cz+ax-by)}=\dfrac{n}{z(ax+by-cz)}$.

We have $\dfrac{\dfrac{x}{l}}{mb+nc-la}=\dfrac{\dfrac{y}{m}}{nc+la-mb}=\dfrac{\dfrac{z}{n}}{la+mb-nc}$

$$=\frac{\dfrac{y}{m}+\dfrac{z}{n}}{2la}$$

$=$ two similar expressions;

$$\therefore \frac{ny+mz}{a}=\frac{lz+nx}{b}=\frac{mx+ly}{c}.$$

Multiply the first of these fractions above and below by x, the second by y, and the third by z; then

$$\frac{nxy + mxz}{ax} = \frac{lyz + nxy}{by} = \frac{mxz + lyz}{cz}$$

$$= \frac{2lyz}{by + cz - ax}$$

$$= \text{two similar expressions;}$$

$$\therefore \quad \frac{l}{x\,(by + cz - ax)} = \frac{m}{y\,(cz + ax - by)} = \frac{n}{z\,(ax + by - cz)}.$$

16. If we have *two* equations containing *three* unknown quantities in the first degree, such as

$$a_1 x + b_1 y + c_1 z = 0 \qquad \qquad \text{...(1)},$$

$$a_2 x + b_2 y + c_2 z = 0 \qquad \qquad \text{...(2)}$$

we cannot solve these completely; but by writing them in the form

$$a_1 \left(\frac{x}{z} \right) + b_1 \left(\frac{y}{z} \right) + c_1 = 0,$$

$$a_2 \left(\frac{x}{z} \right) + b_2 \left(\frac{y}{z} \right) + c_2 = 0,$$

we can, by regarding $\frac{x}{z}$ and $\frac{y}{z}$ as the unknowns, solve in the ordinary way and obtain

$$\frac{x}{z} = \frac{b_1 c_2 - b_2 c_1}{a_1 b_2 - a_2 b_1}, \ \frac{y}{z} = \frac{c_1 a_2 - c_2 a_1}{a_1 b_2 - a_2 b_1};$$

or, more symmetrically,

$$\frac{x}{b_1 c_2 - b_2 c_1} = \frac{y}{c_1 a_2 - c_2 a_1} = \frac{z}{a_1 b_2 - a_2 b_1}. \qquad \text{...(3)}$$

It thus appears that when we have two equations of the type represented by (1) and (2) we may always by the above formula write down the *ratios* $x : y : z$ in terms of the coefficients of the equations by the following rule :

Write down the coefficients of x, y, z in order, beginning with those of y; and repeat these as in the diagram.

Multiply the coefficients across in the way indicated by the arrows, remembering that in forming the products any one obtained by descending is positive, and any one obtained by ascending is negative. The three results

$$b_1 c_2 - b_2 c_1, \ c_1 a_2 - c_2 a_1, \ a_1 b_2 - a_2 b_1$$

are proportional to x, y, z respectively.

This is called the **Rule of Cross Multiplication.**

Example 1. Find the ratios of $x : y : z$ from the equations
$$7x = 4y + 8z, \quad 3z = 12x + 11y.$$

By transposition we have
$$7x - 4y - 8z = 0,$$
$$12x + 11y - 3z = 0.$$

Write down the coefficients, thus
$$\begin{array}{cccc} -4 & -8 & 7 & -4 \\ 11 & -3 & 12 & 11, \end{array}$$

whence we obtain the products
$$(-4) \times (-3) - 11 \times (-8), \quad (-8) \times 12 - (-3) \times 7, \quad 7 \times 11 - 12 \times (-4),$$
or
$$100, \; -75, \; 125;$$
$$\therefore \frac{x}{100} = \frac{y}{-75} = \frac{z}{125},$$

that is,
$$\frac{x}{4} = \frac{y}{-3} = \frac{z}{5}.$$

Example 2. Eliminate x, y, z from the equations
$$a_1 x + b_1 y + c_1 z = 0, \qquad \qquad \dots(1)$$
$$a_2 x + b_2 y + c_2 z = 0, \qquad \qquad \dots(2)$$
$$a_3 x + b_3 y + c_3 z = 0. \qquad \qquad \dots(3)$$

From (2) and (3), by cross multiplication,
$$\frac{x}{b_2 c_3 - b_3 c_2} = \frac{y}{c_2 a_3 - c_3 a_2} = \frac{z}{a_2 b_3 - a_3 b_2};$$

denoting each of these ratios by k, by multiplying up, substituting in (1), and dividing out by k, we obtain
$$a_1 (b_2 c_3 - b_3 c_2) + b_1 (c_2 a_3 - c_3 a_2) + c_1 (a_2 b_3 - a_3 b_2) = 0.$$
This relation is called the eliminant of the given equations.

Example 3. Solve the equations
$$ax + by + cz = 0, \qquad \qquad \dots(1)$$
$$x + y + z = 0, \qquad \qquad \dots(2)$$
$$bcx + cay + abz = (b - c)(c - a)(a - b). \qquad \dots(3)$$

From (1) and (2), by cross multiplication,
$$\frac{x}{b - c} = \frac{y}{c - a} = \frac{z}{a - b} = k, \text{ suppose};$$
$$\therefore x = k(b - c), \; y = k(c - a), \; z = k(a - b).$$

Substituting in (3),
$$k\{bc(b - c) + ca(c - a) + ab(a - b)\} = (b - c)(c - a)(a - b),$$
$$k\{-(b - c)(c - a)(a - b)\} = (b - c)(c - a)(a - b);$$
$$\therefore k = -1;$$
whence
$$x = c - b, \; y = a - c, \; z = b - a.$$

17. If in Art. 16 we put $z = 1$, equations (1) and (2) become

$$a_1 x + b_1 y + c_1 = 0,$$
$$a_2 x + b_2 y + c_2 = 0;$$

and (3) becomes

$$\frac{x}{b_1 c_2 - b_2 c_1} = \frac{y}{c_1 a_2 - c_2 a_1} = \frac{1}{a_1 b_2 - a_2 b_1};$$

or

$$x = \frac{b_1 c_2 - b_2 c_1}{a_1 b_2 - a_2 b_1}, \quad y = \frac{c_1 a_2 - c_2 a_1}{a_1 b_2 - a_2 b_1}.$$

Hence any two simultaneous equations involving two unknowns in the first degree may be solved by the rule of cross multiplication.

Example: Solve $5x - 3y - 1 = 0$, $x + 2y = 12$.

By transposition, $\qquad 5x - 3y - 1 = 0,$
$$x + 2y - 12 = 0;$$

$$\therefore \quad \frac{x}{36 + 2} = \frac{y}{-1 + 60} = \frac{1}{10 + 3};$$

whence $\qquad\qquad x = \frac{38}{13}, y = \frac{59}{13}.$

EXAMPLES I

1. Find the ratio compounded of

   (1) the ratio $2a : 3b$, and the duplicate ratio of $9b^2 : ab$

   (2) the subduplicate ratio of $64 : 9$, and the ratio $27 : 56$

   (3) the duplicate ratio of $\dfrac{2a}{b} : \dfrac{\sqrt{6}a^2}{b^2}$, and the ratio $3ax : 2by$.

2. If $x + 7 : 2 (x + 14)$ in the duplicate ratio of $5 : 8$, find x.

3. Find two numbers in the ratio of $7 : 12$ so that the greater exceeds the less by 275.

4. What number must be added to each term of the ratio $5 : 37$ to make it equal to $1 : 3$?

5. If $x : y = 3 : 4$, find the ratio of $7x - 4y : 3x + y$.

6. If $15 (2x^2 - y^2) = 7xy$, find the ratio of $x : y$.

7. If $\dfrac{a}{b} = \dfrac{c}{d} = \dfrac{e}{f}$,

   prove that $\dfrac{2a^4 b^2 + 3a^2 e^2 - 5e^4 f}{2b^6 + 3b^2 f^2 - 5f^5} = \dfrac{a^4}{b^4}.$

8. If $\dfrac{a}{b} = \dfrac{b}{c} = \dfrac{c}{d}$, prove that $\dfrac{a}{d}$ is equal to

$$\sqrt{\dfrac{a^5 + b^2 c^2 + a^3 c^2}{b^4 c + d^4 + b^2 c d^2}}$$

9. If $\dfrac{x}{q + r - p} = \dfrac{y}{r + p - q} = \dfrac{z}{p + q - r}$,
    shew that $(q - r)\, x + (r - p)\, y + (p - q)\, z = 0$.

10. If $\dfrac{y}{x - z} = \dfrac{y + x}{z} = \dfrac{x}{y}$, find the ratios of $x : y : z$.

11. If $\dfrac{y + z}{pb + qc} = \dfrac{z + x}{pc + qa} = \dfrac{x + y}{pa + qb}$,
    shew that $\dfrac{2\,(x + y + z)}{a + b + c} = \dfrac{(b + c)\, x + (c + a)\, y + (a + b)\, z}{bc + ca + ab}$.

12. If $\dfrac{x}{a} = \dfrac{y}{b} = \dfrac{z}{c}$,

    shew that $\dfrac{x^3 + a^3}{x^2 + a^2} + \dfrac{y^3 + b^3}{y^2 + b^2} + \dfrac{z^3 + c^3}{z^2 + c^2} = \dfrac{(x + y + z)^3 + (a + b + c)^3}{(x + y + z)^2 + (a + b + c)^2}$.

13. If $\dfrac{2y + 2z - x}{a} = \dfrac{2z + 2x - y}{b} = \dfrac{2x + 2y - z}{c}$,

    shew that $\dfrac{x}{2b + 2c - a} = \dfrac{y}{2c + 2a - b} = \dfrac{z}{2a + 2b - c}$.

14. If $(a^2 + b^2 + c^2)\,(x^2 + y^2 + z^2) = (ax + by + cz)^2$
    shew that $x : a = y : b = z : c$.

15. If $l\,(my + nz - lx) = m\,(nz + lx - my) = n\,(lx + my - nz)$,
    prove $\dfrac{y + z - x}{l} = \dfrac{z + x - y}{m} = \dfrac{x + y - z}{n}$.

16. Shew that the eliminant of
    $$ax + cy + bz = 0,\ cx + by + az = 0,\ bx + ay + cz = 0,$$
    is $\qquad a^3 + b^3 + c^3 - 3abc = 0.$

17. Eliminate x, y, z from the equations
    $$ax + hy + gz = 0,\ hx + by + fz = 0,\ gx + fy + cz = 0.$$

18. If $x = cy + bz,\ y = az + cx,\ z = bx + ay$,

    shew that $\dfrac{x^2}{1 - a^2} = \dfrac{y^2}{1 - b^2} = \dfrac{z^2}{1 - c^2}$.

19. Given that $a\,(y + z) = x,\ b\,(z + x) = y,\ c\,(x + y) = z$,
    prove that $bc + ca + ab + 2abc = 1$.

Solve the following equations :

20. $3x - 4y + 7z = 0$, $2x - y - 2z = 0$, $3x^3 - y^3 + z^3 = 18$.

21. $x + y = z$, $3x - 2y + 17z = 0$, $x^3 + 3y^3 + 2z^3 = 167$.

22. $7yz + 3zx = 4xy$, $21yz - 3zx = 4xy$, $x + 2y + 3z = 19$.

23. $3x^2 - 2y^2 + 5z^2 = 0$, $7x^2 - 3y^2 - 15z^2 = 0$, $5x - 4y + 7z = 6$.

24. If $\dfrac{l}{\sqrt{a} - \sqrt{b}} + \dfrac{m}{\sqrt{b} - \sqrt{c}} + \dfrac{n}{\sqrt{c} - \sqrt{a}} = 0$,

$$\dfrac{l}{\sqrt{a} + \sqrt{b}} + \dfrac{m}{\sqrt{b} + \sqrt{c}} + \dfrac{n}{\sqrt{c} + \sqrt{a}} = 0,$$

shew that $\dfrac{l}{(a - b)(c - \sqrt{ab})} = \dfrac{m}{(b - c)(a - \sqrt{bc})} = \dfrac{n}{(c - a)(b - \sqrt{ac})}$.

Solve the equations :

25. $ax + by + cz = 0$,
$bcx + cay + abz = 0$,
$xyz + abc\,(a^3x + b^3y + c^3z) = 0$.

26. $ax + by + cz = a^2x + b^2y + c^2z = 0$,
$x + y + z + (b - c)(c - a)(a - b) = 0$.

27. If $a(y + z) = x$, $b(z + x) = y$, $c(x + y) = z$,

prove that $\dfrac{x^2}{a(1 - bc)} = \dfrac{y^2}{b(1 - ca)} = \dfrac{z^2}{c(1 - ab)}$.

28. If $ax + hy + gz = 0$, $hx + by + fz = 0$, $gx + fy + cz = 0$,
prove that

(1) $\dfrac{x^2}{bc - f^2} = \dfrac{y^2}{ca - g^2} = \dfrac{z^2}{ab - h^2}$.

(2) $(bc - f^2)(ca - g^2)(ab - h^2) = (fg - ch)(gh - af)(hf - bg)$.

■ ■ ■

Chapter 2

PROPORTION

18. Definition : When two ratios are equal, the four quantities composing them are said to be **proportionals.** Thus if $\dfrac{a}{b} = \dfrac{c}{d}$, then a, b, c, d are proportionals. This is expressed by saying that a is to b as c is to d, and the proportion is written

$$a : b :: c : d$$

or

$$a : b = c : d.$$

The terms a and d are called the *extremes*, b and c the *means.*

19. *If four quantities are in proportion, the product of the extremes is equal to the product of the means.*

Let a, b, c, d be the proportionals.

Then by definition $\dfrac{a}{b} = \dfrac{c}{d}$;

whence $\qquad\qquad ad = bc.$

Hence if any three terms of a proportion are given, the fourth may be found. Thus if a, c, d are given, then $b = \dfrac{ad}{c}$.

Conversely, if there are any four quantities, a, b, c, d, such that $ad = bc$, then a, b, c, d are proportionals; a and d being the extremes, b and c the means; or vice-versa.

20. Definition : Quantities are said to be in **continued proportion** when the first is to the second, as the second is to the third, as the third to the fourth; and so on. Thus $a, b, c, d, \ldots$ are in continued proportion when

$$\frac{a}{b} = \frac{b}{c} = \frac{c}{d} = \ldots$$

If three quantities a, b, c are in continued proportion, then

$$a : b = b : c;$$

$$\therefore \quad ac = b^2. \qquad\qquad\qquad \text{[Art. 18.]}$$

In this case b is said to be a mean proportional between a and c, and c is said to be a third proportional to a and b.

21. *If three quantities are proportionals the first is to the third in the duplicate ratio of the first to the second.*

Let the three quantities be a, b, c; then $\dfrac{a}{b} = \dfrac{b}{c}$.

Now $$\frac{a}{c} = \frac{a}{b} \times \frac{b}{c} = \frac{a}{b} \times \frac{a}{b} = \frac{a^2}{b^2};$$

that is, $$a : c = a^2 : b^2.$$

It will be seen that this proposition is the same as the *definition* of duplicate ratio given in Euclid, Book V.

22. If $a : b = c : d$ and $e : f = g : h$, then will $ae : bf = cg : dh$.

For $$\frac{a}{b} = \frac{c}{d} \quad \text{and} \quad \frac{e}{f} = \frac{g}{h};$$

$\therefore$ $$\frac{ae}{bf} = \frac{cg}{dh},$$

or $$ae : bf = cg : dh.$$

Cor. If $$a : b = c : d,$$
and $$b : x = d : y,$$
then $$a : x = c : y.$$

This is the theorem known as *ex aequali* in Geometry.

23. If four quantities a, b, c, d form a proportion, many other proportions may be deduced by the properties of fractions. The results of these operations are very useful, and some of them are often quoted by the annexed names borrowed from Geometry.

(1) If $a : b = c : d$, then $b : a = d : c$.   [*Invertendo.*]

For $\dfrac{a}{b} = \dfrac{c}{d}$; therefore $1 \div \dfrac{a}{b} = 1 \div \dfrac{c}{d}$;

that is $$\frac{b}{a} = \frac{d}{c};$$

or $$b : a = d : c.$$

(2) If $a : b = c : d$, then $a : c = b : d$.   [*Alternando.*]

For $ad = bc$; therefore $\dfrac{ad}{cd} = \dfrac{bc}{cd}$;

that is, $$\frac{a}{c} = \frac{b}{d};$$

or $$a : c = b : d.$$

(3) If $a : b = c : d$, then $a + b : b = c + d : d$.   [*Componendo.*]

For $\dfrac{a}{b} = \dfrac{c}{d}$; therefore $\dfrac{a}{b} + 1 = \dfrac{c}{d} + 1$;

that is $$\frac{a + b}{b} = \frac{c + d}{d};$$

or $$a + b : b = c + d : d.$$

(4) If $a : b = c : d$, then $a - b : b = c - d : d.$ [*Dividendo.*]

For $\dfrac{a}{b} = \dfrac{c}{d}$; therefore $\dfrac{a}{b} - 1 = \dfrac{c}{d} - 1$;

that is, $$\dfrac{a - b}{b} = \dfrac{c - d}{d} ;$$

or $$a - b : b = c - d : d.$$

(5) If $a : b = c : d$, then $a + b : a - b = c + d : c - d$

For by (3) $$\dfrac{a + b}{b} = \dfrac{c + d}{d} ,$$

and by (4) $$\dfrac{a - b}{b} = \dfrac{c - d}{d} ;$$

$\therefore$ by division, $$\dfrac{a + b}{a - b} = \dfrac{c + d}{c - d} ;$$

or $$a + b : a - b = c + d : c - d.$$

This proposition is usually quoted as *Componendo and Dividendo.*

Several other proportions may be proved in a similar way.

24. The results of the preceding article are the algebraical equivalents of some of the propositions in the fifth book of Euclid, and the student is advised to make himself familiar with them in their verbal form. For example, *dividendo* may be quoted as follows :

When there are four proportionals, the excess of the first above the second is to the second, as the excess of the third above the fourth is to the fourth.

25. We shall now compare the algebraical definition of proportion with that given in Euclid. .

Euclid's definition is as follows :

Four quantities are said to be proportionals when if *any equimultiples whatever* be taken of the first and third, and also *any equimultiples whatever* of the second and fourth, the multiple of the third is greater than, equal to, or less than the multiple of the fourth, according as the multiple of the first is greater than, equal to, or less than the multiple of the second.

In algebraical symbols the definition may be thus stated :

Four quantities a, b, c, d are in proportion when $pc \gtreqless qd$ according as $pa \gtreqless qb$, p and q being *any positive integers whatever.*

I. To deduce the geometrical definition of proportion from the algebraical definition.

Since $\dfrac{a}{b} = \dfrac{c}{d}$, by multiplying both sides by $\dfrac{p}{q}$, we obtain

$$\frac{pa}{qb} = \frac{pc}{qd};$$

hence, from the properties of fractions,

$$pc \gtreqqless qd \text{ according as } pa \gtreqqless qb,$$

which proves the proposition.

II. To deduce the algebraical definition of proportion from the geometrical definition.

Given that $pc \gtreqqless qd$ according as $pa \gtreqqless qb$, to prove

$$\frac{a}{b} = \frac{c}{d}.$$

If $\dfrac{a}{b}$ is not equal to $\dfrac{c}{d}$, one of them must be the greater. Suppose $\dfrac{a}{b} > \dfrac{c}{d}$; then it will be possible to find some fraction $\dfrac{q}{p}$ which lies between them, q and p being positive integers.

Hence $\qquad\qquad\qquad\qquad \dfrac{a}{b} > \dfrac{q}{p}$ ...(1)

and $\qquad\qquad\qquad\qquad \dfrac{c}{d} < \dfrac{q}{p}$ ...(2)

From (1) $\qquad\qquad\qquad\qquad pa > qb;$

from (2) $\qquad\qquad\qquad\qquad pc < qd;$

and these contradict the hypothesis.

Therefore $\dfrac{a}{b}$ and $\dfrac{c}{d}$ are not unequal; that is $\dfrac{a}{b} = \dfrac{c}{d}$; which proves the proposition.

26. It should be noticed that the geometrical definition of proportion deals with *concrete* magnitudes, such as lines or areas, represented geometrically but not referred to any common unit of measurement. So that Euclid's definition is applicable to incommensurable as well as to commensurable quantities; whereas the algebraical definition, strictly speaking, applies only to commensurable quantities, since it tacitly assumes that a is the same determinate multiple, part, or parts, of b that c is of d. But the proofs which have been given for commensurable quantities will still be true for incommensurables, since the ratio of two incommensurables can always be made to differ from the ratio of two integers *by less than any assignable quantity*. This has been shewn in Art. 7; it may also be proved more generally as in the next article.

27. Suppose that a and b are incommensurable; divide b into m equal parts each equal to β, so that $b = m\beta$, where m is a positive integer. Also suppose β is contained in a more than n times and less than $n + 1$ times;

then
$$\frac{a}{b} > \frac{n\beta}{m\beta} \text{ and } < \frac{(n+1)\beta}{m\beta},$$

that is, $\dfrac{a}{b}$ lies between $\dfrac{n}{m}$ and $\dfrac{n+1}{m}$;

so that $\dfrac{a}{b}$ differs from $\dfrac{n}{m}$ by a quantity less than $\dfrac{1}{m}$. And since we can choose β (our unit of measurement) as small as we please, m can be made as great as we please. Hence $\dfrac{1}{m}$ can be made as small as we please, and two integers n and m can be found whose ratio will express that of a and b to any required degree of accuracy.

28. The propositions proved in Art. 23 are often useful in solving problems. In particular, the solution of certain equations is greatly facilitated by a skilful use of the operations *componendo* and *dividendo*.

Example 1. If $(2ma + 6mb + 3nc + 9nd)(2ma - 6mb - 3nc + 9nd)$
$$= (2ma - 6mb + 3nc - 9nd)(2ma + 6mb - 3nc - 9nd),$$
prove that a, b, c, d are proportionals.

We have $\dfrac{2ma + 6mb + 3nc + 9nd}{2ma - 6mb + 3nc - 9nd} = \dfrac{2ma + 6mb - 3nc - 9nd}{2ma - 6mb - 3nc + 9nd};$

$\therefore$ componendo and dividendo,

$$\frac{2(2ma + 3nc)}{2(6mb + 9nd)} = \frac{2(2ma - 3nc)}{2(6mb - 9nd)}$$

Alternando, $\dfrac{2ma + 3nc}{2ma - 3nc} = \dfrac{6mb + 9nd}{6mb - 9nd}.$

Again, componendo and dividendo,

$$\frac{4ma}{6nc} = \frac{12mb}{18nd};$$

whence $\dfrac{a}{c} = \dfrac{b}{d},$

or $a : b = c : d.$

Example 2. Solve the equation
$$\frac{\sqrt{x+1} + \sqrt{x-1}}{\sqrt{x+1} - \sqrt{x-1}} = \frac{4x-1}{2}.$$

We have, componendo and dividendo,
$$\frac{\sqrt{x+1}}{\sqrt{x-1}} = \frac{4x+1}{4x-3};$$

$$\therefore \qquad \frac{x+1}{x-1} = \frac{16x^2 + 8x + 1}{16x^2 - 24x + 9}.$$

Again, componendo and dividendo,

$$\frac{2x}{2} = \frac{32x^2 - 16x + 10}{32x - 8}$$

$$\therefore \qquad x = \frac{16x^2 - 8x + 5}{16x - 4};$$

whence

$$16x^2 - 4x = 16x^2 - 8x + 5;$$

$$\therefore \qquad x = \frac{5}{4}.$$

EXAMPLES II

1. Find the fourth proportional to $3, 5, 27$.

2. Find the mean proportional between

   (1) 6 and 24 \qquad\qquad (2) $360a^4$ and $250a^2b^2$.

3. Find the third proportional to $\dfrac{x}{y} + \dfrac{y}{x}$ and $\dfrac{x}{y}$.

   If $a : b = c : d$, prove that

4. $a^2c + ac^2 : b^2d + bd^2 = (a + c)^3 : (b + d)^3$.

5. $pa^2 + qb^2 : pa^2 - qb^2 = pc^2 + qd^2 : pc^2 - qd^2$.

6. $a - c : b - d = \sqrt{a^2 + c^2} : \sqrt{b^2 + d^2}$.

7. $\sqrt{a^2 + c^2} : \sqrt{b^2 + d^2} = \sqrt{ac + \dfrac{c^3}{a}} : \sqrt{bd + \dfrac{d^3}{b}}$

   If a, b, c, d are in continued proportion, prove that

8. $a : b + d = c^3 : c^2d + d^3$.

9. $2a + 3d : 3a - 4d = 2a^3 + 3b^3 : 3a^3 - 4b^3$.

10. $(a^2 + b^2 + c^2)(b^2 + c^2 + d^2) = (ab + bc + cd)^2$.

11. If b is a mean proportional between a and c, prove that

$$\frac{a^2 - b^2 + c^2}{a^{-2} - b^{-2} + c^{-2}} = b^4.$$

12. If $a : b = c : d$, and $e : f = g : h$, prove that

$$ae + bf : ae - bf = cg + dh : cg - dh.$$

Solve the equations :

13. $\dfrac{2x^3 - 3x^2 + x + 1}{2x^3 - 3x^2 - x - 1} = \dfrac{3x^3 - x^2 + 5x - 13}{3x^3 - x^2 - 5x + 13}$.

14. $\dfrac{3x^4 + x^2 - 2x - 3}{3x^4 - x^2 + 2x + 3} = \dfrac{5x^4 + 2x^2 - 7x + 3}{5x^4 - 2x^2 + 7x - 3}$.

15. $\dfrac{(m+n)\,x - (a-b)}{(m-n)\,x - (a+b)} = \dfrac{(m+n)\,x + a + c}{(m-n)\,x + a - c}$.

16. If a, b, c, d are proportionals, prove that
$$a + d = b + c + \frac{(a-b)\,(a-c)}{a}.$$

17. If a, b, c, d, e are in continued proportion, prove that
$$(ab + bc + cd + de)^2 = (a^2 + b^2 + c^2 + d^2)\,(b^2 + c^2 + d^2 + e^2).$$

18. If the work done by $x - 1$ men in $x + 1$ days is to the work done by $x + 2$ men in $x - 1$ days in the ratio of $9 : 10$, find x.

19. Find four proportionals such that the sum of the extremes is 21, the sum of the means 19, and the sum of the squares of all four numbers is 442.

20. Two casks A and B were filled with two kinds of sherry, mixed in the cask A in the ratio of $2 : 7$, and in the cask B in the ratio of $1 : 5$. What quantity must be taken from each to form a mixture which shall consist of 10 litres of one kind and 45 litres of the other ?

21. Nine litres are drawn from a vessel full of wine; it is then filled with water, then nine litres of the mixture are drawn, and the vessel is again filled with water. If the quantity of wine now in the vessel be to the quantity of water in it as 16 to 9, how much does the vessel hold ?

22. If four positive quantities are in continued proportion, shew that the difference between the first and last is at least three times as great as the difference between the other two.

23. In England the population increased 15.9 per cent. between 1871 and 1881; if the town population increased 18 per cent. and the country population 4 per cent., compare the town, and country populations in 1871.

24. In a certain country the consumption of tea is five times the consumption of coffee. If a per cent. more tea and b per cent. more coffee were consumed, the aggregate amount consumed would be $7c$ per cent. more; but if b per cent more tea and a per cent. more coffee were consumed, the aggregate amount consumed would be $3c$ per cent. more : compare a and b.

25. Brass is an alloy of copper and zinc; bronze is an alloy containing 80 per cent of copper, 4 of zinc, and 16 of tin. A fused mass of brass and bronze is found to contain 74 per cent of copper, 16 of zinc, and 10 of tin find the ratio of copper to zinc in the composition of brass.

26. A crew can row a certain course up stream in 84 minutes; they can row the same course down stream in 9 minutes less than they could row it in still water : how long would they take to row down with the stream ?

■ ■ ■

Chapter 3

VARIATION

29. Definition : One quantity A is said to **vary directly** as another B, when the two quantities depend upon each other in such a manner that if B is changed, A is changed *in the same ratio*.

Note. The word *directly* is often omitted, and A is said to vary as B.

For instance : if a train moving at a uniform rate travels 40 miles in 60 minutes, it will travel 20 miles in 30 minutes, 80 miles in 120 minutes, and so on ; the distance in each case being increased or diminished in the same ratio as the time. This is expressed by saying that when the velocity is uniform *the distance is proportional to the time*, or *the distance varies as the time*.

30. The symbol $\propto$ is used to denote variation : so that $A \propto B$ is read "*A varies as B*".

31. *If A varies as B, then A is equal to B multiplied by some constant quantity.*

For suppose that $a, a_1, a_2, a_3, ..., b, b_1, b_2, b_3, ...$ are corresponding values of A and B.

Then, by definition, $\dfrac{a}{a_1} = \dfrac{b}{b_1} ; \dfrac{a}{a_2} = \dfrac{b}{b_2} ; \dfrac{a}{a_3} = \dfrac{b}{b_3}$; and so on,

$\therefore \qquad \dfrac{a_1}{b_1} = \dfrac{a_2}{b_2} = \dfrac{a_3}{b_3} = ...,$ each being equal to $\dfrac{a}{b}$.

Hence $\dfrac{\text{any value of } A}{\text{the corresponding value of } B}$ is always the same ;

that is, $\qquad \dfrac{A}{B} = m,$ where m is constant.

$\therefore \qquad A = mB.$

If any pair of corresponding values of A and B are known, the constant m can be determined. For instance, if $A = 3$ when $B = 12$,

we have $\qquad\qquad 3 = m \times 12;$

$\therefore \qquad\qquad\qquad m = \frac{1}{4},$

and $\qquad\qquad\qquad A = \frac{1}{4} B.$

32. Definition : One quantity A is said to **vary inversely** as another B, when A varies *directly* as the reciprocal of B.

Thus if A varies inversely as B, $A = \dfrac{m}{B}$, where m is constant.

The following is an illustration of inverse variation : If 6 men do a certain work in 8 hours, 12 men would do the same work in 4 hours, 2 men in 24 hours ; and so on. Thus it appears that when the number of men is increased, the time is proportionately decreased ; and vice-versa.

Example 1. The cube root of x varies inversely as the square of y ; if $x = 8$ when $y = 3$, find x when $y = 1\frac{1}{2}$.

By supposition $\sqrt[3]{x} = \dfrac{m}{y^2}$, where m is constant.

Putting $x = 8$, $y = 3$, we have $2 = \dfrac{m}{9}$,

$\therefore$ $\qquad\qquad\qquad\qquad m = 18$,

and $\qquad\qquad\qquad\qquad \sqrt[3]{x} = \dfrac{18}{y^2}$;

hence, by putting $y = \dfrac{3}{2}$, we obtain $x = 512$.

Example 2. The square of the time of a planet's revolution varies as the cube of its distance from the Sun ; find the time of Venus' revolution, assuming the distances of the Earth and Venus from the Sun to be $91\frac{1}{4}$ and 66 millions of miles respectively.

Let P be the periodic time measured in days, D the distance in millions of miles ; we have $P^2 \propto D^3$,

or $\qquad\qquad\qquad\qquad P^2 = kD^3$,

where k is some constant.

For the Earth, $\quad 365 \times 365 = k \times 91\frac{1}{4} \times 91\frac{1}{4} \times 91\frac{1}{4}$,

whence $\qquad\qquad\qquad k = \dfrac{4 \times 4 \times 4}{365}$;

$\therefore$ $\qquad\qquad\qquad\qquad P^2 = \dfrac{4 \times 4 \times 4}{365} D^3$.

For Venus, $\qquad\qquad P^2 = \dfrac{4 \times 4 \times 4}{365} \times 66 \times 66 \times 66$;

whence $\qquad\qquad\qquad P = 4 \times 66 \times \sqrt{\dfrac{264}{365}}$

$\qquad\qquad\qquad\qquad\quad = 264 \times \sqrt{0.7233}, \quad$ approximately,

$\qquad\qquad\qquad\qquad\quad = 264 \times 0.85$

$\qquad\qquad\qquad\qquad\quad = 224.4$.

Hence the time of revolution is nearly $224\frac{1}{2}$ days.

33. Definition : One quantity is said to **vary jointly** as a number of others, when it varies directly as their product.

Thus A varies jointly as B and C, when $A = m\,BC$. For instance, the interest on a sum of money varies jointly as the principal, the time, and the rate per cent.

34. Definition : A is said to vary directly as B and inversely as C, when A varies as $\dfrac{B}{C}$.

35. *If A varies as B when C is constant, and A varies as C when B is constant, then will A vary as BC when both B and C vary.*

The variation of A depends partly on that of B and partly on that of C. Suppose these latter variations to take place separately, each in its turn producing its own effect on A ; also let a, b, c be certain simultaneous values of A, B, C.

1. *Let C be constant* while B changes to b ; then A must undergo a partial change and will assume some intermediate value a', where

$$\frac{A}{a'} = \frac{B}{b} \qquad\qquad \text{...(1)}$$

2. *Let B be constant*, that is, let it retain its value b, while C changes to c ; then A must complete its change and pass from its intermediate value a' to its final value a, where

$$\frac{a'}{a} = \frac{C}{c} \qquad\qquad \text{...(2)}$$

From (1) and (2) $\qquad \dfrac{A}{a'} \times \dfrac{a'}{a} = \dfrac{B}{b} \times \dfrac{C}{c}$;

that is, $\qquad\qquad\qquad A = \dfrac{a}{bc} \cdot BC,$

or $\qquad\qquad\qquad\qquad A$ varies as BC.

36. The following are illustrations of the theorem proved in the last article.

The amount of work done by a *given number of men* varies directly as the number of days they work, and the amount of work done *in a given time* varies directly as the number of men ; therefore when the number of days and the number of men are both variable, the amount of work will vary as the product of the number of men and the number of days.

Again, in Geometry the area of a triangle varies directly as its base when the height is constant, and directly as the height when the base is constant ; and when both the height and base are variable, the area varies as the product of the numbers representing the height and the base.

Example. The volume of a right circular cone varies as the square of the radius of the base when the height is constant, and as the height when the base is constant. If the radius of the base is 7 cm and the height 15 cm the volume is 770 cubic cm find the height of a cone whose volume is 132 cubic cm and which stands on a base whose radius is 3 cm.

Let h and r denote respectively the height and radius of the base measured in cm. ; also let V be the volume in cubic cm.

Then $V = mr^2h$, where m is constant.

By supposition, $\qquad 770 = m \times 7^2 \times 15$;

whence $\qquad\qquad\qquad m = \dfrac{22}{21}$;

$\therefore \qquad\qquad\qquad V = \dfrac{22}{21} r^2h.$

$\therefore$ by substituting $V = 132, r = 3$, we get

$$132 = \frac{22}{21} \times 9 \times h \ ;$$

whence $\qquad\qquad\qquad h = 14$;

and therefore the height is 14 cm.

37. The proposition of Art. 35 can easily be extended to the case in which the variation of A depends upon that of more than two variables. Further, the variations may be either direct or inverse. The principle is interesting because of its frequent occurrence in Physical Science. For example, in the theory of gases it is found by experiment that the pressure (p) of a gas varies as the " absolute temperature" (t) when its volume (v) is constant, and that the pressure varies inversely as the volume when the temperature is constant ; that is

$$p \propto t, \text{ when } v \text{ is constant}$$

and $\qquad\qquad p \propto \dfrac{1}{v}$, when t is constant.

From these results we should expect that, when both t and v are variable, we should have the formula

$$p \propto \frac{t}{v}, \text{ or } pv = kt, \text{ where } k \text{ is constant} ;$$

and by actual experiment this is found to be the case.

Example. The duration of a railway journey varies directly as the distance and inversely as the velocity ; the velocity varies directly as the square root of the quantity of coal used per km, and inversely as the number of carriages in the train. In a journey of 50 km. in half an hour with 18 carriages 100 kg. of coal is required ; how much coal will be consumed in a journey of 42 km. in 28 minutes with 16 carriages ?

Let t = the time expressed in hours,

d = the distance in kilometres,

v = the velocity in km per hour,

q = the number of kg of coal used per km

c = the number of carriages.

We have $$t \propto \frac{d}{v},$$

and $$v \propto \frac{\sqrt{q}}{c},$$

whence $$t \propto \frac{cd}{\sqrt{q}},$$

or $$t = \frac{kcd}{\sqrt{q}}, \quad \text{where } k \text{ is constant.}$$

Substituting the values given, we have (since $q = 2$)

$$\frac{1}{2} = \frac{k \times 18 \times 50}{\sqrt{2}};$$

that is, $$k = \frac{1}{\sqrt{2} \times 18 \times 50}.$$

Hence $$t = \frac{cd}{\sqrt{2} \times 18 \times 50 \sqrt{q}}.$$

Substituting now the values of t, c, d given in the second part of the question, we have

$$\frac{28}{60} = \frac{16 \times 42}{\sqrt{2} \times 18 \times 50 \sqrt{q}};$$

that is, $$\sqrt{q} = 4\sqrt{2};$$

whence $$q = 32.$$

Hence the quantity of coal is $42 \times 32 = 1344$ kg.

EXAMPLES III

1. If x varies as y, and $x = 8$ when $y = 15$, find x when $y = 10$.

2. If P varies inversely as Q, and $P = 7$ when $Q = 3$, find P when $Q = 2\frac{1}{3}$.

3. If the square of x varies as the cube of y, and $x = 3$ when $y = 4$, find the value of y when $x = \frac{1}{\sqrt{3}}$.

4. A varies as B and C jointly ; if $A = 2$ when $B = \frac{3}{5}$ and $C = \frac{10}{27}$, find C when $A = 54$ and $B = 3$.

5. If A varies as C, and B varies as C, then $A \pm B$ and $\sqrt{AB}$ will each vary as C.

6. If A varies as BC, then B varies inversely as $\dfrac{C}{A}$.

7. P varies directly as Q and inversely as R ; also $P = \dfrac{2}{3}$ when $Q = \dfrac{3}{7}$ and $R = \dfrac{9}{14}$; find Q when $P = \sqrt{48}$ and $R = \sqrt{75}$.

8. If x varies as y, prove that $x^2 + y^2$ varies as $x^2 - y^2$.

9. If y varies as the sum of two quantities, of which one varies directly as x and the other inversely as x ; and if $y = 6$ when $x = 4$, and $y = 3\frac{1}{3}$ when $x = 3$; find the equation between x and y.

10. If y is equal to the sum of two quantities, one of which varies as x directly, and the other as x^2 inversely ; and if $y = 19$ when $x = 2$, or 3 ; find y in terms of x.

11. If A varies directly as the square root of B and inversely as the cube of C, and if $A = 3$ when $B = 256$, and $C = 2$, find B when $A = 24$ and $C = \dfrac{1}{2}$

12. Given that $x + y$ varies as $z + \dfrac{1}{z}$, and that $x - y$ varies as $z - \dfrac{1}{z}$, find the relation between x and z, provided that $z = 2$ when $x = 3$ and $y = 1$.

13. If A varies as B and C jointly, while B varies as D^2, and C varies inversely as A, shew that A varies as D.

14. If y varies as the sum of three quantities of which the first is constant, the second varies as x, and the third as x^2 ; and if $y = 0$ when $x = 1$, $y = 1$ when $x = 2$, and $y = 4$ when $x = 3$; find y when $x = 7$.

15. When a body falls from rest its distance from the starting point varies as the square of the time it has been falling : if a body falls through 122.6 m in 5 seconds, how far does it fall in 10 seconds ? Also how far does it fall in the 10th second ?

16. Given that the volume of a sphere varies as the cube of its radius, and that when the radius is 3·5 cm the volume is 179.7 cubic cm, find the volume when the radius is 1.75 cm.

17. The weight of a circular disc varies as the square of the radius when the thickness remains the same ; it also varies as the thickness when the radius remains the same. Two discs have

their thicknesses in the ratio of $9:8$; find the ratio of their radii if the weight of the first is twice that of the second.

18. At a certain regatta the number of races on each day varied jointly as the number of days from beginning and end of the regatta up to and including the day in question. On three successive days there were respectively 6, 5 and 3 races. Which days were these, and how long did the regatta last?

19. The price of a diamond varies as the square of its weight. Three rings of equal weight, each composed of a diamond set in gold, have values Rs. a, Rs. b, Rs. c, the diamonds in them weighing 3, 4, 5 carats respectively. Shew that the value of a diamond of one carat is

$$\text{Rs.} \left(\frac{a+c}{2} - b \right),$$

the cost of workmanship being the same for each ring.

20. Two persons are awarded pensions proportion to the square root of the number of years they have served. One has served 9 years longer than the other and receives a pension greater by Rs. 500. If the length of service of the first had exceeded that of the second by $4\frac{1}{4}$ years their pensions would have been in the proportion of $9:8$. How long had they served and what were their respective pensions?

21. The attraction of a planet on its satellites varies directly as the mass (M) of the planet, and inversely as the square of the distance (D); also the square of a satellite's time of revolution varies directly as the distance and inversely as the force of attraction. If m_1, d_1, t_1, and m_2, d_2, t_2, are simultaneous values of M, D, T respectively, prove that

$$\frac{m_1 t_1^2}{m_2 t_2^2} = \frac{d_1^3}{d_2^3}.$$

Hence find the time of revolution of that moon of Jupiter whose distance is to the distance of our Moon as $35:31$, having given that the mass of Jupiter is 343 times that of the Earth, and that the Moon's period is 27.32 days.

22. The consumption of coal by a locomotive varies as the square of the velocity; when the speed is 32 km an hour the consumption of coal per hour is 2 tonnes: if the price of coal be Rs. 10 per tonne, and the other expenses of the engine be Rs. 11.25 nP. an hour, find the least cost of a journey of 100 km.

Chapter 4

ARITHMETICAL PROGRESSION

38. Definition : Quantities are said to be in Arithmetical Progression when they increase or decrease by a *common difference*.

Thus each of the following series forms an Arithmetical Progression :

$$3, 7, 11, 15, \ldots\ldots$$
$$8, 2, -4, -10, \ldots\ldots$$
$$a, a + d, a + 2d, a + 3d, \ldots\ldots$$

The common difference is found by subtracting *any* term of the series from that which *follows* it. In the first of the above examples the common difference is 4; in the second it is -6; in the third it is d.

39. If we examine the series

$$a, a + d, a + 2d, a + 3d, \ldots$$

we notice that *in any term the coefficient of d is always less by one than the number of the term in the series.*

Thus the   3rd term is $a + 2d$;

6th term is $a + 5d$;

20th term is $a + 19d$;

and, generally, the pth term is $a + (p - 1) d$.

If n be the number of terms, and if l denote the last, or nth term, we have

$$l = a + (n - 1) d.$$

40. *To find the sum of a number of terms in Arithmetical Progression.*

Let a denote the first term, d the common difference, and n the number of terms. Also let l denote the last term, and s the required sum; then

$$s = a + (a + d) + (a + 2d) + \ldots + (l - 2d) + (l - d) + l;$$

and, by writing the series in the reverse order,

$$s = l + (l - d) + (l - 2d) + \ldots + (a + 2d) + (a + d) + a.$$

Adding together these two series,

$$2s = (a + l) + (a + l) + (a + l) + \ldots \text{ to } n \text{ terms}$$
$$= n (a + l),$$

$$\therefore \qquad s = \frac{n}{2}(a+l) \qquad \qquad \text{...(1)}$$

$$\text{and} \qquad l = a + (n-1)d \qquad \qquad \text{...(2)}$$

$$\therefore \qquad s = \frac{n}{2}\{2a + (n-1)d\} \qquad \qquad \text{...(3)}$$

41. In the last article we have three useful formulae (1), (2), (3); in each of these any one of the letters may denote the unknown quantity when the three others are known. For instance, in (1) if we substitute given values for s, n, l, we obtain an equation for finding a; and similarly in the other formulae. But it is necessary to guard against a too mechanical use of these general formulae, and it will often be found better to solve simple questions by a mental rather than by an actual reference to the requisite formula.

Example 1. Find the sum of the series $5\frac{1}{2}, 6\frac{3}{4}, 8, \ldots\ldots$ to 17 terms.

Here the common difference is $1\frac{1}{4}$; hence from (3),

$$\begin{aligned}
\text{the sum} &= \frac{17}{2}\left\{2 \times \frac{11}{2} + 16 \times 1\frac{1}{4}\right\} \\
&= \frac{17}{2}(11 + 20) \\
&= \frac{17 \times 31}{2} \\
&= 263\frac{1}{2}.
\end{aligned}$$

Example 2. The first term of a series is 5, the last 45, and the sum 400: find the number of terms, and the common difference.

If n be the number of terms, then from (1)

$$400 = \frac{n}{2}(5 + 45);$$

whence $\qquad n = 16.$

If d be the common difference

$$45 = \text{the 16th term} = 5 + 15d;$$

whence $\qquad d = 2\frac{2}{3}.$

42. If *any two* terms of an Arithmetical Progression be given the series can be completely determined; for the data furnish *two* simultaneous equations, the solution of which will give the first term and the common difference.

Example : The 54th and 4th terms of an A.P. are -61 and 64; find the 23rd term.

If a be the first term, and d the common difference,

$$-61 = \text{the 54}^\text{th}\text{ term} = a + 53d;$$

and $\qquad\qquad 64 = $ the 4th term $= a + 3d;$

whence we obtain $\qquad\qquad d = -\dfrac{5}{2}, a = 71\dfrac{1}{2};$

and $\qquad\qquad$ the 23rd term $= a + 22d = 16\dfrac{1}{2}.$

43. Definition : When three quantities are in Arithmetical Progression the middle one is said to be the **arithmetic mean** of the other two.

Thus a is the arithmetic mean between $a - d$ and $a + d$.

44. *To find the arithmetic mean between two given quantities.*

Let a and b be the two quantities; A the arithmetic mean. Then since a, A, b are in A.P. we must have

$$b - A = A - a,$$

each being equal to the common difference;

whence $\qquad\qquad A = \dfrac{a + b}{2}.$

45. Between two given quantities it is always possible to insert any number of terms such that the whole series thus formed shall be in A.P.; and by an extension of the definition in Art. 43, the terms thus inserted are called the *arithmetic means.*

Example. Insert 20 arithmetic means between 4 and 67.

Including the extremes, the number of terms will be 22; so that we have to find a series of 22 terms in A.P., of which 4 is the first and 67 the last.

Let d be the common difference;

then $\qquad\qquad 67 = $ the 22nd term $= 4 + 21d;$

whence $\qquad d = 3$, and the series is $4, 7, 10, \ldots\ldots, 61, 64, 67;$

and the required means are $7, 10, 13, \ldots\ldots, 58, 61, 64.$

46. *To insert a given number of arithmetic means between two given quantities.*

Let a and b be the given quantities, n the number of means.

Including the extremes the number of terms will be $n + 2$; so that we have to find a series of $n + 2$ terms in A.P., of which a is the first, and b is the last.

Let d be the common difference;

then $\qquad\qquad b = $ the $(n + 2)^{\text{th}}$ term

$\qquad\qquad\qquad = a + (n + 1) d;$

whence $\qquad\qquad d = \dfrac{b - a}{n + 1};$

and the required means are

$$a + \frac{b-a}{n+1}, a + \frac{2(b-a)}{n+1}, \ldots, a + \frac{n(b-a)}{n+1}.$$

Example 1. The sum of three numbers in A.P. is 27, and the sum of their squares is 293 ; find them.

Let a be the middle number, d the common difference ; then the three numbers are $a-d, a, a+d$.

Hence $a - d + a + a + d = 27$;

whence $a = 9$, and the three numbers are $9 - d, 9, 9 + d$.

$\therefore$ $(9-d)^2 + 81 + (9+d)^2 = 293$;

whence $d = \pm 5$;

and the numbers are 4, 9, 14.

Example 2. Find the sum of the first p terms of the series whose n^{th} term is $3n - 1$.

By putting $n = 1$, and $n = p$ respectively, we obtain

$$\text{first term} = 2, \text{ last term} = 3p - 1;$$

$\therefore$ $\text{sum} = \frac{p}{2}(2 + 3p - 1) = \frac{p}{2}(3p + 1).$

EXAMPLES IV. a.

1. Sum $2, 3\frac{1}{4}, 4\frac{1}{2}, \ldots$ to 20 terms.

2. Sum $49, 44, 39, \ldots$ to 17 terms.

3. Sum $\frac{3}{4}, \frac{2}{3}, \frac{7}{12}, \ldots$ to 19 terms.

4. Sum $3, \frac{7}{3}, 1\frac{2}{3}, \ldots$ to n terms.

5. Sum $3.75, 3.5, 3.25, \ldots$ to 16 terms.

6. Sum $-7\frac{1}{2}, -7, -6\frac{1}{2}, \ldots$ to 24 terms.

7. Sum $1.3, -3.1, -7.5, \ldots$ to 10 terms.

8. Sum $\frac{6}{\sqrt{3}}, 3\sqrt{3}, \frac{12}{\sqrt{3}}, \ldots$ to 50 terms.

9. Sum $\frac{3}{\sqrt{5}}, \frac{4}{\sqrt{5}}, \sqrt{5}, \ldots$ to 25 terms.

10. Sum $a - 3b, 2a - 5b, 3a - 7b, \ldots$ to 40 terms.

11. Sum $2a - b, 4a - 3b, 6a - 5b, \ldots$ to n terms.

12. Sum $\frac{a+b}{2}, a, \frac{3a-b}{2}, \ldots$ to 21 terms.

13. Insert 19 arithmetic means between $\frac{1}{4}$ and $-9\frac{3}{4}$.

14. Insert 17 arithmetic means between $3\frac{1}{2}$ and $-41\frac{1}{2}$.

15. Insert 18 arithmetic means between $-35x$ and $3x$.

16. Insert x arithmetic means between x^2 and 1.

17. Find the sum of the first n odd numbers.

18. In an A.P. the first term is 2, the last term 29, the sum 155 ; find the difference.

19. The sum of 15 terms of an A.P. is 600, and the common difference is 5 ; find the first term.

20. The third term of an A.P. is 18, and the seventh term is 30 ; find the sum of 17 terms.

21. The sum of three numbers in A.P. is 27, and their product is 504 ; find them.

22. The sum of three numbers in A.P. is 12, and the sum of their cubes is 408 ; find them.

23. Find the sum of 15 terms of the series whose n^{th} term is $4n + 1$.

24. Find the sum of 35 terms of the series whose p^{th} term is $\frac{p}{7} + 2$.

25. Find the sum of p terms of the series whose n^{th} term is $\frac{n}{a} + b$.

26. Find the sum of n terms of the series

$$\frac{2a^2 - 1}{a}, \ 4a - \frac{3}{a}, \ \frac{6a^2 - 5}{a}, \ \dots$$

---

47. In an Arithmetical Progression when s, a, d are given to determine the values of n we have the quadratic equation

$$s = \frac{n}{2}\{2a + (n-1)\,d\} ;$$

When both roots are positive and integral there is no difficulty in interpreting the result corresponding to each. In some cases a suitable interpretation can be given for a negative value of n.

Example. How many terms of the series $-9, -6, -3, \dots$ must be taken that the sum may be 66 ?

Here $\dfrac{n}{2} \{-18 + (n-1)\,3\} = 66$;

that is, $n^2 - 7n - 44 = 0$,

or $(n-11)(n+4) = 0$;

$\therefore$ $n = 11$ or -4.

If we take 11 terms of the series, we have

$$-9, -6, -3, 0, 3, 6, 9, 12, 15, 18, 21;$$

the sum of which is 66.

If be begin at the *last* of these terms and *count backwards* four terms, the sum is also 66; and thus, although the negative solution does not directly answer the question proposed, we are enabled to give it an intelligible meaning, and we see that it answers a question closely connected with that to which the positive solution applies.

48.   We can justify this interpretation in the general case in the following way.

The equation to determine n is

$$dn^2 + (2a-d)\,n - 2s = 0 \qquad \qquad \dots(1)$$

Since in the case under discussion the roots of this equation have opposite signs, let us denote them by n_1 and $-n_2$. The last term of the series corresponding to n_1 is

$$a + (n_1 - 1)\,d ;$$

if we begin at this term and count *backwards,* the common difference must be denoted by $-d$, and the sum of n_2 terms is

$$\dfrac{n_2}{2} \{2\,(a + \overline{n_1 - 1}\,d) + (n_2 - 1)\,(-d)\} ,$$

and we shall shew that this is equal to s.

For the expression $= \dfrac{n_2}{2} \{2a + (2n_1 - n_2 - 1)\,d\}$

$$= \dfrac{1}{2} \{2an_2 + 2n_1\,n_2 d - n_2\,(n_2 + 1)\,d\}$$

$$= \dfrac{1}{2} \{2n_1\,n_2 d \cdot (d.n_2^2 - 2a - d.n_2)\}$$

$$= \dfrac{1}{2} (4s - 2s) = s,$$

since $-n_2$ satisfies $dn^2 + (2a-d)\,n - 2s = 0$, and $-n_1\,n_2$ is the product of the roots of this equation.

49.   When the value of n is fractional there is no exact number of terms which corresponds to such a solution.

Example : How many terms of the series 26, 21, 16,... must be taken to amount to 74 ?

Here
$$\frac{n}{2}\{52 + (n-1)(-5)\} = 74,$$

that is,
$$5n^2 - 57n + 148 = 0,$$

or
$$(n - 4)(5n - 37) = 0 ;$$

∴
$$n = 4 \text{ or } 7\frac{2}{5}.$$

Thus the number of terms is 4. It will be found that the sum of 7 terms is greater, while the sum of 8 terms is less than 74.

50.   We add some Miscellaneous Examples.

Example 1. The sums of n terms of two arithmetic series are in the ratio of $7n + 1 : 4n + 27$; find the ratio of their 11th terms.

Let the first term and common difference of the two series be a_1, d_1 and a_2, d_2 respectively.

We have
$$\frac{2a_1 + (n-1)d_1}{2a_2 + (n-1)d_2} = \frac{7n+1}{4n+27}.$$

Now we have to find the value of $\dfrac{a_1 + 10d_1}{a_2 + 10d_2}$; hence, by putting $n = 21$, we obtain
$$\frac{2a_1 + 20d_1}{2a_2 + 20d_2} = \frac{148}{111} = \frac{4}{3} ;$$

thus the required ratio 4 : 3.

Example 2. If $S_1, S_2, S_3, ..., S_p$ are the sums of n terms of arithmetic series whose first terms are 1, 2, 3, 4,... and whose common differences are 1, 3, 5, 7, ... ; find the value of
$$S_1 + S_2 + S_3 + ... + S_p.$$

We have
$$S_1 = \frac{n}{2}\{2 + (n-1)\} = \frac{n(n+1)}{2},$$

$$S_2 = \frac{n}{2}\{4 + (n-1)3\} = \frac{n(3n+1)}{2},$$

$$S_3 = \frac{n}{2}\{6 + (n-1)5\} = \frac{n(5n+1)}{2},$$

$$S_p = \frac{n}{2}\{2p + (n-1)(2p-1)\} = \frac{n}{2}\{(2p-1)n + 1\} ;$$

∴ the required sum
$$= \frac{n}{2}\{(n+1) + (3n+1) + ... \overline{(2p-1}\cdot n + 1)\}$$

$$= \frac{n}{2}\{(n + 3n + 5n + ... \overline{2p-1}\cdot n) + p\}$$

$$= \frac{n}{2} \{n(1 + 3 + 5 + \dots \overline{2p-1}) + p\}$$

$$= \frac{n}{2}(np^2 + p)$$

$$= \frac{np}{2}(np + 1).$$

EXAMPLES IV. b.

1. Given $a = -2$, $d = 4$ and $s = 160$, find n.

2. How many terms of the series 12, 16, 20, ... must be taken to make 208 ?

3. In an A.P. the third term is four times the first term, and the sixth term is 17 ; find the series.

4. The 2nd, 31st and last terms of an A.P. are $7\frac{3}{4}$, $\frac{1}{2}$ and $-6\frac{1}{2}$ respectively ; find the first term and the number of terms.

5. The 4th, 42nd, and last terms of an A.P. are 0, -95 and -125 respectively ; find the term and the number of terms.

6. A man arranges to pay off a debt of £3600 by 40 annual instalments which form an arithmetic series. When 30 of the instalments are paid he dies leaving a third of the debt unpaid; find the value of the first instalment.

7. Between two numbers whose sum is $2\frac{1}{6}$ an even number of arithmetic means is inserted ; the sum of these means exceeds their number by unity : how many means are there ?

8. The sum of n terms of series 2, 5, 8, ... is 950; find n.

9. Sum the series $\frac{1}{1 + \sqrt{x}}$, $\frac{1}{1 - x}$, $\frac{1}{1 - \sqrt{x}}$, ... to n terms.

10. If the sum of 7 terms is 49, and the sum of 17 terms is 289, find the sum of n terms.

11. If the pth, q^{th}, r^{th} terms of an A.P. are a, b, c respectively, shew that
$$(q - r)a + (r - p)b + (p - q)c = 0.$$

12. The sum of p terms of an A.P. is q, and the sum of q terms is p ; find the sum of $p + q$ terms.

13. The sum of four integers in A.P. is 24, and their product is 945 ; find them.

14. Divide 20 into four parts which are in A.P., and such that the product of the first and fourth is to the product of the second and third in the ratio of 2 to 3.

15. The pth term of an A.P. is q, and the qth term is p ; find the mth term.

16. How many term of the series 9, 12, 15, ... must be taken to make 306 ?

17. If the sum of n terms of an A.P. is $2n + 3n^2$, find the rth term.

18. If the sum of m terms of an A.P. is to the sum of n terms as m^2 to n^2, shew that the mth term is to the nth term as $2m - 1$ is to $2n - 1$.

19. Prove that the sum of an odd number of terms in A.P. is equal to the middle term multiplied by the number of terms.

20. If $s = n (5n - 3)$ for all values of n, find the pth term.

21. The number of terms in an A.P. is even ; the sum of the odd terms is 24, of the even terms 30, and the last term exceeds the first by $10 \frac{1}{2}$: find the number of terms.

22. There are two sets of numbers each consisting of 3 terms in A.P. and the sum of each set is 15. The common difference of the first set is greater by 1 than the common difference of the second set, and the product of the first set is to the product of the second set as 7 to 8; find the numbers.

23. Find the relation between x and y in order that the rth mean between x and $2y$ may be the same as the rth mean between $2x$ and y, n means being inserted in each case.

24. If the sum of an A.P. is the same for p as for q terms, shew that its sum for $p + q$ terms is zero.

■■■

Chapter 5

GEOMETRICAL PROGRESSION

51. Definition : Quantities are said to be in **Geometrical Progression** when they increase or decrease by a *constant factor*.

Thus each of the following series forms a Geometrical Progression :

$$3, 6, 12, 24, \ldots\ldots$$

$$1, -\frac{1}{3}, \frac{1}{9}, -\frac{1}{27}, \ldots\ldots$$

$$a, ar, ar^2, ar^3, \ldots\ldots$$

The constant factor is also called the *common ratio,* and it is found by dividing *any* term by that which immediately *precedes* it. In the first of the above examples the common ratio is 2, in the second it is $-\frac{1}{3}$; in the third it is r.

52. If we examine the series

$$a, ar, ar^2, ar^3, ar^4, \ldots$$

we notice that in *any term the index of r is always less by one than the number of the term in the series.*

Thus   the 3rd term is ar^2;

the 6th term is ar^5;

the 20th term is ar^{19};

and, generally, the pth term is ar^{p-1}.

If n be the number of terms, and if l denote the last, or n^{th} term, we have

$$l = ar^{n-1}$$

53. Definition : When three quantities are in Geometrical Progression, the middle one is called the geometric mean between the other two.

To find the geometric mean between two given quantities.

Let a and b be the two quantities, G the geometric mean. Then since a, G, b are in GP,

$$\frac{b}{G} = \frac{G}{a},$$

each being equal to the common ratio;

$$\therefore \qquad\qquad G^2 = ab;$$

whence $\qquad\qquad G = \sqrt{ab}$.

54. *To insert a given number of geometric means between two given quantities.*

Let a and b be the given quantities, n the number of means.

In all there will be $n + 2$ terms; so that we have to find a series of $n + 2$ terms in G.P., of which a is the first and b the last.

Let r be the common ratio;

then $\qquad\qquad b =$ the $(n + 2)^{\text{th}}$ term

$$= ar^{n+1};$$

$$\therefore \qquad\qquad r^{n+1} = \frac{b}{a};$$

$$\therefore \qquad\qquad r = \left(\frac{b}{a}\right)^{\frac{1}{n+1}}. \qquad\qquad \ldots(1)$$

Hence the required means are $ar, ar^2, \ldots ar^n$, where r has the value found in (1).

Example: Insert 4 geometric means between 160 and 5.

We have to find 6 terms in G.P. of which 160 is the first, and 5 the sixth.

Let r be the common ratio;

then $5 =$ the sixth term

$$= 160r^5;$$

$$\therefore \qquad\qquad r^5 = \frac{1}{32};$$

whence $\quad r = \frac{1}{2};$

and the means are 80, 40, 20, 10.

55. *To find the sum of a number of terms in Geometrical Progression.*

Let a be the first term, r the common ratio, n the number of terms, and s the sum required. Then

$$s = a + ar + ar^2 + \ldots + ar^{n-2} + ar^{n-1};$$

multiplying every term by r, we have

$$rs = ar + ar^2 + \ldots + ar^{n-2} + ar^{n-1} + ar^n.$$

Hence by subtraction,

$$rs - s = ar^n - a;$$

$$\therefore \qquad\qquad (r - 1)s = a(r^n - 1);$$

$$\therefore \qquad s = \frac{a\,(r^n - 1)}{r - 1}. \qquad \qquad \ldots(1)$$

Changing the signs in numerator and denominator,

$$s = \frac{a\,(1 - r^n)}{1 - r}. \qquad \qquad \ldots(2)$$

Note : It will be found convenient to remember both forms given above for s, using (2) in all cases except when r is *positive and greater than 1*.

Since $ar^{n-1} = l$, the formula (1) may be written

$$s = \frac{rl - a}{r - 1};$$

a form which is sometimes useful.

Example : Sum the series $\dfrac{2}{3}$, -1, $\dfrac{3}{2}$, ... to 7 terms.

The common ratio $= -\dfrac{3}{2}$; hence by formula (2)

$$\text{the sum} = \frac{\dfrac{2}{3}\left\{1 - \left(-\dfrac{3}{2}\right)^7\right\}}{1 + \dfrac{3}{2}}$$

$$= \frac{\dfrac{2}{3}\left\{1 + \dfrac{2187}{128}\right\}}{\dfrac{5}{2}} = \frac{2}{3} \times \frac{2315}{128} \times \frac{2}{5}$$

$$= \frac{463}{96}.$$

56. Consider the series 1, $\dfrac{1}{2}$, $\dfrac{1}{2^2}$, $\dfrac{1}{2^3}$, ...

$$\text{The sum to } n \text{ terms} = \frac{1 - \dfrac{1}{2^n}}{1 - \dfrac{1}{2}}$$

$$= 2\left(1 - \frac{1}{2^n}\right) = 2 - \frac{1}{2^{n-1}}.$$

From this result it appears that however many terms be taken the sum of the above series is always less than 2. Also we see that, by making n sufficiently large, we can make the fraction $\dfrac{1}{2^{n-1}}$ as small as we please. Thus by taking a suficient number of terms the sum can be made to differ by as little as we please from 2.

In the next article a more general case is discussed.

57. From Art. 55 we have $s = \dfrac{a(1 - r^n)}{1 - r}$

$$= \frac{a}{1 - r} - \frac{ar^n}{1 - r}.$$

Suppose r is a proper fraction; then the greater the value of n the smaller is the value of r^n, and consequently of $\dfrac{ar^n}{1 - r}$; and therefore by making n sufficiently large, we can make the sum of n terms of the series differ from $\dfrac{a}{1 - r}$ by as small a quantity as we please.

This result is usually stated thus *the sum of an infinite number of terms of a decreasing Geometrical Progression is* $\dfrac{a}{1 - r}$; *or more briefly, the sum to infinity is* $\dfrac{a}{1 - r}$.

Example 1. Find three numbers in G.P. whose sum is 19, and whose product is 216.

Denote the numbers by $\dfrac{a}{r}$, a, ar; then $\dfrac{a}{r} \times a \times ar = 216$; hence $a = 6$, and the numbers are $\dfrac{6}{r}$, 6, 6r.

$$\therefore \qquad \frac{6}{r} + 6 + 6r = 19;$$

$$\therefore \qquad 6 - 13r + 6r^2 = 0;$$

whence $r = \dfrac{3}{2}$ or $\dfrac{2}{3}$.

Thus the numbers are 4, 6, 9.

Example 2. The sum of an infinite number of terms in G.P. is 15, and the sum of their squares is 45; find the series.

Let a denote the first term, r the common ratio; then the sum of the terms is $\dfrac{a}{1 - r}$; and the sum of their squares is $\dfrac{a^2}{1 - r^2}$.

Hence $\qquad\qquad \dfrac{a}{1 - r} = 15, \qquad\qquad$ ...(1)

$$\frac{a^2}{1 - r^2} = 45. \qquad\qquad \text{...(2)}$$

Dividing (2) by (1) $\dfrac{a}{1+r} = 3,$ ...(3)

and from (1) and (3) $\dfrac{1+r}{1-r} = 5;$

whence $r = \dfrac{2}{3}$, and therefore $a = 5$.

Thus the series is $5, \dfrac{10}{3}, \dfrac{20}{9}, ...$

EXAMPLES V. a.

1.   Sum $\dfrac{1}{2}, \dfrac{1}{3}, \dfrac{2}{9}, ...$ to 7 terms.

2.   Sum $-2, 2\dfrac{1}{2}, -3\dfrac{1}{8}, ...$ to 6 terms.

3.   Sum $\dfrac{3}{4}, 1\dfrac{1}{2}, 3, ...$ to 8 terms.

4.   Sum $2, -4, 8, ...$ to 10 terms.

5.   Sum $16.2, 5.4, 1.8, ...$ to 7 terms.

6.   Sum $1, 5, 25, ...$ to p terms.

7.   Sum $3, -4, \dfrac{16}{3}, ...$ to $2n$ terms.

8.   Sum $1, \sqrt{3}, 3, ...$ to 12 terms.

9.   Sum $\dfrac{1}{\sqrt{2}}, -2, \dfrac{8}{\sqrt{2}}, ...$ to 7 terms.

10. Sum $-\dfrac{1}{3}, \dfrac{1}{2}, -\dfrac{3}{4}, ...$ to 7 terms.

11. Insert 3 geometric means between $2\dfrac{1}{4}$ and $\dfrac{4}{9}$.

12. Insert 5 geometric means between $3\dfrac{5}{9}$ and $40\dfrac{1}{2}$.

13. Insert 6 geometric means between 14 and $-\dfrac{7}{64}$.

Find the sum of the following series to infinity :

14. $\dfrac{8}{5}, -1, \dfrac{5}{8}, ...$

15. $.45, .015, .0005, ...$

16. $1.665, -1.11, .74, ...$

17. $3^{-1}, 3^{-2}, 3^{-3}, ...$

18. $3, \sqrt{3}, 1, ...$

19. $7, \sqrt{42}, 6, \ldots$

20. The sum of the first 6 terms of a G.P. is 9 times the sum of the first 3 terms; find the common ratio.

21. The fifth term of a G.P. is 81, and the second term is 24; find the series.

22. The sum of a G.P. whose common ratio is 3 is 728, and the last term is 486; find the first term.

23. In a G.P. the first term is 7, the last term 448, and the sum 889; find the common ratio.

24. The sum of three numbers in G.P. is 38, and their product is 1728; find them.

25. The continued product of three numbers in G.P. is 216, and the sum of the products of them in pairs is 156; find the numbers.

26. If S_p denote the sum of the series $1 + r^p + r^{2p} + \ldots$ *ad inf.*, and s_p the sum of the series $1 - r^p + r^{2p} - \ldots$ *ad inf.*, prove that
$$S_p + s_p = 2S_{2p}.$$

27. If the pth, q^{th}, r^{th} terms of a G.P. be a, b, c respectively, prove that
$$a^{q-r} b^{r-p} c^{p-q} = 1.$$

28. The sum of an infinite number of terms of a G.P. is 4 and the sum of their cubes is 192; find the series.

58. Recurring decimals furnish a good illustration of infinite Geometrical Progressions.

Example : Find the value of $0.4\overset{..}{2}\overset{.}{3}$.

$$0.4\overset{..}{2}\overset{.}{3} = 0.4232323\ldots$$

$$= \frac{4}{10} + \frac{23}{1000} + \frac{23}{100000} + \ldots$$

$$= \frac{4}{10} + \frac{23}{10^3} + \frac{23}{10^5} + \ldots;$$

that is, $\quad 0.4\overset{..}{2}\overset{.}{3} = \frac{4}{10} + \frac{23}{10^3}\left(1 + \frac{1}{10^2} + \frac{1}{10^4} + \ldots\right)$

$$= \frac{4}{10} + \frac{23}{10^3} \cdot \frac{1}{1 - \dfrac{1}{10^2}}$$

$$= \frac{4}{10} + \frac{23}{10^3} \cdot \frac{100}{99}$$

$$= \frac{4}{10} + \frac{23}{990}$$

$$= \frac{419}{990},$$

which agrees with the values found by the usual arithmetical rule.

59. The general rule for reducing any recurring decimal to a vulgar fraction may be proved by the method employed in the last example; but it is easier to proceed as follows.

To find the value of a recurring decimal.

Let P denote the figures which do not recur, and suppose them p in number; let Q denote the recurring period consisting of q figures; let D denote the value of the recurring decimal; then

$$D = 0.PQQQ \ldots;$$

$$\therefore \qquad 10^p \times D = P.QQQ \ldots;$$

and $\qquad\qquad 10^{p+q} \times D = PQ.QQQ \ldots;$

therefore, by subtraction, $(10^{p+q} - 10^p) D = PQ - P;$

that is, $10^p (10^q - 1) D = PQ - P;$

$$\therefore \qquad\qquad D = \frac{PQ - P}{(10^q - 1) 10^p}.$$

Now $10^q - 1$ is a number consisting of q nines; therefore the denominator consists of q nines followed by p ciphers. Hence we have the following rule for reducing a recurring decimal to a vulgar fraction :

For the numerator subtract the integral number consisting of the non-recurring figures from the integral number consisting of the non-recurring and recurring figures; for the denominator take a number consisting of as many nines as there are recurring figures followed by as many ciphers as there are non-recurring figures.

60. *To find the sum of n terms of the series*

$$a, (a + d) r, (a + 2d) r^2, (a + 3d) r^3, \ldots$$

in which each term is the product of corresponding terms in an arithmetic and geometric series.

Denote the sum by S; then

$$S = a + (a + d) r + (a + 2d) r^2 + \ldots + (a + \overline{n-1}\, d) r^{n-1};$$

$$\therefore \quad rS = ar + (a + d) r^2 + \ldots + (a + \overline{n-2}d) r^{n-1} + (a + \overline{n-1}d) r^n.$$

By subtraction,

$$S (1 - r) = a + (dr + dr^2 + \ldots + dr^{n-1}) - (a + \overline{n-1}d) r^n$$

$$= a + \frac{dr(1 - r^{n-1})}{1 - r} - (a + \overline{n-1}d)\, r^n;$$

$$\therefore \quad S = \frac{a}{1 - r} + \frac{dr(1 - r^{n-1})}{(1 - r)^2} - \frac{(a + \overline{n-1}d)\, r^n}{1 - r},$$

Cor. Write S in the form

$$\frac{a}{1 - r} + \frac{dr}{(1 - r)^2} - \frac{dr^n}{(1 - r)^2} - \frac{(a + \overline{n-1}d)\, r^n}{1 - r};$$

then if $r < 1$, we can make r^n as small as we please by taking n sufficiently great. In this case, *assuming that all the terms which inverse r^n can be made so small that they may be neglected*, we obtain $\dfrac{a}{1 - r} + \dfrac{dr}{(1 - r)^2}$ for the sum to infinity. We shall refer to this point again in Chap. 21.

In summing to infinity series of this class it is usually best to proceed as in the following example.

Example 1. If $x < 1$, find the sum of the series

$$1 + 2x + 3x^2 + 4x^3 + \dots \text{ to infinity.}$$

Let
$$S = 1 + 2x + 3x^2 + 4x^3 + \dots;$$

$$\therefore \quad xS = x + 2x^2 + 3x^3 + \dots;$$

$$\therefore \quad S(1 - x) = 1 + x + x^2 + x^3 + \dots$$

$$= \frac{1}{1 - x};$$

$$\therefore \quad S = \frac{1}{(1 - x)^2}.$$

Example 2. Sum the series $1 + \dfrac{4}{5} + \dfrac{7}{5^2} + \dfrac{10}{5^3} + \dots$ to n terms.

Let
$$S = 1 + \frac{4}{5} + \frac{7}{5^2} + \frac{10}{5^3} + \dots + \frac{3n - 2}{5^{n-1}};$$

$$\therefore \quad \frac{1}{5}S = \frac{1}{5} + \frac{4}{5^2} + \frac{7}{5^3} + \dots + \frac{3n - 5}{5^{n-1}} + \frac{3n - 2}{5^n};$$

$$\therefore \quad \frac{4}{5}S = 1 + \left(\frac{3}{5} + \frac{3}{5^2} + \frac{3}{5^3} + \dots + \frac{3}{5^{n-1}} \right) - \frac{3n - 2}{5^n}$$

$$= 1 + \frac{3}{5} \left(1 + \frac{1}{5} + \frac{1}{5^2} + \dots + \frac{1}{5^{n-2}} \right) - \frac{3n - 2}{5^n}$$

$$= 1 + \frac{3}{5} \cdot \frac{1 - \dfrac{1}{5^{n-1}}}{1 - \dfrac{1}{5}} - \frac{3n - 2}{5^n}$$

$$= 1 + \frac{3}{4}\left(1 - \frac{1}{5^{n-1}}\right) - \frac{3n-2}{5^n}$$

$$= \frac{7}{4} - \frac{12n+7}{4 \cdot 5^n};$$

$$\therefore \quad S = \frac{35}{16} - \frac{12n+7}{16 \cdot 5^{n-1}}.$$

EXAMPLES V. b.

1. Sum $1 + 2a + 3a^2 + 4a^3 + \dots$ to n terms.

2. Sum $1 + \frac{3}{4} + \frac{7}{16} + \frac{15}{64} + \frac{31}{256} + \dots$ to infinity.

3. Sum $1 + 3x + 5x^2 + 7x^3 + 9x^4 + \dots$ to infinity, x being < 1.

4. Sum $1 + \frac{2}{2} + \frac{3}{2^2} + \frac{4}{2^3} + \dots$ to n terms.

5. Sum $1 + \frac{3}{2} + \frac{5}{4} + \frac{7}{8} + \dots$ to infinity.

6. Sum $1 + 3x + 6x^2 + 10x^3 + \dots$ to infinity, x being < 1.

7. Prove that the $(n+1)$th term of a G.P., of which the first term is a and the third term b, is equal to the $(2n+1)$th term of a G.P. of which the first term is a and the fifth term b.

8. The sum of $2n$ terms of a G.P. whose first term is a and common ratio r is equal to the sum of n of a G.P. whose first term is b and common ratio r^2. Prove that b is equal to the sum of the first two terms of the first series.

9. Find the sum of the infinite series
   $$1 + (1+b)\,r + (1+b+b^2)\,r^2 + (1+b+b^2+b^3)\,r^3 + \dots,$$
   r and b being proper fractions.

10. The sum of three numbers in G.P. is 70; if the two extremes be multiplied each by 4, and the mean by 5, the products are in A.P., find the numbers.

11. The first two terms of an infinite G.P. are together equal to 5, and every term is 3 times the sum of all the terms that follow it; find the series.

    Sum the following series :

12. $x + a,\ x^2 + 2a,\ x^3 + 3a \dots$ to n terms.

13. $x(x+y) + x^2(x^2+y^2) + x^3(x^3+y^3) + \ldots$ to n terms.

14. $a + \dfrac{1}{3}, 3a - \dfrac{1}{6}, 5a + \dfrac{1}{12} + \ldots$ to $2p$ terms.

15. $\dfrac{2}{3} + \dfrac{3}{3^2} + \dfrac{2}{3^3} + \dfrac{3}{3^4} + \dfrac{2}{3^5} + \dfrac{3}{3^6} + \ldots$ to infinity.

16. $\dfrac{4}{7} - \dfrac{5}{7^2} + \dfrac{4}{7^3} - \dfrac{5}{7^4} + \dfrac{4}{7^5} - \dfrac{5}{7^6} + \ldots$ to infinity.

17. If a, b, c, d be in G.P., prove that
$$(b-c)^2 + (c-a)^2 + (d-b)^2 = (a-d)^2.$$

18. If the arithmetic mean between a and b is twice as great as the geometric mean, shew that $a : b = 2 + \sqrt{3} : 2 - \sqrt{3}$.

19. Find the sum of n terms of the series, the rth terms of which is
$$(2r+1)\,2^r.$$

20. Find the sum of $2n$ terms of a series of which every even term is a times the term before it, and every odd term c times the term before it, the first term being unity.

21. If S_n denote the sum of n terms of a G.P. whose first term is a, and common ratio r, find the sum of $S_1, S_3, S_5, \ldots, S_{2n-1}$.

22. If $S_1, S_2, S_3, \ldots, S_p$ are the sums of infinite geometric series, whose first terms are $1, 2, 3, \ldots, p$, and whose common ratios are
$$\dfrac{1}{2}, \dfrac{1}{3}, \dfrac{1}{4}, \cdots \dfrac{1}{p+1} \text{ respectively,}$$
prove that $S_1 + S_2 + S_3 + \ldots + S_p = \dfrac{p}{2}(p+3)$.

23. If $r < 1$ and positive and m is a positive integer, shew that $(2m+1)\,r^m\,(1-r) < 1 - r^{2m+1}$.

Hence shew that nr^n is indefinitely small when n is indefinitely great.

■ ■ ■

Chapter 6

HARMONICAL PROGRESSION. THEOREMS CONNECTED WITH THE PROGRESSIONS.

61. Definition : Three quantities a, b, c are said to be in **Harmonical Progression** when $\dfrac{a}{c} = \dfrac{a-b}{b-c}$.

Any number of quantities are said to be in Harmonical Progression when every three consecutive terms are in Harmonical Progression.

62. *The reciprocals of quantities in Harmonical Progression are in Arithmetical Progression.*

By definition, if a, b, c are in Harmonical Progression,

$$\frac{a}{c} = \frac{a-b}{b-c};$$

∴ $$a(b-c) = c(a-b),$$

dividing every term by abc,

$$\frac{1}{c} - \frac{1}{b} = \frac{1}{b} - \frac{1}{a},$$

which proves the proposition.

63. Harmonical properties are chiefly interesting because of their importance in Geometry and in the Theory of Sound; in Algebra the proposition just proved is the only one of any importance. There is no general formula for the sum of any number of quantities in Harmonical Progression. Questions in H.P. are generally solved by inverting the terms, and making use of the properties of the corresponding AP.

64. *To find the harmonic mean between two given quantities.*

Let a, b be the two quantities, H their harmonic mean; then $\dfrac{1}{a}, \dfrac{1}{H}, \dfrac{1}{b}$ are in A.P.;

∴ $$\frac{1}{H} - \frac{1}{a} = \frac{1}{b} - \frac{1}{H},$$

$$\frac{2}{H} = \frac{1}{a} + \frac{1}{b},$$

$$H = \frac{2ab}{a+b}.$$

Example : Insert 40 harmonic means between 7 and $\frac{1}{6}$.

Here 6 is the 42nd term of an A.P. whose first term is $\frac{1}{7}$; let d be the common difference; then

$$6 = \frac{1}{7} + 41d; \text{ whence } d = \frac{1}{7}.$$

Thus the arithmetic means are $\frac{2}{7}, \frac{3}{7}, \ldots, \frac{41}{7}$; and therefore the harmonic

means are $3\frac{1}{2}, 2\frac{1}{3}, \ldots, \frac{7}{41}$.

65. If A, G, H be the arithmetic, geometric, and harmonic means between a and b, we have proved

$$A = \frac{a+b}{2} \qquad \qquad \text{...(1)}$$

$$G = \sqrt{ab} \qquad \qquad \text{...(2)}$$

$$H = \frac{2ab}{a+b} \qquad \qquad \text{...(3)}$$

Therefore $\qquad AH = \frac{a+b}{2} \cdot \frac{2ab}{a+b} = ab = G^2;$

that is, G is the geometric mean between A and H.

From these results we see that

$$A - G = \frac{a+b}{2} - \sqrt{ab} = \frac{a+b-2\sqrt{ab}}{2} = \left(\frac{\sqrt{a}-\sqrt{b}}{\sqrt{2}} \right)^2;$$

which is positive if a and b are positive' therefore *the arithmetic mean of any two positive quantities is greater than their geometric mean.*

Also from the equation $G^2 = AH$, we see that G is intermediate in value between A and H; and it has been proved that $A > G$, therefore $G > H$; that is, *the arithmetic, geometric, and harmonic means between any two positive quantities are in descending order of magnitude.*

66. Miscellaneous questions in the Progressions afford scope for skill and ingenuity, the solution being often neatly effected by some special artifice. The student will find the following hints useful.

1. If the same quantity be added to, or subtracted from, all the terms of an A.P., the resulting terms will form an A.P., with the same common difference as before. [Art. 38.]

2. If all the terms of an A.P., be multiplied or divided by the same quantity, the resulting terms will form an A.P., but with a new common difference. [Art. 38.]

3. If all the terms of a G.P. be multiplied or divided by the same quantity, the resulting terms will form a G.P. with the same common ratio as before. [Art. 51.]

4. If $a, b, c, d, \ldots$ are in G.P., they are also in *continued proportion*, since, by definition,

$$\frac{a}{b} = \frac{b}{c} = \frac{c}{d} = \ldots = \frac{1}{r}.$$

Conversely, a series of quantities in continued proportion may be represented by $x, xr, xr^2, \ldots$.

Example 1. If a^2, b^2, c^2 are in A.P., shew that $b + c, c + a, a + b$ are in H.P.

By adding $ab + ac + bc$ to each term, we see that

$$a^2 + ab + ac + bc, \ b^2 + ba + bc + ac, \ c^2 + ca + cb + ab \text{ are in A.P.,}$$

that is $(a + b)(a + c), (b + c)(b + a), (c + a)(c + b)$ are in A.P.,

$\therefore$ dividing each term by $(a + b)(b + c)(c + a)$,

$$\frac{1}{b+c}, \frac{1}{c+a}, \frac{1}{a+b} \text{ are in A.P.,}$$

that is, $b + c, c + a, a + b$ are in H.P.,

Example 2. If l the last term, d the common difference, and s the sum of n terms of an A.P. be connected by the equation $8ds = (d + 2l)^2$, prove that $d = 2a$.

Since the given relation is true for any number of terms, put $n = 1$; then

$$a = l = s.$$

Hence by substitution, $8ad = (d + 2a)^2$,

or $(d - 2a)^2 = 0;$

$\therefore$ $d = 2a.$

Example 3. If the pth, qth, rth, sth terms of an A.P. are in G.P., show that $p - q, q - r, r - s$ are in G.P.

With the usual notation we have

$$\frac{a + (p-1)d}{a + (q-1)d} = \frac{a + (q-1)d}{a + (r-1)d} = \frac{a + (r-1)d}{a + (s-1)d} \qquad \text{[Art. 66. (4)]}$$

$\therefore$ each of these ratios

$$= \frac{\{a + (p-1)d\} - \{a + (q-1)d\}}{\{a + (q-1)d\} - \{a + (r-1)d\}} = \frac{\{a + (q-1)d\} - \{a + (r-1)d\}}{\{a + (r-1)d\} - \{a + (s-1)d\}}$$

$$= \frac{p-q}{q-r} = \frac{q-r}{r-s}.$$

Hence $p - q, q - r, r - s$ are in G.P.

67. The numbers 1, 2, 3, ... are often referred to as the *natural numbers*; the nth term of the series is n, and the sum of the first n terms is $\dfrac{n}{2}(n+1)$.

68. *To find the sum of the squares of the first n natural numbers.*

Let the sum be denoted by S; then

$$S = 1^2 + 2^2 + 3^2 + \dots + n^2.$$

We have $n^3 - (n-1)^3 = 3n^2 - 3n + 1$;

and by changing n into $n-1$,

$$(n-1)^3 - (n-2)^3 = 3(n-1)^2 - 3(n-1) + 1;$$

similarly $(n-2)^3 - (n-3)^3 = 3(n-2)^2 - 3(n-2) + 1;$

$$\dots\dots\dots\dots\dots\dots\dots\dots\dots$$

$$3^3 - 2^3 = 3 \cdot 3^2 - 3 \cdot 3 + 1;$$

$$2^3 - 1^3 = 3 \cdot 2^2 - 3 \cdot 2 + 1;$$

$$1^3 - 0^3 = 3 \cdot 1^2 - 3 \cdot 1 + 1.$$

Hence, by addition,

$$n^3 = 3(1^2 + 2^2 + 3^2 + \dots + n^2) - 3(1 + 2 + 3 + \dots + n) + n$$

$$= 3S - \frac{3n(n+1)}{2} + n.$$

$\therefore \quad 3S = n^3 - n + \dfrac{3n(n+1)}{2}$

$$= n(n+1)(n-1+\tfrac{3}{2});$$

$\therefore \quad S = \dfrac{n(n+1)(2n+1)}{6}.$

69. *To find the sum of the cubes of the first n natural numbers.*

Let the sum be denoted by S; then

$$S = 1^3 + 2^3 + 3^3 + \dots + n^3.$$

We have $n^4 - (n-1)^4 = 4n^3 - 6n^2 + 4n - 1$;

$$(n-1)^4 - (n-2)^4 = 4(n-1)^3 - 6(n-1)^2 + 4(n-1) - 1;$$

$$(n-2)^4 - (n-3)^4 = 4(n-2)^3 - 6(n-2)^2 + 4(n-2) - 1;$$

$$\dots\dots\dots\dots\dots\dots\dots\dots\dots$$

$$3^4 - 2^4 = 4 \cdot 3^3 - 6 \cdot 3^2 + 4 \cdot 3 - 1;$$

$$2^4 - 1^4 = 4 \cdot 2^3 - 6 \cdot 2^2 + 4 \cdot 2 - 1;$$

$$1^4 - 0^4 = 4 \cdot 1^3 - 6 \cdot 1^2 + 4 \cdot 1 - 1.$$

Hence, by addition,

$$n^4 = 4S - 6(1^2 + 2^2 + \ldots + n^2) + 4(1 + 2 + \ldots + n) - n;$$

$$\therefore \quad 4S = n^4 + n + 6(1^2 + 2^2 + \ldots + n^2) - 4(1 + 2 + \ldots + n)$$

$$= n^4 + n + n(n + 1)(2n + 1) - 2n(n + 1)$$

$$= n(n + 1)(n^2 - n + 1 + 2n + 1 - 2)$$

$$= n(n + 1)(n^2 + n);$$

$$\therefore \quad S = \frac{n^2(n + 1)^2}{4} = \left(\frac{n(n + 1)}{2}\right)^2$$

Thus *the sum of the cubes of the first n natural numbers is equal to the square of the sum of these numbers.*

The formulae of this and the two preceding articles may be applied to find the sum of the squares, and the sum of the cubes of the terms of the series

$$a, a + d, a + 2d, \ldots$$

70. In referring to the results we have just proved it will be convenient to introduce a notation which the student will frequently meet with in Higher Mathematics. We shall denote the series.

$$1 + 2 + 3 + \ldots + n \qquad \text{by } \Sigma n;$$

$$1^2 + 2^2 + 3^2 + \ldots + n^2 \qquad \text{by } \Sigma n^2;$$

$$1^3 + 2^3 + 3^3 + \ldots + n^3 \qquad \text{by } \Sigma n^3;$$

where Σ placed before a term signifies the sum of all terms of which that term is the general type.

Example 1. Sum the series

$$1.2 + 2.3 + 3.4 + \ldots \text{ to } n \text{ terms.}$$

The nth term $= n(n + 1) = n^2 + n$; and by writing down each term in a similar form we shall have two columns, one consisting of the first n natural numbers, and the other of their squares.

$$\therefore \quad \text{the sum} = \Sigma n^2 + \Sigma n$$

$$= \frac{n(n + 1)(2n + 1)}{6} + \frac{n(n + 1)}{2}$$

$$= \frac{n(n + 1)}{2}\left\{\frac{2n + 1}{3} + 1\right\}$$

$$= \frac{n(n + 1)(n + 2)}{3}.$$

Example 2. Sum to n terms the series whose nth term is $2^{n-1} + 8n^3 - 6n^2$.

Let the sum be denoted by S; then

$$S = \Sigma 2^{n-1} + 8\Sigma n^3 - 6\Sigma n^2$$

$$= \frac{2^n - 1}{2 - 1} + \frac{8n^2 (n+1)^2}{4} - \frac{6n (n+1) (2n+1)}{6}$$

$$= 2^n - 1 + n (n+1) \{2n (n+1) - (2n+1)\}$$

$$= 2^n - 1 + n (n+1) (2n^2 - 1).$$

EXAMPLES VI. a.

1. Find the fourth term in each of the following series :

(1) $2, 2\frac{1}{2}, 3\frac{1}{3}, \ldots$

(2) $2, 2\frac{1}{2}, 3, \ldots$

(3) $2, 2\frac{1}{2}, 3\frac{1}{8}, \ldots$

2. Insert two harmonic means between 5 and 11.

3. Insert four harmonic means between $\frac{2}{3}$ and $\frac{2}{13}$.

4. If 12 and $9\frac{3}{5}$ are the geometric and harmonic means, respectively, between two numbers, find them.

5. If the harmonic mean between two quantities is to their geometric means as 12 to 13, prove that the quantities are in the ratio of 4 to 9.

6. If a, b, c be in H.P., shew that
$$a : a - b = a + c : a - c.$$

7. If the mth term of a H.P. be equal to n, and the nth term be equal to m, prove that the $(m + n)$th term is equal to $\frac{mn}{m + n}$.

8. If the pth, q^{th}, r^{th} terms of a H.P. be a, b, c respectively, prove that
$$(q - r) bc + (r - p) ca + (p - q) ab = 0.$$

9. If b is the harmonic mean between a and c, prove that
$$\frac{1}{b - a} + \frac{1}{b - c} = \frac{1}{a} + \frac{1}{c}.$$

Find the sum of n terms of the series whose n^{th} term is

10. $3n^2 - n.$ 11. $n^3 + \frac{3}{2} n.$ 12. $n (n + 2).$

13. $n^2 (2n + 3)$ 14. $3^n - 2^n.$ 15. $3 (4^n + 2n^2) - 4n^3.$

16. If the $(m + 1)^{th}$, $(n + 1)^{th}$, and $(r + 1)^{th}$ terms of an A.P. are in G.P., and m, n, r are in H.P., shew that the ratio of the common difference to the first term in the A.P. is $-\dfrac{2}{n}$.

17. If l, m, n are three numbers in G.P., prove that the first term of an A.P. whose l^{th}, m^{th}, and n^{th} terms are in H.P. is to the common difference as $m + 1$ to 1.

18. If the sum of n terms of a series be $a + bn + cn^2$, find the nth term and the nature of the series.

19. Find the sum of n terms of the series whose n^{th} term is
$$4n \, (n^2 + 1) - (6n^2 + 1).$$

20. If between any two quantities there be inserted two arithmetic means A_1, A_2; two geometric means G_1, G_2; and two harmonic means H_1, H_2; shew that $G_1 G_2 : H_1 H_2 = A_1 + A_2 : H_1 + H_2$.

21. If p be the first of n arithmetic means between two numbers, and q the first of n harmonic means between the same two numbers, prove that the value of q cannot lie between p and $\left(\dfrac{n+1}{n-1}\right)^2 p$.

22. Find the sum of the cubes of the terms of an A.P., and shew that it is exactly divisible by the sum of the terms.

Piles of Shot and Shells

71. *To find the number of shot arranged in a complete pyramid on a square base.*

Suppose that each side of the base contains n shot; then the number of shot in the lowest layer is n^2; in the next it is $(n - 1)^2$; in the next $(n - 2)^2$; and so on, up to a single shot at the top.

$\therefore$
$$S = n^2 + (n - 1)^2 + (n - 2)^2 + \ldots + 1$$
$$= \frac{n \, (n + 1) \, (2n + 1)}{6} \qquad \text{[Art. 68.]}$$

72. *To find the number of shot arranged in a complete pyramid the base of which is an equilateral triangle.*

Suppose that each side of the base contains n shot; then the number of shot in the lowest layer is

$$n + (n - 1) + (n - 2) + \ldots + 1;$$

that is, $\dfrac{n(n+1)}{2}$ or $\dfrac{1}{2}(n^2 + n)$.

In this result write $n - 1, n - 2, \ldots$ for n, and we thus obtain the number of shot in the 2nd, 3rd, … layers.

$$\therefore \quad S = \tfrac{1}{2}(\Sigma n^2 + \Sigma n)$$

$$= \frac{n(n+1)(n+2)}{6} \qquad \text{[Art. 70.]}$$

73. *To find the number of shot arranged in a complete pyramid the base of which is a rectangle.*

Let m and n be the number of shot in the long and short side respectively of the base.

The top layer consists of a single row of $m - (n - 1)$, or $m - n + 1$ shot;

in the next layer the number is $2(m - n + 2)$;

in the next layer the number is $3(m - n + 3)$;

and so on;

in the lowest layer the number is $n(m - n + n)$.

$$\therefore \quad S = (m - n + 1) + 2(m - n + 2) + 3(m - n + 3) + \ldots + n(m - n + n)$$

$$= (m - n)(1 + 2 + 3 + \ldots + n) + (1^2 + 2^2 + 3^2 + \ldots + n^2)$$

$$= \frac{(m - n)\, n(n+1)}{2} + \frac{n(n+1)(2n+1)}{6}$$

$$= \frac{n(n+1)}{6}\{3(m - n) + 2n + 1\}$$

$$= \frac{n(n+1)(3m - n + 1)}{6}$$

74. *To find the number of shot arranged in an incomplete pyramid the base of which is a rectangle.*

Let a and b denote the number of shot in the two sides of the top layer, n the number of layers.

In the top layer the number of shot is ab;

in the next layer the number is $(a + 1)(b + 1)$;

in the next layer the number is $(a + 2)(b + 2)$; and so on;

in the lowest layer the number is $(a + \overline{n - 1})(b + \overline{n - 1})$

or $ab + (a + b)(n - 1) + (n - 1)^2.$

$$\therefore \quad S = abn + (a + b) \, \Sigma \, (n - 1) + \Sigma \, (n - 1)^2$$

$$= abn + \frac{(n - 1) \, n \, (a + b)}{2} + \frac{(n - 1) \, n \, (2. \, \overline{n - 1} + 1)}{6}$$

$$= \frac{n}{6} \, \{6ab + 3 \, (a + b) \, (n - 1) + (n - 1) \, (2n - 1)\}.$$

75. In numerical examples it is generally easier to use the following method.

Example : Find the number of shot in an incomplete square pile of 16 courses, having 12 shot in each side of the top.

If we place on the given pile a square pile having 11 shot in each side of the base, we obtain a complete square pile of 27 courses

and number of shot in the complete pile $= \dfrac{27 \times 28 \times 55}{6} = 6930$; [Art. 71.]

also number of shot in the added pile $= \dfrac{11 \times 12 \times 23}{6} = 506$;

$\therefore$ number of shot in the incomplete pile $= 6424$.

EXAMPLES VI. b.

Find the number of shot in

1. A square pile, having 15 shot in each side of the base.

2. A triangular pile, having 18 shot in each side of the base.

3. A rectangular pile, the length and the breadth of the base containing 50 and 28 shot respectively.

4. An incomplete triangular pile, a side of the base having 25 shot, and a side of the top 14.

5. An incomplete square pile of 27 courses, having 40 shot in each side of the base.

6. The number of shot in a complete rectangular pile is 24395; if there are 34 shot in the breadth of the base, how many are there in its length ?

7. The number of shot in the top layer of a square pile is 169, and in the lowest layer is 1089; how many shot does the pile contain ?

8. Find the number of shot in a complete rectangular pile of 15 courses, having 20 shot in the longer side of its base.

9. Find the number of shot in an incomplete rectangular pile, the number of shot in the sides of its upper course being 11 and 18, and the number in the shorter side of its lowest course being 30.

10. What is the number of shot required to complete a rectangular pile having 15 and 6 shot in the longer and shorter side, respectively, of its upper course ?

11. The number of shot in a triangular pile is greater by 150 than half the number of shot in a square pile, the number of layers in each being the same; find the number of shot in the lowest layer of the triangular pile.

12. Find the number of shot in an incomplete square pile of 16 courses when the number of shot in the upper course is 1005 less than in the lowest course.

13. Shew that the number of shot in a square pile is one-fourth the number of shot in a triangular pile of double the number of courses.

14. If the number of shot in a triangular pile is to the number of shot in a square pile of double the number of courses as 13 to 175; find the number of shot in each pile.

15. The value of a triangular pile of 16 lb. shot is £ 51; if the value of iron be 10s. 6d. per cwt., find the number of shot in the lowest layer.

16. If from a complete square pile of n courses a triangular pile of the same number of courses be formed; shew that the remaining shot will be just sufficient to form another triangular pile, and find the number of shot in its side.

■ ■ ■

Chapter 7

SCALES OF NOTATION

76. The ordinary numbers with which we are acquainted in Arithmetic are expressed by means of multiples of powers of 10; for instance

$$25 = 2 \times 10 + 5;$$

$$4705 = 4 \times 10^3 + 7 \times 10^2 + 0 \times 10 + 5$$

This method of representing numbers is called the common or denary scale of notation, and ten is said to be the radix of the scale. The symbols employed in this system of notation are the nine digits and zero.

In like manner any number other than ten may be taken as the radix of a scale of notation; thus if 7 is the radix, a number expressed by 2453 represents $2 \times 7^3 + 4 \times 7^2 + 5 \times 7 + 3$; and in this scale no digit higher than 6 can occur.

Again in a scale whose radix is denoted by r the above number 2453 stands for $2r^3 + 4r^2 + 5r + 3$. More generally, if in the scale whose radix is r we denote the digits, beginning with that in the units' place, by $a_0, a_1, a_2, ..., a_n$; then the number so formed will be represented by

$$a_n r^n + a_{n-1} r^{n-1} + a_{n-2} r^{n-2} + ... + a_2 r^2 + a_1 r + a_0,$$

where the coefficients $a_n, a_{n-1}, ..., a_0$ are integers, all less than r, of which any one or more after the first may be zero.

Hence in this scale the digits are r in number, their values ranging from 0 to $r-1$.

77. The names Binary, Ternary, Quaternary, Quinary, Senary, Septenary, Octenary, Nonary, Denary, Undenary and Duodenary are used to denote the scales corresponding to the values *two, three, ... twelve* of the radix.

In the undenary, duodenary, ... scales we shall require symbols to represent the digits which are greater than nine. It is unusual to consider any scale higher than that with radix twelve; when necessary we shall employ the symbols t, e, T as digits to denote 'ten', 'eleven' and 'twelve.'

It is especially worthy of notice that in every scale 10 is the symbol not for 'ten', but for the radix itself.

78. The ordinary operations of Arithmetic may be performed in any scale; but, bearing in mind that the successive powers of the radix are no longer powers of ten, in determining the *carrying figures* we must not divide by ten, but by the radix of the scale in question.

Example 1. In the scale of eight subtract 371532 from 530225, and multiply the difference by 27.

$$
\begin{array}{cc}
530225 & 136473 \\
371532 & 27 \\
\hline
136473 & 1226235 \\
       & 275166 \\
       \cline{2-2}
       & 4200115
\end{array}
$$

Explanation : After the first figure of the subtraction, since we cannot take 3 from 2 we add 8; thus we have to take 3 from ten, which leaves 7; then 6 from ten, which leaves 4; then 2 from eight which leaves 6; and so on.

Again, in multiplying by 7, we have

$$3 \times 7 = \text{twenty one} = 2 \times 8 + 5;$$

we therefore, put down 5 and carry 2.

Next $7 \times 7 + 2 = \text{fifty one} = 6 \times 8 + 3;$

put down 3 and carry 6; and so on, until the multiplication is completed.

In the addition,

$$3 + 6 = \text{nine} = 1 \times 8 + 1;$$

we therefore put down 1 and carry 1.

Similarly $\qquad 2 + 6 + 1 = \text{nine} = 1 \times 8 + 1;$

and $\qquad\qquad 6 + 1 + 1 = \text{eight} = 1 \times 8 + 0;$

and so on.

Example 2. Divide 15*et*20 by 9 in the scale of twelve.

$$9)\ \underline{15et20} $$
$$1ee96\ldots6$$

Explanation : Since $15 = 1 \times T + 5 = \text{seventeen} = 1 \times 9 + 8,$

we put down 1 and carry 8.

Also $\qquad 8 \times T + e = \text{one hundred and seven} = e \times 9 + 8;$

we therefore put down *e* and carry 8; and so on.

Example 3. Find the square root of 442641 *in the scale of seven.*

$$
\begin{array}{r|l}
 & 442641(546 \\
 & 34 \\
\cline{2-2}
134 & 1026 \\
 & 602 \\
\cline{2-2}
1416 & 12441 \\
 & 12441
\end{array}
$$

EXAMPLES VII. a.

1. Add together 23241, 4032, 300421 in the scale of five.

2. Find the sum of the nonary numbers 303478, 150732, 264305.

3. Subtract 1732765 from 3673124 in the scale of eight.

4. From $3te756$ take $2e46t2$ in the duodenary scale.

5. Divide the difference between 1131315 and 235143 by 4 in the scale of six.

6. Multiply 6431 by 35 in the scale of seven.

7. Find the product of the nonary numbers 4685, 3483.

8. Divide 102432 by 36 in the scale of seven.

9. In the ternary scale subtract 121012 from 11022201, and divide the result by 1201.

10. Find the square root of 300114 in the quinary scale.

11. Find the square of $tttt$ in the scale of eleven.

12. Find the G.C.M of 2541 and 3102 in the scale of seven.

13. Divide 14332216 by 6541 in the septenary scale.

14. Subtract 20404020 from 103050301 and find the square root of the result in the octenary scale.

15. Find the square root of $eet001$ in the scale of twelve.

16. The following numbers are in the scale of six, find by the ordinary rules, without transforming to the denary scale;
    (1) the G.C.M of 31141 and 3102;
    (2) the L.C.M of 23, 24, 30, 32, 40, 41, 43, 50.

79. *To express a given intergral number in any proposed scale.*

Let N be the given number, and r the radix of the proposed scale.

Let $a_0, a_1, a_2, \ldots a_n$ be the required digits by which N is to be expressed, beginning with that in the units' place; then

$$N = a_n r^n + a_{n-1} r^{n-1} + \ldots + a_2 r^2 + a_1 r + a_0$$

We have now to find the values of $a_0, a_1, a_2, \ldots a_n$.

Divide N by r, then the remainder is a_0, and the quotient is

$$a_n r^{n-1} + a_{n-1} r^{n-2} + \ldots + a_2 r + a_1.$$

If this quotient is divided by r, the remainder is a_1;

If the next quotient .... a_2;

and so on, until there is no further quotient.

Thus all the required digits $a_0, a_1, a_2, \ldots a_n$ are determined by successive divisions by the radix of the proposed scale.

Example 1. Express the denary number 5213 in the scale of seven.

$$
\begin{array}{r}
7)\ 5213 \\
\hline
7)\ 744\ ......5 \\
\hline
7)\ 106\ ......2 \\
\hline
7)\ 15\ .....1 \\
\hline
2\ 1
\end{array}
$$

Thus $5213 = 2 \times 7^4 + 1 \times 7^3 + 1 \times 7^2 + 2 \times 7 + 5$;
and the number required is 21125.

Example 2. Transform 21125 from scale seven to scale eleven.

$$
\begin{array}{r}
e)\ 21125 \\
\hline
e)\ 1244\ ......t \\
\hline
e)\ 61\ ....0 \\
\hline
3\ ......t
\end{array}
$$

∴ the required number is $3t0t$.

Explanation : In the first line of work

$$21 = 2 \times 7 + 1 = \text{fifteen} = 1 \times e + 4;$$

therefore on dividing by e we put down 1 and carry 4.

Next $\quad 4 \times 7 + 1 = \text{twenty nine} = 2 \times e + 7;$

therefore we put down 2 and carry 7; and so on.

Example 3. Reduce 7215 from scale twelve to scale ten by working a scale ten, and verify the result by working in the scale twelve.

In scale of ten $\left\{ \begin{array}{r} 7215 \\ 12 \\ \hline 86 \\ 12 \\ \hline 1033 \\ 12 \\ \hline 12401 \end{array} \right.$
$\left. \begin{array}{r} t)\ 7215 \\ \hline t)\ 874......1 \\ \hline t)\ t4......0 \\ \hline t)\ 10......4 \\ \hline 1......2 \end{array} \right\}$ In scale of twelve

Thus the result is 12401 in each case.

Explanation : 7215 in scale twelve means $7 \times 12^3 + 2 \times 12^2 + 1 \times 12 + 5$ in scale ten. The calculation is most readily effected by writing this expression in the form $[\{(7 \times 12 + 2)\} \times 12 + 1] \times 12 + 5$; thus we multiply 7 by 12 and add 2 to the product; then we multiply 86 by 12 and add 1 to the product; then 1033 by 12 and add 5 to the product.

80. Hitherto we have only discussed whole numbers; but fractions may also be expressed in any scale of notation; thus

·25 in scale ten denotes $\dfrac{2}{10} + \dfrac{5}{10^2}$;

·25 in scale six denotes $\dfrac{2}{6} + \dfrac{5}{6^2}$;

25 in scale r denotes $\dfrac{2}{r} + \dfrac{5}{r^2}$.

Fractions thus expressed in a form analogous to that of ordinary decimal fractions are called radix-fractions, and the point is called the radix-point. The general type of such fractions in scale r is

$$\frac{b_1}{r} + \frac{b_2}{r^2} + \frac{b_3}{r^3} + \ldots;$$

where $b_1, b_2, b_3, \ldots$ are integers, all less than r, of which any one or more may be zero.

81.   *To express a given radix fraction in any proposed scale.*

Let F be the given fraction, and r the radix of the proposed scale.

Let $b_1, b_2, b_3, \ldots$ be the required digits beginning from the left; then

$$F = \frac{b_1}{r} + \frac{b_2}{r^2} + \frac{b_3}{r^3} + \ldots$$

We have now to find the values of $b_1, b_2, b_3, \ldots$

Multiply both sides of the equation by r; then

$$rF = b_1 + \frac{b_2}{r} + \frac{b_3}{r^2} + \ldots;$$

Hence, b_1 is equal to the integral part of rF; and, if we denote the fractional part by F_1, we have

$$F_1 = \frac{b_2}{r} + \frac{b_3}{r^2} + \ldots$$

Multiply again by r; then, as before, b_2 is the integral part of rF_1; and similarly by successive multiplications by r, each of the digits may be found, and the fraction expressed in the proposed scale.

If in the successive multiplications by r any one of the products is an integer the process terminates at this stage, and the given fraction can be expressed by a finite number of digits. But if none of the products is an integer the process will never terminate, and in this case the digits recur, forming a radix fraction analogous to a recurring decimal.

Example 1.   Express $\dfrac{13}{16}$ as a radix fraction in scale six.

$$\frac{13}{16} \times 6 = \frac{13 \times 3}{8} = 4 + \frac{7}{8};$$

$$\frac{7}{8} \times 6 = \frac{7 \times 3}{4} = 5 + \frac{1}{4};$$

$$\frac{1}{4} \times 6 = \frac{1 \times 3}{2} = 1 + \frac{1}{2};$$

$$\frac{1}{2} \times 6 = 3.$$

$\therefore$ the required fraction $= \dfrac{4}{6} + \dfrac{5}{6^2} + \dfrac{1}{6^3} + \dfrac{3}{6^4}$

$$= .4513.$$

Example 2. Transform 16064.24 from scale eight to scale five.

We must treat the integral and the fractional parts separately,

5) 16064	0.24
5) 2644......0	5
5) 440......4	1.44
5) 71......3	5
5) 13......2	2.64
2 1	5
	4.04
	5
	0.24

After this the digits in the fractional part recur; hence the required number is 212340.1240.

82. *In any scale of notation of which the radix is r, the sum of the digits of any whole number divided by $r-1$ will leave the same remainder as the whole number divided by $r-1$.*

Let N denote the number, $a_0, a_1, a_2, \ldots a_n$ the digits beginning with that in the units place, and S the sum of the digits; then

$$N = a_0 + a_1 r + a_2 r^2 + \ldots + a_{n-1} r^{n-1} + a_n r^n;$$
$$S = a_0 + a_1 + a_2 + \ldots + a_{n-1} + a_n$$

$\therefore \quad N - S = a_1(r-1) + a_2(r^2-1) + \ldots + a_{n-1}(r^{n-1}-1) + a_n(r^n-1)$

Now every term on the right hand side is divisible by $r-1$;

$\therefore \qquad \dfrac{N-S}{r-1} = $ an integer;

that is, $\qquad \dfrac{N}{r-1} = I + \dfrac{S}{r-1}$,

where I is some integer; which proves the proposition.

Hence a number in scale r will be divisible by $r-1$ when the sum of its digits is divisible by $r-1$.

83. By taking $r = 10$ we learn from the above proposition that a number divided by 9 will leave the same remainder as the sum of its digits divided by 9. The rule known as "casting out the nines" for testing the accuracy of multiplication is founded on this property.

The rule may be thus explained :

Let two numbers be represented by $9a + b$ and $9c + d$, and their product by P; then

$$P = 81ac + 9bc + 9ad + bd.$$

Hence $\dfrac{P}{9}$ has the same remainder as $\dfrac{bd}{9}$; and therefore the *sum of the digits of P*, when divided by 9, gives the same remainder as the *sum of the digits of bd*, when divided by 9. If on trial this should not be the case, the multiplication must have been incorrectly performed. In practice b and d are readily found from the sums of the digits of the two numbers to be multiplied together.

Example : Can the product of 31256 and 8427 be 263395312 ?

The sums of the digits of the multiplicand, multiplier, and product are 17, 21, and 34 respectively; again, the sums of the digits of these three numbers are 8, 3 and 7, whence $bd = 8 \times 3 = 24$, which has 6 for the sum of the digits; thus we have two different remainder, 6 and 7, and the multiplication is incorrect.

84. *If N denote any number in the scale of r, and D denote the difference, supposed positive, between the sums of the digits in the odd and the even places; then $N - D$ or $N + D$ is a multiple of $r + 1$.*

Let $a_0, a_1, a_2, \ldots a_n$ denote the digits beginning with that in the units' place; then

$$N = a_0 + a_1 r + a_2 r^2 + a_3 r^3 + \ldots + a_{n-1} r^{n-1} + a_n r^n$$

$$\therefore \quad N - a_0 + a_1 - a_2 + a_3 - \ldots = a_1 (r+1) + a_2 (r^2 - 1) + a_3 (r^3 + 1) + \ldots ;$$

and the last term on the right will be $a_n (r^n + 1)$ or $a_n (r^n - 1)$ according as n is odd or even. Thus every term on the right is divisible by $r + 1$; hence

$$\frac{N - (a_0 - a_1 + a_2 - a_3 + \ldots)}{r + 1} = \text{an integer.}$$

Now $a_0 - a_1 + a_2 - a_3 + \ldots = \pm D$;

$$\therefore \qquad \frac{N \mp D}{r + 1} \text{ is an integer;}$$

which proves the proposition.

Cor. If the sum of the digits in the even places is equal to the sum of the digits in the odd places, $D = 0$, and N is divisible by $r + 1$.

Example 1. Prove that 4.41 is a square number in any scale of notation whose radix is greater than 4.

Let r be the radix; then

$$4.41 = 4 + \frac{4}{r} + \frac{1}{r^2} = \left(2 + \frac{1}{r}\right)^2;$$

thus the given number is the square of 2.1.

Example 2. In what scale is the denary number 2.4375 represented by 2.13 ?

Let r be the scale; then

$$2 + \frac{1}{r} + \frac{3}{r^2} = 2.4375 = 2\frac{7}{16};$$

whence $\qquad 7r^2 - 16r - 48 = 0;$

that is, $\qquad (7r + 12)(r - 4) = 0.$

Hence the radix is 4.

Sometimes it is best to use the following method.

Example 3. In what scale will the nonary number 25607 be expressed by 101215 ?

The required scale must be less than 9, since the new number *appears* the greater; also it must be greater than 5; therefore the required scale must be 6, 7 or 8; and *by trial* we find that it is 7.

EXAMPLES VII. b.

1. Express 4954 in the scale of seven.

2. Express 624 in the scale of five.

3. Express 206 in the binary scale.

4. Express 1458 in the scale of three.

5. Express 5381 in powers of nine.

6. Transform 212231 from scale four to scale five.

7. Express the duodenary number 398e in powers of 10.

8. Transform 6t12 from scale twelve to scale eleven.

9. Transform 213014 from the senary to the nonary scale.

10. Transform 23861 from scale nine to scale eight.

11. Transform 400803 from the nonary to the quinary scale.

12. Express the septenary number 20665152 in powers of 12.

13. Transform $ttteee$ from scale twelve to the common scale.

14. Express $\frac{3}{10}$ as a radix fraction in the septenary scale.

15. Transform 17.15625 from scale ten to scale twelve.

16. Transform 200.211 from the ternary to the nonary scale.

17.   Transform 71.03 from the duodenary to the octenary scale.

18.   Express the septenary fraction $\dfrac{1552}{2626}$ as a denary vulgar fraction in its lowest terms.

19.   Find the denary value of the septenary numbers $.\overset{.}{4}$ and $.\overset{..}{42}$.

20.   In what scale is the denary number 182 denoted by 222 ?

21.   In what scale is the denary fraction $\dfrac{25}{128}$ denoted by 0.0302 ?

22.   Find the radix of the scale in which 554 represents the square of 24.

23.   In what scale is 511197 denoted by 1746335 ?

24.   Find the radix of the scale in which the numbers denoted by 479, 698, 907 are in arithmetical progression.

25.   In what scale are the radix-fractions .16, .20, .28 in geometric progression ?

26.   The number 212542 is in the scale of six; in what scale will it be denoted by 17486 ?

27.   Shew that 148.84 is a perfect square in every scale in which the radix is greater than eight.

28.   Shew that 1234321 is a perfect square in any scale whose radix is greater than 4; and that the square root is always expressed by the same four digits.

29.   Prove that 1.331 is a perfect cube in any scale whose radix is greater than three.

30.   Find which of the weights 1, 2, 4, 8, 16, ... lbs. must be used to weigh one ton.

31.   Find which of the weights 1, 3, 9, 27, 81, ... lbs. must be used to weigh ten thousand lbs., not more than one of each kind being used but in either scale that is necessary.

32.   Shew that 1367631 is a perfect cube in every scale in which the radix is greater than seven.

33.   Prove that in the ordinary scale a number will be divisible by 8 if the number formed by its last three digits is divisible by eight.

34.   Prove that the square of $rrrr$ in the scale of s is $rrrq0001$, where q, r, s are any three consecutive integers.

35. If any number N be taken in the scale r, and a new number N' be formed by altering the order of its digits in any way, shew that the difference between N and N' is divisible by $r - 1$.

36. If a number has an even number of digits, shew that it is divisible by $r + 1$ if the digits equidistant from each end are the same.

37. If in the ordinary scale S_1 be the sum of the digits of a number N, and $3S_2$ be the sum of the digits of the number $3N$, prove that the difference between S_1 and S_2 is a multiple of 3.

38. Shew that in the ordinary scale any number formed by writing down three digits and then repeating them in the same order is a multiple of 7, 11 and 13.

39. In a scale whose radix is odd, shew that the sum of the digits of any number will be odd if the number be odd, and even if the number be even.

40. If n be odd, and a number in the denary scale be formed by writing down n digits and then repeating them in the same order, shew that it will be divisible by the number formed by the n digits, and also 9090...9091 containing $n - 1$ digits.

■■■

Chapter 8

SURDS AND IMAGINARY QUANTITIES

85. In the *Elementary Algebra,* Art. 272, it is proved that the denominator of any expression of the form $\dfrac{a}{\sqrt{b} + \sqrt{c}}$ can be rationalised by multiplying the numerator and the denominator by $\sqrt{b} - \sqrt{c}$, the surd *conjugate* to the denominator.

Similarly, in the case of a fraction of the form $\dfrac{a}{\sqrt{b} + \sqrt{c} + \sqrt{d}}$, where the denominator involves three quadratic surds, we may by two operations render that denominator rational.

For, first multiply both numerator and denominator by $\sqrt{b} + \sqrt{c} - \sqrt{d}$; the denominator becomes $(\sqrt{b} + \sqrt{c})^2 - (\sqrt{d})^2$ or $b + c - d + 2\sqrt{bc}$. Then multiply both numerator and denominator by $(b + c - d) - 2\sqrt{bc}$; the denominator becomes $(b + c - d)^2 - 4bc$, which is a rational quantity.

Example : Simplify $\dfrac{12}{3 + \sqrt{5} - 2\sqrt{2}}$.

$$\text{The expression} = \frac{12\,(3 + \sqrt{5} + 2\sqrt{2})}{(3 + \sqrt{5})^2 - (2\sqrt{2})^2}$$

$$= \frac{12(3 + \sqrt{5} + 2\sqrt{2})}{6 + 6\sqrt{5}}$$

$$= \frac{2\,(3 + \sqrt{5} + 2\sqrt{2})\,(\sqrt{5} - 1)}{(\sqrt{5} + 1)\,(\sqrt{5} - 1)}$$

$$= \frac{2 + 2\sqrt{5} + 2\sqrt{10} - 2\sqrt{2}}{2}$$

$$= 1 + \sqrt{5} + \sqrt{10} - \sqrt{2}.$$

86. *To find the factor which will rationalise any given binomial surd.*

Case I. Suppose the given surd is $\sqrt[p]{a} - \sqrt[q]{b}$.

Let $\sqrt[p]{a} = x$, $\sqrt[q]{b} = y$, and let n be the L.C.M of p and q; then x^n and y^n are both rational.

Now $x^n - y^n$ is divisible by $x - y$ for all values of n, and

$$x^n - y^n = (x - y)\,(x^{n-1} + x^{n-2}\,y + x^{n-3}\,y^2 + \ldots + y^{n-1}).$$

Thus the rationalising factor is

$$x^{n-1} + x^{n-2}y + x^{n-3}y^2 + \ldots + y^{n-1};$$

and the rational product is $x^n - y^n$.

Case II. Suppose the given surd is $\sqrt[p]{a} + \sqrt[q]{b}$.

Let x, y, n have the same meanings as before; then

(1) If n is even, $x^n - y^n$ is divisible by $x + y$, and

$$x^n - y^n = (x + y)(x^{n-1} - x^{n-2}y + \ldots + xy^{n-2} - y^{n-1})$$

Thus the rationalising factor is

$$x^{n-1} - x^{n-2}y + \ldots + xy^{n-2} - y^{n-1};$$

and the rational product is $x^n - y^n$.

(2) If n is odd, $x^n + y^n$ is divisible by $x + y$, and

$$x^n + y^n = (x + y)(x^{n-1} - x^{n-2}y + \ldots - xy^{n-2} + y^{n-1})$$

Thus the rationalising factor is

$$x^{n-1} - x^{n-2}y + \ldots - xy^{n-2} + y^{n-1};$$

and the rational product is $x^n + y^n$.

Example 1. Find the factor which will rationalise $\sqrt{3} + \sqrt[3]{5}$.

Let $x = 3^{1/2}$, $y = 5^{1/3}$; then x^6 and y^6 are both rational, and

$$x^6 - y^6 = (x + y)(x^5 - x^4y + x^3y^2 - x^2y^3 + xy^4 - y^5);$$

thus, substituting for x and y, the required factor is

$$3^{5/2} - 3^{4/2} \cdot 5^{1/3} + 3^{3/2} \cdot 5^{2/3} - 3^{2/2} \cdot 5^{3/3} + 3^{1/2} \cdot 5^{4/3} - 5^{5/3},$$

or $3^{5/2} - 9 \cdot 5^{1/3} + 3^{3/2} \cdot 5^{2/3} - 15 + 3^{1/2} \cdot 5^{4/3} - 5^{5/3};$

and the rational product is $3^{6/2} - 5^{6/3} = 3^3 - 5^2 = 2$.

Example 2. Express $\left(5^{1/2} + 9^{1/8}\right) \div \left(5^{1/2} - 9^{1/8}\right)$ as an equivalent fraction with a rational denominator.

To rationalise the denominator, which is equal to $5^{1/2} - 3^{1/4}$, put $5^{1/2} = x$, $3^{1/4} = y$; then since $x^4 - y^4 = (x - y)(x^3 + x^2y + xy^2 + y^3)$

the required factor is $5^{3/2} + 5^{2/2} \cdot 3^{1/4} + 5^{1/2} \cdot 3^{2/4} + 3^{3/4};$

and the rational denominator is $5^{4/2} - 3^{4/4} = 5^2 - 3 = 22$.

$\therefore$ the expression

$$= \frac{(5^{1/2} + 3^{1/4})(5^{3/2} + 5^{2/2} \cdot 3^{1/4} + 5^{1/2} \cdot 3^{2/4} + 3^{3/4})}{22}$$

$$= \frac{5^{4/2} + 2 \cdot 5^{3/2} \cdot 3^{1/4} + 2 \cdot 5^{2/2} \cdot 3^{2/4} + 2 \cdot 5^{1/2} \cdot 3^{3/4} + 3^{4/4}}{22}$$

$$= \frac{14 + 5^{3/2} \cdot 3^{1/4} + 5 \cdot 3^{1/2} + 5^{1/2} \cdot 3^{3/4}}{11}$$

87. We have shewn in the *Elementary Algebra*, Art. 277, how to find the square root of a binomial quadratic surd. We may sometimes extract the square root of an expression containing more than two quadratic surds, such as $a + \sqrt{b} + \sqrt{c} + \sqrt{d}$.

Assume $\sqrt{a + \sqrt{b} + \sqrt{c} + \sqrt{d}} = \sqrt{x} + \sqrt{y} + \sqrt{z}$;

∴ $a + \sqrt{b} + \sqrt{c} + \sqrt{d} = x + y + z + 2\sqrt{xy} + 2\sqrt{xz} + 2\sqrt{yz}$

If then $2\sqrt{xy} = \sqrt{b}, 2\sqrt{xz} = \sqrt{c}, 2\sqrt{yz} = \sqrt{d}$,

and if, at the same time, the values of x, y, z thus found satisfy $x + y + z = a$, we shall have obtained the required root.

Example : Find the square root of $21 - 4\sqrt{5} + 8\sqrt{3} - 4\sqrt{15}$.

Assume $\sqrt{21 - 4\sqrt{5} + 8\sqrt{3} - 4\sqrt{15}} = \sqrt{x} + \sqrt{y} - \sqrt{z}$;

∴ $21 - 4\sqrt{5} + 8\sqrt{3} - 4\sqrt{15} = x + y + z + 2\sqrt{xy} - 2\sqrt{xz} - 2\sqrt{yz}$.

Put $2\sqrt{xy} = 8\sqrt{3}, 2\sqrt{xz} = 4\sqrt{15}, 2\sqrt{yz} = 4\sqrt{5}$;

by multiplication, $xyz = 240$; that is $\sqrt{xyz} = 4\sqrt{15}$;

whence it follows that $\sqrt{x} = 2\sqrt{3}, \sqrt{y} = 2, \sqrt{z} = \sqrt{5}$.

And since these values satisfy the equation $x + y + z = 21$, the required root is $2\sqrt{3} + 2 - \sqrt{5}$.

88. If $\sqrt[3]{a + \sqrt{b}} = x + \sqrt{y}$, then will $\sqrt[3]{a - \sqrt{b}} = x - \sqrt{y}$.

For, by cubing, we obtain

$$a + \sqrt{b} = x^3 + 3x^2\sqrt{y} + 3xy + y\sqrt{y}.$$

Equating rational and irrational parts, we have

$$a = x^3 + 3xy, \quad \sqrt{b} = 3x^2\sqrt{y} + y\sqrt{y};$$

∴ $a - \sqrt{b} = x^3 - 3x^2\sqrt{y} + 3xy - y\sqrt{y}$;

that is, $\sqrt[3]{a - \sqrt{b}} = x - \sqrt{y}$.

Similarly, by the help of the Binomial Theorem, Chap. 13, it may be proved that if

$$\sqrt[n]{a + \sqrt{b}} = x + \sqrt{y}, \text{ then } \sqrt[n]{a - \sqrt{b}} = x - \sqrt{y},$$

where n is any positive integer.

89. By the following method the cube root of an expression of the form $a \pm \sqrt{b}$ may sometimes be found.

Suppose $\sqrt[3]{a + \sqrt{b}} = x + \sqrt{y}$;

then $\sqrt[3]{a - \sqrt{b}} = x - \sqrt{y}$;

∴ $\sqrt[3]{a^2 - b} = x^2 - y$ ...(1)

Again, as in the last article,

$$a = x^3 + 3xy \qquad \qquad ... (2)$$

The values of x and y have to be determined from (1) and (2).

In (1) suppose that $\sqrt[3]{a^2 - b} = c$; then by substituting for y in (2) we obtain

$$a = x^3 + 3x\,(x^2 - c);$$

that is, $\qquad 4x^3 - 3cx = a.$

If from this equation the value of x can be determined by trial, the value of y is obtained from $y = x^2 - c$.

Note : We do not here assume $\sqrt{x} + \sqrt{y}$ for the cube root, as in the extraction of the square root; for with this assumption, on cubing we should have

$$a + \sqrt{b} = x\sqrt{x} + 3x\sqrt{y} + 3y\sqrt{x} + y\sqrt{y}$$

and since every term on the right hand side is irrational we cannot equate rational and irrational parts.

Example : Find the cube root of $72 - 32\sqrt{5}$.

Assume $\qquad \sqrt[3]{72 - 32\sqrt{5}} = x - \sqrt{y};$

then $\qquad \sqrt[3]{72 + 32\sqrt{5}} = x + \sqrt{y}$

By multiplication, $\sqrt[3]{5184 - 1024 \times 5} = x^2 - y;$

that is, $\qquad 4 = x^2 - y \qquad \qquad \ldots(1)$

Again $\qquad 72 - 32\sqrt{5} = x^3 - 3x^2\sqrt{y} + 3xy - y\sqrt{y};$

whence $\qquad 72 = x^3 + 3xy \qquad \qquad \ldots(2)$

From (1) and (2), $\qquad 72 = x^3 + 3x\,(x^2 - 4);$

that is, $\qquad x^3 - 3x = 18.$

By *trial*, we find that $x = 3$; hence $y = 5$, and the cube root is $3 - \sqrt{5}$.

90. When the binomial whose cube root we are seeking consists of *two* quadratic surds, we proceed as follows.

Example : Find the cube root of $9\sqrt{3} + 11\sqrt{2}$.

$$\sqrt[3]{9\sqrt{3} + 11\sqrt{2}} = \sqrt[3]{3\sqrt{3}\left(3 + \frac{11}{3}\sqrt{\frac{2}{3}}\right)}$$

$$= \sqrt{3}\ \sqrt[3]{3 + \frac{11}{3}\sqrt{\frac{2}{3}}}$$

By proceeding as in the last article, we find that

$$\sqrt[3]{3 + \frac{11}{3}\sqrt{\frac{2}{3}}} = 1 + \sqrt{\frac{2}{3}};$$

$\therefore$ the required cube root $= \sqrt{3}\left(1 + \sqrt{\dfrac{2}{3}}\right) = \sqrt{3} + \sqrt{2}.$

91. We add a few harder examples in surds.

Example 1. *Express with rational denominator* $\dfrac{4}{\sqrt[3]{9} - \sqrt[3]{3} + 1}$

The expression $= \dfrac{4}{3^{2/3} - 3^{1/3} + 1}$

$= \dfrac{4\,(3^{1/3} + 1)}{(3^{1/3} + 1)\,(3^{2/3} - 3^{1/3} + 1)}$

$= \dfrac{4\,(3^{1/3} + 1)}{3 + 1} = 3^{1/3} + 1.$

Example 2. *Find the square root of*

$$\frac{3}{2}\,(x - 1) + \sqrt{2x^2 - 7x - 4}.$$

The expression $= \dfrac{1}{2}\,\{3x - 3 + 2\,\sqrt{(2x + 1)\,(x - 4)}\}$

$= \dfrac{1}{2}\,\{(2x + 1) + (x - 4) + 2\,\sqrt{(2x + 1)\,(x - 4)}\,\};$

hence, by inspection, the square root is

$$\frac{1}{\sqrt{2}}\,(\sqrt{2x + 1} + \sqrt{x - 4}).$$

Example 3. *Given* $\sqrt{5} = 2.23607$, *find the value of*

$$\frac{\sqrt{3 - \sqrt{5}}}{\sqrt{2} + \sqrt{7 - 3\sqrt{5}}}.$$

Multiplying numerator and denominator by $\sqrt{2}$,

the expression $= \dfrac{\sqrt{6 - 2\sqrt{5}}}{2 + \sqrt{14 - 6\sqrt{5}}}$

$= \dfrac{\sqrt{5} - 1}{2 + 3 - \sqrt{5}}$

$= \dfrac{1}{\sqrt{5}} = \dfrac{\sqrt{5}}{5} = 0.44721.$

EXAMPLES VIII. a.

Express as equivalent fractions with rational denominator :

1. $\dfrac{1}{1 + \sqrt{2} - \sqrt{3}}$

2. $\dfrac{\sqrt{2}}{\sqrt{2} + \sqrt{3} - \sqrt{5}}$

3. $\dfrac{1}{\sqrt{a} + \sqrt{b} + \sqrt{a + b}}$

4. $\dfrac{2\,\sqrt{a} + 1}{\sqrt{a - 1} - \sqrt{2a} + \sqrt{a + 1}}$

5. $\dfrac{\sqrt{10} + \sqrt{5} - \sqrt{3}}{\sqrt{3} + \sqrt{10} - \sqrt{5}}$

6. $\dfrac{(\sqrt{3} + \sqrt{5})\,(\sqrt{5} + \sqrt{2})}{\sqrt{2} + \sqrt{3} + \sqrt{5}}$

Find a factor which will rationalise :

7. $\sqrt[3]{3} - \sqrt{2}$

8. $\sqrt[6]{5} + \sqrt[3]{2}$

9. $a^{1/6} + b^{1/4}$

10. $\sqrt[3]{3} - 1$

11. $2 + \sqrt[4]{7}$

12. $\sqrt[3]{5} - \sqrt[4]{3}$

Express with rational denominator :

13. $\dfrac{\sqrt[3]{3} - 1}{\sqrt[3]{3} + 1}$

14. $\dfrac{\sqrt[6]{9} - \sqrt[6]{8}}{\sqrt[6]{9} + \sqrt[6]{8}}$

15. $\dfrac{\sqrt{2} \cdot \sqrt[3]{3}}{\sqrt[3]{3} + \sqrt{2}}$

16. $\dfrac{\sqrt[3]{3}}{\sqrt{3} + \sqrt[6]{9}}$

17. $\dfrac{\sqrt{8} + \sqrt[3]{4}}{\sqrt{8} - \sqrt[3]{4}}$

18. $\dfrac{\sqrt[6]{27}}{3 - \sqrt[6]{9}}$

Find the square root of :

19. $16 - 2\sqrt{20} - 2\sqrt{28} + 2\sqrt{35}$

20. $24 + 4\sqrt{15} - 4\sqrt{21} - 2\sqrt{35}$

21. $6 + \sqrt{12} - \sqrt{24} - \sqrt{8}$

22. $5 - \sqrt{10} - \sqrt{15} + \sqrt{6}$

23. $a + 3b + 4 + 4\sqrt{a} - 4\sqrt{3b} - 2\sqrt{3ab}$

24. $21 + 3\sqrt{8} - 6\sqrt{3} - 6\sqrt{7} - \sqrt{24} - \sqrt{56} + 2\sqrt{21}.$

Find the cube root of :

25. $10 + 6\sqrt{3}$

26. $38 + 17\sqrt{5}$

27. $99 - 70\sqrt{2}$

28. $38\sqrt{14} - 100\sqrt{2}$

29. $54\sqrt{3} + 41\sqrt{5}$

30. $135\sqrt{3} - 87\sqrt{6}$

Find the square root of :

31. $a + x + \sqrt{2ax + x^2}$

32. $2a - \sqrt{3a^2 - 2ab - b^2}$

33. $1 + a^2 + (1 + a^2 + a^4)^{1/2}$

34. $1 + (1 - a^2)^{-1/2}$

35. If $a = \dfrac{1}{2 - \sqrt{3}}$, $b = \dfrac{1}{2 + \sqrt{3}}$, find the value of $7a^2 + 11ab - 7b^2$.

36. If $x = \dfrac{\sqrt{3} - \sqrt{2}}{\sqrt{3} + \sqrt{2}}$, $y = \dfrac{\sqrt{3} + \sqrt{2}}{\sqrt{3} - \sqrt{2}}$, find the value of $3x^2 - 5xy + 3y^2$.

Find the value of :

37. $\dfrac{\sqrt{26 - 15\sqrt{3}}}{5\sqrt{2} - \sqrt{38 + 5\sqrt{3}}}.$

38. $\sqrt{\dfrac{6 + 2\sqrt{3}}{33 - 19\sqrt{3}}}.$

39. $(28 - 10\sqrt{3})^{1/2} - (7 + 4\sqrt{3})^{-1/2}.$

40. $(26 + 15\sqrt{3})^{2/3} - (26 + 15\sqrt{3})^{-2/3}.$

41. Given $\sqrt{5} = 2.23607$, find the value of

$$\frac{10\sqrt{2}}{\sqrt{18} - \sqrt{3 + \sqrt{5}}} - \frac{\sqrt{10} + \sqrt{18}}{\sqrt{8} + \sqrt{3 - \sqrt{5}}}.$$

42. Divide $x^3 + 1 + 3x \sqrt[3]{2}$ by $x - 1 + \sqrt[3]{2}$.

43. Find the cube root of $9ab^2 + (b^2 + 24a^2) \sqrt{b^2 - 3a^2}$.

44. Evaluate $\dfrac{\sqrt{x^2 - 1}}{x - \sqrt{x^2 - 1}}$, when $2x = \sqrt{a} + \dfrac{1}{\sqrt{a}}$.

IMAGINARY QUANTITIES

92. Although from the rule of signs it is evident that a negative quantity cannot have a real square root, yet imaginary quantities represented by symbols of the form $\sqrt{-a}, \sqrt{-1}$ are of frequent occurrence in mathematical investigations, and their use leads to valuable results. We therefore proceed to explain in what sense such roots are to be regarded.

When the quantity under the radical sign is negative, we can no longer consider the symbol $\sqrt{}$ as indicating a possible arithmetical operation; but just as $\sqrt{a}$ may be defined as a symbol which obeys the relation $\sqrt{a} \times \sqrt{a} = a$, so we shall define $\sqrt{-a}$ to be such that $\sqrt{-a} \times \sqrt{-a} = -a$, and we shall accept the meaning to which this assumption leads us.

It will be found that this definition will enable us to bring imaginary quantities under the dominion of ordinary algebraical rules, and that through their use results may be obtained which can be relied on with as much certainty as others which depend solely on the use of real quantities.

93. By definition, $\sqrt{-1} \times \sqrt{-1} = -1$.

$\therefore \qquad \sqrt{a} \cdot \sqrt{-1} \times \sqrt{a} \cdot \sqrt{-1} = a(-1);$

that is, $\qquad (\sqrt{a} \cdot \sqrt{-1})^2 = -a.$

Thus the product $\sqrt{a} \cdot \sqrt{-1}$ may be regarded as equivalent to the imaginary quantity $\sqrt{-a}$.

94. It will generally be found convenient to indicate the imaginary character of an expression by the presence of the symbol $\sqrt{-1}$; thus

$$\sqrt{-4} = \sqrt{4 \times (-1)} = 2\sqrt{-1}.$$
$$\sqrt{-7a^2} = \sqrt{7a^2 \times (-1)} = a\sqrt{7}\sqrt{-1}.$$

95. We shall always consider that, in the absence of any statement to the contrary, of the signs which may be prefixed before a radical the positive sign is to be taken. But in the use of imaginary quantities there is one point of importance which deserves notice.

Since $(-a) \times (-b) = ab$,

by taking the square root, we have

$$\sqrt{-a} \times \sqrt{-b} = \pm \sqrt{ab}.$$

Thus in forming the product of $\sqrt{-a}$ and $\sqrt{-b}$ it would appear that either of the signs $+$ or $-$ might be placed before $\sqrt{ab}$. This is not the case, for

$$\sqrt{-a} \times \sqrt{-b} = \sqrt{a} \cdot \sqrt{-1} \times \sqrt{b} \cdot \sqrt{-1}$$
$$= \sqrt{ab} \, (\sqrt{-1})^2$$
$$= -\sqrt{ab}.$$

96. It is usual to apply the term 'imaginary' to all expressions which are not wholly real. Thus $a + b\sqrt{-1}$ may be taken as the general type of all imaginary expressions. *Here a and b are real quantities, but not necessarily rational.*

97. In dealing with imaginary quantities we apply the laws of combination which have been proved in the case of other surd quantities.

Example 1. $a + b\sqrt{-1} \pm (c + d\sqrt{-1}) = a \pm c + (b \pm d)\sqrt{-1}.$

Example 2. The product of $a + b\sqrt{-1}$ and $c + d\sqrt{-1}$.

$$= (a + b\sqrt{-1})(c + d\sqrt{-1})$$
$$= ac - bd + (bc + ad)\sqrt{-1}.$$

98. If $a + b\sqrt{-1} = 0$, then $a = 0$, and $b = 0$.

For, if $a + b\sqrt{-1} = 0$,

then $b\sqrt{-1} = -a$;

$\therefore \qquad -b^2 = a^2;$

$\therefore \qquad a^2 + b^2 = 0.$

Now a^2 and b^2 are both positive, therefore their sum cannot be zero unless each of them is separately zero; that is, $a = 0$, and $b = 0$.

99. If $a + b\sqrt{-1} = c + d\sqrt{-1}$, then $a = c$, and $b = d$.

For, by transposition, $a - c + (b - d)\sqrt{-1} = 0$;

therefore, by the last article, $a - c = 0$, and $b - d = 0$;

that is $\qquad a = c$, and $b = d$.

Thus in order that two imaginary expressions may be equal it is necessary and sufficient that the real parts should be equal and the imaginary parts should be equal.

100. Definition : When two imaginary expressions differ only in the sign of the imaginary part they are said to be **conjugate.**

Thus $a - b\sqrt{-1}$ is conjugate to $a + b\sqrt{-1}$.

Similarly $\sqrt{2} + 3\sqrt{-1}$ is conjugate to $\sqrt{2} - 3\sqrt{-1}$.

101.   *The sum and the product of two conjugate imaginary expressions are both real.*

For $a + b\sqrt{-1} + a - b\sqrt{-1} = 2a$.

Again $(a + b\sqrt{-1})(a - b\sqrt{-1}) = a^2 - (-b^2)$

$$= a^2 + b^2.$$

102.   Definition : The positive value of the square root of $a^2 + b^2$ is called the modulus of each of the conjugate expressions

$$a + b\sqrt{-1} \text{ and } a - b\sqrt{-1}.$$

103.   *The modulus of the product of two imaginary expressions is equal to the product of their moduli.*

Let the two expressions be denoted by $a + b\sqrt{-1}$ and $c + d\sqrt{-1}$.

Then their product $= ac - bd + (ad + bc)\sqrt{-1}$, which is an imaginary expression whose modulus

$$= \sqrt{(ac - bd)^2 + (ad + bc)^2}$$
$$= \sqrt{a^2c^2 + b^2d^2 + a^2d^2 + b^2c^2}$$
$$= \sqrt{(a^2 + b^2)(c^2 + d^2)}$$
$$= \sqrt{a^2 + b^2} \times \sqrt{c^2 + d^2} ;$$

which proves the proposition.

104.   If the denominator of a fraction is of the form $a + b\sqrt{-1}$, it may be rationalised by multiplying the numerator and the denominator by the conjugate expression $a - b\sqrt{-1}$.

For instance

$$\frac{c + d\sqrt{-1}}{a + b\sqrt{-1}} = \frac{(c + d\sqrt{-1})(a - b\sqrt{-1})}{(a + b\sqrt{-1})(a - b\sqrt{-1})}$$

$$= \frac{ac + bd + (ad - bc)\sqrt{-1}}{a^2 + b^2}$$

$$= \frac{ac + bd}{a^2 + b^2} + \frac{ad - bc}{a^2 + b^2}\sqrt{-1}.$$

Thus by reference to Art. 97, we see that the *sum, difference, product, and quotient of two imaginary expressions is in each case an imaginary expression of the same form.*

105.   *To find the square root of $a + b\sqrt{-1}$.*

Assume $\sqrt{a + b + \sqrt{-1}} = x + y\sqrt{-1},$

where x and y are real quantities.

By squaring, $a + b\sqrt{-1} = x^2 - y^2 + 2xy\sqrt{-1}$;
therefore, by equating real and imaginary parts,

$$x^2 - y^2 = a \qquad \ldots(1)$$
$$2xy = b \qquad \ldots(2)$$

$\therefore \qquad (x^2 + y^2)^2 = (x^2 - y^2)^2 + (2xy)^2$

$$= a^2 + b^2;$$

$\therefore \qquad x^2 + y^2 = \sqrt{a^2 + b^2} \qquad \ldots(3)$

From (1) and (3), we obtain

$$x^2 = \frac{\sqrt{a^2 + b^2} + c}{2}, \; y^2 = \frac{\sqrt{a^2 + b^2} - a}{2};$$

$\therefore \qquad x = \pm \left\{ \dfrac{\sqrt{a^2 + b^2} + a}{2} \right\}^{1/2}, \; y = \pm \left\{ \dfrac{\sqrt{a^2 + b^2} - a}{2} \right\}^{1/2}.$

Thus the required root is obtained.

Since x and y are real quantities, $x^2 + y^2$ is positive, and therefore in (3) the positive sign must be prefixed before the quantity $\sqrt{a^2 + b^2}$.

Also from (2) we see that the product xy must have the same as b; hence x and y must have like signs if b is positive, and unlike signs if b is negative.

Example 1. Find the square root of $-7 - 24\sqrt{-1}$.

Assume $\qquad \sqrt{-7 - 24\sqrt{-1}} = x + y\sqrt{-1}$;

then $\qquad -7 - 24\sqrt{-1} = x^2 - y^2 + 2xy\sqrt{-1}$;

$\therefore \qquad x^2 - y^2 = -7 \qquad \ldots(1)$

and $\qquad 2xy = -24$

$\therefore \qquad (x^2 + y^2)^2 = (x^2 - y^2)^2 + (2xy)^2$

$$= 49 + 576 = 625$$

$\therefore \qquad x^2 + y^2 = 25 \qquad \ldots(2)$

From (1) and (2), $x^2 = 9$ and $y^2 = 16$;

$\therefore \qquad x = \pm 3, \; y = \pm 4.$

Since the product xy is negative, we must take

$$x = 3, y = -4; \text{ or } x = -3, y = 4$$

Thus the roots are $3 - 4\sqrt{-1}$ and $-3 + 4\sqrt{-1}$;

that is, $\sqrt{-7 - 24\sqrt{-1}} = \pm(3 - 4\sqrt{-1})$.

Example 2. To find the value of $\sqrt[4]{-64a^4}$.

$$\sqrt[4]{-64a^4} = \sqrt{\pm 8a^2 \sqrt{-1}}$$

$$= 2a\sqrt{2}\sqrt{\pm\sqrt{-1}}.$$

It remains to find the value of $\sqrt{\pm\sqrt{-1}}$.

Assume $\qquad\qquad \sqrt{+\sqrt{-1}} = x + y\sqrt{-1}$;

then $\qquad\qquad\quad +\sqrt{-1} = x^2 - y^2 + 2xy\sqrt{-1}$;

∴ $\qquad\qquad\qquad x^2 - y^2 = 0$ and $2xy = 1$;

whence $x = \dfrac{1}{\sqrt{2}}, y = \dfrac{1}{\sqrt{2}}$; or $x = -\dfrac{1}{\sqrt{2}}, y = -\dfrac{1}{\sqrt{2}}$;

∴ $\qquad\qquad \sqrt{+\sqrt{-1}} = \pm\dfrac{1}{\sqrt{2}}(1 + \sqrt{-1})$

Similarly $\qquad \sqrt{-\sqrt{-1}} = \pm\dfrac{1}{\sqrt{2}}(1 - \sqrt{-1})$

∴ $\qquad\qquad \sqrt{\pm\sqrt{-1}} = \pm\dfrac{1}{\sqrt{2}}(1 \pm \sqrt{-1})$;

and finally $\sqrt[4]{-64a^4} = \pm 2a(1 \pm \sqrt{-1})$.

106. The symbol $\sqrt{-1}$ is often represented by the letter i; but until the student has had a little practice in the use of imaginary quantities he will find it easier to retain the symbol $\sqrt{-1}$. It is useful to notice the successive powers of $\sqrt{-1}$ or i; thus

$$(\sqrt{-1})^1 = \sqrt{-1}, \qquad i = i;$$
$$(\sqrt{-1})^2 = -1, \qquad i^2 = -1;$$
$$(\sqrt{-1})^3 = -\sqrt{-1}, \qquad i^3 = -i;$$
$$(\sqrt{-1})^4 = 1, \qquad i^4 = 1;$$

and since each power is obtained by multiplying the one before it by $\sqrt{-1}$, or i, we see that the results must now recur.

107. We shall now investigate the properties of certain imaginary quantities which are of very frequent occurrence.

Suppose $x = \sqrt[3]{1}$; then $x^3 = 1$, or $x^3 - 1 = 0$;

that is, $\qquad\qquad (x-1)(x^2 + x + 1) = 0$

∴ $\qquad\qquad$ either $x - 1 = 0$, or $x^2 + x + 1 = 0$;

whence $\qquad\qquad x = 1$, or $x = \dfrac{-1 \pm \sqrt{-3}}{2}$.

It may be shewn by actual involution that each of these values when cubed is equal to unity. Thus unity has three cube roots,

$$1, \frac{-1 + \sqrt{-3}}{2}, \frac{-1 - \sqrt{-3}}{2};$$

two of which are imaginary expressions.

Let us denote these by α and β; then since they are the roots of the equation

$$x^2 + x + 1 = 0,$$

their product is equal to unity;

that is, $\qquad \alpha\,\beta = 1;$

$\therefore \qquad\qquad \alpha^3\beta = \alpha^2;$

that is, $\qquad\qquad \beta = \alpha^2$, since $\alpha^3 = 1$.

Similarly we may shew that $\alpha = \beta^2$.

108. Since *each of the imaginary roots is the square of the other*, it is usual to denote the three cube roots of unity by $1, \omega, \omega^2$.

Also ω satisfies the equation $x^2 + x + 1 = 0$;

$\therefore \qquad\qquad 1 + \omega + \omega^2 = 0;$

that is, the *sum of the three cube roots of unity is zero.*

Again, $\qquad\qquad \omega \cdot \omega^2 = \omega^3 = 1;$

therefore, (1) *the product of the two imaginary roots is unity;*

(2) *every integral power of ω^3 is unity.*

109. It is useful to notice that the successive positive integral powers of ω are $1, \omega$ and ω^2; for, if n be a multiple of 3, it must be of the form $3m$; and $\omega^n = \omega^{3m} = 1$.

If n be not a multiple of 3, it must be of the form $3m + 1$ or $3m + 2$.

If $n = 3m + 1$, $\qquad \omega^n = \omega^{3m+1} = \omega^{3m} \cdot \omega = \omega$

If $n = 3m + 2$, $\qquad \omega^n = \omega^{3m+2} = \omega^{3m} \cdot \omega^2 = \omega^2$.

110. We now see that every quantity has three cube roots, two of which are imaginary. For the cube roots of a^3 are those of $a^3 \times 1$, and therefore are $a, a\omega, a\omega^2$. Similarly the cube roots of 9 are $\sqrt[3]{9}, \omega\sqrt[3]{9}, \omega^2\sqrt[3]{9}$ where $\sqrt[3]{9}$ is the cube root found by the ordinary arithmetical rule. In future, unless otherwise stated, the symbol $\sqrt[3]{a}$ will always be taken to denote the arithmetical cube root of a.

Example 1. Reduce $\dfrac{(2 + 3\sqrt{-1})^2}{2 + \sqrt{-1}}$ to the form $A + B\sqrt{-1}$.

The expression $= \dfrac{4 - 9 + 12\sqrt{-1}}{2 + \sqrt{-1}}$

$= \dfrac{(-5 + 12\sqrt{-1})(2 - \sqrt{-1})}{(2 + \sqrt{-1})(2 - \sqrt{-1})}$

$= \dfrac{-10 + 12 + 29\sqrt{-1}}{4 + 1}$

$= \dfrac{2}{5} + \dfrac{29}{5}\sqrt{-1};$

which is of the required form.

Example 2. Resolve $x^3 + y^3$ into three factors of the first degree.

Since, $x^3 + y^3 = (x + y)(x^2 - xy + y^2)$

$x^3 + y^3 = (x + y)(x + \omega y)(x + \omega^2 y);$

for $\omega + \omega^2 = -1$, and $\omega^3 = 1.$

Example 3. Shew that

$$(a + \omega b + \omega^2 c)(a + \omega^2 b + \omega c) = a^2 + b^2 + c^2 - bc - ca - ab$$

In the product of $a + \omega b + \omega^2 c$ and $a + \omega^2 b + \omega c,$

the coefficients of b^2 and c^2 are ω^3, or 1 :

the coefficient of $bc = \omega^2 + \omega^4 = \omega^2 + \omega = -1;$

the coefficients of ca and $ab = \omega^2 + \omega = -1;$

$\therefore$ $(a + \omega b + \omega^2 c)(a + \omega^2 b + \omega c) = a^2 + b^2 + c^2 - bc - ca - ab.$

Example 4. Shew that

$$(1 + \omega - \omega^2)^3 - (1 - \omega + \omega^2)^3 = 0$$

Since $1 + \omega + \omega^2 = 0$, we have

$$(1 + \omega - \omega^2)^3 - (1 - \omega + \omega^2)^3 = (-2\omega^2)^3 - (-2\omega)^3$$
$$= -8\omega^6 + 8\omega^3$$
$$= -8 + 8 = 0.$$

EXAMPLE VIII. b.

1. Multiply $2\sqrt{-3} + 3\sqrt{-2}$ by $4\sqrt{-3} - 5\sqrt{-2}.$

2. Multiply $3\sqrt{-7} - 5\sqrt{-2}$ by $3\sqrt{-7} + 5\sqrt{-2}.$

3. Multiply $e^{\sqrt{-1}} + e^{-\sqrt{-1}}$ by $e^{\sqrt{-1}} - e^{-\sqrt{-1}}.$

4. Multiply $x - \dfrac{1 + \sqrt{-3}}{2}$ by $x - \dfrac{1 - \sqrt{-3}}{2}.$

Express with rational denominator :

5. $\dfrac{1}{3 - \sqrt{-2}}$

6. $\dfrac{3\sqrt{-2} + 2\sqrt{-5}}{3\sqrt{-2} - 2\sqrt{-5}}$

7. $\dfrac{3 + 2\sqrt{-1}}{2 - 5\sqrt{-1}} + \dfrac{3 - 2\sqrt{-1}}{2 + 5\sqrt{-1}}$

8. $\dfrac{a + x\sqrt{-1}}{a - x\sqrt{-1}} - \dfrac{a - x\sqrt{-1}}{a + x\sqrt{-1}}$

9. $\dfrac{(x + \sqrt{-1})^2}{x - \sqrt{-1}} - \dfrac{(x - \sqrt{-1})^2}{x + \sqrt{-1}}$

10. $\dfrac{(a + \sqrt{-1})^3 - (a - \sqrt{-1})^3}{(a + \sqrt{-1})^2 - (a - \sqrt{-1})^2}$

11. Find the value of $(-\sqrt{-1})^{4n+3}$, when n is a positive integer.

12. Find the square of $\sqrt{9 + 40\sqrt{-1}} + \sqrt{9 - 40\sqrt{-1}}.$

Find the square root of

13. $-5 + 12\sqrt{-1}$

14. $-11 - 60\sqrt{-1}$

15. $-47 + 8\sqrt{-3}$

16. $-8\sqrt{-1}$

17. $a^2 - 1 + 2a\sqrt{-1}$

18. $4ab - 2(a^2 - b^2)\sqrt{-1}$

Express in the form $A + iB$

19. $\dfrac{3 + 5i}{2 - 3i}$

20. $\dfrac{\sqrt{3} - i\sqrt{2}}{2\sqrt{3} - i\sqrt{2}}$

21. $\dfrac{1 + i}{1 - i}$

22. $\dfrac{(1 + i)^2}{3 - i}$

23. $\dfrac{(a + ib)^2}{a - ib} - \dfrac{(a - ib)^2}{a + ib}$

If $1, \omega, \omega^2$ are the three cube roots of unity, prove

24. $(1 + \omega^2)^4 = \omega$

25. $(1 - \omega + \omega^2)(1 + \omega - \omega^2) = 4$

26. $(1 - \omega)(1 - \omega^2)(1 - \omega^4)(1 - \omega^5) = 9$

27. $(2 + 5\omega + 2\omega^2)^6 = (2 + 2\omega + 5\omega^2)^6 = 729$

28. $(1 - \omega + \omega^2)(1 - \omega^2 + \omega^4)(1 - \omega^4 + \omega^8) \ldots$ to $2n$ factors $= 2^{2n}$.

29. Prove that
$$x^3 + y^3 + z^3 - 3xyz = (x + y + z)(x + y\omega + z\omega^2)(x + y\omega^2 + z\omega)$$

30. If $x = a + b,\ y = a\omega + b\omega^2,\ z = a\omega^2 + b\omega$,
shew that

(1) $xyz = a^3 + b^3$.

(2) $x^2 + y^2 + z^2 = 6ab$

(3) $x^3 + y^3 + z^3 = 3(a^3 + b^3)$.

31. If $ax + cy + bz = X,\ cx + by + az = Y,\ bx + ay + cz = Z$,
shew that $(a^2 + b^2 + c^2 - bc - ca - ab)(x^2 + y^2 + z^2 - yz - zx - xy)$
$= X^2 + Y^2 + Z^2 - YZ - XZ - XY$.

Chapter 9

THE THEORY OF QUADRATIC EQUATIONS

111. After suitable reduction every quadratic equation may be written in the form

$$ax^2 + bx + c = 0, \qquad \qquad \text{...(1)}$$

and the solution of the equation is

$$x = \frac{-b \pm \sqrt{b^2 - 4ac}}{2a}. \qquad \qquad \text{...(2)}$$

We shall now prove some important propositions connected with the roots and coefficients of the equations of which (1) is the type.

112. *A quadratic equation cannot have more than two roots.*

For, if possible, let the equation $ax^2 + bx + c = 0$ have three *different* roots α, β, γ. Then since each of these values must satisfy the equation, we have

$$a\alpha^2 + b\alpha + c = 0, \qquad \qquad \text{...(1)}$$

$$a\beta^2 + b\beta + c = 0, \qquad \qquad \text{...(2)}$$

$$a\gamma^2 + b\gamma + c = 0. \qquad \qquad \text{...(3)}$$

From (1) and (2), by subtraction,

$$a(\alpha^2 - \beta^2) + b(\alpha - \beta) = 0;$$

divide out by $\alpha - \beta$ which, by hypothesis, is not zero; then

$$a(\alpha + \beta) + b = 0.$$

Similarly from (2) and (3)

$$a(\beta + \gamma) + b = 0;$$

∴ by subtraction $\qquad a(\alpha - \gamma) = 0;$

which is impossible, since, by hypothesis, a is not zero, and α is not equal to γ. Hence there cannot be three different roots.

113. In Art. 111 let the two roots in (2) be denoted by α and β, so that

$$\alpha = \frac{-b + \sqrt{b^2 - 4ac}}{2a}, \quad \beta = \frac{-b - \sqrt{b^2 - 4ac}}{2a};$$

then we have the following results :

(1) If $b^2 - 4ac$ (the quantity under the radical) is positive, α and β are real and unequal.

(2) If $b^2 - 4ac$ is zero, α and β are real and equal, each reducing in this case to $-\dfrac{b}{2a}$

(3) If $b^2 - 4ac$ is negative, α and β are imaginary and unequal.

(4) If $b^2 - 4ac$ is a perfect square, α and β are rational and unequal.

By applying these tests the nature of the roots of any quadratic may be determined without solving the equation :

Example 1. Shew that the equation $2x^2 - 6x + 7 = 0$ cannot be satisfied by any real values of x.

Here $a = 2$, $b = -6$, $c = 7$; so that

$$b^2 - 4ac = (-6)^2 - 4 \cdot 2 \cdot 7 = -20.$$

Therefore the roots are imaginary.

Example 2. If the equation $x^2 + 2(k + 2)x + 9k = 0$ has equal roots, find k. The condition for equal roots gives

$$(k + 2)^2 = 9k,$$

$$k^2 - 5k + 4 = 0,$$

$$(k - 4)(k - 1) = 0;$$

$\therefore$ $\qquad\qquad\qquad k = 4$, or 1.

Example 3. Shew that the roots of the equation

$$x^2 - 2px + p^2 - q^2 + 2qr - r^2 = 0$$

are rational.

The roots will be rational provided $(-2p)^2 - 4(p^2 - q^2 + 2qr - r^2)$ is a perfect square. But this expression reduces to $4(q^2 - 2qr + r^2)$, or $4(q - r)^2$. Hence the roots are rational.

114. Since $\alpha = \dfrac{-b + \sqrt{b^2 - 4ac}}{2a}$, $\beta = \dfrac{-b - \sqrt{b^2 - 4ac}}{2a}$,

we have by addition

$$\alpha + \beta = \frac{-b + \sqrt{b^2 - 4ac} - b - \sqrt{b^2 - 4ac}}{2a}$$

$$= -\frac{2b}{2a} = -\frac{b}{a} \qquad\qquad \ldots(1)$$

and by multiplication we have

$$\alpha\beta = \frac{(-b + \sqrt{b^2 - 4ac})(-b - \sqrt{b^2 - 4ac})}{4a^2}$$

$$= \frac{(-b)^2 - (b^2 - 4ac)}{4a^2}$$

$$= \frac{4ac}{4a^2} = \frac{c}{a} . \qquad \qquad \qquad \qquad \dots(2)$$

By writing the equation in the form

$$x^2 + \frac{b}{a} x + \frac{c}{a} = 0,$$

these results may also be expressed as follows.

In a quadratic equation *where the coefficient of the first term is unity,*

(i) the sum of the roots is equal to the coefficient of x with its sign changed

(ii) the product of the roots is equal to the third term.

Note : In any equation the term which does not contain the unknown quantity is frequently called *the absolute term.*

115.   Since $-\dfrac{b}{a} = \alpha + \beta$, and $\dfrac{c}{a} = \alpha\beta$,

the equation $x^2 + \dfrac{b}{a} x + \dfrac{c}{a} = 0$ may be written

$$x^2 - (\alpha + \beta) x + \alpha\beta = 0 \qquad \qquad \dots(1)$$

Hence any quadratic may also be expressed in the form

$$x^2 - (\text{sum of roots}) x + \text{product of roots} = 0 \qquad \dots(2)$$

Again, from (1) we have

$$(x - \alpha)(x - \beta) = 0 \qquad \qquad \dots(3)$$

We may now easily form an equation with given roots.

Example 1. Form the equation whose roots are 3 and –2.

The equation is $\qquad (x - 3)(x + 2) = 0,$

or $\qquad\qquad\qquad x^2 - x - 6 = 0.$

When the roots are irrational it is easier to use the following method.

Example 2. Form the equation whose roots are $2 + \sqrt{3}$ and $2 - \sqrt{3}$.

We have sum of roots = 4,

product of roots = 1;

$\therefore$ the equation is $x^2 - 4x + 1 = 0,$

by using formula (2) of the present article.

116.   By a method analogous to that used in Example 1 of the last article we can form an equation with three or more given roots.

Example 1. Form the equation whose roots are 2, –3 and $\dfrac{7}{5}$.

The required equation must be satisfied by each of the following suppositions :

$$x - 2 = 0, x + 3 = 0, x - \frac{7}{5} = 0;$$

therefore the equation must be

$$(x - 2)(x + 3)\left(x - \frac{7}{5}\right) = 0;$$

that is, $$(x - 2)(x + 3)(5x - 7) = 0,$$

or $$5x^3 - 2x^2 - 37x + 42 = 0.$$

Example 2. Form the equation whose roots are $0, \pm u, \dfrac{c}{b}$.

The equation has to be satisfied by

$$x = 0, \quad x = a, \quad x = -a, \quad x = \frac{c}{b};$$

therefore it is

$$x(x + a)(x - a)\left(x - \frac{c}{b}\right) = 0;$$

that is, $$x(x^2 - a^2)(bx - c) = 0,$$

or $$bx^4 - cx^3 - a^2 bx^2 + a^2 cx = 0.$$

117. The results of Art. 114 are most important, and they are generally sufficient to solve problems connected with the roots of quadratics. In such questions *the roots should never be considered singly,* but use should be made of the relations obtained by writing down the sum of the roots, and their product, in terms of the coefficients of the equation.

Example 1. If α *and* β are the roots of $x^2 - px + q = 0$, find the value of (1) $\alpha^2 + \beta^2$, (2) $\alpha^3 + \beta^3$.

We have $\alpha + \beta = p$,

$$\alpha\beta = q.$$

$\therefore$ $$\alpha^2 + \beta^2 = (\alpha + \beta)^2 - 2\alpha\beta$$

$$= p^2 - 2q.$$

Again, $\alpha^3 + \beta^3 = (\alpha + \beta)(\alpha^2 + \beta^2 - \alpha\beta)$

$$= p\{(\alpha + \beta)^2 - 3\alpha\beta\}$$

$$= p(p^2 - 3q).$$

Example 2. If α, β are the roots of the equation $lx^2 + mx + n = 0$, find the equation whose roots are $\dfrac{\alpha}{\beta}, \dfrac{\beta}{\alpha}$.

We have sum of roots $= \dfrac{\alpha}{\beta} + \dfrac{\beta}{\alpha} = \dfrac{\alpha^3 + \beta^2}{\alpha\beta}$

product of roots $= \dfrac{\alpha}{\beta} \cdot \dfrac{\beta}{\alpha} = 1;$

$\therefore$ by Art. 115 the required equation is

$$x^2 - \left(\frac{\alpha^2 + \beta^2}{\alpha\beta}\right)x + 1 = 0,$$

or $\alpha\beta x^2 - (\alpha^2 + \beta^2)\, x + \alpha\beta = 0.$

As in the last example $\alpha^2 + \beta^2 = \dfrac{m^2 - 2nl}{l^2}$, and $\alpha\beta = \dfrac{n}{l}$.

$\therefore$ the equation is $\dfrac{n}{l}\, x^2 - \dfrac{m^2 - 2nl}{l^2}\, x + \dfrac{n}{l} = 0,$

or $nlx^2 - (m^2 - 2nl)\, x + nl = 0.$

Example 3. When $x = \dfrac{3 + 5\sqrt{-1}}{2}$, find the value of $2x^3 + 2x^2 - 7x + 72$;

and shew that it will be unaltered if $\dfrac{3 - 5\sqrt{-1}}{2}$ be substituted for x.

Form the quadratic equation whose roots are $\dfrac{3 \pm 5\sqrt{-1}}{2}$;

the sum of the roots $= 3$;

the product of the roots $= \dfrac{17}{2}$;

hence the equation is $2x^2 - 6x + 17 = 0$;

$\therefore$ $2x^2 - 6x + 17$ is a quadratic *expression* which vanishes for *either* of the values

$$\frac{3 \pm 5\sqrt{-1}}{2}.$$

Now $2x^3 + 2x^2 - 7x + 72 = x\,(2x^2 - 6x + 17) + 4\,(2x^2 - 6x + 17) + 4$

$= x \times 0 + 4 \times 0 + 4$

$= 4;$

which is the numerical value of the expression in each of the supposed cases.

118.   *To find the condition that the roots of the equation* $ax^2 + bx + c = 0$ *should be* (1) *equal in magnitude and opposite in sign,* (2) *reciprocals.*

The roots will be equal in magnitude and opposite in sign if their sum is zero; hence the required condition is

$$-\frac{b}{a} = 0, \text{ or } b = 0.$$

Again, the roots will be reciprocals when their product is unity; hence we must have

$$\frac{c}{a} = 1, \text{ or } c = a.$$

The first of these results is of frequent occurrence in Analytical Geometry, and the second is a particular case of a more general condition applicable to equations of any degree.

Example : Find the condition that the roots of $ax^2 + bx + c = 0$ may be (1) both positive, (2) opposite in sign, but the greater of them negative.

We have $$\alpha + \beta = -\frac{b}{a}, \quad \alpha\beta = \frac{c}{a}.$$

(1) If the roots are both positive, $\alpha\beta$ is positive, and therefore c and a have like signs.

Also, since $\alpha + \beta$ is positive, $\frac{b}{a}$ is negative; therefore b and a have unlike signs.

Hence the required condition is that the signs of a and c should be like, and opposite to the sign of b.

(2) If the roots are of opposite signs, $\alpha\beta$ is negative, and therefore c and a have unlike signs.

Also since $\alpha + \beta$ has the sign of the greater root it is negative, and therefore $\frac{b}{a}$ is positive; therefore b and a have like signs.

Hence the required condition is that the signs of a and b should be like and opposite to the sign of c.

EXAMPLES IX. a.

Form the equations whose roots are

1. $-\dfrac{4}{5}, \dfrac{3}{7}$.
2. $\dfrac{m}{n}, -\dfrac{n}{m}$.
3. $\dfrac{p-q}{p+q}, -\dfrac{p+q}{p-q}$.

4. $7 \pm 2\sqrt{5}$.
5. $\pm 2\sqrt{3} - 5$.
6. $-p \pm 2\sqrt{2}q$.

7. $-3 \pm 5i$.
8. $-a \pm ib$.
9. $\pm i(a - b)$.

10. $-3, \dfrac{2}{3}, \dfrac{1}{2}$.
11. $\dfrac{a}{2}, 0, -\dfrac{2}{a}$.
12. $2 \pm \sqrt{3}, 4$.

13. Prove that the roots of the following equations are real :
   (1) $x^2 - 2ax + a^2 - b^2 - c^2 = 0$,
   (2) $(a - b + c)x^2 + 4(a - b)x + (a - b - c) = 0$.

14. If the equation $x^2 - 15 - m(2x - 8) = 0$ has equal roots, find the values of m.

15. For what values of m will the equation
$$x^2 - 2x(1 + 3m) + 7(3 + 2m) = 0$$
have equal roots ?

16. For what value of m will the equation
$$\frac{x^2 - bx}{ax - c} = \frac{m - 1}{m + 1}$$
have roots equal in magnitude but opposite in sign ?

17. Prove that the roots of the following equations are rational :

(1) $(a + c - b) x^2 + 2cx + (b + c - a) = 0$,

(2) $abc^2x^2 + 3a^2cx + b^2cx - 6a^2 - ab + 2b^2 = 0$.

If α, β are the roots of the equation $ax^2 + bx + c = 0$, find the values of

18. $\dfrac{1}{\alpha^2} + \dfrac{1}{\beta^2}$.　　　　19. $\alpha^4\beta^7 + \alpha^7\beta^4$.　　　　20. $\left(\dfrac{\alpha}{\beta} - \dfrac{\beta}{\alpha}\right)^2$

Find the value of :

21. $x^3 + x^2 - x + 22$ when $x = 1 + 2i$.

22. $x^3 - 3x^2 - 8x + 15$ when $x = 3 + i$.

23. $x^3 - ax^2 + 2a^2x + 4a^3$ when $\dfrac{x}{a} = 1 - \sqrt{-3}$,

24. If α and β are the roots of $x^2 + px + q = 0$, form the equation whose roots are $(\alpha - \beta)^2$ and $(\alpha + \beta)^2$.

25. Prove that the roots of $(x - a)(x - b) = h^2$ are always real.

26. If x_1, x_2 are the roots of $ax^2 + bx + c = 0$, find the value of

(1) $(ax_1 + b)^{-2} + (ax_2 + b)^{-2}$,

(2) $(ax_1 + b)^{-3} + (ax_2 + b)^{-3}$.

27. Find the condition that one root of $ax^2 + bx + c = 0$ shall be n times the other.

28. If α, β are the roots of $ax^2 + bx + c = 0$, form the equation whose roots are $\alpha^2 + \beta^2$ and $\alpha^{-2} + \beta^{-2}$.

29. Form the equation whose roots are the squares of the sum and of the difference of the roots of

$$2x^2 + 2(m + n)x + m^2 + n^2 = 0.$$

30. Discuss the signs of the roots of the equation

$$px^2 + qx + r = 0.$$

119. The following example illustrates a useful application of the results proved in Art. 113.

Example : If x is a real quantity, prove that the expression $\dfrac{x^2 + 2x - 11}{2(x - 3)}$

can have all numerical values except such as lie between 2 and 6.

Let the given expression be represented by y, so that

$$\frac{x^2 + 2x - 11}{2(x-3)} = y;$$

then multiplying up and transposing, we have

$$x^2 + 2x(1-y) + 6y - 11 = 0.$$

This is a quadratic equation, and in order that x may have real values $4(1-y)^2 - 4(6y-11)$ must be positive; or dividing by 4 and simplifying, $y^2 - 8y + 12$ must be positive; that is, $(y-6)(y-2)$ must be positive. Hence the factors of this product must be both positive, or both negative. In the former case y is greater than 6; in the latter y is less than 2. Therefore y cannot lie between 2 and 6, but may have any other value.

In this example it will be noticed that the *quadratic expression* $y^2 - 8y + 12$ is positive so long as y does not lie between the roots of the corresponding *quadratic equation* $y^2 - 8y + 12 = 0$.

This is a particular case of the general proposition investigated in the next article.

120. *For all real values of x the expression $ax^2 + bx + c$ has the same sign as a, except when the roots of the equation $ax^2 + bx + c = 0$ are real and unequal, and x has a value lying between them.*

Case I. Suppose that the roots of the equation

$$ax^2 + bx + c = 0$$

are real; denote them by α and β, and let α be the greater.

Then
$$ax^2 + bx + c = a\left(x^2 + \frac{b}{a}x + \frac{c}{a}\right)$$

$$= a\{x^2 - (\alpha+\beta)x + \alpha\beta\}$$

$$= a(x-\alpha)(x-\beta).$$

Now if x is greater than α, the factors $x-\alpha, x-\beta$ are both positive; and if x is less than β, the factors $x-\alpha, x-\beta$ are both negative; therefore in each case the expression $(x-\alpha)(x-\beta)$ is positive, and $ax^2 + bx + c$ has the same sign as a. But if x has a value lying between α and β, the expression $(x-\alpha)(x-\beta)$ is negative, and the sign of $ax^2 + bx + c$ is opposite to that of a.

Case II. If α and β are equal, then

$$ax^2 + bx + c = a(x-\alpha)^2,$$

and $(x-\alpha)^2$ is positive for all real values of x; hence $ax^2 + bx + c$ has the same sign as a.

Case III. Suppose that the equation $ax^2 + bx + c = 0$ has imaginary roots; then

$$ax^2 + bx + c = a\left\{x^2 + \frac{b}{a}x + \frac{c}{a}\right\}$$

$$= a\left\{\left(x + \frac{b}{2a}\right)^2 + \frac{4ac - b^2}{4a^2}\right\}.$$

But $b^2 - 4ac$ is negative since the roots are imaginary; hence $\frac{4ac - b^2}{4a^2}$ is positive, and the expression

$$\left(x + \frac{b}{2a}\right)^2 + \frac{4ac - b^2}{4a^2}$$

is positive for all real values of x; therefore $ax^2 + bx + c$ has the same sign as a. This establishes the proposition.

121. From the preceding article it follows that the expression $ax^2 + bx + c$ will always have the same sign whatever real value x may have, provided that $b^2 - 4ac$ is negative or zero; and if this condition is satisfied the expression is positive or negative according as a is positive or negative.

Conversely, in order that the expression $ax^2 + bx + c$ may be always positive, $b^2 - 4ac$ must be negative or zero, and a must be positive; and in order that $ax^2 + bx + c$ may be always negative $b^2 - 4ac$ must be negative or zero, and a must be negative.

Example : Find the limits between which a must lie in order that

$$\frac{ax^2 - 7x + 5}{5x^2 - 7x + a}$$

may be capable of all values, x being any real quantity.

Put $\dfrac{ax^2 - 7x + 5}{5x^2 - 7x + a} = y;$

then $(a - 5y)x^2 - 7x(1 - y) + (5 - ay) = 0.$

In order that the values of x found from this quadratic may be real, the expression

$49(1 - y)^2 - 4(a - 5y)(5 - ay)$ must be positive,

that is, $(49 - 20a)y^2 + 2(2a^2 + 1)y + (49 - 20a)$ must be positive;

hence $(2a^2 + 1)^2 - (49 - 20a)^2$ must be negative or zero, and $49 - 20a$ must be positive.

Now $(2a^2 + 1)^2 - (49 - 20a)^2$ is negative or zero, according as

$2(a^2 - 10a + 25) \times 2(a^2 + 10a - 24)$ is negative or zero;

that is, according as $4(a-5)^2(a+12)(a-2)$ is negative or zero.

This expression is negative as long as a lies between 2 and -12, and for such values $49 - 20a$ is positive; the expression is zero when $a = 5, -12$, or 2, but $49 - 20a$ is negative when $a = 5$. Hence the limiting values are 2 and -12, and a may have any intermediate value.

EXAMPLES IX. b.

1. Determine the limits between which n must lie in order that the equation

$$2ax(ax + nc) + (n^2 - 2)c^2 = 0$$

may have real roots.

2. If x be real, prove that $\dfrac{x}{x^2 - 5x + 9}$ must lie between 1 and $-\dfrac{1}{11}$.

3. Shew that $\dfrac{x^2 - x + 1}{x^2 + x + 1}$ lies between 3 and $\dfrac{1}{3}$ for all real values of x.

4. If x be real, prove that $\dfrac{x^2 + 34x - 71}{x^2 + 2x - 7}$ can have no value between 5 and 9.

5. Find the equation whose roots are $\dfrac{\sqrt{a}}{\sqrt{a} \pm \sqrt{a-b}}$.

6. If α, β are roots of the equation $x^2 - px + q = 0$, find the value of

   (1) $\alpha^2(\alpha^2\beta^{-1} - \beta) + \beta^2(\beta^2\alpha^{-1} - \alpha)$,

   (2) $(\alpha - p)^{-4} + (\beta - p)^{-4}$.

7. If the roots of $lx^2 + nx + n = 0$ be in the ratio of $p : q$ prove that

$$\sqrt{\frac{p}{q}} + \sqrt{\frac{q}{p}} + \sqrt{\frac{n}{l}} = 0.$$

8. If x be real, the expression $\dfrac{(x + m)^2 - 4mn}{2(x - n)}$ admits of all values except such as lie between $2n$ and $2m$.

9. If the roots of the equation $ax^2 + 2bx + c = 0$ be α and β, and those of the equation $Ax^2 + 2Bx + C = 0$ be $\alpha + \delta$ and $\beta + \delta$, prove that

$$\frac{b^2 - ac}{a^2} = \frac{B^2 - AC}{A^2}$$

10. Shew that the expression $\dfrac{px^2 + 3x - 4}{p + 3x - 4x^2}$ will be capable of all values when x is real, provided that p has any value between 1 and 7.

11. Find the greatest value of $\dfrac{x + 2}{2x^2 + 3x + 6}$ for real values of x.

12. Shew that if x is real, the expression
$$(x^2 - bc)(2x - b - c)^{-1}$$
has no real values between b and c.

13. If the roots of $ax^2 + 2bx + c = 0$ be possible and different, then the roots of
$$(a + c)(ax^2 + 2bx + c) = 2(ac - b^2)(x^2 + 1)$$
will be impossible, and *vice-versa*.

14. Shew that the expression $\dfrac{(ax - b)(dx - c)}{(bx - a)(cx - d)}$ will be capable of all values when x is real, if $a^2 - b^2$ and $c^2 - d^2$ have the same sign.

*122. We shall conclude this chapter with some miscellaneous theorems and examples. It will be convenient here to introduce a phraseology and notation which the student will frequently meet with in his mathematical reading.

Definition : Any expression which involves x, and whose value is dependent on that of x, is called a function of x. Functions of x are usually denoted by symbols of the form $f(x)$, $F(x)$, $\phi(x)$.

Thus the equation $y = f(x)$ may be considered as equivalent to a statement that any change made in the value of x will produce a consequent change in y, and *vice-versa*. The quantities x and y are called variables, and are further distinguished as the independent variable and the dependent variable.

An *independent variable* is a quantity which may have any value we choose to assign to it, and the corresponding *dependent variable* has its value determined as soon as the value of the independent variable is known.

*123. An expression of the form
$$p_0 x^n + p_1 x^{n-1} + p_2 x^{n-2} + \ldots + p_{n-1} x + p_n$$

where n is a positive integer, and the coefficients $p_0, p_1, p_2, ..., p_n$ do not involve x, is called a rational and integral algebraical function of x. In the present chapter we shall confine our attention to functions of this kind.

*124.   A function is said to be linear when it contains no higher power of the variable than the first; thus $ax + b$ is a linear function of x. A function is said to be **quadratic** when it contains no higher power of the variable than the second; thus $ax^2 + bx + c$ is a quadratic function of x. Functions of the *third, fourth,...* degrees are those in which the highest power of the variable is respectively the *third, fourth,...* . Thus in the last article the expression is a function of x of the nth degree.

*125.   The symbol $f(x, y)$ is used to denote a function of two variables x and y; thus $ax + by + c$, and $ax^2 + bxy + cy^2 + dx + ey + f$ are respectively linear and quadratic functions of x, y.

The *equations* $f(x) = 0, f(x, y) = 0$ are said to be linear, quadratic,... according as the *functions* $f(x), f(x, y)$ are linear, quadratic,... .

*126.   We have proved in Art. 120 that the *expression* $ax^2 + bx + c$ admits of being put in the form $a(x - \alpha)(x - \beta)$, where α and β are the roots of the *equation* $ax^2 + bx + c = 0$.

Thus a quadratic expression $ax^2 + bx + c$ is capable of being resolved into two rational factors of the first degree, whenever the equation $ax^2 + bx + c = 0$ has rational roots; that is, when $b^2 - 4ac$ is a perfect square.

*127.   *To find the condition that a quadratic function of x, y, may be resolved into two linear factors.*

Denote the function by $f(x, y)$ where

$$f(x, y) = ax^2 + 2hxy + by^2 + 2gx + 2fy + c.$$

Write this in descending powers of x, and equate it to zero; thus

$$ax^2 + 2x(hy + g) + by^2 + 2fy + c = 0.$$

Solving this quadratic in x we have

$$x = \frac{-(hy + g) \pm \sqrt{(hy + g)^2 - a(by^2 + 2fy + c)}}{a},$$

or $ax + hy + g = \pm \sqrt{y^2(h^2 - ab) + 2y(hg - af) + (g^2 - ac)}.$

Now in order that $f(x, y)$ may be the product of two linear factors of the form $px + qy + r$, the quantity under the radical must be a perfect square; hence

$$(hg - af)^2 = (h^2 - ab)(g^2 - ac).$$

Transposing and dividing by a, we obtain

$$abc + 2fgh - af^2 - bg^2 - ch^2 = 0;$$

which is the condition required.

This proposition is of great importance in Analytical Geometry.

*128. To find the condition that the equations

$$ax^2 + bx + c = 0, \quad a'x^2 + b'x + c' = 0$$

may have a common root.

Suppose these equations are both satistied by $x = \alpha$; then

$$a\alpha^2 + b\alpha + c = 0,$$

$$a'\alpha^2 + b'\alpha + c' = 0;$$

∴ by cross multiplication

$$\frac{\alpha^2}{bc' - b'c} = \frac{\alpha}{ca' - c'a} = \frac{1}{ab' - a'b}.$$

To eliminate α, square the second of these equal ratios and equate it to the product of the other two; thus

$$\frac{\alpha^2}{(ca' - c'a)^2} = \frac{\alpha^2}{(bc' - b'c)} \cdot \frac{1}{(ab' - a'b)};$$

∴

$$(ca' - c'a)^2 = (bc' - b'c)(ab' - a'b),$$

which is the condition required.

It is easy to prove that this is the condition that the two quadratic functions $ax^2 + bxy + cy^2$ and $a'x^2 + b'xy + c'y^2$ may have a common linear factor.

EXAMPLES IX. c.

1. For what values of m will the expression

$$y^2 + 2xy + 2x + my - 3$$

be capable of resolution into two rational factors ?

2. Find the values of m which will make $2x^2 + mxy + 3y^2 - 5y - 2$ equivalent to the product of two linear factors.

3. Shew that the expression

$$A\,(x^2 - y^2) - xy\,(B - C)$$

always admits of two real linear factors.

4. If the equations
$$x^2 + px + q = 0,\ x^2 + p'x + q' = 0$$
have a common root, shew that it must be equal to
$$\frac{pq' - p'q}{q - q'} \quad \text{or} \quad \frac{q - q'}{p' - p}.$$

5. Find the condition that the expressions
$$lx^2 + mxy + ny^2,\ l'x^2 + m'xy + n'y^2$$
may have a common linear factor.

6. If the expression
$$3x^2 + 2Pxy + 2y^2 + 2ax - 4y + 1$$
can be resolved into linear factors, prove that P must be one of the roots of the equation $P^2 + 4aP + 2a^2 + 6 = 0$.

7. Find the condition that the expressions
$$ax^2 + 2hxy + by^2,\ a'x^2 + 2h'xy + b'y^2$$
may be respectively divisible by factors of the form $y - mx,\ my + x$.

8. Shew that in the equation
$$x^2 - 3xy + 2y^2 - 2x - 3y - 35 = 0,$$
for every real value of x there is a real value of y, and for every real value of y there is a real value of x.

9. If x and y are two real quantities connected by the equation
$$9x^2 + 2xy + y^2 - 92x - 20y + 244 = 0,$$
then will x lie between 3 and 6, and y between 1 and 10.

10. If $(ax^2 + bx + c)\,y + a'x^2 + b'x + c' = 0$, find the condition that x may be a rational function of y.

■ ■ ■

Chapter 10

MISCELLANEOUS EQUATIONS

129. In this chapter we propose to consider some miscellaneous equations; it will be seen that many of these can be solved by the ordinary rules for quadratic equations, but others require some special artifice for their solution.

Example 1. Solve $8x^{\frac{3}{2n}} - 8x^{-\frac{3}{2n}} = 63$.

Multiply by $x^{\frac{3}{2n}}$ and transpose; thus

$$8x^{\frac{3}{n}} - 63x^{\frac{3}{2n}} - 8 = 0;$$
$$(x^{3/2n} - 8)(8x^{3/2n} + 1) = 0;$$
$$x^{\frac{3}{2n}} = 8, \quad \text{or} \quad -\frac{1}{8};$$
$$x = (2^3)^{\frac{2n}{3}}, \quad \text{or} \quad \left(-\frac{1}{2^3}\right)^{\frac{2n}{3}};$$
$$\therefore \quad x = 2^{2n}, \quad \text{or} \quad \frac{1}{2^{2n}}.$$

Example 2. Solve $2\sqrt{\dfrac{x}{a}} + 3\sqrt{\dfrac{a}{x}} = \dfrac{b}{a} + \dfrac{6a}{b}$.

Let $\sqrt{\dfrac{x}{a}} = y$; then $\sqrt{\dfrac{a}{x}} = \dfrac{1}{y}$;

$$\therefore \quad 2y + \frac{3}{y} = \frac{b}{a} + \frac{6a}{b};$$
$$2aby^2 - 6a^2y - b^2y + 3ab = 0;$$
$$(2ay - b)(by - 3a) = 0;$$
$$y = \frac{b}{2a}, \quad \text{or} \quad \frac{3a}{b};$$
$$\therefore \quad \frac{x}{a} = \frac{b^2}{4a^2}, \quad \text{or} \quad \frac{9a^2}{b^2};$$

that is,
$$x = \frac{b^2}{4a}, \quad \text{or} \quad \frac{9a^3}{b^2}.$$

Example 3. Solve $(x-5)(x-7)(x+6)(x+4) = 504$.

We have $(x^2 - x - 20)(x^2 - x - 42) = 504;$

which, being arranged as a quadratic in $x^2 - x$, gives

$$(x^2 - x)^2 - 62 (x^2 - x) + 336 = 0;$$

$$\therefore \qquad (x^2 - x - 6) (x^2 - x - 56) = 0;$$

$$\therefore \qquad x^2 - x - 6 = 0, \text{ or } x^2 - x - 56 = 0;$$

whence $x = 3, -2, 8, -7.$

130.   Any equation which can be thrown into the form

$$ax^2 + bx + c + p \sqrt{ax^2 + bx + c} = q$$

may be solved as follows.

Putting $y = \sqrt{ax^2 + bx + c}$, we obtain

$$y^2 + py - q = 0.$$

Let α and β be the roots of this equation, so that

$$\sqrt{ax^2 + bx + c} = \alpha, \ \sqrt{ax^2 + bx + c} = \beta;$$

from these equations we shall obtain *four* values of x.

When no sign is prefixed to a radical it is usually understood that it is to be taken as positive; hence, if α and β are both positive, all the four values of x satisfy the *original* equation. If however α or β is negative, the roots found from the resulting quadratic will satisfy the equation

$$ax^2 + bx + c - p \sqrt{ax^2 + bx + c} = q,$$

but not the original equation.

Example : Solve $x^2 - 5x + 2 \sqrt{x^2 - 5x + 3} = 12.$

Add 3 to each side; then

$$x^2 - 5x + 3 + 2 \sqrt{x^2 - 5x + 3} = 15.$$

Putting $\sqrt{x^2 - 5x + 3} = y$, we obtain $y^2 + 2y - 15 = 0$; whence $y = 3$ or -5. Thus $\sqrt{x^2 - 5x + 3} = +3$, or $\sqrt{x^2 - 5x + 3} = -5.$

Squaring, and solving the resulting quadratics, we obtain from the first $x = 6$ or -1; and from the second $x = \dfrac{5 \pm \sqrt{113}}{2}$. The first pair of values satisfies the given equation, but the second pair satisfies the equation

$$x^2 - 5x - 2 \sqrt{x^2 - 5x + 3} = 12.$$

131.   Before clearing an equation of radicals it is advisable to examine whether any common factor can be removed by division.

Example : Solve $\sqrt{x^2 - 7ax + 10a^2} - \sqrt{x^2 + ax - 6a^2} = x - 2a.$

We have

$$\sqrt{(x - 2a) (x - 5a)} - \sqrt{(x - 2a) (x + 3a)} = x - 2a.$$

The factor $\sqrt{x - 2a}$ can now be removed from every term;

$\therefore$ $\qquad\qquad \sqrt{x-5a}-\sqrt{x+3a}=\sqrt{x-2a};$

$$x-5a+x+3a-2\sqrt{(x-5a)(x+3a)}=x-2a;$$

$$x=2\sqrt{x^2-2ax-15a^2};$$

$$3x^2-8ax-60a^2=0;$$

$$(x-6a)(3x+10a)=0;$$

$$x=6a, \quad \text{or} \quad -\frac{10a}{3}.$$

Also by equating to zero the factor $\sqrt{x-2a}$, we obtain $x=2a$.

On trial it will be found that $x=6a$ does not satisfy the equation; thus the roots are $-\dfrac{10a}{3}$ and $2a$.

The student may compare a similar question discussed in the *Elementary Algebra*. Art. 281.

132. The following artifice is sometimes useful.

Example : Solve $\sqrt{3x^2-4x+34}+\sqrt{3x^2-4x-11}=9$ ...(1)

We have *identically*

$$(3x^2-4x+34)-(3x^2-4x-11)=45 \qquad\qquad ...(2)$$

Divide each member of (2) by the corresponding member of (1); thus

$$\sqrt{3x^2-4x+34}-\sqrt{3x^2-4x-11}=5 \qquad\qquad ...(3)$$

Now (2) is an *identical equation* true for *all* values of x, whereas (1) is an equation which is true only for certain values of x; hence also equation (3) is only true for these values of x.

From (1) and (3) by addition

$$\sqrt{3x^2-4x+34}=7;$$

whence $\qquad x=3, \quad \text{or} \quad -\dfrac{5}{3}.$

133. The solution of an equation of the form

$$ax^4 \pm bx^3 \pm cx^2 \pm bx + a = 0,$$

in which the coefficients of terms equidistant from the beginning and end are equal, can be made to depend on the solution of a quadratic. Equations of this type are known as *reciprocal equations,* and are so named because they are not altered when x is changed into its reciprocal $\dfrac{1}{x}$.

For a more complete discussion of reciprocal equations the student is referred to Arts. 568–570.

Example : Solve $12x^4-56x^3+89x^2-56x+12=0.$

Dividing by x^2 and rearranging,

$$12\left(x^2 + \frac{1}{x^2}\right) - 56\left(x + \frac{1}{x}\right) + 89 = 0.$$

Put $x + \dfrac{1}{x} = z$; then $x^2 + \dfrac{1}{x^2} = z^2 - 2$;

$\therefore$ $\qquad\qquad\qquad 12\,(z^2 - 2) - 56z + 89 = 0;$

whence we obtain $\qquad\qquad z = \dfrac{5}{2},$ or $\dfrac{13}{6}.$

$\therefore$ $\qquad\qquad\qquad x + \dfrac{1}{x} = \dfrac{5}{2},$ or $\dfrac{13}{6}.$

By solving these equations we find that $x = 2, \dfrac{1}{2}, \dfrac{3}{2}, \dfrac{2}{3}.$

134. The following equation though not *reciprocal* may be solved in a similar manner.

Example: Solve $6x^4 - 25x^3 + 12x^2 + 25x + 6 = 0.$

We have $\qquad 6\left(x^2 + \dfrac{1}{x^2}\right) - 25\left(x - \dfrac{1}{x}\right) + 12 = 0;$

whence $\qquad 6\left(x - \dfrac{1}{x}\right)^2 - 25\left(x - \dfrac{1}{x}\right) + 24 = 0;$

$\therefore$ $\qquad 2\left(x - \dfrac{1}{x}\right) - 3 = 0,$ or $3\left(x - \dfrac{1}{x}\right) - 8 = 0;$

whence we obtain $\quad x = 2, -\dfrac{1}{2}, 3, -\dfrac{1}{3}.$

135. When one root of a quadratic equation is obvious by inspection, the other root may often be readily obtained by making use of the properties of the roots of quadratic equations proved in Art. 114.

Example: Solve $(1 - a^2)(x + a) - 2a(1 - x^2) = 0.$

This is a quadratic, one of whose roots is clearly a.

Also, since the equation may be written

$$2ax^2 + (1 - a^2)\,x - a\,(1 + a^2) = 0,$$

the product of the roots is $-\dfrac{1 + a^2}{2}$; and therefore the other root is $-\dfrac{1 + a^2}{2a}.$

EXAMPLES X. a.

[*When any of the roots satisfy a modified form of the equation, the student should examine the particular arrangement of the signs of the radicals to which each solution applies.*]

Solve the following equations:

1. $x^{-2} - 2x^{-1} = 8.$ $\qquad\qquad$ **2.** $9 + x^{-4} = 10x^{-2}.$

3. $2\sqrt{x} + 2x^{-\frac{1}{2}} = 5.$

4. $6x^{\frac{3}{4}} = 7x^{\frac{1}{4}} - 2x^{-\frac{1}{4}}.$

5. $x^{\frac{2}{n}} + 6 = 5x^{\frac{1}{n}}.$

6. $3x^{\frac{1}{2n}} - x^{\frac{1}{n}} - 2 = 0.$

7. $5\sqrt{\dfrac{3}{x}} + 7\sqrt{\dfrac{x}{3}} = 22\frac{2}{3}.$

8. $\sqrt{\dfrac{x}{1-x}} + \sqrt{\dfrac{1-x}{x}} = 2\frac{1}{6}.$

9. $6\sqrt{x} = 5x^{-\frac{1}{2}} - 13.$

10. $1 + 8x^{\frac{6}{5}} + 9\sqrt[5]{x^3} = 0.$

11. $3^{2x} + 9 = 10 \cdot 3^x.$

12. $5(5^x + 5^{-x}) = 26.$

13. $2^{2x+3} + 1 = 32 \cdot 2^x.$

14. $2^{2x+3} - 57 = 65(2^x - 1).$

15. $\sqrt{2^x} + \dfrac{1}{\sqrt{2^x}} = 2.$

16. $\dfrac{3}{\sqrt{2x}} - \dfrac{\sqrt{2x}}{5} = 5\frac{9}{10}.$

17. $(x-7)(x-3)(x+5)(x+1) = 1680.$

18. $(x+9)(x-3)(x-7)(x+5) = 385.$

19. $x(2x+1)(x-2)(2x-3) = 63.$

20. $(2x-7)(x^2-9)(2x+5) = 91.$

21. $x^2 + 2\sqrt{x^2 + 6x} = 24 - 6x.$

22. $3x^2 - 4x + \sqrt{3x^2 - 4x - 6} = 18.$

23. $3x^2 - 7 + 3\sqrt{3x^2 - 16x + 21} = 16x.$

24. $8 + 9\sqrt{(3x-1)(x-2)} = 3x^2 - 7x.$

25. $\dfrac{3x-2}{2} + \sqrt{2x^2 - 5x + 3} = \dfrac{(x+1)^2}{3}.$

26. $7x - \dfrac{\sqrt{3x^2 - 8x + 1}}{x} = \left(\dfrac{8}{\sqrt{x}} + \sqrt{x}\right)^2.$

27. $\sqrt{4x^2 - 7x - 15} - \sqrt{x^2 - 3x} = \sqrt{x^2 - 9}.$

28. $\sqrt{2x^2 - 9x + 4} + 3\sqrt{2x - 1} = \sqrt{2x^2 + 21x - 11}.$

29. $\sqrt{2x^2 + 5x - 7} + \sqrt{3(x^2 - 7x + 6)} - \sqrt{7x^2 - 6x - 1} = 0.$

30. $\sqrt{a^2 + 2ax - 3x^2} - \sqrt{a^2 + ax - 6x^2} = \sqrt{2a^2 + 3ax - 9x^2}.$

31. $\sqrt{2x^2 + 5x - 2} - \sqrt{2x^2 + 5x - 9} = 1.$

32. $\sqrt{3x^2 - 2x + 9} + \sqrt{3x^2 - 2x - 4} = 13.$

33. $\sqrt{2x^2 - 7x + 1} - \sqrt{2x^2 - 9x + 4} = 1.$

34. $\sqrt{3x^2 - 7x - 30} - \sqrt{2x^2 - 7x - 5} = x - 5.$

35. $x^4 + x^3 - 4x^2 + x + 1 = 0.$ **36.** $x^4 + \dfrac{8}{9}x^2 + 1 = 3x^3 + 3x.$

37. $x^4 + 1 - 3(x^3 + x) = 2x^2.$

38. $10(x^4 + 1) - 63x(x^2 - 1) + 52x^2 = 0.$

39. $\dfrac{x + \sqrt{12a - x}}{x - \sqrt{12a - x}} = \dfrac{\sqrt{a} + 1}{\sqrt{a} - 1}.$ **40.** $\dfrac{a + 2x + \sqrt{a^2 - 4x^2}}{a + 2x - \sqrt{a^2 - 4x^2}} = \dfrac{5x}{a}.$

41. $\dfrac{x + \sqrt{x^2 - 1}}{x - \sqrt{x^2 - 1}} - \dfrac{x - \sqrt{x^2 - 1}}{x + \sqrt{x^2 - 1}} = 8x\sqrt{x^2 - 3x + 2}.$

42. $\sqrt{x^2 + x} + \dfrac{\sqrt{x - 1}}{\sqrt{x^3 - x}} = \dfrac{5}{2}.$ **43.** $\dfrac{x^3 + 1}{x^2 - 1} = x + \sqrt{\dfrac{6}{x}}.$

44. $2^{x^2} : 2^{2x} = 8 : 1.$ **45.** $a^{2x}(a^2 + 1) = (a^{3x} + a^x)\,a.$

46. $\dfrac{8\sqrt{x - 5}}{3x - 7} = \dfrac{\sqrt{3x - 7}}{x - 5}.$

47. $\dfrac{18(7x - 3)}{2x + 1} = \dfrac{250\sqrt{2x + 1}}{3\sqrt{7x - 3}}.$

48. $(a + x)^{2/3} + 4(a - x)^{2/3} = 5(a^2 - x^2)^{1/3}.$

49. $\sqrt{x^2 + ax - 1} - \sqrt{x^2 + bx - 1} = \sqrt{a} - \sqrt{b}.$

50. $\dfrac{x + \sqrt{x^2 - 1}}{x - \sqrt{x^2 - 1}} + \dfrac{x - \sqrt{x^2 - 1}}{x + \sqrt{x^2 - 1}} = 98.$

51. $x^4 - 2x^3 + x = 380.$ **52.** $27x^3 + 21x + 8 = 0.$

136. We shall now discuss some simultaneous equations of two unknown quantities.

Example 1. Solve $x + 2 + y + 3 + \sqrt{(x + 2)(y + 3)} = 39.$

$$(x + 2)^2 + (y + 3)^2 + (x + 2)(y + 3) = 741.$$

Put $x + 2 = u$, and $y + 3 = v$; then

$$u + v + \sqrt{uv} = 39, \qquad \qquad \dots(1)$$

$$u^2 + v^2 + uv = 741, \qquad \qquad \dots(2)$$

hence, from (1) and (2), we obtain by division,

$$u + v - \sqrt{uv} = 19 \qquad \qquad \dots(3)$$

From (1) and (3), $u + v = 29;$

and $\sqrt{uv} = 10,$

or $uv = 100;$

whence $u = 25,$ or $4;$ $v = 4,$ or $25;$

thus $x = 23,$ or $2;$ $y = 1,$ or $22.$

Example 2. Solve $\qquad x^4 + y^4 = 82,$ ...(1)

$$x - y = 2. \qquad \qquad ...(2)$$

Put $\quad x = u + v$, and $y = u - v$;

then from (2) we obtain $v = 1$.

Substituting in (1), $(u + 1)^4 + (u - 1)^4 = 82$;

$\therefore \qquad\qquad\qquad 2\,(u^4 + 6u^2 + 1) = 82$;

$$u^4 + 6u^2 - 40 = 0;$$

whence $\qquad\qquad\qquad u^2 = 4$, or -10;

and $\qquad\qquad\qquad u = \pm\,2$, or $\pm\,\sqrt{-10}$.

Thus , $\qquad\qquad\qquad x = 3, -1, 1 \pm \sqrt{-10}$;

$$y = 1, -3, -1 \pm \sqrt{-10}.$$

Example 3. Solve $\qquad \dfrac{2x + y}{3x - y} - \dfrac{x - y}{x + y} = 2\,\dfrac{8}{15},$ ...(1)

$$7x + 5y = 29. \qquad\qquad ...(2)$$

From (1), $15\,(2x^2 + 3xy + y^2 - 3x^2 + 4xy - y^2) = 38\,(3x^2 + 2xy - y^2)$;

$\therefore \qquad\qquad\qquad 129x^2 - 29xy - 38y^2 = 0$;

$\therefore \qquad\qquad\qquad (3x - 2y)\,(43x + 19y) = 0$.

Hence $\qquad\qquad\qquad 3x = 2y,$ ...(3)

or $\qquad\qquad\qquad 43x = -19y.$ ...(4)

From (3), $\qquad\qquad \dfrac{x}{2} = \dfrac{y}{3} = \dfrac{7x + 5y}{29}$

$$= 1, \text{ by equation (2)}$$

$\therefore \qquad\qquad\qquad x = 2, y = 3.$

Again, from (4), $\qquad \dfrac{x}{19} = \dfrac{y}{-43} = \dfrac{7x + 5y}{-82}$

$$= -\dfrac{29}{82}, \text{ by equation (2)}$$

$\therefore \qquad\qquad\qquad x = -\dfrac{551}{82}, y = \dfrac{1247}{82}.$

Hence $x = 2, y = 3$; or $x = -\dfrac{551}{82}, y = \dfrac{1247}{82}.$

Example 4. *Solve* $\qquad 4x^3 + 3x^2 y + y^3 = 8,$

$$2x^3 - 2x^2 y + xy^2 = 1.$$

Put $y = mx$, and substitute in both equations. Thus

$$x^3\,(4 + 3m + m^3) = 8 \qquad ...(1)$$

$$x^3\,(2 - 2m + m^2) = 1 \qquad ...(2)$$

$\therefore \qquad\qquad\qquad \dfrac{4 + 3m + m^3}{2 - 2m + m^2} = 8;$

$$m^3 - 8m^2 + 19m - 12 = 0;$$

that is, $\qquad (m-1)(m-3)(m-4) = 0;$

$\therefore \qquad\qquad m = 1,\ \text{or}\ 3,\ \text{or}\ 4.$

(i) Take $m = 1$, and substitute in either (1) or (2).

From (2), $x^3 = 1$; $\therefore x = 1$;

and $y = mx = x = 1$.

(ii) Take $m = 3$; and substitute in (2);

thus $\qquad 5x^3 = 1$; $\therefore x = \sqrt[3]{\dfrac{1}{5}}$;

and $\qquad y = mx = 3x = 3\sqrt[3]{\dfrac{1}{5}}$.

(iii) Take $m = 4$; we obtain

$$10x^3 = 1; \quad \therefore x = \sqrt[3]{\dfrac{1}{10}};$$

and $\qquad\qquad\qquad y = mx = 4x = 4\sqrt[3]{\dfrac{1}{10}}$.

Hence the complete solution is

$$x = 1,\ \sqrt[3]{\dfrac{1}{5}},\ \sqrt[3]{\dfrac{1}{10}}.$$

$$y = 1,\ 3\sqrt[3]{\dfrac{1}{5}},\ 4\sqrt[3]{\dfrac{1}{10}}.$$

Note : The above method of solution may always be used when the equations are *of the same degree and homogeneous*

Example 5. *Solve* $\qquad 31x^2y^2 - 7y^4 - 112xy + 64 = 0 \qquad$ ...(1)

$$x^2 - 7xy + 4y^2 + 8 = 0 \qquad\qquad ...(2)$$

From (2) we have $-8 = x^2 - 7xy + 4y^2$; and substituting in (1),

$$31x^2y^2 - 7y^4 + 14xy(x^2 - 7xy + 4y^2) + (x^2 - 7xy + 4y^2)^2 = 0;$$

$\therefore \quad 31x^2y^2 - 7y^4 + (x^2 - 7xy + 4y^2)(14xy + x^2 - 7xy + 4y^2) = 0;$

$\therefore \qquad\qquad\qquad 31x^2y^2 - 7y^4 + (x^2 + 4y^2)^2 - (7xy)^2 = 0;$

that is, $\qquad\qquad x^4 - 10x^2y^2 + 9y^4 = 0 \qquad\qquad$ ...(3)

$\therefore \qquad\qquad (x^2 - y^2)(x^2 - 9y^2) = 0;$

hence $\qquad\qquad x = \pm y,\ \text{or}\ x = \pm 3y.$

Taking these cases in succession and substituting in (2), we obtain

$$x = y = \pm 2;$$

$$x = -y = \pm\sqrt{-\dfrac{2}{3}};$$

$$x = \pm 3,\ y = \pm 1;$$

$$x = \pm 3 \sqrt{-\frac{4}{17}}, \quad y = \mp \sqrt{-\frac{4}{17}}.$$

Note : It should be observed that equation (3) is *homogeneous*. The method here employed by which one equation is made homogeneous by a suitable combination with the other is a valuable artifice. It is especially useful in Analytical Geometry.

Example 6. Solve $(x+y)^{\frac{2}{3}} + 2(x-y)^{\frac{2}{3}} = 3(x^2 - y^2)^{\frac{1}{3}}$ ...(1)

$$3x - 2y = 13 \qquad \qquad \text{...(2)}$$

Divide each term of (1) by $(x^2 - y^2)^{\frac{1}{3}}$, or $(x+y)^{\frac{1}{3}}(x-y)^{\frac{1}{3}}$;

$$\therefore \qquad \left(\frac{x+y}{x-y}\right)^{\frac{1}{3}} + 2\left(\frac{x-y}{x+y}\right)^{\frac{1}{3}} = 3.$$

This equation is a quadratic in $\left(\dfrac{x+y}{x-y}\right)^{\frac{1}{3}}$, from which we easily find,

$$\left(\frac{x+y}{x-y}\right)^{\frac{1}{3}} = 2 \quad \text{or} \quad 1; \text{whence} \frac{x+y}{x-y} = 8 \quad \text{or} \quad 1;$$

$$\therefore \qquad 7x = 9y, \quad \text{or} \quad y = 0.$$

Combining these equations with (2), we obtain

$$x = 9, y = 7; \quad \text{or} \quad x = \frac{13}{3}, y = 0.$$

EXAMPLES X. b.

Solve the following equations :

1. $3x - 2y = 7, \quad xy = 20.$

2. $5x - y = 3, \quad y^2 - 6x^2 = 25.$

3. $4x - 3y = 1, \quad 12xy + 13y^2 = 25.$

4. $x^4 + x^2 y^2 + y^4 = 931, \quad x^2 - xy + y^2 = 19.$

5. $x^2 + xy + y^2 = 84, \quad x - \sqrt{xy} + y = 6.$

6. $x + \sqrt{xy} + y = 65, \quad x^2 + xy + y^2 = 2275.$

7. $x + y = 7 + \sqrt{xy}, \quad x^2 + y^2 = 133 - xy.$

8. $3x^2 - 5y^2 = 7, \quad 3xy - 4y^2 = 2.$

9. $5y^2 - 7x^2 = 17, \quad 5xy - 6x^2 = 6.$

10. $3x^2 + 165 = 16xy, \quad 7xy + 3y^2 = 132.$

11. $3x^2 + xy + y^2 = 15, \quad 31xy - 3x^2 - 5y^2 = 45.$

12. $x^2 + y^2 - 3 = 3xy, \quad 2x^2 - 6 + y^2 = 0.$

13. $x^4 + y^4 = 706, \quad x + y = 8$

14. $x^4 + y^4 = 272, \quad x - y = 2$

15. $x^5 - y^5 = 992, \quad x - y = 2.$

16. $x + \dfrac{4}{y} = 1, \quad y + \dfrac{4}{x} = 25.$

17. $\dfrac{x^2}{y} + \dfrac{y^2}{x} = \dfrac{9}{2}, \quad \dfrac{3}{x+y} = 1.$

18. $\dfrac{x}{2} + \dfrac{y}{5} = 5, \quad \dfrac{2}{x} + \dfrac{5}{y} = \dfrac{5}{6}.$

19. $x + y = 1072, \quad x^{\frac{1}{3}} + y^{\frac{1}{3}} = 16.$

20. $xy^{\frac{1}{2}} + yx^{\frac{1}{2}} = 20, \quad x^{\frac{3}{2}} + y^{\frac{3}{2}} = 65$

21. $x^{\frac{1}{2}} + y^{\frac{1}{2}} = 5, \quad 6\left(x^{-\frac{1}{2}} + y^{-\frac{1}{2}} \right) = 5.$

22. $\sqrt{x+y} + \sqrt{x-y} = 4, \quad x^2 - y^2 = 9.$

23. $y + \sqrt{x^2 - 1} = 2, \quad \sqrt{x+1} - \sqrt{x-1} = \sqrt{y}.$

24. $\sqrt{\dfrac{x}{y}} + \sqrt{\dfrac{y}{x}} = \dfrac{10}{3}, \quad x + y = 10$

25. $\dfrac{\sqrt{x} - \sqrt{y}}{\sqrt{x} + \sqrt{y}} + \dfrac{\sqrt{x} + \sqrt{y}}{\sqrt{x} - \sqrt{y}} = \dfrac{17}{4}, \quad x^2 + y^2 = 706.$

26. $x^2 + 4y^2 - 15x = 10(3y - 8), \quad xy = 6.$

27. $x^2 y^2 + 400 = 41xy, \quad y^2 = 5xy - 4x^2.$

28. $4x^2 + 5y = 6 + 20xy - 25y^2 + 2x, \quad 7x - 11y = 17.$

29. $9x^2 + 33x - 12 = 12xy - 4y^2 + 22y, \quad x^2 - xy = 18.$

30. $(x^2 - y^2)(x - y) = 16xy, \quad (x^4 - y^4)(x^2 - y^2) = 640x^2 y^2.$

31. $2x^2 - xy + y^2 = 2y, \quad 2x^2 + 4xy = 5y.$

32. $\dfrac{x^3 + y^3}{(x+y)^2} + \dfrac{x^3 - y^3}{(x-y)^2} = \dfrac{43x}{8}, \quad 5x - 7y = 4.$

33. $y(y^2 - 3xy - x^2) + 24 = 0, \quad x(y^2 - 4xy + 2x^2) + 8 = 0.$

34. $3x^3 - 8xy^2 + y^3 + 21 = 0, \quad x^2(y - x) = 1.$

35. $y^2(4x^2 - 108) = x(x^3 - 9y^3), \quad 2x^2 + 9xy + y^2 = 108.$

36. $6x^4 + x^2 y^2 + 16 = 2x(12x + y^3), \quad x^2 + xy - y^2 = 4.$

37. $x(a+x) = y(b+y), \quad ax+by = (x+y)^2.$

38. $xy+ab = 2ax, \quad x^2y^2 + a^2b^2 = 2b^2y^2.$

39. $\dfrac{x-a}{a^2} + \dfrac{y-b}{b^2} = \dfrac{1}{x-b} - \dfrac{1}{y-a} - \dfrac{1}{a-b} = 0.$

40. $bx^3 = 10a^2bx + 3a^3y, \quad ay^3 = 10ab^2y + 3b^3x.$

41. $2a\left(\dfrac{x}{y} - \dfrac{y}{x}\right) + 4a^2 = 4x^2 + \dfrac{xy}{2a} - \dfrac{y^2}{a^2} = 1.$

137. Equations involving three or more unknown quantities can only be solved in special cases. We shall here consider some of the most useful methods of solution.

Example 1. Solve $\qquad\qquad x+y+z = 13 \qquad\qquad\qquad …(1)$
$$x^2 + y^2 + z^2 = 65 \qquad\qquad …(2)$$
$$xy = 10 \qquad\qquad …(3)$$

From (2) and (3), $\qquad\qquad (x+y)^2 + z^2 = 85.$

Put u for $x+y$; then this equation becomes

$$u^2 + z^2 = 85.$$

Also from (1), $\qquad\qquad\qquad u+z = 13;$

whence we obtain $u = 7$ or $6; z = 6$ or $7.$

Thus we have $\qquad \left.\begin{array}{l} x+y = 7, \\ xy = 10 \end{array}\right\}$ and $\left.\begin{array}{l} x+y = 6, \\ xy = 10 \end{array}\right\}$

Hence the solutions are

$$\left.\begin{array}{l} x = 5,\text{ or }2, \\ y = 2,\text{ or }5, \\ z = 6; \end{array}\right\} \text{ and } \left.\begin{array}{l} x = 3 \pm \sqrt{-1}, \\ y = 3 \mp \sqrt{-1}, \\ z = 7. \end{array}\right\}$$

Example 2. Solve $\qquad (x+y)(x+z) = 30,$
$$(y+z)(y+x) = 15,$$
$$(z+x)(z+y) = 18.$$

Write u, v, w for $y+z, z+x, x+y$ respectively; thus

$$vw = 30,\ wu = 15,\ uv = 18 \qquad\qquad …(1)$$

Multiplying these equations together, we have

$$u^2v^2w^2 = 30 \times 15 \times 18 = 15^2 \times 6^2;$$

$\therefore \qquad\qquad\qquad\qquad uvw = \pm 90.$

Combining this result with each of the equations in (1), we have

$\qquad u = 3, v = 6, w = 5;$ or $u = -3, v = -6, w = -5;$

$$\therefore \left.\begin{array}{l} y+z = 3, \\ z+x = 6, \\ x+y = 5 \end{array}\right\} \text{ and } \left.\begin{array}{l} y+z = -3, \\ z+x = -6, \\ x+y = -5 \end{array}\right\}$$

whence $\qquad x = 4, y = 1, z = 2;$ or $x = -4, y = -1, z = -2.$

Example 3. Solve

$$y^2 + yz + z^2 = 49 \qquad \ldots(1),$$
$$z^2 + zx + x^2 = 19 \qquad \ldots(2),$$
$$x^2 + xy + y^2 = 39 \qquad \ldots(3).$$

Subtracting (2) from (1)

$$y^2 - x^2 + z(y - x) = 30;$$

that is,

$$(y - x)(x + y + z) = 30 \qquad \ldots(4)$$

Similarly from (1) and (3)

$$(z - x)(x + y + z) = 10 \qquad \ldots(5)$$

Hence from (4) and (5), by division

$$\frac{y - x}{z - x} = 3;$$

whence

$$y = 3z - 2x.$$

Substituting in equation (3), we obtain

$$x^2 - 3xz + 3z^2 = 13.$$

From (2),

$$x^2 + xz + z^2 = 19.$$

Solving these homogeneous equations as in Example 4, Art. 136, we obtain

$$x = \pm 2, z = \pm 3; \text{ and therefore } y = \pm 5;$$
$$x = \pm \frac{11}{\sqrt{7}}, z = \pm \frac{1}{\sqrt{7}}; \text{ and therefore } y = \mp \frac{19}{\sqrt{7}}$$

Example 4. Solve $x^2 - yz = a^2, y^2 - zx = b^2, z^2 - xy = c^2$.

Multiply the equations by y, z, x respectively and add; then

$$c^2 x + a^2 y + b^2 z = 0 \qquad \ldots(1)$$

Multiply the equations by z, x, y respectively and add; then

$$b^2 x + c^2 y + a^2 z = 0 \qquad \ldots(2)$$

From (1) and (2) by cross multiplication,

$$\frac{x}{a^4 - b^2 c^2} = \frac{y}{b^4 - c^2 a^2} = \frac{z}{c^4 - a^2 b^2} = k \text{ suppose.}$$

Substitute in any one of the given equations; then

$$k^2 (a^6 + b^6 + c^6 - 3a^2 b^2 c^2) = 1;$$

$$\therefore \quad \frac{x}{a^4 - b^2 c^2} = \frac{y}{b^4 - c^2 a^2} = \frac{z}{c^4 - a^2 b^2} = \pm \frac{1}{\sqrt{a^6 + b^6 + c^6 - 3a^2 b^2 c^2}}.$$

EXAMPLES X. c.

Solve the following equations :

1. $9x + y - 8z = 0, \quad 4x - 8y + 7z = 0, \quad yz + zx + xy = 47.$

2. $3x + y - 2z = 0, \quad 4x - y - 3z = 0, \quad x^3 + y^3 + z^3 = 467.$

3. $x - y - z = 2, \quad x^2 + y^2 - z^2 = 22, \quad xy = 5.$

4. $x + 2y - z = 11$, $x^2 - 4y^2 + z^2 = 37$, $xz = 24$.

5. $x^2 + y^2 - z^2 = 21$, $3xz + 3yz - 2xy = 18$, $x + y - z = 5$.

6. $x^2 + xy + xz = 18$, $y^2 + yz + yx + 12 = 0$, $z^2 + zx + zy = 30$.

7. $x^2 + 2xy + 3xz = 50$, $2y^2 + 3yz + yx = 10$, $3z^2 + zx + 2zy = 10$,

8. $(y - z)(z + x) = 22$, $(z + x)(x - y) = 33$, $(x - y)(y - z) = 6$.

9. $x^2 y^2 z^2 u = 12$, $x^2 y^2 zu = 8$, $x^2 yz^2 u^2 = 1$, $3xy^2 z^2 u^2 = 4$.

10. $x^3 y^2 z = 12$, $x^3 yz^3 = 54$, $x^7 y^3 z^2 = 72$.

11. $xy + x + y = 23$, $xz + x + z = 41$, $yz + y + z = 27$.

12. $2xy - 4x + y = 17$, $3yz + y - 6z = 52$, $6xz + 3z + 2x = 29$.

13. $xz + y = 7z$, $yz + x = 8z$, $x + y + z = 12$.

14. $x^3 + y^3 + z^3 = a^3$, $x^2 + y^2 + z^2 = a^2$, $x + y + z = a$.

15. $x^2 + y^2 + z^2 = yz + zx + xy = a^2$, $3x - y + z = a\sqrt{3}$.

16. $x^2 + y^2 + z^2 = 21a^2$, $yz + zx - xy = 6a^2$, $3x + y - 2z = 3a$.

INDETERMINATE EQUATIONS

138. Suppose the following problem were proposed for solution :

A person spends Rs. 461 in buying horses and cows; if each horse costs Rs. 23 and each cow Rs. 16, how many of each does he buy ?

Let x, y be the number of horses and cows respectively; then

$$23x + 16y = 461.$$

Here we have *one* equation involving *two* unknown quantities, and it is clear that by ascribing any value we please to x, we can obtain a corresponding value for y; thus it would appear at first sight that the problem admits of an infinite number of solutions. But it is clear from the nature of the question that x and y must be positive integers; and with this restriction, as we shall see later, the number of solutions is limited.

If the number of unknown quantities is greater than the number of independent equations, there will be an unlimited number of solutions, and the equations are said to be indeterminate. In the present section we shall only discuss the simplest kinds of indeterminate equations, confining our attention to *positive integral values* of the unknown quantities; it will be seen that this restriction enables us to express the solutions in a very simple form.

The general theory of indeterminate equations will be found in Chap. 26.

Example 1. Solve $7x + 12y = 220$ in positive integers.

Divide throughout by 7, the smaller coefficient; thus

$$x + y + \frac{5y}{7} = 31 + \frac{3}{7};$$

$$\therefore \qquad x + y + \frac{5y - 3}{7} = 31 \qquad \qquad \dots(1)$$

Since x and y are to be integers, we must have

$$\frac{5y - 3}{7} = \text{integer};$$

and therefore

$$\frac{15y - 9}{7} = \text{integer};$$

that is

$$2y - 1 + \frac{y - 2}{7} = \text{integer};$$

and therefore $\qquad \frac{y - 2}{7} = \text{integer} = p \text{ (suppose)}.$

$$\therefore \qquad \qquad y - 2 = 7p,$$

or $\qquad \qquad \qquad y = 7p + 2 \qquad \qquad \dots(2)$

Substituting this value of y in (1),

$$x + 7p + 2 + 5p + 1 = 31;$$

that is $\qquad \qquad \qquad x = 28 - 12p \qquad \qquad \dots(3)$

If in these results we give to p any integral value, we obtain corresponding integral values of x and y; but if $p > 2$, we see from (3) that x is negative; and if p is a negative integer, y is negative. Thus the only *positive integral* values of x and y are obtained by putting $p = 0, 1, 2$.

The complete solution may be exhibited as follows :

$$\left. \begin{array}{llll} p = 0, & 1, & 2, \\ x = 28, & 16, & 4, \\ y = 2, & 9, & 16. \end{array} \right\}$$

Note : When we obtained $\frac{5y - 3}{7} = \text{integer}$, we multiplied by 3 *in order to make the coefficient of y differ by unity from a multiple of 7*. A similar artifice should always be employed before introducing a symbol to denote the integer.

Example 2. Solve in positive integers, $14x - 11y = 29 \qquad \dots(1)$

Divide by 11, the smaller coefficient; thus

$$x + \frac{3x}{11} - y = 2 + \frac{7}{11};$$

$$\therefore \qquad \frac{3x - 7}{11} = 2 - x + y = \text{integer};$$

hence

$$\frac{12x - 28}{11} = \text{integer};$$

that is

$$x - 2 + \frac{x - 6}{11} = \text{integer};$$

$$\therefore \qquad \frac{x - 6}{11} = \text{integer} = p \text{ suppose};$$

and from (1), $\therefore \quad x = 11p + 6$ }
                                          $y = 14p + 5$ }

This is called the *general solution* of the equation, and by giving to p any positive integral value or zero, we obtain positive integral values of x and y; thus we have

$$p = 0, \quad 1, \quad 2, \quad 3, \dots$$
$$x = 6, \quad 17, \quad 28, \quad 39, \dots$$
$$y = 5, \quad 19, \quad 33, \quad 47, \dots$$

the number of solutions being infinite.

Example 3. In how many ways can Rs. 5 be paid in 25 nP. and 10nP pieces ?

Let x be the number of 25 nP. pieces and y the number of 10 nP. pieces; then

$$25x + 10y = 500$$

$$\therefore \qquad x + \frac{2}{5} y = 20$$

So, $$x = 20 - \frac{2}{5} y.$$

Now $y + \frac{2}{5} y$ must be integers and solutions are obtained by ascribing to y integer values which make $\frac{2}{5} y$ integral, viz., 5, 10, 15, 20, ... 45. The number of ways is therefore 9.

If however, the sum may be paid *either* in 25 nP. or 10 nP. pieces only, y may also have the values 0 and 50.

If $y = 0$, the sum is paid entirely in 25 nP. pieces and if $y = 50$ the sum is paid entirely in 10 nP. pieces.

Thus if zero values of x and y are admissible, the number of ways is 11.

Example 4. The expenses of a party numbering 43 were Rs. 2.29 nP; if each man paid 10 nP., each woman 5 nP., and each child 2 nP., how many were there of each ?

Let x, y, z denote the number of men, women, and children, respectively then we have

$$x + y + z = 43 \qquad \qquad \dots(1)$$
$$10x + 5y + 2z = 229.$$

Eliminating z, we obtain

$$8x + 3y = 143$$

The general solution of this equation is

$$x = 3p + 1,$$
$$y = 45 - 8p;$$

Hence by substituting in (1), we obtain

$$z = 5p - 3.$$

Here p cannot be negative or zero, but may have positive integral values from 1 to 5. Thus

$$p = 1, \quad 2, \quad 3, \quad 4, \quad 5;$$
$$x = 4, \quad 7, \quad 10, \quad 13, \quad 16;$$
$$y = 37, \quad 29, \quad 21, \quad 13, \quad 5;$$
$$z = 2, \quad 7, \quad 12, \quad 17, \quad 22.$$

EXAMPLES X. d.

Solve in positive integers :

1. $3x + 8y = 103$.   **2.** $5x + 2y = 53$.   **3.** $7x + 12y = 152$.

4. $13x + 11y = 414$. **5.** $23x + 25y = 915$. **6.** $41x + 47y = 2191$.

Find the general solution in positive integers, and the least values of x and y which satisfy the equations :

7. $5x - 7y = 3$.   **8.** $6x - 13y = 1$.   **9.** $8x - 21y = 33$.

10. $17y - 13x = 0$.   **11.** $19y - 23x = 7$.   **12.** $77y - 30x = 295$.

13. A farmer spends £ 752 in buying horses and cows; if each horse costs £ 37 and each cow £ 23, how many of each does he buy ?

14. In how many ways can £ 5 be paid in shillings and sixpences, including zero solutions ?

15. Divide 81 into two parts so that one may be a multiple of 8 and the other of 5.

16. What is the simplest way for a person who has only guineas to pay 10s. 6d. to another who has only half-crowns ?

17. Find a number which being divided by 39 gives a remainder 16, and by 56 a remainder 27. How many such numbers are there ?

18. What is the smallest number of florins that must be given to discharge a debt of £ 1. 6s. 6d., if the change is to be paid in half crowns only ?

19. Divide 136 into two parts one of which when divided by 5 leaves remainder 2, and the other divided by 8 leaves remainder 3.

20. I buy 40 animals consisting of rams at £ 4, pigs at £ 2, and oxen at £ 17 : if I spend £ 301, how many of each do I buy ?

21. In my pocket I have 27 coins, which are sovereigns, half-crowns or shillings, and the amount I have is £ 5.0s. 6d.; how many coins of each sort have I ?

■ ■ ■

Chapter 11

PERMUTATIONS AND COMBINATIONS

139. Each of the *arrangements* which can be made by taking some or all of a number of things is called a **permutation.**

Each of the *groups* or *selections* which can be made by taking some or all of a number of things is called a **combination.**

Thus the *permutations* which can be made by taking the letters *a, b, c, d* two at a time are twelve in number, namely,

$$ab, \ ac, \ ad, \ bc, \ bd, \ cd,$$
$$ba, \ ca, \ da, \ cb, \ db, \ dc;$$

each of these presenting a different *arrangement* of two letters.

The *combinations* which can be made by taking the letters *a, b, c, d* two at a time are six in number : namely,

$$ab, \ ac, \ ad, \ bc, \ bd, \ cd;$$

each of these presenting a different *selection* two letters.

From this it appears that in forming *combinations* we are only concerned with the number of things each selection contains ; whereas in forming *permutations* we have also to consider the order of the things which make up each arrangement; for instance, if from four letters *a, b, c, d* we make a selection of three, such as *abc*, this single combination admits of being arranged in the following ways :

$$abc, acb, bca, bac, cab, cba,$$

and so gives rise to six different permutations.

140. Before discussing the general propositions of this chapter there is an important principle which we proceed to explain and illustrate by a few numerical examples.

If one operation can be performed in m ways, and (when it has been performed in any one of these ways) a second operation can then be performed in n ways, the number of ways of performing the two operations will be m × n.

If the first operation be performed in *any one* way, we can associate with this any of the *n* ways of performing the second operation; and thus we shall have *n*-ways of performing the two operations without considering more than *one* way of performing the first; and so corresponding to *each* of the m ways of performing the first operation, we shall have n ways of performing the two; hence altogether the number of ways in which the two operations can be performed is represented by the product $m \times n$.

Example 1. There are 10 steamers plying between Liverpool and Dublin; in how many ways can a man go from Liverpool to Dublin and return by a different steamer ?

There are *ten* ways of making the first passage; and with each of these there is a choice of *nine* ways of returning (since the man is not to come back by the same steamer); hence the number of ways of making the two journeys is 10×9, or 90.

This principle may easily be extended to the case in which there are more than two operations each of which can be performed in a given number of ways.

Example 2. Three travellers arrive at a town where there are four hotels; in how many ways can they take up their quarters, each at a different hotel ?

The first traveller has choice of four hotels, and when he has made his selection in any one way, the second traveller has a choice of three; therefore the first two can make their choice in 4×3 ways; and with any one such choice the third traveller can select his hotel in 2 ways; hence the required number of ways is $4 \times 3 \times 2$, or 24.

141. *To find the number of permutations of n dissimilar things taken r at a time.*

This is the same thing as finding the number of ways in which we can fill up r places when we have n different things at our disposal.

The first place may be filled up in n ways, for any one of the n things may be taken; when it has been filled up in any one of these ways, the second place can then be filled up in $n - 1$ ways; and since each way of filling up the first place can be associated with each way of filling up the second, the number of ways in which the first two places can be filled up is given by the product $n(n - 1)$. And when the first two places have been filled up in any way, the third place can be filled up in $n - 2$ ways. And reasoning as before, the number of ways in which three places can be filled up in $n(n - 1)(n - 2)$.

Proceeding thus, and noticing that a new factor is introduced with each new place filled up, and that at any stage the number of factors is the same as the number of places filled up, we shall have the number of ways in which r places can be filled up equal to

$$n(n - 1)(n - 2) \ldots \text{ to } r \text{ factors;}$$

and the rth factor is

$$n - (r - 1), \text{ or } n - r + 1.$$

Therefore the number of permutations of n things taken r at a time is

$$n (n-1) (n-2) \ldots (n-r+1).$$

Cor. The number of permutations of n things taken all at a time is

$$n (n-1) (n-2) \ldots \text{to } n \text{ factors,}$$

or $\qquad\qquad n (n-1) (n-2) \ldots 3 \cdot 2 \cdot 1.$

It is usual to denote this product by the symbol $n\,!$, which is read "factorial n." Also $n\,!$ is sometimes used for $n\,!$.

142. We shall in future denote the number of permutations of n things taken r at a time by the symbol $^{n}P_{r}$, so that

$$^{n}P_{r} = n (n-1) (n-2) \ldots (n-r+1);$$

also $\qquad\qquad\qquad ^{n}P_{n} = n\,!.$

In working numerical examples it is useful to notice that the suffix in the symbol $^{n}P_{r}$ always denotes the number of factors in the formula we are using.

143. The number of permutations of n things taken r at a time may also be found in the following manner.

Let $^{n}P_{r}$ represent the number of permutations of n things taken r at a time.

Suppose we form all the permutations of n things taken $r-1$ at a time; the number of these will be $^{n}P_{r-1}$.

With *each of these* put one of the remaining $n-r+1$ things. Each time we do this we shall get one permutation of n things r at a time; and therefore the whole number of the permutations of n things r at a time is $^{n}P_{r-1} \times (n-r+1)$; that is,

$$^{n}P_{r} = {}^{n}P_{r-1} \times (n-r+1).$$

By writing $r-1$ for r in this formula, we obtain

$$^{n}P_{r-1} = {}^{n}P_{r-2} \times (n-r+2),$$

similarly, $\qquad ^{n}P_{r-2} = {}^{n}P_{r-3} \times (n-r+3),$

$$\ldots\ldots\ldots\ldots\ldots\ldots\ldots\ldots$$

$$^{n}P_{3} = {}^{n}P_{2} \times (n-2),$$

$$^{n}P_{2} = {}^{n}P_{1} \times (n-1),$$

$$^{n}P_{1} = n.$$

Multiply together the vertical columns and cancel like factors from each side, and we obtain

$$^{n}P_{r} = n (n-1) (n-2) \ldots (n-r+1).$$

Example 1. Four persons enter a railway carriage in which there are six seats; in how many ways can they take their places ?

The first person may seat himself in 6 ways; and then the second person in 5; the third in 4; and the fourth in 3; and since each of these ways may be associated with each of the others, the required answer is $6 \times 5 \times 4 \times 3$, or 360.

Example 2. How many different numbers can be formed by using six out of the nine digits 1, 2, 3, ... 9 ?

Here we have 9 different things and we have to find the number of permutations of them taken 6 at a time;

$\therefore$ the required result $= {}^9P_6$

$$= 9 \times 8 \times 7 \times 6 \times 5 \times 4$$

$$= 60480.$$

144. *To find the number of combinations of n dissimilar things taken r at a time.*

Let ${}^nC_r$ denote the required number of combinations.

Then each of these combinations consists of a group of r dissimilar things which can be arranged among themselves in $\lfloor r$ ways [Art. 142.]

Hence ${}^nC_r \times r$! is equal to the number of *arrangements* of n things taken r at a time; that is ,

$$\quad {}^nC_r \times r! = {}^nP_r$$

$$= n (n-1) (n-2) \ldots (n-r+1);$$

$$\therefore \quad {}^nC_r = \frac{n (n-1) (n-2) \ldots (n-r+1)}{r!} \qquad \ldots(1)$$

Cor. This formula for ${}^nC_r$ may also be written in a different form; for if we multiply the numerator and the denominator by $(n-r)$! we obtain

$$\frac{n (n-1) (n-2) \ldots (n-r+1) \times (n-r)!}{r! (n-r)!}$$

The numerator now consists of the product of all the natural numbers from n to 1;

$$\therefore \qquad {}^nC_r = \frac{n!}{r! (n-r)!} \qquad \ldots(2)$$

It will be convenient to remember both these expressions for ${}^nC_r$, using (1) in all cases where a numerical result is required, and (2) when it is sufficient to leave it in an algebraical shape.

Note. If in formula (2) we put $r = n$, we have

$$ {}^nC_n = \frac{n!}{n! \, 0!} = \frac{1}{0!} ;$$

but $^{n}C_{n} = 1$, so that if the formula is to be true for $r = n$, the symbol $0\,!$ must be considered as equivalent to 1.

Example. From 12 books in how many ways can a selection of 5 be made, (1) when one specified book is always included, (2) when one specified book is always excluded ?

(1) Since the specified book is to be included in every selection, we have only to choose 4 out of the remaining 11.

Hence the number of ways $= {}^{11}C_{4}$

$$= \frac{11 \times 10 \times 9 \times 8}{1 \times 2 \times 3 \times 4}$$

$$= 330.$$

(2) Since the specified book is always to be excluded, we have to select the 5 books out of the remaining 11.

Hence the number of ways $= {}^{11}C_{5}$

$$= \frac{11 \times 10 \times 9 \times 8 \times 7}{1 \times 2 \times 3 \times 4 \times 5}$$

$$= 462.$$

145. *The number of combinations of n things r at a time is equal to the number of combinations of n things n − r at a time.*

In making all the possible combinations of n things, to each group of r things we select, there is left a corresponding group of $n - r$ things; that is, the number of combinations of n things r at a time is the same as the number of combinations of n things $n - r$ at a time;

$$\therefore \qquad {}^{n}C_{r} = {}^{n}C_{n-r}.$$

The proposition may also be proved as follows :

$$^{n}C_{n-r} = \frac{n\,!}{(n-r)\,!\,[n-(n-r)]\,!} \qquad \text{[Art. 144.]}$$

$$= \frac{n\,!}{(n-r)\,!\,r\,!}$$

$$= {}^{n}C_{r}.$$

Such combinations are called *complementary*.

Note. Put $r = n$, then $^{n}C_{0} = {}^{n}C_{n} = 1$.

The result we have just proved is useful in enabling us to abridge arithmetical work.

Example. Out of 14 men in how many ways can an eleven be chosen ?

The required number $= {}^{14}C_{11}$

$$= {}^{14}C_{3}$$

$$= \frac{14 \times 13 \times 12}{1 \times 2 \times 3}$$

$$= 364.$$

If we had made use of the formula $^{14}C_{11}$, we should have had to reduce an expression whose numerator and denominator each contained 11 factors.

146. *To find the number of ways in which $m + n$ things can be divided into two groups containing m and n things respectively.*

This is clearly equivalent to finding the number of combinations of $m + n$ things m at a time, for every time we select one group of m things we leave a group of n things behind.

Thus the required number $= \dfrac{(m+n)\,!}{m\,!\,n\,!}$.

Note. If $n = m$, the groups are equal, and in this case the number of *different* ways of subdivision is $\dfrac{2m\,!}{m\,!\,m\,!\,2\,!}$; for in any one way it is possible to interchange the two groups without obtaining a new distribution.

147. *To find the number of ways in which $m + n + p$ things can be divided into three groups containing m, n, p things severally.*

First divide $m + n + p$ things into two groups containing m and $n + p$ things respectively : the number of ways in which this can be done is

$$\frac{(m+n+p)\,!}{m\,!\,(n+p)\,!}.$$

Then the number of ways in which the group of $n + p$ things can be divided into two groups containing n and p things respectively is

$$\frac{(n+p)\,!}{n\,!\,p\,!}.$$

Hence the number of ways in which the subdivision into three groups containing m, n, p things can be made is

$$\frac{(m+n+p)\,!}{m\,!\,(n+p)\,!} \times \frac{(n+p)\,!}{n\,!\,p\,!} \quad \text{or} \quad \frac{(m+n+p)\,!}{m\,!\,n\,!\,p\,!}.$$

Note. If we put $n = p = m$, we obtain $\dfrac{3m\,!}{m\,!\,m\,!\,m\,!}$; but this formula regards as different all the possible orders in which the three groups can occur in any one mode of subdivision, and since there are $3\,!$ such orders corresponding to each mode of subdivision the number of *different ways* in which subdivision into three *equal* groups can be made is $\dfrac{3m\,!}{m\,!\,m\,!\,m\,!\,3\,!}.$

Example. The number of ways in which 15 recruits can be divided into three equal groups is $\dfrac{15\,!}{5\,!\,5\,!\,5\,!\,3\,!}$; and the number of ways in which they can be drafted into three different regiments, five into each, is $\dfrac{15\,!}{5\,!\,5\,!\,5\,!}.$

148. In the example which follow it is important to notice that the formula for *permutations* should not be used until the suitable *selections* required by the question have been made.

Example 1. From 7 Englishmen and 4 Americans a committee of 6 is to be formed; in how many ways can this be done, (1) when the committee contains exactly 2 Americans, (2) at least 2 Americans ?

(1) We have to choose 2 Americans and 4 Englishmen.

The number of ways in which the Americans can be chosen is $^4C_2$; and the number of ways in which the Englishmen can be chosen is $^7C_4$. Each of the first groups can be associated with each of the second; hence

the required number of ways $= {}^4C_2 \times {}^7C_4$

$$= \frac{4!}{2!2!} \times \frac{7!}{4!3!}$$

$$= \frac{7!}{2!2!3!} = 210.$$

(2) The committee may contain 2, 3, or 4 Americans.

We shall exhaust all the suitable combinations by forming all the groups containing 2 Americans and 4 Englishmen; then 3 Americans and 3 Englishmen; and lastly 4 Americans and 2 Englishmen.

The *sum* of the three results will give the answer. Hence the required number of ways $= {}^4C_2 \times {}^7C_4 + {}^4C_2 \times {}^7C_3 + {}^4C_4 \times {}^7C_2$

$$= \frac{4!}{2!2!} \times \frac{7!}{4!3!} + \frac{4!}{3!} \times \frac{7!}{3!4!} + 1 \times \frac{7!}{2!5!}$$

$$= 210 + 140 + 21 = 371.$$

In this Example we have only to make use of the suitable formulae for *combinations*, for we are not concerned with the possible arrangements of the members of the committee among themselves.

Example 2. Out of 7 consonants and 4 vowels, how many words can be made each containing 3 consonants and 2 vowels ?

The number of ways of choosing the three consonants is $^7C_3$, and the number of ways of choosing the 2 vowels is $^4C_2$; and since each of the first groups can be associated with each of the second, the number of combined groups, each containing 3 consonants and 2 vowels, is $^7C_3 \times {}^4C_2$.

Further, each of these groups contains 5 letters, which may be arranged among themselves in 5 ! ways. Hence

the required number of words $= {}^7C_3 \times {}^4C_2 \times 5!$

$$= \frac{7!}{3!4!} \times \frac{4!}{2!2!} \times 5!$$

$$= 5 \times 7!$$

$$= 25200.$$

Example 3. How many words can be formed out of the letters article. so that the vowels occupy the even places ?

Here we have to put the 3 vowels in 3 specified places, and the 4 consonants in the 4 remaining places; the first operation can be done in 3 ! ways, and the second in 4 ! Hence

the required number of words $= 3 ! \times 4 !$

$$= 144$$

In this Example the formula for permutations is immediately applicable, because by the statement of the question there is but one way of choosing the vowels, and one way of choosing the consonants.

EXAMPLES XI. a.

1. In how many ways can a consonant and a vowel be chosen out of the letters of the word *courage* ?

2. There are 8 candidates for a Classical, 7 for a Mathematical, and 4 for a Natural Science Scholarship. In how many ways can the Scholarships be awarded ?

3. Find the value of $^{8}P_{7}$, $^{25}P_{5}$, $^{24}C_{4}$, $^{19}C_{14}$.

4. How many different arrangements can be made by taking 5 of the letters of the word *equation* ?

5. If four times the number of permutations of n things 3 together is equal to five times the number of permutations of $n-1$ things 3 together, find n.

6. How many permutations can be made out of the letters of the word *triangle* ? How many of these will begin with t and end with e ?

7. How many different selections can be made by taking four of the digits 3, 4, 7, 5, 8, 1 ? How many different numbers can be formed with four of these digits ?

8. If $^{2n}C_{3} : {}^{n}C_{2} = 44 : 3$, find n.

9. How many changes can rung with a peal of 5 bells ?

10. How many changes can be rung with a peal of 7 bells, the tenor always being last ?

11. On how many nights may a watch of 4 men be drafted from a crew of 24, so that no two watches are identical ? On how many of these would any one man be taken ?

12. How many arrangements can be made out of the letters of the word *draught*, the vowels never being separated ?

13. In a town council there are 25 councillors and 10 aldermen; how many committees can be formed each consisting of 5 councillors and 3 aldermen ?

14. Out of the letters A, B, C, p, q, r how many arrangements can be made (1) beginning with a capital, (2) beginning and ending with a capital ?

15. Find the number of combinations of 50 things 46 at a time.

16. If $^nC_{12} = {}^nC_8$, find $^nC_{17}$, $^{22}C_n$.

17. In how many ways can the letters of the word *vowels* be arranged, if the letters oe can only occupy odd places ?

18. From 4 officers and 8 privates, in how many ways can 6 be chosen (1) to include exactly one officer, (2) to include at least one officer ?

19. In how many ways can a party of 4 or more be selected from 10 persons ?

20. If $^{18}C_r = {}^{18}C_{r+2}$, find $^rC_5$.

21. Out of 25 consonants and 5 vowels how many words can be formed each consisting of 2 consonants and 3 vowels ?

22. In a library there are 20 Latin and 6 Greek books; in how many ways can a group of 5 consisting of 3 Latin and 2 Greek books be placed on a shelf ?

23. In how many ways can 12 things be divided equally among 4 persons ?

24. From 3 capitals, 5 consonants, and 4 vowels, how many words can be made, each containing 3 consonants and 2 vowels, and beginning with a capital ?

25. At an election three districts are to be canvassed by 10, 15, and 20 men respectively. If 45 men volunteer, in how many ways can they be allotted to the different districts ?

26. In how many ways can 4 Latin and 1 English book be placed on a shelf so that the English book is always in the middle, the selection being made from 7 Latin and 3 English books ?

27. A boat is to be manned by eight men, of whom 2 can only row on bow side and 1 can only row on stroke side; in how many ways can the crew be arranged ?

28. There are two works each of 3 volumes, and two works each of 2 volumes; in how many ways can the 10 books be placed on a shelf so that volumes of the same work are not separated ?

29. In how many ways can 10 examination papers be arranged so that the best and worst papers never come together ?

30. An eight-oared boat is to manned by a crew chosen from 11 men, of whom 3 can steer but cannot row, and the rest can row but cannot steer. In how many ways can the crew be arranged, if two of the men can only row on bow side ?

31. Prove that the number of ways in which p positive and n negative signs may be placed in a row so that no two negative signs shall be together is $^{p+1}C_n$.

32. If $^{56}P_{r+6} : {}^{54}P_{r+3} = 30800 : 1$, find r.

33. How many different signals can be made by hoisting 6 differently coloured flags one above the other, when any number of them may be hoisted at once ?

34. If $^{28}C_{2r} : {}^{24}C_{2r-4} = 225 : 11$, find r.

149. Hitherto, in the formulae we have proved, the things have been regarded as *unlike*. Before considering cases in which some one or more sets of things may be *like*, it is necessary to point out exactly in what sense the words *like* and *unlike* are used when we speak of things being *dissimilar, different, unlike,* we imply that the things are *visibly unlike,* so as to be easily distinguishable from each other. On the other hand we shall always use the term *like* things to denote such as are alike to the eye and cannot be distinguished from each other. For instance, in Ex. 2 Art. 148, the consonants and the vowels may be said each to consist of a group of things united by a common characteristic, and thus in a certain sense to be of the same kind; but they cannot be regarded as *like* things, because there is an individuality existing among the things of each group which makes them easily distinguishable from each other. Hence, in the final stage of the example we considered each group to consist of five *dissimilar* things and therefore capable of 5 ! arrangements among themselves. [Art. 141 Cor.]

150. Suppose we have to find all the possible ways of arranging 12 books on a shelf, 5 of them being Latin, 4 English, and the remainder in different languages.

The books in each language may be regarded as belonging to one class, united by a common characteristic; but if they were distinguishable from each other, the number of permutations would be 12 !, since for the purpose of arrangement among themselves they are essentially different.

If, however, the books in the same language are not distinguishable from each other, we should have to find the number of ways in which 12 things can be arranged among themselves, when 5 of them are exactly alike of one kind, and 4 exactly alike of a second kind : a problem which is not directly included in any of the cases we have previously considered.

151.　*To find the number of ways in which n things may be arranged among themselves, taking them all at a time, whem p of the things are exactly alike of one kind, q of them exactly alike of another kind, r of them exactly alike of a third kind, and the rest all different.*

Let there be n letters; suppose p of them to be a, q of them to be b, r of them to be c, and the rest to be unlike.

Let x be the required number of permutations; then if the p letters a were replaced by p unlike letters different from any of the rest, from any one of the x permutations, without altering the position of any of the remaining letters, we could form p ! new permutations. Hence if this change were made in each of the x permutations we should obtain $x \times (p\,!)$ permutations.

Similarly, if the q letters b were replaced by q unlike letters, the number of permutations would be

$$x \times (p\,!) \times (q\,!).$$

In like manner, by replacing the r letters c by r unlike letters, we should finally obtain $x \times (p\,!) \times (q\,!) \times r\,!$ permutations.

But the things are now all different, and therefore admit of n ! permutations among themselves. Hence

$$x \times (p\,!) \times (q\,!) \times r\,! = n\,!;$$

that is,　　　　　　　　　$$x = \frac{n\,!}{p\,!\,q\,!\,r\,!}\,;$$

which is the required number of permutations.

Any case in which the things are not all different may be treated similarly.

Example 1.　How many different permutations can be made out of the letters of the word assassination taken all together ?

We have here 13 letters of which 4 are s, 3 are a, 2 are i, and 2 are n. Hence the number of permutations

$$= \frac{13!}{4!\,3!\,2!\,2!}$$

$$= 13 \cdot 11 \cdot 10 \cdot 9 \cdot 8 \cdot 7 \cdot 3 \cdot 5$$

$$= 1001 \times 10800 = 10810800.$$

Example 2. How many numbers can be formed with the digits 1, 2, 3, 4, 3, 2, 1 so that the odd digits always occupy the odd places ?

The odd digits 1, 3, 3, 1 can be arranged in their four places in

$$\frac{4!}{2!\,2!} \text{ ways} \qquad\qquad …(1)$$

The even digits 2, 4, 2 can be arranged in their three places in

$$\frac{3!}{2!} \text{ ways} \qquad\qquad …(2)$$

Each of the ways in (1) can be associated with each of the ways in (2). Hence the required number $= \dfrac{4!}{2!\,2!} \times \dfrac{3!}{2!} = 6 \times 3 = 18.$

152. *To find the number of permutations of n things r at a time, when each thing may be repeated once, twice, … up to r times in any arrangement.*

Here we have to consider the number of ways in which r places can be filled up when we have n different things at our disposal, each of the n things being used as often as we please in any arrangement.

The first place may be filled up in n ways, and, when it has been filled up in any one way, the second place may also be filled up in n ways, since we are not precluded from using the same thing again. Therefore the number of ways in which the first two places can be filled up is $n \times n$ or n^2. The third place can also be filled up in n ways, and therefore the first three places in n^3 ways.

Proceeding in this manner, and noticing that at any stage the index of n is always the same as the number of places filled up, we shall have the number of ways in which the r places can be filled up equal to n^r.

Example. In how many ways can 5 prizes be given away to 4 boys, when each boy is eligible for all the prizes ?

Any one of the prizes can be given in 4 ways; and then any one of the remaining prizes can also be given in 4 ways, since it may be obtained by the boy who has already received a prize. Thus two prizes can be given away in 4^2 ways, three prizes in 4^3 ways, and so on. Hence the 5 prizes can be given away in 4^5, or 1024 ways.

153. *To find the total number of ways in which it is possible to make a selection by taking some or all of n things.*

Each thing may be dealt with in two ways, for it may either be taken or left; and since either way of dealing with any one thing may be associated with either way of dealing with each one of the others, the number of ways of dealing with the n things is

$$2 \times 2 \times 2 \times 2 \ldots \text{ to } n \text{ factors.}$$

But this includes the case in which all the things are left, therefore, rejecting this case, the total number of ways is $2^n - 1$.

This is often spoken of as "the total number of combinations" of n things.

Example. A man has 6 friends; in how many ways may he invite one or more of them to dinner ?

He has to select some or all of his 6 friends; and therefore the number of ways is $2^6 - 1$, or 63.

This result can be verified in the following manner.

The guests may be invited singly, in twos, threes, ...; therefore the number of selections

$$= {}^6C_1 + {}^6C_2 + {}^6C_3 + {}^6C_4 + {}^6C_5 + {}^6C_6$$
$$= 6 + 15 + 20 + 15 + 6 + 1 = 63.$$

154. *To find for what value of r the number of combinations of n things r at a time is greatest.*

Since $\qquad {}^nC_r = \dfrac{n(n-1)(n-2) \ldots (n-r+2)(n-r+1)}{1 \cdot 2 \cdot 3 \ldots (r-1)\,r}$,

and $\qquad {}^nC_{r-1} = \dfrac{n(n-1)(n-2) \ldots (n-r+2)}{1 \cdot 2 \cdot 3 \ldots (r-1)}$;

$\therefore \qquad {}^nC_r = {}^nC_{n-1} \times \dfrac{n-r+1}{r}$.

The multiplying factor $\dfrac{n-r+1}{r}$ may be written $\dfrac{n+1}{r} - 1$, which shews that it decreases as r increases. Hence as r receives the values $1, 2, 3, \ldots$ in succession, ${}^nC_r$ is continually increased until $\dfrac{n+1}{r} - 1$ becomes equal to 1 or less than 1.

Now, $\qquad\qquad\qquad \dfrac{n+1}{r} - 1 > 1,$

so long as $\qquad\qquad\qquad \dfrac{n+1}{r} > 2;$

that is, $\qquad\qquad\qquad \dfrac{n+1}{2} > r.$

We have to choose the greatest value of r consistent with this inequality.

(1)   Let n be even, and equal to $2m$; then

$$\frac{n+1}{2} = \frac{2m+1}{2} = m + \frac{1}{2};$$

and for all values of r up to m inclusive this is greater than r. Hence by putting $r = m = \dfrac{n}{2}$, we find that the greatest number of combinations is $^{n}C_{n/2}$.

(2) Let n be odd and equal to $2m + 1$; then

$$\frac{n+1}{2} = \frac{2m+2}{2} = m + 1;$$

and for all values of r up to m inclusive this is greater than r; but when $r = m + 1$ the multiplying factor becomes equal to 1, and $^{n}C_{m+1} = {}^{n}C_{m}$; that is, $^{n}C_{\frac{n+1}{2}} = {}^{n}C_{\frac{n-1}{2}}$;

and therefore the number of combinations is greatest when the things are taken $\dfrac{n+1}{2}$, or $\dfrac{n-1}{2}$ at a time; the result being the same in the two cases.

155. The formula for the number of combinations of n things r at a time may be found without assuming the formula for the number of permutations.

Let $^{n}C_{r}$ denote the number of combinations of n things taken r at a time; and let the n things be denoted by the letters $a, b, c, d, \ldots$.

Take away a; then with the remaining letters we can form $^{n-1}C_{r-1}$ combinations of $n - 1$ letters taken $r - 1$ at a time. With each of these write a; thus we see that of the combinations of n things r at a time, the number of those which contain a is $^{n-1}C_{r-1}$; similarly the number of those which contain b is $^{n-1}C_{r-1}$; and so for each of the n letters.

Therefore $n \times {}^{n-1}C_{r-1}$ is equal to the number of combinations r at a time which contain a, together with those that contain b, those that contain c, and so on.

But by forming the combinations in this manner, each particular one will be repeated r times. For instance, if $r = 3$, the combination abc will be found among those containing a, among those containing b, and among those containing c. Hence

$$^{n}C_{r} = {}^{n-1}C_{r-1} \times \frac{n}{r}.$$

By writing $n-1$ and $r-1$ instead of n and r respectively,

$$^{n-1}C_{r-1} = {}^{n-2}C_{r-2} \times \frac{n-1}{r-1}.$$

Similarly, $$^{n-2}C_{r-2} = {}^{n-3}C_{r-3} \times \frac{n-2}{r-2},$$

....

$$^{n-r+2}C_2 = {}^{n-r+1}C_1 \times \frac{n-r+2}{2};$$

and finally $$^{n-r+1}C_1 = n-r+1.$$

Multiply together the vertical columns and cancel like factors from each side; thus

$$^{n}C_r = \frac{n(n-1)(n-2)\ldots(n-r+1)}{r(r-1)(r-2)\ldots 1}.$$

156. *To find the total number of ways in which it is possible to make a selection by taking some or all out of $p+q+r+\ldots$ things, where of p are alike of one kind, q alike of a second kind, r alike of a third kind; and so on.*

The p things may be disposed of in $p+1$ ways; for we may take $0, 1, 2, 3, \ldots p$ of them. Similarly the q things may be disposed of in $q+1$ ways; the r things in $r+1$ ways; and so on.

Hence the number of ways in which all the things may be disposed of is $(p+1)(q+1)(r+1)\ldots$

But this includes the case in which none of the things are taken; therefore, rejecting this case, the total number of ways is

$$(p+1)(q+1)(r+1)\ldots -1.$$

157. A general formula expressing the number of permutations, or combinations, of n things taken r at a time, when the things are not all different, may be somewhat complicated; but a particular case may be solved in the following manner.

Example. Find the number of ways in which (1) a selection, (2) an arrangement, of four letters can be made from the letters of the word proportion.

There are 10 letters of six different sorts, namely

$$o, o, o; p, p; r, r; t; i; n.$$

In finding groups of four these may be classified as follows :

(1) Three alike, one different.
(2) Two alike, two others alike.
(3) Two alike, the other two different.
(4) All four different.

(1) The selection can be made in 5 ways; for each of the five letters, p, r, t, i, n, can be taken with the single group of the three like letters o.

(2) The selection can be made in $^3C_2$ ways; for we have to choose two out of the three pairs $o, o; p, p; r, r$. This gives 3 selections.

(3) The selection can be made in 3×10 ways; for we select one of the 3 pairs, and then two from the remaining 5 letters. This gives 30 selections.

(4) This selection can be made in $^6C_4$ ways as we have to take 4 different letters to choose from the six o, p, r, t, i, n. This gives 15 selections.

Thus the total number of selections is $5 + 3 + 30 + 15$; that is, 53.

In finding the different arrangements of 4 letters we have to permute in all possible ways each of the foregoing groups.

(1) gives rise to $5 \times \dfrac{4!}{3!}$, or 20 arrangements.

(2) gives rise to $3 \times \dfrac{4!}{2!2!}$, or 18 arrangements.

(3) gives rise to $30 \times \dfrac{4!}{2!}$, or 360 arrangements.

(4) gives rise to $15 \times 4!$, or 360 arrangements.

Thus the total number of arrangements is
$$20 + 18 + 360 + 360; \text{ that is, } 758.$$

EXAMPLES XI. b.

1. Find the number of arrangements that can be made out of the letters of the words

    (1) *independence*,   (2) *superstitious*,   (3) *institutions*.

2. In how many ways can 17 billiard balls be arranged, if 7 of them are black, 6 red, and 4 white?

3. A room is to be decorated with fourteen flags; if 2 of them are blue, 3 red, 2 white, 3 green, 2 yellow, and 2 purple, in how many ways can they be hung?

4. How many numbers greater than a million can be formed with the digits 2, 3, 0, 3, 4, 2, 3?

5. Find the number of arrangements which can be made out of the letters of the word *algebra*, without altering the relative positions of vowels and consonants.

6. On three different days a man has to drive to a railway station and he can choose from 5 conveyances; in how many ways can he make the three journeys?

7. I have counters of n different colours, red, white, blue, ...; in how many ways can I make an arrangement consisting of r

counters, supposing that there are at least r of each different colour ?

8. In a steamer there are stalls for 12 animals, and there are cows, horses, and calves (not less than 12 of each) ready to be shipped; in how many ways can the shipload be made ?

9. In how many ways can n things be given to p persons, when there is no restriction as to the number of things each may receive ?

10. In how many ways can five things be divided between two persons ?

11. How many different arrangements can be made out of the letters in the expression $a^3b^2c^4$ when written at full length ?

12. A letter lock consists of three rings each marked with fifteen different letters; find in how many ways it is possible to make an unsuccessful attempt to open the lock.

13. Find the number of triangles which can be formed by joining three angular points of a quindecagon.

14. A library has a copies of one book, b copies of each of two books, c copies of each of three books, and single copies of d books. In how many ways can these books be distributed, if all are out at once ?

15. How many numbers less than 10000 can be made with the eight digits 1, 2, 3, 0, 4, 5, 6, 7 ?

16. In how many ways can the following prizes be given away to a class of 20 boys : first second Classical, first and second Mathematical, first Science, and first French ?

17. A telegraph has 5 arms and each arm is capable of 4 distinct positions, including the position of rest; what is the total number of signals that can be made ?

18. In how many ways can 7 persons form a ring ? In how many ways can 7 Englishmen and 7 Americans sit down at a round table, no two Americans being together ?

19. In how many ways is it possible to draw a sum of money from a bag containing a sovereign, a half- sovereign, a crown, a florin, a shilling, a penny, and a farthing ?

20. From 3 cocoa nuts, 4 apples, and 2 oranges, how many selections of fruit can be made, taking at least one of each kind ?

21. Find the number of different ways of dividing mn things into n equal groups.

22. How many signals can be made by hoisting 4 flags of different colours one above the other, when any number of them may be hoisted at once ? How many with 5 flags ?.

23. Find the number of permutations which can be formed out of the letters of the word *series* taken three together ?

24. There are p points in a plane, no three of which are in the same straight line with the exception of q, which are all in the same straight line; find the number (1) of straight lines, (2) of triangles which result from joining them.

25. There are p points in space, no four of which are in the same plane with the exception of q, which are all in the same plane; find how many planes there are each containing three of the points.

26. There are n different books and p copies of each ; find the number of ways in which a selection can be made from them.

27. Find the number of selections and of arrangements that can be made by taking 4 letters from word *expression*.

28. How many permutations of 4 letters can be made out of the letters of the word *examination* ?

29. Find the sum of all numbers greater than 10000 formed by using the digits 1, 3, 5, 7, 9, no digit being repeated in any number.

30. Find the sum of all numbers greater than 10000 formed by using the digits 0, 2, 4, 6, 8, no digit being repeated in any number.

31. If of $p + q + r$ things p be alike, and q be alike, and the rest different, shew that the total number of combinations is

$$(p + 1) (q + 1) 2^{r} - 1.$$

32. Shew that the number of permutations which can be formed from $2n$ letters which are either a's or b's is greatest when the number of a's is equal to the number of b's.

33. If the $n + 1$ numbers $a, b, c, d, \ldots$ be all different, and each of them a prime number, prove that the number of different factors of the expression $a^{m}bcd \ldots$ is $(m + 1) 2^{n} - 1$.

Chapter 12

MATHEMATICAL INDUCTION

158. Many important mathematical formulae are not easily demonstrated by a direct mode of proof; in such cases we frequently find it convenient to employ a method of proof known as mathematical induction, which we shall now illustrate.

Example 1. Suppose it is required to prove that the sum of the cubes of the first n natural numbers is equal to $\left\{ \dfrac{n(n+1)}{2} \right\}^2$.

We can easily see by trial that the statement is true in simple cases, such as when $n = 1$, or 2, or 3; and from this we might be led to *conjecture* that the formula was true in all cases. Assume that it is true when n terms are taken; that is, suppose

$$1^3 + 2^3 + 3^3 + \dots \text{ to } n \text{ terms} = \left\{ \frac{n(n+1)}{2} \right\}^2.$$

Add the $(n+1)^{\text{th}}$ term, that is, $(n+1)^3$ to each side; then $1^3 + 2^3 + 3^3 + \dots$ to

$$n+1 \text{ terms} = \left\{ \frac{n(n+1)}{2} \right\}^2 + (n+1)^3$$

$$= (n+1)^2 \left(\frac{n^2}{4} + n + 1 \right)$$

$$= \frac{(n+1)^2 (n^2 + 4n + 4)}{4}$$

$$= \left\{ \frac{(n+1)(n+2)}{2} \right\}^2 ;$$

which is *of the same form* as the result we assumed to be true for n terms, $n+1$ taking the place of n; in other words, if the result is true when we take a certain number of terms, whatever that number may be, it is true when we increase that number by one; but we see that it is true when 3 terms are taken; therefore it is true when 4 terms are taken; it is therefore true when 5 terms are taken; and so on. Thus the result is true universally.

Example 2. To determine the product of n binomial factors of the form $x + a$.

By actual multiplication we have

$$(x+a)(x+b)(x+c) = x^3 + (a+b+c)x^2 + (ab+bc+ca)x + abc;$$

$$(x+a)(x+b)(x+c)(x+d) = x^4 + (a+b+c+d)x^3$$

$$+ (ab+ac+ad+bc+bd+cd)x^2 + (abc+abd+acd+bcd)x + abcd.$$

In these results we observe that the following laws hold :

1. The number of terms on the right is one more than the number of binomial factors on the left.

2. The index of x in the first term is the same as the number of binomial factors; and in each of the other terms the index is one less than that of the preceding term.

3. The coefficient of the first term is unity; the coefficient of the second term is the sum of the letters $a, b, c, \ldots$; the coefficient of the third term is the sum of the products of these letters taken two at a time; the coefficient of the fourth term is the sum of their products taken three at a time; and so on; the last term is the product of all the letters.

Assume that these laws hold in the case of $n - 1$ factors; that is, suppose

$$(x + a)(x + b) \ldots (x + h) = x^{n-1} + p_1 x^{n-2} + p_2 x^{n-3} + p_3 x^{n-4} +$$
$$\ldots + p_{n-1},$$

where
$$p_1 = a + b + c + \ldots h$$
$$p_2 = ab + ac + \ldots + ah + bc + bd + \ldots;$$
$$p_3 = abc + abd + \ldots;$$
$$\ldots\ldots\ldots\ldots\ldots\ldots$$
$$p_{n-1} = abc \ldots h.$$

Multiply both sides by another factor $x + k$; thus

$$(x + a)(x + b) \ldots (x + h)(x + k)$$
$$= x^n + (p_1 + k) x^{n-1} + (p_2 + p_1 k) x^{n-2}$$
$$+ (p_3 + p_2 k) x^{n-3} + \ldots + p_{n-1} k.$$

Now
$$p_1 + k = (a + b + c + \ldots + h) + k$$
$$= \text{sum of all the } n \text{ letters } a, b, c, \ldots k;$$
$$p_2 + p_1 k = p_2 + k(a + b + \ldots + h)$$
$$= \text{sum of the products taken two at a time of all the}$$
$$n \text{ letters } a, b, c, \ldots k;$$
$$p_3 + p_2 k = p_3 + k(ab + ac + \ldots + ah + bc + \ldots)$$
$$= \text{sum of the products taken three at a time of all}$$
$$\text{the } n \text{ letters } a, b, c, \ldots k;$$
$$p_{n-1} k = \text{product of all the } n \text{ letters } a, b, c, \ldots k.$$

If therefore the laws hold when $n - 1$ factors are multiplied together, they hold in the case of n factors. But we have seen that they hold in the case of 4 factors; therefore they hold for 5 factors; therefore also for 6 factors; and so on; thus they hold universally. Therefore

$$(x + a)(x + b)(x + c) \ldots (x + k) = x^n + S_1 x^{n-1} + S_2 x^{n-2} + S_3 x^{n-3} + \ldots + S_n$$

where $S_1 = $ the sum of all the n letters $a, b, c \ldots k$;

$S_2 = $ the sum of the product taken two at a time of these n letters.

$$\ldots\ldots\ldots\ldots\ldots\ldots\ldots$$

$S_n = $ the product of all the n letters.

159. Theorems relating to divisibility may often be established by induction.

Example. Shew that $x^n - 1$ is divisible by $x - 1$ for all positive integral values of n.

By division
$$\frac{x^n - 1}{x - 1} = x^{n-1} + \frac{x^{n-1} - 1}{x - 1};$$

if therefore $x^{n-1} - 1$ is divisible by $x - 1$, then $x^n - 1$ is also divisible by $x - 1$. But $x^2 - 1$ is divisible by $x - 1$; therefore $x^3 - 1$ is divisible by $x - 1$; therefore $x^4 - 1$ is divisible by $x - 1$, and so on; hence the proposition is established.

Other examples of the same kind will be found in the chapter on the *Theory of Numbers*.

160. From the foregoing examples it will be seen that the only theorems to which induction can be applied are those which admit of successive cases corresponding to the order of the natural numbers $1, 2, 3, \ldots n$.

EXAMPLES XII

Prove by induction :

1. $1 + 3 + 5 + \ldots + (2n - 1) = n^2$.

2. $1^2 + 2^2 + 3^2 + \ldots + n^2 = \frac{1}{6} n (n + 1) (2n + 1)$

3. $2 + 2^2 + 2^3 + \ldots + 2^n = 2 (2^n - 1)$.

4. $\dfrac{1}{1 \cdot 2} + \dfrac{1}{2 \cdot 3} + \dfrac{1}{3 \cdot 4} + \ldots$ to n terms $= \dfrac{n}{n + 1}$.

5. Prove by induction that $x^n - y^n$ is divisible by $x + y$ when n is even.

Chapter 13

BINOMIAL THEOREM.
POSITIVE INTEGRAL INDEX

161. It may be shewn by actual multiplication that

$$(x + a)(x + b)(x + c)(x + d)$$
$$= x^4 + (a + b + c + d)x^3 + (ab + ac + ad + bc + bd + cd)x^2$$
$$+ (abc + abd + acd + bcd)x + abcd \qquad \qquad ...(1)$$

We may, however, write down this result by inspection; for the complete product consists of the sum of a number of partial products each of which is formed by multiplying together four letters, *one* being taken from *each* of the four factors. If we examine the way in which the various partial products are formed, we see that

(1)   the term x^4 is formed by taking the letter x out of each of the factors.

(2)   the terms involving x^3 are formed by taking the letter x out of *any three* factors, in every way possible, and *one* of the letters a, b, c, d out of the remaining factor.

(3)   the terms involving x^2 are formed by taking the letter x out of *any two* factors, in every way possible, and two of the letters a, b, c, d out of the remaining factors.

(4)   the terms involving x are formed by taking the letter x out of *any one* factor, and *three* of the letters a, b, c, d out of the remaining factors

(5)   the term independent of x is the product of all the letters a, b, c, d.

Example 1. $(x - 2)(x + 3)(x - 5)(x + 9)$
$$= x^4 + (-2 + 3 - 5 + 9)x^3 + (-6 + 10 - 18 - 15 + 27 - 45)x^2$$
$$+ (30 - 54 + 90 - 135)x + 270$$
$$= x^4 + 5x^3 - 47x^2 - 69x + 270.$$

Example 2.   Find the coefficient of x^3 in the product
$$(x - 3)(x + 5)(x - 1)(x + 2)(x - 8).$$

The terms involving x^3 are formed by multiplying together the x in *any three* of the factors, and *two* of the numerical quantities out of the two remaining factors; hence the coefficient is equal to the sum of the products of the quantities $-3, 5, -1, 2, -8$ taken two at a time.

Thus the required coefficient

$$= -15 + 3 - 6 + 24 - 5 + 10 - 40 - 2 + 8 - 16$$
$$= -39.$$

162. If in equation (1) of the preceding article we suppose $b = c = d = a$, we obtain

$$(x + a)^4 = x^4 + 4ax^3 + 6a^2x^2 + 4a^3x + a^4.$$

The method here exemplified of deducing a particular case from a more general result is one of frequent occurrence in Mathematics; for it often happens that it is more easy to prove a general proposition than it is to prove a particular case of it.

We shall in the next article employ the same method to prove a formula known as the Binomial Theorem, by which any binomial of the form $x + a$ can be raised to any assigned positive integral power.

163.   *To find the expansion of $(x + a)^n$ when n is a positive integer.*

Consider the expression

$$(x + a)(x + b)(x + c) \ldots (x + k),$$

the number of factors being n.

The expansion of this expression is the continued product of the n factors, $x + a, x + b, x + c, \ldots, x + k$, and every term in the expansion is of n dimensions, being a product formed by multiplying together n letters, *one* taken from each of these n factors.

The highest power of x is x^n, and is formed by taking the letter x from *each* of the n factors.

The terms involving x^{n-1} are formed by taking the letter x from any $(n - 1)$ of the factors and *one* of the letters $a, b, c, \ldots k$ from the remaining factor; thus the coefficient of x^{n-1} in the final product is the sum of the letters $a, b, c, \ldots k$; denote it by S_1.

The terms involving x^{n-2} are formed by taking the letter x from *any* $n - 2$ of the factors, and two of the letters $a, b, c, \ldots k$ from the two remaining factors; thus the coefficient of x^{n-2} in the final product is the sum of the products of the letters $a, b, c, \ldots k$ taken two at a time; denote it by S_2.

And, generally, the terms involving x^{n-r} are formed by taking the letter x from *any* $n - r$ of the factors, and r of the letters $a, b, c, \ldots k$ from the r remaining factors; thus the coefficient of x^{n-r} in the final product is the sum of the products of the letters $a, b, c, \ldots k$ taken r at a time; denote it by S_r.

The last term in the product is $abc \ldots k$; denote it by S_n.

Hence $(x + a)(x + b)(x + c) \ldots (x + k)$

$$= x^n + S_1 x^{n-1} + S_2 x^{n-2} + \ldots + S_r x^{n-r} + \ldots + S_{n-1} x + S_n.$$

In S_1 the *number of terms* is n; in S_2 *the number of terms* is the same as the number of combinations of n things 2 at a time; that is $^nC_2$; in S_3 *the number of terms is* $^nC_3$; and so on.

Now suppose $b, c, \ldots k$, each equal to a; then S_1 becomes $^nC_1 a$; S_2 becomes $^nC_2 a^2$; S_3 becomes $^nC_3 a^3$; and so on; thus

$$(x+a)^n = x^n + {}^nC_1 ax^{n-1} + {}^nC_2 a^2 x^{n-2} + {}^nC_3 a^3 x^{n-3} + \ldots + {}^nC_n a^n;$$

substituting for $^nC_1, {}^nC_2, \ldots$ we obtain

$$(x+a)^n = x^n + nax^{n-1} + \frac{n(n-1)}{1\cdot2} a^2 x^{n-2}$$
$$+ \frac{n(n-1)(n-2)}{1\cdot2\cdot3} a^3 x^{n-3} + \ldots + a^n,$$

the series containing $n + 1$ terms.

This is the *Binomial Theorem*, and the expression on the right is said to be the expansion of $(x + a)^n$.

164. The Binomial Theorem may also be proved as follows :

By induction we can find the product of the n factors $x + a, x + b, x + c \ldots x + k$ as explained in Art. 158, Ex. 2; We can then deduce the expansion of $(x + a)^n$ as in Art. 163.

165. The coefficients in the expansion of $(x + a)^n$ are very conveniently expressed by the symbols $^nC_1, {}^nC_2, {}^nC_3, \ldots {}^nC_n$. We shall, however, sometimes further abbreviate them by omitting n, and writing $C_1, C_2, C_3, \ldots C_n$. With this notation we have

$$(x+a)^n = x^n + C_1 ax^{n-1} + C_2 a^2 x^{n-2} + C_3 a^3 x^{n-3} + \ldots + C_n a^n.$$

If we write $-a$ in the place of a, we obtain

$$(x-a)^n = x^n + C_1 (-a) x^{n-1} + C_2 (-a)^2 x^{n-2} + C_3 (-a)^3 x^{n-3}$$
$$+ \ldots + C_n (-a)^n$$
$$= x^n - C_1 ax^{n-1} + C_2 a^2 x^{n-2} - C_3 a^3 x^{n-3} + \ldots + (-1)^n C_n a^n.$$

Thus the terms in the expansion of $(x + a)^n$ and $(x - a)^n$ are numerically the same, but in $(x - a)^n$ they are alternately positive and negative , and the last term is positive or negative according as n is even or odd.

Example 1. Find the expansion of $(x + y)^6$.

By the formula,

$$(x + y)^6 = x^6 + {}^6C_1\, x^5 y + {}^6C_2\, x^4 y^2 + {}^6C_3\, x^3 y^3 + {}^6C_4\, x^2 y^4 + {}^6C_5\, xy^5 + {}^6C_6\, y^6$$
$$= x^6 + 6x^5 y + 15x^4 y^2 + 20x^3 y^3 + 15x^2 y^4 + 6xy^5 + y^6,$$

on calculating the values of ${}^6C_1, {}^6C_2, {}^6C_3, \ldots$.

Example 2. Find the expansion of $(a - 2x)^7$

$$(a - 2x)^7 = a^7 - {}^7C_1\, a^6\, (2x) + {}^7C_2\, a^5\, (2x)^2 - {}^7C_3\, a^4\, (2x)^3 + \ldots \text{ to 8 terms.}$$

Now remembering that ${}^nC_r = {}^nC_{n-r}$, after calculating the coefficients up to ${}^7C_3$, the rest may be written down at once; for ${}^7C_4 = {}^7C_3;\; {}^7C_5 = {}^7C_2$, and so on.

Hence $(a - 2x)^7 = a^7 - 7a^6\, (2x) + \dfrac{7\cdot 6}{1\cdot 2}\, a^5\, (2x)^2 - \dfrac{7\cdot 6\cdot 5}{1\cdot 2\cdot 3}\, a^4\, (2x)^3 + \ldots$

$$= a^7 - 7a^6\, (2x) + 21a^5\, (2x)^2 - 35a^4\, (2x)^3 + 35a^3\, (2x)^4$$
$$\qquad\qquad - 21a^2\, (2x)^5 + 7a\, (2x)^6 - (2x)^7$$
$$= a^7 - 14a^6 x + 84a^5 x^2 - 280a^4 x^3 + 560a^3 x^4 - 672\, a^2 x^5 + 448ax^6 - 128x^7.$$

Example 3. Find the value of

$$(a + \sqrt{a^2 - 1})^7 + (a - \sqrt{a^2 - 1})^7.$$

We have here the sum of two expansions whose terms are numerically the same; but in the second expansion the second, fourth sixth, and eighth terms are negative, and therefore destroy the corresponding terms of the first expansion. Hence the value

$$= 2\,\{a^7 + 21a^5\, (a^2 - 1) + 35a^3\, (a^2 - 1)^2 + 7a\, (a^2 - 1)^3\}$$
$$= 2a\, (64a^6 - 112a^4 + 56a^2 - 7).$$

166. In the expansion of $(x + a)^n$, the coefficient of the second term is ${}^nC_1$; of the third term is ${}^nC_2$; of the fourth term is ${}^nC_3$; and so on; the suffix in each term being one less than the number of the term to which it applies; hence ${}^nC_r$ is the coefficient of the $(r + 1)^{\text{th}}$ term. This is called the **general term,** because by giving to r different numerical values any of the coefficients may be found from ${}^nC_r$; and by giving to x and a their appropriate indices any assigned term may be obtained.

Thus the $(r + 1)^{\text{th}}$ term may be written

$$^nC_r \, x^{n-r} a^r, \text{ or } \frac{n\,(n-1)\,(n-2)\,\ldots\,(n-r+1)}{r\,!}\,x^{n-r}a^r.$$

In applying this formula to any particular case, it should be observed that *the index of* a *is the same as the suffix of* C, *and that the sum of the indices of* x *and* a *is* n

Example 1. Find the fifth term of $(a + 2x^3)^{17}$.

The required term $= \, ^{17}C_4 \, a^{13} \, (2x^3)^4$

$$= \frac{17\cdot16\cdot15\cdot14}{1\cdot2\cdot3\cdot4} \times 16a^{13}\,x^{12}$$

$$= 38080a^{13}\,x^{12}.$$

Exmple 2. Find the fourteenth term of $(3 - a)^{15}$.

The required term $= \, ^{15}C_{13}\,(3)^2\,(-a)^{13}$

$$= \, ^{15}C_2 \times (-9a^{13}) \hspace{2cm} \text{[Art. 145.]}$$

$$= -945a^{13}.$$

167. The simplest form of the binomial theorem is the expansion of $(1 + x)^n$. This is obtained from the general formula of Art. 163, by writing 1 in the place of x, and x in the place of a. Thus

$$(1+x)^n = 1 + \,^nC_1\,x + \,^nC_2\,x^2 + \ldots + \,^nC_r\,x^r + \ldots \,^nC_n\,x^n$$

$$= 1 + nx + \frac{n\,(n-1)}{1\cdot2}\,x^2 + \ldots x^n;$$

the general term being

$$\frac{n\,(n-1)\,(n-2)\,\ldots\,(n-r+1)}{r\,!}\,x^r.$$

The expansion of a binomial may always be made to depend upon the case in which the first term is unity; thus

$$(x+y)^n = \left\{ x\left(1 + \frac{y}{x}\right)\right\}^n$$

$$= x^n\,(1+z)^n, \text{ where } z = \frac{y}{x}.$$

Example 1. Find the coefficient of x^{16} in the expansion of $(x^2 - 2x)^{10}$.

We have $\quad (x^2 - 2x)^{10} = x^{20}\left(1 - \frac{2}{x}\right)^{10};$

and, since x^{20} multiplies every term in the expansion of $\left(1 - \dfrac{2}{x}\right)^{10}$, we have in this expansion to seek the coefficient of the term which contains $\dfrac{1}{x^4}$.

Hence the required coefficient $= \, ^{10}C_4\,(-2)^4$

$$= \frac{10 \cdot 9 \cdot 8 \cdot 7}{1 \cdot 2 \cdot 3 \cdot 4} \times 16$$

$$= 3360.$$

In some cases the following method is simpler.

Example 2. Find the coefficient of x^r in the expansion of $\left(x^2 + \dfrac{1}{x^3} \right)^n$.

Suppose that x^r occurs in the $(p+1)^{\text{th}}$ term.

The $(p+1)^{\text{th}}$ term $= {}^nC_p (x^2)^{n-p} \left(\dfrac{1}{x^3} \right)^p$

$$= {}^nC_p x^{2n-5p}.$$

But this term contains x^r, and therefore $2n - 5p = r$, or $p = \dfrac{2n-r}{5}$.

Thus the required coefficient $= {}^nC_p = {}^nC_{\frac{2n-r}{5}}$

$$= \frac{n!}{\left(\dfrac{1}{5}(2n-r) \right)! \left(\dfrac{1}{5}(3n+r) \right)!}.$$

Unless $\dfrac{2n-r}{5}$ is a positive integer there will be no term containing x^r in the expansion.

168. In Art. 163 we deduced the expansion of $(x+a)^n$ from the product of n factors $(x+a)(x+b) \dots (x+k)$, and the method of proof there given is valuable in consequence of the wide generality of the results obtained. But the following shorter proof of the Binomial Theorem should be noticed.

It will be seen in Chap. 15. that a similar method is used to obtain the general term of the expansion of

$$(a_1 + b + c + \dots)^n.$$

169. *To prove the Binomial theorem.*

The expansion of $(x+a)^n$ is the product of n factors, each equal to $x + a$, and every term in the expansion is of n dimensions, being a product formed by multiplying together n letters, *one* taken from each of the n factors. Thus each term involving $x^{n-r}a^r$ is obtained by taking a out of *any* r of the factors, and x out of the remaining $n-r$ factors. Therefore the number of terms which involve $x^{n-r}a^r$ must be equal to the number of ways in which r things can be selected out of n; that is, the coefficient of $x^{n-r}a^r$ is ${}^nC_r$, and by giving to r the values $0., 1, 2, 3, \dots, n$ in succession we obtain the coefficients of all the terms. Hence

$$(x+a)^n = x^n + {}^nC_1 x^{n-1}a + {}^nC_2 x^{n-2}a^2 + \dots + {}^nC_r x^{n-r}a^r + \dots + a^n$$

since ${}^nC_0$ and ${}^nC_n$ are each equal to unity.

EXAMPLES XIII. a.

Expand the following binomials :

1. $(x-3)^5$.

2. $(3x+2y)^4$.

3. $(2x-y)^5$.

4. $(1-3a^2)^6$.

5. $(x^2+x)^5$.

6. $(1-xy)^7$.

7. $\left(2 - \dfrac{3x^2}{2}\right)^4$.

8. $\left(3a - \dfrac{2}{3}\right)^6$.

9. $\left(1 + \dfrac{x}{2}\right)^7$.

10. $\left(\dfrac{2}{3}x - \dfrac{3}{2x}\right)^6$.

11. $\left(\dfrac{1}{2} + a\right)^8$.

12. $\left(1 - \dfrac{1}{x}\right)^{10}$.

Write down and simplify :

13. The 4th term of $(x-5)^{13}$.

14. The 10th term of $(1-2x)^{12}$.

15. The 12th term of $(2x-1)^{13}$.

16. The 28th term of $(5x+8y)^{30}$.

17. The 4th term of $\left(\dfrac{a}{3} + 9b\right)^{10}$.

18. The 5th term of $\left(2a - \dfrac{b}{3}\right)^8$.

19. The 7th term of $\left(\dfrac{4x}{5} - \dfrac{5}{2x}\right)^9$.

20. The 5th term of $\left(\dfrac{x^{3/2}}{a^{1/2}} - \dfrac{y^{5/2}}{b^{3/2}}\right)^8$.

Find the value of

21. $(x+\sqrt{2})^4 + (x-\sqrt{2})^4$.

22. $(\sqrt{x^2-a^2}+x)^5 - (\sqrt{x^2-a^2}-x)^5$.

23. $(\sqrt{2}+1)^6 - (\sqrt{2}-1)^6$.

24. $(2-\sqrt{1-x})^6 + (2+\sqrt{1-x})^6$.

25. Find the middle term of $\left(\dfrac{a}{x} + \dfrac{x}{a}\right)^{10}$.

26. Find the middle term of $\left(1 - \dfrac{x^2}{2}\right)^{14}$.

27. Find the coefficient of x^{18} in $\left(x^2 + \dfrac{3a}{x}\right)^{15}$.

28. Find the coefficient of x^{18} in $(ax^4 - bx)^9$.

29. Find the coefficients of x^{32} and x^{-17} in $\left(x^4 - \dfrac{1}{x^3}\right)^{15}$.

30. Find the two middle terms of $\left(3a - \dfrac{a^3}{6}\right)^9$.

31. Find the term independent of x in $\left(\dfrac{3}{2} x^2 - \dfrac{1}{3x} \right)^9$.

32. Find the 13th term of $\left(9x - \dfrac{1}{3\sqrt{x}} \right)^{18}$

33. If x^r occurs in the expansion of $\left(x + \dfrac{1}{x} \right)^n$, find its coefficient.

34. Find the term independent of x in $\left(x - \dfrac{1}{x^2} \right)^{3n}$

35. If x^p occurs in the expansion of $\left(x^2 + \dfrac{1}{x} \right)^{2n}$, prove that its coefficient is $\dfrac{2n\,!}{\left(\dfrac{1}{3}(4n-p) \right)! \left(\dfrac{1}{3}(2n+p) \right)!}$

170. *In the expansion of* $(1+x)^n$ *the coefficients of terms equidistant from the beginning and end are equal.*

The coefficient of the $(r+1)^{\text{th}}$ term from the beginning is $^n C_r$.

The $(r+1)^{\text{th}}$ term from the end has $n+1-(r+1)$, or $n-r$ terms before it; therefore counting from the beginning it is the $(n-r+1)^{\text{th}}$ term, and its coefficient is $^n C_{n-r}$, which has been shewn to be equal to $^n C_r$.[Art. 145.] Hence the proposition follows.

171. *To find the greatest coefficient in the expansion of* $(1+x)^n$.

The coefficient of the general term of $(1+x)^n$ is $^n C_r$; and we have only to find for what value of r this is greatest.

By Art. 154, when n is even, the greatest coefficient is $^n C_{\frac{n}{2}}$; and when n is odd, it is $^n C_{\frac{n-1}{2}}$, or $^n C_{\frac{n+1}{2}}$; these two coefficients being equal.

172. *To find the greatest term in the expansion of* $(x+a)^n$.

We have $(x+a)^n = x^n \left(1 + \dfrac{a}{x} \right)^n$;

therefore, since x^n multiplies every term in $\left(1 + \dfrac{a}{x} \right)^n$, it will be sufficient to find the greatest term in this latter expansion.

Let the rth and $(r+1)^{\text{th}}$ be any two consecutive terms. The $(r+1)^{\text{th}}$ term is obtained by multiplying the rth term by $\dfrac{n-r+1}{r} \cdot \dfrac{a}{x}$; that is, by

$$\left(\frac{n+1}{r}-1\right)\frac{a}{x}.$$ [Art. 166.]

The factor $\dfrac{n+1}{r}-1$ decreases as r increases; hence the $(r+1)^{\text{th}}$ term is not always greater than the rth term, but only until $\left(\dfrac{n+1}{r}-1\right)\dfrac{a}{x}$ becomes equal to 1, or less than 1.

Now,
$$\left(\frac{n+1}{r}-1\right)\frac{a}{x}>1,$$

so long as
$$\frac{n+1}{r}-1>\frac{x}{a};$$

that is,
$$\frac{n+1}{r}>\frac{x}{a}+1,$$

or
$$\frac{n+1}{\frac{x}{a}+1}>r \qquad\qquad \dots(1)$$

If $\dfrac{n+1}{\frac{x}{a}+1}$ be an integer, denote it by p; then if $r=p$ the multiplying factor becomes 1, and the $(p+1)^{\text{th}}$ term is equal to the pth; and these are greater than any other term.

If $\dfrac{n+1}{\frac{x}{a}+1}$ be not an integer, denote its integral part by q; then the greatest value of r consistent with (1) is q; hence the $(q+1)^{\text{th}}$ term is the greatest.

Since we are only concerned with the *numerically greatest term*, the investigation will be the same for $(x-a)^n$; therefore in any numerical example it is unnecessary to consider the sign of the second term of the binomial. Also it will be found best to work each example independently of the general formula.

Example 1. If $x=\dfrac{1}{3}$, find the greatest term in the expansion of $(1+4x)^8$.

Denote the rth and $(r+1)^{\text{th}}$ terms by T_r and T_{r+1} respectively; then

$$T_{r+1}=\frac{8-r+1}{r}\cdot 4x\times T_r$$

$$= \frac{9-r}{r} \times \frac{4}{3} \times T_r;$$

hence $\qquad T_{r+1} > T_r,$

so long as $\qquad \dfrac{9-r}{r} \times \dfrac{4}{3} > 1;$

that is $\qquad 36 - 4r > 3r,$

or $\qquad\qquad 36 > 7r.$

The greatest value of r consistent with this is 5; hence the greatest term is the sixth, and its value

$$= {}^8C_5 \times \left(\frac{4}{3}\right)^5 = {}^8C_3 \times \left(\frac{4}{3}\right)^5 = \frac{57344}{243}.$$

Example 2. Find the greatest term in the expansion of $(3 - 2x)^9$ when $x = 1.$

$$(3 - 2x)^9 = 3^9 \left(1 - \frac{2x}{3}\right)^9;$$

thus it will be sufficient to consider the expansion of

$$\left(1 - \frac{2x}{3}\right)^9.$$

Here, $\qquad T_{r+1} = \dfrac{9 - r + 1}{r} \cdot \dfrac{2x}{3} \times T_r, \text{ numerically,}$

$$= \frac{10 - r}{r} \times \frac{2}{3} \times T_r;$$

hence $\qquad T_{r+1} > T_r,$

so long as $\qquad \dfrac{10 - r}{r} \times \dfrac{2}{3} > 1;$

that is, $\qquad\qquad 20 > 5r.$

Hence for all values of r up to 3, we have $T_{r+1} > T_r;$ but if $r = 4$, then $T_{r+1} = T_r$, and these are the greatest terms. Thus the 4th and 5th terms are numerically equal and greater than any other term, and their value

$$= 3^9 \times {}^9C_3 \times \left(\frac{2}{3}\right)^3 = 3^6 \times 84 \times 8 = 489888.$$

173. *To find the sum of the coefficients in the expansion of* $(1 + x)^n.$

In the identity $(1 + x)^n = 1 + C_1 x + C_2 x^2 + C_3 x^3 + \ldots + C_n x^n,$
Put $x = 1$; thus

$$2^n = 1 + C_1 + C_2 + C_3 + \ldots + C_n$$
$$= \text{sum of the coefficients.}$$

Cor. $\qquad C_1 + C_2 + C_3 + \ldots + C_n = 2^n - 1;$

that is "total number of combinations of n things" is $2^n - 1$. [Art. 153.]

174. *To prove that in the expansion of $(1 + x)^n$, the sum of the coefficients of the odd terms is equal to the sum of the coefficients of the even terms.*

In the identity $(1 + x)^n = 1 + C_1 x + C_2 x^2 + C_3 x^3 + \ldots + C_n x^n$,

put $x = -1$; thus

$$0 = 1 - C_1 + C_2 - C_3 + C_4 - C_5 + \ldots;$$

$\therefore$

$$1 + C_2 + C_4 + \ldots = C_1 + C_3 + C_5 + \ldots$$

$$= \frac{1}{2} \text{ (sum of all the coefficients)}$$

$$= 2^{n-1}.$$

175. The Binomial Theorem may also be applied to expand expressions which contain more than two terms.

Example. Find the expansion of $(x^2 + 2x - 1)^3$.

Regarding $2x - 1$ as a single term, the expansion

$$= (x^2)^3 + 3 (x^2)^2 (2x - 1) + 3x^2 (2x - 1)^2 + (2x - 1)^3.$$

$$= x^6 + 6x^5 + 9x^4 - 4x^3 - 9x^2 + 6x - 1, \text{ on reduction.}$$

176. The following example is instructive.

Example. If $(1 + x)^n = c_0 + c_1 x + c_2 x^2 + \ldots + c_n x^n$,

find the value of $c_0 + 2c_1 + 3c_2 + 4c_3 + \ldots (n + 1) c_n$ ...(1),

and $c_1^2 + 2c_2^2 + 3c_3^2 + \ldots + nc_n^2$ ...(2).

The series $(1) = (c_0 + c_1 + c_2 + \ldots + c_n) + (c_1 + 2c_2 + 3c_3 + \ldots + nc_n)$

$$= 2^n + n \left\{ 1 + (n - 1) + \frac{(n - 1) (n - 2)}{1 \cdot 2} + \ldots + 1 \right\}$$

$$= 2^n + n (1 + 1)^{n-1}$$

$$= 2^n + n \cdot 2^{n-1}$$

To find the value of the series (2), we proceed thus :

$$c_1 x + 2c_2 x^2 + 3c_3 x^3 + \ldots + nc_n x^n$$

$$= nx \left\{ 1 + (n - 1) x + \frac{(n - 1) (n - 2)}{1 \cdot 2} x^2 + \ldots + x^{n-1} \right\}$$

$$= nx (1 + x)^{n-1};$$

hence, by changing x into $\dfrac{1}{x}$, we have

$$\frac{c_1}{x} + \frac{2c_2}{x^2} + \frac{3c_3}{x^3} + \ldots + \frac{nc_n}{x^n} = \frac{n}{x} \left(1 + \frac{1}{x} \right)^{n-1}$$ ...(3),

Also $c_0 + c_1 x + c_2 x^2 + \ldots + c_n x^n = (1 + x)^n$ ...(4).

If we multiply together the two series on the left-hand sides of (3) and (4), we see that in the product the term independent of x is the series (2); hence the series (2) = term independent of x in

$$\frac{n}{x}(1+x)^n\left(1+\frac{1}{x}\right)^{n-1}$$

= term independent of x in $\dfrac{n}{x^n}(1+x)^{2n-1}$

= coefficient of x^n in $n(1+x)^{2n-1}$

= $n \times {}^{2n-1}C_n$

= $\dfrac{(2n-1)!}{(n-1)!\,(n-1)!}$.

EXAMPLES XIII. b.

In the following expansions find which is the greatest term :

1. $(x-y)^{30}$ when $x=11, y=4$.   **2.** $(2x-3y)^{28}$ when $x=9, y=4$.

3. $(2a+b)^{14}$ when $a=4, b=5$.   **4.** $(3+2x)^{15}$ when $x=\dfrac{5}{2}$.

In the following expansions find the value of the greatest term :

5. $(1+x)^n$ when $x=\dfrac{2}{3}$, $n=6$.

6. $(a+x)^n$ when $a=\dfrac{1}{2}$, $x=\dfrac{1}{3}$, $n=9$.

7. Shew that the coefficient of the middle term of $(1+x)^{2n}$ is equal to the sum of the coefficients of the middle terms of $(1+x)^{2n-1}$.

8. If A be the sum of the odd terms and B the sum of the even terms in the expansion of $(x+a)^n$, prove that $A^2-B^2=(x^2-a^2)^n$.

9. The $2^{\text{nd}}, 3^{\text{rd}}, 4^{\text{th}}$ terms in the expansion of $(x+y)^n$ are $240, 720, 1080$ respectively; find x, y, n.

10. Find the expansion of $(1+2x-x^2)^4$.

11. Find the expansion of $(3x^2-2ax+3a^2)^3$.

12. Find the rth term from the end in $(x+a)^n$.

13. Find the $(p+2)^{\text{th}}$ term from the end in $\left(x-\dfrac{1}{x}\right)^{2n+1}$.

14. In the expansion of $(1+x)^{43}$ the coefficients of the $(2r+1)^{\text{th}}$ and the $(r+2)^{\text{th}}$ terms are equal; find r.

15. Find the relation between r and n in order that the coefficients of the $3r^{\text{th}}$ and $(r+2)^{\text{th}}$ terms of $(1+x)^{2n}$ may be equal.

16. Shew that the middle term in the expansion of $(1+x)^{2n}$ is
$$\frac{1 \cdot 3 \cdot 5 \ldots (2n-1)}{n!} 2^n x^n.$$

If $c_0, c_1, c_2, \ldots c_n$ denote the coefficients in the expansion of $(1+x)^n$, prove that

17. $c_1 + 2c_2 + 3c_3 + \ldots + nc_n = n \cdot 2^{n-1}$.

18. $c_0 + \dfrac{c_1}{2} + \dfrac{c_2}{3} + \ldots + \dfrac{c_n}{n+1} = \dfrac{2^{n+1}-1}{n+1}$.

19. $\dfrac{c_1}{c_0} + \dfrac{2c_2}{c_1} + \dfrac{3c_3}{c_2} + \ldots + \dfrac{{}^n c_n}{c_{n-1}} = \dfrac{n(n+1)}{2}$

20. $(c_0 + c_1)(c_1 + c_2) \ldots (c_{n-1} + c_n) = \dfrac{c_1 c_2 \ldots c_n (n+1)^n}{n!}$.

21. $2c_0 + \dfrac{2^2 c_1}{2} + \dfrac{2^3 c_2}{3} + \dfrac{2^4 c_3}{4} + \ldots + \dfrac{2^{n+1} c_n}{n+1} = \dfrac{3^{n+1}-1}{n+1}$.

22. $c_0^2 + c_1^2 + c_2^2 + \ldots + c_n^2 = \dfrac{2n!}{n! \, n!}$.

23. $c_0 c_r + c_1 c_{r+1} + c_2 c_{r+2} + \ldots + c_{n-r} c_n = \dfrac{2n!}{(n-r)! \, (n+r)!}$.

Chapter 14

BINOMIAL THEOREM.
ANY INDEX.

177. In the last chapter we investigated the Bionomial Theorem when the index was any positive integer; we shall now consider whether the formulae there obtained hold in the case of negative and fractional values of the index.

Since, by Art. 167, every binomial may be reduced to one common type, it will be sufficient to confine our attention to binomials of the form $(1 + x)^n$.

By actual evolution, we have

$$(1 + x)^{1/2} = \sqrt{1 + x} = 1 + \frac{1}{2}x - \frac{1}{8}x^2 + \frac{1}{16}x^3 - \ldots;$$

and by actual division,

$$(1 - x)^{-2} = \frac{1}{(1 - x)^2} = 1 + 2x + 3x^2 + 4x^3 + \ldots;$$

[Compare Ex. 1, Art. 60.]

and in each of these series the number of terms is unlimited.

In these cases we have by independent processes obtained an expansion for each of the expressions $(1 + x)^{1/2}$ and $(1 + x)^{-2}$. We shall presently prove that they are only particular cases of the general formula for the expansion of $(1 + x)^n$, where n is any rational quantity.

This formula was discovered by Newton.

178. Suppose we have two expressions arranged in ascending powers of x, such as

$$1 + mx + \frac{m(m-1)}{1 \cdot 2}x^2 + \frac{m(m-1)(m-2)}{1 \cdot 2 \cdot 3}x^3 + \ldots \qquad \ldots(1)$$

and $$1 + nx + \frac{n(n-1)}{1 \cdot 2}x^2 + \frac{n(n-1)(n-2)}{1 \cdot 2 \cdot 3}x^3 + \ldots \qquad \ldots(2)$$

The product of these two expressions will be a series in ascending powers of x; denote it by

$$1 + Ax + Bx^2 + Cx^3 + Dx^4 + \ldots;$$

then it is clear that $A, B, C, \ldots$ are functions of m and n, and therefore the actual values of $A, B, C, \ldots$ in any particular case will depend upon the values of m and n in that case. But the way in which the coefficients of the powers of x in (1) and (2) combine to give $A, B, C, \ldots$ is quite independent of m and n; in other words, *whatever values m and n may have, $A, B, C, \ldots$ preserve the same invariable form.* If therefore we can determine the form of $A, B, C, \ldots$ for any value of m and n, we conclude that $A, B, C, \ldots$ will have the same form *for all values* of m and n.

The principle here explained is often referred to as an example of "the permanence of equivalent forms;" in the present case we have only to recognise the fact that in *any algebraical product* the *form* of the result will be the same whether the quantities involved are whole numbers, or fractions; positive, or negative.

We shall make use of this principle in the general proof of the Binomial Theorem for any index. The proof which we give is due to Euler.

179. *To prove the Binomial Theorem when the index is a positive fraction.*

Whatever be the value of m, *positive or negative, integral or fractional,* let the symbol $f(m)$ stand for the series

$$1 + mx + \frac{m(m-1)}{1 \cdot 2} x^2 + \frac{m(m-1)(m-2)}{1 \cdot 2 \cdot 3} x^3 + \ldots;$$

then $f(n)$ will stand for the series

$$1 + nx + \frac{n(n-1)}{1 \cdot 2} x^2 + \frac{n(n-1)(n-2)}{1 \cdot 2 \cdot 3} x^3 + \ldots$$

If we multiply these two series together the product will be another series in ascending powers of x, whose *coefficients will be unaltered in form whatever* m *and* n *may be.*

To determine this *invariable form of the product* we may give to m and n any values that are most convenient; for this purpose suppose that m and n are positive integers. In this case $f(m)$ is the expanded form of $(1+x)^m$, and $f(n)$ is the expanded form of $(1+x)^n$; and therefore

$$f(m) \times f(n) = (1+x)^m \times (1+x)^n = (1+x)^{m+n},$$

but when m and n are positive integers the expansion of $(1+x)^{m+n}$ is

$$1 + (m+n)x + \frac{(m+n)(m+n-1)}{1 \cdot 2} x^2 + \ldots$$

This then is the *form* of the product of $f(m) \times f(n)$ *in all cases*, whatever the values of m and n may be; and in agreement with our previous notation it may be denoted by $f(m+n)$; therefore for all values of m and n.

$$f(m) \times f(n) = f(m+n).$$

Also $\qquad f(m) \times f(n) \times f(p) = f(m+n) \times f(p)$

$$= f(m+n+p) \text{ similarly.}$$

Proceeding in this way we may shew that

$$f(m) \times f(n) \times f(p) \dots \text{ to } k \text{ factors} = f(m+n+p+ \dots \text{ to } k \text{ terms}).$$

Let each of these quantities $m, n, p, \dots$ be equal to $\dfrac{h}{k}$, where h and k are positive integers;

$$\therefore \qquad \left\{ f\left(\frac{h}{k} \right) \right\}^{k} = f(h);$$

but since h is a positive integer, $f(h) = (1+x)^{h}$;

$$\therefore \qquad (1+x)^{h} = \left\{ f\left(\frac{h}{k} \right) \right\}^{h};$$

$$\therefore \qquad (1+x)^{h/k} = f\left(\frac{h}{k} \right);$$

but $f\left(\dfrac{h}{k} \right)$ stands for the series

$$1 + \frac{h}{k} x + \frac{\dfrac{h}{k}\left(\dfrac{h}{k} - 1 \right)}{1 \cdot 2} x^{2} + \dots;$$

$$\therefore \qquad (1+x)^{h/k} = 1 + \frac{h}{k} x + \frac{\dfrac{h}{k}\left(\dfrac{h}{k} - 1 \right)}{1 \cdot 2} x^{2} + \dots,$$

which proves the Binomial Theorem for any positive fractional index.

180. *To prove the Binomial Theorem when the index is any negative quantity.*

It has been proved that

$$f(m) \times f(n) = f(m+n)$$

for all values of m and n. Replacing m by $-n$ (where n is positive), we have

$$f(-n) \times f(n) = f(-n+n)$$

$$= f(0)$$

$$= 1.$$

Since all terms of the series except the first vanish;

$$\therefore \qquad \frac{1}{f(n)} = f(-n);$$

but $f(n) = (1+x)^n$, for *any positive* value of n;

$$\therefore \qquad \frac{1}{(1+x)^n} = f(-n),$$

or $\qquad\qquad (1+x)^{-n} = f(-n).$

But $f(-n)$ stands for the series

$$1 + (-n)x + \frac{(-n)(-n-1)}{1\cdot2}x^2 + \ldots;$$

$$\therefore \qquad (1+x)^{-n} = 1 + (-n)x + \frac{(-n)(-n-1)}{1\cdot2}x^2 + \ldots;$$

which proves the Binomial Theorem for any negative index. Hence the theorem is completely established.

181. The proof contained in the two preceding articles may not appear wholly satisfactory, and will probably present some difficulties to the student. There is only one point to which we shall now refer.

In the expression for $f(m)$ the number of terms is finite when m is a positive integer, and unlimited in all other cases. See Art. 182. It is therefore necessary to enquire in what sense we are to regard the statement that $f(m) \times f(n) = f(m+n)$. It will be seen in Chapter 21., that when $x < 1$, each of the series $f(m)$, $f(n)$, $f(m+n)$ is *convergent*, and $f(m+n)$ is the true arithmetical equivalent of $f(m) \times f(n)$. But when $x > 1$, all these series are divergent, and we only assert that if we multiply the series denoted by $f(m)$ by the series denoted by $f(n)$, the first r terms of the product will agree with the first r terms of $f(m+n)$, whatever finite value r may have.   [See Art. 308.]

Example 1. Expand $(1-x)^{3/2}$ to four terms.

$$(1-x)^{\frac{3}{2}} = 1 + \frac{3}{2}(-x) + \frac{\frac{3}{2}\left(\frac{3}{2}-1\right)}{1\cdot2}(-x)^2 + \frac{\frac{3}{2}\left(\frac{3}{2}-1\right)\left(\frac{3}{2}-2\right)}{1\cdot2\cdot3}(-x)^3 + \ldots$$

$$= 1 - \frac{3}{2}x + \frac{3}{8}x^2 + \frac{1}{16}x^3 + \ldots$$

Example 2. Expand $(2+3x)^{-4}$ to four terms.

$$(2+3x)^{-4} = 2^{-4}\left(1 + \frac{3x}{2}\right)^{-4}$$

$$= \frac{1}{2^4}\left[1 + (-4)\left(\frac{3x}{2}\right) + \frac{(-4)(-5)}{1\cdot2}\left(\frac{3x}{2}\right)^2 + \frac{(-4)(-5)(-6)}{1\cdot2\cdot3}\left(\frac{3x}{2}\right)^3 + \ldots\right]$$

$$= \frac{1}{16}\left(1 - 6x + \frac{45}{2}x^2 - \frac{135}{2}x^3 + \ldots\right)$$

182. In finding the general term we must now use the formula.

$$\frac{n(n-1)(n-2) \ldots (n-r+1)}{r!} x^r$$

written in full; for the symbol ^nC_r can no longer be employed when n is fractional or negative.

Also the coefficient of the general term can never vanish unless one of the factors of its numerator is zero; the series will therefore stop at the rth term, when $n - r + 1$ is zero; that is, when $r = n + 1$; but since r is a positive integer this equality can never hold except when the index n is positive and integral. Thus the expansion by the Binomial Theorem extends to $n + 1$ terms when n is a positive integer, and to an infinite number of terms in all other cases.

Example 1. Find the general term in the expansion of $(1 + x)^{\frac{1}{2}}$.

$$\text{The } (r+1)^{th} \text{ term} = \frac{\frac{1}{2}\left(\frac{1}{2}-1\right)\left(\frac{1}{2}-2\right) \ldots \left(\frac{1}{2}-r+1\right)}{r!} x^r$$

$$= \frac{1(-1)(-3)(-5) \ldots (-2r+3)}{2^r r!} x^r.$$

The number of factors in the numerator is r, and $r - 1$ of these are negative; therefore, by taking -1 out of each of these negative factors, we may write the above expression

$$(-1)^{r-1} \frac{1 \cdot 3 \cdot 5 \ldots (2r-3)}{2^r r!} x^r.$$

Example 2. Find the general term in the expansion of $(1 - nx)^{1/n}$.

$$\text{The } (r+1)^{th} \text{ term} = \frac{\frac{1}{n}\left(\frac{1}{n}-1\right)\left(\frac{1}{n}-2\right) \ldots \left(\frac{1}{n}-r+1\right)}{r!} (-nx)^r$$

$$= \frac{1(1-n)(1-2n) \ldots (1-\overline{r-1}\cdot n)}{n^r r!} (-1)^r n^r x^r$$

$$= (-1)^r \frac{1(1-n)(1-2n) \ldots (1-\overline{r-1}\cdot n)}{r!} x^r$$

$$= (-1)^r (-1)^{r-1} \frac{(n-1)(2n-1) \ldots (\overline{r-1}\cdot n - 1)}{r!} x^r$$

$$= -\frac{(n-1)(2n-1) \ldots (\overline{r-1}\cdot n - 1)}{r!} x^r,$$

since $\qquad (-1)^r (-1)^{r-1} = (-1)^{2r-1} = -1.$

Example 3. Find the general term in the expansion of $(1 - x)^{-3}$.

$$\text{The } (r+1)^{th} \text{ term} = \frac{(-3)(-4)(-5) \ldots (-3-r+1)}{r!} (-x)^r$$

$$= (-1)^r \frac{3 \cdot 4 \cdot 5 \ldots (r+2)}{r!} (-1)^r x^r$$

$$= (-1)^{2r} \frac{3 \cdot 4 \cdot 5 \ldots (r+2)}{1 \cdot 2 \cdot 3 \ldots r} x^r$$

$$= \frac{(r+1)(r+2)}{1 \cdot 2} x^r,$$

by removing like factors from the numerator and denominator.

EXAMPLES XIV. a.

Expand to 4 terms the following expressions :

1. $(1+x)^{\frac{1}{2}}$

2. $(1+x)^{\frac{3}{2}}$

3. $(1-x)^{\frac{2}{5}}$

4. $(1+x^2)^{-2}$

5. $(1-3x)^{\frac{1}{3}}$

6. $(1-3x)^{-\frac{1}{3}}$

7. $(1+2x)^{-\frac{1}{2}}$

8. $\left(1+\dfrac{x}{3}\right)^{-3}$.

9. $\left(1+\dfrac{2x}{3}\right)^{\frac{3}{2}}$

10. $\left(1+\dfrac{1}{2}a\right)^{-4}$

11. $(2+x)^{-3}$

12. $(9+2x)^{\frac{1}{2}}$

13. $(8+12a)^{\frac{2}{3}}$

14. $(9-6x)^{-\frac{3}{2}}$

15. $(4a-8x)^{-\frac{1}{2}}$

Write down and simplify :

16. The 8th term of $(1+2x)^{-\frac{1}{2}}$.

17. The 11th term of $(1-2x^3)^{\frac{11}{2}}$.

18. The 10th term of $(1+3a^2)^{\frac{16}{3}}$.

19. The 5th term of $(3a-2b)^{-1}$.

20. The $(r+1)^{\text{th}}$ term of $(1-x)^{-2}$.

21. The $(r+1)^{\text{th}}$ term of $(1-x)^{-4}$.

22. The $(r+1)^{\text{th}}$ term of $(1+x)^{\frac{1}{2}}$.

23. The $(r+1)^{\text{th}}$ term of $(1+x)^{\frac{11}{3}}$.

24. The 14th term of $(2^{10}-2^7 x)^{13/2}$.

25. The 7th term of $(3^8+6^4 x)^{\frac{11}{4}}$.

183.   If we expand $(1 - x)^{-2}$ by the Binomial Theorem, we obtain
$$(1 - x)^{-2} = 1 + 2x + 3x^2 + 4x^3 + \ldots;$$
but, by referring to Art. 60, we see that this result is only true when x is less than 1. This leads us to enquire whether we are always justified in assuming the truth of the statement
$$(1 + x)^n = 1 + nx + \frac{n(n-1)}{1 \cdot 2} x^2 + \ldots,$$
and, if not, under what conditions the expansion of $(1 + x)^n$ may be used as its true equivalent.

Suppose, for instance, that $n = -1$; then we have
$$(1 - x)^{-1} = 1 + x + x^2 + x^3 + x^4 + \ldots \qquad \ldots(1)$$
in this equation put $x = 2$; we then obtain
$$(-1)^{-1} = 1 + 2 + 2^2 + 2^3 + 2^4 + \ldots$$
This contradictory result is sufficient to shew that we cannot take
$$1 + nx + \frac{n(n-1)}{1 \cdot 2} x^2 + \ldots$$
as the true arithmetical equivalent of $(1 + x)^n$ in all cases.

Now from the formula for the sum of a geometrical progression, we know that the sum of the first r terms of the series (1)
$$= \frac{1 - x^r}{1 - x} = \frac{1}{1 - x} - \frac{x^r}{1 - x};$$
and, when x is numerically less than 1, by taking r sufficiently large we can make $\dfrac{x^r}{1 - x}$ as small as we please; that is, by taking a sufficient number of terms the sum can be made to differ as little as we please from $\dfrac{1}{1 - x}$. But when x is numerically greater than 1, the value of $\dfrac{x^r}{1 - x}$ increases with r, and therefore no such approximation to the value of $\dfrac{1}{1 - x}$ is obtained by taking any number of terms of the series
$$1 + x + x^2 + x^3 + \ldots$$

It will be seen in the chapter on Convergency and Divergency of Series that the expansion by the Binomial Theorem of $(1 + x)^n$ in ascending powers of x is always arithmetically intelligible when x is less than 1.

But if x is greater than 1, then since the general term of the series
$$1 + nx + \frac{n(n-1)}{1 \cdot 2} x^2 + \ldots$$

contains x^r, it can be made greater than any finite quantity by taking r sufficiently large; in which case there is no limit to the value of the above series; and therefore the expansion of $(1+x)^n$ as an infinite series in ascending powers of x has no meaning arithmetically intelligible when x is greater than 1.

184. We may remark that we can always expand $(x+y)^n$ by the Binomial Theorem; for we may write the expression in either of the two following forms:

$$x^n \left(1 + \frac{y}{x} \right)^n, \; y^n \left(1 + \frac{x}{y} \right)^n;$$

and we obtain the expansion from the first or second of these according as x is greater or less than y.

185. *To find in its simplest form the general term in the expansion of* $(1-x)^{-n}$.

The $(r+1)^{\text{th}}$ term

$$= \frac{(-n)(-n-1)(-n-2) \dots (-n-r+1)}{r\,!} (-x)^r$$

$$= (-1)^r \frac{n(n+1)(n+2) \dots (n+r-1)}{r\,!} (-1)^r x^r$$

$$= (-1)^{2r} \frac{n(n+1)(n+2) \dots (n+r-1)}{r\,!} x^r$$

$$= \frac{n(n+1)(n+2) \dots (n+r-1)}{r\,!} x^r.$$

From this it appears that every term in the expansion of $(1-x)^{-n}$ is positive.

Although the general term in the expansion of any binomial may always be found as explained in Art. 182, it will be found more expeditious in practice to use the above form of the general term in all cases where the index is negative, retaining the form

$$\frac{n(n-1)(n-2) \dots (n-r+1)}{r\,!} x^r$$

only in the case of positive indices.

Example : Find the general term in the expansion of $\dfrac{1}{\sqrt[3]{1-3x}}$.

$$\frac{1}{\sqrt[3]{1-3x}} = (1-3x)^{-\frac{1}{3}}.$$

The $(r+1)^{\text{th}}$ term

$$= \frac{\frac{1}{3}\left(\frac{1}{3}+1\right)\left(\frac{1}{3}+2\right)\left(\frac{1}{3}+r-1\right)}{r\,!}(3x)^r$$

$$= \frac{1 \cdot 4 \cdot 7 \dots (3r-2)}{3^r\,r\,!}\, 3^r x^r$$

$$= \frac{1 \cdot 4 \cdot 7 \dots (3r-2)}{r\,!}\, x^r.$$

If the given expression had been $(1+3x)^{-\frac{1}{3}}$ we should have used the same formula for the general term, replacing $3x$ by $-3x$.

186.   The following expansions should be remembered :

$$(1-x)^{-1} = 1 + x + x^2 + x^3 + \dots + x^r + \dots$$

$$(1-x)^{-2} = 1 + 2x + 3x^2 + 4x^3 + \dots + (r+1)x^r + \dots$$

$$(1-x)^{-3} = 1 + 3x + 6x^2 + 10x^3 + \dots + \frac{(r+1)(r+2)}{1 \cdot 2}x^r + \dots$$

187.   The general investigation of the greatest term in the expansion of $(1+x)^n$, when n is unrestricted in value, will be found in Art. 189; but the student will have no difficulty in applying to any numerical example the method explained in Art. 172.

Example :   Find the greatest term in the expansion of $(1+x)^{-n}$ when $x = \dfrac{2}{3}$, and $n = 20$.

We have
$$T_{r+1} = \frac{n+r-1}{r} \cdot x \times T_r, \text{ numerically,}$$

$$= \frac{19+r}{r} \times \frac{2}{3} \times T_r;$$

$\therefore$
$$T_{r+1} > T_r,$$

So long as
$$\frac{2(19+r)}{3r} > 1;$$

that is,
$$38 > r.$$

Hence for all values of r up to 37, we have $T_{r+1} > T_r$; but if $r = 38$ then $T_{r+1} = T_r$, and these are the greatest terms. Thus the 38th and 39th terms are equal numerically and greater than any other term.

188.   Some useful applications of the Binomial Theorem are explained in the following examples.

Example 1.   Find the first three terms in the expansion of
$$(1+3x)^{\frac{1}{2}}(1-2x)^{-\frac{1}{3}}.$$

Expanding the two binomials as far as the term containing x^2, we have

$$\left(1+\frac{3}{2}x-\frac{9}{8}x^2-\ldots\right)\left(1+\frac{2}{3}x+\frac{8}{9}x^2+\ldots\right)$$

$$=1+x\left(\frac{3}{2}+\frac{2}{3}\right)+x^2\left(\frac{8}{9}+\frac{3}{2}\cdot\frac{2}{3}-\frac{9}{8}\right)\ldots$$

$$=1+\frac{13}{6}x+\frac{55}{72}x^2.$$

If in this Example $x=.002$, so that $x^2=.000004$, we see that the third term is a decimal fraction beginning with 5 ciphers. If therefore we were required to find the numerical value of the given expression correct to 5 places of decimals it would be sufficient to substitute .002 for x in $1+\frac{13}{6}x$, neglecting the term involving x^2.

Example 2. When x is so small that its square and higher powers may be neglected, find the value of

$$\frac{\left(1+\frac{2}{3}x\right)^{-5}+\sqrt{4+2x}}{\sqrt{(4+x)^3}}$$

Since x^2 and the higher powers may be neglected, it will be sufficient to retain the first two terms in the expansion of each binomial.

Therefore the expression $\;=\dfrac{\left(1+\frac{2}{3}x\right)^{-5}+2\left(1+\frac{x}{2}\right)^{\frac{1}{2}}}{8\left(1+\frac{x}{4}\right)^{\frac{3}{2}}}$

$$=\frac{\left(1-\frac{10}{3}x\right)+2\left(1+\frac{1}{4}x\right)}{8\left(1+\frac{3}{8}x\right)}$$

$$=\frac{1}{8}\left(3-\frac{17}{6}x\right)\left(1+\frac{3}{8}x\right)^{-1}$$

$$=\frac{1}{8}\left(3-\frac{17}{6}x\right)\left(1-\frac{3}{8}x\right)$$

$$=\frac{1}{8}\left(3-\frac{95}{24}x\right),$$

the term involving x^2 being neglected.

Example 3. Find the value of $\dfrac{1}{\sqrt{47}}$ to four places of decimals.

$$\frac{1}{\sqrt{47}}=(47)^{-\frac{1}{2}}=(7^2-2)^{-\frac{1}{2}}=\frac{1}{7}\left(1-\frac{2}{7^2}\right)^{-\frac{1}{2}}$$

$$= \frac{1}{7}\left(1 + \frac{1}{7^2} + \frac{3}{2} \cdot \frac{1}{7^4} + \frac{5}{2} \cdot \frac{1}{7^6} + \dots\right)$$

$$= \frac{1}{7} + \frac{1}{7^3} + \frac{3}{2} \cdot \frac{1}{7^5} + \frac{5}{2} \cdot \frac{1}{7^7} + \dots$$

To obtain the values of the several terms we proceed as follows :

$$7\,)\,1$$
$$7\,\overline{)\,0.142857} \quad \dots\dots = \frac{1}{7},$$
$$7\,\overline{)\,0.020408}$$
$$7\,\overline{)\,0.002915} \quad \dots\dots = \frac{1}{7^3},$$
$$7\,\overline{)\,0.000416}$$
$$0.000059 \quad \dots\dots = \frac{1}{7^5};$$

and we can see that the term $\dfrac{5}{2} \cdot \dfrac{1}{7^7}$ is a decimal fraction beginning with 5 ciphers.

$$\therefore \qquad \frac{1}{\sqrt{47}} = 0.142857 + 0.002915 + 0.000088$$

$$= 0.14586,$$

and this result is correct to at least four places of decimals.

Example 4. Find the cube root of 126 to 5 places of decimals.

$$(126)^{1/3} = (5^3 + 1)^{1/3}$$

$$= 5\left(1 + \frac{1}{5^3}\right)^{\frac{1}{3}}$$

$$= 5\left(1 + \frac{1}{3} \cdot \frac{1}{5^3} - \frac{1}{9} \cdot \frac{1}{5^6} + \frac{5}{81} \cdot \frac{1}{5^9} - \dots\right)$$

$$= 5 + \frac{1}{3} \cdot \frac{1}{5^2} - \frac{1}{9} \cdot \frac{1}{5^5} + \frac{1}{81} \cdot \frac{1}{5^7} - \dots$$

$$= 5 + \frac{1}{3} \cdot \frac{2^2}{10^2} - \frac{1}{9} \cdot \frac{2^5}{10^5} + \frac{1}{81} \cdot \frac{2^7}{10^7} - \dots$$

$$= 5 + \frac{0.04}{3} - \frac{0.00032}{9} + \frac{0.0000128}{81} - \dots$$

$$= 5 + 0.013333\dots - 0.000035\dots + \dots$$

$$= 5.01329, \text{ to five places of decimals.}$$

EXAMPLES XIV. b.

Find the $(r+1)^{\text{th}}$ term in each of the following expansions :

1. $(1+x)^{-1/2}$.   2. $(1-x)^{-5}$.   3. $(1+3x)^{1/3}$.

4. $(1+x)^{-\frac{2}{3}}$.　　5. $(1+x^2)^{-3}$.　　6. $(1-2x)^{-\frac{3}{2}}$.

7. $(a+bx)^{-1}$.　　8. $(2-x)^{-2}$.　　9. $\sqrt[3]{(a^3-x^3)^2}$.

10. $\dfrac{1}{\sqrt{1+2x}}$.　　11. $\dfrac{1}{\sqrt[3]{(1-3x)^2}}$.　　12. $\dfrac{1}{\sqrt[n]{a^n-nx}}$.

Find the greatest term in each of the following expansions :

13. $(1+x)^{-7}$ when $x=\dfrac{4}{15}$.　　14. $(1+x)^{\frac{21}{2}}$ when $x=\dfrac{2}{3}$.

15. $(1-7x)^{-\frac{11}{4}}$ when $x=\dfrac{1}{8}$.

16. $(2x+5y)^{12}$ when $x=8$ and $y=3$.

17. $(5-4x)^{-7}$ when $x=\dfrac{1}{2}$.

18. $(3x^2+4y^3)^{-n}$ when $x=9$, $y=2$, $n=15$.

Find to five places of decimals the value of

19. $\sqrt{98}$.　　20. $\sqrt[3]{998}$.　　21. $\sqrt[3]{1003}$.

22. $\sqrt[4]{2400}$.　　23. $\dfrac{1}{\sqrt[3]{128}}$.　　24. $\left(1\dfrac{1}{250}\right)^{\frac{1}{3}}$.

25. $(630)^{-\frac{3}{4}}$.　　26. $\sqrt[5]{3128}$.

If x be so small that its square and higher powers may be neglected, find the value of

27. $(1-7x)^{\frac{1}{3}}(1+2x)^{-\frac{3}{4}}$.　　28. $\sqrt{4-x}\cdot\left(3-\dfrac{x}{2}\right)^{-1}$.

29. $\dfrac{(8+3x)^{\frac{2}{3}}}{(2+3x)\sqrt{4-5x}}$.　　30. $\dfrac{\left(1+\dfrac{2}{3}x\right)^{-5}\times(4+3x)^{\frac{1}{2}}}{(4+x)^{\frac{3}{2}}}$.

31. $\dfrac{\sqrt[4]{1-\dfrac{3}{5}x}+\left(1+\dfrac{5}{6}x\right)^{-6}}{\sqrt[3]{1+2x}+\sqrt[5]{1-\dfrac{x}{2}}}$.　　32. $\dfrac{\sqrt[3]{8+3x}-\sqrt[5]{1-x}}{(1+5x)^{\frac{3}{5}}+\left(4+\dfrac{x}{2}\right)^{\frac{1}{2}}}$.

33. Prove that the coefficient of x^r in the expansion of $(1-4x)^{-\frac{1}{2}}$ is $\dfrac{(2r)!}{(r!)^2}$.

34. Prove that $(1 + x)^n = 2^n \left\{ 1 - n \dfrac{1-x}{1+x} + \dfrac{n(n+1)}{1 \cdot 2} \left(\dfrac{1-x}{1+x} \right)^2 \cdots \right\}.$

35. Find the first three terms in the expansion of

$$\frac{1}{(1+x)^2 \sqrt{1+4x}}.$$

36. Find the first three terms in the expansion of

$$\frac{(1+x)^{\frac{3}{4}} + \sqrt{1+5x}}{(1-x)^2}.$$

37. Shew that the nth coefficient in the expansion of $(1-x)^{-n}$ is double of the $(n-1)^{\text{th}}$.

189. *To find the numerically greatest term in the expansion of* $(1 + x)^n$, *for any rational value of n.*

Since we are only concerned with the *numerical* value of the greatest term, we shall consider x throughout as positive.

Case I : Let n be a positive integer.

The $(r+1)^{\text{th}}$ term is obtained by multiplying the rth term by $\dfrac{n-r+1}{r} \cdot x$; that is, by $\left(\dfrac{n+1}{r} - 1 \right) x$; and therefore the terms continue to increase so long as

$$\left(\frac{n+1}{r} - 1 \right) x > 1;$$

that is,

$$\frac{(n+1)x}{r} > 1 + x,$$

or

$$\frac{(n+1)x}{1+x} > r.$$

If $\dfrac{(n+1)x}{1+x}$ be an integer, denote it by p; then if $r = p$, the multiplying factor is 1, and the $(p+1)^{\text{th}}$ term is equal to the pth, and these are greater than any other term.

If $\dfrac{(n+1)x}{1+x}$ be not an integer, denote its integral part by q; then the greatest value of r is q, and the $(q+1)^{\text{th}}$ term is the greatest.

Case II : Let n be a positive fraction.

As before, the $(r+1)^{\text{th}}$ term is obtained by multiplying the rth term by $\left(\dfrac{n+1}{r} - 1 \right) x.$

(1) If x be greater than unity, by increasing r the above multiplier can be made as near as we please to $-x$; so that after a certain term each term is nearly x times the preceding term numerically, and thus the terms increase continually, and there is no greatest term.

(2) If x be less than unity we see that the multiplying factor continues positive, and decreases until $r > n + 1$, and from this point it becomes negative but always remains less than 1 numerically; therefore there will be a greatest term.

As before, the multiplying factor will be greater than 1

so long as $\dfrac{(n+1)\,x}{1+x} > r.$

If $\dfrac{(n+1)\,x}{1+x}$ be an integer, denote it by p; then, as in Case I., the $(p+1)^{\text{th}}$ term is equal to the pth, and these are greater than any other term.

If $\dfrac{(n+1)\,x}{1+x}$ be not an integer, let q be its integral part; then the $(q+1)^{\text{th}}$ term is the greatest.

Case III : Let n be negative.

Let $n = -m$, so that m is positive; then the numerical value of the multiplying factor is $\dfrac{m+r-1}{r} \cdot x$; that is

$$\left(\frac{m-1}{r}+1\right)x.$$

(1) If α be greater than unity we may shew, as in Case II., that there is no greatest term.

(2) If x be less than unity, the multiplying factor will be greater than 1, so long as

$$\left(\frac{m-1}{r}+1\right)x > 1;$$

that is $\dfrac{(m-1)\,x}{r} > 1 - x,$

or $\dfrac{(m-1)\,x}{1-x} > r.$

If $\dfrac{(m-1)\,x}{1-x}$ be a positive integer, denote it by p; then the $(p+1)^{\text{th}}$ term is equal to the pth term, and these are greater than any other term.

If $\dfrac{(m-1)\,x}{1-x}$ be positive but not an integer, let q be its integral part; then the $(q+1)^{\text{th}}$ term is the greatest.

If $\dfrac{(m-1)\,x}{1-x}$ be negative, then m is less than unity; and by writing

the multiplying factor in the form $\left(1-\dfrac{1-m}{r}\right)x$, we see that it is

always less than 1 : hence each term is less than the preceding, and consequently the first term is the greatest.

190. *To find the number of homogeneous products of r dimensions that can be formed out of the n letters a, b., c, ... and their powers.*

By division, or by the Binomial Theorem, we have

$$\frac{1}{1-ax} = 1 + ax + a^2x^2 + a^3x^3 + \dots,$$

$$\frac{1}{1-bx} = 1 + bx + b^2x^2 + b^3x^3 + \dots,$$

$$\frac{1}{1-cx} = 1 + cx + c^2x^2 + c^3x^3 + \dots,$$

$$\dots\dots\dots\dots\dots$$

Hence, by multiplication,

$$\frac{1}{1-ax} \cdot \frac{1}{1-bx} \cdot \frac{1}{1-cx} \dots$$

$$= (1 + ax + a^2x^2 + \dots)(1 + bx + b^2x^2 + \dots)(1 + cx + c^2x^2 + \dots) \dots$$

$$= 1 + x(a+b+c+\dots) + x^2(a^2 + ab + ac + b^2 + bc + c^2 + \dots) + \dots$$

$$= 1 + S_1x + S_2x^2 + S_3x^3 + \dots \text{ suppose;}$$

where $S_1, S_2, S_3, \dots$ are the *sums* of the homogeneous products of *one, two, three,* ... dimensions that can be formed of $a, b, c, \dots$ and their powers.

To obtain the *number* of these products, put $a, b, c, \dots$ each equal to 1; each term in $S_1, S_2, S_3, \dots$ now becomes 1, and the values of $S_1, S_2, S_3, \dots$ so obtained give the number of the homogeneous products of *one, two, three,* ... dimensions.

Also $\quad \dfrac{1}{1-ax} \cdot \dfrac{1}{1-bx} \cdot \dfrac{1}{1-cx} \dots$

becomes $\dfrac{1}{(1-x)^n}$ or $(1-x)^{-n}$.

Hence S_r = coefficient of x^r in the expansion of $(1-x)^{-n}$

$$= \frac{n(n+1)(n+2)\dots(n+r-1)}{r!}$$

$$= \frac{(n+r-1)!}{r!(n-1)!}$$

191. *To find the number of terms in the expansion of any multinomial when the index is a positive integer.*

In the expansion of $(a_1 + a_2 + a_3 + \ldots + a_r)^n$,

every term is of n dimensions; therefore the number of terms is the same as the number of homogeneous products of n dimensions that can be formed out of the r quantities $a_1, a_2, \ldots, a_r$, and their powers; and therefore by the preceding article is equal to

$$\frac{(r+n-1)!}{n!(r-1)!}$$

192. From the result of Art. 190 we may deduce a theorem relating to the number of combinations of n things.

Consider n letters $a, b, c, d, \ldots$; then if we were to write down all the homogeneous products of r dimensions which can be formed of these letters and their powers, every such product would represent one of the combinations, r at a time, of the n letters, when any one of the letters might occur once, twice, thrice, ... up to r times.

Therefore the number of combinations of n things r at a time when repetitions are allowed is equal to the number of homogeneous products of r dimensions which can be formed out of n letters, and therefore equal to $\dfrac{(n+r-1)!}{r!(n-1)!}$, or $^{n+r-1}C_r$.

That is, the number of combinations of n things r at a time when repetitions are allowed is equal to the number of combinations of $n+r-1$ things r at a time when repetitions are excluded.

193. We shall conclude this chapter with a few miscellaneous examples.

Example 1. Find the coefficient of x^r in the expansion of $\dfrac{(1-2x)^2}{(1+x)^3}$.

The expression $= (1 - 4x + 4x^2)(1 + p_1x + p_2x^2 + \ldots + p_rx^r + \ldots)$ suppose.

The coefficient of x^r will be obtained by multiplying p_r, p_{r-1}, p_{r-2} by $1, -4, 4$ respectively, and adding the results; hence the required coefficient $= p_r - 4p_{r-1} + 4p_{r-2}$.

But $\qquad p_r = (-1)^r \dfrac{(r+1)(r+2)}{2}$ [Ex. 3, Art. 182.]

Hence the required coefficient

$$= (-1)^r \frac{(r+1)(r+2)}{2} - 4(-1)^{r-1} \frac{r(r+1)}{2} + 4(-1)^{r-2} \frac{(r-1)r}{2}$$

$$= \frac{(-1)^r}{2}[(r+1)(r+2) + 4r(r+1) + 4r(r-1)]$$

$$= \frac{(-1)^r}{2}(9r^2 + 3r + 2).$$

Example 2. Find the value of the series

$$2 + \frac{5}{2!\cdot3} + \frac{5\cdot7}{3!\cdot3^2} + \frac{5\cdot7\cdot9}{4!\cdot3^3} + \dots$$

The expression $= 2 + \dfrac{3\cdot5}{2!}\cdot\dfrac{1}{3^2} + \dfrac{3\cdot5\cdot7}{3!}\cdot\dfrac{1}{3^3} + \dfrac{3\cdot5\cdot7\cdot9}{4!}\cdot\dfrac{1}{3^4} + \dots$

$$= 2 + \frac{\frac{3}{2}\cdot\frac{5}{2}}{2!}\cdot\frac{2^2}{3^2} + \frac{\frac{3}{2}\cdot\frac{5}{2}\cdot\frac{7}{2}}{3!}\cdot\frac{2^3}{3^3} + \frac{\frac{3}{2}\cdot\frac{5}{2}\cdot\frac{7}{2}\cdot\frac{9}{2}}{4!}\cdot\frac{2^4}{3^4} + \dots$$

$$= 1 + \frac{\frac{3}{2}}{1}\cdot\frac{2}{3} + \frac{\frac{3}{2}\cdot\frac{5}{2}}{2!}\cdot\left(\frac{2}{3}\right)^2 + \frac{\frac{3}{2}\cdot\frac{5}{2}\cdot\frac{7}{2}}{3!}\cdot\left(\frac{2}{3}\right)^3 + \dots$$

$$= \left(1 - \frac{2}{3}\right)^{-\frac{3}{2}} = \left(\frac{1}{3}\right)^{-\frac{3}{2}}$$

$$= 3^{\frac{3}{2}} = 3\sqrt{3}.$$

Example 3. If n is any positive integer, shew that the integral part of $(3 + \sqrt{7})^n$ is an odd number.

Suppose I to denote the integral and f the fractional part of $(3 + \sqrt{7})^n$. Then

$$I + f = 3^n + C_1 3^{n-1}\sqrt{7} + C_3 3^{n-2}7 + C_3 3^{n-3}(\sqrt{7})^3 + \dots \qquad \dots(1)$$

Now $3 - \sqrt{7}$ is positive and less than 1, therefore $(3 - \sqrt{7})^n$ is a proper fraction; denote it by f';

$$\therefore \qquad f' = 3^n - C_1 3^{n-1}\sqrt{7} + C_2 3^{n-2}7 - C_3 3^{n-3}(\sqrt{7})^3 + \dots \qquad \dots(2).$$

Add together (1) and (2); the irrational terms disappear, and we have

$$I + f + f' = 2(3^n + C_2 3^{n-2}7 + \dots)$$

$$= \text{an even integer.}$$

But since f and f' are proper fractions their sum must be 1;

$$\therefore \qquad I = \text{an odd integer.}$$

EXAMPLES XIV. c.

Find the coefficient of

1. x^{100} in the expansion of $\dfrac{3-5x}{(1-x)^2}$.

2. a^{12} in the expansion of $\dfrac{4 + 2a - a^2}{(1+a)^3}$.

3. x^n in the expansion of $\dfrac{3x^2 - 2}{x + x^2}$.

4. Find the coefficient of x^n in the expansion of $\dfrac{2 + x + x^2}{(1+x)^3}$.

5. Prove that
$$1 - \frac{1}{2}\cdot\frac{1}{2} + \frac{1\cdot 3}{2\cdot 4}\cdot\frac{1}{2^2} - \frac{1\cdot 3\cdot 5}{2\cdot 4\cdot 6}\cdot\frac{1}{2^3} + \frac{1\cdot 3\cdot 5\cdot 7}{2\cdot 4\cdot 6\cdot 8}\cdot\frac{1}{2^4} - \cdots = \sqrt{\frac{2}{3}}.$$

6. Prove that
$$\sqrt{8} = 1 + \frac{3}{4} + \frac{3\cdot 5}{4\cdot 8} + \frac{3\cdot 5\cdot 7}{4\cdot 8\cdot 12} + \cdots$$

7. Prove that
$$1 + \frac{2n}{3} + \frac{2n\,(2n+2)}{3\cdot 6} + \frac{2n\,(2n+2)\,(2n+4)}{3\cdot 6\cdot 9} + \cdots$$
$$= 2^n \left\{ 1 + \frac{n}{3} + \frac{n\,(n+1)}{3\cdot 6} + \frac{n\,(n+1)\,(n+2)}{3\cdot 6\cdot 9} + \cdots \right\}.$$

8. Prove that
$$7^n \left\{ 1 + \frac{n}{7} + \frac{n\,(n-1)}{7\cdot 14} + \frac{n\,(n-1)\,(n-2)}{7\cdot 14\cdot 21} + \cdots \right\}$$
$$= 4^n \left\{ 1 + \frac{n}{2} + \frac{n\,(n+1)}{2\cdot 4} + \frac{n\,(n+1)\,(n+2)}{2\cdot 4\cdot 6} + \cdots \right\}.$$

9. Prove that approximately, when x is very small,
$$\frac{3\left(x + \dfrac{4}{9}\right)^{1/2}\left(1 - \dfrac{3}{4}x^2\right)^{1/3}}{2\left(1 + \dfrac{9}{16}x\right)^2} = 1 - \frac{307}{256}x^2.$$

10. Shew that the integral part of $(5 + 2\sqrt{6})^n$ is odd, if n be a positive integer.

11. Shew that the integral part of $(8 + 3\sqrt{7})^n$ is odd, if n be a positive integer.

12. Find the coefficient of x^n in the expansion of $(1 - 2x + 3x^2 - 4x^3 + \cdots)^{-n}$.

13. Shew that the middle term of $\left(x + \dfrac{1}{x}\right)^{4n}$ is equal to the coefficient of x^n in the expansion of $(1 - 4x)^{-\left(n + \frac{1}{2}\right)}$.

14. Prove that the expansion of $(1 - x^3)^n$ may be put into the form

$$(1 - x)^{3n} + 3nx (1 - x)^{3n - 2} + \frac{3n (3n - 3)}{1 \cdot 2} x^2 (1 - x)^{3n - 4} + \ldots$$

15. Prove that the coefficient of x^n in the expansion $\dfrac{1}{1 + x + x^2}$ is 1, 0, -1 according as n is of the form $3m$, $3m - 1$, or $3m + 1$.

16. In the expansion of $(a + b + c)^3$ find (1) the number of terms, (2) the sum of the coefficients of the terms.

17. Prove that if n be an even integer,

$$\frac{1}{1 ! (n - 1) !} + \frac{1}{3 ! (n - 3) !} + \frac{1}{5 ! (n - 5) !} + \ldots + \frac{1}{(n - 1) ! 1 !} = \frac{2^{n - 1}}{n !}.$$

18. If $c_0, c_1, c_2, \ldots, c_n$ are the coefficients in the expansion of $(1 + x)^n$, when n is a positive integer, prove that

(1) $c_0 - c_1 + c_2 - c_3 + \ldots + (-1)^r c_r = (-1)^r \dfrac{n ! - 1}{r ! (n - r - 1) !}$.

(2) $c_0 - 2c_1 + 3c_2 - 4c_3 + \ldots + (-1)^n (n + 1) c_n = 0$.

(3) $c_0^2 - c_1^2 + c_2^2 - c_3^2 + \ldots + (-1)^n c_n^2 = 0$, or $(-1)^{\frac{n}{2}} c_{\frac{n}{2}}$,

according as n is odd or even.

19. If s_n denote the sum of the first n natural numbers, prove that

(1) $(1 - x)^{-3} = s_1 + s_2 x + s_3 x^2 + \ldots + s_n x^{n - 1} + \ldots$

(2) $2 (s_1 s_{2n} + s_2 s_{2n - 1} + \ldots + s_n s_{n + 1}) = \dfrac{2n + 4}{5 ! (2n - 1) !}$.

20. If $q_n = \dfrac{1 \cdot 3 \cdot 5 \cdot 7 \ldots (2n - 1)}{2 \cdot 4 \cdot 6 \cdot 8 \ldots 2n}$, prove that

(1) $q_{2n + 1} + q_1 q_{2n} + q_2 q_{2n - 1} + \ldots + q_{n - 1} q_{n + 2} + q_n q_{n + 1} = \dfrac{1}{2}$.

(2) $2 \{ q_{2n} - q_1 q_{2n - 1} + q_2 q_{2n - 2} + \ldots + (-1)^{n - 1} q_{n - 1} q_{n + 1} \}$
                 $= q_n + (-1)^{n - 1} q_n^2$.

21. Find the sum of the products, two at a time, of the coefficients in the expansion of $(1+x)^n$, when n is a positive integer.

22. If $(7+4\sqrt{3})^n = p + \beta$, where n and p are positive integers, and β a proper fraction, shew that $(1-\beta)(p+\beta)=1$.

23. If $c_0, c_1, c_2, \ldots c_n$ are the coefficients in the expansion of $(1+x)^n$, where n is a positive integer, shew that

$$c_1 - \frac{c_2}{2} + \frac{c_3}{3} - \ldots + \frac{(-1)^{n-1}c_n}{n} = 1 + \frac{1}{2} + \frac{1}{3} + \ldots + \frac{1}{n}.$$

■ ■ ■

Chapter 15

MULTINOMIAL THEOREM

194. We have already seen in Art. 175, how we may apply the Binomial Theorem to obtain the expansion of a multinomial expression. In the present chapter our object is not so much to obtain the complete expansion of a multinomial as to find the coefficient of any assigned term.

Example : Find the coefficient of $a^4 b^2 c^3 d^5$ in the expansion of

$$(a + b + c + d)^{14}.$$

The expansion is the product of 14 factors each equal to $a + b + c + d$, and every term in the expansion is of 14 dimensions, being a product formed by taking one letter out of each of these factors. Thus to form the term $a^4 b^2 c^3 d^5$, we take a out of any *four* of the fourteen factors, b out of any *two* of the remaining ten, c out of any *three* of the remaining eight. But the number of ways in which this can be done is clearly equal to the number of ways of arranging 14 letters when four of them must be a, two b, three c, and five d; that is, equal to

$$\frac{14\,!}{4\,!\,2\,!\,3\,!\,5\,!} \qquad \text{[Art. 151.]}$$

This is therefore the number of times in which the term $a^4 b^2 c^3 d^5$ appears in the final product, and consequently the coefficient required is 2522520.

195. *To find the coefficient of any assigned term in the expansion of* $(a + b + c + d + \ldots)^p$, *where p is a positive integer.*

The expansion is the product of p factors each equal to $a + b + c + d + \ldots$, and every term in the expansion is formed by taking one letter out of each of these p factors; and therefore the number of ways in which any term $a^{\alpha} b^{\beta} c^{\gamma} d^{\delta} \ldots$ will appear in the final product is equal to the number of ways of arranging p letters when α of them must be a, β must be b, γ must be c; and so on. That is,

the coefficient of $\quad a^{\alpha} b^{\beta} c^{\gamma} d^{\delta} \quad$ is $\dfrac{p\,!}{\alpha\,!\,\beta\,!\,\gamma\,!\,\delta\,!\,\ldots}$,

where $\qquad \alpha + \beta + \gamma + \delta + \ldots = p$.

Cor : In the expansion of

$$(a + bx + cx^2 + dx^3 + \ldots)^p,$$

the term involving $a^{\alpha} b^{\beta} c^{\gamma} d^{\delta} \ldots$ is

$$\frac{p!}{\alpha!\,\beta!\,\gamma!\,\delta!\,\ldots}\,a^{\alpha}\,(bx)^{\beta}\,(cx^2)^{\gamma}\,(dx^3)^{\delta}\,\ldots,$$

or

$$\frac{p!}{\alpha!\,\beta!\,\gamma!\,\delta!\,\ldots}\,a^{\alpha}b^{\beta}c^{\gamma}d^{\delta}\,\ldots\,x^{\beta+2\gamma+3\delta+\ldots},$$

where $\qquad \alpha+\beta+\gamma+\delta+\ldots=p.$

This may be called *the general term* of the expansion.

Example. Find the coefficient of x^5 in the expansion of $(a+bx+cx^2)^9$.

The general term of the expansion is

$$\frac{9!}{\alpha!\,\beta!\,\gamma!}\,a^{\alpha}b^{\beta}\,c^{\gamma}\,x^{\beta+2\gamma} \qquad \ldots(1)$$

where $\qquad \alpha+\beta+\gamma=9.$

We have to obtain by trial all the positive integral values of β and γ which satisfy the equation $\beta+2\gamma=5$; the values of α can then be found from the equation

$$\alpha+\beta+\gamma=9.$$

Putting $\gamma=2$, we have $\beta=1$, and $\alpha=6$;

putting $\gamma=1$, we have $\beta=3$, and $\alpha=5$;

putting $\gamma=0$, we have $\beta=5$, and $\alpha=4$.

The required coefficient will be the sum of the corresponding values of the expression (1).

Therefore the coefficient required

$$=\frac{9!}{6!\,2!}\,a^6bc^2+\frac{9!}{5!\,3!}\,a^5b^3c+\frac{9!}{4!\,5!}\,a^4b^5$$

$$=252a^6bc^2+504a^5b^3c+126a^4b^5.$$

196. *To find the general term in the expansion of*

$$(a+bx+cx^2+dx^3+\ldots)^n,$$

where n is any rational quantity.

By the Binomial Theorem, the general term is

$$\frac{n\,(n-1)\,(n-2)\,\ldots\,(n-p+1)}{p!}\,a^{n-p}\,(bx+cx^2+dx^3+\ldots)^p,$$

where p is a positive integer.

And, by Art. 195, the general term of the expansion of

$$(bx+cx^2+dx^3+\ldots)^p$$

is

$$\frac{p!}{\beta!\,\gamma!\,\delta!\,\ldots}\,b^{\beta}c^{\gamma}d^{\delta}\,\ldots\,x^{\beta+2\gamma+3\delta+\ldots},$$

where $\beta,\gamma,\delta\ldots$ are positive integers whose sum is p.

Hence the general term in the expansion of the given expression is

$$\frac{n\,(n-1)\,(n-2)\,...\,(n-p+1)}{\beta\,!\,\gamma\,!\,\delta\,!\,...}\,a^{n-p}\,b^{\beta}c^{\gamma}d^{\delta}\,...\,x^{\beta+2\gamma+3\delta+\,...},$$

where $\beta+\gamma+\delta+\,...\,=p.$

197.   Since $(a+bx+cx^2+dx^3+\,...)^n$ may be written in the form

$$a^n\left(1+\frac{b}{a}\,x+\frac{c}{a}\,x^2+\frac{d}{a}\,x^3+\,...\right)^n,$$

it will be sufficient to consider the case in which the first term of the multinomial is unity.

Thus the general term of

$$(1+bx+cx^2+dx^3+\,...)^n$$

is $\dfrac{n\,(n-1)\,(n-2)\,...\,(n-p+1)}{\beta\,!\,\gamma\,!\,\delta\,!}\,b^{\beta}c^{\gamma}d^{\delta}\,...\,x^{\beta+2\gamma+3\delta+\,...}$

where $\beta+\gamma+\delta+\,...\,=p.$

Example : Find the coefficient of x^3 in the expansion of

$$(1-3x-2x^2+6x^3)^{\frac{2}{3}}.$$

The general term is

$$\frac{\frac{2}{3}\left(\frac{2}{3}-1\right)\left(\frac{2}{3}-2\right)...\left(\frac{2}{3}-p+1\right)}{\beta\,!\,\gamma\,!\,\delta\,!}\,(-3)^{\beta}\,(-2)^{\gamma}\,(6)^{\delta}\,x^{\beta+2\gamma+3\delta} \qquad ...(1)$$

We have to obtain by trial all the positive integral values of β, γ, δ which satisfy the equation $\beta+2\gamma+3\delta=3$; and then p is found from the equation $p=\beta+\gamma+\delta$. The required coefficient will be the sum of the corresponding values of the expression (1).

In finding β, γ, δ, ... it will be best to commence by giving to δ successive integral values beginning with the greatest admissible. In the present case the values are found to be

$$\delta=1,\quad \gamma=0,\quad \beta=0,\quad p=1;$$
$$\delta=0,\quad \gamma=1,\quad \beta=1,\quad p=2;$$
$$\delta=0,\quad \gamma=0,\quad \beta=3,\quad p=3.$$

Substituting these values in (1) the required coefficient

$$=\left(\frac{2}{3}\right)(6)+\left(\frac{2}{3}\right).\left(-\frac{1}{3}\right)(-3)\,(-2)+\frac{\frac{2}{3}\left(-\frac{1}{3}\right)\left(-\frac{4}{3}\right)}{3\,!}\,(-3)^3$$

$$=4-\frac{4}{3}-\frac{4}{3}=\frac{4}{3}.$$

198. Sometimes it is more expeditious to use the Binomial Theorem.

Example. Find the coefficient of x^4 in the expansion of $(1 - 2x + 3x^2)^{-3}$.

The required coefficient is found by picking out the coefficient of x^4 from the first few terms of the expansion of $(1 - 2x + 3x^2)^{-3}$ by the Binomial Theorem; that is, from

$$1 + 3(2x - 3x^2) + 6(2x - 3x^2)^2 + 10(2x - 3x^2)^3 + 15(2x - 3x^2)^4;$$

we stop at this term for all the other terms involve powers of x higher than x^4.

The required coefficient $= 6 \cdot 9 + 10 \cdot 3(2)^2(-3) + 15(2)^4$
$$= -66.$$

EXAMPLES. XV.

Find the coefficient of

1. $a^2 b^3 c^4 d$ in the expansion of $(a - b - c + d)^{10}$.

2. $a^2 b^5 d$ in the expansion of $(a + b - c - d)^8$.

3. $a^3 b^3 c$ in the expansion of $(2a + b + 3c)^7$.

4. $x^2 y^3 z^4$ in the expansion of $(ax - by + cz)^9$.

5. x^3 in the expansion of $(1 + 3x - 2x^2)^3$.

6. x^4 in the expansion of $(1 + 2x + 3x^2)^{10}$.

7. x^6 in the expansion of $(1 + 2x - x^2)^5$.

8. x^8 in the expansion of $(1 - 2x + 3x^2 - 4x^3)^4$;

Find the coefficient of

9. x^{23} in the expansion of $(1 - 2x + 3x^2 - x^4 - x^5)^5$.

10. x^5 in the expansion of $(1 - 2x + 3x^2)^{-\frac{1}{2}}$.

11. x^3 in the expansion of $(1 - 2x + 3x^2 - 4x^3)^{\frac{1}{2}}$.

12. x^8 in the expansion of $\left(1 - \dfrac{x^2}{3} + \dfrac{x^4}{9}\right)^{-2}$.

13. x^4 in the expansion of $(2 - 4x + 3x^2)^{-2}$.

14. x^6 in the expansion of $(1 + 4x^2 + 10x^4 + 20x^6)^{-\frac{3}{4}}$.

15. x^{12} in the expansion of $(3 - 15x^3 + 18x^6)^{-1}$.

16. Expand $(1 - 2x - 2x^2)^{\frac{1}{4}}$ as far as x^2.

17. Expand $(1 + 3x^2 - 6x^3)^{-\frac{2}{3}}$ as far as x^5.

18. Expand $(8 - 9x^3 + 18x^4)^{\frac{4}{3}}$ as far as x^8.

19. If $(1 + x + x^2 + \ldots + x^p)^n = a_0 + a_1 x + a_2 x^2 + \ldots + a_{np} x^{np}$,
    prove that

    (1) $a_0 + a_1 + a_2 + \ldots + a_{np} = (p + 1)^n$.

    (2) $a_1 + 2a_2 + 3a_3 + \ldots + np \cdot a_{np} = \dfrac{1}{2} np \, (p + 1)^n$.

20. If $a_0, a_1, a_2, a_3, \ldots$ are the coefficients in order of the expansion
    of $(1 + x + x^2)^n$; prove that

    $$a_0^2 - a_1^2 + a_2^2 - a_3^2 + \ldots + (-1)^{n-1} a_{n-1}^2 = \frac{1}{2} a_n \{1 - (-1)^n a_n\}.$$

21. If the expansion of $(1 + x + x^2)^n$
    be $a_0 + a_1 x + a_2 x^2 + \ldots + a_r x^r + \ldots + a_{2n} x^{2n}$,
    shew that

    $$a_0 + a_3 + a_6 + \ldots = a_1 + a_4 + a_7 + \ldots = a_2 + a_5 + a_8 + \ldots = 3^{n-1}.$$

    ■■■

Chapter 16

LOGARITHMS

199. Definition : The **logarithm** of any number to a given **base** is the index of the power to which the base must be raised in order to equal the given number. Thus if $a^x = N$, x is called the logarithm of N to the base a.

Examples : (1) Since $3^4 = 81$, the logarithm of 81 to base 3 is 4.

(2) Since $10^1 = 10$, $10^2 = 100$, $10^3 = 1000$, ...

the natural numbers 1, 2, 3, ... are respectively the logarithms of 10, 100, 1000, ... to base 10.

200. The logarithm of N to base a is usually written $\log_a N$, so that the same meaning is expressed by the two equations

$$a^x = N; \quad x = \log_a N.$$

From these equations we deduce

$$N = a^{\log_a N},$$

an identity which is sometimes useful.

Example : Find the logarithm of $32\sqrt[5]{4}$ to base $2\sqrt{2}$.

Let x be the required logarithm; then,

by definition,
$$(2\sqrt{2})^x = 32\sqrt[5]{4};$$

$\therefore$
$$\left(2 \cdot 2^{\frac{1}{2}} \right)^x = 2^5 \cdot 2^{\frac{2}{5}};$$

$\therefore$
$$2^{\frac{3}{2}x} = 2^{5 + \frac{2}{5}};$$

hence, by equating the indices, $\dfrac{3}{2} x = \dfrac{27}{5};$

$\therefore$
$$x = \frac{18}{5} = 3 \cdot 6,$$

201. When it is understood that a particular system of logarithms is in use, the suffix denoting the base is omitted. Thus in arithmetical calculations in which 10 is the base, we usually write $\log 2$, $\log 3$, ... instead of $\log_{10} 2$, $\log_{10} 3$, ...

Any number might be taken as the base of logarithms, and corresponding to any such base a system of logarithms of all numbers could be found. But before discussing the logarithmic systems commonly used, we shall prove some general propositions which are true for all logarithms independently of any particular base.

202. *The logarithm of 1 is 0.*

For $a^0 = 1$ for all values of a; therefore $\log 1 = 0$, whatever the base may be.

203. *The logarithm of the base itself is 1.*

For $a^1 = a$; therefore $\log_a a = 1$.

204. *To find the logarithm of a product.*

Let MN be the product; let a be the base of the system, and suppose

$$x = \log_a M, \quad y = \log_a N;$$

So that $\qquad a^x = M, \qquad a^y = N.$

Thus the product $\quad MN = a^x \times a^y = a^{x+y};$

whence, by definition, $\log_a MN = x + y$

$$= \log_a M + \log_a N.$$

Similarly $\quad \log_a MNP = \log_a M + \log_a N + \log_a P;$

and so on for any number of factors.

> *Example:* $\qquad \log 42 = \log(2 \times 3 \times 7)$
> $$= \log 2 + \log 3 + \log 7.$$

205. *To find the logarithm of a fraction.*

Let $\dfrac{M}{N}$ be the fraction, and suppose

$$x = \log_a M, \quad y = \log_a N;$$

So that $\qquad a^x = M, a^y = N.$

Thus the fraction $\dfrac{M}{N} = \dfrac{a^x}{a^y}$

$$= a^{x-y};$$

whence, by definition, $\log_a \dfrac{M}{N} = x - y$

$$= \log_a M - \log_a N.$$

> *Example:* $\log\left(4\dfrac{2}{7}\right) = \log \dfrac{30}{7}$
> $$= \log 30 - \log 7$$
> $$= \log(2 \times 3 \times 5) - \log 7$$
> $$= \log 2 + \log 3 + \log 5 - \log 7.$$

206. *To find the logarithm of a number raised to any power, integral or fractional.*

Let $\log_a (M^p)$ be required, and suppose

$$x = \log_a M, \text{ so that } a^x = M;$$

then
$$M^p = (a^x)^p$$
$$= a^{px};$$

whence, by definition, $\log_a (M^p) = px;$

that is
$$\log_a (M^p) = p \log_a M.$$

Similarly,
$$\log_a \left(M^{\frac{1}{r}} \right) = \frac{1}{r} \log_a M.$$

207. It follows from the results we have proved that

(1) the logarithm of a product is equal to the sum of the logarithms of its factors;

(2) the logarithm of a fraction is equal to the logarithm of the numerator diminished by the logarithm of the denominator;

(3) the logarithm of the pth power of a number is p times the logarithm of the number;

(4) the logarithm of the rth root of a number is equal to $\frac{1}{r}$ th of the logarithm of the number.

Also we see that by the use of logarithms the operations of multiplication and division may be replaced by those of addition and subtraction; and the operations of involution and evolution by those of multiplication and division.

Example 1. Express the logarithm of $\dfrac{\sqrt{a^3}}{c^5 b^2}$ in terms of $\log a, \log b$ and $\log c$.

$$\log \frac{\sqrt{a^3}}{c^5 b^2} = \log \frac{a^{\frac{3}{2}}}{c^5 b^2}$$

$$= \log a^{\frac{3}{2}} - \log (c^5 b^2)$$

$$= \frac{3}{2} \log a - (\log c^5 + \log b^2)$$

$$= \frac{3}{2} \log a - 5 \log c - 2 \log b.$$

Example 2. Find x from the equation $a^x \cdot c^{-2x} = b^{3x+1}$.

Taking logarithms of both sides, we have

$$x \log a - 2x \log c = (3x+1) \log b;$$

$\therefore$ $\qquad x (\log a - 2 \log c - 3 \log b) = \log b;$

$\therefore$ $\qquad x = \dfrac{\log b}{\log a - 2 \log c - 3 \log b}.$

EXAMPLES XVI. a.

Find the logarithms of

1. 16 to base $\sqrt{2}$, and 1728 to base $2\sqrt{3}$.

2. 125 to base $5\sqrt{5}$, and 0·25 to base 4.

3. $\dfrac{1}{256}$ to base $2\sqrt{2}$, and 0·3 to base 9.

4. 0·0625 to base 2, and 1000 to base 0·01.

5. 0·0001 to base 0·001, and 0·1 to base $9\sqrt{3}$.

6. $\sqrt[4]{a^{\frac{8}{5}}}, \dfrac{1}{a^{\frac{1}{2}}}, \sqrt[3]{a^{-\frac{15}{2}}}$ to base a.

7. Find the value of

$$\log_8 128, \ \log_6 \frac{1}{216}, \ \log_{27} \frac{1}{81}, \ \log_{343} 49.$$

Express the following seven logarithms in terms of $\log a$, $\log b$, and $\log c$,

8. $\log (\sqrt{a^2 b^3})^6$.

9. $\log (\sqrt[3]{a^2} \times \sqrt[2]{b^3})$.

10. $\log \sqrt[9]{a^{-4} b^3}$.

11. $\log (\sqrt{a^{-2} b} \times \sqrt[3]{ab^{-3}})$.

12. $\log \left(\sqrt[3]{a^{-1} \sqrt{b^3}} \div \sqrt{b^3 \sqrt{a}} \right)$.

13. $\log \dfrac{\sqrt[3]{ab^{-1} c^{-2}}}{(a^{-1} b^{-2} c^{-4})^{\frac{1}{6}}}$.

14. $\log \left\{ \left(\dfrac{bc^{-2}}{b^{-4} c^3} \right)^{-3} \div \left(\dfrac{b^{-1} c}{b^2 c^{-3}} \right)^5 \right\}$.

15. Shew that $\log \dfrac{\sqrt[4]{5} \cdot \sqrt[10]{2}}{\sqrt[3]{18 \cdot \sqrt{2}}} = \dfrac{1}{4} \log 5 - \dfrac{2}{5} \log 2 - \dfrac{2}{3} \log 3$.

16. Simplify $\log \sqrt[4]{729 \ \sqrt[3]{9^{-1} \cdot 27^{-\frac{4}{3}}}}$

17. Prove that $\log \dfrac{75}{16} - 2 \log \dfrac{5}{9} + \log \dfrac{32}{243} = \log 2$.

Solve the following equations :

18. $a^x = cb^x$.

19. $a^{2x} \cdot b^{3x} = c^5$.

20. $\dfrac{a^{x-1}}{b^{x-1}} = c^{2x}$.

21. $\left. \begin{aligned} a^{2x} \cdot b^{3y} &= m^5 \\ a^{3x} \cdot b^{2y} &= m^{10} \end{aligned} \right\}$

22. If $\log (x^2 y^3) = a$, and $\log \dfrac{x}{y} = b$, find $\log x$ and $\log y$.

23. If $a^{3-x} \cdot b^{5x} = a^{x+6} \cdot b^{3x}$ shew that $x \log \left(\dfrac{b}{a} \right) = \log a$.

24. Solve the equation
$$(a^4 - 2a^2 b^2 + b^4)^{x-1} = (a-b)^{2x} (a+b)^{-2}.$$

COMMON LOGARITHMS

208. Logarithms to the base 10 are called Common Logarithms; this system was first introduced, in 1615, by Briggs, a contemporary of Napier, the inventor of logarithms.

From the equation $10^x = N$, it is evident that common logarithms will not in general be integral, and that they will not always be positive.

For instance $3154 > 10^3$ and $< 10^4$;

∴ $\log 3154 = 3 + a$ fraction.

Again, $0.06 > 10^{-2}$ and $< 10^{-1}$;

∴ $\log 0.06 = -2 + a$ fraction.

209. Definition : The integral part of a logarithm is called the characteristic, and the decimal part is called the mantissa.

The characteristic of the logarithm of any number to the base 10 can be written down by inspection, as we shall now shew.

210. *To determine the characteristic of the logarithm of any number greater than unity.*

Since $10^1 = 10,$

$$10^2 = 100,$$

$$10^3 = 1000,$$

....

it follows that a number with two digits in its integral part lies between 10^1 and 10^2; a number with three digits in its integral part lies between 10^2 and 10^3; and so on. Hence a number with n digits in its integral part lies between 10^{n-1} and 10^n.

Let N be a number whose integral part contains n digits; then
$$N = 10^{(n-1)+\text{a fraction}};$$
$\therefore$ $\log N = (n-1) + \text{a fraction}.$

Hence the characteristic is $n-1$; that is, *the characteristic of the logarithm of a number greater than unity is less by one than the number of digits in its integral part, and is positive.*

211. *To determine the characteristic of the logarithm of a decimal fraction.*

Since $10^0 = 1,$
$$10^{-1} = \frac{1}{10} = 0\cdot1,$$
$$10^{-2} = \frac{1}{100} = 0\cdot01,$$
$$10^{-3} = \frac{1}{1000} = 0\cdot001,$$

....

it follows that a decimal with one cipher immediately after the decimal point, such as $0\cdot0324$, being greater than $0\cdot01$ and less than $0\cdot1$, lies between 10^{-2} and 10^{-1}; a number with two ciphers after the decimal point lies between 10^{-3} and 10^{-2}; and so on. Hence a decimal fraction with n ciphers immediately after the decimal point lies between $10^{-(n+1)}$ and 10^{-n}.

Let D be a decimal beginning with n ciphers; then
$$D = 10^{-(n+1)+\text{a fraction}};$$
$\therefore$ $\log D = -(n+1) + \text{a fraction}.$

Hence the characteristic is $-(n+1)$; that is, *the characteristic of the logarithm of a decimal fraction is greater by unity than the number of ciphers immediately after the decimal point, and is negative.*

212. The logarithms to base 10 of all integers from 1 to 200000 have been found and tabulated; in most Tables they are given to seven places of decimals. This is the system in practical use, and it has two great advantages :

(1) From the results already proved it is evident that the characteristics can be written down by inspection, so that only the mantissae have to be registered in the Tables.

(2) The mantissae are the same for the logarithms of all numbers which have the same significant digits; so that it is sufficient to tabulate the mantissae of the logarithms of *integers*.

This proposition we proceed to prove.

213. Let N be any number, then since multiplying or dividing by a power of 10 merely alters the position of the decimal point without changing the sequence of figures, it follows that $N \times 10^p$ and $N \div 10^q$, where p and q are any integers, are numbers whose significant digits are the same as those of N.

Now $\qquad\qquad \log (N \times 10^p) = \log N + p \log 10$
$$= \log N + p \qquad\qquad ...(1)$$

Again, $\qquad\qquad \log (N \div 10^q) = \log N - q \log 10$
$$= \log N - q \qquad\qquad ...(2)$$

In (1) an integer is added to $\log N$, and in (2) an integer is subtracted from $\log N$; that is, the mantissa or decimal portion of the logarithm remains unaltered.

In this and the three preceding articles the mantissae have been supposed positive. In order to secure the advantages of Briggs' system, we arrange our work so as *always to keep the mantissa positive*, so that when the mantissa of any logarithm has been taken from the Tables the characteristic is prefixed with its appropriate sign according to the rules already given.

214. In the case of a negative logarithm the minus sign is written *over the characteristic*, and not before it, to indicate that the characteristic alone is negative, and not the whole expression. Thus $\bar{4}.30103$, the logarithm of 0.0002, is equivalent to $-4 + 0.30103$, and must be distinguished from -4.30103, an expression in which both the integer and the decimal are negative. In working with negative logarithms an arithmetical artifice will sometimes be necessary in order to make the mantissa positive. For instance, a result such as -3.69897, in which the whole expression is negative, may be transformed by subtracting 1 from the characteristic and adding 1 to the mantissa. Thus

$$-3.69897 = -4 + (1 - .69897) = \bar{4}.30103.$$

Other cases will be noticed in the Examples.

Example 1. Required the logarithm of 0.0002432.

In the Tables we find that 3859636 is the mantissa of log 2432 (the decimal point as well as the characteristic being omitted); and by Art. 211, the characteristic of the logarithm of the given number is -4;

$\therefore \qquad\qquad\qquad \log 0.0002432 = \bar{4}.3859636.$

Example 2.   Find the value of $\sqrt[5]{.00000165}$, given
log 165 = 2.2174839, log 697424 = 5.8434968.

Let x denote the value required; then

$$\log x = \log (0.00000165)^{\frac{1}{5}} = \frac{1}{5} \log (0.00000165)$$

$$= \frac{1}{5} (\bar{6}.2174839);$$

the mantissa of log 0.00000165 being the same as that of log 165, and the characteristic being prefixed by the rule.

Now $\dfrac{1}{5} (\bar{6}.2174839) = \dfrac{1}{5} (\overline{10} + 4.2174839)$

$$= \bar{2}.8434968$$

and 0.8434968 is the mantissa of log 697424; hence x is a number consisting of these same digits but with one cipher after the decimal point. [Art. 211.]

Thus $x = 0.0697424$.

215.   The method of calculating logarithms will be explained in the next chapter, and it will there be seen that they are first found to another base, and then transformed into common logarithms to base 10.

It will therefore be necessary to investigate a method for transforming a system of logarithms having a given base to a new system with a different base.

216.   Suppose that the logarithms of all numbers to base a are known and tabulated, it is required to find the logarithms to base b.

Let N be any number whose logarithm to base b is required.

Let $y = \log_b N$, so that $b^y = N$;

$\therefore$ $\log_a (b^y) = \log_a N$;

that is $y \log_a b = \log_a N$;

$\therefore$ $y = \dfrac{1}{\log_a b} \times \log_a N,$

or $\log_b N = \dfrac{1}{\log_a b} \times \log_a N$ ...(1)

Now since N and b are given, $\log_a N$ and $\log_a b$ are known from the Tables, and thus $\log_b N$ may be found.

Hence it appears that to transform logarithms from base a to base b we have only to multiply them all by $\dfrac{1}{\log_a b}$; this is a constant quantity and is given by the Tables; it is known as the *modulus*.

217. In equation (1) of the preceding article put a for N; thus

$$\log_b a = \frac{1}{\log_a b} \times \log_a a = \frac{1}{\log_a b};$$

∴ $$\log_b a \times \log_a b = 1.$$

This result may also be proved directly as follows :

Let $x = \log_a b$, so that $a^x = b$;

then by taking logarithms to base b, we have

$$x \log_b a = \log_b b = 1;$$

∴ $$\log_a b \times \log_b a = 1.$$

218. The following examples will illustrate the utility of logarithms in facilitating arithmetical calculation; but for information as to the use of Logarithmic Tables the reader is referred to works on Trigonometry.

Example 1. Given $\log 3 = 0.4771213$, find

$$\log \left\{ (2.7)^3 \times (0.81)^{\frac{4}{5}} \div (90)^{\frac{5}{4}} \right\}.$$

The required value $= 3 \log \dfrac{27}{10} + \dfrac{4}{5} \log \dfrac{81}{100} - \dfrac{5}{4} \log 90$

$$= 3 (\log 3^3 - 1) + \frac{4}{5} (\log 3^4 - 2) - \frac{5}{4} (\log 3^2 + 1)$$

$$= \left(9 + \frac{16}{5} - \frac{5}{2} \right) \log 3 - \left(3 + \frac{8}{5} + \frac{5}{4} \right)$$

$$= \frac{97}{10} \log 3 - 5 \frac{17}{20}$$

$$= 4.6280766 - 5.85$$

$$= \overline{2}.7780766.$$

The student should notice that the logarithm of 5 and its powers can always be obtained from $\log 2$; thus

$$\log 5 = \log \frac{10}{2} = \log 10 - \log 2 = 1 - \log 2.$$

Example 2. Find the number of digits in 875^{16}, given
$$\log 2 = 0.3010300, \log 7 = 0.8450980.$$

$$\log (875^{16}) = 16 \log (7 \times 125)$$

$$= 16 (\log 7 + 3 \log 5)$$

$$= 16 (\log 7 + 3 - 3 \log 2)$$

$$= 16 \times 2.9420080$$

$$= 47.072128;$$

hence the number of digits is 48.

Example 3. *Given* log 2 *and* log 3, *find to two places of decimals the value of* x *from the equation*

$$6^{3-4x} \cdot 4^{x+5} = 8.$$

Taking logarithms of both sides, we have

$$(3-4x)\log 6 + (x+5)\log 4 = \log 8;$$

∴　　$(3-4x)(\log 2 + \log 3) + (x+5)\, 2\log 2 = 3\log 2;$

∴　　$x(-4\log 2 - 4\log 3 + 2\log 2) = 3\log 2 - 3\log 2 - 3\log 3 - 10\log 2;$

∴
$$x = \frac{10\log 2 + 3\log 3}{2\log 2 + 4\log 3}$$
$$= \frac{4.4416639}{2.5105452}$$
$$= 1.77\ldots$$

EXAMPLES XVI. b.

1. Find by inspection, the characteristics of the logarithms of 21735, 23.8, 350, 0.035, 0.2, 0.87, 0.875.

2. The mantissa of log 7623 is 0.8821259; write down the logarithms of 7.623, 762.3, .007623, 762300, .000007623.

3. How many digits are there in the integral part of the numbers whose logarithms are respectively

   　　　　4.30103, 1.4771213, 3.69897, 0.56515

4. Give the position of the first significant figure in the numbers whose logarithms are

   　　$\bar{2}.7781513,\ 0.6910815,\ \bar{5}.4871384.$

   Given　log 2 = 0.3010300,　log 3 = 0.4771213,　log 7 = 0.8450980, find the value of

5. log 64.　　　　　6. log 86　　　　　7. log 0·128

8. log 0.0125.　　　9. log 14·4.　　　10. $\log 4\frac{2}{3}.$

11. $\log \sqrt[3]{12}.$　　　12. $\log \sqrt{\dfrac{35}{27}}.$　　　13. $\log \sqrt[4]{0.0105}.$

14. Find the seventh root of 0.00324, having given that
    　　　　log 44092388 = 7.6443636.

15. Given　log 194.8445 = 2.2896883, find the eleventh root of $(39.2)^2$.

16. Find the product of 37.203, 3.7203, 0.0037203, 372030, having given that
    　　　　log 37.203 = 1.5705780, and log 1915631 = 6·2823120.

17. Given log 2 and log 3, find $\log \sqrt[3]{\left(\dfrac{3^2 5^4}{\sqrt{2}}\right)}$.

18. Given log 2 and log 3, find $\log (\sqrt[3]{48} \times 108^{\frac{1}{4}} \div \sqrt[12]{6})$.

19. Calculate to six decimal places the value of
$$\sqrt[3]{\left(\dfrac{294 \times 125}{42 \times 32}\right)^2};$$
given log 2, log 3, log 7; also log 9076.226 = 3.9579053.

20. Calculate to six places of decimals the value of
$$(330 \div 49)^4 \div \sqrt[3]{22 \times 70};$$
given log 2, log 3, log 7; also
log 11 = 1.0413927, and log 17814.1516 = 4.2507651.

21. Find the number of digits in $3^{12} \times 2^8$.

22. Shew that $\left(\dfrac{21}{20}\right)^{100}$ is greater than 100.

23. Determine how many ciphers there are between the decimal point and the first significant digit in $\left(\dfrac{1}{2}\right)^{1000}$

Solve the following equations, having given log 2, log 3, and log 7.

24. $3^{x-2} = 5$.   25. $5^x = 10^3$.   26. $5^{5-3x} = 2^{x+2}$.

27. $21^x = 2^{2x+1} \cdot 5^x$.   28. $2^x \cdot 6^{x-2} = 5^{2x} \cdot 7^{1-x}$

29. $\left.\begin{array}{l} 2^{x+y} = 6^y \\ 3^x = 3 \cdot 2^{y+1} \end{array}\right\}$.   30. $\left.\begin{array}{l} 3^{1-x-y} = 4^{-y} \\ 2^{2x-1} = 3^{3y-x} \end{array}\right\}$.

31. Given $\log_{10} 2 = 0.30103$, find $\log_{25} 200$.

32. Given $\log_{10} 2 = 0.30103$, $\log_{10} 7 = 0.84509$, find $\log_7 \sqrt{2}$ and $\log_{\sqrt{2}} 7$.

Chapter 17

EXPONENTIAL AND LOGARITHMIC SERIES

219. In Chap. 16. it was stated that the logarithms in common use were not found directly, but that logarithms are first found to another base, and then transformed to base 10.

In the present chapter we shall prove certain formulae known as the Exponential and Logarithmic Series, and give a brief explanation of the way in which they are used in constructing a table of logarithms.

220. *To expand a^x in ascending powers of x.*

By the Binomial Theorem, *if* n *is greater than* 1,

$$\left(1 + \frac{1}{n}\right)^{nx} = 1 + nx \cdot \frac{1}{n} + \frac{nx\,(nx-1)}{2!} \cdot \frac{1}{n^2} + \frac{nx\,(nx-1)\,(nx-2)}{3!} \cdot \frac{1}{n^3} + \dots$$

$$= 1 + x + \frac{x\left(x - \frac{1}{n}\right)}{2!} + \frac{x\left(x - \frac{1}{n}\right)\left(x - \frac{2}{n}\right)}{3!} + \qquad \dots(1)$$

By putting $x = 1$, we obtain

$$\left(1 + \frac{1}{n}\right)^n = 1 + 1 + \frac{1 - \frac{1}{n}}{2!} + \frac{\left(1 - \frac{1}{n}\right)\left(1 - \frac{2}{n}\right)}{3!} + \qquad \dots(2)$$

But $\left(1 + \dfrac{1}{n}\right)^{nx} = \left\{\left(1 + \dfrac{1}{n}\right)^n\right\}^x$;

hence the series (1) is the xth power of the series (2); that is,

$$1 + x + \frac{x\left(x - \frac{1}{n}\right)}{2!} + \frac{x\left(x - \frac{1}{n}\right)\left(x - \frac{2}{n}\right)}{3!} + \dots$$

$$= \left\{1 + 1 + \frac{1 - \frac{1}{n}}{2!} + \frac{\left(1 - \frac{1}{n}\right)\left(1 - \frac{2}{n}\right)}{3!} + \dots\right\}^x$$

and this is true however great n may be. If therefore n be indefinitely increased we have

$$1 + x + \frac{x^2}{2!} + \frac{x^3}{3!} + \frac{x^4}{4!} + \dots = \left(1 + 1 + \frac{1}{2!} + \frac{1}{3!} + \frac{1}{4!} + \dots\right)^x.$$

The series $1 + 1 + \frac{1}{2!} + \frac{1}{3!} + \frac{1}{4!} + \dots$ is usually denoted by e; hence

$$e^x = 1 + x + \frac{x^2}{2!} + \frac{x^3}{3!} + \frac{x^4}{4!} + \dots$$

Write cx for x, then

$$e^{cx} = 1 + cx + \frac{c^2 x^2}{2!} + \frac{c^3 x^3}{3!} + \dots$$

Now let $e^c = a$, so that $c = \log_e a$; by substituting for c we obtain

$$a^x = 1 + x \log_e a + \frac{x^2 (\log_e a)^2}{2!} + \frac{x^3 (\log_e a)^3}{3!} + \dots$$

This is the *Exponential Theorem*.

Cor. When n is infinite, the *limit* of $\left(1 + \frac{1}{n}\right)^n = e$. [See Art. 266.]

Also as in the preceding investigation, it may be shewn that when n is indefinitely increased,

$$\left(1 + \frac{x}{n}\right)^n = 1 + x + \frac{x^2}{2!} + \frac{x^3}{3!} + \frac{x^4}{4!} + \dots;$$

that is, when n is infinite, the limit of $\left(1 + \frac{x}{n}\right)^n = e^x$.

By putting $\frac{x}{n} = -\frac{1}{m}$, we have

$$\left(1 - \frac{x}{n}\right)^n = \left(1 + \frac{1}{m}\right)^{-mx} = \left\{\left(1 + \frac{1}{m}\right)^m\right\}^{-x}$$

Now m is infinite when n is infinite;

thus the limit of $\qquad \left(1 - \frac{x}{n}\right)^n = e^{-x}.$

Hence the limit of $\qquad \left(1 - \frac{1}{n}\right)^n = e^{-1}.$

221. In the preceding article no restriction is placed upon the value of x; also since $\frac{1}{n}$ is less than unity, the expansions we have used give results arithmetically intelligible. [Art. 183.]

But there is another point in the foregoing proof which deserves notice. We have assumed that when n is infinite the limit of

$$\frac{x\left(x - \dfrac{1}{n}\right)\left(x - \dfrac{2}{n}\right) \cdots \left(x - \dfrac{r-1}{n}\right)}{r!} \text{ is } \frac{x^r}{r!}$$

for all values of r.

Let us denote the value of

$$\frac{x\left(x - \dfrac{1}{n}\right)\left(x - \dfrac{2}{n}\right) \cdots \left(x - \dfrac{r-1}{n}\right)}{r!} \text{ by } u,$$

Then

$$\frac{u_r}{u_{r-1}} = \frac{1}{r}\left(x - \frac{r-1}{n}\right) = \frac{x}{r} - \frac{1}{n} + \frac{1}{nr}.$$

Since n is infinite, we have

$$\frac{u_r}{u_{r-1}} = \frac{x}{r}; \text{ that is, } u_r = \frac{x}{r}\, u_{r-1}.$$

It is clear that the limit of u_2 is $\dfrac{x^2}{2!}$; hence the limit of u_3 is $\dfrac{x^3}{3!}$; that of u_4 is $\dfrac{x^4}{4!}$; and generally that of u_r is $\dfrac{x^r}{r!}$.

222. The series

$$1 + 1 + \frac{1}{2!} + \frac{1}{3!} + \frac{1}{4!} + \cdots,$$

which we have denoted by e, is very important as it is the base to which logarithms are first calculated. Logarithms to this base are known as the Napierian system, so named after Napier their inventor. They are also called *natural* logarithms from the fact that they are the first logarithms which naturally come into consideration in algebraical investigations.

When logarithms are used in theoretical work it is to be remembered that the base e is always understood, just as in arithmetical work the base 10 is invariably employed.

From the series the approximate value of e can be determined to any required degree of accuracy; to 10 places of decimals it is found to be 2.7182818284.

Example 1. Find the sum of the infinite series

$$1 + \frac{1}{2!} + \frac{1}{4!} + \frac{1}{6!} + \cdots$$

We have $e = 1 + 1 + \dfrac{1}{2!} + \dfrac{1}{3!} + \dfrac{1}{4!} + \ldots$;

and by putting $x = -1$ in the series for e^x,

$$e^{-1} = 1 - 1 + \dfrac{1}{2!} - \dfrac{1}{3!} + \dfrac{1}{4!} - \ldots$$

∴ $\qquad e + e^{-1} = 2\left(1 + \dfrac{1}{2!} + \dfrac{1}{4!} + \dfrac{1}{6!} + \ldots\right)$

hence the sum of the series is $\dfrac{1}{2}(e + e^{-1})$.

Example 2. Find the coefficient of x^r in the expansion of $\dfrac{1 - ax - x^2}{e^x}$.

$$\dfrac{1 - ax - x^2}{e^x} = (1 - ax - x^2)\,e^{-x}$$

$$= (1 - ax - x^2)\left\{1 - x + \dfrac{x^2}{2!} - \dfrac{x^3}{3!} + \ldots + \dfrac{(-1)^r x^r}{r!} + \ldots\right\}.$$

The coefficient required $= \dfrac{(-1)^r}{r!} - \dfrac{(-1)^{r-1} a}{(r-1)!} - \dfrac{(-1)^{r-2}}{(r-2)!}$

$$= \dfrac{(-1)^r}{r!}\{1 + ar - r(r-1)\}$$

223. *To expand* $\log_e(1 + x)$ *in ascending powers of* x.

From Art. 220,

$$a^y = 1 + y\log_e a + \dfrac{y^2(\log_e a)^2}{2!} + \dfrac{y^3(\log_e a)^3}{3!} + \ldots$$

In this series write $1 + x$ for a; thus

$$(1 + x)^y = 1 + y\log_e(1 + x) + \dfrac{y^2}{2!}\{\log_e(1 + x)\}^2 + \dfrac{y^3}{3!}\{\log_e(1 + x)\}^3 + \ldots (1)$$

Also by the Binomial Theorem, when $x < 1$ we have

$$(1 + x)^y = 1 + yx + \dfrac{y(y-1)}{2!}x^2 + \dfrac{y(y-1)(y-2)}{3!}x^3 + \qquad \ldots(2)$$

Now in (2) the coefficient of y is

$$x + \dfrac{(-1)}{1 \cdot 2}x^2 + \dfrac{(-1)(-2)}{1 \cdot 2 \cdot 3}x^3 + \dfrac{(-1)(-2)(-3)}{1 \cdot 2 \cdot 3 \cdot 4}x^4 + \ldots;$$

that is, $\quad x - \dfrac{x^2}{2} + \dfrac{x^3}{3} - \dfrac{x^4}{4} + \ldots$

Equate this to the coefficient of y in (1); thus we have

$$\log_e(1 + x) = x - \dfrac{x^2}{2} + \dfrac{x^3}{3} - \dfrac{x^4}{4} + \ldots$$

This is known as the *Logarithmic Series*.

Example. If $x < 1$, expand $\{\log_e (1 + x)\}^2$ in ascending powers of x.

By equating the coefficients of y^2 in the series (1) and (2), we see that the required expansion is double the coefficient of y^2 in

$$\frac{y (y - 1)}{1 \cdot 2} x^2 + \frac{y (y - 1) (y - 2)}{1 \cdot 2 \cdot 3} x^3 + \frac{y (y - 1) (y - 2) (y - 3)}{1 \cdot 2 \cdot 3 \cdot 4} x^4 + \ldots;$$

that is, double the coefficient of y in

$$\frac{y - 1}{1 \cdot 2} x^2 + \frac{(y - 1) (y - 2)}{1 \cdot 2 \cdot 3} x^3 + \frac{(y - 1) (y - 2) (y - 3)}{1 \cdot 2 \cdot 3 \cdot 4} x^4 + \ldots$$

Thus $\quad \{\log_e (1 + x)\}^2 = 2 \left\{ \dfrac{1}{2} x^2 - \dfrac{1}{3} \left(1 + \dfrac{1}{2} \right) x^3 + \dfrac{1}{4} \left(1 + \dfrac{1}{2} + \dfrac{1}{3} \right) x^4 - \ldots \right\}.$

224. Except when x is very small the series for $\log_e (1 + x)$ is of little use for numerical calculations. We can, however, deduce from it other series by the aid of which Tables of Logarithms may be constructed.

By writing $\dfrac{1}{n}$ for x we obtain $\log_e \dfrac{n + 1}{n}$; hence

$$\log_e (n + 1) - \log_e n = \frac{1}{n} - \frac{1}{2n^2} + \frac{1}{3n^3} - \ldots \qquad \ldots(1)$$

By writing $-\dfrac{1}{n}$ for x we obtain $\log_e \dfrac{n - 1}{n}$; hence, by changing signs on both sides of the equation,

$$\log_e n - \log_e (n - 1) = \frac{1}{n} + \frac{1}{2n^2} + \frac{1}{3n^3} + \ldots \qquad \ldots(2)$$

From (1) and (2) by addition,

$$\log_e (n + 1) - \log_e (n - 1) = 2 \left(\frac{1}{n} + \frac{1}{3n^3} + \frac{1}{5n^5} + \ldots \right) \qquad \ldots(3)$$

From this formula by putting $n = 3$ we obtain $\log_e 4 - \log_e 2$, that is $\log_e 2$; and by effecting the calculation we find that the value of $\log_e 2 = 0.69314718 \ldots$; whence $\log_e 8$ is known.

Again by putting $n = 9$ we obtain $\log_e 10 - \log_e 8$; whence we find $\log_e 10 = 2.30258509 \ldots$

To convert Napierian logarithms into logarithms to base 10 we multiply by $\dfrac{1}{\log_e 10}$ which is the *modulus* [Art 216] of the common system and its value is $\dfrac{1}{2.30258509 \ldots}$, or $0.43429448 \ldots$; we shall denote this modulus by μ.

In the *Proceedings of the Royal Society of London*, Vol. XXVII. page 88, Professor J. C. Adams has given the values of e, μ, $\log_e 2$, $\log_e 3$, $\log_e 5$ to more than 260 places of decimals.

225. If we multiply the above series throughout by μ, we obtain formulae adapted to the calculation of *common logarithms*.

Thus from (1) $\mu \log_e (n + 1) - \mu \log_e n = \dfrac{\mu}{n} - \dfrac{\mu}{2n^2} + \dfrac{\mu}{3n^3} - \ldots;$

that is,

$$\log_{10} (n + 1) - \log_{10} n = \frac{\mu}{n} - \frac{\mu}{2n^2} + \frac{\mu}{3n^3} - \ldots \qquad \ldots(1)$$

Similarly from (2),

$$\log_{10} n - \log_{10} (n - 1) = \frac{\mu}{n} + \frac{\mu}{2n^2} + \frac{\mu}{3n^3} + \ldots \qquad \ldots(2)$$

From either of the above results we see that if the logarithm of one of two consecutive numbers be known, the logarithm of the other may be found, and thus a table of logarithms can be constructed.

It should be remarked that the above formulae are only needed to calculate the logarithms of *prime* numbers, for the logarithm of a *composite* number may be obtained by adding together the logarithms of its component factors.

In order to calculate the logarithm of any one of the smaller prime numbers, we do not usually substitute the number in either of the formulae (1) or (2), but we endeavour to find some value of n by which division may be easily performed, and such that either $n + 1$ or $n - 1$ contains the given number as a factor. We then find $\log (n + 1)$ or $\log (n - 1)$ and deduce the logarithm of the given number.

Example 4. Calculate $\log 2$ and $\log 3$, given $\mu = 0.43429448$.

By putting $n = 10$ in (2), we have the value of $\log 10 - \log 9$; thus
$$1 - 2 \log 3 = 0.043429448 + 0.002171472 + 0.000144765 + 0.000010857$$
$$+ 0.000000868 + 0.000000072 + 0.000000006;$$
$$1 - 2 \log 3 = 0.045757488,$$
$$\log 3 = 0.477121256.$$

Putting $n = 80$ in (1), we obtain $\log 81 - \log 80$; thus
$$4 \log 3 - 3 \log 2 - 1 = 0.005428681 - 0.000033929 + 0.000000283$$
$$- 0.000000003;$$
$$3 \log 2 = 0.908485024 - 0.005395032.$$
$$\log 2 = 0.301029997.$$

In the next article we shall give another series for $\log_e (n + 1) - \log_e n$ which is often useful in the construction of Logarithmic Tables. For further information on the subject the reader is referred to Mr. Glaisher's article on *Logarithms* in the *Encyclopedia Britannica*.

226.   In Art. 223 we have proved that

$$\log_e (1 + x) = x - \frac{x^2}{2} + \frac{x^3}{3} - \ldots;$$

changing x into $- x$, we have

$$\log_e (1 - x) = - x - \frac{x^2}{2} - \frac{x^3}{3} - \ldots$$

By subtraction,

$$\log_e \frac{1 + x}{1 - x} = 2 \left(x + \frac{x^3}{3} + \frac{x^5}{5} + \ldots \right)$$

Put $\dfrac{1 + x}{1 - x} = \dfrac{n + 1}{n}$, so that $x = \dfrac{1}{2n + 1}$; we thus obtain

$$\log_e (n + 1) - \log_e n = 2 \left\{ \frac{1}{2n + 1} + \frac{1}{3 (2n + 1)^3} + \frac{1}{5 (2n + 1)^5} + \ldots \right\}$$

Note : This series converges very rapidly, but in practice is not always so convenient as the series in Art. 224.

227.   The following examples illustrate the subject of the chapter.

Example 1. If α, β are the roots of the equation $ax^2 + bx + c = 0$, shew that

$$\log (a - bx + cx^2) = \log a + (\alpha + \beta) x - \frac{\alpha^2 + \beta^2}{2} x^2 + \frac{\alpha^3 + \beta^3}{3} x^3 - \ldots$$

Since $\alpha + \beta = - \dfrac{b}{a}$, $\alpha\beta = \dfrac{c}{a}$, we have

$$a - bx + cx^2 = a \{1 + (\alpha + \beta) x + \alpha\beta x^2\}$$
$$= a (1 + \alpha x) (1 + \beta x).$$

$\therefore$ $\log (a - bx + cx^2) = \log a + \log (1 + \alpha x) + \log (1 + \beta x)$

$$= \log a + \alpha x - \frac{\alpha^2 x^2}{2} + \frac{\alpha^3 x^3}{3} - \ldots + \beta x - \frac{\beta^2 x^2}{2} + \frac{\beta^3 x^3}{3} - \ldots$$

$$= \log a + (\alpha + \beta) x - \frac{\alpha^2 + \beta^2}{2} x^2 + \frac{\alpha^3 + \beta^3}{3} x^3 - \ldots$$

Example 2. Prove that the coefficient of x^n in the expansion of $\log (1 + x + x^2)$ is $- \dfrac{2}{n}$ or $\dfrac{1}{n}$ according as n is or is not a multiple of 3.

$$\log (1 + x + x^2) = \log \frac{1 - x^3}{1 - x} = \log (1 - x^3) - \log (1 - x)$$

$$= - x^3 - \frac{x^6}{2} - \frac{x^9}{3} - \ldots - \frac{x^{3r}}{r} - \ldots + \left(x + \frac{x^2}{2} + \frac{x^3}{3} + \ldots + \frac{x^r}{r} + \ldots \right)$$

If n is a multiple of 3, denote it by $3r$; then the coefficient of x^n is $-\dfrac{1}{r}$ from the first series, together with $\dfrac{1}{3r}$ from the second series; that is, the coefficient is $-\dfrac{3}{n} + \dfrac{1}{n}$, or $-\dfrac{2}{n}$.

If n is not a multiple of 3, x^n does not occur in the first series, therefore the required coefficient is $\dfrac{1}{n}$.

228. *To prove that e is incommensurable.*

For if not, let $e = \dfrac{m}{n}$, where m and n are positive integers;

then $\qquad \dfrac{m}{n} = 1 + 1 + \dfrac{1}{2!} + \dfrac{1}{3!} + \dots + \dfrac{1}{n!} + \dfrac{1}{(n+1)!} + \dots$

multiply both sides by $n!$;

$\therefore \qquad m(n-1)! = \text{integer} + \dfrac{1}{n+1} + \dfrac{1}{(n+1)(n+2)}$

$$+ \dfrac{1}{(n+1)(n+2)(n+3)} + \dots$$

But $\qquad \dfrac{1}{n+1} + \dfrac{1}{(n+1)(n+2)} + \dfrac{1}{(n+1)(n+2)(n+3)} + \dots$

is a proper fraction, for it is greater than $\dfrac{1}{n+1}$ and less than the geometrical progression

$$\dfrac{1}{n+1} + \dfrac{1}{(n+1)^2} + \dfrac{1}{(n+1)^3} + \dots;$$

that is, less than $\dfrac{1}{n}$; hence an integer is equal to an integer plus a fraction, which is absurd; therefore e is incommensurable.

EXAMPLES XVII

1. Find the value of $1 - \dfrac{1}{2} + \dfrac{1}{3} - \dfrac{1}{4} + \dfrac{1}{5} - \dfrac{1}{6} + \dots$

2. Find the value of
$$\dfrac{1}{2} - \dfrac{1}{2 \cdot 2^2} + \dfrac{1}{3 \cdot 2^3} - \dfrac{1}{4 \cdot 2^4} + \dfrac{1}{5 \cdot 2^5} - \dots$$

3. Shew that
$$\log_e(n+a) - \log_e(n-a) = 2\left(\dfrac{a}{n} + \dfrac{a^3}{3n^3} + \dfrac{a^5}{5n^5} + \dots\right)$$

4. If $y = x - \dfrac{x^2}{2} + \dfrac{x^3}{3} - \dfrac{x^4}{4} + \ldots$,

   shew that $x = y + \dfrac{y^2}{2!} + \dfrac{y^3}{3!} + \ldots$

5. Shew that

   $$\dfrac{a-b}{a} + \dfrac{1}{2}\left(\dfrac{a-b}{a}\right)^2 + \dfrac{1}{3}\left(\dfrac{a-b}{a}\right)^3 + \ldots = \log_e a - \log_e b.$$

6. Find the Napierian logarithm of $\dfrac{1001}{999}$ correct to sixteen places

   of decimals.

7. Prove that $e^{-1} = 2\left(\dfrac{1}{3!} + \dfrac{2}{5!} + \dfrac{3}{7!} + \ldots\right)$

8. Prove that

   $$\log_e (1+x)^{1+x} (1-x)^{1-x} = 2\left(\dfrac{x^2}{1 \cdot 2} + \dfrac{x^4}{3 \cdot 4} + \dfrac{x^6}{5 \cdot 6} + \ldots\right)$$

9. Find the value of $x^2 - y^2 + \dfrac{1}{2!}(x^4 - y^4) + \dfrac{1}{3!}(x^6 - y^6) + \ldots$

10. Find the numerical values of the common logarithms of 7, 11 and 13; given $\mu = 0.43429448$, $\log 2 = 0.30103000$.

11. Shew that if ax^2 and $\dfrac{a}{x^2}$ are each less than unity

$a\left(x^2 + \dfrac{1}{x^2}\right) - \dfrac{a^2}{2}\left(x^4 + \dfrac{1}{x^4}\right) + \dfrac{a^3}{3}\left(x^6 + \dfrac{1}{x^6}\right) - \ldots = \log_e\left(1 + ax^2 + a^2 + \dfrac{a}{x^2}\right)$

12. Prove that

    $$\log_e (1 + 3x + 2x^2) = 3x - \dfrac{5x^2}{2} + \dfrac{9x^3}{3} - \dfrac{17x^4}{4} + \ldots;$$

    and find the general term of the series.

13. Prove that

    $$\log_e \dfrac{1+3x}{1-2x} = 5x - \dfrac{5x^2}{2} + \dfrac{35x^3}{3} - \dfrac{65x^4}{4} + \ldots;$$

    and find the general term of the series.

14. Expand $\dfrac{e^{5x} + e^x}{e^{3x}}$ in a series of ascending powers of x.

15. Express $\dfrac{1}{2}(e^{ix} + e^{-ix})$ in ascending powers of x, where $i = \sqrt{-1}$.

16. Shew that

$$\log_e (x + 2h) = 2 \log_e (x + h) - \log_e x - \left\{ \frac{h^2}{(x+h)^2} + \frac{h^4}{2(x+h)^4} + \frac{h^6}{3(x+h)^6} + \dots \right\}$$

17. If α and β be the roots of $x^2 - px + q = 0$, shew that

$$\log_e (1 + px + qx^2) = (\alpha + \beta) x - \frac{\alpha^2 + \beta^2}{2} x^2 + \frac{\alpha^3 + \beta^3}{3} x^3 - \dots$$

18. If $x < 1$, find the sum of the series

$$\frac{1}{2} x^2 + \frac{2}{3} x^3 + \frac{3}{4} x^4 + \frac{4}{5} x^5 + \dots$$

19. Shew that

$$\log_e \left(1 + \frac{1}{n} \right)^n = 1 - \frac{1}{2(n+1)} - \frac{1}{2 \cdot 3 (n+1)^2} - \frac{1}{3 \cdot 4 (n+1)^3} - \dots$$

20. If $\log_e \dfrac{1}{1 + x + x^2 + x^3}$ be expanded in a series of ascending powers of x, shew that the coefficient of x^n is $-\dfrac{1}{n}$ if n be odd, or of the form $4m + 2$, and $\dfrac{3}{n}$ if n be of the form $4m$.

21. Shew that

$$1 + \frac{2^3}{2!} + \frac{3^3}{3!} + \frac{4^3}{4!} + \dots = 5e.$$

22. Prove that

$$2 \log_e n - \log_e (n + 1) - \log_e (n - 1) = \frac{1}{n^2} + \frac{1}{2n^4} + \frac{1}{3n^6} + \dots$$

23. Shew that $\dfrac{1}{n+1} + \dfrac{1}{2(n+1)^2} + \dfrac{1}{3(n+1)^3} + \dots$

$$= \frac{1}{n} - \frac{1}{2n^2} + \frac{1}{3n^3} - \dots$$

24. If $\log_e \dfrac{9}{10} = -a$, $\log_e \dfrac{24}{25} = -b$, $\log_e \dfrac{81}{80} = c$, shew that

$\log_e 2 = 7a - 2b + 3c$, $\log_e 3 = 11a - 3b + 5c$, $\log_e 5 = 16a - 4b + 7c$;

and calculate $\log_e 2$, $\log_e 3$, $\log_e 5$ to 8 places of decimals.

■■■

Chapter 18

INTEREST AND ANNUITIES

229. In this chapter we shall explain how the solution of questions connected with Interest and Discount may be simplified by the use of algebraical formulae.

We shall use the terms *Interest, Discount, Present Value* in their ordinary arithmetical sense; but instead of taking as the rate of interest the interest on £100 for one year, we shall find it more convenient to take the interest on £1 for one year.

230. *To find the interest and amount of a given sum in a given time at simple interest.*

Let P be the principal in pounds, r the interest of £1 for one year, n the number of years, I the interest, and M the amount.

The interest of P for one year is Pr, and therefore for n years is Pnr; that is,

$$I = Pnr \qquad \qquad \ldots(1)$$

Also $\qquad\qquad M = P + I;$

that is, $\qquad\qquad M = P(1 + nr) \qquad\qquad \ldots(2)$

From (1) and (2) we see that if of the quantities P, n, r, I or P, n, r, M any three be given the fourth may be found.

231. *To find the present value and discount of a given sum due in a given time, allowing simple interest.*

Let P be the given sum, V the present value, D the discount, r the interest of £1 for one year, n the number of years.

Since V is the sum which put out to interest at the present time will in n years amount to P, we have

$$P = V(1 + nr)$$

$$\therefore \qquad V = \frac{P}{1 + nr};$$

And $\qquad\qquad D = P - V = P - \frac{P}{1 + nr};$

$$\therefore \qquad D = \frac{Pnr}{1 + nr}.$$

Note : The value of D given by this equation is called the *true discount.* But in practice when a sum of money is paid before it is due, it is customary to deduct the *interest* on the debt instead of the true discount, and the money so deducted is called the *banker's discount;* so that

Banker's Discount $= Pnr$.

$$\text{True Discount} = \frac{Pnr}{1+nr}$$

Example 1. The difference between the true discount and the banker's discount on £1900 paid 4 months before it is due is $6s$. $8d$.; find the rate per cent., simple interest being allowed.

Let r denote the interest on £1 for one year; then the banker's discount is $\dfrac{1900r}{3}$, and the true discount is $\dfrac{\dfrac{1900r}{3}}{1+\dfrac{1}{3}r}$.

$$\therefore \qquad \frac{1900r}{3} - \frac{\dfrac{1900r}{3}}{1+\dfrac{1}{3}r} = \frac{1}{3};$$

whence

$$1900r^2 = 3 + r;$$

$$\therefore \qquad r = \frac{1 \pm \sqrt{1+22800}}{3800} = \frac{1 \pm 151}{3800}.$$

Rejecting the negative value, we have $r = \dfrac{152}{3800} = \dfrac{1}{25}$;

$$\therefore \qquad \text{rate per cent} = 100r = 4.$$

232. *To find the interest and amount of a given sum in a given time at compound interest.*

Let P denote the principal, R the amount of £1 in one year, n the number of year, I the interest and M the amount.

The amount of P at the end of the first year is PR; and since this is the principal for the second year, the amount at the end of the second year is $PR \times R$ or PR^2. Similarly the amount at the end of the third year is PR^3, and so on; hence the amount in n years is PR^n; that is,

$$M = PR^n;$$

$$\therefore \qquad I = P(R^n - 1).$$

Note : If r denote the interest on £1 for one year, we have
$$R = 1 + r.$$

233. In business transactions when the time contains a fraction of a year it is usual to allow *simple* interest for the fraction of the year. Thus the amount of £1 in $\dfrac{1}{2}$ year is reckoned $1 + \dfrac{r}{2}$; and the amount of P in $4\dfrac{2}{3}$ years at compound interest is $PR^4\left(1+\dfrac{2}{3}r\right)$. Similarly the amount of P in $n+\dfrac{1}{m}$ years is $PR^n\left(1+\dfrac{r}{m}\right)$.

If the interest is payable more than once a year there is a distinction between the *nominal annual rate* of interest and that actually received, which may be called the *true annual rate;* thus if the interest is payable twice a year, and if r is the *nominal* annual rate of interest, the amount of £1 in half a year is $1 + \dfrac{r}{2}$, and therefore in the whole year the amount of £1 is $\left(1 + \dfrac{r}{2}\right)^2$, or $1 + r + \dfrac{r^2}{4}$; so that the *true* annual rate of interest is $r + \dfrac{r^2}{4}$.

234. If the interest is payable q times a year, and if r is the nominal annual rate, the interest on £1 for each interval is $\dfrac{r}{q}$, and therefore the amount of P in n years, or qn intervals, is $P\left(1 + \dfrac{r}{q}\right)^{qn}$.

In this case the interest is said to be "converted into principal" q times a year.

If the interest is convertible into principal every moment, then q becomes infinitely great. To find the value of the amount, put $\dfrac{r}{q} = \dfrac{1}{x}$, so that $q = rx$; thus

$$\text{the amount} = P\left(1 + \frac{r}{q}\right)^{qn} = P\left(1 + \frac{1}{x}\right)^{xnr} = P\left\{\left(1 + \frac{1}{x}\right)^x\right\}^{nr}$$

$$= Pe^{nr}, \text{[Art. 220. Cor.,]}$$

since x is infinite when q is infinite.

235. *To find the present value and discount of a given sum due in a given time, allowing compound interest.*

Let P be the given sum, V the present value, D the discount, R the amount of £1 for one year, n the number of years

Let V is the sum which, put out to interest at the present time, will in n years amount to P, we have

$$P = VR^n;$$

$$\therefore \qquad V = \frac{P}{R^n} = PR^{-n},$$

and $\qquad\qquad D = P\left(1 - R^{-n}\right).$

Example : The present value of £672 due in a certain time is £126; if compound interest at $4\dfrac{1}{6}$ per cent. be allowed, find the time; having given

$$\log 2 = 0.30103; \quad \log 3 = 0.47712.$$

Here $r = \dfrac{4\frac{1}{6}}{100} = \dfrac{1}{24}$ and $R = \dfrac{25}{24}$.

Let n be the number of years; then

$$672 = 126 \left(\dfrac{25}{24} \right)^{n};$$

$\therefore$ $\qquad n \log \dfrac{25}{24} = \log \dfrac{672}{126},$

or $\qquad n \log \dfrac{100}{96} = \log \dfrac{16}{3};$

$\therefore$ $\qquad n (\log 100 - \log 96) = \log 16 - \log 3,$

$$n = \dfrac{4 \log 2 - \log 3}{2 - 5 \log 2 - \log 3}$$

$$n = \dfrac{0.72700}{0.01773} = 41, \text{ very nearly;}$$

thus the time is very nearly 41 years.

EXAMPLES XVIII. a.

When required the following logarithms may be used.

$\qquad \log 2 = 0.3010300, \quad \log 3 = 0.4771213,$
$\qquad \log 7 = 0.8450\,980 \quad \log 11 = 1.0413927.$

1. Find the amount of £100 in 50 years, at 5 per cent. compound interest; given log 114.674 = 2.0594650.

2. At simple interest the interest on a certain sum of money is £90, and the discount on the same sum for the same time and at the same rate is £80; find the sum.

3. In how many years will a sum of money double itself at 5 per cent. compound interest ?

4. Find, correct to a farthing, the present value of £10000 due 8 years hence at 5 per cent. compound interest; given
$\qquad$ log 67683.94 = 4.8304856.

5. In how many years will £1000 become £2500 at 10 per cent. compound interest ?

6. Shew that at simple interest the discount is half the harmonic mean between the sum due and the interest on it.

7. Shew that money will increase more than a hundredfold in a century at 5 per cent compound interest.

8. What sum of money at 6 per cent. compound interest will amount to £1000 in 12 years ? Given

$$\log 106 = 2.0253059, \quad \log 49697 = 4.6963292.$$

9. A man borrows £600 from a money-lender, and the bill is renewed every half-year at an increase of 18 per cent : what time will elapse before it reaches £6000 ? Given $\log 118 = 2.071882$.

10. What is the amount of a farthing in 200 years at 6 per cent. compound interest ? Given $\log 106 = 2.0253059$, $\log 115.1270 = 2.0611800$.

ANNUITIES

236. An **annuity** is a fixed sum paid periodically under certain stated conditions; the payment may be made either once a year or at more frequent intervals. Unless it is otherwise stated we shall suppose the payments annual.

An **annuity certain** is an annuity payable for a fixed term of years independent of any contingency; a life annuity is an annuity which is payable during the lifetime of a person, or of the survivor of a number of persons.

A **deferred annuity**, or **reversion**, is an annuity which does not begin until after the lapse of a certain number of years; and when the annuity is deferred for n years, it is said to commence after n years, and the first payment is made at the end of $n + 1$ years.

If the annuity is to continue for ever it is called a **perpetuity;** if it does not commence at once it is called a **deferred perpetuity.**

An annuity left unpaid for a certain number of years is said to be forborne for that number of years.

237. *To find the amount of an annuity left unpaid for a given number of years, allowing simple interest.*

Let A be the annuity, r the interest of £1 for one year, n the number of years, M the amount.

At the end of the first year A is due, and the amount of this sum in the remaining $n - 1$ years is $A + (n - 1) rA$; at the end of the second year another A is due, and the amount of this sum in the remaining $(n - 2)$ years is $A + (n - 2) rA$; and so on. Now M is the sum of all these amounts;

$$\therefore \qquad M = \{A + (n - 1) rA\} + \{A + (n - 2) rA\} + \dots + (A + rA) + A,$$

the series consisting of n terms;

$\therefore \qquad M = nA + (1 + 2 + 3 + \ldots + \overline{n-1})\,rA$

$$= nA + \frac{n\,(n-1)}{2}\,rA.$$

238. *To find the amount of an annuity left unpaid for a given number of years, allowing compound interest.*

Let A be the annuity, R the amount of £1 for one year, n the number of years, M the amount.

At the end of the first year A is due, and the amount of this sum in the remaining $n-1$ years is AR^{n-1}; at the end of the second year another A is due, and the amount of this sum in the remaining $n-2$ years is AR^{n-2}; and so on.

$\therefore \qquad M = AR^{n-1} + AR^{n-2} + \ldots + AR^2 + AR + A$

$$= A\,(1 + R + R^2 + \ldots \text{ to } n \text{ terms})$$

$$= A\,\frac{R^n - 1}{R - 1}.$$

239. In finding the present value of annuities it is always customary to reckon compound interest; the results obtained when simple interest is reckoned being contradictory and untrustworthy. On this point and for further information on the subject of annuities the reader may consult the Text-books of the Institute of Actuaries, Parts I. and II., and the article *Annuities* in the *Encyclopcedia Britannica*.

240. *To find the present value of an annuity to continue for a given number of years, allowing compound interest.*

Let A be the annuity, R the amount of £1 in one year, n the number of years, V the required present value.

The present value of A due in 1 year is AR^{-1};

the present value of A due in 2 years is AR^{-2};

the present value of A due in 3 years is AR^{-3};

and so on. [Art. 235.]

Now V is the sum of the present values of the different payments;

$\therefore \qquad V = AR^{-1} + AR^{-2} + AR^{-3} + \ldots \text{ to } n \text{ terms}$

$$= AR^{-1}\frac{1 - R^{-n}}{1 - R^{-1}}$$

$$= A\,\frac{1 - R^{-n}}{R - 1}$$

Note. This result may also be obtained by dividing the value of M, given in Art. 238, by R^n. [Art 232.]

Cor. If we make n infinite we obtain for the present value of a *perpetuity*

$$V = \frac{A}{R-1} = \frac{A}{r}.$$

241. If mA is the present value of an annuity A, the annuity is said to be worth m years' purchase.

In the case of a perpetual annuity $mA = \dfrac{A}{r}$; hence

$$m = \frac{1}{r} = \frac{100}{\text{rate per cent.}} ;$$

that is, the number of years' purchase of a perpetual annuity is obtained by dividing 100 by the rate per cent.

As instances of perpetual annuities we may mention the income arising from investments in irredeemable Stocks such as many Government Securities, Corporation Stocks, and Railway Debentures. A good test of the credit of a Government is furnished by the number of years' purchase of its Stocks; thus the $2\frac{1}{2}$ p.c. Consols at 90 are worth 36 years' purchase; Egyptian 4 p.c. Stock at 96 is worth 24 years' purchase; while Austrian 5 p.c. Stock at 80 is only worth 16 years' purchase.

242. *To find the present value of a deferred annuity to commence at the end of p years and to continue for n years, allowing compound interest.*

Let A be the annuity, R the amount of £1 in one year, V the present value.

The first payment is made at the end of $(p + 1)$ years. [Art. 236.]

Hence the present values of the first, second, third, ... payments are respectively.

$$AR^{-(p+1)}, AR^{-(p+2)}, AR^{-(p+3)}, \ldots$$

$$\therefore \quad V = AR^{-(p+1)} + AR^{-(p+2)} + AR^{-(p+3)} + \ldots \text{ to } n \text{ terms}$$

$$= AR^{-(p+1)}\frac{1-R^{-n}}{1-R^{-1}}$$

$$= \frac{AR^{-p}}{R-1} - \frac{AR^{-p-n}}{R-1}.$$

Cor. The present value of a *deferred perpetuity* to commence after p years is given by the formula

$$V = \frac{AR^{-p}}{R-1}.$$

243. A freehold estate is an estate which yields a perpetual annuity called the *rent*; and thus the value of the estate is equal to the present value of a perpetuity equal to the rent.

It follows from Art. 241 that if we know the number of years' purchase that a tenant pays in order to buy his farm, we obtain the rate per cent. at which interest is reckoned by dividing 100 by the number of years, purchase.

Example : The reversion after 6 years of a freehold estate is bought for £20000; what rent ought the purchaser to receive, reckoning compound interest at 5 per cent ? Given log 1.05 = 0.0211893, log 1.340096 = 0.1271358.

The rent is equal to the annual value of the perpetuity, deferred for 6 years, which may be purchased for £20000.

Let £A be the value of the annuity; then since $R = 1.05$, we have

$$20000 = \frac{A \times (1.05)^{-6}}{0.05};$$

$$\therefore \qquad A \times (1.05)^{-6} = 1000;$$
$$\log A - 6 \log 1.05 = 3,$$
$$\log A = 3.1271358 = \log 1340.096.$$
$$\therefore \qquad A = 1340.096, \text{ and the rent is £1340. } 1s . 11d.$$

244. Suppose that a tenant by paying down a certain sum has obtained a lease of an estate for $p + q$ years, and that when q years have elapsed he wishes to renew the lease for a term $p + n$ years ; the sum that he must pay is called the fine for renewing n years of the lease.

Let A be the annual value of the estate; then since the tenant has paid for p of the $p + n$ years, the fine must be equal to the present value of a deferred annuity A, to commence after p years and to continue for n years; that is,

$$\text{the fine} = \frac{AR^{-p}}{R-1} - \frac{AR^{-p-n}}{R-1}. \qquad \text{[Art. 242.]}$$

EXAMPLES XVIII. b.

The interest is supposed compound unless the contrary is stated.

1. The amount of an annuity of £120 which is left unpaid for 5 years is £672; find the rate per cent allowing simple interest.

2. Find the amount of an annuity of £100 in 20 years, allowing compound interest at $4\frac{1}{2}$ per cent. Given

   log 1.045 = 0.0191163,   log 24.117 = 1.3823260.

.3. A freehold estate is bought for £2750; at what rent should it be let so that the owner may receive 4 per cent. on the purchase money ?

4. A freehold estate worth £120 a year is sold for £4000; find the rate of interest.

5. How many years' purchase should be given for a freehold estate, interest being calculated at $3\frac{1}{2}$ per cent ?

6. If a perpetual annuity is worth 25 years' purchase, find the amount of an annuity of Rs. 625 to continue for 2 year.

7. If a perpetual annuity is worth 20 years' purchase, find the annuity to continue for 3 years which can be purchased for Rs. 2522.

8. When the rate of interest is 4 per cent, find what sum must be paid now to receive a freehold estate of Rs. 400 a year 10 years hence; having   given   log 104 = 2.0170333,   log 6.75565 = 0.8296670.

9. Find what sum will amount to Rs. 500 in 50 years at 2 per cent. interest being payable every moment; given $e^{-1} = 0.3678$.

10. If 25 years' purchase must be paid for an annuity to continue n years, and 30 years' purchase for an annuity to continue $2n$ years, find the rate per cent.

11. A man borrows Rs. 5000 at 4 per cent. compound interest; if the principal and interest are to be repaid by 10 equal annual instalments, find the amount of each instalment; having given

   log 1.04 = 0.0170333   and   log 675565 = 5.829667.

12. A man has a capital of Rs. 20000 for which he receives interest at 5 per cent; if he spends Rs. 1800 every year, shew that he will be ruined before the end of the 17th year; having given
   log 2 = 0.3010300, log 3 = 0.4771213, log 7 = 0.8450980.

13. The annual rent of an estate is Rs. 500; if it is let on a lease of 20 years, calculate the fine to be paid to renew the lease when 7 years have elapsed allowing interest at 6 per cent.; having given

   log 106 = 2.0253059, log 4.688385 = 0.6710233,
   log 3.118042 = 0.4938820.

14. If a, b, c years' purchase must be paid for an annuity to continue $n, 2n, 3n$ years respectively; shew that

$$a^2 - ab + b^2 = ac.$$

15. What is the present worth of a perpetual annuity of Rs. 100 payable at the end of the first year, Rs. 200 at the end of the second, Rs. 300 at the end of the third, and so on, increasing Rs. 100 each year; interest being taken at 5 per cent. per annum ?

■■■

Chapter 19

INEQUALITIES

245. Any quantity a is said to be greater than another quantity b when $a - b$ is positive; thus 2 is greater than -3, because $2 - (-3)$, or 5 is positive. Also b is said to be less than a when $b - a$ is negative; thus -5 is less than -2, because $-5 - (-2)$, or -3 is negative.

In accordance with this definition, zero must be regarded as greater than any negative quantity.

In the present chapter we shall suppose (unless the contrary is directly stated) that the letters always denote real and positive quantities.

246. If $a > b$, then it is evident that
$$a + c > b + c;$$
$$a - c > b - c;$$
$$ac > bc;$$
$$\frac{a}{c} > \frac{b}{c};$$

that is, *an inequality will still hold after each side has been increased, diminished, multiplied, or divided by the same positive quantity.*

247. If $a - c > b$,
by adding c to each side,
$$a > b + c;$$
which shews that *in an inequality any term may be transposed from one side to the other if its sign be changed.*

If $a > b$, then evidently $b < a$;

that is, *if the sides of an inequality be transposed, the sign of inequality must be reversed.*

If $a > b$, then $a - b$ is positive, and $b - a$ is negative that is, $-a - (-b)$ is negative, and therefore
$$-a < -b;$$
hence, *if the signs of all the terms of an inequality be changed, the sign of inequality must be reversed.*

Again, if $a > b$, then $-a < -b$, and therefore
$$-ac < -bc;$$

that is, *if the sides of an inequality be multiplied by the same negative quantity, the sign of inequality must be reversed.*

248.   If $a_1 > b_1, a_2 > b_2, a_3 > b_3, ..., a_m > b_m$, it is clear that

$$a_1 + a_2 + a_3 + ... + a_m > b_1 + b_2 + b_3 + ... + b_m;$$

and $$a_1 a_2 a_3 ... a_m > b_1 b_2 b_3 ... b_m.$$

249.   If $a > b$, and if p, q are positive integers, then $\sqrt[q]{a} > \sqrt[q]{b}$ or $a^{\frac{1}{q}} > b^{\frac{1}{q}}$; and therefore $a^{\frac{p}{q}} > b^{\frac{p}{q}}$; that is, $a^n > b^n$, where n is any positive quantity.

Further, $\dfrac{1}{a^n} < \dfrac{1}{b^n}$; that is $a^{-n} < b^{-n}$

250.   The square of every real quantity is positive, and therefore greater than zero. Thus $(a - b)^2$ is positive;

∴ $$a^2 - 2ab + b^2 > 0;$$

∴ $$a^2 + b^2 > 2ab.$$

Similarly $$\frac{x+y}{2} > \sqrt{xy};$$

that is, *the arithmetic mean of two positive quantities is greater than their geometric mean.*

The inequality becomes an equality when the quantities are equal.

251.   The results of the preceding article will be found very useful, especially in the case of inequalities in which the letters are involved symmetrically.

Example 1. If a, b, c denote positive quantities, prove that

$$a^2 + b^2 + c^2 > bc + ca + ab;$$

and $2 (a^3 + b^3 + c^3) > bc (b + c) + ca (c + a) + ab (a + b).$

For $b^2 + c^2 > 2bc$ ...(1);

$$c^2 + a^2 > 2ca;$$

$$a^2 + b^2 > 2ab;$$

whence by addition $a^2 + b^2 + c^2 > bc + ca + ab.$

It may be noticed that this result is true for *any* real values of a, b, c.

•   Again, from (1) $b^2 - bc + c^2 > bc$ ...(2)

∴ $b^3 + c^3 > bc (b + c)$ ...(3)

By writing down the two similar inequalities and adding, we obtain

$$2 (a^3 + b^3 + c^3) > bc (b + c) + ca (c + a) + ab (a + b).$$

It should be observed that (3) is obtained from (2) by introducing the factor $b + c$, and that if this factor be negative the inequality (3) will no longer hold.

Example 2. If x may have any real value find which is the greater, $x^3 + 1$ or $x^2 + x$.

$$x^3 + 1 - (x^2 + x) = x^3 - x^2 - (x - 1)$$
$$= (x^2 - 1)(x - 1)$$
$$= (x - 1)^2 (x + 1).$$

Now $(x - 1)^2$ is positive, hence

$$x^3 + 1 > \text{ or } < x^2 + x$$

according as $x + 1$ is positive or negative; that is, according as $x >$ or < -1.

If $x = -1$, the inequality becomes an equality.

252.   Let a and b be two positive quantities, S their sum and P their product; then from the identity

$$4ab = (a + b)^2 - (a - b)^2,$$

we have

$$4P = S^2 - (a - b)^2, \text{ and } S^2 = 4P + (a - b)^2.$$

Hence, if S is given, P is greatest when $a = b$; and if P is given, S is least when

$$a = b;$$

that is, *if the sum of two positive quantities is given, their product is greatest when they are equal; and if the product of two positive quantities is given, their sum is least when they are equal.*

253.   *To find the greatest value of a product the sum of whose factors is constant.*

Let there be n factors $a, b, c, \ldots k$, and suppose that their sum is constant and equal to s.

Consider the product $abc \ldots k$, and suppose that a and b are any two unequal factors. If we replace the two unequal factors a, b by the two equal factors $\dfrac{a + b}{2}, \dfrac{a + b}{2}$ the product is increased while the sum remains unaltered; hence *so long as the product contains two unequal factors it can be increased without altering the sum of the factors;* therefore the product is greatest when all the factors are equal. In this case the value of each of the n factors is $\dfrac{s}{n}$, and the greatest value of the product is $\left(\dfrac{s}{n}\right)^n$, or

$$\left(\frac{a+b+c+\ldots+k}{n}\right)^n$$

Cor. If $a, b, c, \ldots k$ are *unequal*,

$$\left(\frac{a+b+c+\ldots+k}{n}\right)^n > abc \ldots k;$$

that is, $\qquad \dfrac{a+b+c+\ldots+k}{n} > (abc \ldots k)^{\frac{1}{n}}.$

By an extension of the meaning of the terms *arithmetic mean* and *geometric mean* this result is usually quoted as follows :

the arithmetic mean of any number of positive quantities is greater than the geometric mean.

Example : Shew that $(1^r + 2^r + 3^r + \ldots + n^r)^n > n^n (n!)^r$;
where r is any real quantity.

Since $\qquad \dfrac{1^r + 2^r + 3^r + \ldots + n^r}{n} > (1^r \cdot 2^r \cdot 3^r \ldots n^r)^{\frac{1}{n}};$

$\therefore \qquad \left(\dfrac{1^r + 2^r + 3^r + \ldots + n^r}{n}\right)^n > 1^r \cdot 2^r \cdot 3^r \ldots n^r, \text{ that is, } > (n!)^r;$

whence we obtain the result required.

254. *To find the greatest value of $a^m b^n c^p \ldots$ when $a + b + c + \ldots$ is constant; $m, n, p, \ldots$ being positive integers.*

Since $m, n, p, \ldots$ are constants, the expression $a^m b^n c^p \ldots$ will be greatest when $\left(\dfrac{a}{m}\right)^m \left(\dfrac{b}{n}\right)^n \left(\dfrac{c}{p}\right)^p \ldots$ is greatest. But this last expression is the product of $m + n + p + \ldots$ factors whose sum is $m\left(\dfrac{a}{m}\right) + n\left(\dfrac{b}{n}\right) + p\left(\dfrac{c}{p}\right) + \ldots$, or $a + b + c + \ldots$, and therefore constant. Hence $a^m b^n c^p \ldots$ will be greatest when the factors

$$\frac{a}{m}, \frac{b}{n}, \frac{c}{p}, \ldots$$

are all equal, that is, when

$$\frac{a}{m} = \frac{b}{n} = \frac{c}{p} = \ldots = \frac{a+b+c+\ldots}{m+n+p+\ldots}.$$

Thus the greatest value is

$$m^m n^n p^p \ldots \left(\frac{a+b+c+\ldots}{m+n+p+\ldots}\right)^{m+n+p+\ldots}$$

Example : Find the greatest value of $(a + x)^3 (a - x)^4$ for any real value of x numerically less than a.

The given expression is greatest when $\left(\dfrac{a + x}{3} \right)^3 \left(\dfrac{a - x}{4} \right)^4$ is greatest; but

the sum of the factors of this expression is $3 \left(\dfrac{a + x}{3} \right) + 4 \left(\dfrac{a - x}{4} \right)$, or $2a$; hence

$(a + x)^3 (a - x)^4$ is greatest when $\dfrac{a + x}{3} = \dfrac{a - x}{4}$, or $x = -\dfrac{a}{7}$.

Thus the greatest value is $\dfrac{6^3 \cdot 8^4}{7^7} a^7$.

255. The determination of *maximum* and *minimum* values may often be more simply effected by the solution of a quadratic equation than by the foregoing methods. Instances of this have already occurred in Chap. 9; we add a further.

Example : Divide an odd integer into two integral parts whose product is a maximum.

Denote the integer by $2n + 1$; the two parts by x and $2n + 1 - x$; and the product by y; then $(2n + 1) x - x^2 = y$; whence

$$2x = (2n + 1) \pm \sqrt{(2n + 1)^2 - 4y};$$

but the quantity under the radical must be positive, and therefore y cannot be greater than $\dfrac{1}{4} (2n + 1)^2$, or $n^2 + n + \dfrac{1}{4}$; and since y is integral its greatest value must be $n^2 + n$; in which case $x = n + 1$, or n; thus the two parts are n and $n + 1$.

256. Sometimes we may use the following method.

Example : Find the minimum value of $\dfrac{(a + x)(b + x)}{c + x}$

Put $c + x = y$; then

$$\text{the expression} = \frac{(a - c + y)(b - c + y)}{y}$$

$$= \frac{(a - c)(b - c)}{y} + y + a - c + b - c$$

$$= \left(\frac{\sqrt{(a - c)(b - c)}}{\sqrt{y}} - \sqrt{y} \right)^2 + a - c + b - c + 2 \sqrt{(a - c)(b - c)}.$$

Hence the expression is a minimum when the square term is zero; that is when $y = \sqrt{(a - c)(b - c)}$.

Thus the minimum value is

$$a - c + b - c + 2 \sqrt{(a - c)(b - c)};$$

and the corresponding value of x is $\sqrt{(a - c)(b - c)} - c$.

EXAMPLES XIX. a.

1. Prove that $(ab + xy)(ax + by) > 4abxy$.

2. Prove that $(b + c)(c + a)(a + b) > 8abc$.

3. Shew that the sum of any real positive quantity and its reciprocal is never less than 2.

4. If $a^2 + b^2 = 1$, and $x^2 + y^2 = 1$, shew that $ax + by < 1$.

5. If $a^2 + b^2 + c^2 = 1$, and $x^2 + y^2 + z^2 = 1$, shew that $ax + by + cz < 1$

6. If $a > b$, shew that $a^a b^b > a^b b^a$, and $\log \dfrac{b}{a} < \log \dfrac{1+b}{1+a}$.

7. Shew that $(x^2 y + y^2 z + z^2 x)(xy^2 + yz^2 + zx^2) > 9x^2 y^2 z^2$.

8. Find which is the greater $3ab^2$ or $a^3 + 2b^3$.

9. Prove that $a^3 b + ab^3 < a^4 + b^4$.

10. Prove that $6abc < bc(b + c) + ca(c + a) + ab(a + b)$.

11. Shew that $b^2 c^2 + c^2 a^2 + a^2 b^2 > abc(a + b + c)$.

12. Which is the greater x^3 or $x^2 + x + 2$ for positive values of x?

13. Shew that $x^3 + 13a^2 x > 5ax^2 + 9a^3$, if $x > a$.

14. Find the greatest value of x in order that $7x^2 + 11$ may be greater than $x^3 + 17x$.

15. Find the minimum value of $x^2 - 12x + 40$, and the maximum value of $24x - 8 - 9x^2$.

16. Shew that $(n!)^2 > n^n$, and $2 \cdot 4 \cdot 6 \ldots 2n < (n + 1)^n$.

17. Shew that $(x + y + z)^3 > 27xyz$.

18. Shew that $n^n > 1 \cdot 3 \cdot 5 \ldots (2n - 1)$.

19. If n be a positive integer greater than 2, shew that
$$2^n > 1 + n\sqrt{2^{n-1}}.$$

20. Shew that $(n!)^3 < n^n \left(\dfrac{n+1}{2} \right)^{2n}$.

21. Shew that
(1) $(x + y + z)^3 > 27(y + z - x)(z + x - y)(x + y - z)$.
(2) $xyz > (y + z - x)(z + x - y)(x + y - z)$.

22. Find the maximum value of $(7 - x)^4 (2 + x)^5$ when x lies between 7 and -2.

23. Find the minimum value of $\dfrac{(5 + x)(2 + x)}{1 + x}$

*257. *To prove that if a and b are positive and unequal,*
$\dfrac{a^m + b^m}{2} > \left(\dfrac{a + b}{2}\right)^m$, *except when m is a positive proper fraction.*

We have $a^m + b^m = \left(\dfrac{a + b}{2} + \dfrac{a - b}{2}\right)^m + \left(\dfrac{a + b}{2} - \dfrac{a - b}{2}\right)^m$; and since

$\dfrac{a - b}{2}$ is less than $\dfrac{a + b}{2}$, we may expand each of these expressions in

ascending powers of $\dfrac{a - b}{2}$. [Art. 184.]

$$\therefore \quad \frac{a^m + b^m}{2} = \left(\frac{a + b}{2}\right)^m + \frac{m(m - 1)}{1 \cdot 2}\left(\frac{a + b}{2}\right)^{m - 2}\left(\frac{a - b}{2}\right)^2$$
$$+ \frac{m(m - 1)(m - 2)(m - 3)}{1 \cdot 2 \cdot 3 \cdot 4}\left(\frac{a + b}{2}\right)^{m - 4}\left(\frac{a - b}{2}\right)^4 + \cdots$$

(1) If m is a positive integer, or any negative quantity, all the terms on the right are positive, and therefore

$$\frac{a^m + b^m}{2} > \left(\frac{a + b}{2}\right)^m.$$

(2) If m is positive and less than 1, all the terms on the right after the first are negative, and therefore

$$\frac{a^m + b^m}{2} < \left(\frac{a + b}{2}\right)^m.$$

(3) If $m > 1$ and positive, put $m = \dfrac{1}{n}$ where $n < 1$; then

$$\left(\frac{a^m + b^m}{2}\right)^{\frac{1}{m}} = \left(\frac{a^{\frac{1}{n}} + b^{\frac{1}{n}}}{2}\right)^n;$$

$$\therefore \quad \left(\frac{a^m + b^m}{2}\right)^{\frac{1}{m}} > \frac{\left(a^{\frac{1}{n}}\right)^n + \left(b^{\frac{1}{n}}\right)^n}{2}, \text{ by (2);}$$

$$\therefore \quad \left(\frac{a^m + b^m}{2}\right)^{\frac{1}{m}} > \frac{a + b}{2}.$$

$$\therefore \quad \frac{a^m + b^m}{2} > \left(\frac{a + b}{2}\right)^m$$

Hence the proposition is established. If $m = 0$, or 1, the inequality becomes an equality.

*258. *If there are n positive quantities a, b, c, ... k, then*

$$\frac{a^m + b^m + c^m + ... + k^m}{n} > \left(\frac{a + b + c + ... + k}{n}\right)^m$$

unless m is a positive proper fraction.

Suppose m to have any value not lying between 0 and 1.

Consider the expression $a^m + b^m + c^m + ... + k^m$, and suppose that a and b are unequal; if we replace a and b by the two equal quantities $\frac{a+b}{2}, \frac{a+b}{2}$, the value of $a + b + c + ... + k$ remains unaltered, but the value of $a^m + b^m + c^m + ... + k^m$ is diminished, since

$$a^m + b^m > 2\left(\frac{a+b}{2}\right)^m.$$

Hence so long as any two of the quantities $a, b, c, ... k$ are unequal the expression $a^m + b^m + c^m + ... + k^m$ can be diminished without altering the value of $a + b + c + ... + k$; and therefore the value of $a^m + b^m + c^m + ... + k^m$ will be least when all the quantities $a, b, c, ... k$ are equal. In this case each of the quantities is equal to

$$\frac{a + b + c + ... + k}{n};$$

and the value of $a^m + b^m + c^m + ... + k^m$ then becomes

$$n\left(\frac{a + b + c + ... + k}{n}\right)^m$$

Hence when $a, b, c, ... k$ are unequal,

$$\frac{a^m + b^m + c^m + ... + k^m}{n} > \left(\frac{a + b + c + ... + k}{n}\right)^m.$$

If m lies between 0 and 1 we may in a similar manner prove that the sign of inequality in the above result must be reversed.

The proposition may be stated verbally as follows :

The arithmetic mean of the mth powers of n positive quantities is greater than the mth power of their arithmetic mean in all case except when m lies between 0 and 1.

*259. *If a and b are positive integers, and a > b, and if x be a positive quantity,*

$$\left(1 + \frac{x}{a}\right)^a > \left(1 + \frac{x}{b}\right)^b$$

For $\left(1 + \dfrac{x}{a}\right)^a = 1 + x + \left(1 - \dfrac{1}{a}\right)\dfrac{x^2}{2!} + \left(1 - \dfrac{1}{a}\right)\left(1 - \dfrac{2}{a}\right)\dfrac{x^3}{3!} + \qquad ...(1)$

the series consisting of $a + 1$ terms; and

$\left(1 + \dfrac{x}{b}\right)^b = 1 + x + \left(1 - \dfrac{1}{b}\right)\dfrac{x^2}{2!} + \left(1 - \dfrac{1}{b}\right)\left(1 - \dfrac{2}{b}\right)\dfrac{x^3}{3!} + \qquad ...(2)$

the series consisting of $b + 1$ terms.

After the second term, each term of (1) is greater than the corresponding term of (2); moreover the number of terms in (1) is greater than the number of terms in (2); hence the proposition is established.

*260. *To prove that* $\sqrt[x]{\dfrac{1+x}{1-x}} > \sqrt[y]{\dfrac{1+y}{1-y}}$, *if x and y are proper fractions and positive, and x > y.*

For $\qquad \sqrt[x]{\dfrac{1+x}{1-x}} >$ or $< \sqrt[y]{\dfrac{1+y}{1-y}}$,

according as $\dfrac{1}{x} \log \dfrac{1+x}{1-x} >$ or $< \dfrac{1}{y} \log \dfrac{1+y}{1-y}$.

But $\qquad \dfrac{1}{x} \log \dfrac{1+x}{1-x} = 2\left(1 + \dfrac{x^2}{3} + \dfrac{x^4}{5} + ...\right),$ [Art. 226];

and $\qquad \dfrac{1}{y} \log \dfrac{1+y}{1-y} = 2\left(1 + \dfrac{y^2}{3} + \dfrac{y^4}{5} + ...\right).$

$\therefore \qquad \dfrac{1}{x} \log \dfrac{1+x}{1-x} > \dfrac{1}{y} \log \dfrac{1+y}{1-y}$,

and thus the proposition is proved.

*261. *To prove that* $(1+x)^{1+x}(1-x)^{1-x} > 1$, *if x < 1, and to deduce that*
$a^a b^b > \left(\dfrac{a+b}{2}\right)^{a+b}$

Denote $(1+x)^{1+x}(1-x)^{1-x}$ by P; then

$\log P = (1+x)\log(1+x) + (1-x)\log(1-x)$

$= x\{\log(1+x) - \log(1-x)\} + \log(1+x) + \log(1-x)$

$= 2x\left(x + \dfrac{x^3}{3} + \dfrac{x^5}{5} + ...\right) - 2\left(\dfrac{x^2}{2} + \dfrac{x^4}{4} + \dfrac{x^6}{6} + ...\right)$

$= 2\left(\dfrac{x^2}{1\cdot 2} + \dfrac{x^4}{3\cdot 4} + \dfrac{x^6}{5\cdot 6} + ...\right)$

Hence $\log P$ is positive, and therefore $P > 1$;

that is $(1+x)^{1+x}(1-x)^{1-x} > 1$.

In this result put $x = \dfrac{z}{u}$, where $u > z$; then

$$\left(1 + \frac{z}{u}\right)^{1 + \frac{z}{u}}\left(1 - \frac{z}{u}\right)^{1 - \frac{z}{u}} > 1;$$

$\therefore \qquad \left(\dfrac{u+z}{u}\right)^{u+z}\left(\dfrac{u-z}{u}\right)^{u-z} > 1^u, \text{ or } 1;$

$\therefore \qquad (u+z)^{u+z}(u-z)^{u-z} > u^{2u}.$

Now put $\quad u + z = a, u - z = b$, so that $u = \dfrac{a+b}{2}$;

$\therefore \qquad a^a b^b > \left(\dfrac{a+b}{2}\right)^{a+b}$

EXAMPLES XIX. b.

1. Shew that $27\,(a^4 + b^4 + c^4) > (a + b + c)^4$.

2. Shew that $n\,(n+1)^3 < 8\,(1^3 + 2^3 + 3^3 + \ldots + n^3)$.

3. Shew that the sum of the mth powers of the first n even numbers is greater than $n\,(n+1)^m$, if $m > 1$.

4. If α and β are positive quantities, and $\alpha > \beta$, shew that
$$\left(1 + \frac{1}{\alpha}\right)^\alpha > \left(1 + \frac{1}{\beta}\right)^\beta.$$

    Hence shew that if $n > 1$ the value of $\left(1 + \dfrac{1}{n}\right)^n$ lies between 2 and 2.718 …

5. If a, b, c are in descending order of magnitude, shew that
$$\left(\frac{a+c}{a-c}\right)^a < \left(\frac{b+c}{b-c}\right)^b.$$

6. Shew that $\left(\dfrac{a+b+c+\ldots+k}{n}\right)^{a+b+c+\ldots+k} < a^a b^b c^c \ldots k^k.$

7. Prove that $\dfrac{1}{m}\log(1 + a^m) < \dfrac{1}{n}\log(1 + a^n)$, if $m > n$.

8. If n is a positive integer and $x < 1$, shew that
$$\frac{1 - x^{n+1}}{n+1} < \frac{1 - x^n}{n}.$$

9. If a, b, c are in H.P. and $n > 1$, shew that $a^n + c^n > 2b^n$.

10. Find the maximum value of $x^3 (4a - x)^5$ if x is positive and less than $4a$; and the maximum value of $x^{\frac{1}{2}} (1 - x)^{\frac{1}{3}}$ when x is a proper fraction.

11. If x is positive, shew that $\log (1 + x) < x$ and $> \dfrac{x}{1 + x}$.

12. If $x + y + z = 1$, shew that the least value of $\dfrac{1}{x} + \dfrac{1}{y} + \dfrac{1}{z}$ is 9; and that $(1 - x) (1 - y) (1 - z) > 8xyz$.

13. Shew that $(a + b + c + d) (a^3 + b^3 + c^3 + d^3) > (a^2 + b^2 + c^2 + d^2)^2$.

14. Shew that the expressions
$$a (a - b) (a - c) + b (b - c) (b - a) + c (c - a) (c - b)$$
and $\quad a^2 (a - b) (a - c) + b^2 (b - c) (b - a) + c^2 (c - a) (c - b)$
are both positive.

15. Shew that $(x^m + y^m)^n < (x^n + y^n)^m$, if $m > n$.

16. Shew that $a^b b^a < \left(\dfrac{a + b}{2} \right)^{a + b}$.

17. If a, b, c denote the sides of a triangle, shew that
(1) $a^2 (p - q) (p - r) + b^2 (q - r) (q - p) + c^2 (r - p) (r - q)$ cannot be negative; p, q, r being any real quantities;
(2) $a^2 yz + b^2 zx + c^2 xy$ cannot be positive, if $x + y + z = 0$.

18. Shew that $1 ! 3 ! 5 ! \ldots (2n - 1) ! > (n !)^n$

19. If $a, b, c, d, \ldots$ are p positive integers, whose sum is equal to n, shew that the least value of
$$a ! b ! c ! d ! \ldots \text{ is } (q !)^{p - r} (q + 1) !,$$
where q is the quotient and r the remainder when n is divided by p.

■ ■ ■

Chapter 20

LIMITING VALUES AND VANISHING FRACTIONS

262. If a be a constant finite quantity, the fraction $\dfrac{a}{x}$ can be made as small as we please by sufficiently increasing x; that is, we can make $\dfrac{a}{x}$ approximate to zero as nearly as we please by taking x large enough; this is usually abbreviated by saying, "when x is infinite the limit of $\dfrac{a}{x}$ is zero."

Again, the fraction $\dfrac{a}{x}$ increases as x decreases, and by making x as small as we please we can make $\dfrac{a}{x}$ as large as we please; thus when x is zero $\dfrac{a}{x}$ has no finite limit; this is usually expressed by saying, "when x is zero the limit of $\dfrac{a}{x}$ is infinite."

263. When we say that a quantity *increases without limit* or *is infinite*, we mean that we can suppose the quantity to become greater than any quantity we can name.

Similarly when we say that a quantity *decreases without limit*, we mean that we can suppose the quantity to become smaller than any quantity we can name.

The symbol ∞ is used to denote the value of any quantity which is indefinitely increased, and the symbol 0 is used to denote the value of any quantity which is indefinitely diminished.

264. The two statements of Art. 262 may now be written symbolically as follows :

$$\text{if } x \text{ is } \infty, \text{ then } \frac{a}{x} \text{ is } 0;$$

$$\text{if } x \text{ is } 0, \text{ then } \frac{a}{x} \text{ is } \infty.$$

But in making use of such concise modes of expression, it must be remembered that they are only convenient abbreviations of fuller verbal statements.

265. The student will have had no difficulty in understanding the use of the word *limit*, wherever we have already employed it; by as a clear conception of the ideas conveyed by the words *limit* and *limiting value* is necessary in the higher branches of Mathematics we proceed to explain more precisely their use and meaning.

266. Definition. If $y = f(x)$, and if when x approaches a value a, the function $f(x)$ can be made to differ by as little as we please from a fixed quantity b, then b is called the limit of y when $x = a$.

For instance, if S denote the sum of n terms of the series

$$1 + \frac{1}{2} + \frac{1}{2^2} + \frac{1}{2^3} + \ldots; \text{ then } S = 2 - \frac{1}{2^{n-1}}. \qquad \text{[Art. 56.]}$$

Here S is a function of n, and $\dfrac{1}{2^{n-1}}$ can be made as small as we please by increasing n; that is, the limit of S is 2 when n is infinite.

267. We shall often have occasion to deal with expressions consisting of a series of terms arranged according to powers of some common letter, such as

$$a_0 + a_1 x + a_2 x^2 + a_3 x^3 + \ldots$$

where the coefficients $a_0, a_1, a_2, a_3, \ldots$ are finite quantities independent of x, and the number of terms may be limited or unlimited

It will therefore be convenient to discuss some propositions connected with the limiting values of such expressions under certain conditions.

268. *The limit of the series*

$$a_0 + a_1 x + a_2 x^2 + a_3 x^3 + \ldots$$

when x is indefinitely diminished is a_0.

Suppose that the series consists of an *infinite* number of terms.

Let b be the greatest of the coefficients $a_1, a_2, a_3, \ldots$; and let us denote the given series by $a_0 + S$; then

$$S < bx + bx^2 + bx^3 + \ldots;$$

and if $x < 1$, we have $S < \dfrac{bx}{1-x}$.

Thus when x is indefinitely diminished, S can be made as small as we please; hence the limit of the given series is a_0.

If the series consists of a *finite* number of terms, S is less than in the case we have considered, hence *a fortiori* the proposition is true.

269.   *In the series*

$$a_0 + a_1 x + a_2 x^2 + a_3 x^3 + \ldots,$$

by taking x small enough we may make any term as large as we please compared with the sum of all that follow it; and by taking x large enough we may make any term as large as we please compared with the sum of all that precede it.

The ratio of the term $a_n x^n$ to the sum of all that follow it is

$$\frac{a_n x^n}{a_{n+1} x^{n+1} + a_{n+2} x^{n+2} + \ldots}, \text{ or } \frac{a_n}{a_{n+1} x + a_{n+2} x^2 + \ldots};$$

When x is indefinitely small the denominator can be made as small as we please; that is, the fraction can be made as large as we please.

Again, the ratio of the term $a_n x^n$ to the sum of all that precede it is

$$\frac{a_n x^n}{a_{n-1} x^{n-1} + a_{n-2} x^{n-2} + \ldots}, \text{ or } \frac{a_n}{a_{n-1} y + a_{n-2} y^2 + \ldots};$$

where $y = \dfrac{1}{x}$.

When x is indefinitely large, y is indefinitely small; hence, as in the previous case, the fraction can be made as large as we please.

270.   The following particular form of the foregoing proposition is very useful.

In the expression

$$a_n x^n + a_{n-1} x^{n-1} + \ldots + a_1 x + a_0,$$

consisting of a finite number of terms in *descending* powers of x, by taking x small enough the last term a_0 can be made as large as we please compared with the sum of all the terms that precede it, and by taking x large enough the first term $a_n x^n$ can be made as large as we please compared with the sum of all that follow it.

Example 1. By taking n large enough we can make the first term of $n^4 - 5n^3 - 7n + 9$ as large as we please compared with the sum of all the other terms; that is, we may take the first term n^4 as the equivalent of the whole expression, with an error as small as we please provided n be taken large enough.

Example 2. Find the limit of $\dfrac{3x^3 - 2x^2 - 4}{5x^3 - 4x + 8}$ when (1) x is infinite; (2) x is zero.

(1) In the numerator and denominator we may disregard all terms but the first; hence the limit is $\dfrac{3x^3}{5x^3}$, or $\dfrac{3}{5}$.

(2) When x is indefinitely small the limit is $\dfrac{-4}{8}$, or $-\dfrac{1}{2}$.

Example 3. Find the limit of $\sqrt[x]{\dfrac{1+x}{1-x}}$ when x is zero.

Let P denote the value of the given expression; by taking logarithms we have

$$\log P = \frac{1}{x}\{\log(1+x) - \log(1-x)\}$$

$$= 2\left(1 + \frac{x^2}{3} + \frac{x^4}{5} + \dots\right) \qquad \text{[Art. 226.]}$$

Hence the limit of $\log P$ is 2, and therefore the value of the limit required is e^2.

VANISHING FRACTIONS

271. Suppose it is required to find the limit of

$$\frac{x^2 + ax - 2a^2}{x^2 - a^2}$$

when $x = a$.

If we put $x = a + h$, then h will approach the value zero as x approaches the value a.

Substituting $a + h$ for x,

$$\frac{x^2 + ax - 2a^2}{x^2 - a^2} = \frac{3ah + h^2}{2ah + h^2} = \frac{3a + h}{2a + h},$$

and when h is indefinitely small the limit of this expression is $\dfrac{3}{2}$.

There is however another way of regarding the question; for

$$\frac{x^2 + ax - 2a^2}{x^2 - a^2} = \frac{(x-a)(x+2a)}{(x-a)(x+a)} = \frac{x+2a}{x+a},$$

and if we *now* put $x = a$ the value of the expression is $\dfrac{3}{2}$, as before.

If in the given expression $\dfrac{x^2 + ax - 2a^2}{x^2 - a^2}$ we put $x = a$ *before*

simplification it will be found that it assumes the form $\dfrac{0}{0}$, the value of

which is indeterminate; also we see that it has this form in consequence of the factor $x - a$ appearing in both numerator and denominator. Now we cannot divide by a *zero factor*, but as long as x is not absolutely equal to a the factor $x - a$ may be removed, and we then find that the nearer x approaches to the value a, the nearer does

the value of the fraction approximate to $\dfrac{3}{2}$, or in accordance with the

definition of Art. 266,

when $x = a$, the limit of $\dfrac{x^2 + ax - 2a^2}{x^2 - a^2}$ is $\dfrac{3}{2}$.

272. If $f(x)$ and $\phi(x)$ are two functions of x, each of which becomes

equal to zero for some particular value a of x, the fraction $\dfrac{f(a)}{\phi(a)}$ takes

the form $\dfrac{0}{0}$, and is called a **Vanishing Fraction.**

Example 1. If $x = 3$, find the limit of
$$\frac{x^3 - 5x^2 + 7x - 3}{x^3 - x^2 - 5x - 3}.$$

When $x = 3$, the expression reduces to the indeterminate form $\dfrac{0}{0}$; but by

removing the factor $x - 3$ from numerator and denominator, the fraction

becomes $\dfrac{x^2 - 2x + 1}{x^2 + 2x + 1}$. When $x = 3$ this reduces to $\dfrac{1}{4}$, which is therefore the

required limit.

Example 2. The fraction $\dfrac{\sqrt{3x - a} - \sqrt{x + a}}{x - a}$ becomes $\dfrac{0}{0}$ when $x = a$.

To find its limit, multiply numerator and denominator by the surd conjugate to $\sqrt{3x - a} - \sqrt{x + a}$; the fraction then becomes

$$\frac{(3x - a) - (x + a)}{(x - a)(\sqrt{3x - a} + \sqrt{x + a})}, \text{ or } \frac{2}{\sqrt{3x - a} + \sqrt{x + a}};$$

whence by putting $x = a$ we find that the limit is $\dfrac{1}{\sqrt{2a}}$.

Example 3. The fraction $\dfrac{1 - \sqrt[3]{x}}{1 - \sqrt[5]{x}}$ becomes $\dfrac{0}{0}$ when $x = 1$.

To find its limit, put $x = 1 + h$ and expand by the Binomial Theorem. Thus the fraction

$$= \frac{1-(1+h)^{\frac{1}{3}}}{1-(1+h)^{\frac{1}{5}}} = \frac{1-\left(1+\frac{1}{3}h-\frac{1}{9}h^2+\ldots\right)}{1-\left(1+\frac{1}{5}h-\frac{2}{25}h^2+\ldots\right)}$$

$$= \frac{-\frac{1}{3}+\frac{1}{9}h-\ldots}{-\frac{1}{5}+\frac{2}{25}h-\ldots}$$

Now $h = 0$ when $x = 1$; hence the required limit is $\frac{5}{3}$.

273. Sometimes the roots of an equation assume an indeterminate form in consequence of some relation subsisting between the coefficients of the equation.

For example, if $ax + b = cx + d$,

$$(a-c)x = d-b,$$

$$x = \frac{d-b}{a-c}.$$

But if $c = a$, then x becomes $\frac{d-b}{0}$, or ∞; that is, the root of a simple equation is indefinitely great if the coefficient of x is indefinitely small.

274. The solution of the equations

$$ax + by + c = 0, \quad a'x + b'y + c' = 0$$

is

$$x = \frac{bc'-b'c}{ab'-a'b}, \quad y = \frac{ca'-c'a}{ab'-a'b}.$$

If $ab' - a'b = 0$, then x and y are both infinite. In this case $\frac{a'}{a} = \frac{b'}{b} = m$ suppose; by substituting for a', b', the second equation becomes $ax + by + \frac{c'}{m} = 0$.

If $\frac{c'}{m}$ is not equal to c, the two equations $ax + by + c = 0$ and $ax + by + \frac{c'}{m} = 0$ differ only in their absolute terms, and being *inconsistent* cannot be satisfied by any finite values of x and y.

If $\frac{c'}{m}$ is equal to c, we have $\frac{a'}{a} = \frac{b'}{b} = \frac{c'}{c}$ and the two equations are now identical.

Here, since $bc' - b'c = 0$ and $ca' - c'a = 0$ the values of x and y each assume the form $\dfrac{0}{0}$, and the solution is *indeterminate*. In fact, in the present case we have really only *one* equation involving *two* unknowns, and such an equation may be satisfied by an unlimited number of values.

The reader who is acquainted with Analytical Geometry will have no difficulty in interpreting these results in connection with the geometry of the straight line.

275. We shall now discuss some peculiarities which may arise in the solution of a quadratic equation.

Let the equation be
$$ax^2 + bx + c = 0.$$

If $c = 0$, then
$$ax^2 + bx = 0;$$

whence $x = 0$, or $-\dfrac{b}{a}$;

that is, one of the roots is zero and the other is finite.

If $b = 0$, the roots are equal in magnitude and opposite in sign. [Art. 118.]

If $a = 0$, the equation reduces to $bx + c = 0$; and it appears that in this case the quadratic furnishes only one root, namely $-\dfrac{c}{b}$. But every quadratic equation has two roots, and in order to discuss the value of the other root we proceed as follows.

Write $\dfrac{1}{y}$ for x in the original equation and clear of fractions; thus
$$cy^2 + by + a = 0.$$

Now put $a = 0$, and we have
$$cy^2 + by = 0;$$

the solution of which is $y = 0$, or $-\dfrac{b}{c}$; that is, $x = \infty$, or $-\dfrac{c}{b}$.

Hence, *in any quadratic equation one root will become infinite if the coefficient of x^2 becomes zero.*

This is the form in which the result will be most frequently met with in other branches of higher Mathematics, but the student should notice that it is merely a convenient abbreviation of the following fuller statement:

In the equation $ax^2 + bx + c = 0$, if a is very small one root is very large, and as a is indefinitely diminished this root becomes indefinitely great. In this case the finite root approximates to $-\dfrac{c}{b}$ as its limit.

The cases in which more than one of the coefficients vanish may be discussed in a similar manner.

EXAMPLES XX

Find the limits of the following expressions,

(1) when $x = \infty$,   (2) when $x = 0$.

1. $\dfrac{(2x-3)(3-5x)}{7x^2 - 6x + 4}$ **2.** $\dfrac{(3x^2 - 1)^2}{x^4 + 9}$.

3. $\dfrac{(3 + 2x^3)(x-5)}{(4x^3 - 9)(1 + x)}$ **4.** $\dfrac{(x-3)(2-5x)(3x+1)}{(2x-1)^3}$

5. $\dfrac{1-x^2}{2x^3 - 1} \div \dfrac{1-x}{2x^2}$ **6.** $\dfrac{(3-x)(x+5)(2-7x)}{(7x-1)(x+1)^3}$.

Find the limits of

7. $\dfrac{x^3 + 1}{x^2 - 1}$, when $x = -1$.   **8.** $\dfrac{a^x - b^x}{x}$, when $x = 0$.

9. $\dfrac{e^x - e^{-x}}{\log(1 + x)}$, when $x = 0$.

10. $\dfrac{e^{mx} - e^{ma}}{x - a}$, when $x = a$.

11. $\dfrac{\sqrt{x} - \sqrt{2a} + \sqrt{x - 2a}}{\sqrt{x^2 - 4a^2}}$, when $x = 2a$.

12. $\dfrac{\log((1 + x^2 + x^4))}{3x^2(1 - 2x)}$, when $x = 0$.

13. $\dfrac{1 - x + \log x}{1 - \sqrt{2x - x^2}}$, when $x = 1$.

14. $\dfrac{(a^2 - x^2)^{\frac{1}{2}} + (a - x)^{\frac{3}{2}}}{(a^3 - x^3)^{\frac{1}{2}} + (a - x)^{\frac{1}{2}}}$, when $x = a$.

15. $\dfrac{\sqrt{a^2 + ax + x^2} - \sqrt{a^2 - ax + x^2}}{\sqrt{a + x} - \sqrt{a - x}}$, when $x = 0$.

16. $\left\{\left(\dfrac{n+1}{n}\right)^n - \dfrac{n+1}{n}\right\}^{-n}$, when $n = \infty$.

17. $n \log \dfrac{e}{\left(1 + \dfrac{1}{n}\right)^{n-1}}$, when $n = \infty$.

18. $\sqrt[x]{\dfrac{a + x}{u - x}}$, when $x = 0$.

Chapter 21

CONVERGENCY AND DIVERGENCY OF SERIES

276. An expression in which the successive terms are formed by some regular law is called a series; if the series terminate at some assigned term it is called a finite series; if the number of terms is unlimited, it is called an infinite series.

In the present chapter we shall usually denote a series by an expression of the form

$$u_1 + u_2 + u_3 + \ldots + u_n + \ldots$$

277. Suppose that we have a series consisting of n terms. The sum of the series will be a function of n; if n increases indefinitely, the sum either tends to become equal to a certain finite *limit*, or else it becomes infinitely great.

An infinite series is said to be convergent when the sum of the first n terms cannot numerically exceed some finite quantity however great n may be.

A infinite series is said to be divergent when the sum of the first n terms can be made numerically greater than any finite quantity by taking n sufficienty great.

278. If we can find the sum of the first n terms of a given series, we may ascertain whether it is convergent or divergent by examining whether the series remains finite, or becomes infinite, when n is made indefinitely great.

For example, the sum of the first n terms of the series

$$1 + x + x^2 + x^3 + \ldots \text{ is } \frac{1-x^n}{1-x}.$$

If x is numerically less than 1, the sum approaches to the finite limit $\frac{1}{1-x}$, and the series is therefore convergent.

If x is numerically greater than 1, the sum of the first n terms is $\frac{x^n - 1}{x - 1}$, and by taking n sufficiently great, this can be made greater than any finite quantity; thus the series is divergent.

If $x = 1$, the sum of the first n terms is n, and therefore the series is divergent.

If $x = -1$, the series becomes

$$1 - 1 + 1 - 1 + 1 - 1 + \ldots$$

The sum of an even number of terms is 0, while the sum of an odd number of terms is 1; and thus the sum oscillates between the values 0 and 1. This series belongs to a class which may be called *oscillating* or *periodic convergent series*.

279.   There are many cases in which we have no method of finding the sum of the first n terms of series. We proceed therefore to investigate rules by which we can test the convergency or divergency of a given series without effecting its summation.

280.   *An infinite series in which the terms are alternately positive and negative is convergent if each term is numerically less than the preceding term and if the terms decrease indefinitely.*

Let the series be denoted by

$$u_1 - u_2 + u_3 - u_4 + u_5 - u_6 + \ldots$$

where

$$u_1 > u_2 > u_3 > u_4 > u_5 \ldots$$

The given series may be written in each of the following forms :

$$(u_1 - u_2) + (u_3 - u_4) + (u_5 - u_6) + \ldots \qquad \ldots(1),$$

$$u_1 - (u_2 - u_3) - (u_4 - u_5) - (u_6 - u_7) - \ldots \qquad \ldots(2).$$

From (1) we see that the sum of any number of terms is a positive quantity; and from (2) that the sum of any number of terms is less than u_1; hence the sum of the series is finite.

Also as $u_n = s_n - s_{n-1}$ and the limiting values of s_n and s_{n-1} are the same when n (and therefore $n - 1$) $\to \infty$, it follows that $u_n = 0$ when n is infinite.

Care must be taken not to regard this theorem as always showing convergency. Its converse is not necessarily true as is shown in Art. 290 (II).

281.   For example, the series

$$1 - \frac{1}{2} + \frac{1}{3} - \frac{1}{4} + \frac{1}{5} - \frac{1}{6} + \ldots$$

is convergent. By putting $x = 1$ in Art. 223. we see that its sum is $\log_e 2$.

Again, in the series

$$1 - 3x + \frac{3 \cdot 4}{1 \cdot 2} x^2 - \frac{3 \cdot 4 \cdot 5}{1 \cdot 2 \cdot 3} x^3 + \frac{3 \cdot 4 \cdot 5 \cdot 6}{1 \cdot 2 \cdot 3 \cdot 4} x^4 - \ldots,$$

the numerical part of each term is greater than in the preceding term, but the increase becomes less rapid as more and more terms are taken. If $0 < x < 1$, the powers of x decrease, and though the values of the terms may increase at first, a stage will be reached when the increase in the numerical coefficients is offset by the decrease in the powers of x. Hence afterwards the values of the terms continue to decrease indefinitely and the series is convergent.

282. *An infinite series in which all the terms are of the same sign is divergent if each term is greater than some finite quantity however small.*

For if each term is greater than some finite quantity a, the sum of the first n terms is greater than na.; and this, by taking n sufficiently great, can be made to exceed any finite quantity.

283. Before proceeding to investigate further tests of convergency and divergency, we shall lay down two important principles, which may almost be regarded as axioms.

I. If a series is convergent it will remain convergent, and if divergent it will remain divergent, when we add or remove any *finite* number of its terms; for the sum of these terms is a finite quantity.

II. If a series in which all the terms are positive is convergent, then the series is convergent when some or all of the terms are negative; for the sum is clearly greatest when all of the terms have the same sign.

We shall suppose that all the terms are positive, unless the contrary is stated.

284. *An infinite series is convergent if from and after some fixed term the ratio of each term to the preceding term is numerically less than some quantity which is itself numerically less than unity.*

Let the series beginning from the fixed term be denoted by

$$u_1 + u_2 + u_3 + u_4 + \ldots;$$

and let

$$\frac{u_2}{u_1} < r, \frac{u_3}{u_2} < r, \frac{u_4}{u_3} < r, \ldots;$$

where $r < 1$.

Then

$$u_1 + u_2 + u_3 + u_4 + \ldots$$

$$= u_1 \left(1 + \frac{u_2}{u_1} + \frac{u_3}{u_2} \cdot \frac{u_2}{u_1} + \frac{u_4}{u_3} \cdot \frac{u_3}{u_2} \cdot \frac{u_2}{u_1} + \ldots \right)$$

$$< u_1 (1 + r + r^2 + r^3 + \ldots);$$

that is, $< \dfrac{u_1}{1 - r}$, since $r < 1$.

Hence the given series is convergent.

285.   In the enunciation of the preceding article the student should notice the significance of the words "from and after a fixed term."

Consider the series

$$1 + 2x + 3x^2 + 4x^3 + \ldots + nx^{n-1} + \ldots$$

Here $\dfrac{u_n}{u_{n-1}} = \dfrac{nx}{n-1} = \left(1 + \dfrac{1}{n-1} \right) x;$

and by taking n sufficiently large we can make this ratio approximate to x as nearly as we please, and the ratio of each term to the preceding term will ultimately be x. Hence if $x < 1$ the series is convergent.

But the ratio $\dfrac{u_n}{u_{n-1}}$ will not be less than 1, until $\dfrac{nx}{n-1} < 1$; that is,

until $n > \dfrac{1}{1 - x}$.

Here we have a case of a convergent series in which the terms may increase up to a certain point and then begin to decrease.

For example, if $x = \dfrac{99}{100}$, then $\dfrac{1}{1 - x} = 100$, and the terms do not begin to decrease until after the 100th term.

286.   *An infinite series in which all the terms are of the same sign as divergent if from and after some fixed term the ratio of each term to the preceding term is greater than unity, or equal to unity*

Let the fixed term be denoted by u_1. If the ratio is equal to unity, each of the succeeding terms is equal to u_1, and the sum of n terms is equal to nu_1; hence the series is divergent.

If the ratio is greater than unity, each of the terms after the fixed term is greater than u_1, and the sum of n terms is greater than nu_1; hence the series is divergent.

287.   In the practical application of these tests, to avoid having to ascertain the particular term after which each term is greater or less

than the preceding term, it is convenient to find the limit of $\dfrac{u_n}{u_{n-1}}$

when n is indefinitely increased; let this limit be denoted by λ.

If $\lambda < 1$, the series is convergent.   [Art. 284.]

If $\lambda > 1$, the series is divergent.   [Art. 286.]

If $\lambda = 1$, the series may be either convergent or divergent, and a further test will be required; for it may happen that

$$\frac{u_n}{u_{n-1}} < 1 \text{ but continually approaching to 1 as its limit when } n \text{ is}$$

indefinitely increased. In this case we cannot name any finite quantity r which is itself less than 1 and yet greater than λ.

Hence the test of Art. 284 fails. If, however, $\dfrac{u_n}{u_{n-1}} > 1$ but continually approaching to 1 as its limit, the series is divergent by Art. 286.

We shall use "$\underset{n=\infty}{Lim} \dfrac{u_n}{u_{n-1}}$" as an abbreviation of the words "the limit of $\dfrac{u_n}{u_{n-1}}$ when n is infinite."

Example 1. Find whether the series whose nth term is $\dfrac{(n+1)\,x^n}{n^2}$ is convergent or divergent.

Here $\dfrac{u_n}{u_{n-1}} = \dfrac{(n+1)\,x^n}{n^2} \div \dfrac{n x^{n-1}}{(n-1)^2} = \dfrac{(n+1)\,(n-1)^2}{n^3} \cdot x;$

$\therefore$ $$\underset{n=\infty}{Lim}\ \frac{u_n}{u_{n-1}} = x;$$

hence   if $x < 1$ the series is convergent;

if $x > 1$ the series is divergent.

If $x = 1$, then $\underset{n=\infty}{Lim} \dfrac{u_n}{u_{n-1}} = 1$, and a further test is required.

Example 2. Is the series

$$1^2 + 2^2 x + 3^2 x^2 + 4^2 x^3 + \ldots$$

convergent or divergent ?

Here $\underset{n=\infty}{Lim} \dfrac{u_n}{u_{n-1}} = \underset{n=\infty}{Lim} \dfrac{n^2 x^{n-1}}{(n-1)^2 x^{n-2}} = x.$

Hence if $x < 1$ the series is convergent;

if $x > 1$ the series is divergent.

If $x = 1$ the series becomes $1^2 + 2^2 + 3^2 + 4^2 + \ldots$, and is obviously divergent.

Example 3. In the series

$$a + (a+d)\,r + (a+2d)\,r^2 + \ldots + (a + \overline{n-1} \cdot d)\,r^{n-1} + \ldots;$$

$$Lim_{n=\infty} \frac{u_n}{u_{n-1}} = Lim_{n=\infty} \frac{a+(n-1)d}{a+(n-2)d} \cdot r = r;$$

thus if $r < 1$ the series is convergent, and the sum is finite. [See Art. 50, Cor.]

288. *If there are two infinite series in each of which all the terms are positive and if the ratio of the corresponding terms in the two series is always finite, the two series are both convergent, or both divergent.*

Let the two infinite series be denoted by

$$u_1 + u_2 + u_3 + u_4 + ...,$$

and

$$v_1 + v_2 + v_3 + v_4 + ...$$

The value of the fraction

$$\frac{u_1 + u_2 + u_3 + ... + u_n}{v_1 + v_2 + v_3 + ... + v_n}$$

lies between the greatest and least of the fractions

$$\frac{u_1}{v_1}, \frac{u_2}{v_2}, ... \frac{u_n}{v_n}, \qquad \text{[Art. 14.]}$$

and is therefore a *finite* quantity, L say;

$$\therefore \qquad u_1 + u_2 + u_3 + ... + u_n = L(v_1 + v_2 + v_3 + ... + v_n).$$

Hence if one series is finite in value, so is the other; if one series is infinite in value, so is the other; which proves the proposition.

289. The application of this principle is very important for by means of it we can compare a given series with an *auxiliary series* whose convergency or divergency has been already established. The series discussed in the next article will frequently be found useful as an auxiliary series.

290. *The infinite series*

$$\frac{1}{1^p} + \frac{1}{2^p} + \frac{1}{3^p} + \frac{1}{4^p} + ...$$

is always divergent except when p is positive and greater than 1.

Case I. Let $p > 1$.

The first term is 1; the next two terms together are less than $\dfrac{2}{2^p}$;

the following four terms together are less than $\dfrac{4}{4^p}$; the following eight

terms together are less than $\dfrac{8}{8^p}$; and so on. Hence the series is less

than $1 + \dfrac{2}{2^p} + \dfrac{4}{4^p} + \dfrac{8}{8^p} + ...;$

that is, less than a geometrical progression whose common ratio $\dfrac{2}{2^p}$ is less than 1, since $p > 1$; hence the series is convergent.

Case II. Let $p = 1$.

The series now becomes $1 + \dfrac{1}{2} + \dfrac{1}{3} + \dfrac{1}{4} + \dfrac{1}{5} + \dots$

The third and fourth terms together are greater then $\dfrac{2}{4}$ or $\dfrac{1}{2}$; the following four terms together are greater than $\dfrac{4}{8}$ or $\dfrac{1}{2}$; the following eight terms together are greater than $\dfrac{8}{16}$ or $\dfrac{1}{2}$; and so on. Hence the series is greater than

$$1 + \frac{1}{2} + \frac{1}{2} + \frac{1}{2} + \frac{1}{2} + \dots,$$

and is therefore divergent.   [Art. 286.]

Case III. Let $p < 1$, or negative.

Each term is now greater than the corresponding term in Case II., therefore the series is divergent.

Hence the series is always divergent except in the case when p is positive and greater than unity.

Example. Prove that the series

$$\frac{2}{1} + \frac{3}{4} + \frac{4}{9} + \dots + \frac{n+1}{n^2} + \dots$$

is divergent.

Compare the given series with $1 + \dfrac{1}{2} + \dfrac{1}{3} + \dots + \dfrac{1}{n} + \dots$

Thus if u_n and v_n denote the nth terms of the given series and the auxiliary series respectively, we have

$$\frac{u_n}{v_n} = \frac{n+1}{n^2} \div \frac{1}{n} = \frac{n+1}{n};$$

hence $\underset{n=\infty}{Lim} \dfrac{u_n}{v_n} = 1$, and therefore the two series are both convergent or both divergent. But the auxiliary series is divergent, therefore also the given series is divergent.

This completes the solution of Example 1. Art. 287.

291. In the application of Art. 288 it is necessary that the limit of $\dfrac{u_n}{v_n}$ should be finite; this will be the case if we find our auxiliary series in the following way :

Take u_n, the nth term of the given series and retain only the highest powers of n. Denote the result by v_n; then the limit of $\dfrac{u_n}{v_n}$ is finite by Art. 270, and v_n may be taken as the nth term of the auxiliary series.

Example 1. Shew that the series whose n^{th} term is

$$\frac{\sqrt[3]{2n^2 - 1}}{\sqrt[4]{3n^3 + 2n + 5}} \quad \text{is divergent.}$$

As n increases, u_n approximates to the value

$$\frac{\sqrt[3]{2n^2}}{\sqrt[4]{3n^3}}, \text{ or } \frac{\sqrt[3]{2}}{\sqrt[4]{3}} \cdot \frac{1}{n^{1/12}}$$

Hence, if $v_n = \dfrac{1}{n^{1/12}}$, we have $\underset{n=\infty}{Lim} \dfrac{u_n}{v_n} = \dfrac{\sqrt[3]{2}}{\sqrt[4]{3}}$, which is a finite quantity; therefore the series whose n^{th} term is $\dfrac{1}{n^{1/12}}$ may be taken as the auxiliary series. But this series is divergent [Art. 290]; therefore the given series is divergent.

Example 2. Find whether the series in which

$$u_n = \sqrt[3]{n^3 + 1} - n$$

is convergent or divergent.

Here

$$u_n = n\left(\sqrt[3]{1 + \frac{1}{n^3}} - 1 \right)$$

$$= n\left(1 + \frac{1}{3n^3} - \frac{1}{9n^6} + \dots - 1 \right)$$

$$= \frac{1}{3n^2} - \frac{1}{9n^5} + \dots$$

If we take $v_n = \dfrac{1}{n^2}$, we have

$$\frac{u_n}{v_n} = \frac{1}{3} - \frac{1}{9n^3} + \dots$$

$\therefore \quad Lim \dfrac{u_n}{v_n} = \dfrac{1}{3}.$

But the auxiliary series

$$\frac{1}{1^2} + \frac{1}{2^2} + \frac{1}{3^2} + \dots \frac{1}{n^2} + \dots$$

is convergent, therefore the given series is convergent.

292. *To shew that the expansion of* $(1 + x)^n$ *by the Binomial Theorem is convergent when* $x < 1$.

Let u_r, u_{r+1} represent the rth and $(r+1)^{th}$ terms of the expansion; then

$$\frac{u_{r+1}}{u_r} = \frac{n-r+1}{r}\, x.$$

When $r > u + 1$, this ratio is negative; that is, from this point the terms are alternately positive and negative when x is positive, and always of the same sign when x is negative.

Now when r is infinite, $\underset{n=\infty}{Lim}\ \dfrac{u_{r+1}}{u_r} = x$ numerically; therefore since $x < 1$ the series is convergent if all the terms are of the same sign; and therefore *a fortiori* it is convergent when some of the terms are positive and some negative. [Art. 283.]

293. *To shew that the expansion of* a^x *in ascending powers of* x *is convergent for every value of* x.

Here $\dfrac{u_n}{u_{n-1}} = \dfrac{x \log_e a}{n-1}$; and therefore $\underset{n=\infty}{Lim}\ \dfrac{u_n}{u_{n-1}} < 1$ whatever be the value of x; hence the series is convergent.

294. *To shew that the expansion of* $\log(1 + x)$ *in ascending powers of* x *is convergent when* x *is numerically less than* 1.

Here the numerical value of $\dfrac{u_n}{u_{n-1}} = \dfrac{n-1}{n}\, x$, which in the limit is equal to x; hence the series is convergent when x is less than 1.

If $x = 1$, the series becomes $1 - \dfrac{1}{2} + \dfrac{1}{3} - \dfrac{1}{4} + \dots$, and is convergent. [Art. 280.]

If $x = -1$, the series becomes $-1 - \dfrac{1}{2} - \dfrac{1}{3} - \dfrac{1}{4} - \dots$, and is divergent. [Art. 290.] This shews that the logarithm of zero is infinite and negative, as is otherwise evident from the equation $e^{-\infty} = 0$.

295. The results of the two following examples are important, and will be required in the course of the present chapter.

Example 1. Find the limit of $\dfrac{\log x}{x}$ when x is infinite.

Put $x = e^y$; then

$$\frac{\log x}{x} = \frac{y}{e^v} = \frac{y}{1 + y + \dfrac{y^2}{2!} + \dfrac{y^3}{3!} + \dots}$$

$$= \frac{1}{\dfrac{1}{y} + 1 + \dfrac{y}{2!} + \dfrac{y^2}{3!} + \dots};$$

also when x is infinite y is infinite; hence the value of the fraction is zero.

Example 2. Shew that when n is infinite the limit of $nx^n = 0$, when $x < 1$.

Let $x = \dfrac{1}{y}$; so that $y > 1$;

also $\quad$ let $y^n = z$, so that $n \log y = \log z$; then

$$nx^n = \frac{n}{y^n} = \frac{1}{z} \cdot \frac{\log z}{\log y} = \frac{1}{\log y} \cdot \frac{\log z}{z}.$$

Now when n is infinite z is infinite, and $\dfrac{\log z}{z} = 0$; also $\log y$ is finite;

therefore $\qquad Lim \; nx^n = 0.$

296. It is sometimes necessary to determine whether the product of an infinite number of factors is finite or not.

Suppose the product to consist of n factors and to be denoted by

$$u_1 \, u_2 \, u_3 \dots u_n;$$

then if as n increases indefinitely $u_n < 1$, the product will ultimately be zero, and if $u_n > 1$ the product will be infinite; hence in order that the product may be finite, u_n must tend to the limit 1.

Writing $1 + v_n$ for u_n, the product becomes

$$(1 + v_1)(1 + v_2)(1 + v_3) \dots (1 + v_n).$$

Denote the product by P and take logarithms; then

$$\log P = \log(1 + v_1) + \log(1 + v_2) + \dots + \log(1 + v_n) \qquad \dots(1),$$

and in order that the product may be finite this series must be convergent.

Choose as an auxiliary series

$$v_1 + v_2 + v_3 + \dots + v_n \qquad \dots(2)$$

Now $\qquad Lim \; \dfrac{\log(1 + v_n)}{v_n} = Lim \left(\dfrac{v_n - \dfrac{1}{2} v_n^2 + \dots}{v_n} \right) = 1,$

since the limit of v_n is 0 when the limit of u_n is 1.

Hence if (2) is convergent, (1) is convergent, and the given product finite.

Example. Shew that the limit, when n is infinite, of

$$\frac{1}{2} \cdot \frac{3}{2} \cdot \frac{3}{4} \cdot \frac{5}{4} \cdot \frac{5}{6} \cdot \frac{7}{6} \cdots \frac{2n-1}{2n} \cdot \frac{2n+1}{2n}$$

is finite.

The product consists of $2n$ factors : denoting the successive pairs by $u_1, u_2, u_3, \ldots$ and the product by P, we have

$$P = u_1 u_2 u_3 \ldots u_n;$$

where

$$u_n = \frac{2n-1}{2n} \cdot \frac{2n+1}{2n} = 1 - \frac{1}{4n^2};$$

but $\log P = \log u_1 + \log u_2 + \log u_3 + \ldots + \log u_n$ ...(1).

and we have to shew that this series is finite.

Now $\log u_n = \log\left(1 - \frac{1}{4n^2}\right) = -\frac{1}{4n^2} - \frac{1}{32n^4} - \ldots;$

therefore as in Ex. 2, Art. 291, the series is convergent, and the given product is finite.

297. In mathematical investigations infinite series occur so frequently that the necessity of determining their convergency or divergency is very important; and unless we take care that the series we use are convergent, we may be led to absurd conclusions. [See Art. 183.]

For example, if we expand $(1 - x)^{-2}$ by the Binomial Theorem, we find

$$(1 - x)^{-2} = 1 + 2x + 3x^2 + 4x^3 + \ldots$$

But if we obtain the sum of n terms of this series as explained in Art. 60, it appears that

$$1 + 2x + 3x^2 + \ldots + nx^{n-1} = \frac{1 - x^n}{(1 - x)^2} - \frac{nx^n}{1 - x};$$

whence

$$\frac{1}{(1 - x)^2} = 1 + 2x + 3x^2 + \ldots + nx^{n-1} + \frac{x^n}{(1 - x)^2} + \frac{nx^n}{1 - x}.$$

By making n infinite, we see that $\dfrac{1}{(1 - x)^2}$ can only be regarded as

the true equivalent of the infinite series

$$1 + 2x + 3x^2 + 4x^3 + \ldots$$

when $\dfrac{x^n}{(1-x)^2} + \dfrac{nx^n}{1-x}$ vanishes.

If n is infinite, this quantity becomes infinite when $x = 1$, or $x > 1$, and diminishes indefinitely when $x < 1$, [Art. 295], so that it is only when $x < 1$ that we can assert that

$$\frac{1}{(1-x)^2} = 1 + 2x + 3x^2 + 4x^3 + \dots \text{ to inf.;}$$

and we should be led to erroneous conclusions if we were to use the expansion of $(1-x)^{-2}$ by the Binomial Theorem as if it were true for all values of x. In other words, we can introduce the infinite series $1 + 2x + 3x^2 + \dots$ into our reasoning without error if the series is convergent, but we cannot do so when the series is divergent.

The difficulties of divergent series have compelled a distinction to be made between a series and its *algebraical equivalent*. For example, if we divide 1 by $(1-x)^2$, we can always obtain as many terms as we please of the series

$$1 + 2x + 3x^2 + 4x^3 + \dots$$

whatever x may be, and so in a certain sense $\dfrac{1}{(1-x)^2}$ may be called its *algebraical equivalent*; yet, as we have seen, the equivalence does not really exist except when the series is convergent. It is therefore more appropriate to speak of $\dfrac{1}{(1-x)^2}$ as the *generating function* of the series

$$1 + 2x + 3x^2 + \dots$$

being that function which when developed by ordinary algebraical rules will give the series in question.

The use of the term *generating function* will be more fully explained in the chapter on Recurring Series.

EXAMPLES XXI. a.

Find whether the following series are convergent or divergent :

1. $\dfrac{1}{x} - \dfrac{1}{x+a} + \dfrac{1}{x+2a} - \dfrac{1}{x+3a} + \dots,$

   x and a being positive quantities.

2. $\dfrac{1}{1\cdot2} + \dfrac{1}{2\cdot3} + \dfrac{1}{3\cdot4} + \dfrac{1}{4\cdot5} + \dots$

3. $\dfrac{1}{xy} - \dfrac{1}{(x+1)(y+1)} + \dfrac{1}{(x+2)(y+2)} - \dfrac{1}{(x+3)(y+3)} + \ldots$

x and y being positive quantities.

4. $\dfrac{x}{1\cdot2} + \dfrac{x^2}{2\cdot3} + \dfrac{x^3}{3\cdot4} + \dfrac{x^4}{4\cdot5} + \ldots$

5. $\dfrac{x}{1\cdot2} + \dfrac{x^2}{3\cdot4} + \dfrac{x^3}{5\cdot6} + \dfrac{x^4}{7\cdot8} + \ldots$

6. $1 + \dfrac{2^2}{2\,!} + \dfrac{3^2}{3\,!} + \dfrac{4^2}{4\,!} + \ldots$

7. $\sqrt{\dfrac{1}{2}} + \sqrt{\dfrac{2}{3}} + \sqrt{\dfrac{3}{4}} + \sqrt{\dfrac{4}{5}} + \ldots$

8. $1 + 3x + 5x^2 + 7x^3 + 9x^4 + \ldots$

9. $\dfrac{2}{1^p} + \dfrac{3}{2^p} + \dfrac{4}{3^p} + \dfrac{5}{4^p} + \ldots$

10. $1 + \dfrac{x}{2} + \dfrac{x^2}{5} + \dfrac{x^3}{10} + \ldots + \dfrac{x^n}{n^2+1} + \ldots$

11. $x + \dfrac{3}{5}x^2 + \dfrac{8}{10}x^3 + \dfrac{15}{17}x^4 + \ldots + \dfrac{n^2-1}{n^2+1}x^n + \ldots$

12. $1 + \dfrac{2}{5}x + \dfrac{6}{9}x^2 + \dfrac{14}{17}x^3 + \ldots + \dfrac{2^n-2}{2^n+1}x^{n-1} + \ldots$

13. $\dfrac{1}{1^p} + \dfrac{1}{3^p} + \dfrac{1}{5^p} + \dfrac{1}{7^p} + \ldots$

14. $2x + \dfrac{3x^2}{8} + \dfrac{4x^3}{27} + \ldots + \dfrac{(n+1)x^n}{n^3} + \ldots$

15. $\left(\dfrac{2^2}{1^2} - \dfrac{2}{1}\right)^{-1} + \left(\dfrac{3^3}{2^3} - \dfrac{3}{2}\right)^{-2} + \left(\dfrac{4^4}{3^4} - \dfrac{4}{3}\right)^{-3} + \ldots$

16. $1 + \dfrac{1}{2^2} + \dfrac{2^2}{3^3} + \dfrac{3^3}{4^4} + \dfrac{4^4}{5^5} + \ldots$

17. Test the series whose general terms are

(1) $\sqrt{n^2+1} - n$.   (2) $\sqrt{n^4+1} - \sqrt{n^4-1}$.

18. Test the series

(1) $\dfrac{1}{x} + \dfrac{1}{x+1} + \dfrac{1}{x+2} + \dfrac{1}{x+3} + \ldots,$

(2) $\dfrac{1}{x} + \dfrac{1}{x-1} + \dfrac{1}{x+1} + \dfrac{1}{x-2} + \dfrac{1}{x+2} + \ldots$

x being a positive fraction.

19. Shew that the series

$$1 + \frac{2^p}{2!} + \frac{3^p}{3!} + \frac{4^p}{4!} + \ldots$$

is convergent for all values of p.

20. Shew that the infinite series

$$u_1 + u_2 + u_3 + u_4 + \ldots$$

is convergent or divergent according as $Lim \sqrt[n]{u_n}$ is <1, or >1.

21. Shew that the product

$$\frac{2}{1} \cdot \frac{2}{3} \cdot \frac{4}{3} \cdot \frac{4}{5} \cdot \frac{6}{5} \ldots \frac{2n-2}{2n-3} \cdot \frac{2n-2}{2n-1} \cdot \frac{2n}{2n-1}$$

is finite when n is infinite.

22. Shew that when $x = 1$, no term in the expansion of $(1+x)^n$ is infinite, except when n is negative and numerically greater than unity.

*298. The tests of convergency and divergency we have given in Arts. 287, 291 are usually sufficient. The theorem proved in the next article enables us by means of the auxiliary series.

$$\frac{1}{1^p} + \frac{1}{2^p} + \frac{1}{3^p} + \ldots + \frac{1}{n^p} + \ldots$$

to deduce additional tests which will sometimes be found convenient.

*299. *If u_n, v_n are the general terms of two infinite series in which all the terms are positive, then the u-series will be convergent when the v-series is convergent if after some particular term $\dfrac{u_n}{u_{n-1}} < \dfrac{v_n}{v_{n-1}}$; and the u-series will be divergent when the v-series is divergent if $\dfrac{u_n}{u_{n-1}} > \dfrac{v_n}{v_{n-1}}$.*

Let us suppose that u_1 and v_1 are the particular terms.

Case I. Let $\dfrac{u_2}{u_1} < \dfrac{v_2}{v_1}, \dfrac{u_3}{u_2} < \dfrac{v_3}{v_2}, \ldots;$ then

$$u_1 + u_2 + u_3 + \ldots$$

$$= u_1 \left(1 + \frac{u_2}{u_1} + \frac{u_3}{u_2} \cdot \frac{u_2}{u_1} + \ldots \right)$$

$$< u_1 \left(1 + \frac{v_2}{v_1} + \frac{v_3}{v_2} \cdot \frac{v_2}{v_1} + \ldots \right);$$

that is,
$$< \frac{u_1}{v_1} (v_1 + v_2 + v_3 + \ldots).$$

Hence, if the v-series is convergent the u-series is also convergent.

Case II. Let $\dfrac{u_2}{u_1} > \dfrac{v_2}{v_1}, \dfrac{u_3}{u_2} > \dfrac{v_3}{v_2} \ldots$; then

$$u_1 + u_2 + u_3 + \ldots$$

$$= u_1 \left(1 + \frac{u_2}{u_1} + \frac{u_3}{u_2} \cdot \frac{u_2}{u_1} + \ldots \right)$$

$$> u_1 \left(1 + \frac{v_2}{v_1} + \frac{v_3}{v_2} \cdot \frac{v_2}{v_1} + \ldots \right);$$

that is,
$$> \frac{u_1}{v_1} (v_1 + v_2 + v_3 + \ldots).$$

Hence, if the v-series is divergent the u-series is also divergent.

*300. We have seen in Art. 287 that a series is convergent or divergent according as the limit of the ratio of the nth term to the *preceding* term is less than 1, or greater than 1. In the remainder of the chapter we shall find it more convenient to use this test in the equivalent form :

A series is convergent or divergent according as the limit of the ratio of the nth term to the *succeeding* term is greater than 1, or less than 1; that is, according as $Lim \dfrac{u_n}{u_{n+1}} > 1$, or < 1.

Similarly the theorem of the preceding article may be enunciated :

The u-series will be convergent when the v-series is convergent provided that $Lim \dfrac{u_n}{u_{n+1}} > Lim \dfrac{v_n}{v_{n+1}}$; and the u-series will be divergent when the v-series is divergent provided that

$$Lim \frac{u_n}{u_{n+1}} < Lim \frac{v_n}{v_{n+1}}.$$

*301. *The series whose general term is u_n is convergent or divergent according as* $Lim \left\{ n \left(\dfrac{u_n}{u_{n+1}} - 1 \right) \right\} > 1$, *or* < 1.

Let us compare the given series with the auxiliary series whose general term v_n is $\dfrac{1}{n^p}$.

When $p > 1$ the auxiliary series is convergent, and in this case the given series is convergent if

$$\frac{u_n}{u_{n+1}} > \frac{(n+1)^p}{n^p}, \text{ or } \left(1 + \frac{1}{n}\right)^p;$$

that is, if

$$\frac{u_n}{u_{n+1}} > 1 + \frac{p}{n} + \frac{p(p-1)}{2n^2} + \dots;$$

$$n\left(\frac{u_n}{u_{n+1}} - 1\right) > p + \frac{p(p-1)}{2n} + \dots;$$

that is, if

$$Lim\left\{n\left(\frac{u_n}{u_{n+1}} - 1\right)\right\} > p.$$

But the auxiliary series is convergent if p is greater than 1 by a finite quantity however small; hence the first part of the proposition is established.

When $p < 1$ the auxiliary series is divergent, and by proceeding as before we may prove the second part of the proposition.

Example. Find whether the series

$$\frac{x}{1} + \frac{1}{2} \cdot \frac{x^3}{3} + \frac{1 \cdot 3}{2 \cdot 4} \cdot \frac{x^5}{5} + \frac{1 \cdot 3 \cdot 5}{2 \cdot 4 \cdot 6} \cdot \frac{x^7}{7} + \dots$$

is convergent or divergent.

Here, $Lim \dfrac{u_n}{u_{n+1}} = \dfrac{1}{x^2}$, hence if $x < 1$ the series is convergent, and if $x > 1$ the series is divergent.

It $x = 1$, $Lim \dfrac{u_n}{u_{n+1}} = 1$. In this case

$$u_n = \frac{1 \cdot 3 \cdot 5 \dots (2n-3)}{2 \cdot 4 \cdot 6 \dots (2n-2)} \cdot \frac{1}{2n-1},$$

and

$$\frac{u_n}{u_{n+1}} = \frac{2n(2n+1)}{(2n-1)(2n-1)};$$

$$\therefore \quad n\left(\frac{u_n}{u_{n+1}} - 1\right) = \frac{n(6n-1)}{(2n-1)^2};$$

$$\therefore \quad Lim\left\{n\left(\frac{u_n}{u_{n+1}} - 1\right)\right\} = \frac{3}{2};$$

hence when $x = 1$ the series is convergent.

*302. *The series whose general term is u_n is convergent or divergent, according as* $Lim\left(n \log \dfrac{u_n}{u_{n+1}}\right) > 1$, *or* < 1.

Let us compare the given series with the series whose general term is $\dfrac{1}{n^p}$.

When $p > 1$ the auxiliary series is convergent, and in this case the given series is convergent if

$$\frac{u_n}{u_{n+1}} > \left(1 + \frac{1}{n}\right)^p;$$ [Art. 300.]

that is, if $\log \dfrac{u_n}{u_{n+1}} > p \log \left(1 + \dfrac{1}{n}\right);$

or   if $\log \dfrac{u_n}{u_{n+1}} > \dfrac{p}{n} - \dfrac{p}{2n^2} + \ldots;$

that is, if $Lim \left(n \log \dfrac{u_n}{u_{n+1}}\right) > p.$

Hence the first part of the proposition is established.

When $p < 1$ we proceed in a similar manner; in this case the auxiliary series is divergent.

Example. Find whether the series

$$x + \frac{2^2 x^2}{2!} + \frac{3^3 x^3}{3!} + \frac{4^4 x^4}{4!} + \frac{5^5 x^5}{5!} + \ldots$$

is convergent or divergent.

Here $\dfrac{u_n}{u_{n+1}} = \dfrac{n^n x^n}{n!} \div \dfrac{(n+1)^{n+1} x^{n+1}}{(n+1)!} = \dfrac{n^n}{(n+1)^n x} = \dfrac{1}{\left(1 + \dfrac{1}{n}\right)^n x};$

$\therefore$ $Lim \dfrac{u_n}{u_{n+1}} = \dfrac{1}{ex}$ [Art. 220 Cor.].

Hence if $x < \dfrac{1}{e}$ the series is convergent, if $x > \dfrac{1}{e}$ the series is divergent.

If $x = \dfrac{1}{e}$, then $\dfrac{u_n}{u_{n+1}} = \dfrac{e}{\left(1 + \dfrac{1}{n}\right)^n};$

$\therefore$ $\log \dfrac{u_n}{u_{n+1}} = \log e - n \log \left(1 + \dfrac{1}{n}\right)$

$$= 1 - n\left(\frac{1}{n} - \frac{1}{2n^2} + \frac{1}{3n^3} - \ldots\right)$$

$$= \frac{1}{2n} - \frac{1}{3n^2} + \ldots;$$

$\therefore$ $n \log \dfrac{u_n}{u_{n+1}} = \dfrac{1}{2} - \dfrac{1}{3n} + \ldots,$

$$\therefore \qquad Lim\left(n\log\frac{u_n}{u_{n+1}}\right)=\frac{1}{2};$$

hence when $x=\dfrac{1}{e}$ the series is divergent.

*303. If $Lim\dfrac{u_n}{u_{n+1}}=1$, and also $Lim\left\{n\left(\dfrac{u_n}{u_{n+1}}-1\right)\right\}=1$, the tests given in Arts. 300, 301 are not applicable.

To discover a further test we shall make use of the auxiliary series whose general term is $\dfrac{1}{n(\log n)^p}$. In order to establish the convergency or divergency of this series we need the theorem proved in the next article.

*304. *If $\phi(n)$ is positive for all positive integral values of n and continually diminishes as n increases, and if a be any positive integer, then the two infinite series.*

$$\phi(1)+\phi(2)+\phi(3)+\dots+\phi(n)+\dots,$$

and $\qquad a\phi(a)+a^2\phi(a^2)+a^3\phi(a^3)+\dots+a^n\phi(a^n)+\dots,$

and both convergent, or both divergent.

In the first series let us consider the terms

$$\phi(a^k+1),\ \phi(a^k+2);\ \phi(a^k+3),\dots\ \phi(a^{k+1}) \qquad \dots(1)$$

biginning with the term which follows $\phi(a^k)$.

The number of these terms is $a^{k+1}-a^k$, or $a^k(a-1)$, and each of them is greater than $\phi(a^{k+1})$; hence their sum is greater than $a^k(a-1)\phi(a^{k+1})$; that is, greater than

$$\frac{a-1}{a}\times a^{k+1}\phi(a^{k+1}).$$

By giving to k in succession the values 0, 1, 2, 3, ...we have

$$\phi(2)+\phi(3)+\phi(4)+\dots+\phi(a)>\frac{a-1}{a}\times a\phi(a);$$

$$\phi(a+1)+\phi(a+2)+\phi(a+3)+\dots+\phi(a^2)>\frac{a-1}{a}\times a^2\phi(a^2);$$

$$\dots\dots\dots\dots\dots\dots\dots\dots\dots\dots\dots\dots\dots$$

therefore, by addition, $S_1-\phi(1)>\dfrac{a-1}{a}S_2,$

where S_1, S_2 denote the sums of the first and second series respective¹y; therefore if the second series is divergent so also is the first.

Again, each term of (1) is less than $\phi(a^k)$. and therefore the sum of the series is less than $(a-1) \times a^k \phi(a^k)$.

By given to k in succession the values $0, 1, 2, 3, \ldots$ we have
$$\phi(2) + \phi(3) + \phi(4) + \ldots + \phi(a) < (a-1) \times \phi(1);$$
$$\phi(a+1) + \phi(a+2) + \phi(a+3) + \ldots + \phi(a^2) < (a-1) \times a\phi(a);$$
$$\ldots\ldots\ldots\ldots\ldots\ldots\ldots\ldots\ldots\ldots\ldots\ldots\ldots\ldots\ldots\ldots$$
therefore, by addition
$$S_1 - \phi(1) < (a-1)\{S_2 + \phi(1)\};$$
hence if the second series is convergent so also is the first.

Note. To obtain the general term of the second series we take $\phi(n)$ the general term of the first series, write a^n instead of n and multiply by a^n.

*305. *The series*
$$1 + \frac{1}{2(\log 2)^p} + \frac{1}{3(\log 3)^p} + \ldots + \frac{1}{n(\log n)^p} +$$
is convergent if $p > 1$, and divergent if $p = 1$, or $p < 1$.

By the preceding article the series will be convergent or divergent for the same values of p as the series whose general term is
$$a^n \times \frac{1}{a^n (\log a^n)^p}, \text{ or } \frac{1}{(n \log a)^p}, \text{ or } \frac{1}{(\log a)^p} \times \frac{1}{n^p}.$$

The constant factor $\dfrac{1}{(\log a)^p}$ is common to every term; therefore the given series will be convergent or divergent for the same values of p as the series whose general term is $\dfrac{1}{n^p}$. Hence the required result follows. [Art. 290.]

*306. *The series whose general term is u_n is convergent or divergent according as $Lim\left[\left\{n\left(\dfrac{u_n}{u_{n+1}} - 1\right) - 1\right\}\log n\right] > 1, \text{ or } < 1.$*

Let us compare the given series with the series
$$1 + \frac{1}{2(\log 2)^p} + \frac{1}{3(\log 3)^p} + \ldots + \frac{1}{n(\log n)^p} + \ldots$$

When $p > 1$ the auxiliary series is convergent, and in this case the given series is convergent by Art. 299, if
$$\frac{u_n}{u_{n+1}} > \frac{(n+1)\{\log(n+1)\}^p}{n(\log n)^p}. \qquad \ldots(1).$$

Not when n is very large,

$$\log (n + 1) = \log n + \log \left(1 + \frac{1}{n} \right) = \log n + \frac{1}{n} \text{, nearly;}$$

Hence the condition (1) becomes

$$\frac{u_n}{u_{n+1}} > \left(1 + \frac{1}{n} \right) \left(1 + \frac{1}{n \log n} \right)^p ;$$

that is,

$$\frac{u_n}{u_{n+1}} > \left(1 + \frac{1}{n} \right) \left(1 + \frac{p}{n \log n} \right);$$

that is,

$$\frac{u_n}{u_{n+1}} > 1 + \frac{1}{n} + \frac{p}{n \log n} ;$$

or

$$n \left(\frac{u_n}{u_{n+1}} - 1 \right) > 1 + \frac{p}{\log n} ;$$

or

$$\left\{ n \left(\frac{u_n}{u_{n+1}} - 1 \right) - 1 \right\} \log n > p.$$

Hence the first part of the proposition is established. The second part may be proved in the manner indicated in Art. 301.

Example. Is the series

$$1 + \frac{2^2}{3^2} + \frac{2^2 \cdot 4^2}{3^2 \cdot 5^2} + \frac{2^2 \cdot 4^2 \cdot 6^2}{3^2 \cdot 5^2 \cdot 7^2} + \dots$$

convergent or divergent ?

Here

$$\frac{u_n}{u_{n+1}} = \frac{(2n + 1)^2}{(2n)^2} = 1 + \frac{1}{n} + \frac{1}{4n^2} \qquad \dots(1)$$

$\therefore$ $\displaystyle \operatorname{Lim} \frac{u_n}{u_{n+1}} = 1$, and we proceed to the next test.

From (1),

$$n \left(\frac{u_n}{u_{n+1}} - 1 \right) = 1 + \frac{1}{4n} \qquad \dots(2)$$

$\therefore$ $\displaystyle \operatorname{Lim} \left\{ n \left(\frac{u_n}{u_{n+1}} - 1 \right) \right\} = 1$, and we pass to the next test.

From (2), $\left\{ n \left(\dfrac{u_n}{u_{n+1}} - 1 \right) - 1 \right\} \log n = \dfrac{\log n}{4n}$;

$\therefore$

$$\operatorname{Lim} \left[\left\{ n \left(\frac{u_n}{u_{n+1}} - 1 \right) - 1 \right\} \log n \right] = 0,$$

since $\displaystyle \operatorname{Lim} \frac{\log n}{n} = 0$ [Art. 295]; hence the given series is divergent.

*307. We have shewn in Art. 183 that the use of divergent series in mathematical reasoning may lead to erroneous results. But even when the infinite series are convergent it is necessary to exercise caution in using them.

For instance, the series

$$1 - x + \frac{x^2}{\sqrt[4]{2}} - \frac{x^3}{\sqrt[4]{3}} + \frac{x^4}{\sqrt[4]{4}} - \frac{x^5}{\sqrt[4]{5}} + \dots$$

is convergent when $x = 1$. [Art. 280.] But if we multiply the series by itself, the coefficient of x^{2n} in the product is

$$\frac{1}{\sqrt[4]{2n}} + \frac{1}{\sqrt[4]{2n-1}} + \frac{1}{\sqrt[4]{2}.\sqrt[4]{2n-2}} + \dots + \frac{1}{\sqrt[4]{r}\,\sqrt[4]{2n-r}} + \dots + \frac{1}{\sqrt[4]{2n}}.$$

Denote this by a_{2n}; then since

$$\frac{1}{\sqrt[4]{r}\,\sqrt[4]{2n-r}} > \frac{1}{\left(\sqrt[4]{n}\right)^2}, \text{ or } \frac{1}{\sqrt{n}},$$

$a_{2n} > \dfrac{2n+1}{\sqrt{n}}$, and is therefore infinite when n is infinite.

If $x = 1$, the product becomes

$$a_0 - a_1 + a_2 - a_3 + \dots + a_{2n} - a_{2n+1} + a_{2n+2} - \dots,$$

and since the terms $a_{2n}, a_{2n+1}, a_{2n+2} \dots$ are infinite, the series has no arithmetical meaning.

This leads us to enquire under what conditions the product of two infinite convergent series is also convergent.

*308.   Let us denote the two infinite series

$$a_0 + a_1 x + a_2 x^2 + a_3 x^3 + \dots a_{2n} x^{2n} + \dots,$$
$$b_0 + b_1 x + b_2 x^2 + b_3 x^3 + \dots + b_{2n} x^{2n} + \dots$$

by A and B respectively.

If we multiply these series together we obtain a result of the form

$$a_0 b_0 + (a_1 b_0 + a_0 b_1)\, x + (a_2 b_0 + a_1 b_1 + a_0 b_2)\, x^2 + \dots$$

Suppose this series to be *continued to infinity* and let us denote it by C; then we have to examine under what conditions C may be regarded as the true arithmetical equivalent of the product AB.

First suppose that all the terms in A and B are positive.

Let A_{2n}, B_{2n}, C_{2n} denote the series formed by taking the first $2n + 1$ terms of A, B, C respectively.

If we multiply together the two series A_{2n}, B_{2n}, the coefficient of each power of x in their product is equal to the coefficient of the like power of x in C as far as the term x^{2n}; but in $A_{2n} B_{2n}$ there are terms containing powers of x higher than x^{2n}, whilst x^{2n} is the highest power of x in C_{2n}; hence

$$A_{2n} B_{2n} > C_{2n}.$$

If we form the product $A_n B_n$ the last term is $a_n b_n x^{2n}$; but C_{2n} includes all the terms in the product and some other terms besides; hence

$$C_{2n} > A_n B_n.$$

Thus C_{2n} is intermediate in value between $A_n B_n$ and $A_{2n} B_{2n}$, whatever be the value of n.

Let A and B be *convergent* series; put

$$A_n = A - X, B_n = B - Y,$$

where X and Y are the remainders after $n + 1$ terms of the series have been taken; then when n is infinite X and Y are both indefinitely small.

∴ $$A_n B_n = (A - X)(B - Y) = AB - BX - AY + XY;$$

therefore the limit of $A_n B_n$ is AB, since A and B are both finite.

Similarly, the limit of $A_{2n} B_{2n}$ is AB.

Therefore C which is the limit of C_{2n} must be equal to AB since it lies between the limits of $A_n B_n$ and $A_{2n} B_{2n}$.

Next suppose the terms in A and B are not all of the same sign.

In this case the inequalities $A_{2n} B_{2n} > C_{2n} > A_n B_n$ are not necessarily true, and we cannot reason as in the former case.

Let us denote the aggregates of the positive terms in the two series by P, P' respectively, and the aggregates of the negative terms by N, N'; so that

$$A = P - N, B = P' - N'.$$

Then if each of the expressions P, P', N, N' represents a convergent series, the equation

$$AB = PP' - NP' - PN' + NN',$$

has a meaning perfectly intelligible, for each of the expressions PP', NP', PN', NN' is a convergent series, by the former part of the proposition; and thus the product of the two series A and B is convergent series.

Hence *the product of two series will be convergent provided that the sum of all the terms of the same sign in each is a convergent series.*

But if each of the expressions P, N, P', N' represents a divergent series (as in the preceding article, where also $P' = P$ and $N' = N$), then all the expressions PP', NP', PN', NN' are divergent series. When this is the case, a careful investigation is necessary in each particular example in order to ascertain whether the product is convergent or not.

EXAMPLES XXI. b.

Find whether the following series are convergent or divergent :

1. $1 + \dfrac{1}{2} \cdot \dfrac{x^2}{4} + \dfrac{1 \cdot 3 \cdot 5}{2 \cdot 4 \cdot 6} \cdot \dfrac{x^4}{8} + \dfrac{1 \cdot 3 \cdot 5 \cdot 7 \cdot 9}{2 \cdot 4 \cdot 6 \cdot 8 \cdot 10} \cdot \dfrac{x^6}{12} + \dots$

2. $1 + \dfrac{3}{7} x + \dfrac{3 \cdot 6}{7 \cdot 10} x^2 + \dfrac{3 \cdot 6 \cdot 9}{7 \cdot 10 \cdot 13} x^3 + \dfrac{3 \cdot 6 \cdot 9 \cdot 12}{7 \cdot 10 \cdot 13 \cdot 16} x^4 + \dots$

3. $x^2 + \dfrac{2^2}{3 \cdot 4} x^4 + \dfrac{2^2 \cdot 4^2}{3 \cdot 4 \cdot 5 \cdot 6} x^6 + \dfrac{2^2 \cdot 4^2 \cdot 6^2}{3 \cdot 4 \cdot 5 \cdot 6 \cdot 7 \cdot 8} x^8 + \dots$

4. $1 + \dfrac{2x}{2!} + \dfrac{3^2 x^2}{3!} + \dfrac{4^3 x^3}{4!} + \dfrac{5^4 x^4}{5!} + \dots$

5. $1 + \dfrac{1}{2} x + \dfrac{2!}{3^2} x^2 + \dfrac{3!}{4^3} x^3 + \dfrac{4!}{5^4} x^4 + \dots$

6. $\dfrac{1^2}{2^2} + \dfrac{1^2 \cdot 3^2}{2^2 \cdot 4^2} x + \dfrac{1^2 \cdot 3^2 \cdot 5^2}{2^2 \cdot 4^2 \cdot 6^2} x^2 + \dots$

7. $1 + \dfrac{a(1-a)}{1^2} + \dfrac{(1+a) a (1-a)(2-a)}{1^2 \cdot 2^2}$

   $\dfrac{(2+a)(1+a) a (1-a)(2-a)(3-a)}{1^2 \cdot 2^2 \cdot 3^2} + \dots$

   a being a proper fraction

8. $\dfrac{a+x}{1} + \dfrac{(a+2x)^2}{2!} + \dfrac{(a+3x)^3}{3!} + \dots$

9. $1 + \dfrac{\alpha \cdot \beta}{1 \cdot \gamma} x + \dfrac{\alpha(\alpha+1)\beta(\beta+1)}{1 \cdot 2 \cdot \gamma(\gamma+1)} x^2$

   $+ \dfrac{\alpha(\alpha+1)(\alpha+2)\beta(\beta+1)(\beta+2)}{1 \cdot 2 \cdot 3 \cdot \gamma(\gamma+1)(\gamma+2)} x^3 + \dots$

10. $x^2 (\log 2)^q + x^3 (\log 3)^q + x^4 (\log 4)^q + \dots$

11. $1 + a + \dfrac{a(a+1)}{1 \cdot 2} + \dfrac{a(a+1)(a+2)}{1 \cdot 2 \cdot 3} + \dots$

12. If $\dfrac{u_n}{u_{n+1}} = \dfrac{n^k + A n^{k-1} + B n^{k-2} + C n^{k-3} + \dots}{n^k + a n^{k-1} + b n^{k-2} + c n^{k-3+\dots}}$, where k is a

    positive integer, shew that the series $u_1 + u_2 + u_3 + \dots$ is
    convergent if $A - a - 1$ is positive, and divergent if $A - a - 1$ is
    negative or zero.

Chapter 22

UNDETERMINED COEFFICIENTS

309. In Art. 230 of the *Elementary Algebra*, it was proved that if any rational integral function of x vanishes when $x = a$, it is divisible by $x - a$. [See also Art. 514. Cor.]

Let
$$p_0 x^n + p_1 x^{n-1} + p_2 x^{n-2} + \dots + p_n$$
be a rational integral function of x of n dimensions, which vanishes when x is equal to each of the unequal quantities
$$a_1, a_2, a_3, \dots a_n.$$

Denote the function by $f(x)$; then since $f(x)$ is divisible by $x - a_1$, we have
$$f(x) = (x - a_1)(p_0 x^{n-1} + \dots),$$
the quotient being of $n - 1$ dimensions.

Similarly, since $f(x)$ is divisible by $x - a_2$, we have
$$p_0 x^{n-1} + \dots = (x - a_2)(p_0 x^{n-2} + \dots),$$
the quotient being of $n - 2$ dimensions; and
$$p_0 x^{n-2} + \dots = (x - a_3)(p_0 x^{n-3} + \dots).$$

....

Proceeding in this way, we shall finally obtain after n divisions
$$f(x) = p_0 (x - a_1)(x - a_2)(x - a_3) \dots (x - a_n).$$

310. *If a rational integral function of n dimensions vanishes for more than n values of the variable, the coefficient of each power of the variable must be zero.*

Let the function be denoted by $f(x)$, where
$$f(x) = p_0 x^n + p_1 x^{n-1} + p_2 x^{n-2} + \dots + p_n;$$
and suppose that $f(x)$ vanishes when x is equal to each of the unequal values $a_1, a_2, a_3, \dots a_n$; then
$$f(x) = p_0 (x - a_1)(x - a_2)(x - a_3) \dots (x - a_n).$$

Let c be another value of x which makes $f(x)$ vanish; then since $f(c) = 0$, we have

$$p_0 (c - a_1) (c - a_2) (c - a_3) \dots (c - a_n) = 0;$$

and therefore $p_0 = 0$, since, by hypothesis, none of the other factors is equal to zero. Hence $f(x)$ reduces to

$$p_1 x^{n-1} + p_2 x^{n-2} + p_3 x^{n-3} + \dots + p_n.$$

By hypothesis this expression vanishes for more than n values of x, and therefore $p_1 = 0$.

In a similar manner we may shew that each of the coefficients $p_2, p_3, \dots p_n$ must be equal to zero.

This result may also be enunciated as follows :

If a rational integral function of n dimensions vanishes for more than n values of the variable, it must vanish for every value of the variable.

Cor. If the *function f (x)* vanishes for more than n values of x, the *equation f (x) = 0* has more than n roots.

Hence also, *if an equation of n dimensions has more than n roots it is an identity.*

Example : Prove that

$$\frac{(x-b)(x-c)}{(a-b)(a-c)} + \frac{(x-c)(x-a)}{(b-c)(b-a)} + \frac{(x-a)(x-b)}{(c-a)(c-b)} = 1.$$

This equation is of *two* dimensions, and it is evidently satisfied by each of the *three* values a, b, c; hence it is an identity.

311. If two rational integral functions of n dimensions are equal for more than n values of the variable, they are equal for every value of the variable.

Suppose that the two functions

$$p_0 x^n + p_1 x^{n-1} + p_2 x^{n-2} + \dots + p_n,$$

$$q_0 x^n + q_1 x^{n-1} + q_2 x^{n-2} + \dots + q_n,$$

are equal for more than n values of x; then the expression

$$(p_0 - q_0) x^n + (p_1 - q_1) x^{n-1} + (p_2 - q_2) x^{n-2} + \dots + (p_n - q_n)$$

vanishes for more than n values of x; and therefore, by the preceding article,

$$p_0 - q_0 = 0, p_1 - q_1 = 0, p_2 - q_2 = 0, \dots p_n - q_n = 0;$$

that is,

$$p_0 = q_0, p_1 = q_1, p_2 = q_2, \dots p_n = q_n.$$

Hence the two expressions are *identical*, and therefore are equal for every value of the variable. Thus *if two rational integral functions are identically equal, we may equate the coefficients of the like powers of the variable.*

This is the principle we assumed in the *Elementary Algebra*, Art. 227.

Cor. This proposition still holds if one of the functions is of lower dimensions than the other. For instance, if

$$p_0 x^n + p_1 x^{n-1} + p_2 x^{n-2} + p_3 x^{n-3} + \ldots + p_n$$
$$= q_2 x^{n-2} + q_3 x^{n-3} + \ldots + q_n,$$

we have only to suppose that in the above investigation $q_0 = 0$, $q_1 = 0$, and then we obtain

$$p_0 = 0, \; p_1 = 0, \; p_2 = q_2, \; p_3 = q_3, \; \ldots \; p_n = q_n.$$

312. The theorem of the preceding article is usually referred to as the *Principle of Undetermined Coefficients.* The application of this principle is illustrated in the following examples.

Example 1. Find the sum of the series
$$1 \cdot 2 + 2 \cdot 3 + 3 \cdot 4 + \ldots + n \,(n+1).$$

Assume that
$$1 \cdot 2 + 2 \cdot 3 + 3 \cdot 4 + \ldots + n \,(n+1) = A + Bn + Cn^2 + Dn^3 + En^4 + \ldots,$$
where $A, B, C, D, E, \ldots$ are quantities independent of n, whose values have to be determined.

Change n into $n+1$; then
$$1 \cdot 2 + 2 \cdot 3 + \ldots + n \,(n+1) + (n+1)\,(n+2)$$
$$= A + B\,(n+1) + C\,(n+1)^2 + D\,(n+1)^3 + E\,(n+1)^4 + \ldots$$

By subtraction,
$$(n+1)\,(n+2) = B + C\,(2n+1) + D\,(3n^2 + 3n + 1)$$
$$+ E\,(4n^3 + 6n^2 + 4n + 1)$$

This equation being true for all integral values of n, the coefficients of the respective powers of n on each side must be equal; thus E and all succeeding coefficients must be equal to zero, and
$$3D = 1; \; 3D + 2C = 3; \; D + C + B = 2;$$

whence
$$D = \frac{1}{3}, \; C = 1, \; B = \frac{2}{3}.$$

Hence the sum $= A + \dfrac{2n}{3} + n^2 + \dfrac{1}{3} n^3$.

To find A, put $n = 1$; the series then reduces to its first term, and
$$2 = A + 2, \text{ or } A = 0.$$

Hence $1 \cdot 2 + 2 \cdot 3 + 3 \cdot 4 + \ldots + n\,(n+1) = \dfrac{1}{3} n\,(n+1)\,(n+2)$.

Note : It will be seen from this example that when the nth term is a rational integral function of n, it is sufficient to assume for the sum a function of n which is of one dimension higher than the nth term of the series.

Example 2. Find the conditions that $x^3 + px^2 + qx + r$ may be divisible by

$$x^2 + ax + b.$$

Assume $x^3 + px^2 + qx + r = (x + k)(x^2 + ax + b).$

Equating the coefficients of the like powers of x, we have

$$k + a = p,\ ak + b = q,\ kb = r.$$

From the last equation $k = r/b$; hence by substitution we obtain

$$\frac{r}{b} + a = p, \text{ and } \frac{ar}{b} + b = q;$$

that is, $r = b(p - a),$ and $ar = b(q - b);$

which are the conditions required.

EXAMPLES XXII. a.

Find by the method of Undetermined Coefficients the sum of

1. $1^2 + 3^2 + 5^2 + 7^2 + \ldots$ to n terms.

2. $1 \cdot 2 \cdot 3 + 2 \cdot 3 \cdot 4 + 3 \cdot 4 \cdot 5 + \ldots$ to n terms.

3. $1 \cdot 2^2 + 2 \cdot 3^2 + 3\ 4^2 + 4 \cdot 5^2 + \ldots$ to n terms.

4. $1^3 + 3^3 + 5^3 + 7^3 + \ldots$ to n terms.

5. $1^4 + 2^4 + 3^4 + 4^4 + \ldots$ to n terms.

6.   Find the condition that $x^3 - 3px + 2q$ may be divisible by a factor of the form $x^2 + 2ax + a^2$.

7.   Find the conditions that $ax^3 + bx^2 + cx + d$ may be a perfect cube.

8.   Find the conditions that $a^2x^4 + bx^3 + cx^2 + dx + f^2$ may be a perfect square.

9.   Prove that $ax^2 + 2bxy + cy^2 + 2dx + 2ey + f$ is a perfect square, if $b^2 = ac,\ d^2 = af,\ e^2 = cf.$

10.   If $ax^3 + bx^2 + cx + d$ is divisible by $x^2 + h^2$, prove that $ad = bc$.

11.   If $x^5 - 5qx + 4r$ is divisible by $(x - c)^2$, shew that $q^5 = r^4$.

12.   Prove the identities :

(1) $\dfrac{a^2(x - b)(x - c)}{(a - b)(a - c)} + \dfrac{b^2(x - c)(x - a)}{(b - c)(b - a)} + \dfrac{c^2(x - a)(x - b)}{(c - a)(c - b)} = x^2.$

(2) $\dfrac{(x-b)(x-c)(x-d)}{(a-b)(a-c)(a-d)} + \dfrac{(x-c)(x-d)(x-a)}{(b-c)(b-d)(b-a)}$

$\qquad + \dfrac{(x-d)(x-a)(x-b)}{(c-d)(c-a)(c-b)} + \dfrac{(x-a)(x-b)(x-c)}{(d-a)(d-b)(d-c)} = 1.$

13. Find the condition that

$$ax^2 + 2hxy + by^2 + 2gx + 2fy + c$$

may be the product of two factors of the form

$$px + qy + r, \; p'x + q'y + r'$$

14. If $\xi = lx + my + nz$, $\eta = nx + ly + mz$, $\zeta = mx + ny + lz$, and if the same equations are true for all values of x, y, z when ξ, η, ζ are interchanged with x, y, z respectively, shew that

$$l^2 + 2mn = 1, \; m^2 + 2ln = 0, \; n^2 + 2lm = 0.$$

15. Shew that the sum of the products $n - r$ together of the n quantities $a, a^2, a^3, \ldots a^n$ is

$$\dfrac{(a^{r+1} - 1)(a^{r+2} - 1) \ldots (a^n - 1)}{(a - 1)(a^2 - 1) \ldots (a^{n-r} - 1)} \; a^{\frac{1}{2}(n-r)(n-r+1)}.$$

313. *If the infinite series $a_0 + a_1x + a_2x^2 + a_3x^3 + \ldots$ is equal to zero for every finite value of x for which the series is convergent, then each coefficient must be equal to zero identically.*

Let the series be denoted by S, and let S_1 stand for the expression $a_1 + a_2x + a_3x^2 + \ldots$; then $S = a_0 + xS_1$, and therefore, by hypothesis, $a_0 + xS_1 = 0$ for all finite values of x. But since S is convergent, S_1 cannot exceed some finite limit; therefore by taking x small enough xS_1 may be made as small as we please. In this case the limit of S is a_0; but S is *always* zero, therefore a_0 must be equal to zero identically.

Removing the term a_0, we have $xS_1 = 0$ for all finite values of x; that is, $a_1 + a_2x + a_3x^2 + \ldots$ vanishes for all finite values of x.

Similarly, we may prove in succession that each of the coefficients $a_1, a_2, a_3, \ldots$ is equal to zero identically.

314. *If two infinite series are equal to one another for every finite value of the variable for which both series are convergent, the coefficients of like powers of the variable in the two series are equal.*

Suppose that the two series are denoted by

$$a_0 + a_1x + a_2x^2 + a_3x^3 + \ldots$$

and

$$A_0 + A_1x + A_2x^2 + A_3x^3 + \ldots;$$

then the expression

$$a_0 - A_0 + (a_1 - A_1)\, x + (a_2 - A_2)\, x^2 + (a_3 - A_3)\, x^3 + \ldots$$

vanishes for all values of x within the assigned limits; therefore by the last article

$$a_0 - A_0 = 0, \quad a_1 - A_1 = 0, \quad a_2 - A_2 = 0, \quad a_3 - A_3 = 0, \ldots$$

that is, $a_0 = A_0,\ a_1 = A_1,\ a_2 = A_2,\ a_3 = A_3, \ldots;$

which proves the proposition.

Example 1. Expand $\dfrac{2 + x^2}{1 + x - x^2}$ in a series of ascending powers of x as far as the term involving x^5.

Let
$$\frac{2 + x^2}{1 + x - x^2} = a_0 + a_1 x + a_2 x^2 + a_3 x^3 + \ldots,$$

where $a_0, a_1, a_2, a_3, \ldots$ are constants whose values are to be determined; then

$$2 + x^2 = (1 + x - x^2)\,(a_0 + a_1 x + a_2 x^2 + a_3 x^3 + \ldots).$$

In this equation we may equate the coefficients of like powers of x on each side. On the right-hand side the coefficient of x^n is $a_n + a_{n-1} - a_{n-2}$, and therefore, since x^2 is the highest power of x on the left, for all values of $n > 2$ we have

$$a_n + a_{n-1} - a_{n-2} = 0;$$

this will suffice to find the successive coefficients after the first three have been obtained. To determine these we have the equations

$$a_0 = 2, \quad a_1 + a_0 = 0, \quad a_2 + a_1 - a_0 = 1;$$

whence
$$a_0 = 2, \quad a_1 = -2, \quad a_2 = 5.$$

Also
$$a_3 + a_2 - a_1 = 0, \text{ whence } a_3 = -7;$$
$$a_4 + a_3 - a_2 = 0, \text{ whence } a_4 = 12;$$

and
$$a_5 + a_4 - a_3 = 0, \text{ whence } a_5 = -19;$$

thus
$$\frac{2 + x^n}{1 + x - x^2} = 2 - 2x + 5x^2 - 7x^3 + 12x^4 - 19x^5 + \ldots$$

Example 2. Prove that if n and r are positive integers

$$n^r - n\,(n-1)^r + \frac{n\,(n-1)}{2!}\,(n-2)^r - \frac{n\,(n-1)\,(n-2)}{3!}\,(n-3)^r + \ldots$$

is equal to 0 if r be less than n, and to $n!$ if $r = n$.

We have $(e^x - 1)^n = \left(x + \dfrac{x^2}{2!} + \dfrac{x^3}{3!} + \dfrac{x^4}{4!} + \ldots \right)^n$

$$= x^n + \text{terms containing higher powers of } x \qquad \ldots(1)$$

Again, by the Binomial Theorem,

$$(e^x - 1)^n = e^{nx} - n e^{(n-1)x} + \frac{n\,(n-1)}{1\cdot2}\, e^{(n-2)x} - \ldots, \qquad \ldots(2)$$

By expanding each of the terms e^{nx}, $e^{(n-1)x}$, we find that the coefficient of x^r in (2) is

$$\frac{n^r}{r!} - n \cdot \frac{(n-1)^r}{r!} + \frac{n(n-1)}{2!} \cdot \frac{(n-2)^r}{r!} - \frac{n(n-1)(n-2)}{3!} \cdot \frac{(n-3)^r}{r!} + \dots$$

and by equating the coefficients of x^r in (1) and (2) the result follows.

Example 3. If $y = ax + bx^2 + cx^3 + \dots$

express x in ascending powers of y as far as the term involving y^3.

Assume $\quad x = py + qy^2 + ry^3 + \dots,$

and substitute in the given series; thus

$$y = a(py + qy^2 + ry^3 + \dots) + b(py + qy^2 + \dots)^2 + c(py + qy^2 + \dots)^3 + \dots$$

Equating coefficients of like powers of y, we have

$$ap = 1; \text{ whence } p = \frac{1}{a}.$$

$$aq + bp^2 = 0; \text{ whence } q = -\frac{b}{a^3}.$$

$$ar + 2bpq + cp^3 = 0; \text{ whence } r = \frac{2b^2}{a^5} - \frac{c}{a^4}.$$

Thus $\quad x = \dfrac{y}{a} - \dfrac{by^2}{a^3} + \dfrac{(2b^2 - ac)y^3}{a^5} + \dots$

This is an example of *Reversion of Series.*

Cor. If the series for y be given in the form

$$y = k + ax + bx^2 + cx^3 + \dots$$

put $\qquad y - k = z;$

then $\qquad z = ax + bx^2 + cx^3 + \dots;$

from which x may be expanded in ascending powers of z, that is of $y - k$.

EXAMPLES XXII. b.

Expand the following expressions in ascending powers of x as far as x^3.

1. $\dfrac{1 + 2x}{1 - x - x^2}.$ 2. $\dfrac{1 - 8x}{1 - x - 6x^2}.$ 3. $\dfrac{1 + x}{2 + x + x^2}.$

4. $\dfrac{3 + x}{2 - x - x^2}.$ 5. $\dfrac{1}{1 + ax - ax^2 - x^3}.$

6. Find a and b so that the nth term in the expansion of $\dfrac{a + bx}{(1 - x)^2}$ may be $(3n - 2)x^{n-1}$.

7. Find a, b, c so that the coefficient of x^n in the expansion of $\dfrac{a + bx + cx^2}{(1 - x)^3}$ may be $n^2 + 1$.

8. If $y^2 + 2y = x(y + 1)$, shew that one value of y is $\dfrac{1}{2} x + \dfrac{1}{8} x^2 - \dfrac{1}{128} x^4 + \ldots$

9. If $cx^3 + ax - y = 0$, shew that one value of x is

$$\frac{y}{a} - \frac{cy^3}{a^4} + \frac{3c^2 y^5}{a^7} - \frac{12c^3 y^7}{a^{10}} \ldots$$

Hence shew that $x = 0.00999999$ is an approximate solution of the equation $x^3 + 100x - 1 = 0$. To how many places of decimals is the result correct?

10. In the expansion of $(1 + x)(1 + ax)(1 + a^2 x)(1 + a^3 x) \ldots$, the number of factors being infinite, and $a < 1$, shew that the coefficient of x^r is

$$\frac{1}{(1 - a)(1 - a^2)(1 - a^3) \ldots (1 - a^r)} a^{\frac{1}{2} r(r-1)}.$$

11. When $a < 1$, find the coefficient of x^n in the expansion of

$$\frac{1}{(1 - ax)(1 - a^2 x)(1 - a^3 x) \ldots \text{ to inf.}}$$

12. If n is a positive integer, shew that

(1) $n^{n+1} - n(n-1)^{n+1} + \dfrac{n(n-1)}{2!} (n-2)^{n+1} - \ldots = \dfrac{1}{2} n(n+1)!$;

(2) $n^n - (n+1)(n-1)^n + \dfrac{(n+1)n}{2!} (n-2)^n - \ldots = 1$;

the series in each case being extended to n terms; and

(3) $1^n - n 2^n + \dfrac{n(n-1)}{1 \cdot 2} 3^n - \ldots = (-1)^n n!$;

(4) $(n+p)^n - n(n+p-1)^n + \dfrac{n(n-1)}{2!} (n+p-2)^n - \ldots = n!$;

the series in the last two cases being extended to $n + 1$ terms.

Chapter 23

PARTIAL FRACTIONS

315. In elementary Algebra, a group of fractions connected by the signs of addition and subtraction is reduced to a more simple form by being collected into one single fraction whose denominator is the lowest common denominator of the given fractions. But the converse process of separating a fraction into a group of simpler, or *partial*, fractions is often required. For example, if we wish to expand $\dfrac{3-5x}{1-4x+3x^2}$ in a series of ascending powers of x, we might use the method of Art. 314, Ex. 1, and so obtain as many terms as we please. But if we wish to find the general term of the series this method is inapplicable, and it is simpler to express the given fraction in the equivalent form $\dfrac{1}{1-x}+\dfrac{2}{1-3x}$. Each of the expressions $(1-x)^{-1}$ and $(1-3x)^{-1}$ can now be expanded by the Binomial Theorem, and the general term obtained.

316. In the present chapter we shall give some examples illustrating the decomposition of a rational fraction into partial fractions. For a fuller discussion of the subject the reader is referred to Serret's *Cours d'Algebre Superieure*, or to treatises on the Integral Calculus. In these works it is proved that any rational fraction may be resolved into a series of partial fractions; and that to any linear factor $x-a$ in the denominator there corresponds a partial fraction of the form $\dfrac{A}{x-a}$; to any linear factor $x-b$ occurring *twice* in the denominator there correspond *two* partial fractions, $\dfrac{B_1}{x-b}$ and $\dfrac{B_3}{(x-b)^3}$. If $x-b$ occurs *three* times, there is an additional fraction $\dfrac{B_2}{(x-b)^2}$; and so on. To any quadratic factor x^2+px+q there corresponds a partial fraction of the form $\dfrac{Px+Q}{x^2+px+q}$; if the factor x^2+px+q occurs twice, there is a second partial fraction $\dfrac{P_1x+Q_1}{(x^2+px+q)^2}$; and so on.

Here the quantities $A_1, B_1, B_2, B_3, \ldots P, Q, P_1, Q_1$ are all independent of x.

We shall make use of these results in the examples that follow.

Example 1. Separate $\dfrac{5x - 11}{2x^2 + x - 6}$ into partial fractions.

Since the denominator $2x^2 + x - 6 = (x + 2)(2x - 3)$, we assume

$$\frac{5x - 11}{2x^2 + x - 6} = \frac{A}{x + 2} + \frac{B}{2x - 3},$$

where A and B are quantities independent of x whose values have to be determined.

Clearing of fractions,

$$5x - 11 = A(2x - 3) + B(x + 2).$$

Since this equation is identically true, we may equate coefficients of like powers of x; thus

$$2A + B = 5, \; -3A + 2B = -11;$$

whence

$$A = 3, B = -1.$$

$\therefore \qquad \dfrac{5x - 11}{2x^2 + x - 6} = \dfrac{3}{x + 2} - \dfrac{1}{2x - 3}.$

Example 2. Resolve $\dfrac{mx + n}{(x - a)(x + b)}$ into partial fractions.

Assume

$$\frac{mx + n}{(x - a)(x + b)} = \frac{A}{x - a} + \frac{B}{x + b}.$$

$\therefore \qquad mx + n = A(x + b) + B(x - a). \qquad \ldots(1)$

We might now equate coefficients and find the values of A and B, but it is simpler to proceed in the following manner.

Since A and B are independent of x, we may give to x any value we please.

In (1) put $x - a = 0$, or $x = a$; then

$$A = \frac{ma + n}{a + b};$$

putting $x + b = 0$, or $x = -b$, $B = \dfrac{mb - n}{a + b}$.

$\therefore \qquad \dfrac{mx + n}{(x - a)(x + b)} = \dfrac{1}{a + b}\left(\dfrac{ma + n}{x - a} + \dfrac{mb - n}{x + b}\right).$

Example 3. Resolve $\dfrac{23x - 11x^2}{(2x - 1)(9 - x^2)}$ into partial fractions.

Assume $\dfrac{23x - 11x^2}{(2x - 1)(3 + x)(3 - x)} = \dfrac{A}{2x - 1} + \dfrac{B}{3 + x} + \dfrac{C}{3 - x};$ $\qquad \ldots(1)$

$\therefore \quad 23x - 11x^2 = A(3 + x)(3 - x) + B(2x - 1)(3 - x) + C(2x - 1)(3 + x).$

By putting in succession $2x - 1 = 0, 3 + x = 0, 3 - x = 0$, we find that

$A = 1, B = 4, C = -1.$

$$\therefore \qquad \frac{23x - 11x^2}{(2x - 1)(9 - x^2)} = \frac{1}{2x - 1} + \frac{4}{3 + x} - \frac{1}{3 - x}.$$

Example 4. Resolve $\dfrac{3x^2 + x - 2}{(x - 2)^2 (1 - 2x)}$ into partial fractions.

Assume $\qquad \dfrac{3x^2 + x - 2}{(x - 2)^2 (1 - 2x)} = \dfrac{A}{1 - 2x} + \dfrac{B}{x - 2} + \dfrac{C}{(x - 2)^2}$;

$$\therefore \qquad 3x^2 + x - 2 = A (x - 2)^2 + B (1 - 2x)(x - 2) + C (1 - 2x).$$

Let $1 - 2x = 0$, then $A = -\dfrac{1}{3}$;

let $x - 2 = 0$, then $C = -4$.

To find B, equate the coefficients of x^2; thus

$$3 = A - 2B; \text{ whence } B = -\frac{5}{3}.$$

$$\therefore \qquad \frac{3x^2 + x - 2}{(x - 2)^2 (1 - 2x)} = -\frac{1}{3(1 - 2x)} - \frac{5}{3(x - 2)} - \frac{4}{(x - 2)^2}.$$

Example 5. Resolve $\dfrac{42 - 19x}{(x^2 + 1)(x - 4)}$ into partial fractions.

Assume $\qquad \dfrac{42 - 19x}{(x^2 + 1)(x - 4)} = \dfrac{Ax + B}{x^2 + 1} + \dfrac{C}{x - 4}$;

$$\therefore \qquad 42 - 19x = (Ax + B)(x - 4) + C (x^2 + 1)..$$

Let $x = 4$, then $C = -2$;

equating coefficients of x^2, $\qquad 0 = A + C$, and $A = 2$;

equating the absolute terms, $\qquad 42 = -4B + C$, and $B = -11$,

$$\therefore \qquad \frac{42 - 19x}{(x^2 + 1)(x - 4)} = \frac{2x - 11}{x^2 + 1} - \frac{2}{x - 4}.$$

317. The artifice employed in the following example will sometimes be found useful.

Example : Resolve $\dfrac{9x^3 - 24x^2 + 48x}{(x - 2)^4 (x + 1)}$ into partial fractions.

Assume $\qquad \dfrac{9x^3 - 24x^2 + 48x}{(x - 2)^4 (x + 1)} = \dfrac{A}{x + 1} + \dfrac{f(x)}{(x - 2)^4}$,

where A is some constant, and $f(x)$ a function of x whose value remains to be determined.

$$\therefore \qquad 9x^3 - 24x^2 + 48x = A (x - 2)^4 + (x + 1) f(x).$$

Let $x = -1$, then $A = -1$.

Substituting for A and transposing,

$$(x+1)f(x) = (x-2)^4 + 9x^3 - 24x^2 + 48x = x^4 + x^3 + 16x + 16;$$

$$\therefore \qquad f(x) = x^3 + 16.$$

To determine the partial fractions corresponding to $\dfrac{x^3 + 16}{(x-2)^4}$, put $x - 2 = z$;

then

$$\frac{x^3 + 16}{(x-2)^4} = \frac{(z+2)^3 + 16}{z^4} = \frac{z^3 + 6z^2 + 12z + 24}{z^4}$$

$$= \frac{1}{z} + \frac{6}{z^2} + \frac{12}{z^3} + \frac{24}{z^4}$$

$$= \frac{1}{x-2} + \frac{6}{(x-2)^2} + \frac{12}{(x-2)^3} + \frac{24}{(x-2)^4}.$$

$$\therefore \quad \frac{9x^3 - 24x^2 + 48x}{(x-2)^4(x+1)} = -\frac{1}{x+1} + \frac{1}{x-2} + \frac{6}{(x-2)^2} + \frac{12}{(x-2)^3} + \frac{24}{(x-2)^4}.$$

318. In all the preceding examples the numerator has been of lower dimensions than the denominator; if this is not the case, we divide the numerator by the denominator until a remainder is obtained which is of lower dimensions than the denominator.

Example: Resolve $\dfrac{6x^3 + 5x^2 - 7}{3x^2 - 2x - 1}$ into partial fractions.

By division,

$$\frac{6x^3 + 5x^2 - 7}{3x^2 - 2x - 1} = 2x + 3 + \frac{8x - 4}{3x^2 - 2x - 1};$$

and

$$\frac{8x - 4}{3x^2 - 2x - 1} = \frac{5}{3x + 1} + \frac{1}{x - 1};$$

$$\therefore \quad \frac{6x^3 + 5x^2 - 7}{3x^2 - 2x - 1} = 2x + 3 + \frac{5}{3x + 1} + \frac{1}{x - 1}.$$

319. We shall now explain how resolution into partial fractions may be used to facilitate the expansion of a rational fraction in ascending powers of x.

Example 1. Find the general term of $\dfrac{3x^2 + x - 2}{(x-2)^2(1-2x)}$ when expanded in a series of ascending powers of x.

By Ex. 4, Art. 316, we have

$$\frac{3x^2 + x - 2}{(x-2)^2(1-2x)} = -\frac{1}{3(1-2x)} - \frac{5}{3(x-2)} - \frac{4}{(x-2)^2}$$

$$= -\frac{1}{3(1-2x)} + \frac{5}{3(2-x)} - \frac{4}{(2-x)^2}$$

$$= -\frac{1}{3}(1-2x)^{-1} + \frac{5}{6}\left(1-\frac{x}{2}\right)^{-1} - \left(1-\frac{x}{2}\right)^{-2}.$$

Hence the general term of the expansion is

$$\left(-\frac{2^r}{3} + \frac{5}{6}\cdot\frac{1}{2^r} - \frac{r+1}{2^r}\right)x^r.$$

Example 2. Expand $\dfrac{7+x}{(1+x)(1+x^2)}$ in ascending powers of x and find the general term.

Assume $\qquad \dfrac{7+x}{(1+x)(1+x^2)} = \dfrac{A}{1+x} + \dfrac{Bx+C}{1+x^2}$;

$\therefore \qquad 7+x = A(1+x^2) + (Bx+C)(1+x).$

Let $\quad 1+x = 0$, then $\quad A = 3$;

equating the absolute terms, $\quad 7 = A + C$, whence $C = 4$;

equating the coefficients of x^2, $\quad 0 = A + B$, whence $B = -3$.

$\therefore \qquad \dfrac{7+x}{(1+x)(1+x^2)} = \dfrac{3}{1+x} + \dfrac{4-3x}{1+x^2}$

$$= 3(1+x)^{-1} + (4-3x)(1+x^2)^{-1}$$

$$= 3\{1 - x + x^2 - \dots + (-1)^p x^p + \dots\}$$

$$+ (4-3x)\{1 - x^2 + x^4 - \dots + (-1)^p x^{2p} + \dots\}.$$

To find the coefficient of x^r:

(1) If r is even, the coefficient of x^r in the second series is $4(-1)^{\frac{r}{2}}$; therefore in the expansion the coefficient of x^r is $3 + 4(-1)^{\frac{r}{2}}$.

(2) If r is odd, the coefficient of x^r in the second series is $-3(-1)^{\frac{r-1}{2}}$, and the required coefficient is $3(-1)^{\frac{r+1}{2}} - 3$.

EXAMPLES XXIII

Resolve into partial fractions :

1. $\dfrac{7x-1}{1-5x+6x^2}$.

2. $\dfrac{46+13x}{12x^2-11x-15}$.

3. $\dfrac{1+3x+2x^2}{(1-2x)(1-x^2)}$.

4. $\dfrac{x^2-10x+13}{(x-1)(x^2-5x+6)}$.

5. $\dfrac{2x^3 + x^2 - x - 3}{x\,(x-1)\,(2x+3)}$.

6. $\dfrac{9}{(x-1)\,(x+2)^2}$.

7. $\dfrac{x^4 - 3x^3 - 3x^2 + 10}{(x+1)^2\,(x-3)}$.

8. $\dfrac{26x^2 + 208x}{(x^2+1)\,(x+5)}$.

9. $\dfrac{2x^2 - 11x + 5}{(x-3)\,(x^2+2x-5)}$.

10. $\dfrac{3x^3 - 8x^2 + 10}{(x-1)^4}$.

11. $\dfrac{5x^3 + 6x^2 + 5x}{(x^2-1)\,(x+1)^3}$.

Find the general term of the following expressions when expanded in ascending powers of x.

12. $\dfrac{1 + 3x}{1 + 11x + 28x^2}$.

13. $\dfrac{5x + 6}{(2+x)\,(1-x)}$.

14. $\dfrac{x^2 + 7x + 3}{x^2 + 7x + 10}$.

15. $\dfrac{2x - 4}{(1-x^2)\,(1-2x)}$.

16. $\dfrac{4 + 3x + 2x^2}{(1-x)\,(1+x-2x^2)}$.

17. $\dfrac{3 + 2x - x^2}{(1+x)\,(1-4x)^2}$.

18. $\dfrac{4 + 7x}{(2+3x)\,(1+x)^2}$.

19. $\dfrac{2x + 1}{(x-1)\,(x^2+1)}$.

20. $\dfrac{1 - x + 2x^2}{(1-x)^3}$.

21. $\dfrac{1}{(1-ax)\,(1-bx)\,(1-cx)}$.

22. $\dfrac{3 - 2x^2}{(2 - 3x + x^2)^2}$.

23. Find the sum of n terms of the series

(1) $\dfrac{1}{(1+x)\,(1+x^2)} + \dfrac{x}{(1+x^2)\,(1+x^3)} + \dfrac{x^2}{(1+x^3)\,(1+x^4)} + \dots$

(2) $\dfrac{x\,(1-ax)}{(1+x)\,(1+ax)\,(1+a^2x)} + \dfrac{ax\,(1-a^2x)}{(1+ax)\,(1+a^2x)\,(1+a^3x)} + \dots$

24. When $x < 1$, find the sum of the infinite series

$$\dfrac{1}{(1-x)\,(1-x^3)} + \dfrac{x^2}{(1-x^3)\,(1-x^5)} + \dfrac{x^4}{(1-x^5)\,(1-x^7)} + \dots$$

25. Sum to n terms the series whose p^{th} term is

$$\frac{x^p\,(1 + x^{p+1})}{(1 - x^p)\,(1 - x^{p+1})\,(1 - x^{p+2})}:$$

26. Prove that the sum of the homogeneous products of n dimensions which can be formed of the letters a, b, c and their powers is

$$\frac{a^{n+2}\,(b-c) + b^{n+2}\,(c-a) + c^{n+2}\,(a-b)}{a^2\,(b-c) + b^2\,(c-a) + c^2\,(a-b)}.$$

Chapter 24

RECURRING SERIES

320. A series $u_0 + u_1 + u_2 + u_3 + \ldots$,

in which from and after a certain term each term is equal to the sum of a fixed number of the preceding terms multiplied respectively by certain constants is called a **recurring series**.

321. In the series

$$1 + 2x + 3x^2 + 4x^3 + 5x^4 + \ldots,$$

each term after the second is equal to the sum of the two preceding terms multiplied respectively by the *constants* $2x$, and $-x^2$; these quantities being called constants because they are the same for all values of n. Thus

$$5x^4 = 2x.\, 4x^3 + (-x^2).\, 3x^2;$$

that is,
$$u_4 = 2xu_3 - x^2u_2\,;$$

and generally when n is greater than 1, each term is connected with the two that immediately precede it by the equation

$$u_n = 2xu_{n-1} - x^2 u_{n-2},$$

or
$$u_n - 2xu_{n-1} + x^2 u_{n-2} = 0.$$

In this equation the coefficients of u_n, u_{n-1}, and u_{n-2}, taken with their proper signs, form what is called the **scale of relation**.

Thus the series
$$1 + 2x + 3x^2 + 4x^3 + 5x^4 + \ldots$$
is a recurring series in which the scale of relation is
$$1 - 2x + x^2.$$

322. If the scale of relation of a recurring series is given, any term can be found when a sufficient number of the preceding terms are known. As the method of procedure is the same however many terms the scale of relation may consist of, the following illustration will be sufficient.

If
$$1 - px - qx^2 - rx^3$$
is the scale of relation of the series
$$a_0 + a_1x + a_2x^2 + a_3x^3 + \ldots$$

we have

$$a_n x^n = px \cdot a_{n-1} x^{n-1} + qx^2 \cdot a_{n-2} x^{n-2} + rx^3 \cdot a_{n-3} x^{n-3},$$

or
$$a_n = pa_{n-1} + qa_{n-2} + ra_{n-3};$$

thus any coefficient can be found when the coefficients of the three preceding terms are known.

323. Conversely, if a sufficient number of the terms of a series be given, the scale of relation may be found.

Example : Find the scale of relation of the recurring series

$$2 + 5x + 13x^2 + 35x^3 + \ldots$$

Let the scale of relation be $1 - px - qx^2$; then to obtain p and q we have the equations

$$13 - 5p - 2q = 0, \text{ and } 35 - 13p - 5q = 0;$$

whence $p = 5$, and $q = -6$, thus the scale of relation is

$$1 - 5x + 6x^2.$$

324. If the scale of relation consists of 3 terms it involves 2 constants, p and q; and we must have 2 equations to determine p and q. To obtain the first of these we must know at least 3 terms of the series, and to obtain the second we must have one more term given. Thus to obtain a scale of relation involving two constants we must have at least 4 terms given.

If the scale of relation be $1 - px - qx^2 - rx^3$, to find the 3 constants we must have 3 equations. To obtain the first of these we must know at least 4 terms of the series, and to obtain the other two we must have two more terms given; hence to find a scale of relation involving 3 constants, at least 6 terms of the series must be given.

Generally, to find a scale of relation involving m constants, we must know at least $2m$ consecutive terms.

Conversely, if $2m$ consecutive terms are given, we may assume for the scale of relation

$$1 - p_1 x - p_2 x^2 - p_3 x^3 - \ldots - p_m x^m.$$

325. *To find the sum of n terms of a recurring series.*

The method of finding the sum is the same whatever be the scale of relation; for simplicity we shall suppose it to contain only two constants.

Let the series be

$$a_0 + a_1 x + a_2 x^2 + a_3 x^3 + \ldots \qquad \ldots (1)$$

and let the sum be S; let the scale of relation be $1 - px - qx^2$; so that for every value of n greater than 1, we have

$$a_n - pa_{n-1} - qa_{n-2} = 0.$$

Now $S = a_0 + a_1 x + a_2 x^2 + \ldots + a_{n-1} x^{n-1},$

$-px \, S = -pa_0 x - pa_1 x^2 - \ldots - pa_{n-2} x^{n-1} - pa_{n-1} x^n,$

$-qx^2 S = \qquad\quad - qa_0 x^2 - \ldots - qa_{n-3} x^{n-1} - qa_{n-2} x^n - qa_{n-1} x^{n+1},$

$\therefore \ (1 - px - qx^2) \, S = a_0 + (a_1 - pa_0) \, x - (pa_{n-1} + qa_{n-2}) \, x^n - qa_{n-1} x^{n+1},$

for the coefficient of every other power of x is zero in consequence of the relation

$$a_n - pa_{n-1} - qa_{n-2} = 0.$$

$\therefore \qquad S = \dfrac{a_0 + (a_1 - pa_0) \, x}{1 - px - qx^2} - \dfrac{(pa_{n-1} + qa_{n-2}) \, x^n + qa_{n-1} x^{n+1}}{1 - px - qx^2}.$

Thus the sum of a recurring series is a fraction whose denominator is the scale of relation.

326.   If the second fraction in the result of the last article decreases indefinitely as n increases indefinitely, the sum of an infinite number of terms reduces to $\dfrac{a_0 + (a_1 - pa_0) \, x}{1 - px - qx^2}.$

If we develop this fraction in ascending powers of x as explained in Art. 314, we shall obtain as many terms of the original series as we please; for this reason the expression

$$\frac{a_0 + (a_1 - pa_0) \, x}{1 - px - qx^2}$$

is called the *generating function* of the series.

327.   From the result of Art. 325, we obtain

$$\frac{a_0 + (a_1 - pa_0) \, x}{1 - px - qx^2} = a_0 + a_1 x + a_2 x^2 + + a_{n-1} x^{n-1}$$

$$+ \frac{(pa_{n-1} + qa_{n-2}) \, x^n + qa_{n-1} x^{n+1}}{1 - px - qx^2};$$

from which we see that although the generating function

$$\frac{a_0 + (a_1 - pa_0) \, x}{1 - px - qx^2}$$

may be used to obtain as many terms of the series as we please, it can be regarded as the true equivalent of the infinite series

$$a_0 + a_1x + a_2x^2 + \ldots,$$

only if the remainder

$$\frac{(pa_{n-1} + qa_{n-2})\,x^n + qa_{n-1}\,x^{n+1}}{1 - px - qx^2}$$

vanishes when n is indefinitely increased; in other words only when the series is convergent.

328. When the *generating function* can be expressed as a group of partial fractions the general term of a recurring series may be easily found. Thus, suppose the generating function can be decomposed into the partial fractions

$$\frac{A}{1 - ax} + \frac{B}{1 + bx} + \frac{C}{(1 - cx)^2}.$$

Then the general term is

$$\{Aa^r + (-1)^r Bb^r + (r+1)\,Cc^r\}\,x^r.$$

In this case the sum of n terms may be found without using the method of Art. 325.

Example : Find the generating function, the general term, and the sum to n terms of the recurring series

$$1 - 7x - x^2 - 43x^3 - \ldots$$

Let the scale of relation be $1 - px - qx^2$; then

$$-1 + 7p - q = 0,\ -43 + p + 7q = 0;$$

whence $p = 1$, $q = 6$; and the scale of relation is

$$1 - x - 6x^2.$$

Let S denote the sum of the series; then

$$S = 1 - 7x - x^2 - 43x^3 - \ldots$$
$$-xS = \quad\ -x + 7x^2 + x^3 + \ldots$$
$$-6x^2S = \qquad\quad -6x^2 + 42x^3 + \ldots$$

$$\therefore \qquad (1 - x - 6x^2)\,S = 1 - 8x,$$

$$S = \frac{1 - 8x}{1 - x - 6x^2}\,;$$

which is the generating function.

If we separate $\dfrac{1 - 8x}{1 - x - 6x^2}$ into partial fractions, we obtain

$\dfrac{2}{1 + 2x} - \dfrac{1}{1 - 3x}$; whence the $(r+1)$th or general term is

$$\{(-1)^r\,2^{r+1} - 3^r\}\,x^r.$$

Putting $r = 0, 1, 2, \ldots n - 1$,

the sum to n terms

$$= \{2 - 2^2 x + 2^3 x^2 - \ldots + (-1)^{n-1} 2^n x^{n-1}\} - (1 + 3x + 3^2 x^2$$
$$+ \ldots + 3^{n-1} x^{n-1})$$

$$= \frac{2 + (-1)^{n-1} 2^{n+1} x^n}{1 + 2x} - \frac{1 - 3^n x^n}{1 - 3x}.$$

329. To find the general term and sum of n terms of the recurring series $a_0 + a_1 + a_2 + \ldots$, we have only to find the general term and sum of the series $a_0 + a_1 x + a_2 x^2 + \ldots$, and put $x = 1$ in the results.

Example : Find the general term and sum of n terms of the series
$$1 + 6 + 24 + 84 + \ldots$$

The scale of relation of the series $1 + 6x + 24x^2 + 84x^3 + \ldots$ is $1 - 5x + 6x^2$, and the generating function is $\dfrac{1 + x}{1 - 5x + 6x^2}$.

This expression is equivalent to the partial fractions
$$\frac{4}{1 - 3x} - \frac{3}{1 - 2x}.$$

If these expressions be expanded in ascending powers of x the general term is $(4 \cdot 3^r - 3 \cdot 2^r) x^r$.

Hence the general term of the given series is $4 \cdot 3^r - 3 \cdot 2^r$; and the sum of n terms is $2(3^n - 1) - 3(2^n - 1)$.

330. We may remind the student that in the preceding article the generating function cannot be taken as the sum of the series
$$1 + 6x + 24x^2 + 84x^3 + \ldots$$
except when x has such a value as to make the series convergent. Hence when $x = 1$ (in which case the series is obviously divergent) the generating function is not a true equivalent of the series. But the general term of
$$1 + 6 + 24 + 84 + \ldots$$
is independent of x, and whatever value x may have it will always be the coefficient of x^n in
$$1 + 6x + 24x^2 + 84x^3 + \ldots.$$

We therefore treat this as a convergent series and find its general term in the usual way, and then put $x = 1$.

EXAMPLES XXIV.

Find the generating function and the general term of the following series :

1. $1 + 5x + 9x^2 + 13x^3 + \dots$ **2.** $2 - x + 5x^2 - 7x^3 + \dots$

3. $2 + 3x + 5x^2 + 9x^3 + \dots$ **4.** $7 - 6x + 9x^2 + 27x^4 + \dots$

5. $3 + 6x + 14x^2 + 36x^3 + 98x^4 + 276x^5 + \dots$

Find the nth term and the sum to n terms of the following series :

6. $2 + 5 + 13 + 35 + \dots$ **7.** $-1 + 6x^2 + 30x^3 + \dots$

8. $2 + 7x + 25x^2 + 91x^3 + \dots$

9. $1 + 2x + 6x^2 + 20x^3 + 66x^4 + 212x^5 + \dots$

10. $-\dfrac{3}{2} + 2 + 0 + 8 + \dots$

11. Shew that the series
$$1^2 + 2^2 + 3^2 + 4^2 + \dots + n^2,$$
$$1^3 + 2^3 + 3^3 + 4^3 + \dots + n^3,$$
are recurring series, and find their scales of relation.

12. Shew how to deduce the sum of the first n terms of the recurring series
$$a_0 + a_1x + a_2x^2 + a_3x^3 + \dots$$
from the sum to infinity.

13. Find the sum of $2n + 1$ terms of the series
$$3 - 1 + 13 - 9 + 41 - 53 + \dots$$

14. The scales of the recurring series
$$a_0 + a_1x + a_2x^2 + a_3x^3 + \dots,$$
$$b_0 + b_1x + b_2x^2 + b_3x^3 + \dots,$$
are $1 + px + qx^2$, $1 + rx + sx^2$, respectively; shew that the series whose general term is $(a_n + b_n) x^n$ is a recurring series whose scale is
$$1 + (p + r) x + (q + s + pr) x^2 + (qr + ps) x^3 + qsx^4.$$

15. If a series be formed having for its nth term the sum of n terms of a given recurring series, shew that it will also form a recurring series whose scale of relation will consist of one more term than that of the given series.

Chapter 25

CONTINUED FRACTIONS

331. An expression of the form $a + \cfrac{b}{c + \cfrac{d}{e + \ldots}}$ is called a continued fraction; here the letters $a, b, c, \ldots$ may denoted any quantities whatever, but for the present we shall only consider the simpler form

$a_1 + \cfrac{1}{a_2 + \cfrac{1}{a_3 + \ldots}}$, where $a_1, a_2, a_3, \ldots$ are positive integers. This will be

usually written in the more compact form

$$a_1 + \cfrac{1}{a_2 +} \cfrac{1}{a_3 + \ldots}$$

332. When the number of *quotients* $a_1, a_2, a_3, \ldots$ is finite the continued fraction is said to be *terminating;* if the number of quotients is unlimited the fraction is called an *infinite continued fraction.*

It is possible to reduce every terminating continued fraction to an ordinary fraction by simplifying the fractions in succession beginning from the lowest.

333. *To convert a given fraction into a continued fraction.*

Let $\dfrac{m}{n}$ be the given fraction; divide m by n, let a_1 be the quotient and p the remainder; thus

$$\frac{m}{n} = a_1 + \frac{p}{n} = a_1 + \frac{1}{\dfrac{n}{p}} \, ;$$

divide n by p, let a_2 be the quotient and q the remainder; thus

$$\frac{n}{p} = a_2 + \frac{q}{p} = a_2 + \frac{1}{\dfrac{p}{q}} \, ;$$

divide p by q, let a_3 be the quotient and r the remainder; and so on. Thus

$$\frac{m}{n} = a_1 + \cfrac{1}{a_2 + \cfrac{1}{a_3 + \ldots}} = a_1 + \cfrac{1}{a_2 +} \cfrac{1}{a_3 +} \ldots$$

If m is less than n, the first quotient is zero, and we put

$$\frac{m}{n} = \frac{1}{\dfrac{n}{m}}$$

and proceed as before.

It will be observed that the above process is the same as that of finding the greatest common measure of m and n; hence if m and n are *commensurable* we shall at length arrive at a stage where the division is exact and the process terminates. Thus every fraction whose numerator and denominator are positive integers can be converted into a terminating continued fraction.

Example : Reduce $\dfrac{251}{802}$ to a continued fraction.

Finding the greatest common measure of 251 and 802 by the usual process, we have

$$
\begin{array}{c|c|c|c}
5 & 251 & 802 & 3 \\
6 & 6 & 49 & 8 \\
  &   & 1 &
\end{array}
$$

and the successive quotients are 3, 5, 8, 6; hence

$$\frac{251}{802} = \frac{1}{3+} \frac{1}{5+} \frac{1}{8+} \frac{1}{6}.$$

334. The fractions obtained by stopping at the first, second, third, ... quotients of a continued fraction are called the first, second, third, ... convergents, because, as will be shewn in Art. 339, each successive convergent is a nearer approximation to the true value of the continued fraction than any of the preceding convergents.

335. *To shew that the convergents are alternately less and greater than the continued fraction.*

Let the continued fraction be $a_1 + \dfrac{1}{a_2+} \dfrac{1}{a_3+} \ldots$

The first convergent is a_1, and is too small because the part $\dfrac{1}{a_2+} \dfrac{1}{a_3+} \ldots$ is omitted. The second convergent is $a_1 + \dfrac{1}{a_2}$, and is too great, because the denominator a_2 is too small. The third convergent is $a_1 + \dfrac{1}{a_2+} \dfrac{1}{a_3}$, and is too small because $a_2 + \dfrac{1}{a_3}$ is too great; and so on.

When the given fraction is a proper fraction $a_1 = 0$; if in this case we agree to consider zero as the first convergent, we may enunciate the above results as follows :

The convergents of an odd order are all less, and the convergents of an even order are all greater, than the continued fraction.

336. *To establish the law of formation of the successive convergents.*

Let the continued fraction be denoted by

$$a_1 + \frac{1}{a_2 +} \frac{1}{a_3 +} \frac{1}{a_4 +} \ldots ;$$

then the first three convergents are

$$\frac{a_1}{1}, \quad \frac{a_1 a_2 + 1}{a_2}, \quad \frac{a_3 (a_1 a_2 + 1) + a_1}{a_3 a_2 + 1} ;$$

and we see that the numerator of the third convergent may be formed by multiplying the numerator of the second convergent by the third quotient, and adding the numerator of the first convergent; also that the denominator may be formed in a similar manner.

Suppose that the successive convergents are formed, in a similar way; let the numerators be denoted by $p_1, p_2, p_3, \ldots$ and the denominators by $q_1, q_2, q_3, \ldots$

Assume that the law of formation holds for the nth convergent; that is, suppose

$$p_n = a_n p_{n-1} + p_{n-2}, \ q_n = a_n q_{n-1} + q_{n-2}.$$

The $(n + 1)^{th}$ convergent differs from the nth only in having the quotient $a_n + \dfrac{1}{a_{n+1}}$ in the place of a_n; hence the $(n + 1)^{th}$ convergent

$$= \frac{\left(a_n + \dfrac{1}{a_{n+1}} \right) p_{n-1} + p_{n-2}}{\left(a_n + \dfrac{1}{a_{n+1}} \right) q_{n-1} + q_{n-2}} = \frac{a_{n+1} (a_n p_{n-1} + p_{n-2}) + p_{n-1}}{a_{n+1} (a_n q_{n-1} + q_{n-2}) + q_{n-1}}$$

$$= \frac{a_{n+1} p_n + p_{n-1}}{a_{n+1} q_n + q_{n-1}}, \text{ by supposition.}$$

If therefore, we put

$$p_{n+1} = a_{n+1} p_n + p_{n-1}, \ q_{n+1} = a_{n+1} q_n + q_{n-1},$$

we see that the numerator and denominator of the $(n + 1)^{th}$ convergent follow the law which was supposed to hold in the case of the nth. But the law does hold in the case of the third convergent, hence it holds for the fourth, and so on; therefore, it holds universally.

337. It will be convenient to call a_n the nth *partial* quotient; the *complete* quotient at this stage being $a_n + \dfrac{1}{a_{n+1} +} \dfrac{1}{a_{n+2} +} \ldots$ We shall usually denote the complete quotient at any stage by k.

We have seen that

$$\frac{p_n}{q_n} = \frac{a_n\,p_{n-1} + p_{n-2}}{a_n\,q_{n-1} + q_{n-2}};$$

let the continued fraction be denoted by x; then x differs from $\dfrac{p_n}{q_n}$ only in taking the complete quotient k instead of the partial quotient a_n; thus

$$x = \frac{k\,p_{n-1} + p_{n-2}}{k\,q_{n-1} + q_{n-2}}.$$

338. If $\dfrac{p_n}{q_n}$ be the nth convergent to a continued fraction, then

$$p_n\,q_{n-1} - p_{n-1}\,q_n = (-1)^n$$

Let the continued fraction be denoted by

$$a_1 + \frac{1}{a_2 +}\ \frac{1}{a_3 +}\ \frac{1}{a_4 +}\ \ldots\,;$$

then

$$
\begin{aligned}
p_n\,q_{n-1} - p_{n-1}\,q_n &= (a_n\,p_{n-1} + p_{n-2})\,q_{n-1} - p_{n-1}\,(a_n\,q_{n-1} + q_{n-2}) \\
&= (-1)\,(p_{n-1}\,q_{n-2} - p_{n-2}\,q_{n-1}) \\
&= (-1)^2\,(p_{n-2}\,q_{n-3} - p_{n-3}\,q_{n-2}), \quad \text{similarly,} \\
&= \ldots\ldots\ldots\ldots\ldots\ldots\ldots\ldots\ldots\ldots \\
&= (-1)^{n-2}\,(p_2\,q_1 - p_1\,q_2)
\end{aligned}
$$

But $p_2 q_1 - p_1 q_2 = (a_1 a_2 + 1) - a_1\,a_2 = 1 = (-1)^2$;

hence

$$p_n\,q_{n-1} - p_{n-1}\,q_n = (-1)^n.$$

When the continued fraction is less than unity, this result will still hold if we suppose that $a_1 = 0$, and that the first convergent is zero.

Note : When we are calculating the numerical value of the successive convergents, the above theorem furnishes an easy test of the accuracy of the work.

Cor. 1. Each convergent is in its lowest terms; for if p_n and q_n had a common divisor it would divide $p_n\,q_{n-1} - p_{n-1}\,q_n$, or unity; which is impossible.

Cor. 2. The difference between two successive convergents is a fraction whose numerator is unity; for

$$\frac{p_n}{q_n} \sim \frac{p_{n-1}}{q_{n-1}} = \frac{p_n\,q_{n-1} \sim p_{n-1}\,q_n}{q_n\,q_{n-1}} = \frac{1}{q_n\,q_{n-1}}.$$

EXAMPLES XXV. a.

Calculate the successive convergents to

1. $2 + \cfrac{1}{6+} \cfrac{1}{1+} \cfrac{1}{1+} \cfrac{1}{11+} \cfrac{1}{2}$.

2. $\cfrac{1}{2+} \cfrac{1}{2+} \cfrac{1}{3+} \cfrac{1}{1+} \cfrac{1}{4+} \cfrac{1}{2+} \cfrac{1}{6}$.

3. $3 + \cfrac{1}{3+} \cfrac{1}{1+} \cfrac{1}{2+} \cfrac{1}{2+} \cfrac{1}{1+} \cfrac{1}{9}$.

Express the following quantities as continued fractions and find the fourth convergent to each.

4. $\dfrac{253}{179}$. **5.** $\dfrac{832}{159}$. **6.** $\dfrac{1189}{3927}$. **7.** $\dfrac{729}{2318}$.

8. $\cdot37$. **9.** $1\cdot139$. **10.** $\cdot3029$. **11.** $4\cdot316$.

12. A metre is $39\cdot37079$ inches, shew by the theory of continued fractions that 32 metres is nearly equal to 35 yards.

13. Find a series of fractions converging to $\cdot24226$, the excess in days of the true tropical year over 365 days.

14. A kilometre is very nearly equal to $\cdot62138$ miles; shew that the fractions $\dfrac{5}{8}, \dfrac{18}{29}, \dfrac{23}{37}, \dfrac{64}{103}$ are successive approximations to the ratio of a kilometre to a mile.

15. Two scales of equal length are divided into 162 and 209 equal parts respectively; if their zero points be coincident shew that the 31st division of one nearly coincides with the 40th division of the other.

16. If $\dfrac{n^4 + n^2 - 1}{n^3 + n^2 + n + 1}$ is converted into a continued fraction, shew that the quotients are $n - 1$ and $n + 1$ alternately and find the successive convergents.

17. Shew that

(1) $\dfrac{p_{n+1} - p_{n-1}}{q_{n+1} - q_{n-1}} = \dfrac{p_n}{q_n}$,

(2) $\left(\dfrac{p_{n+2}}{p_n} - 1 \right) \left(1 - \dfrac{p_{n-1}}{p_{n+1}} \right) = \left(\dfrac{q_{n+2}}{q_n} - 1 \right) \left(1 - \dfrac{q_{n-1}}{q_{n+1}} \right)$

18. If $\dfrac{p_n}{q_n}$ is the nth convergent to a continued fraction, and a_n the corresponding quotient, shew that

$$p_{n+2} q_{n-2} \sim p_{n-2} q_{n+2} = a_{n+2} \cdot a_{n+1} \cdot a_n + a_{n+2} + a_n.$$

339.   *Each convergent is nearer to the continued fraction than any of the preceding convergents.*

Let x denote the continued fraction, and $\dfrac{p_n}{q_n}, \dfrac{p_{n+1}}{q_{n+1}}, \dfrac{p_{n+2}}{q_{n+2}}$ three consecutive convergents; then x differs from $\dfrac{p_{n+2}}{q_{n+2}}$ only in taking the complete $(n+2)^{\text{th}}$ quotient in the place of a_{n+2}; denote this by k; thus

$$x = \frac{k\,p_{n+1} + p_n}{k\,q_{n+1} + q_n}\,;$$

$\therefore\qquad x - \dfrac{p_n}{q_n} = \dfrac{k\,(p_{n+1}\,q_n \sim p_n\,q_{n+1})}{q_n\,(k\,q_{n+1} + q_n)} = \dfrac{k}{q_n\,(k\,q_{n+1} + q_n)}\,,$

and $\qquad \dfrac{p_{n+1}}{q_{n+1}} \sim x = \dfrac{p_{n+1}\,q_n \sim p_n\,q_{n+1}}{q_{n+1}\,(k\,q_{n+1} + q_n)} = \dfrac{1}{q_{n+1}\,(k\,q_{n+1} + q_n)}\,.$

Now k is greater than unity, and q_n is less than q_{n+1}; hence on both accounts the difference between $\dfrac{p_{n+1}}{q_{n+1}}$ and x is less than the difference between $\dfrac{p_n}{q_n}$ and x; that is, every convergent is nearer to the continued fraction than the next preceding convergent, and therefore *a fortiori* than any preceding convergent.

Combining the result of this article with that of Art. 335, it follows that

the convergents of an odd order continually increase, but are always less than the continued fraction;

the convergents of an even order continually decrease, but are always greater than the continued fraction.

340.   *To find limits to the error made in taking any convergent for the continued fraction.*

Let $\dfrac{p_n}{q_n}, \dfrac{p_{n+1}}{q_{n+1}}, \dfrac{p_{n+2}}{q_{n+2}}$ be three consecutive convergents, and let k denote the complete $(n+2)^{\text{th}}$ quotient;

then $\qquad\qquad x = \dfrac{k\,p_{n+1} + p_n}{k\,q_{n+1} + q_n}\,,$

$\therefore\qquad x - \dfrac{p_n}{q_n} = \dfrac{k}{q_n\,(k q_{n+1} + q_n)} = \dfrac{1}{q_n\left(q_{n+1} + \dfrac{q_n}{k}\right)}\,.$

Now k is greater than 1, therefore the difference between x and $\frac{p_n}{q_n}$ is less than $\frac{1}{q_n\,q_{n+1}}$, and greater than $\frac{1}{q_n\,(q_{n+1}+q_n)}$.

Again, since $q_{n+1} > q_n$, the error in taking $\frac{p_n}{q_n}$ instead of x is less than $\frac{1}{q_n^2}$ and greater than $\frac{1}{2q_{n+1}^2}$.

341. From the last article it appears that the error in taking $\frac{p_n}{q_n}$ instead of the continued fraction is less than $\frac{1}{q_n\,q_{n+1}}$, or $\frac{1}{q_n\,(a_{n+1}\,q_n + q_{n-1})}$; that is, less than $\frac{1}{a_{n+1}\,q_n^2}$; hence the larger a_{n+1} is, the nearer does $\frac{p_n}{q_n}$ approximate to the continued fraction; therefore, *any convergent which immediately procedes a large quotient is a near approximation to the continued fraction.*

Again, since the error is less than $\frac{1}{q_n^2}$, it follows that in order to find a convergent which will differ from the continued fraction by less than a given quantity $\frac{1}{a}$, we have only to calculate the successive convergents up to $\frac{p_n}{q_n}$, where q_n^2 is greater than a.

342. The properties of continued fractions enable us to find two small integers whose ratio closely approximates to that of two incommensurable quantities, or to that of two quantities whose exact ratio can only be expressed by large integers.

Example : Find a series of fractions approximating to 3·14159.

In the process of finding the greatest common measure of 14159 and 1,00,000, the successive quotients are 7, 15. 1, 25, 1, 7, 4. Thus

$$3\cdot14159 = 3 + \frac{1}{7+} \frac{1}{15+} \frac{1}{1+} \frac{1}{25+} \frac{1}{1+} \frac{1}{7+} \frac{1}{4}.$$

The successive convergents are

$$\frac{3}{1},\ \frac{22}{7},\ \frac{333}{106},\ \frac{355}{113},\ \dots;$$

this last convergents which precedes the large quotient 25 is a very near approximation, the error being less than $\dfrac{1}{25 \times (113)^2}$, and therefore less th

$\dfrac{1}{25 \times (100^2)}$, or ·000004.

343. *Any convergent is nearer to the continued fraction than any other fraction whose denominator is less than that of the convergent.*

Let x be the continued fraction, $\dfrac{p_n}{q_n}, \dfrac{p_{n-1}}{q_{n-1}}$ two consecutive convergents $\dfrac{r}{s}$ a fraction whose denominators is less than q_n.

If possible, let $\dfrac{r}{s}$ be nearer to x than $\dfrac{p_n}{q_n}$, then $\dfrac{r}{s}$ must be nearer to x than $\dfrac{p_{n-1}}{q_{n-1}}$ [Art. 339]; and since x lies between $\dfrac{p_n}{q_n}$ and $\dfrac{p_{n-1}}{q_{n-1}}$, it follows that $\dfrac{r}{s}$ must lies between $\dfrac{p_n}{q_n}$ and $\dfrac{p_{n-1}}{q_{n-1}}$.

Hence $\dfrac{r}{s} \sim \dfrac{p_{n-1}}{q_{n-1}} < \dfrac{p_n}{q_n} \sim \dfrac{p_{n-1}}{q_{n-1}}$, that is $< \dfrac{1}{q_n q_{n-1}}$;

∴ $$r q_{n-1} \sim s p_{n-1} < \frac{s}{q_n} ;$$

that is, an integer less than a fraction; which is impossible. Therefore, $\dfrac{p_n}{q_n}$ must be nearer to the continued fraction than $\dfrac{r}{s}$.

344. *If $\dfrac{p}{q}, \dfrac{p'}{q'}$ be two consecutive convergents to a continued fraction x, then $\dfrac{pp'}{qq'}$ is greater or less than x^2, according as $\dfrac{p}{q}$ is greater or less than $\dfrac{p'}{q'}$.*

Let k be the complete quotient corresponding to the convergent immediately succeeding $\dfrac{p'}{q'}$; then $x = \dfrac{kp' + p}{kq' + q}$

∴ $\dfrac{pp'}{qq'} - x^2 = \dfrac{1}{qq'(kq'+q)^2} \{ pp'(kq'+q)^2 - qq'(kp'+p)^2 \}$

$= \dfrac{(k^2 p'q' - pq)(pq' - p'q)}{qq'(kq'+q)^2}$.

The factor $k^2 p'q' - pq$ is positive, since $p' > p$, $q' > q$, and $k > 1$; hence $\dfrac{pp'}{qq'} >$ or $< x^2$, according as $pq' - p'q$ is positive or negative; that is, according as $\dfrac{p}{q} >$ or $< \dfrac{p'}{q'}$.

Cor. It follows from the above investigation that the expressions $pq' - p'q$, $pp' - qq'x^2$, $p^2 - q^2x^2$, $q'^2x^2 - p'^2$ have the same sign.

EXAMPLES XXV. b.

1. Find limits to the error in taking $\dfrac{222}{203}$ yards as equivalent to a metre, given that a metre is equal to $1 \cdot 0936$ yards.

2. Find an approximation to
$$1 + \frac{1}{3+} \frac{1}{5+} \frac{1}{7+} \frac{1}{9+} \frac{1}{11+} \cdots$$
which differs from the true value by less than $\cdot 0001$.

3. Shew by the theory of continued fractions that $\dfrac{99}{70}$ differs from $1 \cdot 41421$ by a quantity less than $\dfrac{1}{11830}$.

4. Express $\dfrac{a^3 + 6a^2 + 13a + 10}{a^4 + 6a^3 + 14a^2 + 15a + 7}$ as a continued fraction, and find the third convergent.

5. Shew that the difference between the first and n^{th} convergents is numerically equal to
$$\frac{1}{q_1 q_2} - \frac{1}{q_2 q_3} + \frac{1}{q_3 q_4} - \cdots + \frac{(-1)^n}{q_{n-1} q_n}.$$

6. Shew that if a_n is the quotient corresponding to $\dfrac{p_n}{q_n}$,

(1) $\dfrac{p_n}{p_{n-1}} = a_n + \dfrac{1}{a_{n-1}+} \dfrac{1}{a_{n-2}+} \dfrac{1}{a_{n-3}+} \cdots \dfrac{1}{a_3+} \dfrac{1}{a_2+} \dfrac{1}{a_1}$,

(2) $\dfrac{q_n}{q_{n-1}} = a_n + \dfrac{1}{a_{n-1}+} \dfrac{1}{a_{n-2}+} \dfrac{1}{a_{n-3}+} \cdots \dfrac{1}{a_3+} \dfrac{1}{a_2}$.

7. In the continued fraction $\dfrac{1}{a+}\dfrac{1}{a+}\dfrac{1}{a+}\dfrac{1}{a+}\ldots$, shew that

(1) $p_n^2 + p_{n+1}^2 = p_{n-1}\,p_{n+1} + p_n\,p_{n+2}$,

(2) $p_n = q_{n-1}$.

8. If $\dfrac{p_n}{q_n}$ is the nth convergent to the continued fraction

$$\dfrac{1}{a+}\dfrac{1}{b+}\dfrac{1}{a+}\dfrac{1}{b+}\dfrac{1}{a+}\dfrac{1}{b+}\ldots$$

shew that

$$q_{2n} = p_{2n+1},\; q_{2n-1} = \dfrac{a}{b}\,p_{2n}.$$

9. In the continued fraction

$$\dfrac{1}{a+}\dfrac{1}{b+}\dfrac{1}{a+}\dfrac{1}{b+}\ldots,$$

shew that

$$p_{n+2} - (ab+2)\,p_n + p_{n-2} = 0,\quad q_{n+2} - (ab+2)\,q_n + q_{n-2} = 0.$$

10. Shew that

$$a\left(x_1 + \dfrac{1}{ax_2+}\dfrac{1}{x_3+}\dfrac{1}{ax_4+}\ldots \text{ to } 2n \text{ quotients} \right)$$

$$= ax_1 + \dfrac{1}{x_2+}\dfrac{1}{ax_3+}\dfrac{1}{x_4+}\ldots \text{ to } 2n \text{ quotients}.$$

11. If $\dfrac{M}{N},\dfrac{P}{Q},\dfrac{R}{S}$ are the nth, $(n-1)^{\text{th}}$, $(n-2)^{\text{th}}$ convergents to the continued fractions

$$\dfrac{1}{a_1+}\dfrac{1}{a_2+}\dfrac{1}{a_3+}\ldots,\quad \dfrac{1}{a_2+}\dfrac{1}{a_3+}\dfrac{1}{a_4+}\ldots,\quad \dfrac{1}{a_3+}\dfrac{1}{a_4+}\dfrac{1}{a_5+}\ldots,$$

respectively, shew that

$$M = a_2 P + R,\; N = (a_1 a_2 + 1)\,P + a_1 R.$$

12. If $\dfrac{p_n}{q_n}$ is the nth convergent to

$$\dfrac{1}{a+}\dfrac{1}{a+}\dfrac{1}{a+}\ldots,$$

shew that p_n and q_n are respectively the coefficients of x^n in the expansion of

$$\dfrac{x}{1-ax-x^2} \quad \text{and} \quad \dfrac{ax+x^2}{1-ax-x^2}.$$

Hence shew that $p_n = q_{n-1} = \dfrac{\alpha^n - \beta^n}{\alpha - \beta}$, where α, β are the roots

of the equation $t^2 - at - 1 = 0$.

13. If $\dfrac{p_n}{q_n}$ is the nth convergent to

$$\frac{1}{a+}\frac{1}{b+}\frac{1}{a+}\frac{1}{b+} \cdots,$$

shew that p_n and q_n are respectively the coefficients of x^n in
the expansions of

$$\frac{x + bx^2 - x^3}{1 - (ab+2)\,x^2 + x^4} \quad \text{and} \quad \frac{ax + (ab+1)\,x^2 - x^4}{1 - (ab+2)\,x^2 + x^4}.$$

Hence shew that

$$ap_{2n} = bq_{2n-1} = ab\,\frac{\alpha^n - \beta^n}{\alpha - \beta},$$

$$p_{2n+1} = q_n = \frac{\alpha^{n+1} - \beta^{n+1} - (\alpha^n - \beta^n)}{\alpha - \beta},$$

where α, β are the values of x^2 found from the equation

$$1 - (ab+2)\,x^2 - x^4 = 0.$$

■■■

Chapter 26

INDETERMINATE EQUATIONS OF THE FIRST DEGREE

345. In Chap. 10, we have shewn how to obtain the positive integral solutions of indeterminate equations with numerical coefficients; we shall now apply the properties of continued fractions to obtain the general solution of any indeterminate equation of the first degree.

346. Any equation of the first degree involving two unknowns x and y can be reduced to the form $ax \pm by = \pm c$, where a, b, c are positive integers. This equation admits of an unlimited number of solutions; but if the conditions of the problem require x and y to be positive integers, the number of solutions may be limited.

It is clear that the equation $ax + by = -c$ has no positive integral solution; and that the equation $ax - by = -c$ is equivalent to $by - ax = c$; hence it will be sufficient to consider the equations $ax \pm by = c$.

If a and b have a factor m which does not divide c, neither of the equations $ax \pm by = c$ can be satisfied by integral values of x and y; for $ax \pm by$ is divisible by m, whereas c is not.

If a, b, c have a common factor it can be removed by division; so that we shall suppose a, b, c to have no common factor, and that a and b are prime to each other.

347. *To find the general solution in positive integers of the equation*
$$ax - by = c.$$

Let $\dfrac{a}{b}$ be converted into a continued fraction, and let $\dfrac{p}{q}$ denote the convergent just preceding $\dfrac{a}{b}$; then $aq - bp = \pm 1$. [Art. 338.]

I. If $aq - bp = 1$, the given equation may be written
$$ax - by = c \, (aq - bp);$$
$$\therefore \qquad a \, (x - cq) = b \, (y - cp).$$

Now since a and b have no common factor, $x - cq$ must be divisible by b; hence $x - cq = bt$, where t is an integer,

$$\therefore \qquad \frac{x - cq}{b} = t = \frac{y - cp}{a};$$

that is, $\qquad x = bt + cq, \ y = at + cp;$

from which positive integral solutions may be obtained by giving to t any positive integral value, or any negative integral value numerically smaller than the less of the two quantities $\frac{cq}{b}$, $\frac{cp}{a}$; also t may be zero; thus the number of solutions is unlimited.

II. If $aq - bp = -1$, we have

$$ax - by = -c \ (aq - bp),$$

$$\therefore \qquad a \ (x + cq) = b \ (y + cp);$$

$$\therefore \qquad \frac{x + cq}{b} = \frac{y + cp}{a} = t, \text{ an integer;}$$

or $\qquad x = bt - cq, \ y = at - cp;$

from which positive integral solutions may be obtained by giving to t any positive integral value which exceeds the greater of the two quantities $\frac{cq}{b}$, $\frac{cp}{a}$; thus the number of solutions is unlimited.

III. If either a or b is unity, the fraction $\frac{a}{b}$ cannot be converted into a continued fraction with unit numerators, and the investigation fails. In these cases, however, the solutions may be written down by inspection; thus if $b = 1$, the equation becomes $ax - y = c$; whence $y = ax - c$, and the solutions may be found by ascribing to x any positive integral value greater than $\frac{c}{a}$.

Note : It should be observed that the series of values for x and y form two arithmetical progressions in which the common differences are b and c respectively.

Example : Find the general solution in positive integers of $29x - 42y = 5$.

In converting $\frac{42}{29}$ into a continued fraction the convergent just before $\frac{42}{29}$ is $\frac{13}{9}$; we have therefore

$$29 \times 13 - 42 \times 9 = -1;$$

$$\therefore \qquad 29 \times 65 - 42 \times 45 = -5;$$

combining this with the given equation, we obtain

$$29 \ (x + 65) = 42 \ (y + 45);$$

$$\therefore \qquad \frac{x + 65}{42} = \frac{y + 45}{29} = t, \text{ an integer;}$$

hence the general solution is

$$x = 42t - 65, \ y = 29t - 45.$$

348.   *Given one solution in positive integers of the equation* $ax - by = c$, *to find the general solution.*

Let h, k be a solution of $ax - by = c$; then $ah - bk = c$.

$$\therefore \qquad ax - by = ah - bk;$$

$$\therefore \qquad a(x - h) = b(y - k);$$

$$\therefore \qquad \frac{x - h}{b} = \frac{y - k}{a} = t, \text{ an integer;}$$

$$\therefore \qquad x = h + bt, \, y = k + at;$$

which is the general solution.

349.   *To find the general solution in positive integers of the equation*

$$ax + by = c$$

Let $\dfrac{a}{b}$ be converted into a continued fraction, and let $\dfrac{p}{q}$ be the convergent just preceding $\dfrac{a}{b}$; then $aq - bp = \pm 1$.

I. If $aq - bp = 1$, we have

$$ax + by = c(aq - bp);$$

$$\therefore \qquad a(cq - x) = b(y + cp);$$

$$\therefore \qquad \frac{cq - x}{b} = \frac{y + cp}{a} = t, \text{ an integer;}$$

$$\therefore \qquad x = cq - bt, \, y = at - cp;$$

from which positive integral solutions may be obtained by giving to t positive integral values greater than $\dfrac{cp}{a}$ and less than $\dfrac{cq}{b}$. Thus the number of solutions is limited, and if there is no integer fulfilling these conditions there is no solution.

II. If $aq - bp = -1$, we have

$$ax + by = -c(aq - bp);$$

$$\therefore \qquad a(x + cq) = b(cp - y);$$

$$\therefore \qquad \frac{x + cq}{b} = \frac{cp - y}{a} = t, \text{ an integer;}$$

$$\therefore \qquad x = bt - cq, \, y = cp - at;$$

from which positive integral solutions may be obtained by giving to t positive integral values greater than $\dfrac{cq}{b}$ and less than $\dfrac{cp}{a}$. As before, the number of solutions is limited, and there may be no solution.

III. If either a or b is equal to unity, the solution may be found by inspection as in Art. 347.

350.   *Given one solution in positive integers of the equation* $ax + by = c$, *to find the general solution.*

Let h, k be a solution of $ax + by = c$; then $ah + bk = c$.

$\therefore$ $$ax + by = ah + bk;$$

$\therefore$ $$a(x - h) = b(k - y);$$

$\therefore$ $$\frac{x - h}{b} = \frac{k - y}{a} = t, \text{ an integer;}$$

$\therefore$ $$x = h + bt, \ y = k - at;$$

which is the general solution.

351.   *To find the number of solutions in positive integers of the equation*
$$ax + by = c.$$

Let $\dfrac{a}{b}$ be converted into a continued fraction, and let $\dfrac{p}{q}$ be the convergent just preceding $\dfrac{a}{b}$; then $aq - bp = \pm 1$.

I. Let $aq - bp = 1$; then the general solution is
$$x = cq - bt, \ y = at - cp \qquad \qquad \text{[Art. 349.]}$$
Positive integral solutions will be obtained by giving to t positive integral values not greater than $\dfrac{cq}{b}$, and not less than $\dfrac{cp}{a}$.

(i) Suppose that $\dfrac{c}{a}$ and $\dfrac{c}{b}$ are not integers.

Let $$\frac{cp}{a} = m + f, \ \frac{cq}{b} = n + g,$$

where m, n are positive integers and f, g proper fractions; then the least value t can have is $m + 1$, and the greatest value is n; therefore the number of solutions is

$$n - m = \frac{cq}{b} - \frac{cp}{a} + f - g = \frac{c}{ab} + f - g.$$

Now this is an integer, and may be written $\dfrac{c}{ab} + a$ fraction, or $\dfrac{c}{ab} - a$ fraction, according as f is greater or less than g. Thus the number of solutions is the integer nearest to $\dfrac{c}{ab}$, greater or less according as f or g is the greater.

(ii) Suppose that $\dfrac{c}{b}$ is an integer.

In this case $g = 0$, and one value of x is zero. If we include this, the number of solutions is $\dfrac{c}{ab} + f$, which must be an integer. Hence the number of solutions is the greatest integer in $\dfrac{c}{ab} + 1$ or $\dfrac{c}{ab}$, according as we include or exclude the zero solution.

(iii) Suppose that $\dfrac{c}{a}$ is an integer.

In this case $f = 0$, and one value of y is zero. If we include this, the least value of t is m and the greatest is n; hence the number of solutions is $n - m + 1$, or $\dfrac{c}{ab} - y + 1$. Thus the number of solutions is the greatest integer in $\dfrac{c}{ab} + 1$ or $\dfrac{c}{ab}$, according as we include or exclude the zero solution.

(iv) Suppose that $\dfrac{c}{a}$ and $\dfrac{c}{b}$ are both integers.

In this case $f = 0$ and $g = 0$, and both x and y have a zero value. If we include these, the least value t can have is m, and the greatest is n; hence the number of solutions is $n - m + 1$, or $\dfrac{c}{ab} + 1$. If we exclude the zero values the number of solutions is $\dfrac{c}{ab} - 1$.

II. If $aq - bp = -1$, the general solution is
$$x = bt - cq, \quad y = cp - at,$$
and similar results will be obtained.

352. To find the solutions in positive integers of the equation $ax + by + cz = d$, we may proceed as follows.

By transposition $ax + by = d - cz$; from which by giving to z in succession the values $0, 1, 2, 3, \ldots$ we obtain equations of the form $ax + by = c'$, which may be solved as already explained.

353. If we have two simultaneous equations
$$ax + by + cz = d, \quad a'x + b'y + c'z = d',$$
by eliminating one of the unknowns, z say, we obtain an equation of the form $Ax + By = C$. Suppose that $x = f$, $y = g$ is a solution, then the general solution can be written
$$x = f + Bs, \quad y = g - As,$$
where s is an integer.

Substituting these values of x and y in either of the given equations we obtain an equation of the form $Fs + Gz = H$, of which the general solution is

$$s = h + Gt, z = k - Ft \text{ say.}$$

Substituting for s, we obtain

$$x = f + Bh + BGt, y = g - Ah - AGt;$$

and the values of x, y, z are obtained by giving to t suitable integral values.

354. If one solution in positive integers of the equations

$$ax + by + cz = d, a'x + b'y + c'z = d',$$

can be found, the general solution may be obtained as follows.

Let f, g, h be the particular solution; then

$$af + bg + ch = d, a'f + b'g + c'h = d'.$$

By subtraction,

$$a(x - f) + b(y - g) + c(z - h) = 0,$$
$$a'(x - f) + b'(y - g) + c'(z - h) = 0;$$

whence

$$\frac{x - f}{bc' - b'c} = \frac{y - g}{ca' - c'a} = \frac{z - h}{ab' - a'b} = \frac{t}{k},$$

where t is an integer and k is the H.C.F. of the denominators $bc' - b'c, ca' - c'a, ab' - a'b$. Thus the general solution is

$$x = f + (bc' - b'c)\frac{t}{k}, y = g + (ca' - c'a)\frac{t}{k}, z = h + (ab' - a'b)\frac{t}{k}.$$

EXAMPLES XXVI.

Find the general solution and the least positive integral solution of

1. $775x - 711y = 1$ 2. $455x - 519y = 1$ 3. $436x - 393y = 5$

4. In how many ways can £1. 19s. 6d. be paid in florins and half-crowns ?

5. Find the number of solutions in positive integers of
$$11x + 15y = 1031$$

6. Find two fractions having 7 and 9 for their denominators, and such that their sum is $1\frac{10}{63}$.

7. Find two proper fractions in their lowest terms having 12 and 8 for their denominators and such that their difference is $\frac{1}{24}$.

8. A certain sum contains of x pounds y shillings, and it is half of y pounds x shillings; find the sum.

Solve in positive integers :

9.
$$\left. \begin{array}{l} 6x + 7y + 4z = 122 \\ 11x + 8y - 6z = 145 \end{array} \right\}.$$

10.
$$\left. \begin{array}{l} 12x - 11y + 4z = 22 \\ -4x + 5y + z = 17 \end{array} \right\}.$$

11.
$$\left. \begin{array}{l} 20x - 21y = 38 \\ 3y + 4z = 34 \end{array} \right\}.$$

12.
$$\left. \begin{array}{l} 13x + 11z = 103 \\ 7z - 5y = 4 \end{array} \right\}.$$

13. $7x + 4y + 19z = 84.$

14. $23x + 17y + 11z = 130.$

15. Find the general form of all positive integers which divided by 5, 7, 8 leave remainders 3, 2, 5 respectively.

16. Find the two smallest integers which divided by 3, 7, 11 leave remainders 1, 6, 5 respectively.

17. A number of three digits in the septenary scale is represented in the nonary scale by the same three digits in reverse order; if the middle digit in each case is zero, find the value of the number in the denary scale.

18. If the integers 6, a, b are in harmonic progression, find all the possible values of a and b.

19. Two rods of equal length are divided into 250 and 243 equal parts respectively; if their ends be coincident, find the divisions which are the nearest together.

20. Three bells commenced to toll at the same time, and tolled at intervals 23, 29, 34 seconds respectively. The second and third bells tolled 39 and 40 seconds respectively longer than the first; how many times did each bell toll if they all ceased in less than 20 minutes.

21. Find the greatest value of c in order that the equation $7x + 9y = c$ may have exactly six solutions in positive integers.

22. Find the greatest value of c in order that the equation $14x + 11y = c$ may have exactly five solutions in positive integers.

23. Find the limits within which c must lie in order that the equation $19x + 14y = c$ may have six solutions, zero solutions being excluded.

24. Shew that the greatest value of c in order that the equation $ax + by = c$ may have exactly n solutions in positive integers is $(n + 1) ab - a - b$, and that the least value of c is $(n - 1) ab + a + b$, zero solutions being excluded.

Chapter 27

RECURRING CONTINUED FRACTIONS

355. We have seen in Chap. 25. that a *terminating* continued fraction with rational quotients can be reduced to an ordinary fraction with integral numerator and denominator, and therefore, cannot be equal to a surd; but we shall prove that a quadratic surd can be expressed as an *infinite* continued fraction whose quotients recur. We shall first consider a numerical example.

Example : Express $\sqrt{19}$ as a continued fraction, and find a series of fractions approximating to its value.

$$\sqrt{19} = 4 + (\sqrt{19} - 4) = 4 + \frac{3}{\sqrt{19} + 4} \, ;$$

$$\frac{\sqrt{19} + 4}{3} = 2 + \frac{\sqrt{19} - 2}{3} = 2 + \frac{5}{\sqrt{19} + 2} \, ;$$

$$\frac{\sqrt{19} + 2}{5} = 1 + \frac{\sqrt{19} - 3}{5} = 1 + \frac{2}{\sqrt{19} + 3} \, ;$$

$$\frac{\sqrt{19} + 3}{2} = 3 + \frac{\sqrt{19} - 3}{2} = 3 + \frac{5}{\sqrt{19} + 3} \, ;$$

$$\frac{\sqrt{19} + 3}{5} = 1 + \frac{\sqrt{19} - 2}{5} = 1 + \frac{3}{\sqrt{19} + 2} \, ;$$

$$\frac{\sqrt{19} + 2}{3} = 2 \, \frac{\sqrt{19} - 4}{3} = 2 + \frac{1}{\sqrt{19} + 4} \, ;$$

$$\sqrt{19} + 4 = 8 + (\sqrt{19} - 4) = 8 + \dots$$

after this the quotients 2, 1, 3, 1, 2, 8 recur; hence

$$\sqrt{19} = 4 + \frac{1}{2+} \frac{1}{1+} \frac{1}{3+} \frac{1}{1+} \frac{1}{2+} \frac{1}{8+} \dots$$

It will be noticed that the quotients recur as soon as we come to a quotient which is double of the first. In Art. 361 we shall prove that this is always the case.

[**Explanation** : In each of the lines above we perform the same series of operations. For example, consider the second line : we first find the greatest integer in $\frac{\sqrt{19} + 4}{3}$; this is 2, and the remainder is $\frac{\sqrt{19} + 4}{3} - 2$, that is $\frac{\sqrt{19} - 2}{3}$. We then multiply numerator and denominator by the surd conjugate to $\sqrt{19} - 2$, so that after inverting the result $\frac{5}{\sqrt{19} + 2}$; we begin a new line with a rational denominator.]

The first seven convergents formed as explained in Art. 336 are

$$\frac{4}{1}, \frac{9}{2}, \frac{13}{3}, \frac{48}{11}, \frac{61}{14}, \frac{170}{39}, \frac{1421}{326}.$$

The error in taking the last of these is less than $\dfrac{1}{(326)^2}$, and is therefore less than $\dfrac{1}{(320)^2}$ or $\dfrac{1}{102400}$, and a *fortiori* less than $0 \cdot 00001$. Thus the seventh convergent gives the value to at least four places of decimals.

356. *Every periodic continued fraction is equal to one of the roots of quadratic equation of which the coefficients are rational.*

Let x denote the continued fraction, and y the periodic part, and suppose that

$$x = a + \frac{1}{b+} \frac{1}{c+} \cdots \frac{1}{h+} \frac{1}{k+} \frac{1}{y},$$

and

$$y = m + \frac{1}{n+} \cdots \frac{1}{u+} \frac{1}{v+} \frac{1}{y},$$

where $a, b, c, \ldots, h, k, m, n, \ldots, u, v$ are positive integers.

Let $\dfrac{p}{q}, \dfrac{p'}{q'}$ be the convergents to x corresponding to the quotients h, k respectively; then since y is the complete quotient, we have $x = \dfrac{p'y + p}{q'y + q}$; whence $y = \dfrac{p - qx}{q'x - p'}$.

Let $\dfrac{r}{s}, \dfrac{r'}{s'}$ be the convergents to y corresponding to the quotients u, v respectively; then $y = \dfrac{r'y + r}{s'y + s}$.

Substituting for y in terms of x and simplifying we obtain a quadratic of which the coefficients are rational.

The equation $s'y^2 - (s - r')y - r = 0$, which gives the value of y, has its roots real and of opposite signs; if the positive value of y be substituted in $x = \dfrac{p'y + p}{q'y + q}$, on rationalising the denominator the value of x is of the form $\dfrac{A + \sqrt{B}}{C}$, where A, B, C are integers, AB being positive since the value of y is real.

Example : Express $1 + \dfrac{1}{2+} \dfrac{1}{3+} \dfrac{1}{2+} \dfrac{1}{3+} \cdots$ as a surd.

Let x be the value of the continued fraction; then $x - 1 = \dfrac{1}{2+} \dfrac{1}{3 + (x - 1)}$; whence $2x^2 + 2x - 7 = 0$.

The continued fraction is equal to the positive root of this equation, and is therefore, equal to $\dfrac{\sqrt{15}-1}{2}$.

EXAMPLES XXVII. a.

Express the following surds as continued fractions, and find the sixth convergent to each :

1. $\sqrt{3}$.   2. $\sqrt{5}$.   3. $\sqrt{6}$.   4. $\sqrt{8}$.   5. $\sqrt{11}$.

6. $\sqrt{13}$.   7. $\sqrt{14}$.   8. $\sqrt{22}$.   9. $2\sqrt{3}$.   10. $4\sqrt{2}$.

11. $3\sqrt{5}$.   12. $4\sqrt{10}$.   13. $\dfrac{1}{\sqrt{21}}$.   14. $\dfrac{1}{\sqrt{33}}$.   15. $\sqrt{\dfrac{6}{5}}$.

16. $\sqrt{\dfrac{7}{11}}$.

17. Find limits of the error when $\dfrac{268}{65}$ is taken for $\sqrt{17}$.

18. Find limits of the error when $\dfrac{916}{191}$ is taken for $\sqrt{23}$.

19. Find the first convergent to $\sqrt{101}$ that is correct to five places of decimals.

20. Find the first convergent to $\sqrt{15}$ that is correct to five places of decimals.

Express as a continued fraction the positive root of each of the following equations :

21. $x^2 + 2x - 1 = 0$.   22. $x^2 - 4x - 3 = 0$.   23. $7x^2 - 8x - 3 = 0$.

24. Express each root of $x^2 - 5x + 3 = 0$ as a continued fraction.

25. Find the value of $3 + \dfrac{1}{6+} \dfrac{1}{6+} \dfrac{1}{6+} \cdots$

26. Find the value of $\dfrac{1}{1+} \dfrac{1}{3+} \dfrac{1}{1+} \dfrac{1}{3+} \cdots$

27. Find the value of $3 + \dfrac{1}{1+} \dfrac{1}{2+} \dfrac{1}{3+} \dfrac{1}{1+} \dfrac{1}{2+} \dfrac{1}{3+} \cdots$

28. Find the value of $5 + \dfrac{1}{1+} \dfrac{1}{1+} \dfrac{1}{1+} \dfrac{1}{10+} \cdots$

29. Shew that
$$3 + \dfrac{1}{1+} \dfrac{1}{6+} \dfrac{1}{1+} \dfrac{1}{6+} \cdots = 3\left(1 + \dfrac{1}{3+} \dfrac{1}{2+} \dfrac{1}{3+} \dfrac{1}{2+} \cdots\right).$$

30. Find the difference between the infinite continued fractions

$$\frac{1}{1+}\ \frac{1}{3+}\ \frac{1}{5+}\ \frac{1}{1+}\ \frac{1}{3+}\ \frac{1}{5+}\ \cdots,\quad \frac{1}{3+}\ \frac{1}{1+}\ \frac{1}{5+}\ \frac{1}{3+}\ \frac{1}{1+}\ \frac{1}{5+}\ \cdots$$

*357. *To convert a quadratic surd into a continued fraction.*

Let N be a positive integer which is not an exact square, and let a_1 be the greatest integer contained in $\sqrt{N}$; then

$$\sqrt{N} = a_1 + (\sqrt{N} - a_1) = a_1 + \frac{r_1}{\sqrt{N} + a_1}\ ,\ \text{if } r_1 = N - a_1^2.$$

Let b_1 be the greatest integer contained in $\dfrac{\sqrt{N} + a_1}{r_1}$; then

$$\frac{\sqrt{N} + a_1}{r_1} = b_1 + \frac{\sqrt{N} - b_1 r_1 + a_1}{r_1} = b_1 + \frac{\sqrt{N} - a_2}{r_1} = b_1 + \frac{r_2}{\sqrt{N} + a_2}\ ;$$

where $a_2 = b_1 r_1 - a_1$ and $r_1 r_2 = N - a_2^2$.

Similarly

$$\frac{\sqrt{N} + a_2}{r_2} = b_2 + \frac{\sqrt{N} - a_3}{r_2} = b_2 + \frac{r_3}{\sqrt{N} + a_3}\ ;$$

where $a_3 = b_2 r_2 - a_2$ and $r_2 r_3 = N - a_3^2$;

and so on; and generally

$$\frac{\sqrt{N} + a_{n-1}}{r_{n-1}} = b_{n-1} + \frac{\sqrt{N} - a_n}{r_{n-1}} = b_{n-1} + \frac{r_n}{\sqrt{N} + a_n}\ ;$$

where $a_n = b_{n-1} r_{n-1} - a_{n-1}$ and $r_{n-1} r_n = N - a_n^2$.

Hence $\sqrt{N} = a_1 + \dfrac{1}{b_1 +}\ \dfrac{1}{b_2 +}\ \dfrac{1}{b_3 +}\ \dfrac{1}{b_4 +}\ \cdots$;

and thus $\sqrt{N}$ can be expressed as an infinite continued fraction.

We shall presently prove that this fraction consists of recurring periods; it is evident that the period will begin whenever any complete quotient is first repeated.

We shall call the series of quotients

$$\sqrt{N},\ \frac{\sqrt{N} + a_1}{r_1},\ \frac{\sqrt{N} + a_2}{r_2},\ \frac{\sqrt{N} + a_3}{r_3},\ \cdots$$

the first, second, third, fourth … complete quotients.

*358. From the preceding article it appears that the quantities $a_1, r_1, b_1, b_2, b_3 \ldots$ are positive integers; we shall now prove that the quantities $a_2, a_3, a_4, \ldots, r_2, r_3, r_4, \ldots$ are also positive integers.

Let $\dfrac{p}{q}, \dfrac{p'}{q'}, \dfrac{p''}{q''}$ be three consecutive convergents to $\sqrt{N}$, and let

$\dfrac{p''}{q''}$ be the convergent corresponding to the partial quotient b_n. The

complete quotient at this stage is $\dfrac{\sqrt{N} + a_n}{r_n}$; hence

$$\sqrt{N} = \frac{\dfrac{\sqrt{N} + a_n}{r_n}\, p' + p}{\dfrac{\sqrt{N} + a_n}{r_n}\, q' + q} = \frac{p'}{q'}\, \frac{\sqrt{N} + a_n\, p' + r_n\, p}{\sqrt{N} + a_n\, q' + r_n\, q}\,.$$

Clearing of fractions and equating rational and irrational parts, we have

$$a_n\, p' + r_n\, p = N q',\ a_n\, q' + r_n\, q = p';$$

whence $a_n\,(pq' - p'q) = pp' - qq'\,N,\ r_n\,(pq' - p'q) = Nq'^2 - p'^2$.

But $pq' - p'q = \pm 1$, and $pq' - p'q,\ pp' - qq'\,N,\ Nq'^2 - p'^2$ have the same sign [Art. 344]; hence a_n and r_n are positive integers. Since two

convergents procedo the complete quotient $\dfrac{\sqrt{N} + a_2}{r_2}$, this

investigation holds for all values of n greater than 1.

*359.   *To prove that the complete and partial quotients recur.*

In Art. 357 we have proved that $r_n\, r_{n-1} = N - a_n^2$. Also r_n and r_{n-1} are positive integer; hence a_n must be less than $\sqrt{N}$, thus a_n cannot be greater than a_1, and therefore it cannot have any values except 1, 2, 3, ..., a_1; that is, *the number of different values of a_n cannot exceed a_1.*

Again, $a_{n+1} = r_n\, b_n - a_n$, that is $r_n\, b_n = a_n + a_{n+1}$, and therefore $r_n b_n$ cannot be greater than $2a_1$; also b_n is a positive integer; hence r_n cannot be greater than $2a_1$. Thus r_n cannot have any values except 1, 2, 3, ..., $2a_1$; that is, *the number of different values of r_n cannot exceed $2a_1$.*

Thus the complete quotient $\dfrac{\sqrt{N} + a_n}{r_n}$ cannot have more than $2a_1^2$

different values; that is, *some one complete quotient, and therefore all subsequent ones, must recur.*

Also b_n is the greatest integer in $\dfrac{\sqrt{N} + a_n}{r_n}$; hence the *partial quotients must also recur, and the number of partial quotients in each cycle cannot be greater than* $2a_1^2$.

*360. *To prove that* $a_1 < a_n + r_n$.

We have $a_{n-1} + a_n = b_{n-1}\, r_{n-1}$;

$\therefore \qquad a_{n-1} + a_n = \text{or} > r_{n-1}$,

since b_{n-1} is a positive integer;

$\therefore \qquad \sqrt{N} + a_n > r_{n-1}$.

But $N - a_n^2 = r_n\, r_{n-1}$;

$\therefore \qquad \sqrt{N} - a_n < r_n$;

$\therefore \qquad a_1 - a_n < r_n$,

which proves the proposition.

*361. *To shew that the period begins with the second partial quotient and terminates with a partial quotient double of the first.*

Since, as we have seen in Art. 359, a recurrence must take place, let us suppose that the $(n+1)$th complete quotient recurs at the $(s+1)$th; then

$$a_s = a_n,\ r_s = r_n,\ \text{and}\ b_s = b_n;$$

we shall prove that

$$a_{s-1} = a_{n-1},\ r_{s-1} = r_{n-1},\ b_{s-1} = b_{n-1}.$$

We have $r_{s-1}\, r_s = N - a_s^2 = N - a_n^2 = r_{n-1}\, r_n = r_{n-1}\, r_s$;

$\therefore \qquad r_{s-1} = r_{n-1}$.

Again,

$$a_{n-1} + a_n = b_{n-1}\, r_{n-1},\ a_{s-1} + a_s = b_{s-1}\, r_{s-1} = b_{s-1}\, r_{n-1};$$

$\therefore \qquad a_{n-1} - a_{s-1} = r_{n-1}\, (b_{n-1} - b_{s-1})$;

$\therefore \qquad \dfrac{a_{n-1} - a_{s-1}}{r_{n-1}} = b_{n-1} - b_{s-1} = \text{zero, or an integer.}$

But, by Art. 360, $a_1 - a_{n-1} < r_{n-1}$, and $a_1 - a_{s-1} < r_{s-1}$; that is $a_1 - a_{s-1} < r_{n-1}$; therefore, $a_{n-1} - a_{s-1} < r_{n-1}$; hence $\dfrac{a_{n-1} - a_{s-1}}{r_{n-1}}$ is

less than unity, and therefore, must be zero.

Thus $a_{s-1} = a_{n-1}$, and also $b_{s-1} = b_{n-1}$.

Hence if the $(n + 1)$th complete quotient recurs, the nth complete quotient must also recur; therefore, the $(n - 1)$th complete quotient must also recur; and so on.

This proof holds as long as n is not less than 2 [Art. 358], hence the complete quotients recur, beginning with the second quotient $\dfrac{\sqrt{N} + a_1}{r_1}$. It follows therefore that the recurrence begins with the second partial quotient b_1; we shall now shew that it terminates with a partial quotient $2a_1$.

Let $\dfrac{\sqrt{N} + a_n}{r_n}$ be the complete quotient which just preceeds the second complete quotient $\dfrac{\sqrt{N} + a_1}{r_1}$ when it recurs; then $\dfrac{\sqrt{N} + a_n}{r_n}$ and $\dfrac{\sqrt{N} + a_1}{r_1}$ are two consecutive complete quotients; therefore

$$a_n + a_1 = r_n b_n , \ r_n r_1 = N - a_1^2;$$

but $N - a_1^2 = r_1$; hence $r_n = 1$.

Again, $a_1 - a_n < r_n$, that is < 1; hence $a_1 - a_n = 0$, that is

$$a_n = a_1.$$

Also $a_n + a_1 = r_n b_n = b_n$; hence $b_n = 2a_1$; which establishes the proposition.

*362. *To shew that in any period the partial quotients equidistant from the beginning and end are equal, the last partial quotient being excluded.*

Let the last complete quotient be denoted by $\dfrac{\sqrt{N} + a_n}{r_n}$; then

$$r_n = 1, a_n = a_1, b_n = 2a$$

We shall prove that

$$r_{n-1} = r_1, a_{n-1} = a_2, b_{n-1} = b_1;$$
$$r_{n-2} = r_2, a_{n-2} = a_3, b_{n-2} = b_2;$$
$$\cdots\cdots\cdots\cdots\cdots\cdots\cdots\cdots\cdots\cdots\cdots\cdots$$

We have

$$r_{n-1} = r_n r_{n-1} = N - a_n^2 = N - a_1^2 = r_1.$$

Also

$$a_{n-1} + a_1 = a_{n-1} + a_n = r_{n-1} b_{n-1} = r_1 b_{n-1};$$

and

$$a_1 + a_2 = r_1 b_1;$$

$\therefore$ $\qquad a_2 - a_{n-1} = r_1 (b_1 - b_{n-1});$

$\therefore$ $\qquad \dfrac{a_2 - a_{n-1}}{r_1} = b_1 - b_{n-1} = $ zero, or an integer.

But $\dfrac{a_2 - a_{n-1}}{r_1} < \dfrac{a_1 - a_{n-1}}{r_1}$, that is $< \dfrac{a_1 - a_{n-1}}{r_{n-1}}$, which is less than unity; thus $a_2 - a_{n-1} = 0$; hence $a_{n-1} = a_2$, and $b_{n-1} = b_1$.

Similarly $r_{n-2} = r_2$, $a_{n-2} = a_3$, $b_{n-2} = b_2$; and so on.

*363. From the results of Arts. 361, 362, it appears that when a quadratic surd $\sqrt{N}$ is converted into a continued fraction, it must take the following form

$$a_1 + \frac{1}{b_1+} \frac{1}{b_2+} \frac{1}{b_3} + \cdots \frac{1}{b_3+} \frac{1}{b_2+} \frac{1}{b_1+} \frac{1}{2a_1+} \cdots$$

*364. *To obtain the penultimate convergents of the recurring periods.*

Let n be the number of partial quotients in the recurring period; then the penultimate convergents of the recurring periods are the nth, $2n$th, $3n$th, ... convergents; let these be denoted by

$$\frac{p_n}{q_n}, \frac{p_{2n}}{q_{2n}}, \frac{p_{3n}}{q_{3n}}, \ldots \text{ respectively.}$$

Now $\quad \sqrt{N} = a_1 + \dfrac{1}{b_1+} \dfrac{1}{b_2+} \dfrac{1}{b_3+} \cdots \dfrac{1}{b_{n-1}+} \dfrac{1}{2a_1+} \cdots$

so that the partial quotient corresponding to $\dfrac{p_{n+1}}{q_{n+1}}$ is $2a_1$; hence

$$\frac{p_{n+1}}{q_{n+1}} = \frac{2a_1 p_n + p_{n-1}}{2a_1 q_n + q_{n-1}}.$$

The complete quotient at the same stage consists of the period

$$2a_1 + \frac{1}{b_1+} \frac{1}{b_2+} \cdots \frac{1}{b_{n-1}+} \cdots$$

and is therefore, equal to $a_1 + \sqrt{N}$; hence

$$\sqrt{N} = \frac{(a_1 + \sqrt{N}) p_n + p_{n-1}}{(a_1 + \sqrt{N}) q_n + q_{n-1}}.$$

Clearing of fractions and equating rational and irrational parts, we obtain

$$a_1 p_n + p_{n-1} = N q_n, \; a_1 q_n + q_{n-1} = p_n \qquad \ldots(1)$$

Again $\dfrac{p_{2n}}{q_{2n}}$ can be obtained from $\dfrac{p_n}{q_n}$ and $\dfrac{p_{n-1}}{q_{n-1}}$ by taking for the quotient

$$2a_1 + \frac{1}{b_1 +} \ \frac{1}{b_2 +} \cdots \frac{1}{b_{n-1}},$$

which is equal to $a_1 + \dfrac{p_n}{q_n}$. Thus

$$\frac{p_{2n}}{q_{2n}} = \frac{\left(a_1 + \dfrac{p_n}{q_n}\right)p_n + p_{n-1}}{\left(a_1 + \dfrac{p_n}{q_n}\right)q_n + q_{n-1}} = \frac{Nq_n + \dfrac{p_n}{q_n} \cdot p_n}{p_n + \dfrac{p_n}{q_n} \cdot q_n} \cdot \text{ from (1);}$$

$$\therefore \qquad \frac{p_{2n}}{q_{2n}} = \frac{1}{2}\left(\frac{p_n}{q_n} + \frac{Nq_n}{p_n}\right) \qquad\qquad \ldots(2)$$

In like manner we may prove that if $\dfrac{p_{cn}}{q_{cn}}$ is the penultimate convengent in the cth recurring period,

$$a_1 p_{cn} + p_{cn-1} = Nq_{cn}, \ a_1 q_{cn} + q_{cn-1} = p_{cn},$$

and by using these equations, we may obtain $\dfrac{p_{3n}}{q_{3n}}, \dfrac{p_{4n}}{q_{4n}}, \ldots$ successively.

It should be noticed that equation (2) holds for all multiples of n; thus

$$\frac{p_{2cn}}{q_{2cn}} = \frac{1}{2}\left(\frac{p_{cn}}{q_{cn}} + \frac{Nq_{cn}}{p_{cn}}\right);$$

the proof being similar to that already given.

*365.   In Art. 356, we have seen that a periodic continued fraction can be expressed as the root of a quadratic equation with rational coefficients.

Conversely, we might prove by the method of Art. 357 that an expression of the form $\dfrac{A + \sqrt{B}}{C}$, where A, B, C are positive integers, and B not a perfect square, can be converted into a recurring continued fraction. In this case the periodic part will not usually begin with the second partial quotient, nor will the last partial quotient be double the first.

For further information on the subject of recurring continued fractions we refer the student to Serret's *Cours d'Algebre Superieure*, and to a pamphlet on *The Expression of a Quadratic Surd as a Continued Fraction*, by Thomas Muir, M.A., F.R.S.E.

EXAMPLES XXVII. b.

Express the following surds as continued fractions, and find the fourth convergent to each:

1. $\sqrt{a^2+1}$.

2. $\sqrt{a^2-a}$.

3. $\sqrt{a^2-1}$.

4. $\sqrt{1+\dfrac{1}{a}}$.

5. $\sqrt{a^2+\dfrac{2a}{b}}$.

6. $\sqrt{a^2-\dfrac{a}{n}}$.

7. Prove that

$$\sqrt{9a^2+3} = 3a + \frac{1}{2a+} \frac{1}{6a+} \frac{1}{2a+} \frac{1}{6a+} \cdots$$

and find the fifth convergent.

8. Shew that

$$p + \frac{2}{1+} \frac{1}{p+} \frac{1}{1+} \frac{1}{p+} \frac{1}{1+} \cdots = \sqrt{p^2+4p}.$$

9. Shew that

$$p\left(a_1 + \frac{1}{pqa_2+} \frac{1}{a_3+} \frac{1}{pqa_4+} \cdots\right) = pa_1 + \frac{1}{qa_2} + \frac{1}{pa_3} + \frac{1}{qa_4} + \cdots$$

10. If $\sqrt{a^2+1}$ be expressed as a continued fraction, shew that

$$2(a^2+1)q_n = p_{n-1} + p_{n+1}, \ 2p_n = q_{n-1} + q_{n+1}.$$

11. If $\quad x = \dfrac{1}{a_1+} \dfrac{1}{a_2+} \dfrac{1}{a_1+} \dfrac{1}{a_2+} \cdots$

$$y = \frac{1}{2a_1+} \frac{1}{2a_2+} \frac{1}{2a_1+} \frac{1}{2a_2+} \cdots,$$

$$z = \frac{1}{3a_1+} \frac{1}{3a_2+} \frac{1}{3a_1+} \frac{1}{3a_2+} \cdots$$

shew that $x(y^2-z^2) + 2y(z^2-x^2) + 3z(x^2-y^2) = 0$.

12. Prove that

$$\left(a + \frac{1}{b+} \frac{1}{a+} \frac{1}{b+} \frac{1}{a+} \cdots\right)\left(\frac{1}{b+} \frac{1}{a+} \frac{1}{b+} \frac{1}{a+} \cdots\right) = \frac{a}{b}.$$

13. If $\quad x = a + \dfrac{1}{b+} \dfrac{1}{b+} \dfrac{1}{a+} \dfrac{1}{a+} \cdots$

$$y = b + \frac{1}{a+} \frac{1}{a+} \frac{1}{b+} \frac{1}{b+} \cdots$$

shew that $(ab^2+a+b)x - (a^2b+a+b)y = a^2-b^2$.

14. If $\dfrac{p_n}{q_n}$ be the nth convergent to $\sqrt{a^2+1}$, shew that

$$\frac{p_2^2 + p_3^2 + \ldots + p_{n+1}^2}{q_2^2 + q_3^2 + \ldots + q_{n+1}^2} = \frac{p_{n+1}p_{n+2} - p_1p_2}{q_{n+1}q_{n+2} - q_1q_2}.$$

15. Shew that

$$\left(\frac{1}{a+}\,\frac{1}{b+}\,\frac{1}{c+}\,\cdots\right)\left(c+\frac{1}{b+}\,\frac{1}{a+}\,\frac{1}{c+}\,\cdots\right) = \frac{1+bc}{1+ab}.$$

16. If $\dfrac{p_r}{q_r}$ denote the rth convergent to $\dfrac{\sqrt{5}+1}{2}$, shew that

$$p_3 + p_5 + \ldots + p_{2n-1} = p_{2n} - p_2,\ q_3 + q_5 + \ldots + q_{2n-1} = q_{2n} - q_2.$$

17. Shew that the difference of the infinite continued fractions

$$\frac{1}{a+}\,\frac{1}{b+}\,\frac{1}{c+}\,\cdots,\ \frac{1}{b+}\,\frac{1}{a+}\,\frac{1}{c+}\,\cdots,$$

is equal to $\dfrac{a-b}{1+ab}$.

18. If $\sqrt{N}$ is converted into a continued fraction, and if n is the number of quotients in the period, shew that

$$q_{2n} = 2p_n q_n,\ p_{2n} = 2p_n^2 + (-1)^{n+1}.$$

19. If $\sqrt{N}$ be converted into a continued fraction, and if the penultimate convergents in the first, second, ...kth recurring periods be denoted by $n_1, n_2, \ldots, n_k$ respectively, shew that

$$\frac{n_k + \sqrt{N}}{n_k - \sqrt{N}} = \left(\frac{n_1 + \sqrt{N}}{n_1 - \sqrt{N}}\right)^k.$$

■ ■ ■

Chapter 28

INDETERMINATE EQUATIONS OF THE SECOND DEGREE

*366. The solution in positive integers of indeterminate equations of a degree higher than the first, though not of much practical importance, is interesting because of its connection with the *Theory of Numbers*. In the present chapter we shall confine our attention of equations of the second degree involving two variables.

*367. *To shew how to obtain the positive integral values of x and y which satisfy the equation*

$$ax^2 + 2hxy + by^2 + 2gx + 2fy + c = 0,$$

a, b, c, f, g, h being integers.

Solving this equation as a quadratic in x, as in Art. 127, we have

$$ax + hy + g = \pm \sqrt{(h^2 - ab) y^2 + 2 (hg - af) y + (g^2 - ac)} \qquad \ldots(1).$$

Now in order that the values of x and y may be positive integers, the expression under the radical, which we may denote by $py^2 + 2qy + r$, must be a perfect square, that is

$$py^2 + 2qy + r = z^2, \text{ suppose.}$$

Solving this equation as a quadratic in y, we have

$$py + q = \pm \sqrt{q^2 - pr + pz^2};$$

and as before the expression under the radical must be a perfect square; suppose that it is equal to t^2; then

$$t^2 = pz^2 + q^2 - pr,$$

where t and z are variables, and p, q, r are constants.

Unless this equation can be solved in positive integers, the original equation does not admit of a positive integral solution.

We shall return to this point in Art. 374.

If a, b, h are all positive, it is clear that the number of solutions is limited, because for large values of x and y the sign of the expression on the left depends upon that of $ax^2 + 2hxy + by^2$ [Art. 269], and thus cannot be zero for large positive integral values of x and y.

Again, if $h^2 - ab$ is negative, the coefficient of y^2 in (1) is negative, and by similar reasoning we see that the number of solutions is limited.

Example. Solve in positive integers the equation

$$x^2 - 4xy + 6y^2 - 2x - 20y = 29.$$

Solving as a quadratic in x, we have

$$x = 2y + 1 \pm \sqrt{30 + 24y - 2y^2}.$$

But $30 + 24y - 2y^2 = 102 - 2(y-6)^2$; hence $(y-6)^2$ cannot be greater than 51. By trial we find that the expression under the radical becomes a perfect square when $(y-6)^2 = 1$ or 49; thus the positive integral values of y are 5, 7, 13.

When $y = 5$, $x = 21$ or 1; when $y = 7$, $x = 25$ or 5; when $y = 13$, $x = 29$ or 25.

*368. We have seen that the solution in positive integers of the equation

$$ax^2 + 2hxy + by^2 + 2gx + 2fy + c = 0$$

can be made to depend upon the solution of an equation of the form

$$x^2 \pm Ny^2 = \pm a,$$

where N and a are positive integers

The equation $x^2 + Ny^2 = -a$ has no real roots, whilst the equation $x^2 + Ny^2 = a$ has a limited number of solutions, which may be found by trial; we shall therefore confine our attention to equations of the form $x^2 - Ny^2 = \pm a$.

*369. *To shew that the equation $x^2 - Ny^2 = 1$ can always be solved in positive integers.*

Let $\sqrt{N}$ be converted into a continued fraction, and let $\dfrac{p}{q}, \dfrac{p'}{q'}, \dfrac{p''}{q''}$, be any three consecutive convergents; suppose that $\dfrac{\sqrt{N} + a_n}{r_n}$ is the complete quotient corresponding to $\dfrac{p''}{q''}$; then

$$r_n(pq' - p'q) = Nq'^2 - p'^2 \qquad \text{[Art. 358].}$$

But $r_n = 1$ at the end of any period   [Art. 361];

$$\therefore \qquad p'^2 - Nq'^2 = p'q - pq';$$

$\dfrac{p'}{q'}$ being the penultimate convergent of any recurring period.

If the number of quotients in the period is even, $\dfrac{p'}{q'}$ is an even convergent, and is therefore greater than $\sqrt{N}$, and therefore greater than $\frac{p}{q}$; thus $p'q - pq' = 1$. In this case $p'^2 - Nq'^2 = 1$, and therefore $x = p'$, $y = q'$ is a solution of the equation $x^2 - Ny^2 = 1$.

Since $\frac{p'}{q'}$ is the penultimate convergent of any recurring period, the number of solutions is unlimited.

If the number of quotients in the period is odd, the penultimate convergent, in the first period is an *odd* convergent, but the penultimate convergent in the second period is an *even* convergent.

Thus integral solutions will be obtained by putting $x = p'$, $y = q'$, where $\frac{p'}{q'}$ is the penultimate convergent in the second, fourth, sixth, ... recurring periods. Hence also in this case the number of solutions is unlimited.

*370. *To obtain a solution in positive integers of the equation* $x^2 - Ny^2 = -1$.

As in the preceding article, we have

$$p'^2 - Nq'^2 = p'q - pq'.$$

If the number of quotients in the period is *odd*, and if $\frac{p'}{q'}$ is and *odd* penultimate convergent in any recurring period, $\frac{p'}{q'} < \frac{p}{q}$, and therefore $p'q - pq' = -1$.

In this case $p'^2 - Nq'^2 = -1$, and integral solutions of the equation $x^2 - Ny^2 = -1$ will be obtained by putting $x = p'$, $y = q'$, where $\frac{p'}{q'}$ is the penultimate convergent in the first, third, fifth recurring periods.

Example. Solve in positive integers $x^2 - 13y^2 = \pm 1$.

We can shew that $\sqrt{13} = 3 + \dfrac{1}{1+}\dfrac{1}{1+}\dfrac{1}{1+}\dfrac{1}{1+}\dfrac{1}{6+}\ldots$

Here the number of quotients in the period is odd; the penultimate convergent in the period is $\frac{18}{5}$; hence $x = 18$, $y = 5$ is a solution of $x^2 - 13y^2 = -1$.

By Art. 364, the penultimate convergent in the second recurring period is $\frac{1}{2}\left(\frac{18}{5} + \frac{5}{18} \times 13\right)$, that is, $\frac{649}{180}$;

hence $x = 649$, $y = 180$ is a solution of $x^2 - 13y^2 = 1$.

By forming the successive penultimate convergents of the recurring periods we can obtain any number of solutions of the equations

$$x^2 - 13y^2 = -1, \text{ and } x^2 - 13y^2 = +1.$$

*371. When one solution in positive integers of $x^2 - Ny^2 = \pm 1$ has been found we may obtain as many as we please by the following method.

Suppose that $x = h, y = k$ is a solution, h and k being positive integers; then $(h^2 - Nk^2)^n = 1$, where n is any positive integer.

Thus $x^2 - Ny^2 = (h^2 - Nk^2)^n.$

$\therefore$ $(x + y\sqrt{N})(x - y\sqrt{N}) = (h + k\sqrt{N})^n (h - k\sqrt{N})^n.$

Put $x + y\sqrt{N} = (h + k\sqrt{N})^n, (x - y\sqrt{N}) = (h - k\sqrt{N})^n;$

$\therefore$ $2x = (h + k\sqrt{N})^n + (h - k\sqrt{N})^n;$

$$2y\sqrt{N} = (h + k\sqrt{N})^n - (h - k\sqrt{N})^n.$$

The value of x and y so found are positive integers, and by ascribing to n the values 1, 2, 3, ..., as many solutions as we please can be obtained.

Similarly if $x = h, y = k$ is a solution of the equation

$$x^2 - Ny^2 = -1, \text{ and if } n \text{ is any } odd \text{ positive integer,}$$

$$x^2 - Ny^2 = (h^2 - Nk^2)^n.$$

Thus the values of x and y are the same as already found, but n is restricted to the values 1, 3, 5, ...

*372. By putting $x = ax', y = ay'$ the equations $x^2 - Ny^2 = \pm a^2$ become $x'^2 - Ny'^2 = \pm 1$, which we have already shewn how to solve.

*373. We have seen in Art. 369 that

$$p'^2 - Nq'^2 = \pm r_n \ (pq' - p'q) = \pm r_n$$

Hence if a is a denominator of any complete quotient which occurs in converting $\sqrt{N}$ into a continued fraction, and if $\dfrac{p'}{q'}$ is the convergent obtained by stopping short of this complete quotient, one of the equations $x^2 - Ny^2 = \pm a$ is satisfied by the values $x = p', y = q'$.

Again, the odd convergents are all less than $\sqrt{N}$, and the even convergents are all greater than $\sqrt{N}$; hence if $\dfrac{p'}{q'}$ is an even convergent,

$x = p', y = q'$ is a solution of $x^2 - Ny^2 = a$; and if $\dfrac{p'}{q'}$ is an odd convergent,

$x = p', y = q'$ is a solution of $x^2 - Ny^2 = -a$.

*374. The method explained in the preceding article enables up to find a solution of *one* of the equations $x^2 - Ny^2 = \pm a$ only when a is one of the denominators which occurs in the process of converting $\sqrt{N}$ into a continued fraction. For example, if we convert $\sqrt{7}$ into a continued fraction, we shall find that

$$\sqrt{7} = 2 + \frac{1}{1+} \frac{1}{1+} \frac{1}{1+} \frac{1}{4+} \cdots$$

and that the denominators of the complete quotients are 3, 2, 3, 1.

The successive convergents are

$$\frac{2}{1}, \frac{3}{1}, \frac{5}{2}, \frac{8}{3}, \frac{37}{14}, \frac{45}{17}, \frac{82}{31}, \frac{127}{48}, \dots;$$

and if we take the cycle of equations

$$x^2 - 7y^2 = -3, \ x^2 - 7y^2 = 2, \ x^2 - 7y^2 = -3, \ x^2 - 7y^2 = 1,$$

we shall find that they are satisfied by taking

for x the values 2, 3, 5, 8, 37, 45, 82 127, ...

and for y the values 1, 1, 2, 3, 14, 17, 31, 48, ...

*375 It thus appears that the number of cases in which solutions in integers of the equations $x^2 - Ny^2 = \pm a$ can be obtained with certainty is very limited. In a numerical example it may, however, sometimes happen that we can discover by trial a positive integral solution of the equations $x^2 - Ny^2 = \pm a$, when a is not one of the above mentioned denominators; thus we easily find that the equation $x^2 - 7y^2 = 53$ is satisfied by $y = 2, x = 9$.

When one solution in integers has been found, any number of solutions may be obtained as explained in the next article.

*376. Suppose that $x = f, y = g$ is a solution of the equation $x^2 - Ny^2 = a$; and let $x = h, y = k$ be *any* solution of the equation $x^2 - Ny^2 = 1$; then

$$x^2 - Ny^2 = (f^2 - Ng^2)(h^2 - Nk^2)$$
$$= (fh \pm Ngk)^2 - N(fk \pm gh)^2.$$

By putting $x = fh \pm Ngk, y = fk \pm gh,$

and ascribing to h, k their values found as explained in Art. 371, we may obtain any number of solutions.

*377. Hitherto it has been supposed that N is not a perfect square; if, however, N is a perfect square the equation takes the form $x^2 - n^2y^2 = a$, which may be readily solved as follows.

Suppose that $a = bc$, where b and c are two positive integers of which b is the greater; then

$$(x + ny)(x - ny) = bc.$$

Put $x + ny = b$, $x - ny = c$; if the values of x and y found from these equations are integers we have obtained one solution of the equation; the remaining solutions may be obtained by ascribing to b and c all their possible values.

Example. Find two positive integers the difference of whose squares is equal to 60.

Let x, y be the two integers; then $x^2 - y^2 = 60$; that is, $(x + y)(x - y) = 60$.

Now 60 is the product of any of the pair of factors

$$1, 60; 2, 30; 3, 20; 4, 15; 5, 12; 6, 10;$$

and the values required are obtained from the equations

$$x + y = 30, \ x + y = 10,$$
$$x - y = 2; \ x - y = 6;$$

the other equations giving fractional values of x and y.

Thus the numbers are 16, 14; or 8, 2.

Cor. In like manner we may obtain the solution in positive integers of

$$ax^2 + 2hxy + by^2 + 2gx + 2fy + c = k,$$

If the left-hand member can be resolved into rational linear factors.

*378. If in the general equation a, or b, or both, are zero instead of employing the method explained in Art. 367 it is simpler to proceed as in the following example.

Example. Solve in positive integers

$$2xy - 4x^2 + 12x - 5y = 11.$$

Expressing y in terms of x, we have

$$y = \frac{4x^2 - 12x + 11}{2x - 5} = 2x - 1 + \frac{6}{2x - 5}.$$

In order that y may be an integer $\dfrac{6}{2x - 5}$ must be an integer; hence $2x - 5$ must be equal to ± 1, or ± 2, or ± 3, or ± 6.

The cases ± 2, ± 6 may clearly be rejected; hence the admissible values of x are obtained from

$$2x - 5 = \pm 1, \ 2x - 5 = \pm 3$$

whence the values of x are 3, 2, 4, 1.

Taking these values in succession we obtain the solutions

$$x = 3, y = 11; x = 2, y = -3; x = 4, y = 9; x = 1, y = -1;$$

and therefore the admissible solutions are

$$x = 3, y = 11; x = 4, y = 9.$$

*379. The principles already explained enable us to discover for what values of the variables given linear or quadratic functions of x and y become perfect squares. Problem of this kind are sometimes called *Diophantine Problems* because they were first investigated by the Greek mathematician Diophantus about the middle of the fourth century.

Example 1. Find the general expressions for two positive integers which are such that if their product is taken from the sum of their squares the difference is a perfect square.

Denote the integers by x and y; then

$$x^2 - xy + y^2 = z^2 \text{ suppose;}$$

$\therefore$

$$x(x - y) = z^2 - y^2.$$

This equation is satisfied by the suppositions

$$mx = n(z + y), \ n(x - y) = m(z - y),$$

where m and n are positive integers.

Hence $\quad mx - ny - nz = 0, \ nx + (m - n)y - mz + 0.$

From these equations we obtain by cross multiplication

$$\frac{x}{2mn - n^2} = \frac{y}{m^2 - n^2} = \frac{z}{m^2 - mn + n^2};$$

and since the given equation is homogeneous we may take for the general solution

$$x = 2mn - n^2, y = m^2 - n^2, z = m^2 - mn + n^2.$$

Here m and n are any two positive integers, m being the greater; thus if $m = 7, n = 4$, we have

$$z = 40, y = 33, z = 37.$$

Example 2. Find the general expression for three positive integers in arithmetic progression, and such that the sum of every two is a perfect square.

Denote the integers by $x - y, x, x + y$; and let

$$2x - y = p^2, 2x = q^2, 2x + y = r^2;$$

then $\quad\quad\quad\quad\quad\quad p^2 + r^2 = 2q^2$

or $\quad\quad\quad\quad\quad\quad r^2 - q^2 = q^2 - p^2.$

This equation is satisfied by the suppositions,

$$m(r - q) = n(q - p), \ n(r + q) = m(q + p),$$

where m and n are positive integers.

From these equations we obtain by cross multiplication

$$\frac{p}{n^2 + 2mn - m^2} = \frac{q}{m^2 + n^2} = \frac{r}{m^2 + 2mn - n^2}.$$

Hence we may take for general solution

$$p = n^2 + 2mn - m^2, \quad q = m^2 + n^2, \quad r = m^2 + 2mn - n^2;$$

whence $\qquad x = \frac{1}{2}(m^2 + n^2)^2, \quad y = 4mn(m^2 - n^2),$

and the three integers can be found.

From the value of x it is clear that m and n are either both even or both odd; also their values must be such that x is greater than y, that is,

$$(m^2 + n^2)^2 > 8mn(m^2 - n^2),$$

or $\qquad m^3(m - 8n) + 2m^2n^2 + 8mn^3 + n^4 > 0;$

which condition is satisfied if $m > 8n$.

If $m = 9, n = 1$, then $x = 3362, y = 2880$, and the numbers are 482, 3362, 6242. The sums of these taken in pairs are 3844, 6724, 9604, which are the squares of 62, 82, 98 respectively.

EXAMPLES XXVIII

Solve in positive integers :

1. $5x^2 - 10xy + 7y^2 = 77$.

2. $7x^2 - 2xy + 3y^2 = 27$.

3. $y^2 - 4xy + 5x^2 - 10x = 4$.

4. $xy - 2x - y = 8$.

5. $3x + 3xy - 4y = 14$.

6. $4x^2 - y^2 = 315$.

Find the smallest solution in positive integers of

7. $x^2 - 14y^2 = 1$.   8. $x^2 - 19y^2 = 1$.   9. $x^2 = 41y^2 - 1$.

10. $x^2 - 61y^2 + 5 = 0$.   11. $x^2 - 7y^2 - 9 = 0$.

Find the general solution in positive integers of

12. $x^2 - 3y^2 = 1$.   13. $x^2 - 5y^2 = 1$.   14. $x^2 - 17y^2 = -1$.

Find the general values of x and y which make each of the following expressions a perfect square :

15. $x^2 - 3xy + 3y^2$.   16. $x^2 + 2xy + 2y^2$.   17. $5x^2 + y^2$.

18. Find two positive integers such that the square of one exceeds the square of the other by 105.

19. Find a general formula for three integers which may be taken to represent the lengths of the sides of a right-angled triangle.

20. Find a general formula to express two positive integers which are such that the result obtained by adding their product to the sum of their squares is a perfect square.

21. "There came three Dutchmen of my acquaintance to see me, being lately married; they brought their wives with them. The men's names were Hendriek, Claas, and Cornelius; the women's Geertruij, Catriin, and Anna : but I forgot the name of each man's wife. They told me they had been at market to buy hogs; each person bought as many hogs as they gave shillings for one hog; Hendriek bought 23 hogs more than Catriin; and Claas bought 11 more than Geertruij; likewise, each man laid out 3 guineas more than his wife. I desire to know the name of each man's wife." (*Miscellany of Mathematical Problems*, 1743.)

22. Shew that the sum of the first n natural numbers is a perfect square, if n equal to k^2 or $k'^2 - 1$, where k is the numerator of an odd, and k' the numerator of an even convergent to $\sqrt{2}$.

■■■

Chapter 29

SUMMATION OF SERIES

380. Examples of summation of certain series have occurred in previous chapters; it will be convenient here to give a synopsis of the methods of summation which have already been explained.

(i) Arithmetical Progression, Chap. 4.

(ii) Geometrical Progression, Chap. 5.

(iii) Series which are partly arithmetical and partly geometrical, Art. 60.

(iv) Sums of the powers of the Natural Numbers and allied Series, Arts. 68 to 75.

(v) Summation by means of Undetermined Coefficients, Art. 312.

(vi) Recurring Series, Chap. 24.

We now proceed to discuss methods of greater generality; but in the course of the present chapter it will be seen that some of the foregoing methods may still be usefully employed.

381. If the rth term of a series can be expressed as the difference of two quantities one which is the same function of r that the other is of $r-1$, the sum of the series may be readily found.

For let the series be denoted by

$$u_1 + u_2 + u_3 + \dots + u_n,$$

and its sum by S_n, and suppose that any term u_r can be put in the form $v_r - v_{r-1}$; then

$$S_n = (v_1 - v_0) + (v_2 - v_1) + \dots + (v_{n-1} - v_{n-2}) + (v_n - v_{n-1})$$

$$= v_n - v_0.$$

Example. Sum to n terms the series

$$\frac{1}{(1+x)(1+2x)} + \frac{1}{(1-2x)(1+3x)} + \frac{1}{(1+3x)(1+4x)} + \dots$$

If we denote the series by

$$u_1 + u_2 + u_3 + \dots + u_n,$$

we have

$$u_1 = \frac{1}{x}\left(\frac{1}{1+x} - \frac{1}{1+2x}\right),$$

$$u_2 = \frac{1}{x}\left(\frac{1}{1+2x} - \frac{1}{1+3x}\right),$$

$$u_3 = \frac{1}{x}\left(\frac{1}{1+3x} - \frac{1}{1+4x}\right),$$

. . . .

$$u_n = \frac{1}{x}\left(\frac{1}{1+nx} - \frac{1}{1+\overline{n+1}.x}\right),$$

∴ by addition, $$S_n = \frac{1}{x}\left(\frac{1}{1+x} - \frac{1}{1+\overline{n+1}.x}\right)$$

$$= \frac{n}{(1+x)(1+\overline{n+1}.x)}.$$

382. Sometimes a suitable transformation may be obtained by separating u_n into partial fractions by the methods explained in Chap. 23.

Example. Find the sum of

$$\frac{1}{(1+x)(1+ax)} + \frac{a}{(1+ax)(1+a^2x)} + \frac{a^2}{(1+a^2x)(1+a^3x)} + \dots \text{ to } n \text{ terms.}$$

The nth term $= \dfrac{a^{n-1}}{(1+a^{n-1}x)(1+a^nx)} = \dfrac{A}{1+a^{n-1}x} + \dfrac{B}{1+a^nx}$ suppose;

∴ $\quad a^{n-1} = A(1+a^nx) + B(1+a^{n-1}x).$

By putting $1+a^{n-1}x$, $1+a^nx$ equal to zero in succession, we obtain

$$A = \frac{a^{n-1}}{1-a}, \quad B = -\frac{a^n}{1-a}.$$

Hence $$u_1 = \frac{1}{1-a}\left(\frac{1}{1+x} - \frac{a}{1+ax}\right),$$

similarly, $$u_2 = \frac{1}{1-a}\left(\frac{a}{1+ax} - \frac{a^2}{1+a^2x}\right)$$

. . . .

$$u_n = \frac{1}{1-a}\left(\frac{a^{n-1}}{1+a^{n-1}x} - \frac{a^n}{1+a^nx}\right).$$

∴ $$S_n = \frac{1}{1-a}\left(\frac{1}{1+x} - \frac{a^n}{1+a^nx}\right).$$

383. *To find the sum of n terms of a series each term of which is composed of r factors in arithmetical progression, the first factors of the several terms being in the same arithmetical progression.*

Let the series be denoted by $u_1 + u_2 + u_3 + \dots + u_n$, where

$$u_n = (a+nb)(a+\overline{n+1}.b)(a+\overline{n+2}.b) \dots (a+\overline{n+r-1}.b).$$

Replacing n by $n-1$, we have

$$u_{n-1} = (a + \overline{n-1}.\,b)\,(a + nb)\,(a + \overline{n+1}.\,b)$$
$$\dots (a + \overline{n+r-2}.\,b);$$

$$\therefore \quad (a + \overline{n-1}.\,b)\,u_n = (a + \overline{n+r-1}.\,b)\,u_{n-1} = v_n, \text{ say.}$$

Replacing n by $n+1$ we have

$$(a + \overline{n+r}.\,b)\,u_n = v_{n+1};$$

therefore, by subtraction,

$$(r+1)\,b.\,u_n = v_{n+1} - v_n\,.$$

Similarly, $\qquad (r+1)\,b.\,u_{n-1} = v_n - v_{n-1},$

$$\dotfill$$

$$(r+1)\,b.\,u_2 = v_3 - v_2,$$
$$(r+1)\,b.\,u_1 = v_2 - v_1.$$

By addition, $(r+1)\,b.\,S_n = v_{n+1} - v_1;$

that is, $\qquad S_n = \dfrac{v_{n+1} - v_1}{(r+1)\,b}$

$$= \dfrac{(a + \overline{n+r}.\,b)\,u_n}{(r+1)\,b} + C, \quad \text{say;}$$

where C is a quantity independent of n, which may be found by ascribing to n some particular value.

The above result gives us the following convenient rule :

Write down the nth term, affix the next factor at the end divide by the number of factors thus increased and by the common difference, and add a constant.

It may be noticed that $C = -\dfrac{v_1}{(r+1)\,b} = -\dfrac{a}{(r+1)\,b}\,u_1$; it is however better not to quote this result, but to obtain C as above indicated.

Example. Find the sum of n terms of the series

$$1.3.5 + 3.5.7 + 5.7.9 + \dots$$

The nth term is $(2n-1)\,(2n+1)\,(2n+3)$; hence by the rule

$$S_n = \dfrac{(2n-1)\,(2n+1)\,(2n+3)\,(2n+5)}{4.2} + C.$$

To determine C, put $n = 1$; then the series reduces to its first term, and we have $15 = \dfrac{1.3.5.7}{8} + C$; whence $C = \dfrac{15}{8}$;

$$\therefore \quad S_n = \dfrac{(2n-1)\,(2n+1)\,(2n+3)\,(2n+5)}{8} + \dfrac{15}{8}$$

$$= n\,(2n^3 + 8n^2 + 7n - 2), \text{ after reduction.}$$

384. The sum of the series in the preceding article may also be found either by the method of Undetermined Coefficients [Art. 312] or in the following manner.

We have $u_n = (2n - 1)(2n + 1)(2n + 3) = 8n^3 + 12n^2 - 2n - 3$;

$$\therefore \quad S_n = 8\Sigma n^3 + 12\Sigma n^2 - 2\Sigma n - 3n,$$

using the notation of Art. 70;

$$\therefore \quad S_n = 2n^2(n+1)^2 + 2n(n+1)(2n+1) - n(n+1) - 3n$$

$$= n(2n^3 + 8n^2 + 7n - 2).$$

385. It should be noticed that the rule given in Art. 383 is only applicable to cases in which the factors of each term form an arithmetical progression, and the first factors of the several terms are in the *same* arithmetical progression,

Thus the sum of the series

$$1.\,3.\,5 + 2.\,4.\,6 + 3.\,5.\,7 + \ldots \text{ to } n \text{ terms,}$$

may be found by either of the methods suggested in the preceding article, but not directly by the rule of Art.383. Here

$$u_n = n(n+2)(n+4) = n(\overline{n+1}+1)(\overline{n+2}+2)$$

$$= n(n+1)(n+2) + 2n(n+1) + n(n+2) + 2n$$

$$= n(n+1)(n+2) + 3n(n+1) + 3n.$$

The rule can now be applied to each term; thus

$$S_n = \tfrac{1}{4}n(n+1)(n+2)(n+3) + n(n+1)(n+2) + \tfrac{3}{2}n(n+1) + 0$$

$$= \tfrac{1}{4}n(n+1)(n+4)(n+5), \text{ the constant being zero.}$$

386. *To find the sum of n terms of a series each term of which is composed of the reciprocal of the product of r factors in arithmetical progression, the first factors of the several terms being in the same arithmetical progression.*

Let the series be denoted by $u_1 + u_2 + u_3 + \ldots + u_n$, where

$$\frac{1}{u_n} = (a + nb)(a + \overline{n+1}.\,b)(a + \overline{n+2}.\,b)\ldots(a + \overline{n+r-1}.\,b).$$

Replacing n by $n - 1$,

$$\frac{1}{u_{n-1}} = (a + \overline{n-1}.\,b)(a + nb)(a + \overline{n+1}.\,b)\ldots(a + \overline{n+r-2}.\,b);$$

$$\therefore \quad (a + \overline{n+r-1}.\,b)\,u_n = (a + \overline{n-1}.\,b)\,u_{n-1} = v_n, \text{ say}$$

Replacing n by $n + 1$, we have

$$(a + nb)\,u_n = v_{n+1};$$

therefore, by subtraction,

$$(r-1) \, b \, . \, u_n = v_n - v_{n+1}.$$

Similarly $(r-1) \, b \, . \, u_{n-1} = v_{n-1} - v_n,$

$$\dots\dots\dots\dots\dots\dots\dots\dots$$

$$(r-1) \, b \, . \, u_2 = v_2 - v_3,$$

$$(r-1) \, b \, . \, u_1 = v_1 - v_2.$$

By addition, $(r-1) \, b \, . \, S_n = v_1 - v_{n+1};$

that is

$$S_n = \frac{v_1 - v_{n+1}}{(r-1) \, b} = C - \frac{(a+nb) \, u_n}{(r-1) \, b},$$

where C is a quantity independent of n, which may be found by ascribing to n some particular value.

Thus $S_n = C - \dfrac{1}{(r-1) \, b} \cdot \dfrac{1}{(a + \overline{n+1} \, . \, b) \dots (a + \overline{n+r-1} \, . \, b)}$

Hence the sum may be found by the following rule:

Write down the nth term, strike off a factor from the beginning, divide by the number of factors so diminished and by the common difference, change the sign and add a constant.

The value of $C = \dfrac{v_1}{(r-1) \, b} = \dfrac{a+rb}{(r-1) \, b} \, u_1;$ but it is advisable in each case to determine C by ascribing to n some particular value.

Example 1. Find the sum of n terms of the series

$$\frac{1}{1 \, . \, 2 \, . \, 3 \, . \, 4} + \frac{1}{2 \, . \, 3 \, . \, 4 \, . \, 5} + \frac{1}{3 \, . \, 4 \, . \, 5 \, . \, 6} + \dots$$

The nth term is $\dfrac{1}{n \, (n+1) \, (n+2) \, (n+3)};$

hence, by the rule, we have

$$S_n = C - \frac{1}{3 \, (n+1) \, (n+2) \, (n+3)}.$$

put $n=1$, then $\dfrac{1}{1 \, . \, 2 \, . \, 3 \, . \, 4} = C - \dfrac{1}{3 \, . \, 2 \, . \, 3 \, . \, 4}$; whence $C = \dfrac{1}{18}$;

$$\therefore \qquad S_n = \frac{1}{18} - \frac{1}{3 \, (n+1) \, (n+2) \, (n+3)}.$$

By making n indefinitely great, we obtain $S_\infty = \dfrac{1}{18}.$

Example 2. Find the sum to n terms of the series

$$\frac{3}{1 \, . \, 2 \, . \, 4} + \frac{4}{2 \, . \, 3 \, . \, 5} + \frac{5}{3 \, . \, 4 \, . \, 6} + \dots$$

Here the rule is not directly applicable, because although 1, 2, 3, ..., the first factors of the several denominators, are in arithmetical progression, the factors of any one denominator are not. In this example we may proceed as follows :

$$u_n = \frac{n+2}{n\,(n+1)\,(n+3)} = \frac{(n+2)^2}{n\,(n+1)\,(n+2)\,(n+3)}$$

$$= \frac{n\,(n+1)+3n+4}{n\,(n+1)\,(n+2)\,(n+3)}$$

$$= \frac{1}{(n+2)\,(n+3)} + \frac{3}{(n+1)\,(n+2)\,(n+3)} + \frac{4}{n\,(n+1)\,(n+2)\,(n+3)}.$$

Each of these expressions may be taken as the nth term of a series to which the rule is applicable.

$$\therefore \qquad S_n = C - \frac{1}{n+3} - \frac{3}{2\,(n+2)\,(n+3)} - \frac{4}{3\,(n+1)\,(n+2)\,(n+3)} \,;$$

put $n=1$, then

$$\frac{3}{1.\,2.\,4} = C - \frac{1}{4} - \frac{3}{2.\,3.\,4} - \frac{4}{3.\,2.\,3.\,4} \,; \quad \text{whence } C = \frac{29}{36} \,;$$

$$\therefore \qquad S_n = \frac{29}{36} - \frac{1}{n+3} - \frac{3}{2\,(n+2)\,(n+3)} - \frac{4}{3\,(n+1)\,(n+2)\,(n+3)}$$

387. In cases where the methods of Arts. 383, 386 are *directly* applicable, instead of quoting the rules we may always effect the summation in the following way, which is sometimes called the Method of Subtraction.'

Example. Find the sum of n terms of the series

$$2.\,5 + 5.\,8 + 8.\,11 + 11.\,14 + \dots$$

The arithmetical progression in this case is

$$2, 5, 8, 11, 14, \dots$$

In each term of the given series introduce as a new factor the next term of the arithmetical progression; denote this series by S', and the given series by S; then

$$S' = 2.\,5.\,8 + 5.\,8.\,11 + 8.\,11.\,14 + \dots$$
$$+ (3n-1)\,(3n+2)\,(3n+5);$$

$$\therefore \qquad S' - 2.\,5.\,8 = 5.\,8.\,11 + 8.\,11.\,14 + 11.\,14.\,17 + \dots \text{ to } (n-1) \text{ terms.}$$

By subtraction,

$$- 2.\,5.\,8 = 9\,[5.\,8 + 8.11 + 11.\,14 + \dots \text{ to } (n-1) \text{ terms}]$$
$$- (3n-1)\,(3n+2)\,(3n+5),$$

$$- 2.\,5.\,8 = 9\,[S - 2.\,5] - (3n-1)\,(3n+2)\,(3n+5),$$

$$9S = (3n-1)\,(3n+2)\,(3n+5) - 2.\,5.\,8 + 2.\,5.\,9,$$

$$S = n\,(3n^2 + 6n + 1).$$

388. When the nth term of a series is a rational integral function of n it can be expressed in a form which will enable us readily to apply the method given in Art. 383.

For suppose $\phi_1(n)$ is a rational integral function of n of p dimensions, and assume

$$\phi(n) = A + Bn + Cn(n+1) + Dn(n+1)(n+2) + \dots,$$

where $A, B, C, D, \dots$ are undetermined constants $p+1$ in number.

This identity being true for all values of n, we may equate the coefficients of like powers of n; we thus obtain $p+1$ simple equations to determine the $p+1$ constants.

Example. Find the sum of n terms of the series whose general term is

$$n^4 + 6n^3 + 5n^2.$$

Assume

$$n^4 + 6n^3 + 5n^2 = A + Bn + Cn(n+1) + Dn(n+1)(n+2)$$
$$+ En(n+1)(n+2)(n+3);$$

Equating coefficients of like powers of n, since this is an identity, gives

$$A = 0, B = 0, C = -6, D = 0, E = 1. \text{ Thus}$$

$$n^4 + 6n^3 + 5n^2 = n(n+1)(n+2)(n+3) - 6n(n+1).$$

Hence $$S_n = \frac{1}{5}n(n+1)(n+2)(n+3)(n+4) - 2n(n+1)(n+2)$$

$$= \frac{1}{5}n(n+1)(n+2)(n^2+7n+2).$$

POLYGONAL AND FIGURATE NUMBERS

389.   If in the expression $n + \frac{1}{2}n(n-1)b$, which is the sum of n terms of an arthmetical progression whose first term is 1 and common difference b, we give to b the values $0, 1, 2, 3, \dots$, we get

$$n, \ \frac{1}{2}n(n+1), \ n^2, \ \frac{1}{2}n(3n-1), \dots,$$

which are the nth terms of the **Polygonal Numbers** of the second, third, fourth, fifth, ... orders; the first order being that in which each term is unity. The polygonal numbers of the second, third fourth, fifth, ... orders are sometimes called *linear, triangular, square, pentagonal, ...*

390.   *To find the sum of the first n terms of the rth order of polygonal numbers.*

The nth term of the rth order is $n + \frac{1}{2}n(n-1)(r-2)$;

$$\therefore \quad S_n = \Sigma n + \frac{1}{2}(r-2)\Sigma(n-1)n$$

$$= \frac{1}{2}n(n+1) + \frac{1}{6}(r-2)(n-1)n(n+1) \qquad \text{[Art. 383]}$$

$$= \frac{1}{6}n(n+1)\{(r-2)(n-1)+3\}$$

391.   If the sum of n terms of the series

$$1, 1, 1, 1, 1, \dots,$$

be taken as the nth term of a new series, we obtain
$$1, 2, 3, 4, 5, \ldots$$

If again we take $\dfrac{n(n+1)}{2}$, which is the sum of n terms of the last series, as the nth term of a new series, we obtain
$$1, 3, 6, 10, 15, \ldots$$

By proceeding in this way, we obtain a succession of series such that in any one, the nth term is the sum of n terms of the preceding series. The successive series thus formed are known as **Figurate Numbers** of the first, second, third, ... orders.

392. *To find the nth term and the sum of n terms of the rth order of figurate numbers.*

The nth term of the first order is 1; the nth term of the second order is n; the nth term of the third order is Σn, that is $\frac{1}{2} n(n+1)$; the nth term of the fourth order is $\Sigma \dfrac{n(n+1)}{1 . 2}$, that is $\dfrac{n(n+1)(n+2)}{1 . 2 . 3}$; the nth term of the fifth order is $\Sigma \dfrac{n(n+1)(n+2)}{1 . 2 . 3}$, that is $\dfrac{n(n+1)(n+2)(n+3)}{4!}$; and so on.

Thus it is easy to see that the nth term of the rth order is
$$\frac{n(n+1)(n+2) \ldots (n+r-2)}{(r-1)!}, \text{ or } \frac{(n+r-2)!}{(n-1)!(r-1)!}.$$

Again, the sum of n terms of the rth order is
$$\frac{n(n+1)(n+2) \ldots (n+r-1)}{r!}$$
which is the nth term of the $(r+1)^{\text{th}}$ order.

Note. In applying the rule of Art. 383 to find the sum of n terms of any order of figurate numbers, it will be found that the constant is always zero.

393.   The properties of *figurate numbers* are historically interesting on account of the use made of them by Pascal in his *Traite du triangle arithmetique*, published in 1665.

The following table exhibits the *Arithmetical Triangle* in its simplest form

1	1	1	1	1	1	1	1	1	1	...
1	2	3	4	5	6	7	8	9	...	
1	3	6	10	15	21	28	36	...		
1	4	10	20	35	56	84	...			

	5	15	35	70	126	...
1	6	21	56	126	...	
1	7	28	84	...		
1	8	36	...			
1	9	...				
1	...					

Pascal constructed the numbers in the triangle by the following rule :

Each number is the sum of that immediately above it and that immediately to the left of it;

thus $15 = 5 + 10,\ 28 = 7 + 21,\ 126 = 56 + 70.$

From the mode of construction, it follows that the numbers in the successive horizontal rows, or vertical columns, are the figurate numbers of the first, second, third, ... orders.

A line drawn so as to cut off an equal number of units from the top row and the left-hand column is called a *base*, and the bases are numbered beginning from the top left-hand corner. Thus the 6th base is a line drawn through the numbers 1, 5, 10, 10, 5, 1; and it will be observed that there are six of these numbers, and that they are the coefficients of the terms in the expansion of $(1 + x)^5$.

The properties of these numbers were discussed by Pascal with great skill : in particular he used his *Arithmetical Triangle* to develop the theory of Combinations, and to establish some interesting propositions in Probability. The subject is fully treated in Todhunter's *History of Probability*, Chapter 2.

394.   Where no ambiguity exists as to the number of terms in a series, we have used the symbol Σ to indicate summation; but in some cases the following modified notation, which indicates the limits between which the summation is to be effected, will be found more convenient.

Let $\phi(x)$ be any function of x, then $\displaystyle\sum_{x=l}^{x=m} \phi(x)$ denotes the sum of the series of terms obtained from $\phi(x)$ by giving to x all positive integral values from l to m inclusive.

For instance, suppose it is required to find the sum of all the terms of the series obtained from the expression

$$\frac{(p-1)(p-2)\ \dots\ (p-r)}{r!}$$

by giving to p all integral values from $r + 1$ to p inclusive.

Writing the factors of the numerator in ascending order,

the required sum $= \overset{p=p}{\underset{p=r+1}{\Sigma}} \dfrac{(p-r)(p-r+1)\ldots(p-1)}{r!}$

$= \dfrac{1}{r!}\{1.2.3.\ldots r + 2.3.4.\ldots(r+1) +$

$\ldots + (p-r)(p-r+1)\ldots(p-1)\}$

$= \dfrac{1}{r!} \cdot \dfrac{(p-r)(p-r+1)\ldots(p-1)p}{r+1}$,   [Art. 383.]

$= \dfrac{(p-1)(p-2)\ldots(p-r)}{(r+1)!}$.

Since the given expression is zero for all values of p from 1 to r inclusive, we may write the result in the form

$$\overset{p=p}{\underset{p=1}{\Sigma}} \dfrac{(p-1)(p-2)\ldots(p-r)}{r!} = \dfrac{p(p-1)(p-2)\ldots(p-r)}{(r+1)!}.$$

EXAMPLES. XXIX. a.

Sum the following series to n terms :

1. $1.2.3 + 2.3.4 + 3.4.5 + \ldots$

2. $1.2.3.4 + 2.3.4.5 + 3.4.5.6 + \ldots$

3. $1.4.7 + 4.7.10 + 7.10.13 + \ldots$

4. $1.4.7 + 2.5.8 + 3.6.9 + \ldots$

5. $1.5.9 + 2.6.10 + 3.7.11 + \ldots$

Sum the following series to n terms and to infinity :

6. $\dfrac{1}{1.2} + \dfrac{1}{2.3} + \dfrac{1}{3.4} + \ldots$

7. $\dfrac{1}{1.4} + \dfrac{1}{4.7} + \dfrac{1}{7.10} + \ldots$

8. $\dfrac{1}{1.3.5} + \dfrac{1}{3.5.7} + \dfrac{1}{5.7.9} + \ldots$

9. $\dfrac{1}{1.4.7} + \dfrac{1}{4.7.10} + \dfrac{1}{7.10.13} + \ldots$

10. $\dfrac{4}{1.2.3} + \dfrac{5}{2.3.4} + \dfrac{6}{3.4.5} + \ldots$

11. $\dfrac{1}{3.4.5} + \dfrac{2}{4.5.6} + \dfrac{3}{5.6.7} + \ldots$

12. $\dfrac{1}{1.2.3} + \dfrac{3}{2.3.4} + \dfrac{5}{3.4.5} + \dfrac{7}{4.5.6} + \ldots$

Find the sum of n terms of the series :

13. $1 . 3 . 2^2 + 2 . 4 . 3^2 + 3 . 5 . 4^2 + \dots$

14. $(n^2 - 1^2) + 2 (n^2 - 2^2) + 3 (n^2 - 3^2) + \dots$

Find the sum of n terms of the series whose nth term is

15. $n^2 (n^2 - 1).$ **16.** $(n^2 + 5n + 4) (n^2 + 5n + 8).$

17. $\dfrac{n^2 (n^2 - 1)}{4n^2 - 1}.$ **18.** $\dfrac{n^4 + 2n^3 + n^2 - 1}{n^2 + n}.$

19. $\dfrac{n^3 + 3n^2 + 2n + 2}{n^2 + 2n}.$ **20.** $\dfrac{n^4 + n^2 + 1}{n^4 + n}.$

21.   Shew that the nth term of the rth order of figurate numbers is equal to the rth term of the nth order.

22.   If the nth term of the rth order of figurate numbers is equal to the $(n + 2)^{\text{th}}$ term of the $(r - 2)^{\text{th}}$ order, shew that $r = n + 2$.

23.   Shew that the sum of the first n of all the sets of polygonal numbers from the linear to that of the rth order inclusive is

$$\frac{(r - 1) n (n + 1)}{12} (rn - 2n - r + 8).$$

SUMMATION BY THE METHOD OF DIFFERENCES

395.   Let u_n denote some rational integral function of n, and let $u_1, u_2, u_3, u_4, \dots$ denote the values of u_n when for n the values $1, 2, 3, 4, \dots$ are written successively.

We proceed to investigate a method of finding u_n when a certain number of the terms $u_1, u_2, u_3, u_4, \dots$ are given.

From the series $u_1, u_2, u_3, u_4, u_5, \dots$ obtain a second series by subtracting each term from the term which immediately follows it.

The series

$$u_2 - u_1, u_3 - u_2, u_4 - u_3, u_5 - u_4, \dots$$

thus found is called the *series of the first order of differences*, and may be conveniently denoted by

$$\Delta u_1, \Delta u_2, \Delta u_3, \Delta u_4, \dots$$

By subtracting each term of this series from the term that immediately follows it, we have

$$\Delta u_2 - \Delta u_1, \Delta u_3 - \Delta u_2, \Delta u_4 - \Delta u_3, \dots$$

which may be called the *series of the second order of differences*, and denoted by

$$\Delta_1 u_1, \Delta_2 u_2, \Delta_3 u_3, \dots$$

From this series we may proceed to form the *series of the third, fourth, fifth, ... orders of differences, the general* terms of these series being $\Delta_3 u_r, \Delta_4 u_r, \Delta_5 u_r, \ldots$ respectively.

From the law of formation of the series

$$u_1, \quad u_2, \quad u_3, \quad u_4, \quad u_5, \quad u_6, \ldots\ldots$$
$$\Delta u_1, \quad \Delta u_2, \quad \Delta u_3, \quad \Delta u_4, \quad \Delta u_5, \ldots\ldots$$
$$\Delta_2 u_1, \quad \Delta_2 u_2, \quad \Delta_2 u_3, \quad \Delta_2 u_4, \ldots\ldots$$
$$\Delta_3 u_1, \quad \Delta_3 u_2, \quad \Delta_3 u_3, \ldots\ldots$$

it appears that any term in any series is equal to the term immediately preceding it added to the term below it on the left.

Thus $u_2 = u_1 + \Delta u_1$, and $\Delta u_2 = \Delta u_1 + \Delta_2 u_1$.

By addition, since $u_2 + \Delta u_2 = u_3$ we have

$$u_3 = u_1 + 2\Delta u_1 + \Delta_2 u_1$$

In an exactly similar manner by using the second, third, and fourth series in place of the first, second, and third, we obtain

$$\Delta u_3 = \Delta u_1 + 2\Delta_2 u_1 + \Delta_3 u_1.$$

By addition, since $u_3 + \Delta u_3 = u_4$, we have

$$u_4 = u_1 + 3\Delta u_1 + 3\Delta_2 u_1 + \Delta_3 u_1.$$

So far as we have proceeded, the numerical coefficients follow the same law as those of the Binomial theorem. We shall now prove by induction that this will always be the case. For suppose that

$$u_{n+1} = u_1 + n\,\Delta u_1 + \frac{n(n-1)}{1.2}\Delta_2 u_1 + \ldots + {}^nC_r\,\Delta_r u_1 + \ldots + \Delta_n u_1;$$

then by using the second to be $(n+2)$th series in the place of the first to the $(n+1)$th series, we have

$$\Delta u_{n+1} = \Delta u_1 + n\,\Delta_2 u_1 + \frac{n(n-1)}{1.2}\Delta_3 u_1 + \ldots + {}^nC_{r-1}\,\Delta_r u_1 + \ldots + \Delta_{n+1} u_1.$$

By addition, since $u_{n+1} + \Delta u_{n+1} = u_{n+2}$, we obtain

$$u_{n+2} = u_1 + (n+1)\,\Delta u_1 + \ldots + ({}^nC_r + {}^nC_{r-1})\,\Delta_r u_1 + \ldots + \Delta_{n+1} u_1$$

But $${}^nC_r + {}^nC_{r-1} = \left(\frac{n-r+1}{r} + 1\right) \times {}^nC_{r-1} = \frac{n+1}{r} \times {}^nC_{r-1}$$

$$= \frac{(n+1)\,n\,(n-1)\ldots(n+1-r+1)}{1.2.3\ldots(r-1)\,r} = {}^{n+1}C_r.$$

Hence if the law of formation holds for u_{n+1} it also holds for u_{n+2}, but it is true in the case of u_4, therefore it holds for u_5, and therefore universally. Hence

$$u_n = u_1 + (n-1)\,\Delta u_1 + \frac{(n-1)\,(n-2)}{1.2}\,\Delta_2 u_1 + \dots + \Delta_{n-1}\,u_1.$$

396.　To find the sum of n terms of the series

$$u_1, \quad u_2, \quad u_3, \quad u_4, \dots\dots$$

in terms of the differences of u_1.

Suppose the series $u_1, u_2, u_3, \dots$ is the first order of differences of the series

$$v_1, \quad v_2, \quad v_3, \quad v_4, \dots\dots$$

then $v_{n+1} = (v_{n+1} - v_n) + (v_n - v_{n-1}) + \dots + (v_2 - v_1) + v_1$ identically;

$$\therefore \qquad v_{n+1} = u_n + u_{n-1} + \dots + u_2 + u_1 + v_1.$$

Hence in the series

$$0, \quad v_2, \quad v_3, \quad v_4, \quad v_5, \dots\dots$$
$$u_1, \quad u_2, \quad u_3, \quad u_4, \dots\dots$$
$$\Delta u_1, \quad \Delta u_2, \quad \Delta u_3, \dots\dots$$

the law of formation is the same as in the preceding article;

$$\therefore \qquad v_{n+1} = 0 + n u_1 + \frac{n\,(n-1)}{1.2}\,\Delta u_1 + \dots + \Delta_n u_1;$$

that is ,

$$u_1 + u_2 + u_3 + \dots + u_n$$

$$= n u_1 + \frac{n\,(n-1)}{2\,!}\,\Delta u_1 + \frac{n\,(n-1)\,(n-2)}{3\,!}\,\Delta_2 u_1 + \dots + \Delta_n u_1.$$

The formulae of this and the preceding article may be expressed in a slightly different form, as follows: if a is the first term of a given series, $d_1, d_2, d_3, \dots$ the first terms of the successive orders of differences, the nth term of the given series is obtained from the formula

$$a + (n-1)\,d_1 + \frac{(n-1)\,(n-2)}{2\,!}\,d_2 + \frac{(n-1)\,(n-2)\,(n-3)}{3\,!}\,d_3 + \dots;$$

and the sum of n terms is

$$na + \frac{n\,(n-1)}{2\,!}\,d_1 + \frac{n\,(n-1)\,(n-2)}{3\,!}\,d_2$$

$$+ \frac{n\,(n-1)\,(n-2)\,(n-3)}{4\,!}\,d_3 + \dots$$

Example. Find the general term and the sum of n terms of the series

$$12, 40, 90, 168, 280, 432, \dots$$

The successive orders of difference are

$$28, \qquad 50, \qquad 78, \qquad 112, \qquad 152, \ldots\ldots$$
$$22, \qquad 28, \qquad 34, \qquad 40, \ldots\ldots$$
$$6, \qquad 6, \qquad 6, \ldots\ldots$$
$$0, \qquad 0, \ldots\ldots$$

Hence the nth term

$$= 12 + 28\,(n-1) + \frac{22\,(n-1)\,(n-2)}{2!} + \frac{6\,(n-1)\,(n-2)\,(n-3)}{3!}$$

$$= n^3 + 5n^2 + 6n.$$

The sum of n terms may now be found by writing down the value of $\Sigma n^3 + 5\Sigma n^2 + 6\Sigma n$. Or we may use the formula of the present article and obtain

$$S_n = 12n + \frac{28n\,(n-1)}{2!} + \frac{22n\,(n-1)\,(n-2)}{3!} + \frac{6n\,(n-1)\,(n-2)\,(n-3)}{4!}$$

$$= \frac{n}{12}\,(3n^2 + 26n + 69n + 46),$$

$$= \frac{1}{12}\,n\,(n+1)\,(3n^2 + 23n + 46).$$

397. It will be seen that this method of summation will only succeed when the series is such that in forming the orders of differences we eventually come to a series in which all the terms are equal. This will always be the case if the nth term of the series is a rational integral function of n.

For simplicity we will consider a function of three dimensions; the method of proof, however, is perfectly general.

Let the series be

$$u_1 + u_2 + u_3 + \ldots + u_n + u_{n+1} + u_{n+2} + u_{n+3} + \ldots$$

where $u_n = An^3 + Bn^2 + Cn + D$,

and let v_n, w_n, z_n denote the nth term of the first, second, third orders of differences;

then $\qquad v_n = u_{n+1} - u_n = A\,(3n^2 + 3n + 1) + B\,(2n + 1) + C;$

that is, $\qquad v_n = 3An^2 + (3A + 2B)\,n + A + B + C;$

Similarly $\quad w_n = v_{n+1} - v_n = 3A\,(2n + 1) + 3A + 2B$

and $\qquad z_n = w_{n+1} - w_n = 6A.$

Thus the terms in the third order of differences are equal; and generally, if the nth term of the given series is of p dimensions, the terms in the pth order of differences will be equal.

Conversely, if the terms in the pth order of differences are equal, the nth term of the series is a rational integral function of n of p dimensions.

Example. Find the nth term of the series

$$-1, -3, 3, 23, 63, 129, \ldots$$

The successive orders of differences are

-2,	6,	20,	40,	66, ...	
	8,	14,	20,	26, ...	
	6,	6,	6, ...		

Thus the terms in the third order of differences are equal; hence we may assume $u_n = A + Bn + Cn^2 + Dn^3$,

where A, B, C, D have to be determined.

Putting $1, 2, 3, 4$ for n in succession, we have four simultaneous equations, from which we obtain $A = 3, B = -3, C = -2, D = 1$;

hence the general term of the series is $3 - 3n - 2n^2 + n^3$.

398.   *If a_n is a rational integral function of p dimensions in n, the series*

$$a_0 + a_1 x + a_2 x^2 + \ldots + a_n x^n$$

is a recurring series, whose scale of relation is $(1-x)^{p+1}$.

Let S denote the sum of the series; then

$$S(1-x) = a_0 + (a_1 - a_0)x + (a_2 - a_1)x^2 + \ldots + (a_n - a_{n-1})x^n - a_n x^{n+1}$$

$$= a_0 + b_1 x + b_2 x^2 + \ldots + b_n x^n - a_n x^{n+1}, \text{ say;}$$

here $b_n = a_n - a_{n-1}$, so that b_n is of $p-1$ dimensions in n.

Multiplying this last series by $1-x$, we have

$$S(1-x)^2 = a_0 + (b_1 - a_0)x + (b_2 - b_1)x^2 + \ldots$$

$$+ (b_n - b_{n-1})x^n - (a_n + b_n)x^{n+1} + a_n x^{n+2}$$

$$= a_0 + (b_1 - a_0)x + c_2 x^2 + c_3 x^3 + \ldots$$

$$+ c_n x^n - (a_n + b_n)x^{n+1} + a_n x^{n+2}, \text{ say ;}$$

here $c_n = b_n - b_{n-1}$, so that c_n is of $p-2$ dimensions in n.

Hence it follows that after the successive multiplications by $1-x$, the coefficients of x^n in the first, second, third, ... products are general terms in the first, second, third, ... orders of differences of the coefficients.

By hypothesis a_n is a rational integral function of n of p dimensions; therefore after p multiplications by $1-x$ we shall arrive at a series the terms of which, with the exception of p terms at the beginning, and p terms at the end of the series, form a geometrical progression, each of whose coefficients is the same.   [Art. 397.]

Thus $S(1-x)^p = k(x^p + x^{p+1} + \ldots + x^n) + f(x)$, where k is a constant, and $f(x)$ stands for the p terms at the beginning and p terms at the end of the product.

$$\therefore \qquad S(1-x)^p = \frac{k(x^p - x^{n+1})}{1-x} + f(x);$$

that is,

$$S = \frac{kx^p(1 - x^{n-p+1}) + (1-x)f(x)}{(1-x)^{p+1}};$$

thus the series is a recurring series whose scale of relation is $(1-x)^{p+1}$. [Art. 325.]

If the general term is not given, the dimensions of a_n are readily found by the method explained in Art. 397.

Example. Find the generating function of the series

$$3 + 5x + 9x^2 + 15x^3 + 23x^4 + 33x^5 + \ldots$$

Forming the successive orders of differences of the coefficients, we have the series

$$2, 4, 6, 8, 10, \ldots$$
$$2, 2, 2, 2, \ldots;$$

thus the terms in the second order of differences are equal; hence a_n is a rational integral function of n of two dimensions; and therefore the scale of relation is $(1-x)^3$. We have

$$S = 3 + 5x + 9x^2 + 15x^3 + 23x^4 + 33x^5 + \ldots$$
$$-3xS = -9x - 15x^2 - 27x^3 - 45x^4 - 69x^5 - \ldots$$
$$3x^2S = 9x^2 + 15x^3 + 27x^4 + 45x^5 + \ldots$$
$$-x^3S = - 3x^3 - 5x^4 - 9x^5 - \ldots$$

By addition, $(1-x)^3 S = 3 - 4x + 3x^2;$

$$\therefore \qquad S = \frac{3 - 4x + 3x^2}{(1-x)^3}.$$

399. We have seen in Chap. 24, that the generating function of a recurring series is a rational fraction whose denominator is the scale of relation. Suppose that this denominator can be resolved into the factors $(1-ax)(1-bx)(1-cx) \ldots$; then the generating function can be separated into partial fractions of the form

$$\frac{A}{1-ax} + \frac{B}{1-bx} + \frac{C}{1-cx} + \ldots$$

Each of these fractions can be expanded by the Binomial Theorem in the form of a geometrical series; hence in this case the recurring series can be expressed and the sum of a number of geometrical series

If however the scale of relation contains any factor $1 - ax$ more than once, corresponding to this repeated factor there will be partial fractions of the form $\dfrac{A_2}{(1-ax)^2}, \dfrac{A_3}{(1-ax)^3}, \ldots$; which when expanded by the Binomial Theorem do not form geometrical series; hence in this case the recurring series cannot be expressed as the sum of a number of geometrical series.

400. The successive orders of differences of the geometrical progression

$$a, ar, ar^2, ar^3, ar^4, ar^5, \ldots$$

are $a(r-1), a(r-1)r, a(r-1)r^2, a(r-1)r^3, \ldots$

$$a(r-1)^2, a(r-1)^2 r, a(r-1)^2 r^2,$$

....

which are themselves geometrical progressions having the same common ratio r as the original series.

401. Let us consider the series in which

$$u_n = ar^{n-1} + \phi(n),$$

where $\phi(n)$ is a rational integral function of n of p dimensions, and from this series let us form the successive orders of differences.

Each term in any of these orders in the sum of two parts, one arising from terms of the form ar^{n-1}, and the other from terms of the form $\phi(n)$ in the original series. Now since $\phi(n)$ is of p dimensions, the part arising from $\phi(n)$ will be zero in the $(p+1)^{\text{th}}$ and succeeding orders of differences, and therefore these series will be geometrical progressions whose common ratio is r [Art. 400.]

Hence if the first few terms of a series are given, and if the pth order of differences of these terms form a geometrical progression whose common ratio is r, then we may assume that the general term of the given series is $ar^{n-1} + f(n)$, where $f(n)$ is a rational integral function of n of $p-1$ dimensions.

Example. Find the nth term of the series

$$10, 23, 60, 169, 494, \ldots$$

The successive orders of differences are

$$13, 37, 109, 335, \ldots$$

$$24, 72, 216, \ldots$$

Thus the second order of differences is a geometrical progression in which the common ratio is 3; hence we may assume for the general term

$$u_n = a \cdot 3^{n-1} + bn + c.$$

To determine the constants a, b, c make n equal to 1, 2, 3 successively;

then $\qquad$ $a + b + c = 10,\ 3a + 2b + c = 23,\ 9a + 3b + c = 60;$

whence $\qquad$ $a = 6,\ b = 1,\ c = 3.$

Thus $\qquad$ $u_n = 6 \cdot 3^{n-1} + n + 3 = 2 \cdot 3^n + n + 3.$

402. In each of the examples on recurring series that we have just given, on forming the successive orders of differences we have obtained a series the law of which is obvious on inspection, and we have thus been enabled to find a general expression for the nth term of the original series.

If, however, the recurring series is equal to the sum of a number of geometrical progressions whose common ratios are $a, b, c, \ldots$, its general term is of the form $Aa^{n-1} + Bb^{n-1} + Cc^{n-1}$, and therefore the general term in the successive orders of differences is of the same form; that is all the orders of differences follow the same law as the original series. In this case to find the general term of the series we must have recourse to the more general method explained in Chap. 24. But when the coefficients are large the scale of relation is not found without considerable arithmetical labour; hence it is generally worth while to write down a few of the orders of differences to see whether we shall arrive at a series the law of whose terms is evident.

403. We add some examples in further illustration of the preceding principles.

Example 1. Find the sum of n terms of the series

$$\frac{5}{1.2} \cdot \frac{1}{3} + \frac{7}{2.3} \cdot \frac{1}{3^2} + \frac{9}{3.4} \cdot \frac{1}{3^3} + \frac{11}{4.5} \cdot \frac{1}{3^4} + \ldots$$

Here $\qquad$ $u_n = \dfrac{2n+3}{n(n+1)} \cdot \dfrac{1}{3^n}.$

Assuming $\qquad$ $\dfrac{2n+3}{n(n+1)} = \dfrac{A}{n} + \dfrac{B}{n+1},$

we find $A = 3,\ B = -1.$

Hence $\qquad$ $u_n = \left(\dfrac{3}{n} - \dfrac{1}{n+1} \right) \dfrac{1}{3^n} = \dfrac{1}{n} \cdot \dfrac{1}{3^{n-1}} - \dfrac{1}{n+1} \cdot \dfrac{1}{3^n},$

and therefore $\qquad$ $S_n = 1 - \dfrac{1}{n+1} \cdot \dfrac{1}{3^n}.$

Example 2. Find the sum of n terms of the series

$$\frac{1}{3} + \frac{3}{3.7} + \frac{5}{3.7.11} + \frac{7}{3.7.11.15} + \ldots$$

The nth term is $\dfrac{2n-1}{3.7.11 \ldots (4n-5)(4n-1)}.$

Assume

$$\frac{2n-1}{3.7\dots(4n-5)(4n-1)} = \frac{A(n+1)+B}{3.7\dots4n-1} - \frac{An+B}{3.7\dots(4n-5)}.$$

$$\therefore \qquad 2n-1 = An + (A+B) - (An+B)(4n-1).$$

On equating coefficients we have three equations involving the two unknowns A and B, and our assumption will be correct if values of A and B can be found to satisfy all three.

Equating coefficients of n^2, we obtain $A = 0$.

Equating the absolute terms, $-1 = 2B$; that is $B = -\frac{1}{2}$; and it will be found that these values of A and B satisfy the third equation.

$$\therefore \qquad u_n = \frac{1}{2}\cdot\frac{1}{3.7\dots(4n-5)} - \frac{1}{2}\cdot\frac{1}{3.7\dots(4n-5)(4n-1)};$$

hence $\qquad\qquad S_n = \frac{1}{2} - \frac{1}{2}\cdot\frac{1}{3.7.11\dots(4n-1)}.$

Example 3. Sum to n terms the series

$$6.9 + 12.21 + 20.37 + 30.57 + 42.81 + \dots$$

By the method of Art. 396 or that of Art. 397, we find that the nth term of the series $6, 12, 20, 30, 42, \dots$ is $n^2 + 3n + 2$, and the nth term of the series

$$9, 21, 37, 57, 81, \dots \text{ is } 2n^2 + 6n + 1.$$

Hence $\qquad\qquad u_n = (n+1)(n+2)\{2n(n+3)+1\}$

$$= 2n(n+1)(n+2)(n+3) + (n+1)(n+2);$$

$$\therefore \qquad S_n = \frac{2}{5}n(n+1)(n+2)(n+3)(n+4)$$

$$+ \frac{1}{3}(n+1)(n+2)(n+3) - 2.$$

Example 4. Find the sum of n terms of the series

$$2.2 + 6.4 + 12.8 + 20.16 + 30.32 + \dots$$

In the series $2, 6, 12, 20, 30, \dots$ the nth term is $n^2 + n$;

hence $\qquad\qquad u_n = (n^2 + n)2^n.$

Assume $(n^2 + n)2^n = (An^2 + Bn + C)2^n$

$$- \{A(n-1)^2 + B(n-1) + C\}2^{n-1};$$

dividing out by 2^{n-1} and equating coefficients of like powers of n, we have

$$2 = A, \ 2 = 2A + B, \ 0 = C - A + B;$$

whence $A = 2, B = -2, C = 4.$

$$\therefore \qquad u_n = (2n^2 - 2n + 4)2^n - \{2(n-1)^2 - 2(n-1) + 4\}2^{n-1};$$

and $\qquad S_n = (2n^2 - 2n + 4)2^n - 4 = (n^2 - n + 2)2^{n+1} - 4.$

EXAMPLES XXIX. b.

Find the nth term and the sum of n terms of the series :

1. $4, 14, 30, 52, 80, 114, \ldots$

2. $8, 26, 54, 92, 140, 198, \ldots$

3. $2, 12, 36, 80, 150, 252, \ldots$

4. $8, 16, 0, -64, -200, -432, \ldots$

5. $30, 144, 420, 960, 1890, 3360, \ldots$

Find the generating functions of the series :

6. $1 + 3x + 7x^2 + 13x^3 + 21x^4 + 31x^5 + \ldots$

7. $1 + 2x + 9x^2 + 20x^3 + 35x^4 + 54x^5 + \ldots$

8. $2 + 5x + 10x^2 + 17x^3 + 26x^4 + 37x^5 + \ldots$

9. $1 - 3x + 5x^2 - 7x^3 + 9x^4 - 11x^5 + \ldots$

10. $1^4 + 2^4 x + 3^4 x^2 + 4^4 x^3 + 5^4 x^4 + \ldots$

Find the sum of the infinite series :

11. $\dfrac{1 \cdot 2}{3} + \dfrac{2 \cdot 3}{3^2} + \dfrac{3 \cdot 4}{3^3} + \dfrac{4 \cdot 5}{3^4} + \ldots$

12. $1^2 - \dfrac{2^2}{5} + \dfrac{3^2}{5^2} - \dfrac{4^2}{5^3} + \dfrac{5^2}{5^4} - \dfrac{6^2}{5^5} + \ldots$

Find the general term and the sum of n terms of the series :

13. $9, 16, 29, 54, 103, \ldots$

14. $-3, -1, 11, 39, 89, 167, \ldots$

15. $2, 5, 12, 31, 86, \ldots$

16. $1, 0, 1, 8, 29, 80, 193, \ldots$

17. $4, 13, 35, 94, 262, 755, \ldots$

Find the sum of n terms of the series :

18. $1 + 2x + 3x^2 + 4x^3 + 5x^4 + \ldots$

19. $1 + 3x + 6x^2 + 10x^3 + 15x^4 + \ldots$

20. $\dfrac{3}{1 \cdot 2} \cdot \dfrac{1}{2} + \dfrac{4}{2 \cdot 3} \cdot \dfrac{1}{2^2} + \dfrac{5}{3 \cdot 4} \cdot \dfrac{1}{2^3} + \dfrac{6}{4 \cdot 5} \cdot \dfrac{1}{2^4} + \ldots$

21. $\dfrac{1^2}{2 \cdot 3} \cdot 4 + \dfrac{2^2}{3 \cdot 4} \cdot 4^2 + \dfrac{3^2}{4 \cdot 5} \cdot 4^3 + \dfrac{4^2}{5 \cdot 6} \cdot 4^4 + \ldots$

22. $3 \cdot 4 + 8 \cdot 11 + 15 \cdot 20 + 24 \cdot 31 + 35 \cdot 44 + \ldots$

23. $1 \cdot 3 + 4 \cdot 7 + 9 \cdot 13 + 16 \cdot 21 + 25 \cdot 31 + \ldots$

24. $1 \cdot 5 + 2 \cdot 15 + 3 \cdot 31 + 4 \cdot 53 + 5 \cdot 81 + \ldots$

25. $\dfrac{1}{1.3} + \dfrac{2}{1.3.5} + \dfrac{3}{1.3.5.7} + \dfrac{4}{1.3.5.7.9} + \cdots$

26. $\dfrac{1.2}{3!} + \dfrac{2.2^2}{4!} + \dfrac{3.2^3}{5!} + \dfrac{4.2^4}{6!} + \cdots$

27. $2.2 + 4.4 + 7.8 + 11.16 + 16.32 + \cdots$

28. $1.3 + 3.3^2 + 5.3^3 + 7.3^4 + 9.3^5 + \cdots$

29. $\dfrac{1}{2.4} + \dfrac{1.3}{2.4.6} + \dfrac{1.3.5}{2.4.6.8} + \dfrac{1.3.5.7}{2.4.6.8.10} + \cdots$

30. $\dfrac{2}{1.2} + \dfrac{5}{2.3} \cdot 2 + \dfrac{10}{3.4} \cdot 2^2 + \dfrac{17}{4.5} \cdot 2^3 + \cdots$

31. $\dfrac{4}{1.2.3} \cdot \dfrac{1}{3} + \dfrac{5}{2.3.4} \cdot \dfrac{1}{3^2} + \dfrac{6}{3.4.5} \cdot \dfrac{1}{3^3} + \cdots$

32. $\dfrac{1}{3!} + \dfrac{5}{4!} + \dfrac{11}{5!} + \dfrac{19}{6!} + \cdots$

33. $\dfrac{19}{1.2.3} \cdot \dfrac{1}{4} + \dfrac{28}{2.3.4} \cdot \dfrac{1}{8} + \dfrac{39}{3.4.5} \cdot \dfrac{1}{16} + \dfrac{52}{4.5.6} \cdot \dfrac{1}{32} + \cdots$

404. There are many series the summation of which can be brought under no general rule. In some cases a skilful modification of the foregoing methods may be necessary; in others it will be found that the summation depends on the properties of certain known expansions, such as those obtained by the Binomial, Logarithmic, and Exponential Theorems.

Example 1. Find the sum of the infinite series

$$\frac{2}{1!} + \frac{12}{2!} + \frac{28}{3!} + \frac{50}{4!} + \frac{78}{5!} + \cdots$$

The nth term of the series $2, 12, 28, 50, 78, \ldots$ is $3n^2 + n - 2$; hence

$$u_n = \frac{3n^2 + n - 2}{n!} = \frac{3n(n-1) + 4n - 2}{n!}$$

$$= \frac{3}{(n-2)!} + \frac{4}{(n-1)!} - \frac{2}{n!}.$$

Put n equal to $1, 2, 3, 4, \ldots$ in succession; then we have

$$u_1 = 4 - \frac{2}{1!}; \; u_2 = 3 + \frac{4}{1!} - \frac{2}{2!}; \; u_3 = \frac{3}{1!} + \frac{4}{2!} - \frac{2}{3!};$$

and so on.

Whence $S_\infty = 3e + 4e - 2(e - 1) = 5e + 2$.

Example 2. If $(1 + x)^n = c_0 + c_1 x + c_2 x^2 + \ldots + c_n x^n$, find the value of $1^2 c_1 + 2^2 c_2 + 3^2 c_3 + \ldots + n^2 c_n$.

As in Art. 398. we may easily shew that

$$1^2 + 2^2 x + 3^2 x^2 + 4^2 x^3 + \ldots + n^2 x^{n-1} + \ldots = \frac{1+x}{(1-x)^3}$$

Also $c_n + c_{n-1} x + \ldots + c_2 x^{n-2} + c_1 x^{n-1} + c_0 x^n = (1+x)^n$.

Multiply together these two results; then the given series is equal to the coefficient of x^{n-1} in $\dfrac{(1+x)^{n+1}}{(1-x)^3}$, that is, in $\dfrac{(2-1-x)^{n+1}}{(1-x)^3}$.

The only terms containing x^{n-1} in this expansion arise from

$$2^{n+1}(1-x)^{-3} - (n+1)2^n(1-x)^{-2} + \frac{(n+1)n}{2!}2^{n-1}(1-x)^{-1};$$

∴   the given series

$$= \frac{n(n+1)}{2!}2^{n+1} - n(n+1)2^n + \frac{n(n+1)}{2!}2^{n-1}$$

$$= n(n+1)2^{n-3}.$$

Example 3. If $b = a + 1$, and n is a positive integer, find the value of

$$b^n - (n-1)ab^{n-2} + \frac{(n-2)(n-3)}{2!}a^2 b^{n-4}$$

$$- \frac{(n-3)(n-4)(n-5)}{3!}a^3 b^{n-6} + \ldots$$

By the Binomial Theorem, we see that

$$1, \; n-1, \; \frac{(n-3)(n-2)}{2!}, \; \frac{(n-5)(n-4)(n-3)}{3!}, \; \ldots$$

are the coefficients of $x^n, x^{n-2}, x^{n-4}, x^{n-6}, \ldots$ in the expansions of $(1-x)^{-1}$, $(1-x)^{-2}, (1-x)^{-3}, (1-x)^{-4}, \ldots$ respectively. Hence the sum required is equal to the coefficient of x^n in the expansion of the series

$$\frac{1}{1-bx} - \frac{ax^2}{(1-bx)^2} + \frac{a^2 x^4}{(1-bx)^3} - \frac{a^3 x^6}{(1-bx)^4} + \ldots,$$

and although the given expression consists only of a finite number of terms, this series may be considered to extend to infinity.

. But the sum of the series

$$= \frac{1}{1-bx} \div \left(1 + \frac{ax^2}{1-bx}\right) = \frac{1}{1-bx+ax^2}$$

$$= \frac{1}{1-(a+1)x+ax^2}, \text{ since } b = a+1.$$

Hence the given series = coefficient of x^n in $\dfrac{1}{(1-x)(1-ax)}$

$$= \text{ coefficient of } x^n \text{ in } \frac{1}{a-1}\left(\frac{a}{1-ax} - \frac{1}{1-x}\right)$$

$$= \frac{a^{n+1}-1}{a-1}.$$

Example 4. If the series

$$1 + \frac{x^3}{3!} + \frac{x^6}{6!} + \dots, \quad x + \frac{x^4}{4!} + \frac{x^7}{7!} + \dots, \quad \frac{x^2}{2!} + \frac{x^5}{5!} + \frac{x^8}{8!} + \dots,$$

are denoted by a, b, c respectively, shew that

$$a^3 + b^3 + c^3 - 3abc = 1.$$

If ω is an imaginary cube root of unity,

$$a^3 + b^3 + c^3 - 3abc = (a + b + c)(a + \omega b + \omega^2 c)(a + \omega^2 b + \omega c).$$

Now $a + b + c = 1 + x + \dfrac{x^2}{2!} + \dfrac{x^3}{3!} + \dfrac{x^4}{4!} + \dfrac{x^5}{5!} + \dots = e^x;$

and $a + \omega b + \omega^2 c = 1 + \omega x + \dfrac{\omega^2 x^2}{2!} + \dfrac{\omega^3 x^3}{3!} + \dfrac{\omega^4 x^4}{4!} + \dfrac{\omega^5 x^5}{5!} + \dots = e^{\omega x};$

Similarly $a + \omega^2 b + \omega c = e^{\omega^2 x}.$

$$\therefore \qquad a^3 + b^3 + c^3 - 3abc = e^x . e^{\omega x} . e^{\omega^2 x} = e^{(1 + \omega + \omega^2)x}$$

$$= 1. \qquad \text{since } 1 + \omega + \omega^2 = 0.$$

405. *To find the sum of the rth powers of the first n natural numbers.*

Let the sum be denoted by S_n; then

$$S_n = 1^r + 2^r + 3^r + \dots + n^r.$$

Assume that

$$S_n = A_0 n^{r+1} + A_1 n^r + A_2 n^{r-1} + A_3 n^{r-2} + \dots + A_r n + A_{r+1} \dots (1)$$

where $A_0, A_1, A_2, A_3, \dots$ are quantities whose values have to be determined.

Write $n + 1$ in the place of n and subtract; thus

$$(n+1)^r = A_0 \{(n+1)^{r+1} - n^{r+1}\} + A_1 \{(n+1)^r - n^r\}$$

$$+ A_2 \{(n+1)^{r-1} - n^{r-1}\} + A_3 \{(n+1)^{r-2} - n^{r-2}\} + \dots + A_r \dots (2)$$

Expand $(n+1)^{r+1}, (n+1)^r, (n+1)^{r-1}, \dots$ and equate the coefficients of like powers of n. By equating the coefficients of n^r, we have

$$1 = A_0(r+1), \text{ so that } A_0 = \frac{1}{r+1}.$$

By equating the coefficients of n^{r-1}, we have

$$r = \frac{A_0(r+1)r}{2} + A_1 r; \text{ whence } A_1 = \frac{1}{2}.$$

Equate the coefficients of n^{r-p}, substitute for A_0 and A_1, and multiply both sides of the equation by

$$\frac{p\,!}{r\,(r-1)\,(r-2)\,\ldots\,(r-p+1)}\,;$$

we thus obtain

$$1 = \frac{1}{p+1} + \frac{1}{2} + A_2\frac{p}{r} + A_3\frac{p\,(p-1)}{r\,(r-1)} + A_4\frac{p\,(p-1)\,(p-2)}{r\,(r-1)\,(r-2)} + \ldots(3)$$

In (1) write $n-1$ in the place of n and subtract; thus

$$n^r = A_0\,\{n^{r+1} - (n-1)^{r+1}\} + A_1\,\{n^r - (n-1)^r\}$$
$$+ A_2\,\{n^{r-1} - (n-1)^{r-1}\} + \ldots$$

Equate the coefficients of n^{r-p}, and substitute for A_0, A_1; thus

$$0 = \frac{1}{p+1} - \frac{1}{2} + A_2\frac{p}{r} - A_3\frac{p\,(p-1)}{r\,(r-1)} + A_4\frac{p\,(p-1)\,(p-2)}{r\,(r-1)\,(r-2)} - \ldots(4)$$

From (3) and (4), by addition and subtraction,

$$\frac{1}{2} - \frac{1}{p+1} = A_2\frac{p}{r} + A_4\frac{p\,(p-1)\,(p-2)}{r\,(r-1)\,(r-2)} + \ldots \qquad \ldots(5)$$

$$0 = A_3\frac{p\,(p-1)}{r\,(r-1)} + A_5\frac{p\,(p-1)\,(p-2)\,(p-3)}{r\,(r-1)\,(r-2)\,(r-3)} + \ldots \qquad \ldots(6)$$

By ascribing to p in succession the values $2, 4, 6, \ldots$ we see from (6) that each of the coefficients $A_3, A_5, A_7, \ldots$ is equal to zero; and from (5) we obtain

$$A_2 = \frac{1}{6}\cdot\frac{r}{2\,!}\,;\quad A_4 = -\frac{1}{30}\cdot\frac{r\,(r-1)\,(r-2)}{4\,!}\,;$$

$$A_6 = \frac{1}{42}\cdot\frac{r\,(r-1)\,(r-2)\,(r-3)\,(r-4)}{6\,!}\,;\ldots$$

By equating the absolute terms in (2), we obtain

$$1 = A_0 + A_1 + A_2 + A_3 + \ldots + A_r;$$

and by putting $n=1$ in equation (1), we have

$$1 = A_0 + A_1 + A_2 + A_3 + \ldots + A_r + A_{r+1};$$

thus $A_{r+1} = 0$.

406. The result of the preceding article is most conveniently expressed by the formula,

$$S_n = \frac{n^{r+1}}{r+1} + \frac{1}{2}n^r + B_1\frac{r}{2\,!}n^{r-1} - B_3\frac{r\,(r-1)\,(r-2)}{4\,!}n^{r-3}$$
$$+ B_5\frac{r\,(r-1)\,(r-2)\,(r-3)\,(r-4)}{6\,!}n^{r-5} + \ldots,$$

where $\quad B_1 = \frac{1}{6},\ B_3 = \frac{1}{30},\ B_5 = \frac{1}{42},\ B_7 = \frac{1}{30},\ B_9 = \frac{5}{66},\ \ldots$

The quantities B_1, B_3, B_5, ... are known as *Bernoulli's Numbers*; for examples of their application to the summation of other series the advanced student may consult Boole's *Finite Differences*.

Example. Find the value of $1^5 + 2^5 + 3^5 + ... + n^5$.

We have $S_n = \dfrac{n^6}{6} + \dfrac{n^5}{2} + B_1 \dfrac{5}{2!} n^4 - B_3 \dfrac{5 \cdot 4 \cdot 3}{4!} n^2 + C,$

$$= \dfrac{n^6}{6} + \dfrac{n^5}{2} + \dfrac{5n^4}{12} - \dfrac{n^2}{12},$$

the constant being zero.

EXAMPLES XXIX. c.

Find the sum of the following series :

1. $\dfrac{x^3}{3!} + \dfrac{x^5}{5!} + \dfrac{x^7}{7!} + ...$ **2.** $\dfrac{x}{1 \cdot 2} + \dfrac{x^2}{2 \cdot 3} + \dfrac{x^3}{3 \cdot 4} + ...$

3. $x + \dfrac{x^5}{5!} + \dfrac{x^9}{9!} + ...$ **4.** $\dfrac{1}{r!} + \dfrac{2}{(r+1)!} + \dfrac{3}{(r+2)!} + ...$

5. $1 + 2x + \dfrac{2^2 - 1}{2!} \cdot \dfrac{x^2}{1} + \dfrac{3^2 - 1}{3!} \cdot \dfrac{x^3}{2} + \dfrac{4^2 - 1}{4!} \cdot \dfrac{x^4}{3} + ...$

6. $\dfrac{p^r}{r!} + \dfrac{p^{r-1}}{(r-1)!} \cdot \dfrac{q}{1} + \dfrac{p^{r-2}}{(r-2)!} \cdot \dfrac{q^2}{2!} + \dfrac{p^{r-3}}{(r-3)!} \cdot \dfrac{q^3}{3!} + ...$ to $r+1$ terms

7. $\dfrac{n(1+x)}{1+nx} - \dfrac{n(n-1)}{2!} \cdot \dfrac{1+2x}{(1+nx)^2}$

$$+ \dfrac{n(n-1)(n-2)}{3!} \cdot \dfrac{1+3x}{(1+nx)^3} + ... \text{ to } n \text{ terms.}$$

8. $1 + 3\dfrac{2n+1}{2n-1} + 5\left(\dfrac{2n+1}{2n-1}\right)^2 + ...$ to n terms.

9. $1 - \dfrac{n^2}{1^2} + \dfrac{n^2(n^2 - 1^2)}{1^2 \cdot 2^2} - \dfrac{n^2(n^2 - 1^2)(n^2 - 2^2)}{1^2 \cdot 2^2 \cdot 3^2} + ...$ to $n+1$ terms.

10. $(1+2)\log_e 2 + \dfrac{1+2^2}{2!}(\log_e 2)^2 + \dfrac{1+2^3}{3!}(\log_e 2)^3 + ...$

11. $\dfrac{1}{1 \cdot 2 \cdot 3} + \dfrac{1}{3 \cdot 4 \cdot 5} + \dfrac{1}{5 \cdot 6 \cdot 7} + ...$

12. $\dfrac{2}{1!} + \dfrac{3}{2!} + \dfrac{6}{3!} + \dfrac{11}{4!} + \dfrac{18}{5!} + ...$

13. $1 + \dfrac{2x^2}{2!} - \dfrac{x^3}{3!} + \dfrac{7x^4}{4!} - \dfrac{23x^5}{5!} + \dfrac{121x^6}{6!} - ...$

14. Without assuming the formula, find the sum of the series :

(1) $1^6 + 2^6 + 3^6 + \ldots + n^6$.   (2) $1^7 + 2^7 + 3^7 + \ldots + n^7$.

15. Find the sum of $1^3 + 2^3 + \dfrac{3^3}{2!} + \dfrac{4^3}{3!} + \dfrac{5^3}{4!} + \ldots$

16. Shew that the coefficient of x^n in the expansion of

$\dfrac{x}{(1-x)^2 - cx}$ is

$n\left\{1 + \dfrac{n^2 - 1}{3!} c + \dfrac{(n^2 - 1)(n^2 - 4)}{5!} c^2 + \dfrac{(n^2 - 1)(n^2 - 4)(n^2 - 9)}{7!} c^3 + \ldots\right\}$.

17. If n is a positive integer, find the value of

$$2^n - (n-1)2^{n-2} + \dfrac{(n-2)(n-3)}{2!} 2^{n-4}$$
$$- \dfrac{(n-3)(n-4)(n-5)}{3!} 2^{n-6} + \ldots;$$

and if n is a multiple of 3, shew that

$$1 - (n-1) + \dfrac{(n-2)(n-3)}{2!} - \dfrac{(n-3)(n-4)(n-5)}{3!} + \ldots = (-1)^n.$$

18. If n is a positive integer greater than 3, shew that

$$n^3 + \dfrac{n(n-1)}{2!}(n-2)^3 + \dfrac{n(n-1)(n-2)(n-3)}{4!}(n-4)^3 + \ldots$$
$$= n^2(n+3)2^{n-4}.$$

19. Find the sum of n terms of series :

(1) $\dfrac{1}{1 + 1^2 + 1^4} + \dfrac{2}{1 + 2^2 + 2^4} + \dfrac{3}{1 + 3^2 + 3^4} + \ldots$

(2) $\dfrac{5}{1.2} - \dfrac{3}{2.3} + \dfrac{9}{3.4} - \dfrac{7}{4.5} + \dfrac{13}{5.6} - \dfrac{11}{6.7} + \dfrac{17}{7.8} - \ldots$

20. Sum to infinity the series whose nth term is $\dfrac{(-1)^{n+1} x^n}{n(n+1)(n+2)}$.

21. If $(1+x)^n = c_0 + c_1 x + c_2 x^2 + c_3 x^3 + \ldots + c_n x^n$, n being a positive integer, find the value of

$$(n-1)^2 c_1 + (n-3)^2 c_3 + (n-5)^2 c_5 + \ldots$$

22. Find the sum of n terms of the series :

(1) $\dfrac{2}{1.5} - \dfrac{4}{5.7} + \dfrac{8}{7.17} - \dfrac{16}{17.31} + \dfrac{32}{31.65} - \ldots$

(2) $\dfrac{7}{1.2.3} - \dfrac{17}{2.3.4.} + \dfrac{31}{3.4.5} - \dfrac{49}{4.5.6} + \dfrac{71}{5.6.7} - \ldots$

23. Prove that, if $a < 1$, $(1 + ax)(1 + a^3x)(1 + a^5x) \dots$

$$= 1 + \frac{ax}{1 - a^2} + \frac{a^4x^2}{(1 - a^2)(1 - a^4)} + \frac{a^9x^3}{(1 - a^2)(1 - a^4)(1 - a^6)} + \dots$$

24. If A_r is the coefficient of x^r in the expansion of

$$(1 + x)^2 \left(1 + \frac{x}{2}\right)^2 \left(1 + \frac{x}{2^2}\right)^2 \left(1 + \frac{x}{2^3}\right)^2 \dots,$$

prove that $A_r = \dfrac{2^2}{2^r - 1}(A_{r-1} + A_{r-2})$, and $A_4 = \dfrac{1072}{315}$.

25. If n is a multiple of 6, shew that each of the series

$$n - \frac{n(n-1)(n-2)}{3!} \cdot 3 + \frac{n(n-1)(n-2)(n-3)(n-4)}{5!} \cdot 3^2 - \dots,$$

$$n - \frac{n(n-1)(n-2)}{3!} \cdot \frac{1}{3} + \frac{n(n-1)(n-2)(n-3)(n-4)}{5!} \cdot \frac{1}{3^2} - \dots,$$

is equal to zero.

26. If n is a positive integer, shew that

$$(p + q)^n - (n - 1)pq(p + q)^{n-2} + \frac{(n-2)(n-3)}{2!} p^2q^2(p + q)^{n-4} - \dots$$

is equal to $\dfrac{p^{n+1} - q^{n+1}}{p - q}$.

27. If $P_r = (n - r)(n - r + 1)(n - r + 2) \dots (n - r + p - 1)$,
$Q_r = r(r + 1)(r + 2) \dots (r + q - 1)$,

shew that

$$P_1Q_1 + P_2Q_2 + P_3Q_3 + \dots + P_{n-1}Q_{n-1}$$
$$= \frac{p!\, q!\, (n - 1 + p + q)!}{(p + q + 1)!\, (n - 2)!}.$$

28. If n is a multiple of 3, shew that

$$1 - \frac{n-3}{2!} + \frac{(n-4)(n-5)}{3!} - \frac{(n-5)(n-6)(n-7)}{4!} + \dots$$

$$+ (-1)^{r-1} \frac{(n-r-1)(n-r-2) \dots (n-2r+1)}{r!} + \dots,$$

is equal to $\dfrac{3}{n}$ or $-\dfrac{1}{n}$, according as n odd or even.

29. If x is a proper fraction, shew that

$$\frac{x}{1 - x^2} - \frac{x^3}{1 - x^6} + \frac{x^5}{1 - x^{10}} - \dots = \frac{x}{1 + x^2} + \frac{x^3}{1 + x^6} + \frac{x^5}{1 + x^{10}} + \dots$$

Chapter 30

THEORY OF NUMBERS

407. In this chapter we shall use the word *number* as equivalent in meaning to *positive integer*.

A number which is not exactly divisible by any number except itself and unity is called a *prime number*, or a *prime*; a number which is divisible by other numbers besides itself and unity is called a *composite number*; thus 53 is a prime number, and 35 is a composite number. Two numbers which have no common factor except unity are said to be prime to each other; thus 24 is prime to 77.

408. We shall make frequent use of the following elementary propositions, some of which arise so naturally out of the definition of a prime that they may be regarded as axioms.

(i) If a number a divides a product bc and is prime to one factor b, it must divide the other factor c.

For since a divides bc, every factor of a is found in bc; but since a is prime to b, no factor of a is found in b; therefore all the factors of a are found in c; that is, a divides c.

(ii) If a prime number a divides a product $bcd \ldots$ it must divide one of the factors of that product; and therefore if a prime number a divides b^n, where n is any positive integer, it must divide b.

(iii) If a is prime to each of the numbers b and c, it is prime to the product bc. For no factor of a can divide b or c; therefore the product bc is not divisible by any factor of a, that is, a is prime to bc. Conversely if a is prime to bc, it is prime to each of the numbers b and c.

Also if a is prime to each of the numbers $b, c, d, \ldots$, it is prime to the product $bcd \ldots$; and conversely if a is prime to any number, it is prime to every factor of that number.

(iv) If a and b are prime to each other, every positive integral power of a is prime to every positive integral power of b. This follows at once from (iii).

(b) If a is prime to b, the fractions $\dfrac{a}{b}$ and $\dfrac{a^n}{b^m}$ are in their lowest terms, n and m being any positive integers. Also if $\dfrac{a}{b}$ and $\dfrac{c}{d}$ are any two equal fractions, and $\dfrac{a}{b}$ is in its lowest terms, then c and d must be equimultiples of a and b respectively.

409.   *The number of primes is infinite.*

For if not, let p be the greatest prime number; then the product $2 . 3 . 5 . 7 . 11 \ldots p$, in which each factor is a prime number is divisible by each of the factors $2, 3, 5, \ldots p$; and therefore the number formed by adding unity to their product is not divisible by any of these factors; hence it is either a prime number itself or is divisible by some prime number greater than p; in either case p is not the *greatest* prime number, and therefore the number of primes is not limited.

410.   *No rational algebraical formula can represent prime numbers only.*

If possible, let the formula $a + bx + cx^2 + dx^3 + \ldots$ represent prime numbers only, and suppose that when $x = m$ the value of the expression is p, so that

$$p = a + bm + cm^2 + dm^3 + \ldots;$$

when $x = m + np$ the expression becomes

$$a + b\,(m + np) + c\,(m + np)^2 + d\,(m + np)^3 + \ldots,$$

that is, $a + bm + cm^2 + dm^3 + \ldots +$ a multiple of p,

or $p + a$ multiple of p,

thus the expression is divisible by p, and is therefore not a prime number.

411.   *A number can be resolved into prime factors in only one way.*

Let N denote the number; suppose $N = abcd \ldots$, where $a, b, c, d, \ldots$ are prime numbers. Suppose also that $N = \alpha\beta\gamma\delta \ldots$, where $\alpha, \beta, \gamma, \delta, \ldots$ are other prime numbers. Then

$$abcd \ldots = \alpha\beta\gamma\delta \ldots;$$

hence a must divide $abcd \ldots$; but each of the factors of this product is a prime, therefore α must divide one of them, a suppose. But α and a are both prime; therefore α must be equal to a. Hence $bcd \ldots \beta\gamma\delta \ldots$; and as before, β must be equal to one of the factors of bcd ; and so on. Hence the factors in $\alpha\beta\gamma\delta \ldots$, are equal to those in $abcd \ldots$, and therefore N can only be resolved into prime factors in one way.

412.   *To find the number of divisors of a composite number.*

Let N denote the number, and suppose $N = a^p b^q c^r \ldots$, where $a, b, c, \ldots$, are different prime numbers and $p, q, r, \ldots$ are positive integers. Then it is clear that each term of the product

$$(1 + a + a^2 + \ldots + a^p)\,(1 + b + b^2 + \ldots + b^q)\,(1 + c + c^2 + \ldots + c^r) \ldots$$

is a divisor of the given number, and that no other number is a divisor; hence the number of divisors is the number of terms in the product, that is,

$$(p + 1) (q + 1) (r + 1) \dots$$

This includes as divisors, both unity and the number itself.

413. *To find the number of ways in which a composite number can be resolved into two factors.*

Let N denote the number and suppose $N = a^p b^q c^r \dots$, where $a, b, c \dots$ are different prime numbers and $p, q, r \dots$ are positive integers. Then each term of the product

$$(1 + a + a^2 + \dots + a^p) (1 + b + b^2 + \dots + b^q) (1 + c + c^2 + \dots + c^r) \dots$$

is a divisor of N; but there are two divisors corresponding to each way in which N can be resolved into two factors; hence the required number is

$$\frac{1}{2} (p + 1) (q + 1) (r + 1) \dots$$

This supposes N not a perfect square, so that one at least of the quantities $p, q, r \dots$ is an odd number.

If N is a perfect square, one way of resolution into factors is $\sqrt{N} \times \sqrt{N}$, and to this way there corresponds only *one* divisor $\sqrt{N}$. If we exclude this, the number of ways of resolution is

$$\frac{1}{2} \{(p + 1) (q + 1) (r + 1) \dots - 1\}$$

and to this we must add the one way $\sqrt{N} \times \sqrt{N}$; thus we obtain for the required number

$$\frac{1}{2} \{(p + 1) (q + 1) (r + 1) \dots + 1\}.$$

414. *To find the number of ways in which a composite number can be resolved into two factors which are prime to each other.*

As before, let the number $N = a^p b^q c^r \dots$ of the two factors one must contain a^p, for otherwise there would be some power of a in one factor and some power of a in the other factor, and thus the two factors would not be prime to each other. Similarly b^q must ocur in one of the factors only; and so on. Hence the required number is equal to the number of ways in which the product $abc \dots$ can be resolved into two factors; that is, the number of ways is $\frac{1}{2} (1 + 1) (1 + 1) (1 + 1) \dots$ or 2^{n-1}, where n is the number of different prime factors in N.

415. *To find the sum of the divisors of a number.*

Let the number be denoted by $a^p b^q c^r$ ..., as before. Then each term of the product

$$(1 + a + a^2 + ... + a^p)(1 + b + b^2 + ... + b^q)(1 + c + c^2 + ... + c^r) ...$$

is a divisor, and therefore the *sum* of the divisors is equal to this product; that is,

$$\text{the sum required} = \frac{a^{p+1} - 1}{a - 1} \cdot \frac{b^{q+1} - 1}{b - 1} \cdot \frac{c^{r+1} - 1}{c - 1} \cdots$$

Example 1. Consider the number 21600.

Since $21600 = 6^3 \cdot 10^2 = 2^3 \cdot 3^3 \cdot 2^2 \cdot 5^2 = 2^5 \cdot 3^3 \cdot 5^2$,

the number of divisors $= (5 + 1)(3 + 1)(2 + 1) = 72$;

$$\begin{aligned}
\text{the sum of the divisors} &= \frac{2^6 - 1}{2 - 1} \cdot \frac{3^4 - 1}{3 - 1} \cdot \frac{5^3 - 1}{5 - 1} \\
&= 63 \times 40 \times 31 \\
&= 78120.
\end{aligned}$$

Also 21600 can be resolved into two factors prime to each other in 2^{3-1}, or 4 ways.

Example 2. If n is odd show that $n(n^2 - 1)$ is divisible by 24.

We have $n(n^2 - 1) = n(n - 1)(n + 1)$.

Since n is odd, $n - 1$ and $n + 1$ are two consecutive even numbers; hence one of them is divisible by 2 and the other by 4.

Again $n - 1$, n, $n + 1$ are three consecutive numbers; hence one of them is divisible by 3. Thus the given expression is divisible by the product of 2, 3 and 4 that is by 24.

Example 3. Find the highest power of 3 which is contained in 100 !.

Of the first 100 integers, as many are divisible by 3 as the number of times that 3 is contained in 100, that is 33; and the integers are 3, 6, 9, ... 99. Of these, some contain the factor 3 again, namely 9, 18, 27, ... 99, and their number is the quotient of 100 divided by 9. Some again of these last integers contain the factor 3 a third time, namely 27, 54, 81, the number of them being the quotient of 100 by 27. One number only, 81, contains the factor 3 four times.

Hence the highest power required $= 33 + 11 + 3 + 1 = 48$.

This example is a particular case of the theorem investigated in the next article.

416. *To find the highest power of a prime number a which is contained in* n !.

Let the greatest integer contained in $\dfrac{n}{a}, \dfrac{n}{a^2}, \dfrac{n}{a^3}, \ldots$ respectively be denoted by $I\left(\dfrac{n}{a}\right), I\left(\dfrac{n}{a^2}\right), I\left(\dfrac{n}{a^3}\right), \ldots$ Then among the numbers 1, 2, 3, $\ldots n$, there are $I\left(\dfrac{n}{a}\right)$ which contain a at least once, namely the numbers $a, 2a, 3a, 4a, \ldots$ Similarly there are $I\left(\dfrac{n}{a^2}\right)$ which contain a^2 at least once, and $I\left(\dfrac{n}{a^3}\right)$ which contain a^3 at least once; and so on. Hence the highest power of a contained in n ! is

$$I\left(\frac{n}{a}\right) + I\left(\frac{n}{a^2}\right) + I\left(\frac{n}{a^3}\right) + \ldots$$

417. In the remainder of this chapter we shall find it convenient to express a multiple of n by the symbol $M(n)$.

418. *To prove that the product of r consecutive integers is divisible by r !.*

Let P_n stand for the product of r consecutive integers, the least of which is n; then

$$P_n = n\,(n+1)\,(n+2) \ldots (n+r-1),$$

and

$$P_{n+1} = (n+1)\,(n+2)\,(n+3) \ldots (n+r),$$

$\therefore$

$$nP_{n+1} = (n+r)\,P_n = nP_n + rP_n;$$

$\therefore$

$$P_{n+1} - P_n = \frac{P_n}{n} \times r$$

$= r$ times the product of $r-1$ consecutive integers.

Hence if the product of $r-1$ consecutive integers is divisible by $(r-1)$! we have

$$P_{n+1} - P_n = rM\,(r-1)\,!$$
$$= M\,(r)\,!.$$

Now $P_1 = r\,!$, and therefore P_2 is a multiple of $r\,!$; therefore also $P_3, P_4, \ldots$ are multiples of $r\,!$. We have thus proved that if the product of $r-1$ consecutive integers is divisible by $(r-1)\,!$, the product of r consecutive integers is divisible by $r\,!$; but the product of every two consecutive integers is divisible by 2 !; therefore the product of every three consecutive integers is divisible by 3 !; and so on generally.

This proposition may also be proved thus :

By means of Art. 416, we can shew that every prime factor is contained in $(n + r)!$ as often *at least* as it is contained in $n!\,r!$.

This we leave as an exercise to the student.

419. *If p is a prime number, the coefficient of every term in the expansion of $(a + b)^p$, except the first and last, is divisible by p.*

With the exception of the first and last, every term has a coefficient of the form

$$\frac{p\,(p-1)\,(p-2)\,\ldots\,(p-r+1)}{r!}$$

where r may have any integral value not exceeding $p - 1$. Now this expression is an integer; also since p is prime no factor of $r!$ is a divisor of it, and since p is greater than r it cannot divide any factor of $r!$; that is, $(p-1)\,(p-2)\,\ldots\,(p-r+1)$ must be divisible by $r!$. Hence every coefficient except the first and the last is divisible by p.

420. *If p is a prime number, to prove that*

$$(a + b + c + d + \ldots)^p = a^p + b^p + c^p + d^p + \ldots + M\,(p).$$

Write β for $b + c + \ldots$; then by the preceding article

$$(\alpha + \beta)^p = \alpha^p + \beta^p + M\,(p).$$

Again $\qquad \beta^p = (b + c + d + \ldots)^p = (b + \gamma)^p$ suppose;

$$= b^p + \gamma^p + M\,(p).$$

By proceeding in this way we may establish the required result.

421. *[Fermat's Theorem.] If p is a prime number and N is prime to p, then $N^{p-1} - 1$ is a multiple of p.*

We have proved that

$$(a + b + c + d + \ldots)^p = a^p + b^p + c^p + d^p + \ldots + M\,(p);$$

let each of the quantities $a, b, c, d, \ldots$ be equal to unity, and suppose they are N in number; then

$$N^p = N + M\,(p);$$

that is, $N\,(N^{p-1} - 1) = M\,(p)$.

But N is prime to p, and therefore $n^{p-1} - 1$ is a multiple of p.

Cor : Since p is prime, $p - 1$ is an even number except when $p = 2$. Therefore

$$\left(N^{\frac{p-1}{2}} + 1 \right)\left(N^{\frac{p-1}{2}} - 1 \right) = M\,(p).$$

Hence either $N^{\frac{p-1}{2}} + 1$ or $N^{\frac{p-1}{2}} - 1$ is a multiple of p, that is

$N^{\frac{p-1}{2}} = Kp \pm 1$, where K is some positive integer.

422. It should be noticed that in the course of Art. 421 it was shewn that $N^p - N = M(p)$ *whether N is prime to p or not;* this result sometimes more useful than Fermat's theorem.

Example 1. Shew that $n^7 - n$ is divisible by 42.

Since 7 is a prime, $n^7 - n = M(7)$;

also $\qquad n^7 - n = n(n^6 - 1) = n(n+1)(n-1)(n^4 + n^2 + 1)$.

Now $(n-1)n(n+1)$ is divisible by 3 !; hence $n^7 - n$ is divisible by 6×7, or 42.

Example 2. If p is a prime number, shew that the difference of the pth powers of any two numbers exceeds the difference of the numbers by a multiple of p.

Let x, y be the numbers; then

$$x^p - x = M(p) \quad \text{and} \quad y^p - y = M(p),$$

that is, $\qquad\qquad x^p - y^p - (x - y) = M(p)$;

whence we obtain the required result.

Example 3. Prove that every square number is of the form $5n$ or $5n \pm 1$.

If N is not prime to 5, we have $N^2 = 5n$ where n is some positive integer. If N is prime to 5 then $n^4 - 1$ is a multiple of 5 by Fermat's theorem; thus either $N^2 - 1$ or $N^2 + 1$ is a multiple of 5; that is, $N^2 = 5n \pm 1$.

EXAMPLES XXX. a.

1. Find the least multipliers of the numbers 3675, 4374, 18375, 74088 respectively, which will make the products perfect squares.

2. Find the least multipliers of the numbers 7623, 109350, 539539 respectively, which will make the products perfect cubes.

3. If x and y are positive integers, and if $x - y$ is even, shew that $x^2 - y^2$ is divisible by 4.

4. Shew that the difference between any number and its square is even.

5. If $4x - y$ is a multiple of 3, shew that $4x^2 + 7xy - 2y^2$ is divisible by 9.

6. Find the number of divisors of 8064.

7. In how many ways can the number 7056 be resolved into two factors ?

8. Prove that $2^{4n} - 1$ is divisible by 15.

9. Prove that $n(n+1)(n+5)$ is a multiple of 6.

10. Shew that every number and its cube when divided by 6 leave, the same remainder.

11. If n is even, shew that $n(n^2 + 20)$ is divisible by 48.

12. Shew that $n(n^2 - 1)(3n + 2)$ is divisible by 24.

13. If n is greater than 2, shew that $n^5 - 5n^3 + 4n$ is divisible by 120.

14. Prove that $3^{2n} + 7$ is a multiple of 8.

15. If n is a prime number greater than 3, shew that $n^2 - 1$ is a multiple of 24.

16. Shew that $n^5 - n$ is divisible by 30 for all values of n, and by 240 if n is odd.

17. Shew that the difference of the squares of any two prime numbers greater than 6 is divisible by 24.

18. Shew that no square number is of the form $3n - 1$.

19. Shew that every cube number is of the form $9n$ or $9n \pm 1$.

20. Shew that if a cube number is divided by 7, the remainder is 0, 1 or 6.

21. If a number is both square and cube, shew that it is of the form $7n$ or $7n + 1$.

22. Shew that no triangular number can be of the form $3n - 1$.

23. If $2n + 1$ is a prime number, shew that $1^2, 2^2, 3^2, \ldots n^2$ when divided by $2n + 1$ leave different remainders.

24. Shew that $a^x + a$ and $a^x - a$ are always even, whatever a and x may be.

25. Prove that every even power of every odd number is of the form $8r + 1$.

26. Prove that the 12th power of any number is of the form $13n$ or $13n + 1$.

27. Prove that the 8th power of any number is of the form $17n$ or $17n \pm 1$.

28. If n is a prime number greater than 5, shew that $n^4 - 1$ is divisible by 240.

29. If n is any prime number greater than 3, except 7, shew that $n^6 - 1$ is divisible by 168.

30. Shew that $n^{36} - 1$ is divisible by 33744 if n is prime to 2, 3, 19 and 37.

31. When $p + 1$ and $2p + 1$ are both prime numbers, shew that $x^{2p} - 1$ is divisible by $8 (p + 1) (2p + 1)$, if x is prime to 2, $p + 1$, and $2p + 1$.

32. If p is a prime, and x prime to p, shew that $x^{p^r - p^{r-1}} - 1$ is divisible by p^r.

33. If m is a prime number, and a, b two numbers less than m, prove that
$$a^{m-2} + a^{m-3} b + a^{m-4} b^2 + \ldots + b^{m-2}$$
is a multiple of m.

423. If a is any number, then any other number N may be expressed in the form $N = aq + r$, where q is the integral quotient when N is divided by a, and r is a remainder less than a. The number a, to which the other is referred, is sometimes called the *modulus*; and to any given modulus a there are a different *forms* of a number N, each form corresponding to a different value of r. Thus to modulus 3, we have numbers of the form $3q, 3q + 1, 3q + 2$; or, more simply, $3q, 3q \pm 1$, since $3q + 2$ is equal to $3 (q + 1) - 1$. In like manner to modulus 5 any number will be one of the five forms $5q, 5q \pm 1, 5q \pm 2$.

424. If b, c are two integers, which when divided by a leave the same remainder, they are said to be congruent with respect to the modulus a. In this case $b - c$ is a multiple of a, and following the notation of Gauss we shall sometimes express this as follows :
$$b \equiv c \pmod{a}, \quad \text{or} \quad b - c \equiv 0 \pmod{a}.$$
Either of these formulae is called a congruence.

425. *If b, c are congruent with respect to modulus a, then pb and pc are congruent, p being any integer.*

For, by supposition, $b - c = na$, where n is some integer; therefore $pb - pc = pna$; which proves the proposition.

426. *If a is prime to b, and the quantities*
$$a, 2a, 3a, \ldots (b - 1) a$$
are divided by b, the remainders are all different.

For if possible, suppose that two of the quantities ma and $m'a$ when divided by b leave the same remainder r, so that

$$ma = qb + r, \quad m'a = q'b + r;$$

then $\qquad (m - m') a = (q - q') b;$

therefore b divides $(m - m') a$; hence it must divide $m - m'$, since it is prime to a; but this is impossible since m and m' are each less than b.

Thus the remainders are all different, and since none of the quantities is exactly divisible by b, the remainders must be the terms of the series $1, 2, 3, \ldots b - 1$, but not necessarily in this order.

Cor : If a is prime to b, and c is any number, the b terms of the A.P.

$$c, c + a, c + 2a, \ldots, c + (b - 1) a,$$

when divided by b will leave the same remainders as the terms of the series

$$c, c + 1, c + 2, \ldots c + (b - 1),$$

though not necessarily in this order; and therefore the remainders will be $0, 1, 2, \ldots, b - 1$.

427. *If $b_1, b_2, b_3, \ldots$ are respectively congruent to $c_1, c_2, c_3, \ldots$ with regard to modulus a, then the products $b_1 b_2 b_3 \ldots, c_1 c_2 c_3 \ldots$ are also congruent.*

For by supposition,

$$b_1 - c_1 = n_1 a, \quad b_2 - c_2 = n_2 a, \quad b_3 - c_3 = n_3 a, \ldots$$

where $n_1, n_2, n_3 \ldots$ are integers;

$\therefore \qquad b_1 b_2 b_3 \ldots = (c_1 + n_1 a)(c_2 + n_2 a)(c_3 + n_3 a) \ldots$

$$= c_1 c_2 c_3 \ldots + M(a),$$

which proves the proposition.

428. We can now give another proof of Fermat's Theorem.

If p be a prime number and N prime to p, then $N^{p-1} - 1$ is a multiple of p.

Since N and p are prime to each other, the numbers

$$N, 2N, 3N, \ldots (p - 1) N \qquad \ldots(1)$$

when divided by p leave the remainders

$$1, 2, 3, \ldots (p - 1) \qquad \ldots(2)$$

though not necessarily in this order. Therefore the product of all the terms in (1) is congruent to the product of all the terms in (2), p being the modulus.

That is, $(p - 1) ! N^{p-1}$ and $(p - 1) !$ leave the same remainder when divided by p; hence

$$(p - 1) ! (N^{p-1} - 1) = M(p);$$

but $(p - 1) !$ is prime to p; therefore it follows that

$$N^{p-1} - 1 = M(p).$$

429. We shall denote the number of integers less than a number a and prime to it by the symbol $\phi(a)$; thus $\phi(2) = 1$; $\phi(13) = 12$; $\phi(18) = 6$; the integers less than 18 and prime to it being 1, 5, 7, 11, 13, 17. It will be seen that we here consider unity as prime to all numbers.

430. *To shew that if the numbers $a, b, c, d, \ldots$ are prime to each other,*

$$\phi(abcd \ldots) = \phi(a) \cdot \phi(b) \cdot \phi(c) \ldots$$

Consider the product ab; then the first ab numbers can be written in b lines, each line containing a numbers; thus

1,	2,	......	k,	......	a,
$a + 1$,	$a + 2$,	......	$a + k$,	......	$a + a$,
$2a + 1$,	$2a + 2$,	......	$2a + k$,	......	$2a + a$,
......	......	......	......	......	......
$(b-1)a + 1$,	$(b-1)a + 2$,	......	$(b-1)a + k$,	......	$(b-1)a + a$.

Let us consider the vertical column which begins with k; if k is prime to a all the terms of this column will be prime to a; but if k and a have a common divisor, no number in the column will be prime to a. Now the first row contains $\phi(a)$ numbers prime to a; therefore there are $\phi(a)$ vertical columns in each of which every term is prime to a; let us suppose that the vertical column which begins with k is one of these. This column is an A.P., the terms of which when divided by b leave remainders 0, 1, 2, 3, ... $b-1$ [Art. 426 Cor.]; hence the column contains $\phi(b)$ integers prime to b.

Similarly, each of the $\phi(a)$ vertical columns in which every term is prime to a contain $\phi(b)$ integers prime to b; hence in the table there are $\phi(a) \cdot \phi(b)$ integers which are prime to a and also to b, and therefore to ab; that is

$$\phi(ab) = \phi(a) \cdot \phi(b).$$

Therefore $\phi(abcd \ldots) = \phi(a) \cdot \phi(bcd \ldots)$

$$= \phi(a) \cdot \phi(b) \cdot \phi(cd \ldots)$$
$$= \phi(a) \cdot \phi(b) \cdot \phi(c) \cdot \phi(d) \ldots$$

431. *To find the number of positive integers less than a given number, and prime to it.*

Let N denote the number, and suppose that $N = a^p b^q c^r \ldots$, where $a, b, c, \ldots$ are different prime numbers, and $p, q, r \ldots$ positive integers. Consider the factor a^p; of the natural numbers 1, 2, 3, ... $a^p - 1$, a^p, the only ones not prime to a are

$$a, 2a, 3a, \ldots (a^{p-1} - 1)a, (a^{p-1})a$$

and the number of these is a^{p-1}; hence

$$\phi\,(a^p) = a^p - a^{p-1} = a^p\left(1 - \frac{1}{a}\right)$$

Now all the factors $a^p, b^q, c^r, \ldots$ are prime to each other;

$$\therefore \qquad \phi\,(a^p b^q c^r \ldots) = \phi\,(a^p)\,.\,\phi\,(b^q),\,\phi\,(c^r)\,\ldots$$

$$= a^p\left(1 - \frac{1}{a}\right).\,b^q\left(1 - \frac{1}{b}\right).\,c^r\left(1 - \frac{1}{c}\right)\ldots$$

$$= a^p b^q c^r \ldots\left(1 - \frac{1}{a}\right)\left(1 - \frac{1}{b}\right)\left(1 - \frac{1}{c}\right)\ldots;$$

that is, $\qquad \phi\,(N) = N\left(1 - \frac{1}{a}\right)\left(1 - \frac{1}{b}\right)\left(1 - \frac{1}{c}\right)\ldots$

Example : Shew that the sum of all the integers which are less than N and prime to it is $\frac{1}{2}\,N\,\phi\,(N)$.

If x is any integer less than N and prime to it, then $N - x$ is also an integer less than N and prime to it.

Denote the integers by $1, p, q, r, \ldots$, and their sum by S; then

$$S = 1 + p + q + r + \ldots + (N - r) + (N - q) + (N - p) + (N - 1),$$

the series consisting of $\phi\,(N)$ terms.

Writing the series in the reverse order,

$$S = (N - 1) + (N - p) + (N - q) + (N - r) + \ldots + r + q + p + 1;$$

$\therefore$ by addition, $2S = N + N + N + \ldots$ to $\phi\,(N)$ terms;

$$\therefore \qquad\qquad S = \frac{1}{2}\,N\,\phi\,(N).$$

432. From the last article it follows that the number of integers which are less than N and *not* prime to it is

$$N - N\left(1 - \frac{1}{a}\right)\left(1 - \frac{1}{b}\right)\left(1 - \frac{1}{c}\right)\left(1 - \frac{1}{d}\right)\ldots;$$

that is,

$$\frac{N}{a} + \frac{N}{b} + \frac{N}{c} + \ldots - \frac{N}{ab} - \frac{N}{ac} - \frac{N}{bc} - \ldots + \frac{N}{abc} + \ldots$$

Here the term $\dfrac{N}{a}$ gives the number of the integers

$$a,\, 2a,\, 3a,\, \ldots \frac{N}{a}\cdot a$$

which contain a as a factor; the term $\dfrac{N}{ab}$ gives the number of the integers $ab, 2ab, 3ab, \ldots \dfrac{N}{ab}\,ab$, which contain ab as a factor, and so on

Further, every integer is reckoned once, and once only; thus, each multiple of ab will appear once among the multiples of a, once among the multiples of b, and once negatively among the multiples of ab, and is thus reckoned once only. Again, each multiple of abc will appear among the $\dfrac{N}{a}, \dfrac{N}{b}, \dfrac{N}{c}$ terms which are multiples of a, b, c respectively; among the $\dfrac{N}{ab}, \dfrac{N}{ac}, \dfrac{N}{bc}$ terms which are multiples of ab, ac, bc respectively; and among the $\dfrac{N}{abc}$ multiples of abc; that is, since $3 - 3 + 1 = 1$, each multiple of abc occurs once, and once only. Similarly, other cases may be discussed.

433. [Wilson's Theorem.] *If p be a prime number, $1 + (p - 1)!$ is divisible by p.*

By Ex. 2, Art 314 we have

$$(p-1)! = (p-1)^{p-1} - (p-1)(p-2)^{p-1} + \frac{(p-1)(p-2)}{1.2}(p-3)^{p-1}$$
$$- \frac{(p-1)(p-2)(p-3)}{3!}(p-4)^{p-1} + \dots \text{ to } p-1 \text{ terms};$$

and by Fermat's Theorem each of the expressions $(p-1)^{p-1}$, $(p-2)^{p-1}$, $(p-3)^{p-1}$, ... is of the form $1 + M(p)$; thus

$$(p-1)! = M(p) + \left\{ 1 - (p-1) + \frac{(p-1)(p-2)}{1.2} - \dots \text{ to } p-1 \text{ terms} \right\}$$
$$= M(p) + \{(1-1)^{p-1} - (-1)^{p-1}\}$$
$$= M(p) - 1, \quad \text{since } p-1 \text{ is even.}$$

Therefore $1 + (p-1)! = M(p)$.

This theorem is only true when p is prime. For suppose p has a factor q; then q is less than p and must divide $p-1$; hence $1 + (p-1)!$ is not a multiple of q, and therefore not a multiple of p.

Wilson's theorem may also be proved without using the result quoted from Art. 314, as in the following article.

434. [Wilson's theorem.] *If p be a prime number, $1 + (p-1)!$ is divisible by p.*

Let a denote *any one* of the numbers

$$1, 2, 3, 4, \dots (p-1) \qquad \dots(1)$$

then a is prime to p, and if the products

$$1.a, 2.a, 3.a, \dots (p-1)a$$

are divided by p, one and only one of them leaves the remainder 1. [Art. 426.]

Let this be the product ma; then we can shew that the numbers m and a are different unless $a = p - 1$ or 1. For if a^2 were to give remainder 1 on division by p, we should have

$$a^2 - 1 \equiv 0 \ (\text{mod. } p),$$

and since p is prime, this can only be the case when $a + 1 = p$, or $a - 1 = 0$; that is, when $a = p - 1$ or 1.

Hence one and only one of the products $2a$, $3a$, $\ldots$ $(p-2)\,a$ gives remainder 1 when divided by p; that is, for *any one* of the series of numbers in (1), excluding the first and last, it is possible to find *one other*, such that the product of the pair is of the form $M\,(p) + 1$.

Therefore the integers $2, 3, 4, \ldots (p-2)$, the number of which is even, can be associated in pairs such that the product of each pair is of the form $M\,(p) + 1$.

Therefore by multiplying all these pairs together, we have
$$2.\,3.\,4 \ldots (p-2) = M\,(p) + 1;$$
that is, $1.\,2.\,3.\,4 \ldots (p-1) = (p-1)\,\{M\,(p) + 1\};$
whence $\quad (p-1)\,! = M\,(p) + p - 1;$
or $\qquad\qquad 1 + (p-1)\,!$ is a multiple of p.

Cor: If $2p + 1$ is a prime number $(p)^2 + (-1)^r$ is divisible by $2p + 1$.

For by Wilson's theorem $1 + (2p)\,!$ is divisible by $2p + 1$. Put $n = 2p + 1$, so that $p + 1 = n - p$; then
$$(2p)\,! = 1.\,2.\,3.\,4 \ldots p\,(p+1)\,(p+2)\ldots(n-1)$$
$$= 1\,(n-1)\,2\,(n-2)\,3\,(n-3)\ldots p\,(n-p)$$
$$= \text{a multiple of } n + (-1)^r\,(p\,!)^2.$$

Therefore $1 + (-1)^p\,(p\,!)^2$ is divisible by n or $2p + 1$, and therefore $(p\,!)^2 + (-1)^p$ is divisible by $2p + 1$.

435. Many theorems relating to the properties of numbers can be proved by induction.

Example 1. If p is a prime number, $x^p - x$ is divisible by p.

Let $x^p - x$ be denoted by $f(x)$; then
$$f(x+1) - f(x) = (x+1)^p - (x+1) - (x^p - x)$$
$$= px^{p-1} + \frac{p\,(p-1)}{1.\,2}\,x^{p-2} + \ldots + px$$
$$= \text{a multiple of } p, \text{ if } p \text{ is prime [Art. 419.]}$$
$\therefore \quad f(x+1) = f(x) + \text{a multiple of } p.$

If therefore $f(x)$ is divisible by p, so also is $f(x+1)$; but
$$f(2) = 2^p - 2 = (1+1)^p - 2,$$

and this is a multiple of p when p is prime [Art. 419]; therefore $f(3)$ is divisible by p, therefore $f(4)$ is divisible by p, and so on; thus the proposition is true universally.

This furnishes another proof of Fermat's theorem, for if x is prime to p, it follows that $x^{p-1} - 1$ is a multiple of p.

Example 2. Prove that $5^{2n+2} - 24n - 25$ is divisible by 576.

Let $5^{2n+2} - 24n - 25$ be denoted by $f(n)$;

then
$$f(n+1) = 5^{2n+4} - 24(n+1) - 25$$
$$= 5^2 \cdot 5^{2n+2} - 24n - 49;$$

$\therefore \quad f(n+1) - 25f(n) = 25(24n + 25) - 24n - 49$
$$= 576(n+1).$$

Therefore if $f(n)$ is divisible by 576, so also is $f(n+1)$; but by trial we see that the theorem is true when $n = 1$, therefore it is true when $n = 2$, therefore it is true when $n = 3$, and so on; thus it is true universally.

The above result may also be proved as follows :
$$5^{2n+2} - 24n - 25 = 25^{n+1} - 24n - 25$$
$$= 25(1 + 24)^n - 24n - 25$$
$$= 25 + 25 \cdot n \cdot 24 + M(24^2) - 24n - 25$$
$$= 576n + M(576) = M(576).$$

EXAMPLES XXX. b.

1. Shew that $10^n + 3 \cdot 4^{n+2} + 5$ is divisible by 9.

2. Shew that $2 \cdot 7^n + 3 \cdot 5^n - 5$ is a multiple of 24.

3. Shew that $4 \cdot 6^n + 5^{n+1}$ when divided by 20 leaves remainder 3.

4. Shew that $8 \cdot 7^n + 4^{n+2}$ is of the form $24(2r - 1)$.

5. If p is prime, shew that $1 + (2p - 3)!$ is a multiple of p.

6. Shew that $a^{4b+1} - a$ is divisible by 30.

7. Shew that the highest power of 2 contained in $(2^r - 1)!$ is $2^r - r - 1$.

8. Shew that $3^{4n+2} + 5^{2n+1}$ is a multiple of 14.

9. Shew that $3^{2n+5} + 160n^2 - 56n - 243$ is divisible by 512.

10. Prove that the sum of the coefficients of the odd powers of x in the expansion of $(1 + x + x^2 + x^3 + x^4)^{n-1}$, when n is a prime number other than 5, is divisible by n.

11. If n is a prime number greater than 7, shew that $n^6 - 1$ is divisible by 504.

12. If n is an odd number, prove that $n^6 + 3n^4 + 7n^2 - 11$ is a multiple of 128.

13. If p is a prime number, shew that the coefficients of the terms of $(1 + x)^{p-1}$ are alternately greater and less by unity than some multiple of p.

14. If p is a prime, shew that the sum of the $(p-1)$th powers of any p numbers in arithmetical progression, wherein the common difference is not divisible by p, is less by 1 than a multiple of p.

15. Shew that $a^{12} - b^{12}$ is divisible by 91, if a and b are both prime to 91.

16. If p is a prime, shew that $(p - 2r)!\,(2r - 1)! - 1$ is divisible by p.

17. If $n - 1$, $n + 1$ are both prime numbers greater than 5, shew that $n\,(n^2 - 4)$ is divisible by 120, and $n^2\,(n^2 + 16)$ by 720. Also shew that n must be of the form $30t$ or $30t \pm 12$.

18. Shew that the highest power of n which is contained in $(n^r - 1)!$ is equal to $\dfrac{n^r - nr + r - 1}{n - 1}$.

19. If p is a prime number, and a prime to p, and if a square number c^2 can be found such that $c^2 - a$ is divisible by p, shew that $a^{\frac{1}{2}(p-1)} - 1$ is divisible by p.

20. Find the general solution of the congruence
$$98x - 1 \equiv 0 \ (\text{mod. } 139).$$

21. Shew that the sum of the squares of all the numbers less than a given number N and prime to it is

$$\frac{N^3}{3}\left(1 - \frac{1}{a}\right)\left(1 - \frac{1}{b}\right)\left(1 - \frac{1}{c}\right)\ldots + \frac{N}{6}\,(1 - a)\,(1 - b)\,(1 - c)\ldots,$$

and the sum of the cubes is

$$\frac{N^4}{4}\left(1 - \frac{1}{a}\right)\left(1 - \frac{1}{b}\right)\left(1 - \frac{1}{c}\right)\ldots + \frac{N^2}{4}\,(1 - a)\,(1 - b)\,(1 - c)\ldots,$$

$a, b, c \ldots$ being the different prime factors of N.

22. If p and q are any two positive integers, shew that pq ! is divisible by $(p\,!)^q \cdot a\,!$ and by $(q\,!)^p \cdot p\,!$.

23. Shew that the square numbers which are also triangular are given by the squares of the coefficients of the powers of x in the expansion of $\dfrac{1}{1-6x+x^2}$, and that the square numbers which are also pentagonal by the coefficients of the powers of x in the expansion of $\dfrac{1}{1-10x+x^2}$.

24. Shew that the sum of the fourth powers of all the numbers less than N and prime to it is

$$\frac{N^5}{5}\left(1-\frac{1}{a}\right)\left(1-\frac{1}{b}\right)\left(1-\frac{1}{c}\right)\dots + \frac{N^3}{3}(1-a)(1-b)(1-b)\dots$$
$$-\frac{N}{30}(1-a^3)(1-b^3)(1-c^3)\dots,$$

$a, b, c, \dots$ being the different prime factors of N.

25. If $\phi(N)$ is the number of integers which are less than N and prime to it, and if x is prime to N, shew that

$$x^{\phi(N)} - 1 \equiv 0 \ (\text{mod. } N).$$

26. If $d_1, d_2, d_3, \dots$ denote the divisors of a number N, then

$$\phi(d_1) + \phi(d_2) + \phi(d_3) + \dots = N.$$

Shew also that

$$\phi(1)\frac{x}{1+x^2} - \phi(3)\frac{x^3}{1+x^6} + \phi(5)\frac{x^5}{1+x^{10}} - \dots \text{ ad inf.} = \frac{x(1-x^2)}{(1+x^2)^2}.$$

■■■

Chapter 31

THE GENERAL THEORY OF CONTINUED FRACTIONS

*436. In Chapter 25. we have investigated the properties of Continued Fractions of the form $a_1 + \dfrac{1}{a_2+} \dfrac{1}{a_3+} \ldots$, where $a_2, a_3, \ldots$, are positive integers, and a_1 is either a positive integer or zero. We shall now consider continued fractions of a more general type.

*437. The most general form of a continued fraction is $\dfrac{b_1}{a_1 \pm} \dfrac{b_2}{a_2 \pm} \dfrac{b_3}{a_3 \pm} \ldots$, where $a_1, a_2, a_3, \ldots, b_1, b_2, b_3, \ldots$ represent any quantities whatever.

The fractions $\dfrac{b_1}{a_1}, \dfrac{b_2}{a_2}, \dfrac{b_3}{a_3}, \ldots$ are called *components* of the continued fraction. We shall confine our attention to two cases;

(i) that in which the sign before each component is positive;

(ii) that in which the sign is negative.

*438. *To investigate the law of formation of the successive convergents to the continued fraction*

$$\frac{b_1}{a_1+} \frac{b_2}{a_2+} \frac{b_3}{a_3+} \ldots$$

The first three convergents are

$$\frac{b_1}{a_1}, \frac{a_2 b_1}{a_2 a_1 + b_2}, \frac{a_3 \cdot a_2 b_1 + b_3 \cdot b_1}{a_3(a_2 a_1 + b_2) + b_3 \cdot a_1}.$$

We see that the numerator of the third convergent may be formed by multiplying the numerator of the second convergent by a_3, and the numerator of the first by b_3 and adding the results together; also that the denominator may be formed in like manner.

Suppose that the seccessive convergents are formed in a similar way; let the numerators be denoted by $p_1, p_2, p_3 \ldots$, and the denominators by $q_1, q_2, q_3, \ldots$

Assume that the law of formation holds for the nth convergent; that is, suppose

$$p_n = a_n p_{n-1} + b_n p_{n-2}, \quad q_n = a_n q_{n-1} + b_n q_{n-2}.$$

The $(n+1)$th convergent differs from the nth only in having $a_n + \dfrac{b_{n+1}}{a_{n+1}}$ in the place of a_n; hence the $(n+1)$th convergent

$$= \frac{\left(a_n + \dfrac{b_{n+1}}{a_{n+1}}\right) p_{n-1} + b_n p_{n-2}}{\left(a_n + \dfrac{b_{n+1}}{a_{n+1}}\right) q_{n-1} + b_n q_{n-2}} = \frac{p_n + \dfrac{b_{n+1}}{a_{n+1}} p_{n-1}}{q_n + \dfrac{b_{n+1}}{a_{n+1}} q_{n-1}}$$

$$= \frac{a_{n+1} p_n + b_{n+1} p_{n-1}}{a_{n+1} q_n + b_{n+1} q_{n-1}}.$$

If therefore we put

$$p_{n+1} = a_{n+1} p_n + b_{n+1} p_{n-1}, \quad q_{n+1} = a_{n+1} q_n + b_{n+1} q_{n-1},$$

we see that the numerator and denominator of the $(n+1)$th convergent follow the law which was supposed to hold in case of the nth. But the law does hold in the case of the third convergent; hence it holds for the fourth; and so on; therefore it holds universally.

*439. In the case of the continued fraction

$$\frac{b_1}{a_1 -} \frac{b_2}{a_2 -} \frac{b_3}{a_3 -} \ldots,$$

we may prove that

$$p_n = a_n p_{n-1} - b_n p_{n-2}, \quad q_n = a_n q_{n-1} - b_n q_{n-2};$$

a result which may be deduced from that of the preceding article by changing the sign of b_n.

*440. In the continued fraction

$$\frac{b_1}{a_1 +} \frac{b_2}{a_2 +} \frac{b_3}{a_3 +} \ldots,$$

we have seen that

$$p_n = a_n p_{n-1} + b_n p_{n-2}, \quad q_n = a_n q_{n-1} + b_n q_{n-2}.$$

$$\therefore \quad \frac{p_{n+1}}{q_{n+1}} - \frac{p_n}{q_n} = \frac{(a_{n+1} p_n + b_{n+1} p_{n-1}) q_n - (a_{n+1} q_n + b_{n+1} q_{n-1}) p_n}{q_{n+1} q_n}$$

$$= -\frac{b_{n+1} q_{n-1}}{q_{n+1}} \left(\frac{p_n}{q_n} - \frac{p_{n-1}}{q_{n-1}} \right);$$

but $\dfrac{b_{n+1} q_{n-1}}{q_{n+1}} = \dfrac{b_{n+1} q_{n-1}}{a_{n+1} q_n + b_{n+1} q_{n-1}},$

and is therefore a proper fraction; hence $\dfrac{p_{n+1}}{q_{n+1}} - \dfrac{p_n}{q_n}$ is numerically

less than $\dfrac{p_n}{q_n} - \dfrac{p_{n-1}}{q_{n-1}}$, and is of opposite sign.

By reasoning as in Art. 335, we may shew that every convergent of an odd order is greater than the continued fraction, and every convergent of an even order is less than the continued fraction; hence every convergent of an odd order is greater than every convergent of an even order.

Thus $\dfrac{p_{2n+1}}{q_{2n+1}} - \dfrac{p_{2n}}{q_{2n}}$ is positive and less than $\dfrac{p_{2n-1}}{q_{2n-1}} - \dfrac{p_{2n}}{q_{2n}}$; hence

$$\frac{p_{2n+1}}{q_{2n+1}} < \frac{p_{2n-1}}{q_{2n-1}}.$$

Also $\dfrac{p_{2n-1}}{q_{2n-1}} - \dfrac{p_{2n}}{q_{2n}}$ is positive and less than $\dfrac{p_{2n-1}}{q_{2n-1}} - \dfrac{p_{2n-2}}{q_{2n-2}}$; hence

$$\frac{p_{2n}}{q_{2n}} > \frac{p_{2n-2}}{q_{2n-2}}.$$

Hence the convergents of an odd order are all greater than the continued fraction but continually decrease, and the convergents of an even order are all less than the continued fraction but continually increase.

Suppose now that the number of components is infinite, then the convergents of an odd order must tend to some finite limit, and the convergents of an even order must also tend to some finite limit; if these limits are equal the continued fraction tends to *one* definite limit; if they are not equal, the odd convergents tend to one limit, and the even convergents tend to a different limit, and the continued fraction may be said to be *oscillating*; in this case the continued fraction is the symbolical representation of two quantities, one of which is the limit of the odd, and the other that of the even convergents.

*441. *To shew that the continued fraction* $\dfrac{b_1}{a_1 +} \dfrac{b_2}{a_2 +} \dfrac{b_3}{a_3 +} \ldots$ *has a definite*

value if the limit of $\dfrac{a_n a_{n+1}}{b_{n+1}}$ *when n is infinite is greater than zero.*

The continued fraction will have a definite value when n is infinite if the difference of the limits of $\dfrac{p_{n+1}}{q_{n+1}}$ and $\dfrac{p_n}{q_n}$ is equal to zero.

Now $\dfrac{p_{n+1}}{q_{n+1}} - \dfrac{p_n}{q_n} = -\dfrac{b_{n+1}q_{n-1}}{q_{n+1}}\left(\dfrac{p_n}{q_n} - \dfrac{p_{n-1}}{q_{n-1}}\right)$,

whence we obtain

$$\frac{p_{n+1}}{q_{n+1}} - \frac{p_n}{q_n} = (-1)^{n-1}\frac{b_{n+1}q_{n-1}}{q_{n+1}}\cdot\frac{b_n q_{n-2}}{q_n}\cdots\frac{b_4 q_2}{q_4}\cdot\frac{b_3 q_1}{q_3}\left(\frac{p_2}{q_2} - \frac{p_1}{q_1}\right)$$

But $\dfrac{b_{n+1}q_{n-1}}{q_{n+1}} = \dfrac{b_{n+1}q_{n-1}}{a_{n+1}q_n + b_{n+1}q_{n-1}} = \dfrac{1}{\dfrac{a_{n+1}q_n}{b_{n+1}q_{n-1}} + 1}$;

and $\dfrac{a_{n+1}q_n}{b_{n+1}q_{n-1}} = \dfrac{a_{n+1}(a_n q_{n-1} + b_n q_{n-2})}{b_{n+1}q_{n-1}} = \dfrac{a_n a_{n+1}}{b_{n+1}} + \dfrac{a_{n+1}b_n q_{n-2}}{b_{n+1}q_{n-1}}$;

also neither of these terms can be negative; hence if the limit of $\dfrac{a_n a_{n+1}}{b_{n+1}}$ is greater than zero so also is the limit of $\dfrac{a_{n+1}q_n}{b_{n+1}q_{n-1}}$; in which case the limit of $\dfrac{b_{n+1}q_{n-1}}{q_{n+1}}$ is less than 1; and therefore $\dfrac{p_{n+1}}{q_{n+1}} - \dfrac{p_n}{q_n}$ is the limit of the product of an infinite number of proper fractions, and must therefore be equal to zero; that is, $\dfrac{p_{n+1}}{q_{n+1}}$ and $\dfrac{p_n}{q_n}$ tend to the same limit; which proves the proposition.

For example, in the continued fraction

$$\frac{1^2}{3+}\,\frac{2^2}{5+}\,\frac{3^2}{7+}\cdots\frac{n^2}{2n+1+}\cdots,$$

$$Lim\,\frac{a_n a_{n+1}}{b_{n+1}} = Lim\,\frac{(2n+1)(2n+3)}{(n+1)^2} = 4;$$

and therefore the continued fraction tends to a definite limit.

*442. *In the continued fraction* $\dfrac{b_1}{a_1-}\,\dfrac{b_2}{a_2-}\,\dfrac{b_3}{a_3-}\,...$, *if the denominator of every component exceeds the numerator by unity at least, the convergents are positive fractions in ascending order of magnitude.*

By supposition $\dfrac{b_1}{a_1},\dfrac{b_2}{a_2},\dfrac{b_3}{a_3},\,...$ are positive proper fractions in each of which the denominator exceeds the numerator by unity at least. The second convergent is $\dfrac{b_1}{a_1 - \dfrac{b_2}{a_2}}$, and since a_1 exceeds b_1 by unity at least, and $\dfrac{b_2}{a_2}$ is a proper fraction, it follows that $a_1 - \dfrac{b_2}{a_2}$ is greater than b_1; that is, the second convergent is a positive proper fraction. In like manner it may be shewn that $\dfrac{b_2}{a_2 - \dfrac{b_3}{a_3}}$ is a positive proper fraction; denote it by f_1, then the third convergent is $\dfrac{b_1}{a_1 - f_1}$, and is therefore a positive proper fraction. Similarly we may shew that $\dfrac{b_2}{a_2 -}\dfrac{b_3}{a_3 -}\dfrac{b_4}{a_4}$ is a positive proper fraction; hence also the fourth convergent

$$\frac{b_1}{a_1 -}\frac{b_2}{a_2 -}\frac{b_3}{a_3 -}\frac{b_4}{a_4}$$

is a positive proper fraction; and so on.

Again, $p_n = a_n p_{n-1} - b_n p_{n-2}$, $q_n = a_n q_{n-1} - b_n q_{n-2}$;

$$\therefore \quad \frac{p_{n+1}}{q_{n+1}} - \frac{p_n}{q_n} = \frac{b_{n+1} q_{n-1}}{q_{n+1}}\left(\frac{p_n}{q_n} - \frac{p_{n-1}}{q_{n-1}}\right);$$

hence $\dfrac{p_{n+1}}{q_{n+1}} - \dfrac{p_n}{q_n}$ and $\dfrac{p_n}{q_n} - \dfrac{p_{n-1}}{q_{n-1}}$ have the same sign.

But $\dfrac{p_2}{q_2} - \dfrac{p_1}{q_1} = \dfrac{a_2 b_1}{a_1 a_2 - b_2} - \dfrac{b_1}{a_1} = \dfrac{b_1 b_2}{q_1 q_2}$, and is therefore positive;

hence $\dfrac{p_2}{q_2} > \dfrac{p_1}{q_1}, \dfrac{p_3}{q_3} > \dfrac{p_2}{q_2}, \dfrac{p_4}{q_4} > \dfrac{p_3}{q_3}$; and so on; which proves the proposition.

Cor : If the number of the components is infinite, the convergents form an infinite series of proper fractions in ascending order of magnitude; and in this case the continued fraction must tend to a definite limit which cannot exceed unity.

*443.　From the formula

$$p_n = a_n p_{n-1} + b_n p_{n-2}, \quad q_n = a_n q_{n-1} + b_n q_{n-2},$$

we may always determine in succession as many of the convergents as we please. In certain cases, however, a general expression can be found for the nth convergent.

Example : *To find the nth convergent to* $\dfrac{6}{5 -}\dfrac{6}{5 -}\dfrac{6}{5 -}\cdots$

We have $p_n = 5p_{n-1} - 6p_{n-2}$; hence the numerators form a recurring series any three consecutive terms of which are connected by the relation

$$p_n - 5p_{n-1} + 6p_{n-2}.$$

Let $S = p_1 + p_2 x + p_3 x^2 + \ldots + p_n x^{n-1} + \ldots;$

then, as in Art. 325, we have $S = \dfrac{p_1 + (p_2 - 5p_1)\, x}{1 - 5x + 6x^2}.$

But the first two convergents are $\dfrac{6}{5}, \dfrac{30}{19}$;

$\therefore$ $S = \dfrac{6}{1 - 5x + 6x^2} = \dfrac{18}{1 - 3x} - \dfrac{12}{1 - 2x};$

whence $p_n = 18 . 3^{n-1} - 12 . 2^{n-1} = 6\,(3^n - 2^n).$

Similarly if $S' = q_1 + q_2 x + q_3 x^2 + \ldots + q_n x^{n-1} + \ldots$

we find $S' = \dfrac{5 - 6x}{1 - 5x + 6x^2} = \dfrac{9}{1 - 3x} - \dfrac{4}{1 - 2x};$

whence $q_n = 9 . 3^{n-1} - 4 . 2^{n-1} = 3^{n+1} - 2^{n+1}.$

$\therefore$ $\dfrac{p_n}{q_n} = \dfrac{6\,(3^n - 2^n)}{3^{n+1} - 2^{n+1}}.$

This method will only succeed when a_n and b_n are constant for all values of n. Thus in the case of the continued fraction $\dfrac{b}{a+} \dfrac{b}{a+} \dfrac{b}{a+} \ldots$, we may shew that the numerators of the successive convergents are the coefficients of the powers of x in the expansion of $\dfrac{b}{1 - ax - bx^2}$, and the denominators are the coefficients of the powers of x in the expansion of $\dfrac{a + bx}{1 - ax - bx^2}$.

*444. For the investigation of the general values of p_n and q_n the student is referred to works on *Finite Differences*; it is only in special cases that these values can be found by *Algebra*. The following method will sometimes be found useful.

Example : *Find the value of* $\dfrac{1}{1+} \dfrac{2}{2+} \dfrac{3}{3+} \cdots$

The same law of formation holds for p_n and q_n; let us take u_n to denote either of them; then $u_n = n u_{n-1} + n u_{n-2}$

or $u_n - (n+1) u_{n-1} = -(u_{n-1} - n u_{n-2}).$

Similarly, $u_{n-1} - n u_{n-2} = -(u_{n-2} - \overline{n-1}\, u_{n-3}).$

     $\ldots\ldots\ldots\ldots\ldots\ldots\ldots\ldots\ldots\ldots\ldots\ldots\ldots\ldots$

         $u_3 - 4u_2 = -(u_2 - 3u_1);$

whence by multiplication, we obtain

$$u_n - (n+1) u_{n-1} = (-1)^{n-2} (u_2 - 3u_1).$$

The first two convergents are $\dfrac{1}{1}, \dfrac{2}{4}$; hence

$$p_n - (n+1) p_{n-1} = (-1)^{n-1}, \quad q_n - (n+1) q_{n-1} = (-1)^{n-2}.$$

Thus $\quad \dfrac{p_n}{(n+1)!} - \dfrac{p_{n-1}}{n!} = \dfrac{(-1)^{n-1}}{(n+1)!}, \quad \dfrac{q_n}{(n+1)!} - \dfrac{q_{n-1}}{n!} = \dfrac{(-1)^{n-2}}{(n+1)!},$

$$\dfrac{p_{n-1}}{n!} - \dfrac{p_{n-2}}{(n-1)!} = \dfrac{(-1)^{n-2}}{n!}, \quad \dfrac{q_{n-1}}{n!} - \dfrac{q_{n-2}}{(n-1)!} = \dfrac{(-1)^{n-3}}{n!},$$

....

$$\dfrac{p_2}{3!} - \dfrac{p_1}{2!} = -\dfrac{1}{3!}, \quad \dfrac{q_2}{3!} - \dfrac{q_1}{2!} = \dfrac{1}{3!},$$

$$\dfrac{p_1}{2!} = \dfrac{1}{2!}, \quad \dfrac{q_1}{2!} = \dfrac{1}{2} = 1 - \dfrac{1}{2!};$$

whence, by addition

$$\dfrac{p_n}{(n+1)!} = \dfrac{1}{2!} - \dfrac{1}{3!} + \dfrac{1}{4!} - \dots + \dfrac{(-1)^{n-1}}{(n+1)!};$$

$$\dfrac{q_n}{(n+1)!} = 1 - \dfrac{1}{2!} + \dfrac{1}{3!} - \dfrac{1}{4!} + \dots + \dfrac{(-1)^{n-2}}{(n+1)!}.$$

By making n infinite, we obtain

$$Lim \dfrac{p_n}{q_n} = \dfrac{1}{e} \div \left(1 - \dfrac{1}{e} \right) = \dfrac{1}{e-1},$$

which is therefore the value of the given expression.

*445. *If every component of* $\dfrac{b_1}{a_1 +} \dfrac{b_2}{a_2 +} \dfrac{b_3}{a_3 +} \dots$ *is a proper fraction with integral numerator and denominator, the continued fraction is incommensurable.*

For if possible suppose that the continued fraction is commensurable and equal to $\dfrac{B}{A}$, where A and B are positive integers; then $\dfrac{B}{A} = \dfrac{b_1}{a_1 + f_1}$, where f_1 denotes the infinite continued fraction $\dfrac{b_2}{a_2 +} \dfrac{b_3}{a_3 +} \dots$; hence $f_1 = \dfrac{Ab_1 - Ba_1}{B} = \dfrac{C}{B}$ suppose. Now A, B, a_1, b_1 are integers and f_1 is positive, therefore C is a positive integer. Similarly $\dfrac{C}{B} = \dfrac{b_2}{a_2 + f_2}$, where f_2 denotes the infinite continued fraction $\dfrac{b_3}{a_3 +} \dfrac{b_4}{a_4 +} \dots$; hence $f_2 = \dfrac{Bb_2 - Ca_2}{C} = \dfrac{D}{C}$ suppose; and as before, it follows that D is a positive integer; and so on.

Again, $\dfrac{B}{A}, \dfrac{C}{B}, \dfrac{D}{C}, \dots$ are proper fractions; for $\dfrac{B}{A}$ is less than $\dfrac{b_1}{a_1}$,

which is a proper fraction; $\dfrac{C}{B}$ is less than $\dfrac{b_2}{a_2}$; $\dfrac{D}{C}$ is less than $\dfrac{b_3}{a_3}$; and so

on.

Thus $A, B, C, D, \dots$ form an *infinite* series of *positive integers* in *descending* order of magnitude; which is absurd. Hence the given fraction cannot be commensurable.

The above result still holds if some of the components are not proper fractions, provided that from and after a fixed component all the others are proper fractions.

For suppose that $\dfrac{b_n}{a_n}$ and all the succeeding components are proper fractions; thus, as we have just proved, the infinite continued fraction beginning with $\dfrac{b_n}{a_n}$ is incommensurable; denote it by k, then

the complete quotient corresponding to $\dfrac{p_n}{q_n}$ is $\dfrac{k}{1}$, and therefore the

value of the continued fraction is $\dfrac{p_{n-1} + kp_{n-2}}{q_{n-1} + kq_{n-2}}$.

This cannot be commensurable unless $\dfrac{p_{n-1}}{q_{n-1}} = \dfrac{p_{n-2}}{q_{n-2}}$; and this

condition cannot hold unless $\dfrac{p_{n-2}}{q_{n-2}} = \dfrac{p_{n-3}}{q_{n-3}}$, $\dfrac{p_{n-3}}{q_{n-3}} = \dfrac{p_{n-4}}{q_{n-4}}$, $\dots$, and

finally $\dfrac{p_2}{q_2} = \dfrac{p_1}{q_1}$; that is $b_1 b_2 = 0$, which is impossible; hence the given fraction must be incommensurable.

*446. *If every component of* $\dfrac{b_1}{a_1 -} \dfrac{b_2}{a_2 -} \dfrac{b_3}{a_3 -} \dots$ *is a proper fraction with integral numerator and denominator, and if the value of the infinite continued fraction beginning with any component is less than unity, the fraction is incommensurable.*

The demonstration is similar to that of the preceding article.

*EXAMPLES XXXI. a.

1. Shew that in the continued fraction

$$\frac{b_1}{a_1 -} \frac{b_2}{a_2 -} \frac{b_3}{a_3 -} \cdots,$$

$$p_n = a_n p_{n-1} - b_n p_{n-2}, \; q_n = a_n q_{n-1} - b_n q_{n-2}.$$

2. Convert $\left(\dfrac{2x+1}{2x}\right)^2$ into a continued fraction with unit numerators.

3. Shew that

(1) $\sqrt{a^2 + b} = a + \dfrac{b}{2a +} \dfrac{b}{2a +} \cdots,$

(2) $\sqrt{a^2 - b} = a - \dfrac{b}{2a -} \dfrac{b}{2a -} \cdots$

4. In the continued fraction $\dfrac{b_1}{a_1 -} \dfrac{b_2}{a_2 -} \dfrac{b_3}{a_3 -} \cdots,$ if the denominator of every component exceed the numerator by unity at least shew that p_n and q_n increase with n.

5. If $a_1, a_2, a_3, \ldots, a_n$ are in harmonical progression, shew that

$$\frac{a_n}{a_{n-1}} = \frac{1}{2 -} \frac{1}{2 -} \frac{1}{2 -} \cdots \frac{1}{2 -} \frac{a_2}{a_1}.$$

6. Shew that $\left(a + \dfrac{1}{2a +} \dfrac{1}{2a +} \cdots\right)^2 + \left(a - \dfrac{1}{2a -} \dfrac{1}{2a -} \cdots\right)^2 = 2a^2,$

and $\left(a + \dfrac{1}{2a +} \dfrac{1}{2a +} \cdots\right)\left(a - \dfrac{1}{2a -} \dfrac{1}{2a -} \cdots\right) = a^2 - \dfrac{1}{2a^2 -} \dfrac{1}{2a^2 -} \cdots$

7. In the continued fraction

$$\frac{b}{a +} \frac{b}{a +} \frac{b}{a +} \cdots,$$

shew that $p_{n+1} = b q_n, \; b q_{n+1} - a p_{n+1} = b^2 q_{n-1}.$

8. Shew that $\dfrac{b}{a +} \dfrac{b}{a +} \dfrac{b}{a +} \cdots = b \cdot \dfrac{\alpha^x - \beta^x}{\alpha^{x+1} - \beta^{x+1}},$ x being the number of components, and α, β the roots of the equation $k^2 - ak - b = 0.$

9. Prove that the product of the continued fractions

$$a + \frac{1}{b+} \frac{1}{c+} \frac{1}{d+} \frac{1}{a+} \cdots, \; -d + \frac{1}{-c+} \frac{1}{-b+} \frac{1}{-a+} \frac{1}{-d+} \cdots, \text{ is equal}$$

to -1.

Shew that

10. $\dfrac{1}{1-} \dfrac{4}{5-} \dfrac{9}{13-} \dfrac{64}{25-} \cdots \dfrac{(n^2-1)^2}{n^2+(n+1)^2} = \dfrac{(n+1)(n+2)(2n+3)}{6}$.

11. $\dfrac{2}{1-} \dfrac{3}{5-} \dfrac{8}{7-} \cdots \dfrac{n^2-1}{2n+1} = \dfrac{n(n+3)}{2}$.

12. $\dfrac{2}{2-} \dfrac{3}{3-} \dfrac{4}{4-} \cdots \dfrac{n+1}{n+1-} \dfrac{n+2}{n+2} = 1 + 1 + 2! + 3! + \ldots + n!$

13. $\dfrac{1}{1-} \dfrac{1}{3-} \dfrac{2}{4-} \dfrac{3}{5-} = \cdots \dfrac{n-1}{n+1-} \cdots = e - 1$.

14. $\dfrac{4}{1+} \dfrac{6}{2+} \dfrac{8}{3+} \cdots \dfrac{2n+2}{n+} \cdots = \dfrac{2(e^2-1)}{e^2+1}$.

15. $\dfrac{3.3}{1+} \dfrac{3.4}{2+} \dfrac{3.5}{3+} \cdots \dfrac{3(n+2)}{n+} \cdots = \dfrac{6(2e^3+1)}{5e^3-2}$.

16. If $u_1 = \dfrac{a}{b}$, $u_2 = \dfrac{b}{a+b}$, $u_3 = \dfrac{a+b}{a+2b}$, $\ldots$, each successive fraction being formed by taking the denominator and the sum of the numerator and denominator of the preceding fraction for its numerator and denominator respectively, shew that

$$u_n = \frac{\sqrt{5}-1}{2}.$$

17. Prove that the nth convergent to the continued fraction

$$\frac{r}{r+1-} \frac{r}{r+1-} \frac{r}{r+1-} \cdots \text{ is } \frac{r^{n+1}-r}{r^{n+1}-1}.$$

18. Find the value of $\dfrac{a_1}{a_1+1-} \dfrac{a_2}{a_2+1-} \dfrac{a_3}{a_3+1-} \cdots$,

$a_1, a_2, a_3, \ldots$ being positive and greater than unity.

19. Shew that the nth convergent to $1 - \dfrac{1}{4-} \dfrac{1}{4-} \cdots$ is equal to the

$(2n-1)$th convergent to $\dfrac{1}{1+} \dfrac{1}{2+} \dfrac{1}{1+} \dfrac{1}{2+} \cdots$

20. Shew that the $3n$th convergent to

$$\frac{1}{5-} \frac{1}{2-} \frac{1}{1-} \frac{1}{5-} \frac{1}{2-} \frac{1}{1-} \frac{1}{5-} \cdots \text{ is } \frac{n}{3n+1}.$$

21. Shew that $\dfrac{1}{2+}\dfrac{2}{3+}\dfrac{3}{4+}\cdots = \dfrac{3-e}{e-2}$; hence shew that e lies between $2\dfrac{2}{3}$ and $2\dfrac{8}{11}$.

CONVERSION OF SERIES INTO CONTINUED FRACTIONS

*447. It will be convenient here to write the series in the form

$$\frac{1}{u_1} + \frac{1}{u_2} + \frac{1}{u_3} + \ldots + \frac{1}{u_n}.$$

Put

$$\frac{1}{u_r} + \frac{1}{u_{r+1}} = \frac{1}{u_r + x_r};$$

then

$$(u_r + x_r)(u_{r+1} + u_r) = u_r u_{r+1},$$

$$\therefore \qquad x_r = -\frac{u_r^2}{u_r + u_{r+1}}.$$

Hence,

$$\frac{1}{u_1} + \frac{1}{u_2} = \frac{1}{u_1 - \dfrac{u_1^2}{u_1 - u_2}} = \frac{1}{u_1 -} \frac{u_1^2}{u_1 + u}.$$

Similarly, $\dfrac{1}{u_1} + \dfrac{1}{u_2} + \dfrac{1}{u_3} = \dfrac{1}{u_1} + \dfrac{1}{u_2 + x_2} = \dfrac{1}{u_1 -} \dfrac{u_1^2}{u_1 + u_2 + x_2}$.

$$= \frac{1}{u_1 -} \frac{u_1^2}{u_1 + u_2 -} \frac{u_2^2}{u_2 + u_3};$$

and so on; hence generally

$$\frac{1}{u_1} + \frac{1}{u_2} + \frac{1}{u_3} + \ldots + \frac{1}{u_n}$$

$$= \frac{1}{u_1 -} \frac{u_1^2}{u_1 + u_2 -} \frac{u_2^2}{u_2 + u_3 -} \cdots \frac{u_{n-1}^2}{u_{n-1} + u_n}.$$

Example 1. *Express as a continued fraction the series*

$$\frac{1}{a_0} - \frac{x}{a_0 a_1} + \frac{x^2}{a_0 a_1 a_2} - \ldots + (-1)^n \frac{x^n}{a_0 a_1 a_2 \ldots a_n}.$$

Put

$$\frac{1}{a_n} - \frac{x}{a_n a_{n+1}} = \frac{1}{a_n + y_n};$$

then

$$(a_n + y_n)(a_{n+1} - x) = a_n a_{n+1};$$

$$\therefore \qquad y_n = \frac{a_n x}{a_{n+1} - x}.$$

Hence,

$$\frac{1}{a_0} - \frac{x}{a_0 a_1} = \frac{1}{a_0 + y_0} = \frac{1}{a_0 +} \frac{a_0 x}{a_1 - x}$$

Again, $\dfrac{1}{a_0} - \dfrac{x}{a_0 a_1} + \dfrac{x^2}{a_0 a_1 a_2} = \dfrac{1}{a_0} - \dfrac{x}{a_0}\left(\dfrac{1}{a_1} - \dfrac{x}{a_1 a_2}\right) = \dfrac{1}{a_0} - \dfrac{x}{a_0\,(a_1 + y_1)}$

$$= \dfrac{1}{a_0 +} \dfrac{a_0 x}{a_1 + y_1 - x}$$

$$= \dfrac{1}{a_0 +} \dfrac{a_0 x}{a_1 - x +} \dfrac{a_1 x}{a_2 - x}\ ;$$

and generally
$$\dfrac{1}{a_0} - \dfrac{x}{a_0 a_1} + \dfrac{x^2}{a_0 a_1 a_2} - \dots + (-1)^n \dfrac{x^n}{a_0 a_1 a_2 \dots a_n}$$

$$= \dfrac{1}{a_0 +} \dfrac{a_0 x}{a_1 - x +} \dfrac{a_1 x}{a_2 - x +} \dots \dfrac{a_{n-1}\, x}{a_n - x}.$$

Example 2. *Express* $\log(1 + x)$ *as a continued fraction.*

We have $\log(1 + x) = x - \dfrac{x^2}{2} + \dfrac{x^3}{3} - \dfrac{x^4}{4} + \dots$

The required expression is most simply deduced from the continued fraction equivalent to the series

$$\dfrac{x}{a_1} - \dfrac{x^2}{a_2} + \dfrac{x^3}{a_3} - \dfrac{x^4}{a_4} + \dots$$

By putting
$$\dfrac{1}{a_n} - \dfrac{x}{a_{n+1}} = \dfrac{1}{a_n + y_n},$$

we obtain
$$y_n = \dfrac{a_n^2 x}{a_{n+1} - a_n x}\ ;$$

hence we have

$$\dfrac{x}{a_1} - \dfrac{x^2}{a_2} + \dfrac{x^3}{a_3} - \dfrac{x^4}{a_4} + \dots = \dfrac{x}{a_1 +} \dfrac{a_1^2 x}{a_2 - a_1 x +} \dfrac{a_2^2 x}{a_3 - a_2 x +} \dfrac{a_3^2 x}{a_4 - a_3 x +} \dots\ ;$$

∴ $$\log(1 + x) = \dfrac{x}{1 +} \dfrac{1^2 x}{2 - x +} \dfrac{2^2 x}{3 - 2x +} \dfrac{3^2 x}{4 - 3x +} \dots$$

*448. In certain cases we may simplify the components of the continued fraction by the help of the following proposition :

The continued fraction

$$\dfrac{b_1}{a_1 +} \dfrac{b_2}{a_2 +} \dfrac{b_3}{a_3 +} \dfrac{b_4}{a_4 +} \dots$$

is equal to the continued fraction

$$\dfrac{c_1 b_1}{c_1 a_1 +} \dfrac{c_1 c_2 b_2}{c_2 a_2 +} \dfrac{c_2 c_3 b_3}{c_3 a_3 +} \dfrac{c_3 c_4 b_4}{c_4 a_4 +} \dots\ ;$$

where $c_1, c_2, c_3, c_4, \dots$ are any quantities whatever.

Let f_1 denote $\dfrac{b_2}{a_2 +} \dfrac{b_3}{a_3 +} \dots$; then the continued fraction $= \dfrac{b_1}{a_1 + f_1} = \dfrac{c_1 b_1}{c_1 a_1 + c_1 f_1}$.

Let f_2 denote $\dfrac{b_3}{a_3 +} \dfrac{b_4}{a_4 +} \ldots$; then

$$c_1 f_1 = \frac{c_1 b_2}{a_2 + f_2} = \frac{c_1 c_2 b_2}{c_2 a_2 + c_2 f_2}.$$

Similarly, $c_2 f_2 = \dfrac{c_2 c_3 b_3}{c_3 a_3 + c_3 f_3}$; and so on; whence the proposition is established.

*EXAMPLES XXXI. b.

Shew that

1. $\dfrac{1}{u_0} - \dfrac{1}{u_1} + \dfrac{1}{u_2} - \dfrac{1}{u_3} + \ldots + (-1)^n \dfrac{1}{u_n}$

$$= \frac{1}{u_0 +} \frac{u_0^2}{u_1 - u_0 +} \frac{u_1^2}{u_2 - u_1 +} \cdots \frac{u_{n-1}^2}{u_n - u_{n-1}}.$$

2. $\dfrac{1}{a_0} + \dfrac{x}{a_0 a_1} + \dfrac{x^2}{a_0 a_1 a_2} + \ldots + \dfrac{x^n}{a_0 a_1 a_2 \ldots a_n}$

$$= \frac{1}{a_0 -} \frac{a_0 x}{a_1 + x -} \frac{a_1 x}{a_2 + x -} \cdots \frac{a_{n-1} x}{a_n + x}.$$

3. $\dfrac{r-1}{r-2} = \dfrac{r}{r -} \dfrac{r+1}{r+1 -} \dfrac{r+2}{r+2 -} \cdots$

4. $\dfrac{2n}{n+1} = \dfrac{1}{1 -} \dfrac{1}{4 -} \dfrac{1}{1 -} \dfrac{1}{4 -} \ldots$ to n quotients.

5. $1 + \dfrac{1}{2} + \dfrac{1}{3} + \ldots + \dfrac{1}{n+1} = \dfrac{1}{1 -} \dfrac{1}{3 -} \dfrac{4}{5 -} \dfrac{9}{7 -} \cdots \dfrac{n^2}{2n+1}$.

6. $\dfrac{1}{1^2} + \dfrac{1}{2^2} + \ldots + \dfrac{1}{(n+1)^2} = \dfrac{1}{1 -} \dfrac{1^4}{1^2 + 2^2 -} \cdots \dfrac{n^4}{n^2 + (n+1)^2}$.

7. $e^x = 1 + \dfrac{x}{1 -} \dfrac{x}{x+2 -} \dfrac{2x}{x+3 -} \dfrac{3x}{x+4 -} \cdots$

8. $\dfrac{1}{a} - \dfrac{1}{ab} + \dfrac{1}{abc} - \dfrac{1}{abcd} + \ldots = \dfrac{1}{a +} \dfrac{a}{b-1 +} \dfrac{b}{c-1 +} \dfrac{c}{d-1 +} \cdots$

9. $1 + \dfrac{1}{r} + \dfrac{1}{r^4} + \dfrac{1}{r^9} + \dfrac{1}{r^{16}} + \ldots = 1 + \dfrac{1}{r -} \dfrac{r}{r^3 + 1 -} \dfrac{r^3}{r^5 + 1 -} \dfrac{r^5}{r^7 + 1 -} \cdots$

10. $\dfrac{a_1}{a_1+}\dfrac{a_2}{a_2+}\dfrac{a_3}{a_3+}\cdots\dfrac{a_n}{a_n}=\dfrac{1}{1+}\dfrac{1}{a_1+}\dfrac{a_1}{a_2+}\dfrac{a_2}{a_3+}\cdots\dfrac{a_{n-2}}{a_{n-1}}.$

11. If $P=\dfrac{a}{a+}\dfrac{b}{b+}\dfrac{c}{c+}\cdots,\ Q=\dfrac{a}{b+}\dfrac{b}{c+}\dfrac{c}{d+}\cdots,$

shew that $P\,(a+1+Q)=a+Q.$

12. Shew that $\dfrac{1}{q_1}-\dfrac{x}{q_1q_2}+\dfrac{x^2}{q_2q_3}-\dfrac{x^3}{q_3q_4}+\ldots$ is equal to the

continued fraction $\dfrac{1}{a_1+}\dfrac{x}{a_2+}\dfrac{x}{a_3+}\dfrac{x}{a_4+}\ldots,$ where $q_1,\,q_2,\,q_3,\ldots$

are the denominators of the successive convergents.

■■■

Chapter 32

PROBABILITY

449. Definition : If an event can happen in a ways and fail in b ways, and each of these ways is equally likely, the **probability**, or the **chance**, of its happening is $\dfrac{a}{a+b}$, and that of its failing is $\dfrac{b}{a+b}$.

For instance, if in a lottery there are 7 prizes and 25 blanks, the chance that a person holding 1 ticket will win a prize is $\dfrac{7}{32}$, and his chance of not winning is $\dfrac{25}{32}$.

450. The reason for the mathematical definition of probability may be made clear by the following considerations :

If an event can happen in a ways and fail to happen in b ways, and all these ways are equally likely, we can assert that the chance of its happening is to the chance of its failing as a to b. Thus if the chance of its happening is represented by ka, where k is an undetermined constant, then the chance of its failing will be represented by kb.

$\therefore$ chance of happening + chance of failing = $k\,(a + b)$

Now the event is certain to happen or to fail; therefore the sum of the chances of happening and failing must represent *certainty*. If therefore we agree to take certainty as our unit, we have

$$1 = k\,(a + b), \text{ or } k = \frac{1}{a+b} ;$$

$\therefore$ the chance that the even will happen is $\dfrac{a}{a+b}$,

and the chance that the event will not happen is $\dfrac{b}{a+b}$.

Cor. If p is the probability of the happening of an event, the probability of its not happening is $1 - p$.

451. Instead of saying that the chance of the happening of an event is $\dfrac{a}{a+b}$, it is sometimes stated *that the odds are a to b in favour of the event, or b to a against the event.*

452. The definition of probability in Art. 449 may be given in a slightly different form which is sometimes useful. If c is the total number of cases, each being equally likely to occur, and of these a are favourable to the event, then the probability that the event will happen is $\dfrac{a}{c}$, and the probability that it will not happen is $1 - \dfrac{a}{c}$.

Example 1. *What is the chance of throwing a number greater than 4 with an ordinary die whose faces are numbered from 1 to 6 ?*

There are 6 possible ways in which the die can fall, and of these two are favourable to the event required;

therefore the required chance $= \dfrac{2}{6} = \dfrac{1}{3}$.

Example 2. *From a bag containing 4 white and 5 black balls a man draws 3 at random; what are the odds against these being all black ?*

The total number of ways in which 3 balls can be drawn is $^9C_3$, and number of ways of drawing 3 black balls is $^5C_3$; therefore the chance of drawing 3 black balls

$$= \dfrac{^5C_3}{^9C_3} = \dfrac{5.\,4.\,3}{9.\,8.\,7} = \dfrac{5}{42}.$$

Thus the odds against the event are 37 to 5.

Example 3. *Find the chance of throwing at least one ace in a single throw with two dice.*

The possible number of cases is 6×6, or 36.

An ace on one die may be associated with any of the 6 numbers on the other die, and the remaining 5 numbers on the first die may each be associated with the ace on the second die; thus the number of favourable cases is 11.

Therefore the required chance is $\dfrac{11}{36}$.

Or we may reason as follows :

There are 5 ways in which each die can be thrown so as *not* to give an ace; hence 25 throws of the two dice will exclude aces. That is, the chance of *not* throwing one or more aces is $\dfrac{25}{36}$; so that the chance of throwing one ace at

least is $1 - \dfrac{25}{36}$, or $\dfrac{11}{36}$.

Example 4. *Find the chance of throwing more than 15 in one throw with 3 dice.*

A throw amounting to 18 must be made up of 6, 6, 6, and this can occur in 1 way; 17 can be made up of 6, 6, 5 which can occur in 3 ways; 16 may be made up of 6, 6, 4 and 6, 5, 5 each of which arrangements can occur in 3 ways.

Therefore the number of favourable cases is

$$1 + 3 + 3 + 3, \quad \text{or} \quad 10.$$

And the total number of cases is 6^3, or 216;

therefore the required chance $= \dfrac{10}{216} = \dfrac{5}{108}$.

Example 5. *A has 3 shares in a lottery in which there are 3 prizes and 6 blanks; B has 1 share in a lottery in which there is 1 prize and 2 blanks : shew that A's chance of success is to B's as 16 to 7.*

A may draw 3 prizes in 1 way;

he may draw 2 prizes and 1 blank in $\dfrac{3 \cdot 2}{1 \cdot 2} \times 6$ ways;

he may draw 1 prize and 2 blanks in $3 \times \dfrac{6 \cdot 5}{1 \cdot 2}$ ways;

the sum of these numbers is 64, which is the number of ways in which *A* can win a prize. Also he can draw 3 tickets in $\dfrac{9 \cdot 8 \cdot 7}{1 \cdot 2 \cdot 3}$, or 84 ways;

therefore *A*'s chance of success $= \dfrac{64}{84} = \dfrac{16}{21}$.

B's chance of success is clearly $\dfrac{1}{3}$;

therefore *A*'s chance : *B*'s chance $= \dfrac{16}{21} : \dfrac{1}{3}$

$$= 16 : 7.$$

Or we might have reasoned thus : *A* will get all blanks in $\dfrac{6 \cdot 5 \cdot 4}{1 \cdot 2 \cdot 3}$, or 20 ways; the chance of which is $\dfrac{20}{84}$, or $\dfrac{5}{21}$;

therefore *A*'s chance of success $= 1 - \dfrac{5}{21} = \dfrac{16}{21}$.

453. Suppose that there are a number of events $A, B, C, \ldots$, of which one must, and only one can, occur; also suppose that $a, b, c, \ldots$ are the numbers of ways respectively in which these events can happen, and that each of these ways is equally likely to occur; it is required to find the chance of each event.

The total number of equally possible ways is $a + b + c + \ldots$, and of these the number favourable to A is a : hence the chance that A will happen is $\dfrac{a}{a + b + c + \ldots}$. Similarly the chance that B will happen is $\dfrac{b}{a + b + c + \ldots}$; and so on.

454. From the examples we have given it will be seen that the solution of the easier kinds of questions in Probability requires nothing more than a knowledge of the definition of Probability, and the application of the laws of Permutations and Combinations.

EXAMPLES XXXII. a.

1. In a single throw with two dice find the chances of throwing (1) five, (2) six.

2. From a pack of 52 cards two are drawn at random; find the chance that one is a knave and the other a queen.

3. A bag contains 5 white, 7 black, and 4 red balls : find the chance that three balls drawn at random are all white.

4. If four coins are tossed, find the chance that there should be two heads and two tails.

5. One of two events must happen : given that the chance of the one is two-thirds that of the other, find the odds in favour of the other.

6. If from a pack four cards are drawn, find the chance that they will be the four honours of the same suit.

7. Thirteen persons take their places at a round table, shew that it is five to one against two particular persons sitting together.

8. There are three events A, B, C, one of which must, and only one can, happen; the odds are 8 to 3 against A, 5 to 2 against B : find the odds against C.

9. Compare the chances of throwing 4 with one die, 8 with two dice, and 12 with three dice.

10. In shuffling a pack of cards, four are accidentally dropped; find the chance that the missing cards should be one from each suit.

11. A has 3 shares in a lottery containing 3 prizes and 9 blanks; B has 2 shares in a lottery containing 2 prizes and 6 blanks : compare their chances of success.

12. Shew that the chances of throwing six with 4, 3, or 2 dice respectively are as $1 : 6 : 18$.

13. There are three works, one consisting of 3 volumes, one of 4, and the other of 1 volume. They are placed on a shelf at random; prove that the chance that volumes of the same works are all together is $\dfrac{3}{140}$.

14. A and B throw with two dice; if A throws 9, find B's chance of throwing a higher number.

15. The letters forming the word *Clifton* are placed at random in a row : what is the chance that the two vowels come together ?

16. In a hand at whist what is the chance that the 4 kings are held by a specified player ?

17. There are 4 rupees and 3 ten nP.'s placed at random in a line : shew that the chance of the extreme coins being both ten nP.'s is $\dfrac{1}{7}$. Generalize this result in the case of m rupees and n ten nP.'s.

455. We have hitherto considered only those occurrences which in the language of Probability are called *Simple* events. When two or more of these occur in connection with each other, the joint occurrence is called a *Compound* event.

For example, suppose we have a bag containing 5 white and 8 black balls, and two drawings, each of three balls, are made from it successively. If we wish to estimate the chance of drawing first 3 white and then 3 black balls, we should be dealing with compound event.

In such a case the result of the second drawing might or might not be *dependent* on the result of the first. If the balls are not replaced after being drawn, then if the first drawing gives 3 white balls, the ratio of the black to the white balls remaining is greater than if the first drawing had not given three white; thus the chance of drawing 3 black balls at the second trial is affected by the result of the first. But if the balls are replaced after being drawn, it is clear that the result of the second drawing is not in any way affected by the result of the first.

We are thus led to the following definition :

Events are said to be **dependent** or **independent** according as the occurrence of one does or does not affect the occurrence of the others. Dependent events are sometimes said to be *contingent*.

456. *If there are two independent events the respective probabilities of which are known, to find the probability that both will happen.*

Suppose that the first event may happen in a ways and fail in b ways, all these cases being equally likely; and suppose that the second event may happen in a' ways and fail in b' ways, all these ways being equally likely. Each of the $a + b$ cases may be associated with each of the $a' + b'$ cases, to form $(a + b)(a' + b')$ compound cases all equally likely to occur.

In aa' of these both events happen, in bb' of them both fail, in ab' of them the first happens and the second fails and in $a'b$ of them the first fails and the second happens. Thus

$$\frac{aa'}{(a+b)(a'+b')} \text{ is the chance that both events happen;}$$

$$\frac{bb'}{(a+b)(a'+b')} \text{ is the chance that both events fail;}$$

$$\frac{ab'}{(a+b)(a'+b')} \text{ is the chance that the first happens and the}$$

second fails,

$$\frac{a'b}{(a+b)(a'+b')} \text{ is the chance that the first fails and the}$$

second happens.

Thus if the respective chances of two independent events are p and p', the chance that both will happen is pp'. Similar reasoning will apply in the case of any number of independent events. Hence it is easy to see that if $p_1, p_2, p_3, \dots$ are the respective chances that a number of independent events will separately happen, the chance that they will all happen is $p_1 p_2 p_3 \dots$; the chance that the two first will happen and the rest fail is $p_1 p_2 (1 - p_3)(1 - p_4) \dots$; and similarly for any other particular case.

457. If p is the chance that an event will happen in one trial, the chance that it will happen in any assigned succession of r trials is p^r; this follows from the preceding article by supposing

$$p_1 = p_2 = p_3 = \dots = p.$$

To find the chance that some one at least of the events will happen we proceed thus : the chance that all the events fail is $(1 - p_1)(1 - p_2)(1 - p_3) \dots$, and except in this case some one of the events must happen; hence the required chance is

$$1 - (1 - p_1)(1 - p_2)(1 - p_3) \dots$$

Example 1. *Two drawings, each of 3 balls, are made from a bag containing 5 white and 8 black balls, the balls being replaced before the second trial : find the chance that the first drawing will give 3 white, and the second 3 black balls.*

The number of ways in which 3 balls may be drawn is $^{13}C_3$;

.... 3 white .... $^{6}C_3$;

.... 3 black .... $^{8}C_3$.

Therefore the chance of 3 white at the first trial

$$= \frac{5 \cdot 4}{1 \cdot 2} \div \frac{13 \cdot 12 \cdot 11}{1 \cdot 2 \cdot 3} = \frac{5}{143};$$

and the chance of 3 black at the second trial $= \frac{8 \cdot 7 \cdot 6}{1 \cdot 2 \cdot 3} \div \frac{13 \cdot 12 \cdot 11}{1 \cdot 2 \cdot 3} = \frac{28}{143}$;

therefore the chance of the compound event $= \frac{5}{143} \times \frac{28}{143} = \frac{140}{20449}$.

Example 2. *In tossing a coin, find the chance of throwing head and tail alternately in 3 successive trials.*

Here the first throw must give either head or tail; the chance that the second gives the opposite to the first is $\frac{1}{2}$, and the chance that the third throw is the same as the first is $\frac{1}{2}$.

Therefore the chance of the compound event $= \frac{1}{2} \times \frac{1}{2} = \frac{1}{4}$.

Example 3. *Supposing that it is 9 to 7 against a person A who is now 35 years of age living till he is 65, and 3 to 2 against a person B now 45 living till he is 75; find the chance that one at least of these persons will be alive 30 years hence.*

The chance that A will die within 30 years is $\frac{9}{16}$;

the chance that B will die within 30 years is $\frac{3}{5}$;

therefore the chance that both will die is $\frac{9}{16} \times \frac{3}{5}$, or $\frac{27}{80}$;

therefore the chance that both will not be dead, that is that one at least will be alive, is $1 - \frac{27}{80}$, or $\frac{53}{80}$.

458. By a slight modification of the meaning of the symbols in Art. 456, we are enabled to estimate the probability of the concurrence of two *dependent* events. For suppose that *when the first event has happened*, a' denotes the number of ways in which the second event can follow, and b' the number of ways in which it will not follow; then the number of ways in which the two events can happen together is aa', and the probability of their concurrence is $\frac{aa'}{(a+b)(a'+b')}$.

Thus if p is the probability of the first event, and p' the contingent probability that the second will follow, the probability of the concurrence of the two events is pp'.

Example 1. *In a hand at whist find the chance that a specified player holds both the king and queen of trumps.*

Denote the player by A; then the chance that A has the king is clearly $\frac{13}{52}$; for this particular card can be dealt in 52 different ways, 13 of which fall to A.

The chance that, when he has the king, he can also hold the queen is then $\frac{12}{51}$.

for the queen can be dealt in 51 ways, 12 of which fall to A.

Therefore the chance required $= \frac{13}{52} \times \frac{12}{51} = \frac{1}{17}$.

Or we might reason as follows :

The number of ways in which the king and the queen can be dealt to A is equal to the number of permutations of 13 things 2 at a time, or 13 . 12. An l similarly the total number of ways in which the king and queen can be d alt is 52 . 51.

Therefore the chance $= \frac{13 \cdot 12}{52 \cdot 51} = \frac{1}{17}$, as before.

Example 2. *Two drawings, each of 3 balls, are made from a bag containing 5 white and 8 black balls, the balls not being replaced before the second trial : find the chance that the first drawing will give 3 white and the second 3 black balls.*

At the first trial, 3 balls may be drawn in $^{13}C_3$ ways; and 3 white balls may be drawn in $^{5}C_3$ ways;

therefore the chance of 3 white at first trial $= \frac{5 \cdot 4}{1 \cdot 2} \div \frac{13 \cdot 12 \cdot 11}{1 \cdot 2 \cdot 3} = \frac{5}{143}$

When 3 white balls have been drawn and removed, the bag contains 2 white and 8 black balls;

therefore at the second trial 3 balls may be drawn in $^{10}C_3$ ways;

and 3 black balls may be drawn in $^{8}C_3$ ways;

therefore the chance of 3 black at the second trial

$$= \frac{8 \cdot 7 \cdot 6}{1 \cdot 2 \cdot 3} \div \frac{10 \cdot 9 \cdot 8}{1 \cdot 2 \cdot 3} = \frac{7}{15} ;$$

therefore the chance of the compound event

$$= \frac{5}{143} \times \frac{7}{15} = \frac{7}{429}.$$

The student should compare this solution with that of Ex. 1, Art. 457.

459. *If an event can happen in two or more different ways* which are mutually exclusive, *the chance that it will happen is the sum of the chances of its happening in these different ways.*

This is sometimes regarded as a self-evident proposition arising immediately out of the definition of probability. It may, however, be proved as follows :

Suppose the event can happen in two ways which cannot concur; and let $\frac{a_1}{b_1}, \frac{a_2}{b_2}$ be the chances of the happening of the event in these two ways respectively. Then out of $b_1 b_2$ cases there are $a_1 b_2$ in which the event may happen in the first way, and $a_2 b_1$ ways in which the event may happen in the second; *and these ways cannot concur.* Therefore in all, out of $b_1 b_2$ cases there are $a_1 b_2 + a_2 b_1$ cases favourable to the event; hence the chance that the event will happen in one or other of the two ways is

$$\frac{a_1 b_2 + a_2 b_1}{b_1 b_2} = \frac{a_1}{b_1} + \frac{a_2}{b_2}.$$

Similar reasoning will apply whatever be the number of exclusive ways in which the event can happen.

Hence if an event can happen in n ways which are mutually exclusive, and if $p_1, p_2, p_3, \ldots p_n$ are the probabilities that the event will happen in these different ways respectively, the probability that it will happen in some one of these ways is

$$p_1 + p_2 + p_3 + \ldots p_n.$$

Example 1. *Find the chance of throwing 9 at least in a single throw with two dice.*

9 can be made up in 4 ways, and thus the chance of throwing 9 is $\dfrac{4}{36}$.

10 can be made up in 3 ways, and thus the chance of throwing 10 is $\dfrac{3}{36}$.

11 can be made up in 2 ways, and thus the chance of throwing 11 is $\dfrac{2}{36}$.

12 can be made up in 1 way, and thus the chance of throwing 12 is $\dfrac{1}{36}$.

Now the chance of throwing a number not less than 9 is the sum of these separate chances;

∴　the required chance $= \dfrac{4+3+2+1}{36} = \dfrac{5}{18}$.

Example 2. *One purse contains 1 rupee and 3 nP.'s, a second purse contains 2 rupees and 4 nP.'s, and a third contains 3 rupees and 1 nP. If a coin is taken out of one of the purses selected at random, find the chance that it is a rupee.*

Since each purse is equally likely to be taken, the chance of selecting the first is $\dfrac{1}{3}$; and the chance of then drawing a rupee is $\dfrac{1}{4}$; hence the chance of drawing a rupee so far as it depends upon the first purse is $\dfrac{1}{3} \times \dfrac{1}{4}$, or $\dfrac{1}{12}$.

Similarly the chance of drawing a rupee so far as it depends on the second purse is $\dfrac{1}{3} \times \dfrac{2}{6}$, or $\dfrac{1}{9}$; and from the third purse the chance of drawing a rupee is $\dfrac{1}{3} \times \dfrac{3}{4}$, or $\dfrac{1}{4}$;

∴ the required chance $= \dfrac{1}{12} + \dfrac{1}{9} + \dfrac{1}{4} = \dfrac{4}{9}$.

460. In the preceding article we have seen that the probability of an event may sometimes be considered as the sum of the probabilities of two or more separate events; but it is very important to notice that the probability of one or other of a series of events is the sum of the probabilities of the separate events *only when the events are mutually exclusive*, that is, when the occurrence of one is incompatible with the occurrence of any of the others.

Example : *From 20 tickets marked with the first 20 numerals, one is drawn at random; find the chance that it is a multiple of 3 or of 7.*

The chance that the number is a multiple of 3 is $\dfrac{6}{20}$, and the chance that it is a multiple of 7 is $\dfrac{2}{20}$; and *these events are mutually exclusive*, hence the required chance is

$$\frac{6}{20} + \frac{2}{20} \quad \text{or} \quad \frac{2}{5}.$$

But if the question had been : *find the chance that the number is a multiple of 3 or of 5*, it would have been incorrect to reason as follows :

Because the chance that the number is a multiple of 3 is $\dfrac{6}{20}$, and the chance that the number is a multiple of 5 is $\dfrac{4}{20}$, therefore the chance that it is a multiple of 3 or 5 is $\dfrac{6}{20} + \dfrac{4}{20}$, or $\dfrac{1}{2}$. For the number on the ticket might be a multiple *both* of 3 and of 5, so that the two events considered are not mutually exclusive.

461. It should be observed that the distinction between simple and compound events is in many cases a purely artificial one; in fact it often amounts to nothing more than a distinction between two different modes of viewing the same occurrence.

Example : *A bag contains 5 white and 7 black balls; if two balls are drawn what is the chance that one is white and the other black ?*

(i) Regarding the occurrence as a simple event, the chance

$$= (5 \times 7) \div {}^{12}C_2 = \frac{35}{66}.$$

(ii) The occurrence may be regarded as the happening of one or other of the two following compound events :

(1) drawing a white and then a black ball, the chance of which is

$$\frac{5}{12} \times \frac{7}{11} \quad \text{or} \quad \frac{35}{132};$$

(2) drawing a black and then a white ball, the chance of which is

$$\frac{7}{12} \times \frac{5}{11}, \text{ or } \frac{35}{132}.$$

And since these events are mutually exclusive, the required chance

$$= \frac{35}{132} + \frac{35}{132} = \frac{35}{66}.$$

It will be noticed that we have here assumed that the chance of drawing two specified balls successively is the same as if they were drawn simultaneously. A little consideration will shew that this must be the case.

EXAMPLES XXXII. b.

1. What is the chance of throwing an ace in the first only of two successive throws with an ordinary die ?

2. Three cards are drawn at random from an ordinary pack : find the chance that they will consist of a knave, a queen, and a king.

3. The odds against a certain event are 5 to 2, and the odds in favour of another event independent of the former are 6 to 5 : find the chance that one at least of the events will happen.

4. The odds against A solving a certain problem are 4 to 3, and the odds in favour of B solving the same problem are 7 to 5 : what is the chance that the problem will be solved if they both try ?

5. What is the chance of drawing a rupee from a purse one compartment of which contains 3 nP.'s and 2 rupees, and the other 2 rupees and 1 nP. ?

6. A bag contains 17 counters marked with the numbers 1 to 17. A counter is drawn and replaced; a second drawing is then made : what is the chance that the first number drawn is even and the second odd ?

7. Four persons draw each a card from an ordinary pack : find the chance (1) that a card is of each suit, (2) that no two cards are of equal value.

8. Find the chance of throwing six with a single die at least once in five trials.

9. The odds that a book will be favourably reviewed by three independent critics are 5 to 2, 4 to 3 and 3 to 4 respectively; what is the probability that of the three reviews a majority will be favourable ?

10. A bag contains 5 white and 3 black balls, and 4 are successively drawn out and not replaced; what is the chance that they are alternately of different colours ?

11. In three throws with a pair of dice, find the chance of throwing doublets at least once.

12. If 4 whole numbers taken at random are multiplied together shew that the chance that the last digit in the product is 1, 3, 7, or 9 is $\dfrac{16}{625}$.

13. In a purse are 10 coins, all five nP.'s except one which is a rupee; in another are ten coins all five nP.'s. Nine coins are taken from the former purse and put into the latter, and then nine coins are taken from the latter and put into the former : find the chance that the rupee is still in the first purse.

14. If two coins are tossed 5 times, what is the chance that there will be 5 heads and 5 tails ?

15. If 8 coins are tossed, what is the chance that one and only one will turn up head ?

16. A, B, C in order cut a pack of cards, replacing them after each cut, on condition that the first who cuts a spade shall win a prize : find their respective chances.

17. A and B draw from a purse containing 3 rupees and 4 nP.'s; find their respective chances of first drawing a rupee, the coins when drawn not being replaced.

18. A party of n persons sit at a round table, find the odds against two specified individuals sitting next to each other.

19. A is one of 6 horses entered for a race, and is to be ridden by one of two joekeys B and C. It is 2 to 1 that B rides A, in which case all the horses are equally likely to win; if C rides A, his chance is trebled : what are the odds against his winning ?

20. If on an average 1 vessel in every 10 is wrecked, find the chance that out of 5 vessels expected 4 at least will arrive safely.

462. *The probability of the happening of an event in one trial being known, required the probability of its happening once, twice, three times, ... exactly in n trials.*

Let p be the probability of the happening of the event in a single trial, and let $q = 1 - p$; then the probability that the event will happen exactly r times in n trials is the $(r+1)$th term in the expansion of $(q+p)^n$.

For if we select any particular set of r trials out of the total number n, the chance that the event will happen in every one of *these* r trials and fail in all the rest is $p^r q^{n-r}$ [Art. 456], and as a set of r trials can be selected in ^nC_r ways, all of which are equally applicable to the case in point, the required chance is

$$^nC_r p^r q^{n-r}.$$

If we expand $(p+q)^n$ by the Binomial Theorem, we have

$$p^n + {}^nC_1 p^{n-1}q + {}^nC_2 p^{n-2}q^2 + \ldots + {}^nC_{n-r} p^r q^{n-r} + \ldots + q^n;$$

thus the terms of this series will represent respectively the probabilities of the happening of the event exactly n times, $n-1$ times, $n-2$ times, ... in n trials.

463.   If the event happens n times, or fails only once, twice, ... $(n-r)$ times, it happens r times or more; therefore the chance that it happens at *least* r times in n trials is

$$p^n + {}^nC_1 p^{n-1}q + {}^nC_2 p^{n-2}q^2 + \ldots + {}^nC_{n-r} p^r q^{n-r},$$

or   theorem of the first $n-r+1$ terms of the expansion of $(p+q)$.

Example 1. *In four throws with a pair of dice, what is the chance of throwing doublets twice at least ?*

In a single throw the chance of doublets is $\dfrac{6}{36}$, or $\dfrac{1}{6}$; and the chance of failing to throw doublets is $\dfrac{5}{6}$. Now the required event follows if doublets are thrown four times, three times, or twice; therefore the required chance is the sum of the first three terms of the expansion of $\left(\dfrac{1}{6} + \dfrac{5}{6}\right)^4$.

Thus the chance $= \dfrac{1}{6^4}(1 + 4 \cdot 5 + 6 \cdot 5^2) = \dfrac{19}{144}$.

Example 2. *A bag contains a certain number of balls, some of which are white; a ball is drawn and replaced, another is then drawn and replaced; and so on : if p is the chance of drawing a white ball in a single trial. Find the number of white balls that is most likely to have been drawn in n trials.*

The chance of drawing exactly r white balls is $^nC_r p^r q^{n-r}$, and we have to find for what value of r this expression is greatest.

Now $^nC_r p^r q^{n-r} > {}^nC_{r-1} p^{r-1}q^{n-(r-1)}$,

so long as $(n-r+1)p > rq$,

or $(n+1)p > (p+q)r$.

But $p + q = 1$; hence the required value of r is the greatest integer in $p(n+1)$.

If n is such that pn is an integer, the most likely case is that of pn successes and qn failures.

464. Suppose that there are n tickets in a lottery for a prize of £x; then since each ticket is equally likely to win the prize, and a person who possessed all the tickets *must* win, the money value of each ticket is £$\dfrac{x}{n}$; in other words this would be a fair sum to pay for each ticket; hence a person who possessed r tickets might reasonably expect £$\dfrac{rx}{n}$ as the price to be paid for his tickets by any one who wished to buy them; that is, he would estimate £$\dfrac{r}{n}x$ as the worth of his chance. It is convenient then to introduce the following definition :

If p represents a person's chance of success in any venture and M the sum of money which he will receive in case of success, the sum of money denoted by pM is called his **expectation**.

465. In the same way that *expectation* is used in reference to a person, we may conveniently use the phrase *probable value* applied to things.

Example 1. *One purse contains 5 shillings and 1 sovereign : a second purse contains 6 shillings. Two coins are taken from the first and placed in the second : then 2 are taken from the second and placed in the first : find the probable value of the contents of each purse.*

The chance that the sovereign is in the first purse is equal to the sum of the chances that it has moved twice and that it has not moved at all;

that is, the chance $= \dfrac{1}{3} \cdot \dfrac{1}{4} + \dfrac{2}{3} \cdot 1 = \dfrac{3}{4}$.

∴ the chance that the rupee is in the second purse $= \dfrac{1}{4}$.

Hence the probable value of the first purse

$$\frac{3}{4} \text{ of Rs. } 1 \cdot 05 \text{ nP.} + \frac{1}{4} \text{ of 6 nP.'s} = 80\frac{1}{4} \text{ nP.'s.}$$

∴ the probable value of the second purse

$$111 \text{ nP.'s} - 80\frac{1}{4} \text{ nP.'s} = 30\frac{3}{4} \text{ nP.'s.}$$

Or the problem may be solved as follows :
The probable value of the coins removed

$$= \frac{1}{3} \text{ of 105 nP.'s} = 35 \text{ nP.'s.}$$

the probable value of the coins brought back

$$= \frac{1}{4} \text{ of } (6 \text{ nP.'s} + 35 \text{ nP.'s}) = 10\frac{1}{4} \text{ nP.'s}.$$

$\therefore$ the probable value of the first purse

$$= \left(105 - 35 + 10\frac{1}{4}\right) \text{nP.'s} = 80\frac{1}{4} \text{ nP.'s, as before.}$$

Example 2. *A and B throw with one die for a stake of Rs. 11 which is to be won by the player who first throws 6. If A has the first throw, what are their respective expectations ?*

In his first throw A's chance is $\frac{1}{6}$; in his second it is $\frac{5}{6} \times \frac{5}{6} \times \frac{1}{6}$, because each player must have failed once before A can have a second throw; in his third throw his chance is $\left(\frac{5}{6}\right)^4 \times \frac{1}{6}$ because each player must have failed twice; and so on.

Thus A's chance is the sum of the infinite series

$$\frac{1}{6}\left\{ 1 + \left(\frac{5}{6}\right)^2 + \left(\frac{5}{6}\right)^4 + \dots \right\}$$

Similarly B's chance is the sum of the infinite series

$$\frac{5}{6} \cdot \frac{1}{6}\left\{ 1 + \left(\frac{5}{6}\right)^2 + \left(\frac{5}{6}\right)^4 \right\};$$

$\therefore$ A's chance is to B's as 6 is to 5; their respective chances are therefore $\frac{6}{11}$ and $\frac{5}{11}$, and their expectations are Rs. 6 and Rs. 5 respectively.

466.   We shall now give two problems which lead to useful and interesting results.

Example 1. *Two players A and B want respectively m and n points of winning a set of games; their chances of winning a single game are p and q respectively, where the sum of p and q is unity; the stake is to belong to the player who first makes up his set : determine the probabilities in favour of each player.*

Suppose that A wins in exactly $m + r$ games; to do this he must win the last game and $m - 1$ out of the preceding $m + r - 1$ games. The chance of this is $^{m+r-1}C_{m-1}\, p^{m-1}q^r p$, or $^{m+r-1}C_{m-1}\, p^m q^r$.

Now the set will necessarily be decided in $m + n - 1$ games, and A may win his m games in *exactly* m games, or $m + 1$ games, ..., or $m + n - 1$ games; therefore we shall obtain the chance that A wins the set by giving to r the values $0, 1, 2, \dots, n - 1$ in the expression $^{m+r-1}C_{m-1}\, p^m q^r$. Thus A's chance is

$$p^m \left\{ 1 + mq + \frac{m(m+1)}{1.2}q^2 + \dots + \frac{(m+n-2)!}{(m-1)!\,(n-1)!}q^{n-1} \right\};$$

Similarly B's chance is

$$q^n \left\{ 1 + np + \frac{n(n+1)}{1.2}p^2 + \dots + \frac{(m+n-2)!}{(m-1)!\,(n-1)!}p^{m-1} \right\}$$

This question is known as the "Problem of Points," and has engaged the attention of many of the most eminent mathematicians since the time of Pascal. It was originally proposed to Pascal by the Chevalier de Mere in 1654, and was discussed by Pascal and Fermat, but they confined themselves to the case in which the players were supposed to be of equal skill : their results were also exhibited in a different form. The formulae we have given are assigned to Montmort, as they appear for the first time in a work of his published in 1714. The same result was afterwards obtained in different ways by Lagrange and Laplace, and by the latter the problem was treated very fully under various modifications.

Example 2. *There are n dice with f faces marked from 1 to f; if these are thrown at random, what is the chance that the sum of the numbers exhibited shall be equal to p?*

Since any one of the f faces may be exposed on any one of the n dice, the number of ways in which the dice may fall is f^n.

Also the number of ways in which the numbers thrown will have p for their sum is equal to the coefficient of x^p in the expansion of

$$(x^1 + x^2 + x^3 + \ldots + x^f)^n;$$

for this coefficient arises out of the different ways in which n of the indices $1, 2, 3, \ldots, f$ can be taken so as to form p by addition.

Now the above expression $= x^n (1 + x + x^2 + \ldots + x^{f-1})^n$

$$= x^n \left(\frac{1 - x^f}{1 - x} \right)^n.$$

We have therefore to find the coefficient of x^{p-n} in the expansion of

$$(1 - x^f)^n (1 - x)^{-n}.$$

Now $(1 - x^f)^n = 1 - nx^f + \dfrac{n(n-1)}{1.2} x^{2f} - \dfrac{n(n-1)(n-2)}{1.2.3} x^{3f} + \ldots;$

and $\quad (1 - x)^{-n} = 1 + nx + \dfrac{n(n+1)}{1.2} x^2 + \dfrac{n(n+1)(n+2)}{1.2.3} x^3 + \ldots$

Multiply these series together and pick out the coefficient of x^{p-n} in the product; we thus obtain

$$\frac{n(n+1)\ldots(p-1)}{(p-n)!} - n \cdot \frac{n(n+1)\ldots(p-f-1)}{(p-n-f)!}$$
$$+ \frac{n(n-1)}{1.2} \cdot \frac{n(n+1)\ldots(p-2f-1)}{(p-n-2f)!} - \ldots,$$

where the series is to continue so long as no negative factors appear. The required probability is obtained by dividing this series by f^n.

This problem is due to De Moivre and was published by him in 1730; it illustrates a method of frequent utility.

Laplace afterwards obtained the same formula, but in a much more laborious manner; he applied it in an attempt to demonstrate the existence of a primitive cause which has made the planets to move in orbits close to the ecliptic, and in the same direction as the earth round the sun. On this point the reader may consult Todhunter's *History of Probability*, Art. 987.

EXAMPLES XXXII. c.

1. In a certain game A's skill is to B's as 3 to 2 : find the chance of A winning 3 games at least out of 5.

2. A coin whose faces are marked 2, 3 is thrown 5 times : what is the chance of obtaining a total of 12 ?

3. In each of a set of games it is 2 to 1 in favour of the winner of the previous game : what is the chance that the player who wins the first game shall win three at least of the next four ?

4. There are 9 coins in a bag, 5 of which are ruppes and the rest are unknown coins of equal value; find what they must be if the probable value of a draw is 60 nP.

5. A coin is tossed n times, what is the chance that the head will present itself an odd number of times ?

6. From a bag containing 2 rupee pieces and 3 ten nP. pieces a person is allowed to draw 2 coins indiscriminately; find the value of his expectation.

7. Six persons throw for a stake, which is to be won by the one who first throws head with a penny; if they throw in succession, find the chance of the fourth person.

8. Counters marked 1, 2, 3 are placed in a bag, and one is withdrawn and replaced. The operation being repeated three times, what is the chance of obtaining a total of 6 ?

9. A coin whose faces are marked 3 and 5 is tossed 4 times : what are the odds against the sum of the numbers thrown being less than 15 ?

10. Find the chance of throwing 10 exactly in one throw with 3 dice.

11. Two players of equal skill, A and B, are playing a set of games; they leave off playing when A wants 3 points and B wants 2. If the stake is Rs. 16, what share ought each to take ?

12. A and B throw with 3 dice : if A throws 8, what is B's chance of throwing a higher number ?

13. A had in his pocket a rupee and four ten nP. coins; taking out two coins at random he promises to give them to B and C. What is the worth of C's expectation ?

14. In five throws with a single die what is the chance of throwing (1) three aces *exactly*, (2) three aces at least.

15. *A* makes a bet with *B* of Rs. 15 to Rs. 6 that in a single throw with two dice he will throw seven before *B* throws four. Each has a pair of dice and they throw simultaneously until one of them wins, equal throws being disregarded : find *B*'s expectation.

16. A person throws two dice, one the common cube, and the other a regular tetrahedron, the number on the lowest face being taken in the case of the tetrahedron; what is the chance that the sum of the numbers thrown is not less than 5 ?

17. A bag contains a coin of value M, and a number of other coins whose aggregate value is m. A person draws on at a time till he draws the coin M : find the value of his expectation.

18. If $6n$ tickets numbered 0, 1, 2, ... $6n - 1$ are placed in a bag, and three are drawn out, shew that the chance that the sum of the numbers on them is equal to $6n$ is

$$\frac{3n}{(6n - 1)(6n - 2)}.$$

*INVERSE PROBABILITY

*467. In all the cases we have hitherto considered it has been supposed that our knowledge of the causes which may produce a certain event is such as to enable us to determine the chance of the happening of the event. We have now to consider problems of a different character. For example, if it is known that an event has happened in consequence of some one of a certain number of causes, it may be required to estimate the probability of each cause being the true one, and thence to deduce the probability of future events occurring under the operation of the same causes.

*468. Before discussing the general case we shall give a numerical illustration.

Suppose there are two purses, one containing 5 sovereigns and 3 shillings, the other containing 3 sovereigns and 1 shilling, and suppose that a sovereign has been drawn : it is required to find the chance that it came from the first or second purse.

Consider a very large number N of trials; then, since before the event each of the purses is equally likely to be taken, we may assume that the first purse would be chosen in $\frac{1}{2} N$ of the trials, and in $\frac{5}{8}$ of these a sovereign would be drawn; thus a sovereign would be drawn $\frac{5}{8} \times \frac{1}{2} N$, or $\frac{5}{16} N$ times from the first purse.

The second purse would be chosen in $\frac{1}{2} N$ of the trials, and in $\frac{3}{4}$ of these a sovereign would be drawn; thus a sovereign would be drawn $\frac{3}{8} N$ times from the second purse.

Now N is very large but is otherwise an arbitrary number; let us put $N = 16n$; thus a sovereign would be drawn $5n$ times from the first purse, and $6n$ times from the second purse; that is, out of the $11n$ times in which a sovereign is drawn it comes from the first purse $5n$ times, and from the second purse $6n$ times. Hence the probability that the sovereign came from the first purse is $\frac{5}{11}$, and the probability that it came from the second is $\frac{6}{11}$.

*469. It is important that the student's attention should be directed to the nature of the assumption that has been made in the preceding article. Thus, to take a particular instance, although in 60 throws with a perfectly symmetrical die it may not happen that ace is thrown exactly 10 times, yet it will doubtless be at once admitted that if the number of throws is continually increased the ratio of the number of aces to the number of throws will tend more and more nearly to the limit $\frac{1}{6}$. There is no reason why one face should appear oftener than another; hence in the long run the number of times that each of the six faces will have appeared will be approximately equal.

The above instance is a particular case of a general theorem which is due to James Bernoulli, and was first given in the *Ars Conjectandi* published in 1713, eight years after the author's death. Bernoulli's theorem may be enunciated as follows :

If p is the probability that an event happens in a single trial, then if the number of trials is indefinitely increased, it becomes a certainty that the limit of the ratio of the number of successes to the number of trials is equal to p; in other words, if the number of trials is N, the number of successes may be taken to be pN.

See Todhunter's *History of Probability*, Chapter VII. A proof of Bernoulli's theorem is given in the article *Probability* in the *Encyclopaedia Britannica*.

*470. *An observed event has happened through some one of a number of mutually exclusive causes : required to find the probability of any assigned cause being the true one.*

Let there be n causes, and *before the event took place* suppose that the probability of the existence of these causes was estimated at $P_1, P_2, P_3, ..., P_n$. Let p_r denote the probability that when the rth cause exists the event will follow : *after the event has occurred* it is required to find the probability that the rth cause was the true one.

Consider a very great number N of trials; then the first cause exists in P_1N of these, and out of this number the event follows in p_1P_1N; similarly there are p_2P_2N trials in which the event follows from the second cause; and so on for each of the other causes. Hence the number of trials in which the event follows is

$$(p_1P_1 + p_2P_2 + ... + p_nP_n)\,N, \quad \text{or} \quad N\,\Sigma\,(pP);$$

and the number in which the event was due to the rth cause is p_rP_rN; hence *after* the event the probability that the rth cause was the true one is

$$p_rP_rN \div N\,\Sigma\,(pP);$$

that is, the probability that the event was produced by the rth cause is

$$\frac{p_rP_r}{\Sigma\,(pP)}.$$

*471. It is necessary to distinguish clearly between the probability of the existence of the several causes estimated *before* the event, and the probability *after the event has happened* of any assigned cause being the true one. The former are usually called a *priori* probabilities and are represented by $P_1, P_2, P_3, ..., P_n$; the latter are called a *posteriori* probabilities, and if we denote them by $Q_1, Q_2, Q_3, ..., Q_n$, we have proved that

$$Q_r = \frac{p_rP_r}{\Sigma\,(pP)}\,;$$

where p_r denotes the probability of the event on the hypothesis of the existence of the rth cause.

From this result it appears that $\Sigma\,(Q) = 1$, which is otherwise evident as the event has happened from one and only one of the causes.

We shall now give another proof of the theorem of the preceding article which does not depend on the principle enunciated in Art. 469.

*472. *An observed event has happened through some one of a number of mutually exclusive causes : required to find the probability of any assigned cause being the true one.*

Let there be n causes, and *before the event took place* suppose that the probability of the existence of these causes was estimated at $P_1, P_2, P_3, ..., P_n$. Let p_r denote the probability that when the rth cause exists the event will follow; then the *antecedent* probability that the event would follow from the rth cause is $p_r P_r$.

Let Q_r be the a *posteriori* probability that the rth cause was the true one; then the probability that the rth cause was the true one is proportional to the probability that, if in existence, this cause would produce the event;

$$\therefore \qquad \frac{Q_1}{p_1 P_1} = \frac{Q_2}{p_2 P_2} = \cdots = \frac{Q_n}{p_n P_n} = \frac{\Sigma(Q)}{\Sigma(pP)} = \frac{1}{\Sigma(pP)} \ ;$$

$$\therefore \qquad Q_r = \frac{p_r P_r}{\Sigma(pP)}.$$

Hence it appears that in the present class of problems the product $P_r p_r$, will have to be correctly estimated as a first step; in many cases, however, it will be found that $P_1, P_2, P_3, ...$ are all equal, and the work is thereby much simplified.

Example : *There are 3 bags each containing 5 white balls and 2 black balls, and 2 bags each containing 1 white ball and 4 black balls : a black ball having been drawn, find the chance that it came from the first group.*

Of the five bags, 3 belong to the first group and 2 to the second; hence

$$P_1 = \frac{3}{5}, P_2 = \frac{2}{5}.$$

If a bag is selected from the first group the chance of drawing a black ball is $\frac{2}{7}$ · if from the second group the chance is $\frac{4}{5}$; thus $p_1 = \frac{2}{7}, p_2 = \frac{4}{5}$;

$$\therefore \qquad p_1 P_1 = \frac{6}{35}, p_2 P_2 = \frac{8}{25}.$$

Hence the chance that the black ball came from one of the first group is

$$\frac{6}{35} \div \left(\frac{6}{35} + \frac{8}{25} \right) = \frac{15}{43}.$$

*473. When an event has been observed, we are able by the method of Art. 472 to estimate the probability of any particular cause being the true one; we may then estimate the probability of the event happening in a second trial, or we may find the probability of the occurrence of some other event.

For example, p_r is the chance that the event will happen from the rth cause if in existence, and the chance that the rth cause is the true one is Q_r; hence on a second trial the chance that the event will happen from the rth cause is $p_r Q_r$. Therefore the chance that the event will happen from some one of the causes on a second trial is $\Sigma (pQ)$.

Example : *A purse contains 4 coins which are either sovereigns or shillings; 2 coins are drawn and found to be shillings : if these are replaced what is the chance that another drawing will give a sovereign ?*

This question may be interpreted in two ways, which we shall discuss separately.

I. If we consider that all numbers of shillings are *a priori* equally likely, we shall have three hypotheses; for (i) all the coins may be shillings, (ii) three of them may be shillings, (iii) only two of them may be shillings.

Here $$P_1 = P_2 = P_3;$$

also $$p_1 = 1 , p_2 = \frac{1}{2} , p_3 = \frac{1}{6}.$$

Hence probability of first hypothesis $= 1 \div \left(1 + \frac{1}{2} + \frac{1}{6} \right) = \frac{6}{10} = Q_1,$

probability of second hypothesis $= \frac{1}{2} \div \left(1 + \frac{1}{2} + \frac{1}{6} \right) = \frac{3}{10} = Q_2,$

probability of third hypothesis $= \frac{1}{6} \div \left(1 + \frac{1}{2} + \frac{1}{6} \right) = \frac{1}{10} = Q_3.$

Therefore the probability that another drawing will give a sovereign

$$= (Q_1 \times 0) + \left(Q_2 \times \frac{1}{4} \right) + \left(Q_3 \times \frac{2}{4} \right)$$

$$= \frac{1}{4} \cdot \frac{3}{10} + \frac{2}{4} \cdot \frac{1}{10} = \frac{5}{40} = \frac{1}{8}.$$

II. If each coin is equally likely to be a shilling or a sovereign, by taking the terms in the expansion of $\left(\frac{1}{2} + \frac{1}{2} \right)^4$, we see that the chance of four shillings is $\frac{1}{16}$, of three shillings is $\frac{4}{16}$, of two shillings is $\frac{6}{16}$; thus

$$P_1 = \frac{1}{16}, P_2 = \frac{4}{16}, P_3 = \frac{6}{16} ;$$

also, as before, $p_1 = 1, p_2 = \frac{1}{2}, p_3 = \frac{1}{6}.$

Hence $$\frac{Q_1}{6} = \frac{Q_2}{12} = \frac{Q_3}{6} = \frac{Q_1 + Q_2 + Q_3}{24} = \frac{1}{24}.$$

Therefore the probability that another drawing will give a sovereign

$$= (Q_1 \times 0) + \left(Q_2 \times \frac{1}{4} \right) + \left(Q_3 \times \frac{2}{4} \right)$$

$$= \frac{1}{8} + \frac{2}{16} = \frac{1}{4}.$$

*474.   We shall now shew how the theory of probability may be applied to estimate the truth of statements attested by witnesses whose credibility is assumed to be known. We shall suppose that each witness states what he believes to be the truth, whether his statement is the result of observation, or deduction, or experiment; so that any mistake or falsehood must be attributed to errors of judgment and not to wilful deceit.

The class of problems we shall discuss furnishes a useful intellectual exercise, and although the results cannot be regarded as of any practical importance, it will be found that they confirm the verdict of common sense.

*475.   When it is asserted that the probability that a person speaks the truth is p, it is meant that a large number of statements made by him has been examined, and that p is the ratio of those which are true to the whole number.

*476.   Two independent witnesses, A and B, whose probabilities of speaking the truth are p and p' respectively, agree in making a certain statement : what is the probability that the statement is true ?

Here the observed event is the fact that A and B make the same statement. Before the event there are four hypotheses; for A and B may both speak truly; or A may speak truly, B falsely; or A may speak falsely, B truly; or A and B may both speak falsely. The probabilities of these four hypotheses are

$$pp',\ p\,(1-p'),\ p'\,(1-p),\ (1-p)\,(1-p') \text{ respectively.}$$

Hence after the observed event, in which A and B make the same statement, the probability that the statement is true is to the probability that it is false as pp' to $(1-p)\,(1-p')$; that is, the probability that the joint statement is true is

$$\frac{pp'}{pp' + (1-p)\,(1-p')}.$$

Similarly if a third person, whose probability of speaking the truth is p'', makes the same statement, the probability that the statement is true is

$$\frac{pp'p''}{pp'p'' + (1-p)\,(1-p')\,(1-p'')},$$

and so on for any number of persons.

*477.   In the preceding article it has been supposed that we have no knowledge of the event except the statement made by A and B; if we have information from other sources as to the probability of the truth or falsity of the statement, this must be taken into account in estimating the probability of the various hypotheses.

For instance, if A and B agree in stating a fact, of which the *a priori* probability is P, then we should estimate the probability of the truth and falsity of the statement by

$$Ppp' \quad \text{and} \quad (1-P)(1-p)(1-p') \text{ respectively.}$$

Example : *There is a raffle with 12 tickets and two prizes of Rs. 9 and Rs. 6. A, B, C whose probabilities of speaking the truth are* $\dfrac{1}{2}, \dfrac{2}{3}, \dfrac{3}{5}$ *respectively, report the result to D, who holds one ticket. A and B assert that he has won the Rs. 9 prize, and C asserts that he has won the Rs. 6 prize; what is D's expectation ?*

Three cases are possible; D may have won Rs. 9, Rs. 6, or nothing, for A, B, C may all have spoken falsely.

Now with the notation of Art. 472, we have the *a priori* probabilities

$$P_1 = \frac{1}{12}, \ P_2 = \frac{1}{12}, \ P_3 = \frac{10}{12};$$

also $\quad p_1 = \dfrac{1}{2} \times \dfrac{2}{3} \times \dfrac{2}{5} = \dfrac{4}{30}, \ p_2 = \dfrac{1}{2} \times \dfrac{1}{3} \times \dfrac{3}{5} = \dfrac{3}{30}, \ p_3 = \dfrac{1}{2} \times \dfrac{1}{3} \times \dfrac{2}{5} = \dfrac{2}{30};$

$$\therefore \qquad \frac{Q_1}{4} = \frac{Q_2}{3} = \frac{Q_3}{20} = \frac{1}{27};$$

hence D's expectation $= \dfrac{4}{27}$ of Rs. $9 + \dfrac{3}{27}$ of Rs. $6 =$ Rs. 2.

*478. With respect to the results proved in Art. 476, it should be noticed that it was assumed that the statement can be made in two ways only, so that if all the witnesses tell falsehoods they agree in telling the *same* falsehood.

If this is not the case, let us suppose that c is the chance that the two witnesses A and B will agree in telling the same falsehood; then the probability that the statement is true is to the probability that it is false as pp' to $c(1-p)(1-p')$.

As a general rule, it is extremely improbable that two independent witnesses will tell the same falsehood, so that c is usually very small; also it is obvious that the quantity c becomes smaller as the number of witnesses becomes greater. These considerations increase the probability that a statement asserted by two or more independent witnesses is true, even though the credibility of each witness is small.

Example : *A speaks truth 3 times out of 4, and B 7 times out of 10; they both assert that a white ball has been drawn from a bag containing 6 balls all of different colours : find the probability of the truth of the assertion.*

There are two hypotheses; (i) their coincident testimony is true, (ii) it is false.

Here $P_1 = \dfrac{1}{6}$, $P_2 = \dfrac{5}{6}$;

$$p_1 = \frac{3}{4} \times \frac{7}{10}, \; p_2 = \frac{1}{25} \times \frac{1}{4} \times \frac{3}{10};$$

for in estimating p_2 we must take into account the chance that A and B will both select the white ball when it has not been drawn; this chance is

$$\frac{1}{5} \times \frac{1}{5} \quad \text{or} \quad \frac{1}{25}.$$

Now the probabilities of the two hypotheses are as $P_1 p_1$ to $P_2 p_2$, and therefore as 35 to 1; thus the probability that the statement is true is $\dfrac{35}{36}$.

*479. The cases we have considered relate to the probability of the truth of *concurrent* testimony; the following is a case of *traditionary* testimony.

If A states that a certain event took place, having received an account of its occurrence or non-occurrence from B, what is the probability that the event did take place ?

The event happened (1) if they both spoke the truth, (2) if they both spoke falsely; and the event did not happen if only one of them spoke the truth.

Let p, p' denote the probabilities that A and B speak the truth; then the probability that the event did take place is

$$pp' + (1-p)(1-p'),$$

and the probability that it did not take place is

$$p(1-p') + p'(1-p).$$

*480. The solution of the preceding article is that which has usually been given in text-books; but it is open to serious objections, for the assertion that the given event happened if both A and B spoke falsely is not correct except on the supposition that the statement can be made only in two ways. Moreover, although it is expressly stated that A receives his account from B, this cannot generally be taken for granted as it rests on A's testimony.

A full discussion of the different ways of interpreting the question, and of the different solutions to which they lead, will be found in the *Educational Times Reprint*, Vols. XXVII. and XXXII.

*EXAMPLES XXXII. d.

1. There are four balls in a bag, but it is not known of what colours they are; one ball is drawn and found to be white : find the chance that all the balls are white.

2. In a bag there are six balls of unknown colours; three balls are drawn and found to be black; find the chance that no black ball is left in the bag.

3. A letter is known to have come either from London or Clifton; on the postmark only the two consecutive letters ON are legible; what is the chance that it came from London ?

4. Before a race the chances of three runners, A, B, C were estimated to be proportional to 5, 3, 2; but during the race A meets with an accident which reduces his chance to one-third. What are now the respective chances of B and C ?

5. A purse contains n coins of unknown value; a coin drawn at random is found to be a sovereign; what is the chance that it is the only sovereign in the bag ?

6. A man has 10 shillings and one of them is known to have two heads. He takes one at random and tosses it 5 times and it always falls head : what is the chance that it is the shilling with two heads ?

7. A bag contains 5 balls of unknown colour; a ball is drawn and replaced twice, and in each case is found to be red : if two balls are now drawn simultaneously find the chance that both are red.

8. A purse contains five coins, each of which may be a shilling or a sixpence; two are drawn and found to be shillings : find the probable value of the remaining coins.

9. A die is thrown three times and the sum of the three numbers thrown is 15 : find the chance that the first throw was a four.

10. A speaks the truth 3 out of 4 times, and B 5 out of 6 times : what is the probability that they will contradict each other in stating the same fact ?

11. A speaks the truth 2 out of 3 times, and B 4 times out of 5; they agree in the assertion that from a bag containing 6 balls of different colours a red ball has been drawn : find the probability that the statement is true.

12. One of a pack of 52 cards has been lost; from the remainder of the pack two cards are drawn and are found to be spades; find the chance that the missing card is a spade.

13. There is a raffle with 10 tickets and two prizes of value £5 and £1 respectively. A holds one ticket and is informed by B that he has won the £5 prize, while C asserts that he has won the

£ 1 prize : what is A's expectation, if the credibility of B is denoted by $\frac{2}{3}$, and that of C by $\frac{3}{4}$?

14. A purse contains four coins; two coins having been drawn are found to be sovereigns : find the chance (1) that all the coins are sovereigns, (2) that if the coins are replaced another drawing will give a sovereign.

15. P makes a bet with Q of £8 to £120 that three races will be won by the three horses A, B, C against which the betting is 3 to 2, 4 to 1, and 2 to 1 respectively. The first race having been won by A, and it being known that the second race was won either by B, or by a horse D against which the betting was 2 to 1, find the value of P's expectation.

16. From a bag containing n balls, all either white or black, all numbers of each being equally likely, a ball is drawn which turns out to be white; this is replaced, and another ball is drawn, which also turns out to be white. If this ball is replaced, prove that the chance of the next draw giving a black ball is $\frac{1}{2}(n-1)(2n+1)^{-1}$

17. If mn coins have been distributed into m purses, n into each, find (1) the chance that two specified coins will be found in the same purse : and (2) what the chance becomes when r purses have been examined and found not to contain either of the specified coins.

18. A, B are two inaccurate arithmeticians whose chance of solving a given question correctly are $\frac{1}{8}$ and $\frac{1}{12}$ respectively; if they obtain the same result, and if it is 1000 to 1 against their making the same mistake, find the chance that the result is correct.

19. Ten witnesses, each of whom makes but one false statement in six, agree in asserting that a certain event took place; shew that the odds are five to one in favour of the truth of their statement, even although the *a priori* probability of the event is as small as $\frac{1}{5^9+1}$.

LOCAL PROBABILITY : GEOMETRICAL METHODS

*481. The application of Geometry to questions of Probability requires, in general, the aid of the Integral Calculus; there are, however, many easy questions which can be solved by Elementary Geometry.

Example 1. *From each of two equal lines of length l a portion is cut off at random, and removed : what is the chance that the sum of the remainders is less than l ?*

Place the lines parallel to one another, and suppose that after cutting, the right-hand portions are removed. Then the question is equivalent to asking what is the chance that the sum of the right-hand portions is greater than the sum of the left-hand portions. It is clear that the first sum is equally likely to be greater or less than the second; thus the required probability is $\frac{1}{2}$.

Cor : Each of two lines is known to be of length not exceeding l : the chance that their sum is not greater than l is $\frac{1}{2}$.

Example 2. *If three lines are chosen at random, prove that they are just as likely as not to denote the sides of a possible triangle.*

Of three lines one *must* be equal to or greater than each of the other two; denote its length by l. Then all we know of the other two lines is that the length of each lies between 0 and l. But if each of two lines is known to be of random length between 0 and l, it is an even chance that their sum is greater than l. [Ex. 1, Cor.]

Thus the required result follows.

Example 3. *Three tangents are drawn at random to a given circle : shew that the odds are 3 to 1 against the circle being inscribed in the triangle formed by them.*

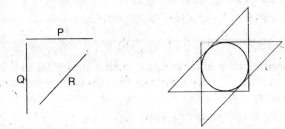

Draw three random lines P, Q, R in the same plane as the circle, and draw to the circle the six tangents parallel to these lines.

Then of the 8 triangles so formed it is evident that the circle will be escribed to 6 and inscribed in 2; and as this is true whatever be the original directions of P, Q, R the required result follows.

*482. Questions in Probability may sometimes be conveniently solved by the aid of Co-ordinate Geometry.

Example : On a rod of length $a + b + c$, lengths a, b are measured at random : find the probability that no point of the measured lines will coincide.

Let AB be the line, and suppose $AP = x$ and $PQ = a$; also let a be measured from P towards B, so that x must be less than $b + c$. Again let $AP' = y$, $P'Q' = b$, and suppose $P'Q'$ measured from P' towards B, then y must be less than $a + c$.

Now in favourable cases we must have $AP' > AQ$, or else $AP > AQ'$,

hence $y > a + x$, or $x > b + y$ ...(1)

Again for all the cases possible, we must have

$$x > 0, \quad \text{and} \quad < b + c \,\Big\}$$
$$y > 0, \quad \text{and} \quad < a + c \,\Big\} \qquad ...(2)$$

Take a pair of rectangular axes and make OX equal to $b + c$, and OY equal to $a + c$.

Draw the line $y = a + x$, represented by TML in the figure; and the line $x = b + y$ represented by KR.

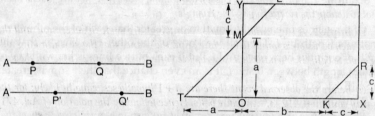

Then YM, KX are each equal to c, OM, OT are each equal to a.

The conditions (1) are only satisfied by points in the triangles MYL and KXR, while the conditions (2) are satisfied by any points within the rectangle OX, OY;

$$\therefore \qquad \text{the required chance} = \frac{c^2}{(a + c)(b + c)}.$$

*483. We shall close this chapter with some Miscellaneous Examples.

Example 1. *A box is divided into m equal compartments into which n balls are thrown at random; find the probability that there will be p compartments each containing a balls, q compartments each containing b balls, r compartments each containing c balls, and so on, where*

$$pa + qb + rc + \ldots = n.$$

Since each of the n balls can fall into any one of the m compartments the total number of cases which can occur is m^n, and these are all equally likely. To determine the number of favourable cases we must find the number of ways in which the n balls can be divided into $p, q, r, \ldots$ parcels containing $a, b, c, \ldots$ balls respectively.

First choose any s of the compartments, where s stands for $p + q + r + \ldots$; the number of ways in which this can be done is

$$\frac{m!}{s!\,(m-s)!} \qquad \qquad \ldots(1)$$

Next subdivide the s compartments into groups containing $p, q, r, \ldots$ severally; by Art. 147, the number of ways in which this can be done is

$$\frac{s!}{p!\,q!\,r!\ldots} \qquad \qquad \ldots(2)$$

Lastly, distribute the n balls into the compartments, putting a into each of the group of p, then b into each of the group of q, c into each of the group of r, and so on. The number of ways in which this can be done is

$$\frac{n!}{(a!)^p\,(b!)^q\,(c!)^r\ldots} \qquad \qquad \ldots(3)$$

Hence the number of ways in which the balls can be arranged to satisfy the required conditions is given by the product of the expressions (1), (2), (3). Therefore the required probability is

$$\frac{m!\,n!}{m^n\,(a!)^p\,(b!)^q\,(c!)^r\ldots p!\,q!\,r!\ldots(m-p-q-r-\ldots)!}$$

Example 2. *A bag contains n balls; k drawings are made in succession, and the ball on each occasion is found to be white : find the chance that the next drawing will give a white ball; (i) when the balls are replaced after each drawing; (ii) when they are not replaced.*

(i) *Before the observed event there are $n+1$ hypotheses, equally likely; for the bag may contain $0, 1, 2, 3, \ldots n$ white balls. Hence following the notation of Art. 471,*

$$P_0 = P_1 = P_2 = P_3 = \ldots = P_n;$$

and
$$p_0 = 0,\; p_1 = \left(\frac{1}{n}\right)^k,\; p_2 = \left(\frac{2}{n}\right)^k;\; p_3 = \left(\frac{3}{n}\right)^k,\; \ldots,\; p_n = \left(\frac{n}{n}\right)^k.$$

Hence after the observed event,

$$Q_r = \frac{r^k}{1^k + 2^k + 3^k + \ldots + n^k}.$$

Now the chance that the next drawing will give a white ball $= \Sigma \dfrac{r}{n} Q_r;$

thus the required chance $= \dfrac{1}{n} \cdot \dfrac{1^{k+1} + 2^{k+1} + 3^{k+1} + \ldots + n^{k+1}}{1^k + 2^k + 3^k + \ldots + n^k};$

and the value of numerator and denominator may be found by Art. 40[r]. In the particular case when $k = 2$.

the required chance $= \dfrac{1}{n} \left\{ \dfrac{n(n+1)}{2} \right\}^2 \div \dfrac{n(n+1)(2n+1)}{6}$

$$= \frac{3(n+1)}{2(2n+1)}.$$

If n is indefinitely large, the chance is equal to the limit, when n is

infinite, of $\dfrac{1}{n} \cdot \dfrac{n^{k+2}}{k+2} \div \dfrac{n^{k+1}}{k+1};$

and thus the chance is $\dfrac{k+1}{k+2}$.

(ii) If the balls are not replaced,

$$p_r = \frac{r}{n} \cdot \frac{r-1}{n-1} \cdot \frac{r-2}{n-2} \cdots \frac{r-k+1}{n-k+1},$$

and

$$Q_r = \frac{p_r}{\Sigma p_r} = \frac{(r-k+1)(r-k+2)\cdots(r-1)\,r}{\displaystyle\sum_{r=0}^{r=n}(r-k+1)(r-k+2)\cdots(r-1)\,r}$$

$$= (k+1)\frac{(r-k+1)(r-k+2)\cdots(r-1)\,r}{(n-k+1)(n-k+2)\cdots(n-1)\,n\,(n+1)}.$$

[Art. 394.]

The chance that the next drawing will give a white ball

$$= \sum_{r=0}^{r=n} \frac{r-k}{n-k} Q_r$$

$$= \frac{k+1}{(n-k)(n-k+1)\cdots n\,(n+1)}\sum_{r=0}^{r=n}(r-k)(r-k+1)\cdots(r-1)\,r$$

$$= \frac{k+1}{(n-k)(n-k+1)\cdots n\,(n+1)} \cdot \frac{(n-k)(n-k+1)\cdots n\,(n+1)}{k+2}$$

$$= \frac{k+1}{k+2},$$

which is independent of the number of balls in the bag at first.

Example 3. *A person writes* n *letters and addresses* n *envelopes; if the letters are placed in the envelopes at random, what is the probability that every letter goes wrong ?*

Let u_n denote the number of ways in which all the letters go wrong, and let *abcd* ... represent that arrangement in which all the letters are in their own envelopes. Now if a in any other arrangement occupies the place of an assigned letter b, this letter must either occupy a's place or some other.

(i) Suppose b occupies a's place. Then the number of ways in which all the remaining $n-2$ letters can be displaced is u_{n-2}, and therefore the numbers of ways in which a may be displaced by interchange with some one of the other $n-1$ letters, and the rest be all displaced is $(n-1)\,u_{n-2}$.

(ii) Suppose a occupies b's place, and b does not occupy a's place. Then in arrangements satisfying the required conditions, since a is fixed in b's place, the letters $b, c, d, \ldots$ must all be displaced, which can be done in u_{n-1} ways; therefore the number of ways in which a occupies the place of another letter but not by interchange with that letter is $(n-1)\,u_{n-1}$;

$\therefore \qquad u_n = (n-1)\,(u_{n-1} + u_{n-2});$

This expression can be rewritten as

$$u_n - n u_{n-1} = (-1)\{u_{n-1} - (n-1)\,u_{n-2}\}$$

$$= (-1)^2\{u_{n-2} - (n-2)\,u_{n-3}\}$$

$$= (-1)^3 \{u_{n-3} - (n-3) u_{n-4}\}$$

and so on until finally this becomes

$$= (-1)^{n-3} \{u_3 - 3u_2\}$$

$$= (-1)^{n-2} \{u_2 - 2u_1\}.$$

But u_2 is clearly 1 and u_1 is 0 by the nature of the problem. Hence

$$u_n = nu_{n-1} + (-1)^{n-2} . 1$$

Also $\qquad nu_{n-1} = n(n-1) u_{n-2} + (-1)^{n-3} . n$

and $\qquad n(n-1) u_{n-2} = n(n-1)(n-2) u_{n-3} + (-1)^{n-4} . n(n-1)$

and so on until finally

$$n(n-1) \dots 4u_3 = n(n-1) \dots 3u_2 + (-1)^3 . n(n-1) \dots 4$$

$$n(n-1) \dots 3u_2 = n(n-1) \dots 2u_1 + (-1)^2 . n(n-1) \dots 3.$$

Using the fact that $u_1 = 0$ and adding, these equations give

$$u_n = \{n(n-1) \dots 3\} - \{n(n-1) \dots 4\} + \{n(n-1) \dots 5\} \dots + (-1)^n . 1.$$

Also the total number of ways of permuting the n letters is $n!$. Thus the probability required is $u_n \div n!$ and this is

$$\frac{1}{2!} - \frac{1}{3!} + \frac{1}{4!} - \frac{1}{5!} + \dots + \frac{(-1)^n}{n!}$$

This problem has been the source of many modifications in the Theory of Probability. It has been discussed by Montmort, De Moivre, Euler and Laplace.

*484. Further reading on the subject of Probability can be found in Whitworth's *Choice and Chance*, Professor Crofton's article in the *Encyclopaedia Britannica* and Todhunter's History of the *Theory of Probability*.

EXAMPLES XXXII. e.

1. What are the odds in favour of throwing at least 7 in a single throw with two dice ?

2. In a purse there are 5 sovereigns and 4 shillings. If they are drawn out one by one, what is the chance that they come out sovereigns and shillings alternately, beginning with a sovereign ?

3. If on an average 9 ships out of 10 return safe to port, what is the chance that out of 5 ships expected at least 3 will arrive ?

4. In a lottery all the tickets are blanks but one; each person draws a ticket, and retains it : shew that each person has an equal chance of drawing the prize.

5.　One bag contains 5 white and 3 red balls, and a second bag contains 4 white and 5 red balls. From one of them, chosen at random, two balls are drawn : find the chance that they are of different colours.

6.　Five persons A, B, C, D, E throw a die in the order named until one of them throws an ace : find their relative chances of winning, supposing the throws to continue till an ace appears.

7.　Three squares of a chess board being chosen at random, what is the chance that two are of one colour and one of another ?

8.　A person throws two dice, one the common cube, and the other a regular tetrahedron, the number on the lowest face being taken in the case of the tetrahedron; find the average value of the throw, and compare the chances of throwing 5, 6, 7.

9.　A's skill is to B's as 1 : 3; to C's as 3 : 2; and to D's as 4 : 3 : find the chance that A in three trials, one with each person, will succeed twice at least.

10.　A certain stake is to be won by the first person who throws an ace with an octahedral die : if there are 4 persons what is the chance of the last ?

11.　Two players A, B of equal skill are playing a set of games; A wants 2 games to complete the set, and B wants 3 games : compare their chances of winning.

12.　A purse contains 3 sovereigns and two shillings : a person drawn one coin in each hand and looks at one of them, which proves to be a sovereign; shew that the other is equally likely to be a sovereign or a shilling.

13.　A and B play for a prize; A is to throw a die first, and is to win if he throws 6. If he fails B is to throw, and to win if he throws 6 or 5. If he fails, A is to throw again and to win with 6 or 5 or 4, and so on : find the chance of each player.

14.　Seven persons draw lots for the occupancy of the six seats in a first class railway compartment : find the chance (1) that two specified persons obtain opposite seats, (2) that they obtain adjacent seats on the same side.

15.　A number consists of 7 digits whose sum is 59; prove that the chance of its being divisible by 11 is $\dfrac{4}{21}$.

16. Find the chance of throwing 12 in a single throw with 3 dice.

17. A bag contains 7 tickets marked with the numbers 0, 1, 2, ..., 6 respectively. A ticket is drawn and replaced; find the chance that after 4 drawings the sum of the numbers drawn is 8.

18. There are 10 tickets, 5 of which are blanks, and the others are marked with the numbers 1, 2, 3, 4, 5 : what is the probability of drawing 10 in three trials, (1) when the tickets are replaced at every trial, (2) if the tickets are not replaced ?

19. If n integers taken at random are multiplied together, shew that the chance that the last digit of the product is 1, 3, 7, or 9 is $\dfrac{2^n}{5^n}$; the chance of its being 2, 4, 6 or 8 is $\dfrac{4^n - 2^n}{5^n}$; of its being 5 is $\dfrac{5^n - 4^n}{10^n}$; and of its being 0 is $\dfrac{10^n - 8^n - 5^n + 4^n}{10^n}$.

20. A purse contains two sovereigns, two shillings and a metal dummy of the same form and size; a person is allowed to draw out one at a time till he draws the dummy : find the value of his expectation.

21. A certain sum of money is to be given to the one of three persons A, B, C who first throws 10 with three dice; supposing them to throw in the order named until the event happens, prove that their chances are respectively

$$\left(\dfrac{8}{13}\right)^2, \dfrac{56}{13^2}, \text{ and } \left(\dfrac{7}{13}\right)^2.$$

22. Two persons, whose probabilities of speaking the truth are $\dfrac{2}{3}$ and $\dfrac{5}{6}$ respectively, assert that a specified ticket has been drawn out of a bag containing 15 tickets : what is the probability of the truth of the assertion ?

23. A bag contains $\dfrac{n(n+1)}{2}$ counters, of which one is marked 1, two are marked 4, three are marked 9, and so on; a person puts in his hand and draws out a counter at random, and is to receive as many shillings as the number marked upon it : find the value of his expectation.

24. If 10 things are distributed among 3 persons, the chance of a particular person having more than 5 of them is $\dfrac{1507}{19683}$.

25. If a rod is marked at random in n points and divided at those points, the chance that none of the parts shall be greater than $\dfrac{1}{n}$ th of the rod is $\dfrac{1}{n^n}$.

26. There are two purses, one containing three sovereigns and a shilling, and the other containing three shillings and a sovereign. A coin is taken from one (it is not known which) and dropped into the other; and then on drawing a coin from each purse, they are found to be two shillings. What are the odds against this happening again if two more are drawn, one from each purse?

27. If a triangle is formed by joining three points taken at random in the circumference of a circle, prove that the odds are 3 to 1 against its being acute-angled.

28. Three points are taken at random on the circumference of a circle : what is the chance that the sum of any two of the arcs so determined is greater than the third?

29. A line is divided at random into three parts, what is the chance that they form the sides of a possible triangle?

30. Of two purses one originally contained 25 sovereigns, and the other 10 sovereigns and 15 shillings. One purse is taken by chance and 4 coins drawn out, which prove to be all sovereigns : what is the chance that this purse contains only sovereigns, and what is the probable value of the next draw from it?

31. On a straight line of length a two points are taken at random; find the chance that the distance between them is greater than b.

32. A straight line of length a is divided into three parts by two points taken at random; find the chance that no part is greater than b.

33. If on a straight line of length $a+b$ two lengths a, b are measured at random, the chance that the common part of these lengths shall not exceed c is $\dfrac{c^2}{ab}$, where c is less than a or

b; also the chance that the smaller length b lies entirely within the larger a is $\dfrac{a-b}{a}$

34. If on a straight line of length $a+b+c$ two lengths a, b are measured at random, the chance of their not having a common part exceeding d is $\dfrac{(c+d)^2}{(c+a)(c+b)}$ where d is less then either a or b,

35. Four passengers, A, B, C, D entire strangers to each other, are travelling in a railway train which contains l first-class, m second-class, and n third-class compartments. A and B are gentlemen whose respective *a priori* chances of travelling first, second, or third class are represented in each instance by λ, μ, ν; C and D are ladies whose similar *a priori* chances are each represented by l, m, n. Prove that, for all values of λ, μ, ν (except in the particular case when $\lambda : \mu : \nu = l : m : n$), A and B are more likely to be found both in the company of the same lady than each with a different one.

■■■

Chapter 33

DETERMINANTS

485. The present chapter is devoted to a brief discussion of determinants and their more elementary properties. The slight introductory sketch here given will enable a student to avail himself of the advantages of determinant notation in Analytical Geometry, and in some other parts of Higher Mathematics; fuller information on this branch of Analysis may be obtained from Dr. Salmon's *Lessons Introductory to the Modern Higher Algebra*, and Muir's *Theory of Determinants*.

486. Consider the two homogeneous linear equations

$$a_1x + b_1y = 0,$$
$$a_2x + b_2y = 0;$$

multiplying the first equation by b_2, the second by b_1, subtracting and dividing by x, we obtain

$$a_1b_2 - a_2b_1 = 0.$$

This result is sometimes written

$$\begin{vmatrix} a_1 & b_1 \\ a_2 & b_2 \end{vmatrix} = 0,$$

and the expression on the left is called **a determinant.** It consists of two rows and two columns, and in its expanded form each term is the product of two quantities; it is therefore, said to be of the *second order*.

The letters a_1, b_1, a_2, b_2 are called the *constituents* of the determinant, and the terms a_1b_2, a_2b_1 are called the *elements*.

487. Since

$$\begin{vmatrix} a_1 & b_1 \\ a_2 & b_2 \end{vmatrix} = a_1b_2 - a_2b_1 = \begin{vmatrix} a_1 & a_2 \\ b_1 & b_2 \end{vmatrix},$$

it follows that *the value of the determinant is not altered by changing the rows into columns, and the columns into rows.*

488. Again, it is easily seen that

$$\begin{vmatrix} a_1 & b_1 \\ a_2 & b_2 \end{vmatrix} = -\begin{vmatrix} b_1 & a_1 \\ b_2 & a_2 \end{vmatrix} \text{ and } \begin{vmatrix} a_1 & b_1 \\ a_2 & b_2 \end{vmatrix} = -\begin{vmatrix} a_2 & b_2 \\ a_1 & b_1 \end{vmatrix};$$

that is, if we interchange two rows or two columns of the determinant, we obtain a determinant which differs from it only in sign.

489. Let us now consider the homogeneous linear equations

$$a_1x + b_1y + c_1z = 0,$$
$$a_2x + b_2y + c_2z = 0,$$
$$a_3x + b_3y + c_3z = 0.$$

By eliminating x, y, z we obtain as in Ex. 2, Art. 16,

$$a_1 (b_2c_3 - b_3c_2) + b_1 (c_2a_3 - c_3a_2) + c_1 (a_2b_3 - a_3b_2) = 0,$$

or

$$a_1 \begin{vmatrix} b_2 & c_2 \\ b_3 & c_3 \end{vmatrix} + b_1 \begin{vmatrix} c_2 & a_2 \\ c_3 & a_3 \end{vmatrix} + c_1 \begin{vmatrix} a_2 & b_2 \\ a_3 & b_3 \end{vmatrix} = 0.$$

This eliminant is usually written

$$\begin{vmatrix} a_1 & b_1 & c_1 \\ a_2 & b_2 & c_2 \\ a_3 & b_3 & c_3 \end{vmatrix} = 0,$$

and the expression on the left being a determinant which consists of three rows and three columns is called a determinant of the *third order*.

490. By a rearrangement of terms the expanded form of the above determinant may be written

$$a_1 (b_2c_3 - b_3c_2) + a_2 (b_3c_1 - b_1c_3) + a_3 (b_1c_2 - b_2c_1),$$

or

$$a_1 \begin{vmatrix} b_2 & b_3 \\ c_2 & c_3 \end{vmatrix} + a_2 \begin{vmatrix} b_3 & b_1 \\ c_3 & c_1 \end{vmatrix} + a_3 \begin{vmatrix} b_1 & b_2 \\ c_1 & c_2 \end{vmatrix} ;$$

hence

$$\begin{vmatrix} a_1 & b_1 & c_1 \\ a_2 & b_2 & c_2 \\ a_3 & b_3 & c_3 \end{vmatrix} = \begin{vmatrix} a_1 & a_2 & a_3 \\ b_1 & b_2 & b_3 \\ c_1 & c_2 & c_3 \end{vmatrix} ;$$

that is, *the value of the determinant is not altered by changing the rows into columns, and the columns into rows.*

491. From the preceding article,

$$\begin{vmatrix} a_1 & b_1 & c_1 \\ a_2 & b_2 & c_2 \\ a_3 & b_3 & c_3 \end{vmatrix} = a_1 \begin{vmatrix} b_2 & c_2 \\ b_3 & c_3 \end{vmatrix} + a_2 \begin{vmatrix} b_3 & c_3 \\ b_1 & c_1 \end{vmatrix} + a_3 \begin{vmatrix} b_1 & c_1 \\ b_2 & c_2 \end{vmatrix}$$

$$= a_1 \begin{vmatrix} b_2 & c_2 \\ b_3 & c_3 \end{vmatrix} - a_2 \begin{vmatrix} b_1 & c_1 \\ b_3 & c_3 \end{vmatrix} + a_3 \begin{vmatrix} b_1 & c_1 \\ b_2 & c_2 \end{vmatrix} \quad \text{...(1)}$$

Also from Art. 489,

$$\begin{vmatrix} a_1 & b_1 & c_1 \\ a_2 & b_2 & c_2 \\ a_3 & b_3 & c_3 \end{vmatrix} = a_1 \begin{vmatrix} b_2 & c_2 \\ b_3 & c_3 \end{vmatrix} - b_1 \begin{vmatrix} a_2 & c_2 \\ a_3 & c_3 \end{vmatrix} + c_1 \begin{vmatrix} a_2 & b_2 \\ a_3 & b_3 \end{vmatrix} \quad \dots(2)$$

We shall now explain a simple method of writing down the expansion of a determinant of the third order, and it should be noticed that it is immaterial whether we develop it from the first row or the first column.

From equation (1), we see that the coefficient of any one of the constituents a_1, a_2, a_3 is that determinant of the second order which is obtained by omitting the row and column in which it occurs. These determinants are called the Minors of the original determinants, and the left-hand side of equation (1) may be written

$$a_1 A_1 - a_2 A_2 + a_3 A_3,$$

where A_1, A_2, A_3 are the minors of a_1, a_2, a_3 respectively.

Again, from equation (2), the determinant is equal to

$$a_1 A_1 - b_1 B_1 + c_1 C_1,$$

where A_1, B_1, C_1 are the minors of a_1, b_1, c_1 respectively.

492. The determinant

$$\begin{vmatrix} a_1 & b_1 & c_1 \\ a_2 & b_2 & c_2 \\ a_3 & b_3 & c_3 \end{vmatrix}$$

$$= a_1 (b_2 c_3 - b_3 c_2) + b_1 (c_2 a_3 - c_3 a_2) + c_1 (a_2 b_3 - a_3 b_2)$$

$$= - b_1 (a_2 c_3 - a_3 c_2) - a_1 (c_2 b_3 - c_3 b_2) - c_1 (b_2 a_3 - b_3 a_2) ;$$

hence

$$\begin{vmatrix} a_1 & b_1 & c_1 \\ a_2 & b_2 & c_2 \\ a_3 & b_3 & c_3 \end{vmatrix} = - \begin{vmatrix} b_1 & a_1 & c_1 \\ b_2 & a_2 & c_2 \\ b_3 & a_3 & c_3 \end{vmatrix}$$

Thus it appears that *if two adjacent columns, or rows, of the determinant are interchanged, the sign of the determinant is changed, but its value remains unaltered.*

If for the sake of brevity we denote the determinant

$$\begin{vmatrix} a_1 & b_1 & c_1 \\ a_2 & b_2 & c_2 \\ a_3 & b_3 & c_3 \end{vmatrix}$$

by $(a_1 b_2 c_3)$, then the result we have just obtained may be written

$$(b_1 a_2 c_3) = - (a_1 b_2 c_3).$$

Similarly we may shew that

$$(c_1a_2b_3) = -(a_1c_2b_3) = +(a_1b_2c_3).$$

493. *If two rows or two columns of the determinant are identical : determinant vanishes.*

For let D be the value of the determinant, then by interchanging two rows or two columns we obtain a determinant whose value is $-D$; but the determinant is unaltered; hence $D = -D$, that is $D = 0$. Thus we have the following equations,

$$a_1A_1 - a_2A_2 + a_3A_3 = D,$$
$$b_1A_1 - b_2A_2 + b_3A_3 = 0,$$
$$c_1A_1 - c_2A_2 + c_3A_3 = 0.$$

494. *If each constituent in any row, or in any column, is multiplied by the same factor, then the determinant is multiplied by that factor.*

For

$$\begin{vmatrix} ma_1 & b_1 & c_1 \\ ma_2 & b_2 & c_2 \\ ma_3 & b_3 & c_3 \end{vmatrix} = ma_1 . A_1 - ma_2 . A_2 + ma_3 . A_3$$

$$= m(a_1A_1 - a_2A_2 + a_3A_3);$$

which proves the proposition.

Cor. If each constituent of one row, or column, is the same multiple of the corresponding constituent of another row, or column, the determinant vanishes.

495. *If each constituent in any row, or column, consists of two terms, then the determinant can be expressed as the sum of two other determinants.*

Thus we have

$$\begin{vmatrix} a_1 + \alpha_1 & b_1 & c_1 \\ a_2 + \alpha_2 & b_2 & c_2 \\ a_3 + \alpha_3 & b_3 & c_3 \end{vmatrix} = \begin{vmatrix} a_1 & b_1 & c_1 \\ a_2 & b_2 & c_2 \\ a_3 & b_3 & c_3 \end{vmatrix} + \begin{vmatrix} \alpha_1 & b_1 & c_1 \\ \alpha_2 & b_2 & c_2 \\ \alpha_3 & b_3 & c_3 \end{vmatrix};$$

for the expression on the left

$$= (\alpha_1 + a_1) A_1 - (a_2 + \alpha_2) A_2 + (a_3 + \alpha_3) A_3$$
$$= (a_1A_1 - a_2A_2 + a_3A_3) + (\alpha_1A_1 - \alpha_2A_2 + \alpha_3A_3);$$

which proves the proposition.

In like manner if each constituent in any one row, or column, consists of m terms, the determinant can be expressed as the sum of m other determinants.

Similarly, we may shew that

$$\begin{vmatrix} a_1 + \alpha_1 & b_1 + \beta_1 & c_1 \\ a_2 + \alpha_2 & b_2 + \beta_2 & c_2 \\ a_3 + \alpha_3 & b_3 + \beta_3 & c_3 \end{vmatrix}$$

$$= \begin{vmatrix} a_1 & b_1 & c_1 \\ a_2 & b_2 & c_2 \\ a_3 & b_3 & c_3 \end{vmatrix} + \begin{vmatrix} a_1 & \beta_1 & c_1 \\ a_2 & \beta_2 & c_2 \\ a_3 & \beta_3 & c_3 \end{vmatrix} + \begin{vmatrix} \alpha_1 & b_1 & c_1 \\ \alpha_2 & b_2 & c_2 \\ \alpha_3 & b_3 & c_3 \end{vmatrix} + \begin{vmatrix} \alpha_1 & \beta_1 & c_1 \\ \alpha_2 & \beta_2 & c_2 \\ \alpha_3 & \beta_3 & c_3 \end{vmatrix}$$

These results may easily be generalised; thus if the constituents of the three columns consist of m, n, p terms respectively, the determinants can be expressed as the sum of mnp determinants.

Example 1. *Shew that* $\begin{vmatrix} b+c & a-b & a \\ c+a & b-c & b \\ a+b & c-a & c \end{vmatrix} = 3abc - a^3 - b^3 - c^3.$

The given determinant

$$= \begin{vmatrix} b & a & a \\ c & b & b \\ a & c & c \end{vmatrix} - \begin{vmatrix} b & b & a \\ c & c & b \\ a & a & c \end{vmatrix} + \begin{vmatrix} c & a & a \\ a & b & b \\ b & c & c \end{vmatrix} - \begin{vmatrix} c & b & a \\ a & c & b \\ b & a & c \end{vmatrix}$$

of these four determinants the first three vanish, Art. 493; thus the expression reduces to the last of the four determinants; hence its value

$$= -\{c(c^2 - ab) - b(ac - b^2) + a(a^2 - bc)\}$$

$$= 3abc - a^3 - b^3 - c^3.$$

Example 2. *Find the value of* $\begin{vmatrix} 67 & 19 & 21 \\ 39 & 13 & 14 \\ 81 & 24 & 26 \end{vmatrix}.$

We have

$$\begin{vmatrix} 67 & 19 & 21 \\ 39 & 13 & 14 \\ 81 & 24 & 26 \end{vmatrix} = \begin{vmatrix} 10+57 & 19 & 21 \\ 0+39 & 13 & 14 \\ 9+72 & 24 & 26 \end{vmatrix} = \begin{vmatrix} 10 & 19 & 21 \\ 0 & 13 & 14 \\ 9 & 24 & 26 \end{vmatrix} + \begin{vmatrix} 57 & 19 & 21 \\ 39 & 13 & 14 \\ 72 & 24 & 26 \end{vmatrix}$$

$$= \begin{vmatrix} 10 & 19 & 21 \\ 0 & 13 & 14 \\ 9 & 24 & 26 \end{vmatrix} = \begin{vmatrix} 10 & 19 & 19+2 \\ 0 & 13 & 13+1 \\ 9 & 24 & 24+2 \end{vmatrix} = \begin{vmatrix} 10 & 19 & 2 \\ 0 & 13 & 1 \\ 9 & 24 & 2 \end{vmatrix}$$

$$= 10 \begin{vmatrix} 13 & 1 \\ 24 & 2 \end{vmatrix} + 9 \begin{vmatrix} 19 & 2 \\ 13 & 1 \end{vmatrix} = 20 - 63 = -43.$$

496. Consider the determinant

$$\begin{vmatrix} a_1 + pb_1 + qc_1 & b_1 & c_1 \\ a_2 + pb_2 + qc_2 & b_2 & c_2 \\ a_3 + pb_3 + qc_3 & b_3 & c_3 \end{vmatrix};$$

as in the last article we can shew that it is equal to

$$\begin{vmatrix} a_1 & b_1 & c_1 \\ a_2 & b_2 & c_2 \\ a_3 & b_3 & c_3 \end{vmatrix} + \begin{vmatrix} pb_1 & b_1 & c_1 \\ pb_2 & b_2 & c_2 \\ pb_3 & b_3 & c_3 \end{vmatrix} + \begin{vmatrix} qc_1 & b_1 & c_1 \\ qc_2 & b_2 & c_2 \\ qc_3 & b_3 & c_3 \end{vmatrix};$$

and the last two of these determinants vanish [Art. 494 Cor.] Thus we see that the given determinant is equal to a new one whose first column is obtained by subtracting from the constituents of the first column of the original determinant equimultiples of the corresponding constituents of the order columns, while the second and third columns remain unaltered.

Conversely,

$$\begin{vmatrix} a_1 & b_1 & c_1 \\ a_2 & b_2 & c_2 \\ a_3 & b_3 & c_3 \end{vmatrix} = \begin{vmatrix} a_1 + pb_1 + qc_1 & b_1 & c_1 \\ a_2 + pb_2 + qc_2 & b_2 & c_2 \\ a_3 + pb_3 + qc_3 & b_3 & c_3 \end{vmatrix};$$

and what has been here proved with reference to the first column is equally true for any of the columns or rows; hence it appears that in reducing a determinant we may replace any one of the rows or columns by a new row or column formed in the following way:

Take the constituents of the row or column to be replaced, and increase or diminish them by any equimultiples of the corresponding constituents of one or more of the other rows or columns.

After a little practice it will be found that determinants may often be quickly simplified by replacing two or more rows or columns simultaneously; for example, it is easy to see that

$$\begin{vmatrix} a_1 + pb_1 & b_1 - qc_1 & c_1 \\ a_2 + pb_2 & b_2 - qc_2 & c_2 \\ a_3 + pb_3 & b_3 - qc_3 & c_3 \end{vmatrix} = \begin{vmatrix} a_1 & b_1 & c_1 \\ a_2 & b_2 & c_2 \\ a_3 & b_3 & c_3 \end{vmatrix};$$

but in any modification of the rule as above enunciated, care must be taken to leave one row or column unaltered.

Thus, if on the left-hand side of the last identity the constituents of the third column were replaced by $c_1 + ra_1, c_2 + ra_2, c_3 + ra_3$ respectively, we should have the former value increased by

$$\begin{vmatrix} a_1 + pb_1 & b_1 - qc_1 & ra_1 \\ a_2 + pb_2 & b_2 - qc_2 & ra_2 \\ a_3 + pb_3 & b_3 - qc_3 & ra_3 \end{vmatrix}$$

and of the four determinants into which this may be resolved there is one which does not vanish, namely

$$\begin{vmatrix} pb_1 & -qc_1 & ra_1 \\ pb_2 & -qc_2 & ra_2 \\ pb_3 & -qc_3 & ra_3 \end{vmatrix}$$

Example 1. Find the value of $\begin{vmatrix} 29 & 26 & 22 \\ 25 & 31 & 27 \\ 63 & 54 & 46 \end{vmatrix}$

The given determinant

$$= \begin{vmatrix} 3 & 26 & -4 \\ -6 & 31 & -4 \\ 9 & 54 & -8 \end{vmatrix} = -3 \times 4 \times \begin{vmatrix} 1 & 26 & 1 \\ -2 & 31 & 1 \\ 3 & 54 & 2 \end{vmatrix} = -12 \times \begin{vmatrix} 1 & 26 & 1 \\ -3 & 5 & 0 \\ 1 & 2 & 0 \end{vmatrix} .$$

$$= -12 \begin{vmatrix} 1 & 1 & 26 \\ 0 & -3 & 5 \\ 0 & 1 & 2 \end{vmatrix} = -12 \begin{vmatrix} -3 & 5 \\ 1 & 2 \end{vmatrix} = 132.$$

[**Explanation :** In the first step of the reduction keep the second column unaltered; for the first new column diminish each constituent of the first column by the corresponding constituent of the second; for the third new column diminish each constituent of the third column by the corresponding constituent of the second. In the second step take out the factors 3 and −4. In the third step keep the first row unaltered; for the second new row diminish the constituents of the second by the corresponding ones of the first; for the third new row diminish the constituents of the third by twice the corresponding constituents of the first. The remaining steps will be easily seen.]

Example 2. Shew that $\begin{vmatrix} a-b-c & 2a & 2a \\ 2b & b-c-a & 2b \\ 2c & 2c & c-a-b \end{vmatrix} = (a+b+c)^3.$

The given determinant

$$= \begin{vmatrix} a+b+c & a+b+c & a+b+c \\ 2b & b-c-a & 2b \\ 2c & 2c & c-a-b \end{vmatrix}$$

$$= (a+b+c) \times \begin{vmatrix} 1 & 1 & 1 \\ 2b & b-c-a & 2b \\ 2c & 2c & c-a-b \end{vmatrix}$$

$$= (a+b+c) \times \begin{vmatrix} 1 & 0 & 0 \\ 2b & -b-c-a & 0 \\ 2c & 0 & -c-a-b \end{vmatrix}$$

$$= (a+b+c) \times \begin{vmatrix} -b-c-a & 0 \\ 0 & -c-a-b \end{vmatrix} = (a+b+c)^3.$$

[**Explanation :** In the first new determinant the first row is the sum of the constituents of the three rows of the original determinant, the second and third rows being unaltered. In the third of the new determinants of the first column remains unaltered, while the second and third columns are obtained by subtracting the constituents of first column from those of the second and third respectively. The remaining transformations are sufficiently obvious.]

497. Before shewing how to express the product of two determinants as a determinant, we shall investigate the value of

$$\begin{vmatrix} a_1\alpha_1 + b_1\beta_1 + c_1\gamma_1 & a_1\alpha_2 + b_1\beta_2 + c_1\gamma_2 & a_1\alpha_3 + b_1\beta_3 + c_1\gamma_3 \\ a_2\alpha_1 + b_2\beta_1 + c_2\gamma_1 & a_2\alpha_2 + b_2\beta_2 + c_2\gamma_2 & a_2\alpha_3 + b_2\beta_3 + c_2\gamma_3 \\ a_3\alpha_1 + b_3\beta_1 + c_3\gamma_1 & a_3\alpha_2 + b_3\beta_2 + c_3\gamma_2 & a_3\alpha_3 + b_3\beta_3 + c_3\gamma_3 \end{vmatrix}$$

From Art. 495, we know that the above determinant can be expressed as the sum of 27 determinants of which it will be sufficient to give the following specimens :

$$\begin{vmatrix} a_1\alpha_1 & a_1\alpha_2 & a_1\alpha_3 \\ a_2\alpha_1 & a_2\alpha_2 & a_2\alpha_3 \\ a_3\alpha_1 & a_3\alpha_2 & a_3\alpha_3 \end{vmatrix}, \quad \begin{vmatrix} a_1\alpha_1 & b_1\beta_2 & c_1\gamma_3 \\ a_2\alpha_1 & b_2\beta_2 & c_2\gamma_3 \\ a_3\alpha_1 & b_3\beta_2 & c_3\gamma_3 \end{vmatrix}, \quad \begin{vmatrix} a_1\alpha_1 & c_1\gamma_2 & b_1\beta_3 \\ a_2\alpha_1 & c_2\gamma_2 & b_2\beta_3 \\ a_3\alpha_1 & c_3\gamma_2 & b_3\beta_3 \end{vmatrix}$$

these are respectively equal to

$$\alpha_1\alpha_2\alpha_3 \begin{vmatrix} a_1 & a_1 & a_1 \\ a_2 & a_2 & a_2 \\ a_3 & a_3 & a_3 \end{vmatrix}, \quad \alpha_1\beta_2\gamma_3 \begin{vmatrix} a_1 & b_1 & c_1 \\ a_2 & b_2 & c_2 \\ a_3 & b_3 & c_3 \end{vmatrix},$$

$$\alpha_1\beta_3\gamma_2 \begin{vmatrix} a_1 & c_1 & b_1 \\ a_2 & c_2 & b_2 \\ a_3 & c_3 & b_3 \end{vmatrix} ;$$

the first of which vanishes; similarly it will be found that 21 out of the 27 determinants vanish. The six determinants that remain are equal to

$$(\alpha_1\beta_2\gamma_3 - \alpha_1\beta_3\gamma_2 + \alpha_2\beta_3\gamma_1 - \alpha_2\beta_1\gamma_3 + \alpha_3\beta_1\gamma_2 - \alpha_3\beta_2\gamma_1) \times$$

$$\begin{vmatrix} a_1 & b_1 & c_1 \\ a_2 & b_2 & c_2 \\ a_3 & b_3 & c_3 \end{vmatrix}$$

that is,

$$\begin{vmatrix} \alpha_1 & \beta_1 & \gamma_1 \\ \alpha_2 & \beta_2 & \gamma_2 \\ \alpha_3 & \beta_3 & \gamma_3 \end{vmatrix} \times \begin{vmatrix} a_1 & b_1 & c_1 \\ a_2 & b_2 & c_2 \\ a_3 & b_3 & c_3 \end{vmatrix} ;$$

hence the given determinant can be expressed as the product of two other determinants.

498. *The product of two determinants is a determinant.*

Consider the two linear equations

$$\left. \begin{array}{c} a_1X_1 + b_1X_2 = 0 \\ a_2X_1 + b_2X_2 = 0 \end{array} \right\} \qquad \ldots(1)$$

where
$$X_1 = \alpha_1 x_1 + \alpha_2 x_2 \atop X_2 = \beta_1 x_1 + \beta_2 x_2 \Bigg\} \qquad \ldots(2)$$

Substituting for X_1 and X_2 in (1), we have

$$(a_1 \alpha_1 + b_1 \beta_1)\, x_1 + (a_1 \alpha_2 + b_1 \beta_2)\, x_2 = 0 \atop (a_2 \alpha_1 + b_2 \beta_1)\, x_1 + (a_2 \alpha_2 + b_2 \beta_2)\, x_2 = 0 \Bigg\} \qquad \ldots(3)$$

In order that equations (3) may simultaneously hold for values of x_1 and x_2 other than zero, we must have

$$\begin{vmatrix} a_1 \alpha_1 + b_1 \beta_1 & a_1 \alpha_2 + b_1 \beta_2 \\ a_2 \alpha_1 + b_2 \beta_1 & a_2 \alpha_2 + b_2 \beta_2 \end{vmatrix} = 0 \qquad \ldots(4)$$

But equations (3) will hold if equations (1) hold, and this will be the case either if

$$\begin{vmatrix} a_1 & b_1 \\ a_2 & b_2 \end{vmatrix} = 0 \qquad \ldots(5)$$

or if $\quad X_1 = 0$ and $X_2 = 0$;

which last condition requires that

$$\begin{vmatrix} \alpha_1 & \beta_1 \\ \alpha_2 & \beta_2 \end{vmatrix} = 0 \qquad \ldots(6)$$

Hence if equations (5) and (6) hold, equation (4) must also hold; and therefore the determinant in (4) must contain as factors the determinants in (5) and (6); and a consideration of the dimensions of the determinants shews that the remaining factor of (4) must be numerical; hence

$$\begin{vmatrix} a_1 & b_1 \\ a_2 & b_2 \end{vmatrix} \times \begin{vmatrix} \alpha_1 & \beta_1 \\ \alpha_2 & \beta_2 \end{vmatrix} = \begin{vmatrix} a_1 \alpha_1 + b_1 \beta_1 & a_1 \alpha_2 + b_1 \beta_2 \\ a_2 \alpha_1 + b_2 \beta_1 & a_2 \alpha_2 + b_2 \beta_2 \end{vmatrix},$$

the numerical factor, by comparing the coefficients of $a_1 b_2 \alpha_1 \beta_2$ on the two sides of the equations, being seen to be unity.

Cor. $\begin{vmatrix} a_1 & b_1 \\ a_2 & b_2 \end{vmatrix}^2 = \begin{vmatrix} a_1^2 + b_1^2 & a_1 a_2 + b_1 b_2 \\ a_1 a_2 + b_1 b_2 & a_2^2 + b_2^2 \end{vmatrix}.$

The above method of proof is perfectly general, and holds whatever be the order of the determinants.

Since the value of a determinant is not altered when we write the rows as columns, and the columns as rows, the product of two determinants may be expressed as a determinant in several ways; but these will all give the same result on expansion.

Example : *Shew that*
$$\begin{vmatrix} A_1 & -B_1 & C_1 \\ -A_2 & B_2 & -C_2 \\ A_3 & -B_3 & C_3 \end{vmatrix} = \begin{vmatrix} a_1 & b_1 & c_1 \\ a_2 & b_2 & c_2 \\ a_3 & b_3 & c_3 \end{vmatrix}^2,$$

the capital letters denoting the minors of the corresponding small letters in the determinant on the right.

Let D, D' denote the determinants on the right and left-hand sides respectively; then

$$DD' = \begin{vmatrix} a_1A_1 - b_1B_1 + c_1C_1 & a_2A_1 - b_2B_1 + c_2C_1 & a_3A_1 - b_3B_1 + c_3C_1 \\ -a_1A_2 + b_1B_2 - c_1C_2 & -a_2A_2 + b_2B_2 - c_2C_2 & -a_3A_2 + b_3B_2 - c_3C_2 \\ a_2A_3 - b_1B_3 + c_1C_3 & a_2A_3 - b_2B_3 + c_2C_3 & a_3A_3 - b_3B_3 + c_3C_3 \end{vmatrix}$$

$$= \begin{vmatrix} D & 0 & 0 \\ 0 & D & 0 \\ 0 & 0 & D \end{vmatrix} ; \qquad \text{[Art. 493]}$$

thus $DD' = D^3$, and therefore, $D' = D^2$.

EXAMPLES XXXIII. a.

Calculate the values of the determinants :

1. $\begin{vmatrix} 1 & 1 & 1 \\ 35 & 37 & 34 \\ 23 & 26 & 25 \end{vmatrix}$
2. $\begin{vmatrix} 13 & 16 & 19 \\ 14 & 17 & 20 \\ 15 & 18 & 21 \end{vmatrix}$
3. $\begin{vmatrix} 13 & 3 & 23 \\ 30 & 7 & 53 \\ 39 & 9 & 70 \end{vmatrix}$

4. $\begin{vmatrix} a & h & g \\ h & b & f \\ g & f & c \end{vmatrix}$
5. $\begin{vmatrix} 1 & z & -y \\ -z & 1 & x \\ y & -x & 1 \end{vmatrix}$
6. $\begin{vmatrix} 1 & 1 & 1 \\ 1 & 1+x & 1 \\ 1 & 1 & 1+y \end{vmatrix}$

7. $\begin{vmatrix} a-b & b-c & c-a \\ b-c & c-a & a-b \\ c-a & a-b & b-c \end{vmatrix}$
8. $\begin{vmatrix} b+c & a & a \\ b & c+a & b \\ c & c & a+b \end{vmatrix}$

If ω is one of the imaginary cube roots of unity, find the value of

9. $\begin{vmatrix} 1 & \omega & \omega^2 \\ \omega & \omega^2 & 1 \\ \omega^2 & 1 & \omega \end{vmatrix}$
10. $\begin{vmatrix} 1 & \omega^3 & \omega^2 \\ \omega^3 & 1 & \omega \\ \omega^2 & \omega & 1 \end{vmatrix}$

11. Eliminate l, m, n from the equations
$$al + cm + bn = 0, \quad cl + bm + an = 0, \quad bl + am + cn = 0.$$
and express the result in the simplest form.

12. Without expanding the determinants, prove that
$$\begin{vmatrix} a & b & c \\ x & y & z \\ p & q & r \end{vmatrix} = \begin{vmatrix} y & b & q \\ x & a & p \\ z & c & r \end{vmatrix} = \begin{vmatrix} x & y & z \\ p & q & r \\ a & b & c \end{vmatrix}$$

13. Solve the equations :

(1) $\begin{vmatrix} a & a & x \\ m & m & m \\ b & x & b \end{vmatrix} = 0.$ (2) $\begin{vmatrix} 15 - 2x & 11 & 10 \\ 11 - 3x & 17 & 16 \\ 7 - x & 14 & 13 \end{vmatrix} = 0.$

Prove the following identities :

14. $\begin{vmatrix} b+c & c+a & a+b \\ q+r & r+p & p+q \\ y+z & z+x & x+y \end{vmatrix} = 2 \begin{vmatrix} a & b & c \\ p & q & r \\ x & y & z \end{vmatrix}$

15. $\begin{vmatrix} 1 & a & a^2 \\ 1 & b & b^2 \\ 1 & c & c^2 \end{vmatrix} = (b-c)(c-a)(a-b).$

16. $\begin{vmatrix} 1 & 1 & 1 \\ a & b & c \\ a^3 & b^3 & c^3 \end{vmatrix} = (b-c)(c-a)(a-b)(a+b+c).$

17. $\begin{vmatrix} x & y & z \\ x^2 & y^2 & z^2 \\ yz & zx & xy \end{vmatrix} = (y-z)(z-x)(x-y)(yz+zx+xy).$

18. $\begin{vmatrix} -2a & a+b & a+c \\ b+a & -2b & b+c \\ c+a & c+b & -2c \end{vmatrix} = 4(b+c)(c+a)(a+b).$

19. $\begin{vmatrix} (b+c)^2 & a^2 & a^2 \\ b^2 & (c+a)^2 & b^2 \\ c^2 & c^2 & (a+b)^2 \end{vmatrix} = 2abc(a+b+c)^3.$

20. Express as a determinant $\begin{vmatrix} 0 & c & b \\ c & 0 & a \\ b & a & 0 \end{vmatrix}^2$

21. Find the condition that the equation $lx + my + nz = 0$ may be satisfied by the three sets of values (a_1, b_1, c_1) (a_2, b_2, c_2) (a_3, b_3, c_3) and shew that it is the same as the condition that the three equations

$$a_1x + b_1y + c_1z = 0, a_2x + b_2y + c_2z = 0, a_3x + b_3y + c_3z = 0$$

may be simultaneously satisfied by l, m, n.

22. Find the value of

$$\begin{vmatrix} a^2+\lambda^2 & ab+c\lambda & ca-b\lambda \\ ab-c\lambda & b^2+\lambda^2 & bc+a\lambda \\ ca+b\lambda & bc-a\lambda & c^2+\lambda^2 \end{vmatrix} \times \begin{vmatrix} \lambda & c & -b \\ -c & \lambda & a \\ b & -a & \lambda \end{vmatrix}$$

23. Prove that $\begin{vmatrix} a+ib & c+id \\ -c+id & a-ib \end{vmatrix} \times \begin{vmatrix} \alpha-i\beta & \gamma-i\delta \\ -\gamma-i\delta & \alpha+i\beta \end{vmatrix}$

where $i = \sqrt{-1}$, can be written in the form

$$\begin{vmatrix} A-iB & C-iD \\ -C-iD & A+iB \end{vmatrix};$$

hence deduce the following theorem, due to Euler;

The product of two sums each of four squares can be expressed as the sum of four squares.

Prove the following identities :

24.
$$\begin{vmatrix} 1 & bc+ad & b^2c^2+a^2d^2 \\ 1 & ca+bd & c^2a^2+b^2d^2 \\ 1 & ab+cd & a^2b^2+c^2d^2 \end{vmatrix}$$

$$= -(b-c)(c-a)(a-b)(a-d)(b-d)(c-d).$$

25.
$$\begin{vmatrix} bc-a^2 & ca-b^2 & ab-c^2 \\ -bc+ca+ab & bc-ca+ab & bc+ca-ab \\ (a+b)(a+c) & (b+c)(b+a) & (c+a)(c+b) \end{vmatrix}$$

$$= 3(b-c)(c-a)(a-b)(a+b+c)(bc+ca+ab).$$

26.
$$\begin{vmatrix} (a-x)^2 & (a-y)^2 & (a-z)^2 \\ (b-x)^2 & (b-y)^2 & (b-z)^2 \\ (c-x)^2 & (c-y)^2 & (c-z)^2 \end{vmatrix}$$

$$= 2(b-c)(c-a)(a-b)(y-z)(z-x)(x-y).$$

27. Find in the form of a determinant the condition that the expression

$$u\alpha^2 + v\beta^2 + w\gamma^2 + 2u'\beta\gamma + 2v'\gamma\alpha + 2w'\alpha\beta$$

may be the product of two factors of the first degree in α, β, γ.

28. Solve the equation :

$$\begin{vmatrix} u+a^2x & w'+abx & v'+acx \\ w'+abx & v+b^2x & u'+bcx \\ v'+acx & u'+bcx & w+c^2x \end{vmatrix} = 0,$$

expressing the result by means of determinants.

499. The properties of determinants may be usefully employed solving simultaneous linear equations.

Let the equations be

$$a_1x + b_1y + c_1z + d_1 = 0,$$
$$a_2x + b_2y + c_2z + d_2 = 0,$$
$$a_3x + b_3y + c_3z + d_3 = 0;$$

multiply them by $A_1, -A_2, A_3$ respectively and add the results, A_1, A_2, A_3 being minors of a_1, a_2, a_3 in the determinant

$$D = \begin{vmatrix} a_1 & b_1 & c_1 \\ a_2 & b_2 & c_2 \\ a_3 & b_3 & c_3 \end{vmatrix}$$

The coefficients of y and z vanish in virtue of the relations proved in Art. 493, and we obtain

$$(a_1A_1 - a_2A_2 + a_3A_3)\, x + (d_1A_1 - d_2A_2 + d_3A_3) = 0.$$

Similarly we may shew that

$$(b_1B_1 - b_2B_2 + b_3B_3)\, y + (d_1B_1 - d_2B_2 + d_3B_3) = 0,$$

and $\quad (c_1C_1 - c_2C_2 + c_3C_3)\, z + (d_1C_1 - d_2C_2 + d_3C_3) = 0.$

Now $\quad a_1A_1 - a_2A_2 + a_3A_3 = -(b_1B_1 - b_2B_2 + b_3B_3)$
$$= c_1C_1 - c_2C_2 + c_3C_3 = D;$$

hence the solution may be written

$$\frac{x}{\begin{vmatrix} d_1 & b_1 & c_1 \\ d_2 & b_2 & c_2 \\ d_3 & b_3 & c_3 \end{vmatrix}} = \frac{-y}{\begin{vmatrix} d_1 & a_1 & c_1 \\ d_2 & a_2 & c_2 \\ d_3 & a_3 & c_3 \end{vmatrix}} = \frac{z}{\begin{vmatrix} d_1 & a_1 & b_1 \\ d_2 & a_2 & b_2 \\ d_3 & a_3 & b_3 \end{vmatrix}} = \frac{-1}{\begin{vmatrix} a_1 & b_1 & c_1 \\ a_2 & b_2 & c_2 \\ a_3 & b_3 & c_3 \end{vmatrix}}$$

or more symmetrically

$$\frac{x}{\begin{vmatrix} b_1 & c_1 & d_1 \\ b_2 & c_2 & d_2 \\ b_3 & c_3 & d_3 \end{vmatrix}} = \frac{-y}{\begin{vmatrix} a_1 & c_1 & d_1 \\ a_2 & c_2 & d_2 \\ a_3 & c_3 & d_3 \end{vmatrix}} = \frac{z}{\begin{vmatrix} a_1 & b_1 & d_1 \\ a_2 & b_2 & d_2 \\ a_3 & b_3 & d_3 \end{vmatrix}} = \frac{-1}{\begin{vmatrix} a_1 & b_1 & c_1 \\ a_2 & b_2 & c_2 \\ a_3 & b_3 & c_3 \end{vmatrix}}.$$

500. Suppose we have the system of four homogeneous linear equations :

$$a_1x + b_1y + c_1z + d_1u = 0,$$
$$a_2x + b_2y + c_2z + d_2u = 0,$$
$$a_3x + b_3y + c_3z + d_3u = 0,$$
$$a_4x + b_4y + c_4z + d_4u = 0.$$

From the last three of these, we have as in the preceding article

$$\frac{x}{\begin{vmatrix} b_2 & c_2 & d_2 \\ b_3 & c_3 & d_3 \\ b_4 & c_4 & d_4 \end{vmatrix}} = \frac{-y}{\begin{vmatrix} a_2 & c_2 & d_2 \\ a_3 & c_3 & d_3 \\ a_4 & c_4 & d_4 \end{vmatrix}} = \frac{z}{\begin{vmatrix} a_2 & b_2 & d_2 \\ a_3 & b_3 & d_3 \\ a_4 & b_4 & d_4 \end{vmatrix}} = \frac{-u}{\begin{vmatrix} a_2 & b_2 & c_2 \\ a_3 & b_3 & c_3 \\ a_4 & b_4 & c_4 \end{vmatrix}}$$

Substituting in the first equation, the eliminant is

$$a_1 \begin{vmatrix} b_2 & c_2 & d_2 \\ b_3 & c_3 & d_3 \\ b_4 & c_4 & d_4 \end{vmatrix} - b_1 \begin{vmatrix} a_2 & c_2 & d_2 \\ a_3 & c_3 & d_3 \\ a_4 & c_4 & d_4 \end{vmatrix} + c_1 \begin{vmatrix} a_2 & b_2 & d_2 \\ a_3 & b_3 & d_3 \\ a_4 & b_4 & d_4 \end{vmatrix}$$

$$- d_1 \begin{vmatrix} a_2 & b_2 & c_2 \\ a_3 & b_3 & c_3 \\ a_4 & b_4 & c_4 \end{vmatrix} = 0.$$

This may be more concisely written in the form

$$\begin{vmatrix} a_1 & b_1 & c_1 & d_1 \\ a_2 & b_2 & c_2 & d_2 \\ a_3 & b_3 & c_3 & d_3 \\ a_4 & b_4 & c_4 & d_4 \end{vmatrix} = 0;$$

the expression on the left being a determinant of the fourth order.

Also we see that the coefficient of a_1, b_1, c_1, d_1 taken with their proper signs are the minors obtained by omitting the row and column which respectively contain these constituents.

501. More generally, if we have n homogeneous linear equations

$$a_1x_1 + b_1x_2 + c_1x_3 + \ldots + k_1x_n = 0,$$
$$a_2x_1 + b_2x_2 + c_2x_3 + \ldots + k_2x_n = 0,$$
$$\ldots\ldots\ldots\ldots\ldots\ldots\ldots\ldots\ldots\ldots\ldots\ldots\ldots$$
$$a_nx_1 + b_nx_2 + c_nx_3 + \ldots + k_nx_n = 0,$$

involving n unknown quantities $x_1, x_2, x_3, \ldots, x_n$, these quantities can be eliminated and the result expressed in the form

$$\begin{vmatrix} a_1 & b_1 & c_1 & \ldots & k_1 \\ a_2 & b_2 & c_2 & \ldots & k_2 \\ \ldots & \ldots & \ldots & \ldots & \ldots \\ a_n & b_n & c_n & \ldots & k_n \end{vmatrix} = 0.$$

The left-hand member of this equation is a determinant which consists of n rows and n columns, and is called a determinant of the nth, order.

The discussion of this more general form of determinant is beyond the scope of the present work; it will be sufficient here to remark that the properties which have been established in the case of determinants of the second and third orders are quite general, and are capable of being extended to determinants of any order.

For example, the above determinant of the nth order is equal to

$$a_1 A_1 - b_1 B_1 + c_1 C_1 - d_1 D_1 + \ldots + (-1)^{n-1} k_1 K_1,$$

or $\qquad a_1 A_1 - a_2 A_2 + a_3 A_3 - a_4 A_4 + \ldots + (-1)^{n-1} a_n A_n$,

according as we develop it from the first row or the first column. Here the capital letters stand for the minors of the constituents denoted by the corresponding small letters, and are themselves determinants of the $(n-1)$th order. Each of these may be expressed as the sum of a number of determinants of the $(n-2)$th order, and so on; and thus the expanded form of the determinant may be obtained.

Although we may always develop a determinant by means of the process described above, it is not always the simplest method, especially when our object is not so much to find the value of the whole determinant, as to find the signs of its several elements.

502. The expanded form of the determinant

$$\begin{vmatrix} a_1 & b_1 & c_1 \\ a_2 & b_2 & c_2 \\ a_3 & b_3 & c_3 \end{vmatrix} = a_1 b_2 c_3 - a_1 b_3 c_2 + a_2 b_3 c_1 - a_2 b_1 c_3 + a_3 b_1 c_2 - a_3 b_2 c_1,$$

and it appears that each element is the product of three factors, one taken from each row, and one from each column; also the signs of half the terms are $+$ and of the other half $-$. The signs of the several elements may be obtained as follows. The first element $a_1 b_2 c_3$, in which the suffixes follow the arithmetical order, is positive; we shall call this the leading element; every other element may be obtained from it by suitably interchanging the suffixes. The sign $+$ or $-$ is to be prefixed to any element according as it can be deduced from the leading element by an even or odd number of permutations of two suffixes; for instance, the element $a_3 b_2 c_1$ is obtained by interchanging the suffixes 1 and 3, therefore, its sign is negative; the element $a_3 b_1 c_2$ is obtained by first interchanging the suffixes 1 and 3, and then the suffixes 1 and 2, hence its sign is positive.

503. The determinant whose leading element is $a_1 b_2 c_3 d_4 \ldots$ may thus be expressed by the notation

$$\Sigma \pm a_1 b_2 c_3 d_4 \ldots,$$

the $\Sigma\pm$ placed before the leading element indicating the aggregate of all the elements which can be obtained from it by suitable interchanges of suffixes and adjustment of signs.

Sometimes the determinant is still more simply expressed by enclosing the leading element within brackets; thus $(a_1b_2c_3d_4 \ldots)$ is used as an abbrevation of $\Sigma\pm a_1b_2c_3d_4 \ldots$

Example : *In the determinant $(a_1b_2c_3d_4e_5)$ what sign is to be prefixed to the element $a_4b_3c_1d_5e_2$?*

From the leading element by permuting the suffixes of a and d we get $a_4b_2c_3d_1e_5$; from this by permuting the suffixes of b and c we have $a_4b_3c_2d_1e_5$; by permuting the suffixes of c and d we have $a_4b_3c_1d_2e_5$; finally by permuting the suffixes of d and e we obtain the required element $a_4b_3c_1d_5e_2$; and since we have made four permutations the sign of the element is positive.

504.   If in Art. 501, each of the constituents $b_1, c_1, \ldots k_1$ is equal to zero the determinant reduces to a_1A_1; in other words it is equal to the product of a_1 and a determinant of the $(n-1)$th order, and we easily infer the following general theorem.

If each of the constituents of the first row or column of a determinant is zero except the first, and if this constituent is equal to m, the determinant is equal to m times that determinant of lower order which is obtained by omitting the first column and first row.

Also since by suitable interchange of rows and columns any constituent can be brought into the first place, it follows that if any row or column has all its constituents except one equal to zero, the determinant can immediately be expressed as a determinant of lower order.

This is sometimes useful in the reduction and simplification of determinants.

Example : *Find the value of*

$$\begin{vmatrix} 30 & 11 & 20 & 38 \\ 6 & 3 & 0 & 9 \\ 11 & -2 & 36 & 3 \\ 19 & 6 & 17 & 22 \end{vmatrix}$$

Diminish each constituent of the first column by twice the corresponding constituent in the second column, and each constituent of the fourth column by three times the corresponding constituent in the second column, and we obtain

$$\begin{vmatrix} 8 & 11 & 20 & 5 \\ 0 & 3 & 0 & 0 \\ 15 & -2 & 36 & 9 \\ 7 & 6 & 17 & 4 \end{vmatrix},$$

and since the second row has three zero constituents this determinant

$$= 3 \begin{vmatrix} 8 & 20 & 5 \\ 15 & 36 & 9 \\ 7 & 17 & 4 \end{vmatrix} = 3 \begin{vmatrix} 8 & 20 & 5 \\ 8 & 19 & 5 \\ 7 & 17 & 4 \end{vmatrix} = 3 \begin{vmatrix} 0 & 1 & 0 \\ 8 & 19 & 5 \\ 7 & 17 & 4 \end{vmatrix} = -3 \begin{vmatrix} 8 & 5 \\ 7 & 4 \end{vmatrix} = 9.$$

505. The following examples shew artifices which are occasionally useful.

Example 1. Prove that

$$\begin{vmatrix} a & b & c & d \\ b & a & d & c \\ c & d & a & b \\ d & c & b & a \end{vmatrix}$$

$$= (a + b + c + d)(a - b + c - d)(a - b - c + d)(a + b - c - d).$$

By adding together all the rows we see that $a + b + c + d$ is a factor of the determinant; by adding together the first and third rows and subtracting from the result the sum of the second and fourth rows we see that $a - b + c - d$ is also a factor; similarly it can be shewn that $a - b - c + d$ and $a + b - c - d$ are factors; the remaining factor is numerical, and, from a comparison of the terms involving a^4 on each side, is easily seen to be unity; hence we have the required result.

Example 2. Prove that

$$\begin{vmatrix} 1 & 1 & 1 & 1 \\ a & b & c & d \\ a^2 & b^2 & c^2 & d^2 \\ a^3 & b^3 & c^3 & d^3 \end{vmatrix} = (a - b)(a - c)(a - d)(b - c)(b - d)(c - d).$$

The given determinant vanishes when $b = a$, for then the first and second columns are identical; hence $a - b$ is a factor of the determinant [Art. 514]. Similarly each of the expressions $a - c$, $a - d$, $b - c$, $b - d$, $c - d$ is a factor of the determinant; the determinant being of six dimensions, the remaining factor must be numerical; and, from a comparison of the terms involving bc^2d^3 on each side, it is easily seen to be unity; hence we obtain the required result.

EXAMPLES XXXIII. b.

Calculate the values of the determinants :

1. $\begin{vmatrix} 1 & 1 & 1 & 1 \\ 1 & 2 & 3 & 4 \\ 1 & 3 & 6 & 10 \\ 1 & 4 & 10 & 20 \end{vmatrix}$

2. $\begin{vmatrix} 7 & 13 & 10 & 6 \\ 5 & 9 & 7 & 4 \\ 8 & 12 & 11 & 7 \\ 4 & 10 & 6 & 3 \end{vmatrix}$

3. $\begin{vmatrix} a & 1 & 1 & 1 \\ 1 & a & 1 & 1 \\ 1 & 1 & a & 1 \\ 1 & 1 & 1 & a \end{vmatrix}$

4. $\begin{vmatrix} 0 & 1 & 1 & 1 \\ 1 & b+c & a & a \\ 1 & b & c+a & b \\ 1 & c & c & a+b \end{vmatrix}$

5. $\begin{vmatrix} 3 & 2 & 1 & 4 \\ 15 & 29 & 2 & 14 \\ 16 & 19 & 3 & 17 \\ 33 & 39 & 8 & 38 \end{vmatrix}.$

6. $\begin{vmatrix} 1+a & 1 & 1 & 1 \\ 1 & 1+b & 1 & 1 \\ 1 & 1 & 1+c & 1 \\ 1 & 1 & 1 & 1+d \end{vmatrix}$

7. $\begin{vmatrix} 0 & x & y & z \\ x & 0 & z & y \\ y & z & 0 & x \\ z & y & x & 0 \end{vmatrix}.$

8. $\begin{vmatrix} 0 & x & y & z \\ -x & 0 & c & b \\ -y & -c & 0 & a \\ -z & -b & -a & 0 \end{vmatrix}.$

9. $\begin{vmatrix} a & b & c & d \\ a & a+b & a+b+c & a+b+c+d \\ a & 2a+b & 3a+2b+c & 4a+3b+2c+d \\ a & 3a+b & 6a+3b+c & 10a+6b+3c+d \end{vmatrix}.$

10. If ω is one of the imaginary cube roots of unity, shew that the square of

$$\begin{vmatrix} 1 & \omega & \omega^2 & \omega^3 \\ \omega & \omega^2 & \omega^3 & 1 \\ \omega^2 & \omega^3 & 1 & \omega \\ \omega^3 & 1 & \omega & \omega^2 \end{vmatrix} = \begin{vmatrix} 1 & 1 & -2 & 1 \\ 1 & 1 & 1 & -2 \\ -2 & 1 & 1 & 1 \\ 1 & -2 & 1 & 1 \end{vmatrix}.$$

hence shew that the value of the determinant on the left is $3\sqrt{-3}$.

11. If $(f^2 - bc) x + (ch - fg) y + (bg - hf) z = 0,$

$\quad (ch - fg) x + (g^2 - ca) y + (af - gh) z = 0,$

$\quad (bg - hf) x + (af - gh) y + (h^2 - ab) z = 0,$

shew that $abc + 2fgh - af^2 - bg^2 - ch^2 = 0.$

Solve the equations ;

12. $x + y + z = 1,$

$\quad ax + by + cz = k,$

$\quad a^2x + b^2y + c^2z = k^2.$

13. $ax + by + cz = k,$

$\quad a^2x + b^2y + c^2z = k^2,$

$\quad a^3x + b^3y + c^3z = k^3.$

14. $x + y + z + u = 1,$

$\quad ax + by + cz + du = k,$

$\quad a^2x + b^2y + c^2z + d^2u = k^2,$

$\quad a^3x + b^3y + c^3z + d^3u = k^3.$

15. Prove that

$$\begin{vmatrix} b+c-a-d & bc-ad & bc(a+d)-ad(b+c) \\ c+a-b-d & ca-bd & ca(b+d)-bd(c+a) \\ a+b-c-d & ab-cd & ab(c+d)-cd(a+b) \end{vmatrix}$$

$$= -2(b-c)(c-a)(a-b)(a-d)(b-d)(c-d).$$

16. Prove that

$$\begin{vmatrix} a^2 & a^2-(b-c)^2 & bc \\ b^2 & b^2-(c-a)^2 & ca \\ c^2 & c^2-(a-b)^2 & ab \end{vmatrix}$$

$$= (b-c)(c-a)(a-b)(a+b+c)(a^2+b^2+c^2).$$

17. Shew that

$$\begin{vmatrix} a & b & c & d & e & f \\ f & a & b & c & d & e \\ e & f & a & b & c & d \\ d & e & f & a & b & c \\ c & d & e & f & a & b \\ b & c & d & e & f & a \end{vmatrix} = \begin{vmatrix} A & B & C \\ C & A & B \\ B & C & A \end{vmatrix},$$

where $A = a^2 - d^2 + 2ce - 2bf,$

$B = e^2 - b^2 + 2ac - 2df,$

$C = c^2 - f^2 + 2ae - 2bd.$

18. If a determinant is of the nth order, and if the constituents of its first, second, third, ... nth rows are the first n figurate numbers of the first, second, third, ... nth orders, shew that its value is unity.

■ ■ ■

Chapter 34

MISCELLANEOUS THEOREMS AND EXAMPLES.

506. We shall begin this chapter with some remarks on the permanence of algebraical form, briefly reviewing the fundamental laws which have been established in the course of the work.

507. In the exposition of algebraical principles we proceed analytically: at the outset we do not lay down new names and new ideas, but we begin from our knowledge of abstract Arithmetic; we prove certain laws of operation which are capable of verification in every particular case, and the *general* theory of these operations constitutes the science of Algebra.

Hence it is usual to speak of *Arithmetical Algebra* and *Symbolical Algebra*, and to make a distinction between them. In the former we define our symbols in a sense arithmetically intelligible, and thence deduce fundamental laws of operation; in the latter we assume the laws of Arithmetical Algebra to be true in all cases, whatever the nature of the symbols may be, and so find out what meaning must be attached to the symbols in order that they may obey these laws. Thus gradually, as we transcend the limits of ordinary Arithmetic, new results spring up, new language has to be employed, and interpretations given to symbols which were not contemplated in the original definitions. At the same time, from the way in which the general laws of Algebra are established, we are assured of their permanence and universality, even when they are applied to quantities not arithmetically intelligible.

508. Confining our attention to positive integral values of the symbols, the following laws are easily established from a *priori* arithmetical definitions.

I. **The Law of Commutation**, which we enunciate as follows :

(i) *Additions and subtractions may be made in any order.*

Thus $\qquad a+b-c = a-c+b = b-c+a.$

(ii) *Multiplications and divisions may be made in any order.*

Thus $\qquad a \times b = b \times a;$

$a \times b \times c = b \times c \times a = a \times c \times b;$ and so on.

$$ab \div c = a \times b \div c = (a \div c) \times b = (b \div c) \times a.$$

II. **The Law of Distribution**, which we enunciate as follows :

Multiplications and divisions may be distributed over additions and subtractions.

Thus
$$(a - b + c)\, m = am - bm + cm,$$
$$(a - b)\,(c - d) = ac - ad - bc + bd.$$

[See *Elementary Algebra*, Arts. 33, 34.]

And since division is the reverse of multiplication, the distributive law for division requires no separate discussion.

III. **The Laws of Indices.**

(i)
$$a^m \times a^n = a^{m+n},$$
$$a^m \div a^n = a^{m-n}.$$

(ii)
$$(a^m)^n = a^{mn}$$

[See *Elementary Algebra*, Art. 233 to 235.]

These laws are *laid down* as fundamental to our subject, having been proved one the supposition that the symbols employed are positive and integral, and that are restricted in such a way that the operations above indicated are arithmetically intelligible. If these conditions do not hold, by the principles of Symbolical Algebra we assume the laws of Arithmetical Algebra to be true in every case and accept the interpretation to which this assumption leads us. By this course we are assured that the laws of Algebraical operation are self-consistent, and that they include in their generality the particular cases of ordinary Arithmetic.

509. From the law of commutation we deduce the rules for the removal and insertion of brackets [*Elementary Algebra*, Arts. 21, 22]; and by the aid of these rules we establish the law of distribution as in Art. 35. For example, it is proved that

$$(a - b)\,(c - d) = ac - ad - bc + bd,$$

with the restriction that a, b, c, d are positive integers, and a greater than b, and c greater than d. Now it is the province of Symbolical Algebra to interpret results like this when all restrictions are removed. Hence by putting $a = 0$, and $c = 0$, we obtain $(-b) \times (-d) = bd$, or *the product of two negative quantities is positive.* Again by putting $b = 0$ and $c = 0$, we obtain $a \times (-d) = -ad$, or *the product of two quantities of opposite signs is negative.*

We are thus led to the *Rule of Sign* as a direct consequence of the law of distribution, and henceforth the rule of signs is included in our fundamental laws of operation.

510. For the way in which the fundamental laws are applied to establish the properties of algebraical fractions, the reader is referred to Chapters 19, 21 and 22 of the *Elementary Algebra*; it will there be seen that symbols and operations to which we cannot give any a *priori* definition are always interpreted so as to make them conform to the laws of Arithmetical Algebra.

511. The laws of indices are fully discussed in Chapter 30 of the *Elementary Algebra*. When m and n are positive integers and $m > n$, we prove directly from the definition of an index that $a^m \times a^n = a^{m+n}$; $a^m \div a^n = a^{m-n}$; $(a^m)^n = a^{mn}$.

We then assume the first of these to be true when the indices are free from al restriction, and in this way we determine meanings for symbols to which our original definition does not apply.

The interpretations for $a^{p/q}, a^0, a^{-n}$ thus derived from the first law are found to be in strict conformity with the other two laws; and henceforth the laws of indices can be applied consistently and with perfect generality.

511. In Chapter 8 we defined the symbol i or $\sqrt{-1}$ as obeying the relation $i^2 = -1$. From this definition and by making i subject to the general laws of Algebra we are enabled to discuss the properties of expressions of the form $a + ib$, in which real and imaginary quantities are combined. Such forms are sometimes called *complex numbers*, and it will be seen by reference to Articles 92 to 105 that if we perform on a *complex number* the operations of addition, subtraction, multiplication, and division, the result is in general itself a complex number.

Also since every rational function involves no operations but those above mentioned, it follows that a rational function of a complex number is in general a complex number.

Expressions of the form a^{x+iy}, $\log(x+iy)$ cannot be fully treated without Trigonometry; but by the aid of De Moivre's theorem, it is easy to shew that such functions can be reduced to complex numbers of the form $A + iB$.

The expression e^{x+iy} is of course included in the more general form a^{x+iy}, but another mode of treating it is worthy of attention.

We have seen in Art. 220 that

$$e^x = \text{Lim}\left(1 + \frac{x}{n}\right)^n, \text{ when } n \text{ is infinite,}$$

x being any real quantity; the quantity e^{x+iy} may be similarly defined by means of the equation

$$e^{x+iy} = Lim \left(1 + \frac{x+iy}{n} \right)^n, \text{ when } n \text{ is infinite,}$$

x and y being any real quantities.

The development of the theory of complex numbers will be found more fully discussed in Chapter V. of Barnard and Child's *Higher Algebra*.

513. We shall now give some theorems and examples illustrating methods which will often be found useful in proving identities, and in the Theory of Equations.

514. *To find the remainder when any rational integral function of x is divided by $x - a$.*

Let $f(x)$ denote any rational integral function of x; divide $f(x)$ by $x - a$ until a remainder is obtained which does not involve x; let Q be the quotient, and R the remainder; then

$$f(x) = Q(x - a) + R.$$

Since R does not involve x it will remain unaltered whatever value we give to x; put $x = a$, then

$$f(a) = Q \times 0 + R;$$

now Q is finite for finite values of x, hence

Cor. If $f(x)$ is exactly divisible by $x - a$, then $R = 0$, that is $f(a) = 0$; hence *if a rational integral function of x vanishes when $x = a$, is divisible by $x - a$.*

515. The proposition contained in the preceding article is so useful that we give another proof of it which has the advantage of exhibiting the form of the quotient.

Suppose that the function is of n dimensions, and let it be denoted by

$$p_0 x^n + p_1 x^{n-1} + p_2 x^{n-2} + p_3 x^{n-3} + \ldots + p_n,$$

then the quotient will be of $n - 1$ dimensions; denote it by

$$q_0 x^{n-1} + q_1 x^{n-2} + q_2 x^{n-3} + \ldots + q_{n-1};$$

let R be the remainder not containing x; then

$$p_0 x^n + p_1 x^{n-1} + p_2 x^{n-2} + p_3 x^{n-3} + \ldots + p_n$$
$$= (x - a)(q_0 x^{n-1} + q_1 x^{n-2} + q_2 x^{n-3} + \ldots + q_{n-1}) + R.$$

Multiplying out and equating the coefficients of like powers of x, we have

$$q_0 = p_0;$$
$$q_1 - aq_0 = p_1, \text{ or } q_1 = aq_0 + p_1;$$
$$q_2 - aq_1 = p_2, \text{ or } q_2 = aq_1 + p_2;$$
$$q_3 - aq_2 = p_3, \text{ or } q_3 = aq_2 + p_3;$$
$$\dots\dots\dots\dots\dots\dots\dots\dots\dots\dots$$
$$R - aq_{n-1} = p_n, \text{ or } R = aq_{n-1} + p_n;$$

thus each successive coefficient in the quotient is formed by multiplying by a the coefficient last formed, and adding the next coefficient in the dividend. The process of finding the successive terms of the quotient and the remainder may be arranged thus :

p_0	p_1	p_2	p_3	p_{n-1}	p_n
	aq_0	aq_1	aq_2	aq_{n-2}	aq_{n-1}
q_0	q_1	q_2	q_3	q_{n-1}	R

Thus $R = aq_{n-1} + p_n = a(aq_{n-2} + p_{n-1}) + p_n = \dots$

$$= p_0 a^n + p_1 a^{n-1} + p_2 a^{n-2} + \dots + p_n.$$

If the divisor is $x + a$ the same method can be used, only in this case the multiplier is $-a$.

Example. *Find the quotient and remainder when*
$$3x^7 - x^6 + 31x^4 + 21x + 5 \text{ is divided by } x + 2.$$

Here the multiplier is -2, and we have

3	-1	0	-31	0	0	21	5
	-6	14	-28	-6	12	-24	6
3	-7	14	3	-6	12	-3	11

Thus the quotient is $3x^6 - 7x^5 + 14x^4 + 3x^3 - 6x^2 + 12x - 3$, and the remainder is 11.

516. In the preceding example the work has been abridged by writing down only the coefficients of the several terms, zero coefficients being used to represent terms corresponding to powers of x which are absent. This method of *Detached Coefficients* may frequently be used to save labour in elementary algebraical processes, particularly when the functions we are dealing with are rational and integral. The following is another illustration.

Example. *Divide* $3x^5 - 8x^4 - 5x^3 + 26x^2 - 33x + 26$ *by*
$$x^3 - 2x^2 - 4x + 8.$$

$$1 + 2 + 4 - 8)\ 3 - 8 - 5 + 26 - 33 + 26\ (3 - 2 + 3$$
$$\underline{\quad 3 + 6 + 12 - 24}$$
$$\underline{\quad -2 + 7 + 2 - 33}$$
$$\underline{\quad -2 - 4 - 8 + 16}$$
$$\underline{\quad 3 - 6 - 17 + 26}$$
$$\underline{\quad 3 + 6 + 12 - 24}$$
$$-5 + 2$$

Thus the quotient is $3x^2 - 2x + 3$ and the remainder is $-5x + 2$.

It should be noticed that in writing down the divisor, the sign of every term *except the first* has been changed; this enables us *to replace the process of subtraction by that of addition* at each successive stage of the work.

517. The work may be still further abridged by the following arrangement, which is known as Horner's *Method of Synthetic Division*.

1	3	− 8	− 5	+ 26	− 33	+ 26
2		6	+ 12	− 24		
4			− 4	− 8	+ 16	
− 8				6	+ 12	− 24
	3	− 2	+ 3	+ 0	− 5	+ 2

[**Explanation** : The column of figures to the left of the vertical line consists of the coefficients of the divisor, the sign of each after the first being changed; the second horizontal line is obtained by multiplying 2, 4, − 8 by 3, the first term of the quotient. We then add the terms in the second column to the right of the vertical line; this gives − 2, which is the coefficient of the second term of the quotient. With the coefficient thus obtained we form the next horizontal line, and add the terms in the third column; this gives 3, which is the coefficient of the third term of the quotient.

By adding up the other columns we get the coefficients of the terms in the remainder.]

Example. *Divide* $6a^5 + 5a^4b - 8a^3b^2 - 6a^2b^3 - 6ab^4$ *by*
$$2a^3 + 3a^2b - b^2 \text{ to four terms in the quotient.}$$

2	6	+ 5	− 8	− 6	− 6		
− 3		− 9	+ 0	+ 3			
0			6	+ 0	− 2		
1				3	+ 0	− 1	
					12	+ 0	− 4
	3	− 2	− 1	+ 0	− 4	+ 11	+ 0	− 4

Thus the quotient is $3a^2 - 2ab - b^2 - 4a^{-2}b^4$, and $11b^5 - 4a^{-2}b^7$ is the remainder.

Here we add the terms in the several columns as before, but each sum has to be divided by 2, the first coefficient in the divisor. When the requisite number of terms in the *quotient* has been so obtained, the remainder is found by merely adding up the rest of the columns, and setting down the results without division.

The student may easily verify this rule by working the division by detached coefficients.

518.   The principle of Art. 514 is often useful in proving algebraical identities; but before giving any illustrations of it we shall make some remarks upon *Symmetrical and Alternating Functions.*

A function is said to be *symmetrical* with respect to its variables when its value is unaltered by the interchange of any pair of them; thus $x + y + z$, $bc + ca + ab$, $x^3 + y^3 + z^3 - xyz$ any symmetrical functions of the first, second , and third degrees respectively.

It is worthy of notice that the only symmetrical function of the first degree in x, y, z is of the form $M(x + y + z)$, where M is independent of x, y, z.

519.   It easily follows from the definition that the sum, difference, product, and quotient of any two symmetrical expressions must also be symmetrical expressions. The recognition of this principle is of great use in checking the accuracy of algebraical work, and in some cases enables us to dispense with much of the labour of calculation.

For example, we know that the expansion of $(x + y + z)^2$ must be a homogeneous function of three dimensions, and therefore of the form
$$x^3 + y^3 + z^3 + A(x^2y + xy^2 + y^2z + yz^2 + z^2x + zx^2) + Bxyz,$$
where A and B are quantities independent of x, y, z.

Put $z = 0$, then $A = 3$, being the coefficient of x^2y in the expansion of $(x + y)^3$.

Put $x = y = z = 1$, and we get $27 = 3 + (3 \times 6) + B$; whence $B = 6$.

Thus $(x + y + z)^3$
$$= x^3 + y^3 + z^3 + 3x^2y + 3xy^2 + 3y^2z + 3yz^2 + 3z^2x + 3zx^2 + 6xyz.$$

520.   A function is said to be *alternating* with respect to its variables, when its sign but not its value is altered by the interchange of any pair of them. Thus $x - y$ and
$$a^2(b - c) + b^2(c - a) + c^2(a - b)$$
are alternating functions.

It is evident that there can be no linear alternating function involving more than two variables, and also that the product of a symmetrical function and an alternating function must be an alternating function.

521. Symmetrical and alternating functions may be concisely denoted by writing down one of the terms and prefixing the symbol Σ; thus Σa stands for the sum of all the terms of which a is the type, Σab stands for the sum of all the terms of which ab is the type; and so on. For instance, if the function involves four letters a, b, c, d,

$$\Sigma a = a + b + c + d;$$
$$\Sigma ab = ab + ac + ad + bc + bd + cd;$$

and so on.

Similarly if the function involves three letters $a, b, c,$

$$\Sigma a^2 (b - c) = a^2 (b - c) + b^2 (c - a) + c^2 (a - b);$$
$$\Sigma a^2 bc = a^2 bc + b^2 ca + c^2 ab;$$

and so on.

It should be noticed that when there are three letters involved $\Sigma a^2 b$ does not consist of three terms, but of six : thus

$$\Sigma a^2 b = a^2 b + a^2 c + b^2 c + b^2 a + c^2 a + c^2 b.$$

The symbol Σ may also be used to imply summation with regard to two or more sets of letters; thus

$$\Sigma yz (b - c) = yz (b - c) + zx (c - a) + xy (a - b).$$

522. The above notation enables us to express in an abridged form the products and powers of symmetrical expressions : thus

$$(a + b + c)^3 = \Sigma a^3 + 3\Sigma a^2 b + 6abc;$$
$$(a + b + c + d)^3 = \Sigma a^3 + 3\Sigma a^2 b + 6\Sigma abc;$$
$$(a + b + c)^4 = \Sigma a^4 + 4\Sigma a^3 b + 6\Sigma a^2 b^2 + 12\Sigma a^2 bc;$$
$$\Sigma a \times \Sigma a^2 = \Sigma a^3 + \Sigma a^2 b.$$

Example 1. *Prove that*

$$(a + b)^5 - a^5 - b^5 = 5ab (a + b) (a^2 + ab + b^2).$$

Denote the expression on the left by E; then E is a function of a which vanishes when $a = 0$; hence a is a factor of E; similarly b is a factor of E. Again E vanishes when $a = -b$, that is $a + b$ is factor of E; and therefore E contains $ab (a + b)$ as a factor. The remaining factor must be of two dimensions, and, since it is symmetrical with respect to a and b, it must be of the form $Aa^2 + Bab + Ab^2$; thus

$$(a + b)^5 - a^5 - b^5 = ab (a + b) (Aa^2 + Bab + Ab^2),$$

where A and B are independent of a and b.

Putting $a = 1$, $b = 1$, we have $15 = 2A + B$;

putting $a = 2$, $b = -1$, we have $15 = 5A - 2B$;

whence $A = 5$, $B = 5$; and thus the required result at once follows.

Example 2. *Find the factors of*

$$(b^3 + c^3)(b - c) + (c^3 + a^3)(c - a) + (a^3 + b^3)(a - b).$$

Denote the expression by E; then E is a function of a which vanishes when $a = b$ and therefore contains $a - b$ as a factor [Art. 514]. Similarly it contains the factors $b - c$ and $c - a$; thus E contains $(b - c)(c - a)(a - b)$ as a factor.

Also since E is of the fourth degree the remaining factor must be of the first degree; and since it is a symmetrical function of a, b, c, it must be of the form $M(a + b + c)$. [Art. 518.]

$$\therefore \qquad E = M(b - c)(c - a)(a - b)(a + b + c).$$

To obtain M we may give to a, b, c any values that we find most convenient; thus by putting $a = 0$, $b = 1$, $c = 2$, we find $M = 1$, and we have the required result.

Example 3. *Shew that*

$$(x + y + z)^5 - x^5 - y^5 - z^5 = 5(y + z)(z + x)(x + y)$$
$$\times (x^2 + y^2 + z^2 + yz + zx + xy).$$

Denote the expression on the left by E; then E vanishes when $y = -z$, and therefore $y + z$ is a factor of E; similarly $z + x$ and $x + y$ are factors; therefore E contains $(y + z)(z + x)(x + y)$ as a factor. Also since E is of the fifth degree the remaining factor is of the second degree, and, since it is symmetrical in x, y, z, it must be of the form

$$A(x^2 + y^2 + z^2) + B(yz + zx + xy).$$

Put $x = y = z = 1$; thus $10 = A + B$;

put $x = 2$, $y = 1$, $z = 0$; thus $35 = 5A + 2B$;

whence $A = B = 5$,

and we have the required result.

523. We collect here for reference a list of identities which are useful in the transformation of algebraical expressions; the student should verify these identities.

$$\Sigma bc(b - c) = -(b - c)(c - a)(a - b).$$

$$\Sigma a^2(b - c) = -(b - c)(c - a)(a - b).$$

$$\Sigma a(b^2 - c^2) = (b - c)(c - a)(a - b).$$

$$\Sigma a^3(b - c) = -(b - c)(c - a)(a - b)(a + b + c).$$

$$a^3 + b^3 + c^3 - 3abc = (a + b + c)(a^2 + b^2 + c^2 - bc - ca - ab).$$

This identity may be given in another form,

$$a^3 + b^3 + c^3 - 3abc = \frac{1}{2}(a+b+c)\{(b-c)^2 + (c-a)^2 + (a-b)^2\}.$$

$$(b-c)^3 + (c-a)^3 + (a-b)^3 = 3(b-c)(c-a)(a-b).$$

$$(a+b+c)^3 - a^3 - b^3 - c^3 = 3(b+c)(c+a)(a+b).$$

$$\Sigma bc(b+c) + 2abc = (b+c)(c+a)(a+b).$$

$$\Sigma a^2(b+c) + 2abc = (b+c)(c+a)(a+b).$$

$$(a+b+c)(bc+ca+ab) - abc = (b+c)(c+a)(a+b).$$

$$2b^2c^2 + 2c^2a^2 + 2a^2b^2 - a^4 - b^4 - c^4$$
$$= (a+b+c)(b+c-a)(c+a-b)(a+b-c).$$

EXAMPLES XXXIV. a.

1. Find the remainder when $3x^5 + 11x^4 + 90x^2 - 19x + 53$ is divided by $x + 5$.

2. Find the equation connecting a and b in order that
$$2x^4 - 7x^3 + ax + b$$
may be divisible by $x - 3$.

3. Find the quotient remainder when
$$x^5 - 5x^4 + 9x^3 - 6x^2 - 16x + 13 \text{ is divided by } x^2 - 3x + 2.$$

4. Find a in order that $x^3 - 7x + 5$ may be a factor of
$$x^5 - 2x^4 - 4x^3 + 19x^2 - 31x + 12 + a.$$

5. Expand $\dfrac{1}{x^4 - 5x^3 + 7x^2 + x - 8}$ in descending powers of x to four terms, and find the remainder.

Find the factors of :

6. $a(b-c)^3 + b(c-a)^3 + c(a-b)^3.$

7. $a^4(b^2 - c^2) + b^4(c^2 - a^2) + c^4(a^2 - b^2).$

8. $(a+b+c)^3 - (b+c-a)^3 - (c+a-b)^3 - (a+b-c)^3.$

9. $a(b-c)^2 + b(c-a)^2 + c(a-b)^2 + 8abc.$

10. $a(b^4 - c^4) + b(c^4 - a^4) + c(a^4 - b^4).$

11. $(bc + ca + ab)^3 - b^3c^3 - c^3a^3 - a^3b^3.$

12. $(a+b+c)^4 - (b+c)^4 - (c+a)^4 - (a+b)^4 + a^4 + b^4 + c^4.$

13. $(a+b+c)^5 - (b+c-a)^5 - (c+a-b)^5 - (a+b-c)^5.$

14. $(x-a)^3(b-c)^3 + (x-b)^3(c-a)^3 + (x-c)^3(a-b)^3.$

Prove the following identities :

15. $\Sigma (b + c - 2a)^3 = 3 (b + c - 2a) (c + a - 2b) (a + b - 2c).$

16. $\dfrac{a (b - c)^2}{(c - a) (a - b)} + \dfrac{b (c - a)^2}{(a - b) (b - c)} + \dfrac{c (a - b)^2}{(b - c) (c - a)} = a + b + c.$

17. $\dfrac{2a}{a + b} + \dfrac{2b}{b + c} + \dfrac{2c}{c + a} + \dfrac{(b - c) (c - a) (a - b)}{(b + c) (c + a) (a + b)} = 3.$

18. $\Sigma a^2 (b + c) - \Sigma a^3 - 2abc = (b + c - a) (c + a - b) (a + b - c).$

19. $\dfrac{a^3 (b + c)}{(a - b) (a - c)} + \dfrac{b^3 (c + a)}{(b - c) (b - a)} + \dfrac{c^3 (a + b)}{(c - a) (c - b)} = bc + ca + ab.$

20. $4\Sigma (b - c) (b + c - 2a)^2 = 9 \Sigma (b - c) (b + c - a)^2.$

21. $(y + z)^2 (z + x)^2 (x + y)^2 = \Sigma x^4 (y + z)^2 + 2 (\Sigma yz)^3 - 2x^2 y^2 z^2.$

22. $\Sigma (ab - c^2) (ac - b^2) = (\Sigma bc) (\Sigma bc - \Sigma a^2).$

23. $abc (\Sigma a)^3 = (\Sigma bc)^3 = abc \Sigma a^3 - \Sigma b^3 c^3 = (a^2 - bc) (b^2 - ca) (c^2 - ab).$

24. $\Sigma (b - c)^3 (b + c - 2a) = 0,$ hence deduce $\Sigma (\beta - \gamma) (\beta + \gamma - 2a)^3 = 0.$

25. $(b + c)^3 + (c + a)^3 + (a + b)^3 - 3 (b + c) (c + a) (a + b)$
$= 2 (a^3 + b^3 + c^3 - 3abc).$

26. If $x = b + c - a, \ y = c + a - b, \ z = a + b - c,$ shew that
$x^3 + y^3 + z^3 - 3xyz = 4 (a^3 + b^3 + c^3 - 3abc).$

27. Prove that the value of $a^3 + b^3 + c^3 - 3abc$ is unaltered if we substitute $s - a, \ s - b, \ s - c$ for $a, \ b, \ c$ respectively , where
$$3s = 2 (a + b + c).$$

Find the value of :

28. $\dfrac{a}{(a - b) (a - c) (x - a)} + \dfrac{b}{(b - c) (b - a) (x - b)}$
$\qquad\qquad + \dfrac{c}{(c - a) (c - b) (x - c)}.$

29. $\dfrac{a^2 - b^2 - c^2}{(a - b) (a - c)} + \dfrac{b^2 - c^2 - a^2}{(b - c) (b - a)} + \dfrac{c^2 - a^2 - b^2}{(c - a) (c - b)}.$

30. $\dfrac{(a + p) (a + q)}{(a - b) (a - c) (a + x)} + \dfrac{(b + p) (b + q)}{(b - c) (b - a) (b + x)}$
$\qquad\qquad + \dfrac{(c + p) (c + q)}{(c - a) (c - b) (c + x)}.$

31. $\Sigma \dfrac{bcd}{(a - b) (a - c) (a - d)}.$ **32.** $\Sigma \dfrac{a^4}{(a - b) (a - c) (a - d)}.$

33. If $x + y + z = s,$ and $xyz = p^2,$ shew that

$$\left(\frac{p}{ys}-\frac{y}{p}\right)\left(\frac{p}{zs}-\frac{z}{p}\right)+\left(\frac{p}{zs}-\frac{z}{p}\right)\left(\frac{p}{xs}-\frac{x}{p}\right)$$
$$+\left(\frac{p}{xs}-\frac{x}{p}\right)\left(\frac{p}{ys}-\frac{y}{p}\right)=\frac{4}{s}.$$

MISCELLANEOUS IDENTITIES.

524.　Many identities can be readily established by making use of the properties of the cube roots of unity; as usual these will be denoted by 1, ω, ω^2.

Example. *Shew that*

$$(x+y)^7 - x^7 - y^7 = 7xy(x+y)(x^2+xy+y^2)^2.$$

The expression, E, on the left vanishes when $x=0$, $y=0$, $x+y=0$; hence it must contain $xy(x+y)$ as a factor.

Putting $x=\omega y$, we have

$$E = \{(1+\omega)^7 - \omega^7 - 1\}y^7 = \{(-\omega^2)^7 - \omega^7 - 1\}y^7$$
$$= (-\omega^2 - \omega - 1)y^7 = 0;$$

hence E contains $x-\omega y$ as a factor; and similarly we may shew that it contains $x-\omega^2 y$ as a factor; that is, E is divisible by

$$(x-\omega y)(x-\omega^2 y), \text{ or } x^2+xy+y^2.$$

Further, E being of seven, and $xy(x+y)(x^2+xy+y^2)$ of five dimensions, the remaining must be of the form $A(x^2+y^2)+Bxy$; thus

$$(x+y)^7 - x^7 - y^7 = xy(x+y)(x^2+xy+y^2)(Ax^2+Bxy+Ay^2).$$

Putting $x=1$, $y=1$, we have　　$21 = 2A+B$;
putting $x=2$, $y=-1$, we have　$21 = 5A-2B$;
whence　　　$A=7$, $B=7$;

$$\therefore \qquad (x+y)^7 - x^7 - y^7 = 7xy(x+y)(x^2+xy+y^2)^2.$$

525.　We know from elementary Algebra that

$$a^3+b^3+c^3-3abc = (a+b+c)(a^2+b^2+c^2-bc-ca-ab);$$

also we have seen in Ex. 3, Art, 110, that

$$a^2+b^2+c^2-bc-ca-ab = (a+\omega b+\omega^2 c)(a+\omega^2 b+\omega c);$$

hence $a^3+b^3+c^3-3abc$ can be resolved into three linear factors; thus

$$a^3+b^3+c^3-3abc = (a+b+c)(a+\omega b+\omega^2 c)(a+\omega^2 b+\omega c).$$

Example. *Shew that the product of*

$$a^3+b^3+c^3-3abc \text{ and } x^3+y^3+z^3-3xyz$$

can be put into the form $A^3+B^3+C^3-3ABC$.

The product $= (a + b + c)(a + \omega b + \omega^2 c)(a + \omega^2 b + \omega c)$

$$\times (x + y + z)(x + \omega y + \omega^2 z)(x + \omega^2 y + \omega z).$$

By taking these six factors in the pairs $(a + b + c)(x + y + z)$;

$$(a + \omega b + \omega^2 c)(x + \omega^2 y + \omega z); \text{ and}$$

$$(a + \omega^2 b + \omega c)(x + \omega y + \omega^2 z),$$

we obtain the three partial products

$$A + B + C, \ A + \omega B + \omega^2 C, \ A + \omega^2 B + \omega C,$$

where $A = ax + by + cz, \ B = bx + cy + az, \ C = cx + ay + bz$.

Thus the product

$$= (A + B + C)(A + \omega B + \omega^2 C)(A + \omega^2 B + \omega C)$$

$$= A^3 + B^3 + C^3 - 3ABC.$$

526. In order to find the values of expressions involving a, b, c when these quantities are connected by the equation $a + b + c = 0$, we might employ the substitution

$$a = h + k, \ b = \omega h + \omega^2 k, \ c = \omega^2 h + \omega k$$

If however the expressions involve a, b, c symmetrically the method exhibited in the following example is preferable.

Example. If $a + b + c = 0$, shew that

$$6(a^5 + b^5 + c^5) = 5(a^3 + b^3 + c^3)(a^2 + b^2 + c^2).$$

We have identically

$$(1 + ax)(1 + bx)(1 + cx) = 1 + px + qx^2 + rx^2.$$

where $p = a + b + c, \ q = bc + ca + ab, \ r = abc$.

Hence, using the condition given,

$$(1 + ax)(1 + bx)(1 + cx) = 1 + qx^2 + rx^2.$$

Taking logarithms and equating the coefficients of x^n, we have

$\dfrac{(-1)^{n-1}}{n}(a^n + b^n + c^n) =$ coefficient of x^n in the expansion of

$\log(1 + qx^2 + rx^3) =$ coefficient of x^n in

$$(qx^2 + rx^3) - \frac{1}{2}(qx^2 + rx^3)^2 + \frac{1}{3}(qx^2 + rx^3)^3 - \dots$$

By putting $n = 2, 3, 5$ we obtain

$$-\frac{a^2 + b^2 + c^2}{2} = q, \quad \frac{a^3 + b^3 + c^3}{3} = r, \quad \frac{a^5 + b^5 + c^5}{5} = -qr;$$

whence $\qquad \dfrac{a^5 + b^5 + c^5}{5} = \dfrac{a^3 + b^3 + c^3}{5} \cdot \dfrac{a^2 + b^2 + c^2}{2},$

and the required result at once follows.

If $a = \beta - \gamma$, $b = \gamma - \alpha$, $c = \alpha - \beta$, the given condition is satisfied; hence we have identically for all values of α, β, γ

$$6\{(\beta - \gamma)^5 + (\gamma - \alpha)^5 + (\alpha - \beta)^5\}$$
$$= 5\{(\beta - \gamma)^3 + (\gamma - \alpha)^3 + (\alpha - \beta)^3\}\{(\beta - \gamma)^2 + (\gamma - \alpha)^2 + (\alpha - \beta)^2\}$$

that is,

$$(\beta - \gamma)^5 + (\gamma - \alpha)^5 + (\alpha - \beta)^5 = 5(\beta - \gamma)(\gamma - \alpha)(\alpha - \beta)$$
$$\times (\alpha^2 + \beta^2 + \gamma^2 - \beta\gamma - \gamma\alpha - \alpha\beta);$$

compare Ex. 3, Art. 522.

EXAMPLES XXXIV. b.

1. If $(a + b + c)^3 = a^3 + b^3 + c^3$, shew that when n is a positive integer $(a + b + c)^{2n + 1} = a^{2n + 1} + b^{2n + 1} + c^{2n + 1}$.

2. Shew that
$$(a + \omega b + \omega^2 c)^2 + (a + \omega^2 b + \omega c)^2$$
$$= (2a - b - c)(2b - c - a)(2c - a - b)$$

3. Shew that $(x + y)^n - x^n - y^n$ is divisible by $xy(x^2 + xy + y^2)$, if n is an odd positive integer not a multiple of 3.

4. Shew that
$$a^3(bz - cy)^3 + b^3(cx - az)^3 + c^3(ay - bx)^3$$
$$= 3abc(bz - cy)(cx - az)(ay - bx).$$

5. Find the value of
$$(b - c)(c - a)(a - b) + (b - \omega c)(c - \omega a)(a - \omega b)$$
$$+ (b - \omega^2 a)(c - \omega^2 a)(a - \omega^2 b)$$

6. Shew that
$$(a^2 + b^2 + c^2 - bc - ca - ab)(x^2 + y^2 + z^2 - yz - zx - xy)$$
may be put into the form $A^2 + B^2 + C^2 - BC - CA - AB$.

7. Shew that $(a^2 + ab + b^2)(x^2 + xy + y^2)$ can be put into the form $A^2 + AB + B^2$, and find the values of A and B.
Shew that

8. $\Sigma(a^2 + 2bc)^3 - 3(a^2 + 2bc)(b^2 + 2ca)(c^2 + 2ab)$
$= (a^3 + b^3 + c^3 - 3abc)^2$.

9. $\Sigma(a^2 - bc)^3 - 3(a^2 - bc)(b^2 - ca)(c^2 - ab) = (a^3 + b^3 + c^3 - 3abc)^2$.

10. $(a^2 + b^2 + c^2)^3 + 2(bc + ca + ab)^3 - 3(a^2 + b^2 + c^2)(bc + ca + ab)^2$
$= (a^3 + b^3 + c^3 - 3abc)^2$.

If $a + b + c = 0$, prove the identities in questions 11 - 17.

11. $2(a^4 + b^4 + c^4) = (a^2 + b^2 + c^2)^2$.

12. $a^5 + b^5 + c^5 = -5abc(bc + ca + ab)$.

13. $a^6 + b^6 + c^6 = 3a^2b^2c^2 - 2(bc + ca + ab)^3$.

14. $3(a^2 + b^2 + c^2)(a^5 + b^5 + c^5) = 5(a^3 + b^3 + c^3)(a^4 + b^4 + c^4)$.

15. $\dfrac{a^7 + b^7 + c^7}{7} = \dfrac{a^5 + b^5 + c^5}{5} \dfrac{a^2 + b^2 + c^2}{2}$

16. $\left(\dfrac{b-c}{a} + \dfrac{c-a}{b} + \dfrac{a-b}{c}\right)\left(\dfrac{a}{b-c} + \dfrac{b}{c-a} + \dfrac{c}{a-b}\right) = 9$.

17. $(b^2c + c^2a + a^2b - 3abc)(bc^2 + ca^2 + ab^2 - 3abc)$
$= (bc + ca + ab)^3 + 27a^2b^2c^2$.

18. $25\{(y-z)^7 + (z-x)^7 + (x-y)^7\}\{(y-z)^3 + (z-x)^3 + (x-y)^3\}$
$= 21\{(y-z)^5 + (z-x)^5 + (x-y)^5\}^2$.

19. $\{(y-z)^2 + (z-x)^2 + (x-y)^2\}^3 - 54(y-z)^2(z-x)^2(x-y)^2$
$= 2(y+z-2x)^2(z+x-2y)^2 \times (x+y-2z)^2$

20. $(b-c)^6 + (c-a)^6 + (a-b)^6 - 3(b-c)^2(c-a)^2(a-b)^2$
$= 2(a^2 + b^2 + c^2 - bc - ca - ab)^3$.

21. $(b-c)^7 + (c-a)^7 + (a-b)^7$
$= 7(b-c)(c-a)(a-b)(a^2 + b^2 + c^2 - bc - ca - ab)^2$.

22. If $a + b + c = 0$, and $x + y + z = 0$, shew that
$4(ax + by + cz)^3 - 3(ax + by + cz)(a^2 + b^2 + c^2)(x^2 + y^2 + z^2)$
$- 2(b-c)(c-a)(a-b)(y-z)(z-x)(x-y) = 54abcxyz$

If $a + b + c + d = 0$, shew that

23. $\dfrac{a^5 + b^5 + c^5 + d^5}{5} = \dfrac{a^3 + b^3 + c^3 + d^3}{3} \cdot \dfrac{a^2 + b^2 + c^2 + d^2}{2}$

24. $(a^3 + b^3 + c^3 + d^3)^2 = 9(bcd + cda + dab + abc)^2$
$= 9(bc - ad)(ca - bd)(ab - cd)$.

25. If $2s = a + b + c$ and $2\sigma^2 = a^2 + b^2 + c^2$, prove that
$\Sigma(s-b)(s-c)(\sigma^2 - a^2) + 5abcs = (s^2 - \sigma^2)(4s^2 + \sigma^2)$.

26. Shew that
$(x^3 + 6x^2y + 3xy^2 - y^3)^3 + (y^3 + 6xy^2 + 3x^2y - x^3)^3$

$$= 27xy\,(x+y)\,(x^2 + xy + y^2)^3.$$

27. Shew that $\Sigma \dfrac{a^5}{(a-b)\,(a-c)\,(a-d)}$

$$= a^2 + b^2 + c^2 + d^2 + ab + ac + ad + bc + bd + cd.$$

28. Resolve into factors

$$2a^2b^2c^2 + (a^3 + b^3 + c^3)\,abc + b^3c^3 + c^3a^3 + a^3b^3.$$

ELIMINATION

527. In Chapter 33 we have seen that the eliminant of a system of linear equations may at once be written down in the form of a determinant. General methods of elimination applicable to equations of any degree will be found discussed in treatises on the Theory of Equations; in particular we may refer the student to Chapters IV. and VI of Dr Salmon's *Lessons Introductory to the Modern Higher Algebra*.and to Chap. XIII of Burnside and Panton's *Theory of Equations.*

These methods, though theoretically complete, are not always the most convenient in practice. We shall therefore only give a brief explanation of the general theory, and shall then illustrate by examples some methods of elimination that are more practically useful.

528. Let us first consider the elimination of one unknown quantity between two equations.

Denot the equations by $f(x) = 0$ and $\phi(x) = 0$, and suppose that, it necessary, the equations have been reduced to a form in which $f(x)$ and $\phi(x)$ represent rational integral functions of x. Since these two functions vanish simultaneously there must be some value of x which satisfies both the given equations; hence the eliminant expresses the condition that must hold between the coefficients in order that the equations may have a common root.

Suppose that $x = \alpha$, $x = \beta$, $x = \gamma$, ... are the roots of $f(x) = 0$, then *one* at least of the quantities $\phi(\alpha), \phi(\beta), \phi(\gamma)$, ... must be equal to zero; hence the eliminant is

$$\phi(\alpha)\,\phi(\beta)\,\phi(\gamma) \ldots = 0.$$

The expression on the left is a symmetrical function of the roots of the equation $f(x) = 0$, and its value can be found by the methods explained in treatises on the *Theory of Equations.*

529. We shall now explain three general methods of elimination : it will be sufficient for our purpose to take a simple example, but it will be seen that in each case the process is applicable to equations of any degree.

The principle illustrated in the following example is due to Euler.

Example. *Eliminate x between the equations*

$$ax^2 + bx^2 + cx + d = 0, fx^2 + gx + h = 0.$$

Let $x + k$ be the factor corresponding to the root common to both equations, and suppose that

$$ax^3 + bx^2 + cx + d = (x + k)(ax^2 + lx + m),$$

and

$$fx^2 + gx + h = (x + k)(fx + n),$$

k, l, m, n being unknown quantities.

From these equations, we have identically

$$(ax^3 + bx^2 + cx + d)(fx + n) = (ax^2 + lx + m)(fx^2 + gx + h).$$

Equating coefficients of like powers of x, we obtain

$$fl + \quad - an + ag - bf = 0,$$
$$gl + fm - bn + ah - cf = 0,$$
$$hl + gm - cn \quad - df = 0,$$
$$hm - dn \quad = 0.$$

From these linear equations by eliminating the unknown quantities l, m, n we obtain the determinant

$$\begin{vmatrix} f & 0 & a & ag - bf \\ g & f & b & ah - cf \\ h & g & c & -df \\ 0 & h & d & 0 \end{vmatrix} = 0.$$

530. The eliminant of the equations $f(x) = 0$, $\phi(x) = 0$ can be very easily expressed as a determinant by Sylvester's *Dialytic Method of Elimination*. We shall take the same example as before.

Example. *Eliminate x between the equations*

$$ax^2 + bx^2 + cx + d = 0, fx^2 + gx + h = 0.$$

Multiply the first equation by x, and the second equation by x and x^2 in succession; we thus have 5 equations between which we can eliminate the 4 quantities x^4, x^3, x^2, x regarded as distinct variables. The equations are

$$ax^3 + bx^2 + cx + d = 0,$$
$$ax^4 + bx^3 + cx^2 + dx \quad = 0,$$
$$fx^2 + gx + h = 0,$$
$$fx^3 + gx^2 + hx \quad = 0,$$
$$fx^4 + gx^3 + hx^2 \quad = 0.$$

Hence the eliminant is
$$\begin{vmatrix} 0 & a & b & c & d \\ a & b & c & d & 0 \\ 0 & 0 & f & g & h \\ 0 & f & g & h & 0 \\ f & g & h & 0 & 0 \end{vmatrix} = 0.$$

531. The principle of the following method is due to Bezout; it has the advantage of expressing the result as a determinant of lower order than either of the determinants obtained by the preceding methods. We shall choose the same example as before, and give Cauchy's mode of conducting the elimination.

Example. *Eliminate x between the equations*
$$ax^3 + bx^2 + cx + d = 0, fx^2 + gx + h = 0.$$

from the equations, we have
$$\frac{a}{f} = \frac{bx^2 + cx + d}{gx^2 + hx},$$
$$\frac{ax + b}{fx + g} = \frac{cx + d}{hx};$$

whence $(ag - bf)\, x^2 + (ah - cf)\, x - df = 0,$

and $(ah - cf)\, x^2 + (bh - cg - df)\, x - dg = 0.$

Combining these two equations with
$$fx^2 + gx + h = 0,$$

and regarding x^2 and x as distinct variables, we obtain for the eliminant
$$\begin{vmatrix} f & g & h \\ ag - bf & ah - cf & -df \\ ah - cf & bh - cg - df & -dg \end{vmatrix} = 0.$$

532. If we have two equations of the form $\phi_1\,(x, y) = 0$, $\phi_2\,(x, y) = 0$, then y may be eliminated by any of the methods already explained; in this case the eliminant will be a function of x.

If we have three equations of the form
$$\phi_1\,(x, y, z) = 0, \;\; \phi_2\,(x, y, z) = 0, \;\; \phi_3\,(x, y, z) = 0,$$

by eliminating z between the first and second equations, and then between the first and third, we obtain two equations of the form
$$\psi_1\,(x, y) = 0, \;\; \psi_2\,(x, y) = 0.$$

If we eliminate y from these equations we have a result of the form $f\,(x) = 0$.

By reasoning in this manner it follows that we can eliminate n variables between $n + 1$ equations.

533. The general methods of elimination already explained may occasionally be employed with advantage, but the eliminants so obtained are rarely in a simple form, and it will often happen that the equations themselves suggest some special mode of elimination. This will be illustrated in the following examples.

Example 1. *Eliminate l, m between the equations*

$$lx + my = a, \ mx - ly = b, \ l^2 + m^2 = 1.$$

By squaring the first two equations and adding,

$$l^2x^2 + m^2x^2 + m^2y^2 + l^2y^2 = a^2 + b^2,$$

that is, $$(l^2 + m^2)(x^2 + y^2) = a^2 + b^2;$$

hence the eliminant is $x^2 + y^2 = a^2 + b^2$.

If $l = \cos\theta$, $m = \sin\theta$, the third equation is satisfied identically; that is, the eliminant of

$$x\cos\theta + y\sin\theta = a, \ x\sin\theta - y\cos\theta = b$$

is $$x^2 + y^2 = a^2 + b^2.$$

Example 2. *Eliminate x, y, z between the equations*

$$y^2 + z^2 = ayz, \ z^2 + x^2 = bzx, \ x^2 + y^2 = cxy.$$

We have $$\frac{y}{z} + \frac{z}{y} = a, \ \frac{z}{x} + \frac{x}{z} = b, \ \frac{x}{y} + \frac{y}{x} = c;$$

by multiplying together these three equations we obtain,

$$2 + \frac{y^2}{z^2} + \frac{z^2}{y^2} + \frac{z^2}{x^2} + \frac{x^2}{z^2} + \frac{x^2}{y^2} + \frac{y^2}{x^2} = abc;$$

hence $$2 + (a^2 - 2) + (b^2 - 2) + (c^2 - 2) = abc;$$

∴ $$a^2 + b^2 + c^2 - 4 = abc.$$

Example 3. *Eliminate x, y between the equations*

$$x^2 - y^2 = px - qy, \ 4xy = qx + py, \ x^2 + y^2 = 1.$$

Multiplying the first equation by x, and the second by y, we obtain

$$x^3 + 3xy^2 = p(x^2 + y^2);$$

hence, by the third equation,

$$p = x^3 + 3xy^2.$$

Similarly, $q = 3x^2y + y^3$.

Thus $$p + q = (x + y)^3, \ p - q = (x - y)^3;$$

∴ $$(p + q)^{2/3} + (p - q)^{2/3} = (x + y)^2 + (x - y)^2$$
$$= 2(x^2 + y^2);$$

∴ $$(p + q)^{2/3} + (p - q)^{2/3} = 2.$$

Example 4. *Eliminate x, y, z between the equations*

$$\frac{y}{z} - \frac{z}{y} = a, \ \frac{z}{x} - \frac{x}{z} = b, \ \frac{x}{y} - \frac{y}{x} = c.$$

We have $a + b + c = \dfrac{x(y^2 - z^2) + y(z^2 - x^2) + z(x^2 - y^2)}{xyz}$

$$= \frac{(y-z)(z-x)(x-y)}{xyz}.$$

If we change the sign of x, the signs of b and c are changed, while the sign of a remains unaltered;

hence $\qquad a-b-c = \dfrac{(y-z)(z+x)(x+y)}{xyz}$.

Similarly, $\qquad b-c-a = \dfrac{(y+z)(z-x)(x+y)}{xyz}$.

and $\qquad c-a-b = \dfrac{(y+z)(z+x)(x-y)}{xyz}$.

$\therefore \quad (a+b+c)(b+c-a)(c+a-b)(a+b-c)$

$$= -\frac{(y^2-z^2)^2(z^2-x^2)^2(x^2-y^2)^2}{x^4 y^4 z^4}$$

$$= -\left(\frac{y}{z}-\frac{z}{y}\right)^2\left(\frac{z}{x}-\frac{x}{z}\right)^2\left(\frac{x}{y}-\frac{y}{x}\right)^2$$

$$= -a^2 b^2 c^2.$$

$\therefore \qquad 2b^2c^2 + 2c^2a^2 + 2a^2b^2 - a^4 - b^4 - c^4 + a^2b^2c^2 = 0.$

EXAMPLES XXXIV. c.

1. Eliminate m from the equations
$$m^2 x - my + a = 0, \quad my + x = 0.$$

2. Eliminate m, n from the equations
$$m^2 x - my + a = 0, \quad n^2 x - ny + a = 0, \quad mn + 1 = 0.$$

3. Eliminate m, n between the equations
$$mx - ny = a(m^2 - n^2), \quad nx + my = 2amn, \quad m^2 + n^2 = 1.$$

4. Eliminate p, q, r from the equations
$$p + q + r = 0, \quad a(qr + rp + pq) = 2a - x,$$
$$apqr = y, \quad qr = -1.$$

5. Eliminate x from the equations
$$ax^2 - 2a^2 x + 1 = 0, \quad a^2 + x^2 - 3ax = 0.$$

6. Eliminate m from the equations
$$y + mx = a(1 + m), \quad my - x = a(1 - m).$$

7. Eliminate x, y, z from the equations
$$yz = a^2, zx = b^2, \quad xy = c^2, \quad x^2 + y^2 + z^2 = d^2.$$

8. Eliminate p, q from the equations
$$x(p+q) = y, \quad p - q = k(1 + pq), \quad xpq = a.$$

9. Eliminate $x, y,$ from the equations
$$x - y = a, \quad x^2 - y^2 = b^2, \quad x^3 - y^3 = c^3.$$

10. Eliminate x, y from the equations
$$x + y = a, \quad x^2 + y^2 = b^2, \quad x^4 + y^4 = c^4.$$

11. Eliminate x, y, z, u from the equations
$$x = by + cz + du, \quad y = cz + du + ax,$$
$$z = du + ax + by, \quad u = ax + by + cz.$$

12. Eliminate x, y, z from the equations
$$x + y + z = 0, \quad x^2 + y^2 + z^2 = a^2,$$
$$x^3 + y^3 + z^3 = b^3, \quad x^5 + y^5 + z^5 = c^5.$$

13. Eliminate x, y, z from the equations
$$\frac{x}{y} + \frac{y}{z} + \frac{z}{x} = a, \quad \frac{x}{z} + \frac{y}{x} + \frac{z}{y} = b, \quad \left(\frac{x}{y} + \frac{y}{z} \right)\left(\frac{y}{z} + \frac{z}{x} \right)\left(\frac{z}{x} + \frac{x}{y} \right) = c,$$

14. Eliminate x, y, z from the equations
$$\frac{x^2(y+z)}{a^3} = \frac{y^2(z+x)}{b^3} = \frac{z^2(x+y)}{c^3} = \frac{xyz}{abc} = 1.$$

15. Eliminate x, y from the equations
$$4(x^2 + y^2) = ax + by, \quad 2(x^2 - y^2) = ax - by, \quad xy = c^2.$$

16. Eliminate x, y, z from the equations
$$(y + z)^2 = 4a^2 yz, \quad (z + x)^2 = 4b^2 zx, \quad (x + y)^2 = 4c^2 xy.$$

17. Eliminate x, y, z from the equations
$$(x + y - z)(x - y + z) = ayz, \quad (y + z - x)(y - z + x) = bzx,$$
$$(z + x - y)(z - x + y) = cxy.$$

18. Eliminate x, y from the equations
$$x^2 y = a, \quad x(x + y) = b, \quad 2x + y = c.$$

19. Shew that $(a + b + c)^3 - 4(b + c)(c + a)(a + b) + 5abc = 0$
is the eliminant of
$$ax^2 + by^2 + cz^2 = ax + by + cz = yz + zx + xy = 0.$$

20. Eliminate x, y from the equations
$$ax^2 + by^2 = ax + by = \frac{xy}{x + y} = c.$$

21. Shew that $b^3 c^3 + c^3 a^3 + a^3 b^3 = 5a^2 b^2 c^2$ is the eliminant of
$$ax + yz = bc, \quad by + zx = ca, \quad cz + xy = ab, \quad xyz = abc$$

22. Eliminate x, y, z from
$$x^2 + y^2 + z^2 = x + y + z = 1,$$
$$\frac{a}{x}(x - p) = \frac{b}{y}(y - q) = \frac{c}{z}(z - r).$$

23. Employ Bezout's method to eliminate x, y from
$$ax^3 + bx^2y + cxy^2 + dy^3 = 0, \ a'x^3 + b'x^2y + c'xy^2 + d'y^3 = 0.$$

■ ■ ■

Chapter 35

THEORY OF EQUATIONS

534. In Chap. 9 we have established certain relations between the roots and the coefficients of quadratic equations. We shall now investigate similar relations which hold in the case of equations of the nth degree, and we shall then discuss some of the more elementary properties in the general theory of equations.

535. Let $p_0x^n + p_1x^{n-1} + p_2x^{n-2} + \ldots + p_{n-1}x + p_n$ be a rational integral function of x of n dimensions, and let us denote it by $f(x)$; then $f(x) = 0$ is the general type of a *rational integral equation* of the nth degree. Dividing throughout by p_0, we see that without any loss of generality we may take

$$x^n + p_1x^{n-1} + p_2x^{n-2} + \ldots + p_{n-1}x + p_n = 0$$

as the type of a rational integral equation of any degree.

Unless otherwise stated the coefficients $p_1, p_2, \ldots, p_n$ will always be supposed rational.

536. Any value of x which makes $f(x)$ vanish is called a root of the equation $f(x) = 0$.

In Art. 514 it was proved that when $f(x)$ is divided by $x - a$, the remainder is $f(a)$; hence if $f(x)$ is divisible by $x - a$ without remainder, a is a root of the equation $f(x) = 0$.

537. We shall assume that every equation of the form $f(x) = 0$ has a root, real or imaginary. The proof of this proposition will be found in treatises on the *Theory of Equations;* it is beyond the range of the present work.

538. *Every equation of the nth degree has n roots, and no more.*

Denote the given equation by $f(x) = 0$, where

$$f(x) = p_0x^n + p_1x^{n-1} + p_2x^{n-2} + \ldots + p_n.$$

The equation $f(x) = 0$ has a root, real or imaginary; let this be denoted by a_1; then $f(x)$ is divisible by $x - a_1$, so that

$$f(x) = (x - a_1)\, \phi_1(x)$$

where $\phi_1(x)$ is a rational integral function of $n-1$ dimensions. Again, the equation $\phi_1(x) = 0$ has a root, real or imaginary; let this be denoted by a_2; then $\phi_1(x)$ is divisible by $x - a_2$, so that

$$\phi_1(x) = (x - a_2)\,\phi_2(x),$$

where $\phi_2(x)$ is a rational integral function of $n - 2$ dimensions.

Thus $f(x) = (x - a_1)(x - a_2)\,\phi_2(x).$

Proceeding in this way, we obtain, as in Art. 309,

$$f(x) = p_0(x - a_1)(x - a_2) \dots (x - a_n).$$

Hence the equation $f(x) = 0$ has n roots, since $f(x)$ vanishes when x has any of the values $a_1, a_2, a_3, \dots, a_n$.

Also the equation cannot have more than n roots; for if x has any value different from any of the quantities $a_1, a_2, a_3, \dots, a_n$, all the factors on the right are different from zero, and therefore $f(x)$ cannot vanish for that value of x.

In the above investigation some of the quantities $a_1, a_2, a_3, \dots, a_n$ may be equal; in this case, however, we shall suppose that the equation has still n roots, although these are not all different.

539.　*To investigate the relations between the roots and the coefficients in any equation.*

Let us denote the equation by

$$x^n + p_1 x^{n-1} + p_2 x^{n-2} + \dots + p_{n-1} x + p_n = 0,$$

and the roots by $a, b, c, \dots k$; then we have identically

$$x^n + p_1 x^{n-1} + p_2 x^{n-2} + \dots + p_{n-1} x + p_n$$
$$= (x - a)(x - b)(x - c) \dots (x - k);$$

hence, with the notation of Art. 163, we have

$$x^n + p_1 x^{n-1} + p_2 x^{n-2} + \dots + p_{n-1} x + p_n$$
$$= x^n - S_1 x^{n-1} + S_2 x^{n-2} - \dots + (-1)^{n-1} S_{n-1} x + (-1)^n S_n.$$

Equating coefficients of like powers of x in this identity,

$-p_1 = S_1 = $ sum of the roots;

$p_2 = S_2 = $ sum of the products of the roots taken two at a time.

$-p_3 = S_3 = $ sum of the products of the roots taken three at a time;

$$\dots\dots\dots\dots\dots\dots\dots\dots\dots\dots\dots\dots\dots\dots\dots\dots\dots\dots\dots\dots\dots\dots\dots\dots\dots$$

$(-1)^n p_n = S_n = $ product of the roots.

If the coefficient of x^n is p_0, then on dividing each term by p_0, the equation becomes

$$x^n + \frac{p_1}{p_0} x^{n-1} + \frac{p_2}{p_0} x^{n-2} + \dots + \frac{p_{n-1}}{p_0} x + \frac{p_n}{p_0} = 0,$$

and, with the notation of Art 521, we have

$$\Sigma a = -\frac{p_1}{p_0}, \ \Sigma ab = \frac{p_2}{p_0}, \ \Sigma abc = -\frac{p_3}{p_0}, \ \dots, abc \dots k = (-1)^n \frac{p_n}{p_0}.$$

Example 1. *Solve the equations*

$$x + ay + a^2 z = a^3, \ x + by + b^2 z = b^3, \ x + cy + c^2 z = c^3.$$

From these equations we see that a, b, c are the values of t which satisfy the cubic equation

$$t^3 - zt^2 - yt - x = 0;$$

hence $\qquad z = a + b + c, \ y = -(bc + ca + ab), \ x = abc.$

Example 2. *If a, b, c are the roots of the equation $x^3 + p_1 x^2 + p_2 x + p_3 = 0$, form the equation whose roots are a^2, b^2, c^2.*

The required equation is $\ (y - a^2)(y - b^2)(y - c^2) = 0,$

or $\qquad (x^2 - a^2)(x^2 - b^2)(x^2 - c^2) = 0,$ if $y = x^2;$

that is, $\qquad (x - a)(x - b)(x - c)(x + a)(x + b)(x + c) = 0.$

But $\qquad (x - a)(x - b)(x - c) = x^3 + p_1 x^2 + p_2 x + p_3;$

hence $\qquad (x + a)(x + b)(x + c) = x^3 - p_1 x^2 + p_2 x - p_3.$

Thus the required equation is

$$(x^3 + p_1 x^2 + p_2 x + p_3)(x^3 - p_1 x^2 + p_2 x - p_3) = 0,$$

or $\qquad (x^3 + p_2 x)^2 - (p_1 x^2 + p_3)^2 = 0,$

or $\qquad x^6 + (2p_2 - p_1^2) x^4 + (p_2^2 - 2p_1 p_3) x^2 - p_3^2 = 0;$

and if we replace x^2 by y, we obtain

$$y^3 + (2p_2 - p_1^2) y^2 + (p_2^2 - 2p_1 p_3) y - p_3^2 = 0.$$

540. The student might suppose that the relations established in the preceding article would enable him to solve any proposed equation; for the number of the relations is equal to the number of the roots. A little reflection will shew that is this not the case; for suppose we eliminate any $n - 1$ of the quantities a, b, c, $\dots$ k and so obtain an equation to determine the remaining one; then since these quantities are involved symmetrically in each of the equations, it is clear that we shall always obtain an equation having the same coefficients; this equation is therefore the original equation with some one of the roots a, b, c, $\dots$ k substituted for x.

Let us take for example the equation

$$x^3 + p_1 x^2 + p_2 x + p_3 = 0;$$

and let a, b, c be the roots; then

$$a + b + c = -p_1,$$
$$ab + ac + bc = p_2,$$
$$abc = -p_3.$$

Multiply these equations by $a^2, -a, 1$ respectively and add; thus

$$a^3 = -p_1a^2 - p_2a - p_3,$$

that is, $\qquad\qquad a^3 + p_1a^2 + p_2a + p_3 = 0,$

which is the original equation with a in the place of x.

The above process of elimination is quite general, and is applicable to equations of any degree.

541. If two or more of the roots of an equation are connected by an assigned relation, the properties proved in Art. 539 will sometimes enable us to obtain the complete solution.

Example 1. *Solve the equation* $4x^3 - 24x^2 + 23x + 18 = 0$, *having given that the roots are in arithmetical progression.*

Denote the roots by $a - b, a, a + b$; then the sum of the roots is $3a$; the sum of the products of the roots two at a time is $3a^2 - b^2$; and the product of the roots is $a(a^2 - b^2)$; hence we have the equations

$$3a = 6, \quad 3a^2 - b^2 = \frac{23}{4}, \quad a(a^2 - b^2) = -\frac{9}{2};$$

from the first equation we find $a = 2$, and from the second $b = \pm\frac{5}{2}$, and since these values satisfy the third, the three equations are consistent. Thus, the roots are $-\frac{1}{2}, 2, \frac{9}{2}$.

Example 2. *Solve the equation* $24x^3 - 14x^2 - 63x + 45 = 0$, *one root being double another.*

Denote the roots by $a, 2a, b$; then we have

$$3a + b = \frac{7}{12}, \quad 2a^2 + 3ab = -\frac{21}{8}, \quad 2a^2b = -\frac{15}{8}.$$

From the first two equations, we obtain

$$8a^2 - 2a - 3 = 0;$$

$$\therefore \qquad a = \frac{3}{4} \text{ or } -\frac{1}{2} \text{ and } b = -\frac{5}{3} \text{ or } \frac{25}{12}.$$

It will be found on trial that the values $a = -\frac{1}{2}, b = \frac{25}{12}$ do not satisfy the third equation $2a^2b = -\frac{15}{8}$; hence we are restricted to the values

$$a = \frac{3}{4}, \quad b = -\frac{5}{3}.$$

Thus the roots are $\frac{3}{4}, \frac{3}{2}, -\frac{5}{3}$.

542. Although we may not be able to find the roots of an equation, we can make use of the relations proved in Art. 539 to determine the values of symmetrical functions of the roots.

Example 1. *Find the sum of the squares and of the cubes of the roots of the equation* $x^3 - px^2 + qx - r = 0$.

Denote the roots by a, b, c; then
$$a + b + c = p, \quad bc + ca + ab = q.$$
Now
$$a^2 + b^2 + c^2 = (a + b + c)^2 - 2(bc + ca + ab)$$
$$= p^2 - 2q.$$

Again, substitute a, b, c for x in the given equation and add; thus
$$a^3 + b^3 + c^3 - p(a^2 + b^2 + c^2) + q(a + b + c) - 3r = 0;$$
$$\therefore \quad a^3 + b^3 + c^3 = p(p^2 - 2q) - pq + 3r$$
$$= p^3 - 3pq + 3r.$$

Example 2. *If a, b, c, d are the roots of*
$$x^4 + px^3 + qx^2 + rx + s = 0,$$
find the value of $\Sigma a^2 b$.

We have
$$a + b + c + d = -p \qquad \qquad \text{...(1)}$$
$$ab + ac + ad + bc + bd + cd = q \qquad \qquad \text{...(2)}$$
$$abc + abd + acd + bcd = -r \qquad \qquad \text{...(3)}$$

From these equations we have
$$-pq = \Sigma a^2 b + 3(abc + abd + acd + bcd)$$
$$= \Sigma a^2 b - 3r;$$
$$\therefore \qquad \Sigma a^2 b = 3r - pq.$$

EXAMPLES XXXV. a.

Form the equation whose roots are :

1. $\dfrac{2}{3}, \dfrac{3}{2}, \pm\sqrt{3}$.

2. $0, 0, 2, 2, -3, -3$.

3. $2, 2, -2, -2, 0, 5$.

4. $a + b, a - b, -a + b, -a - b$.

Solve the equations :

5. $x^4 - 16x^3 + 86x^2 - 176x + 105 = 0$, two roots being 1 and 7.

6. $4x^3 + 16x^2 - 9x - 36 = 0$, the sum of two of the roots being zero.

7. $4x^3 + 20x^2 - 23x + 6 = 0$, two of the roots being equal.

8. $3x^3 - 26x^2 + 52x - 24 = 0$, the roots being in geometrical progression.

9. $2x^3 - x^2 - 22x - 24 = 0$, two of the roots being in the ratio of $3 : 4$.

10. $24x^3 + 46x^2 + 9x - 9 = 0$, one root being double another of the roots.

11. $8x^4 - 2x^3 - 27x^2 + 6x + 9 = 0$, two of the roots being equal but opposite in sign.

12. $54x^3 - 39x^2 - 26x + 16 = 0$, the roots being in geometrical progression.

13. $32x^3 - 48x^2 + 22x - 3 = 0$, the roots being in arithmetical progression.

14. $6x^4 - 29x^3 + 40x^2 - 7x - 12 = 0$, the product of two of the roots being 2.

15. $x^4 - 2x^3 - 21x^2 + 22x + 40 = 0$, the roots being in arithmetical progression.

16. $27x^4 - 195x^3 + 494x^2 - 520x + 192 = 0$, the roots being in geometrical progression.

17. $18x^3 + 81x^2 + 121x + 60 = 0$, one root being half the sum of the other two.

18. If a, b, c are the roots of the equation $x^3 - px^2 + qx - r = 0$, find the value of

    (1) $\dfrac{1}{a^2} + \dfrac{1}{b^2} + \dfrac{1}{c^2}$.   (2) $\dfrac{1}{b^2c^2} + \dfrac{1}{c^2a^2} + \dfrac{1}{a^2b^2}$.

19. If a, b, c are the roots of $x^3 + qx + r = 0$, find the value of
    (1) $(b - c)^2 + (c - a)^2 + (a - b)^2$.
    (2) $(b + c)^{-1} + (c + a)^{-1} + (a + b)^{-1}$.

20. Find the sum of the squares and of the cubes of the roots of $x^4 + qx^2 + rx + s = 0$.

21. Find the sum of the fourth powers of the roots of $x^3 + qx + r = 0$.

543. *In an equation with real coefficients imaginary roots occur in pairs.*

Suppose that $f(x) = 0$ is an equation with real coefficients, and suppose that it has an imaginary root $a + ib$; we shall shew that $a - ib$ is also a root.

The factor of $f(x)$ corresponding to these two roots is

$$(x - a - ib)(x - a + ib), \text{ or } (x - a)^2 + b^2.$$

Let $f(x)$ be divided by $(x-a)^2 + b^2$; denote the quotient by Q, and the remainder, if any, by $Rx + R'$; then

$$f(x) = Q\{(x-a)^2 + b^2\} + Rx + R'.$$

In this identity put $x = a + ib$, then $f(x) = 0$ by hypothesis; also $(x-a)^2 + b^2 = 0$; hence $R(a + ib) + R' = 0$.

Equating to zero the real and imaginary parts,

$$Ra + R' = 0, \ Rb = 0;$$

and b by hypothesis is not zero,

∴ $R = 0$ and $R' = 0$.

Hence $f(x)$ is exactly divisible by $(x-a)^2 + b^2$, that is, by

$$(x - a - ib)(x - a + ib);$$

hence $x = a - ib$ is also a root.

544.   In the preceding article we have seen that if the equation $f(x) = 0$ has a pair of imaginary roots $a \pm ib$, then $(x-a)^2 + b^2$ is a factor of the expression $f(x)$.

Suppose that $a \pm ib$, $c \pm id$, $e \pm ig$, ... are the imaginary roots of the equation $f(x) = 0$, and that $\phi(x)$ is the product of the quadratic factors corresponding to these imaginary roots; then

$$\phi(x) = \{(x-a)^2 + b^2\}\{(x-c)^2 + d^2\}\{(x-e)^2 + g^2\} \dots$$

Now each of these factors is positive for every real value of x; hence $\phi(x)$ is always positive for real values of x.

545.   As in Art 543 we may shew that in an equation with *rational* coefficients, surd roots enter in pairs; that is, if $a + \sqrt{b}$ is a root then $a - \sqrt{b}$ is also a root.

Example 1. *Solve the equation* $6x^4 - 13x^3 - 35x^2 - x + 3 = 0$, *having given that one root is* $2 - \sqrt{3}$.

Since $2 - \sqrt{3}$ is a root, we know that $2 + \sqrt{3}$ is also a root, and corresponding to this pair of roots we have the quadratic factor $x^2 - 4x + 1$.

Also $6x^4 - 13x^3 - 35x^2 - x + 3 = (x^2 - 4x + 1)(6x^2 + 11x + 3)$;

hence the other roots are obtained from

$$6x^2 + 11x + 3 = 0, \quad \text{or} \quad (3x + 1)(2x + 3) = 0;$$

thus the roots are $-\dfrac{1}{3}, -\dfrac{3}{2}, 2 + \sqrt{3}, 2 - \sqrt{3}$.

Example 2. *From the equation of the fourth degree with rational coefficients, one of whose roots is* $\sqrt{2} + \sqrt{-3}$.

Here we must have $\sqrt{2} + \sqrt{-3}, \sqrt{2} - \sqrt{-3}$ as one pair of roots, and $-\sqrt{2} + \sqrt{-3}, -\sqrt{2} - \sqrt{-3}$ as another pair.

Corresponding to the first pair we have the quadratic factor $x^2 - 2\sqrt{2}x + 5$ and corresponding to the second pair we have the quadratic factor $x^2 + 2\sqrt{2}\,x + 5$.

Thus the required equation is

$$(x^2 + 2\sqrt{2}\,x + 5)\,(x^2 - 2\sqrt{2}\,x + 5) = 0,$$

or

$$(x^2 + 5)^2 - 8x^2 = 0,$$

or

$$x^4 + 2x^2 + 25 = 0.$$

Example 3. *Shew that the equation*

$$\frac{A^2}{x-a} + \frac{B^2}{x-b} + \frac{C^2}{x-c} + \ldots + \frac{H^2}{x-h} = k,$$

has no imaginary roots.

If possible let $p + iq$ be a root; then $p - iq$ is also a root. Substitute these values for x and subtract the first result from the second; thus

$$q \left\{ \frac{A^2}{(p-a)^2 + q^2} + \frac{B^2}{(p-b)^2 + q^2} + \frac{C^2}{(p-c)^2 + q^2} + \ldots + \frac{H^2}{(p-h)^2 + q^2} \right\} = 0;$$

which is impossible unless $q = 0$.

546. To determine the nature of some of the roots of an equation it is not always necessary to solve it; for instance, the truth of the following statements will be readily admitted.

(i) If the coefficients are all positive, the equation has no positive root; thus the equation $x^5 + x^3 + 2x + 1 = 0$ cannot have a positive root.

(ii) If the coefficients of the even powers of x are all of one sign, and the coefficients of the odd powers are all of the contrary sign, the equation has no negative root; thus the equation

$$x^7 + x^5 - 2x^4 + x^3 - 3x^2 + 7x - 5 = 0$$

cannot have a negative root.

(iii) If the equation contains only even powers of x and the coefficients are all of the same sign, the equation has no real root; thus the equation $2x^8 + 3x^4 + x^2 + 7 = 0$ cannot have a real root.

(iv) If the equation contains only odd powers of x, and the coefficients are all of the same sign, the equation has no real root except $x = 0$; thus the equation $x^9 + 2x^5 + 3x^3 + x = 0$ has no real root except $x = 0$.

All the foregoing results are included in the theorem of the next article, which is known as Descartes' *Rule of Signs*.

547. *An equation $f(x) = 0$ cannot have more positive roots than there are changes of sign in $f(x)$, and cannot have more negative roots than there are changes of sign in $f(-x)$.*

Suppose that the signs of the terms in a polynomial are $++--+---+-+-$; we shall show that if this polynomial is multiplied by a binomial whose signs are $+-$, there will be at least one more change of sign in the product than in the original polynomial.

Writing down only the signs of the terms in the multiplication, we have

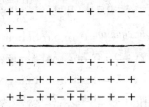

Hence we see that in the product

(i) an ambiguity replaces each continuation of sign in the original polynomial;

(ii) the signs before and after an ambiguity or set of ambiguities are unlike;

(iii) a change of sign is introduced at the end.

Let us take the most unfavourable case and suppose that all the ambiguities are replaced by continuations; from (ii) we see that the number of changes of sign will be the same whether we take the upper or the lower signs; let us take the upper; thus the number of changes of sign cannot be less than in

$$++--+----+-+-+,$$

and this series of signs is the same as in the original polynomial with an additional change of sign at the end.

If then we suppose the factors corresponding to the negative and imaginary roots to be already multiplied together, each factor $x - a$ corresponding to a positive root introduces at least one change of sign; therefore no equation can have more positive roots than it has changes of sign.

Again, the roots of the equation $f(-x) = 0$ are equal to those of $f(x) = 0$ but opposite to them in sign; therefore the negative roots of $f(x) = 0$ are the positive roots of $f(-x) = 0$; but the number of these positive roots cannot exceed the number of changes of sign in $f(-x)$; that is, the number of negative roots of $f(x) = 0$ cannot exceed the number of changes of sign in $f(-x)$.

Example : *Consider the equation* $x^9 + 5x^8 - x^3 + 7x + 2 = 0$.

Here there are two changes of sign, therefore there are at most two positive roots.

Again $f(-x) = -x^9 + 5x^8 + x^3 - 7x + 2$, and here there are three changes of sign, therefore the given equation has at most three negative roots, and therefore it must have at least four imaginary roots.

Examples XXXV. b.

Solve the equations :

1. $3x^4 - 10x^3 + 4x^2 - x - 6 = 0$, one root being $\dfrac{1 + \sqrt{-3}}{2}$

2. $6x^4 - 13x^3 - 35x^2 - x + 3 = 0$, one root being $2 - \sqrt{3}$.

3. $x^4 + 4x^3 + 5x^2 + 2x - 2 = 0$, one root being $-1 + \sqrt{-1}$.

4. $x^4 + 4x^3 + 6x^2 + 4x + 5 = 0$, one root being $\sqrt{-1}$.

5. Solve the equation $x^5 - x^4 + 8x^2 - 9x - 15 = 0$, one root being $\sqrt{3}$ and another $1 - 2\sqrt{-1}$.

Form the equation of lowest dimensions with rational coefficients, one of whose roots is

6. $\sqrt{3} + \sqrt{-2}$.

7. $-\sqrt{-1} + \sqrt{5}$.

8. $-\sqrt{2} - \sqrt{-2}$.

9. $\sqrt{5 + 2\sqrt{6}}$.

10. Form the equation whose roots are $\pm 4\sqrt{3}, 5 \pm 2\sqrt{-1}$.

11. Form the equation whose roots are $1 \pm \sqrt{-2}, 2 \pm \sqrt{-3}$.

12. Form the equation of the eighth degree with rational coefficients one of whose roots is $\sqrt{2} + \sqrt{3} + \sqrt{-1}$.

13. Find the nature of the roots of the equation
$$3x^4 + 12x^2 + 5x - 4 = 0.$$

14. Shew that the equation $2x^7 - x^4 + 4x^3 - 5 = 0$ has at least four imaginary roots.

15. What may be inferred respecting the roots of the equation
$$x^{10} - 4x^6 + x^4 - 2x - 3 = 0 ?$$

16. Find the least possible number of imaginary roots of the equation $x^9 - x^5 + x^4 + x^2 + 1 = 0$.

17. Find the condition that $x^3 - px^2 + qx - r = 0$ may have
(1) two roots equal but of opposite sign;
(2) the roots in geometrical progression.

18. If the roots of the equation $x^4 + px^3 + qx^2 + rx + s = 0$ are in arithmetical progression, shew that $p^3 - 4pq + 8r = 0$; and if they are in geometrical progression, shew that $p^2 s = r^2$.

19. If the roots of the equation $x^n - 1 = 0$ are $1, \alpha, \beta, \gamma, \ldots$, shew that
$$(1 - \alpha)(1 - \beta)(1 - \gamma) \ldots = n.$$

If a, b, c are the roots of the equation $x^3 - px^2 + qx - r = 0$, find the value of

20. $\Sigma a^2 b^2$

21. $(b + c)(c + a)(a + b)$.

22. $\Sigma\left(\dfrac{b}{c} + \dfrac{c}{b}\right)$

23. $\Sigma a^2 b$.

If a, b, c, d are the roots of $x^4 + px^3 + qx^2 + rx + s = 0$, find the value of

24. $\Sigma a^2 bc$.

25. Σa^4.

548. *To find the value of $f(x + h)$, when $f(x)$ is a rational integral function of x.*

Let $\qquad f(x) = p_0 x^n + p_1 x^{n-1} + p_2 x^{n-2} + \ldots + p_{n-1} x + p_n$; then
$$f(x + h) = p_0 (x + h)^n + p_1 (x + h)^{n-1} + p_2 (x + h)^{n-2} + \ldots$$
$$+ p_{n-1}(x + h) + p_n.$$

Expanding each term and arranging the result in ascending powers of h, we have

$$p_0 x^n + p_1 x^{n-1} + p_2 x^{n-2} + \ldots + p_{n-1} x + p_n$$
$$+ h\{np_0 x^{n-1} + (n-1) p_1 x^{n-2} + (n-2) p_2 x^{n-3} + \ldots + p_{n-1}\}$$
$$+ \frac{h^2}{2!}\{n(n-1) p_0 x^{n-2} + (n-1)(n-2) p_1 x^{n-3} + \ldots + 2p_{n-2}\}$$
$$+ \ldots\ldots\ldots\ldots\ldots\ldots\ldots\ldots\ldots\ldots\ldots\ldots\ldots\ldots\ldots\ldots$$
$$+ \frac{h^n}{n!}\{n(n-1)(n-2)\ldots 2.\,1 p_0\}.$$

This result is usually written in the form

$$f(x + h) = f(x) + hf'(x) + \frac{h^2}{2!}f''(x) + \frac{h^3}{3!}f'''(x) + \ldots + \frac{h^n}{n!}f^n(x),$$

and the functions $f'(x), f''(x), f'''(x), \ldots$ are called the *first, second, third, ... derived functions of* $f(x)$.

The student who knows the elements of the Differential Calculus will see that the above expansion of $f(x+h)$ is only a particular case of *Taylor's Theorem;* the functions $f'(x), f''(x), f'''(x)$ may therefore be written down at once by the ordinary rules for differentiation : thus to obtain $f'(x)$ from $f(x)$ we multiply each term in $f(x)$ by the index of x in that term and then diminish the index by unity.

Similarly by successive differentiations we obtain $f''(x)$, $f'''(x), \ldots$

By writing $-h$ in the place of h, we have

$$f(x-h) = f(x) - hf'(x) + \frac{h^2}{2!}f''(x) - \frac{h^3}{3!}f'''(x) + \ldots + (-1)^n \frac{h^n}{n!}f^n(x).$$

The function $f(x+h)$ is evidently symmetrical with respect to x and h; hence

$$f(x+h) = f(h) + xf'(h) + \frac{x^2}{2!}f''(h) + \ldots + \frac{x^n}{n!}f^n(h).$$

Here the expressions $f'(h), f''(h), f'''(h), \ldots$ denote the results obtained by writing h in the place of x in the successive derived functions $f'(x), f''(x), f'''(x), \ldots$

Example : *If* $f(x) = 2x^4 - x^3 - 2x^2 + 5x - 1$, *find the value of* $f(x+3)$.

Here $f(x) = 2x^4 - x^3 - 2x^2 + 5x - 1$, so that $f(3) = 131$;

$$f'(x) = 8x^3 - 3x^2 - 4x + 5, \qquad \text{and } f'(3) = 182;$$

$$\frac{f''(x)}{2!} = 12x^2 - 3x - 2, \quad \text{and} \quad \frac{f''(3)}{2!} = 97;$$

$$\frac{f'''(x)}{3!} = 8x - 1, \quad \text{and} \quad \frac{f'''(3)}{3!} = 23;$$

$$\frac{f^{(iv)}(x)}{4!} = 2.$$

Thus $f(x+3) = 2x^4 + 23x^3 + 97x^2 + 182x + 131$.

The calculation may, however, be effected more systematically by *Horner's process,* as explained in the next article.

549.   Let $f(x) = p_0 x^n + p_1 x^{n-1} + p_2 x^{n-2} + \ldots + p_{n-1}x + p_n;$ put $x = y + h$, and suppose that $f(x)$ then becomes

$$q_0 y^n + q_1 y^{n-1} + q_2 y^{n-2} + \ldots + q_{n-1}y + q_n.$$

Now $y = x - h$; hence we have the identity

$$p_0 x^n + p_1 x^{n-1} + p_2 x^{n-2} + \ldots + p_{n-1}x + p_n$$

$$= q_0 (x - h)^n + q_1 (x - h)^{n - 1} + \ldots + q_{n-1} (x - h) + q_n;$$

therefore q_n is the remainder found by dividing $f(x)$ by $x - h$; also the quotient arising from the division is

$$q_0 (x - h)^{n - 1} + q_1 (x - h)^{n - 2} + \ldots + q_{n-1}.$$

Similarly q_{n-1} is the remainder found by dividing the last expression by $x - h$, and the quotient arising from the division is
$$q_0 (x - h)^{n - 2} + q_1 (x - h)^{n - 3} + \ldots + q_{n-2};$$

and so on. Thus $q_n, q_{n-1}, q_{n-2}, \ldots$ may be found by the rule explained in Art. 515. The last quotient is q_0, and is obviously equal to p_0.

Example : *Find the result of changing x into $x + 3$ in the expression* $2x^4 - x^3 - 2x^2 + 5x - 1$.

Here we divide successively by $x - 3$.

Or more briefly thus :

2	-1	-2	5	-1
	6	15	39	132
	5	13	44	$131 = q_4$
	6	33	138	
	11	46	$182 = q_3$	
	6	51		
	17	$97 = q_2$		
	6			
	$23 = q_1$			

2	-1	-2	5	-1
2	5	13	44	131
2	11	46	182	
2	17	97		
2	23			
2				

Hence the result is $2x^4 + 23x^3 + 97x^2 + 182x + 131$. Compare Art. 548.

It may be remarked that Horner's process is chiefly useful in *numerical work*.

550. *If the variable x changes continuously from a to b the function $f(x)$ will change continuously from $f(a)$ to $f(b)$.*

Let c and $c + h$ be any two values of x lying between a and b. We have

$$f(c + h) - f(c) = h f'(c) + \frac{h^2}{2!} f''(c) + \ldots + \frac{h^n}{n!} f^n(c); x$$

and by taking h small enough the difference between $f(c + h)$ and $f(c)$ can be made as small as we please; hence to a small change in the variable x there corresponds a small change in the function $f(x)$, and therefore as x changes gradually from a to b, the function $f(x)$ changes gradually from $f(a)$ to $f(b)$.

551. It is important to notice that we have not proved that $f(x)$ always increases from $f(a)$ to $f(b)$, or decreases from $f(a)$ to $f(b)$, out that it passes from one value to the other without any sudden change; sometimes it may be increasing and at other times it may be decreasing.

The student who has a knowledge of the elements of Curvetracing will in any particular example find it easy to follow the gradual changes of value of $f(x)$ by drawing the curve $y = f(x)$.

552. *If $f(a)$ and $f(b)$ are of contrary signs then one root of the equation $f(x) = 0$ must lie between a and b.*

As x changes gradually from a to b, the function $f(x)$ changes gradually from $f(a)$ to $f(b)$, and therefore must pass through all intermediate values; but since $f(a)$ and $f(b)$ have contrary signs the value zero must lie between them; that is, $f(x) = 0$ for some value of x between a and b.

It does not follow that $f(x) = 0$ has *only one* root between a and b; neither does it follow that if $f(a)$ and $f(b)$ have the same sign $f(x) = 0$ has no root between a and b.

553. *Every equation of an odd degree has at least one real root whose sign is opposite to that of its last term.*

In the function $f(x)$ substitute for x the values $+\infty, 0, -\infty$ successively, then

$$f(+\infty) = +\infty, f(0) = p_n, f(-\infty) = -\infty$$

If p_n is positive, then $f(x) = 0$ has a root lying between 0 and $-\infty$, and if p_n is negative $f(x) = 0$ has a root lying between 0 and $+\infty$.

554. *Every equation which is of an even degree and has its last term negative has at least two real roots, one positive and one negative.*

For in this case

$$f(+\infty) = +\infty, f(0) = p_n, f(-\infty) = +\infty;$$

but p_n is negative; hence $f(x) = 0$ has a root lying beteeen 0 and $+\infty$, and a root lying between 0 and $-\infty$.

555. *If the expressions $f(a)$ and $f(b)$ have contrary signs, an odd number of roots of $f(x) = 0$ will lie between a and b; and if $f(a)$ and $f(b)$ have the same sign, either no root or an even number of roots will lie between a and b.*

Suppose that a is greater than b, and that $\alpha, \beta, \gamma, \ldots, k$ represent all the roots of $f(x) = 0$ which lie between a and b. Let $\phi(x)$ be the quotient when $f(x)$ is divided by the product $(x - \alpha)(x - \beta)(x - \gamma) \ldots (x - k)$; then

$$f(x) = (x - \alpha)(x - \beta)(x - \gamma) \dots (x - k)\, \phi(x).$$

Hence
$$f(a) = (a - \alpha)(a - \beta)(a - \gamma) \dots (a - k)\, \phi(a).$$
$$f(b) = (b - \alpha)(b - \beta)(b - \gamma) \dots (b - k)\, \phi(b).$$

Now $\phi(a)$ and $\phi(b)$ must be of the same sign, for otherwise a root of the equation $\phi(x) = 0$, and therefore of $f(x) = 0$, would lie between a and b [Art. 552], which is contrary to the hypothesis. Hence if $f(a)$ and $f(b)$ have contrary signs, the expressions

$$(a - \alpha)(a - \beta)(a - \gamma) \dots (a - k),$$
$$(b - \alpha)(b - \beta)(b - \gamma) \dots (b - k),$$

must have contrary signs. Also the factors in the first expression are all positive, and the factors in the second are all negative; hence the number of factors must be odd, that is the number of roots $\alpha, \beta, \gamma, \dots k$ must be odd.

Similarly if $f(a)$ and $f(b)$ have the same sign the number of factors must be even. In this case the given condition is satisfied if $\alpha, \beta, \gamma, \dots k$ are all greater than a, or less than b; thus it does not necessarily follow that $f(x) = 0$ has a root between a and b.

556. If $a, b, c, \dots k$ are the roots of the equation $f(x) = 0$, then
$$f(x) = p_0 (x - a)(x - b)(x - c) \dots (x - k).$$

Here the quantities $a, b, c, \dots k$ are not necessarily unequal. If r of them are equal to a, s to b, t to c, $\dots$, then
$$f(x) = p_0 (x - a)^r (x - b)^s (x - c)^t \dots$$

In this case it is convenient still to speak of the equation $f(x) = 0$ as having n roots, each of the equal roots being considered a distinct root.

557. *If the equation* $f(x) = 0$ *has* r *roots equal to* a, *then the equation* $f'(x) = 0$ *will have* $r - 1$ *roots equal to* a.

Let $\phi(x)$ be the quotient when $f(x)$ is divided by $(x - a)^r$; then
$$f(x) = (x - a)^r\, \phi(x).$$

Write $x + h$ in the place of x; thus
$$f(x + h) = (x - a + h)^r\, \phi(x + h);$$

$\therefore \quad f(x) + hf'(x) + \dfrac{h^2}{2!} f''(x) + \dots$

$$= \{(x - a)^r + r(x - a)^{r-1} h + \dots\} \left\{ \phi(x) + h\phi'(x) + \dfrac{h^2}{2!} \phi''(x) + \dots \right\}.$$

In this identity, by equating the coefficients of h, we have
$$f'(x) = r(x - a)^{r-1} \phi(x) + (x - a)^r \phi'(x).$$

Thus $f'(x)$ contains the factor $x - a$ repeated $f - 1$ times; that is, the equation $f'(x) = 0$ has $r - 1$ roots equal to a.

Similarly we may shew that if the equation $f(x) = 0$ has s roots equal to b, the equation $f'(x) = 0$ has $s - 1$ roots equal to b; and so on.

558. From the foregoing proof we see that if $f(x)$ contains a factor $(x - a)^r$, then $f'(x)$ contains a factor $(x - a)^{r-1}$; and thus $f(x)$ and $f'(x)$ have a common factor $(x - a)^{r-1}$. Therefore if $f(x)$ and $f'(x)$ have no common factor, no factor in $f(x)$ will be repeated; hence *the equation $f(x) = 0$ has or has not equal roots, according as $f(x)$ and $f'(x)$ have or have not a common factor involving x.*

559. From the preceding article it follows that in order to obtain the equal roots of the equation $f(x) = 0$, we must first find the highest common factor of $f(x)$ and $f'(x)$.

Example 1. *Solve the equation* $x^4 - 11x^3 + 44x^2 - 76x + 48 = 0$, *which has equal roots.*

Here
$$f(x) = x^4 - 11x^3 + 44x^2 - 76x + 48,$$
$$f'(x) = 4x^3 - 33x^2 + 88x - 76;$$
and by the ordinary rule we find that the highest common factor of $f(x)$ and $f'(x)$ is $x - 2$; hence $(x - 2)^2$ is a factor of $f(x)$; and
$$f(x) = (x - 2)^2 (x^2 - 7x + 12)$$
$$= (x - 2)^2 (x - 3)(x - 4);$$
thus the roots are 2, 2, 3, 4.

Example 2. *Find the condition that the equation* $ax^3 + 3bx^2 + 3cx + d = 0$ *may have two roots equal.*

In this case the equations $f(x) = 0$, and $f'(x) = 0$, that is
$$ax^3 + 3bx^2 + 3cx + d = 0 \qquad \qquad \text{...(1)}$$
$$ax^2 + 2bx + c = 0 \qquad \qquad \text{...(2)}$$
must have a common root, and the condition required will be obtained by eliminating x between these two equations.

By combining (1) and (2), we have
$$bx^2 + 2cx + d = 0 \qquad \qquad \text{...(3)}$$
From (2) and (3), we obtain
$$\frac{x^2}{2(bd - c^2)} = \frac{x}{bc - ad} = \frac{1}{2(ac - b^2)};$$
thus the required condition is
$$(bc - ad)^2 = 4(ac - b^2)(bd - c^2).$$

560. We have seen that if the equation $f(x) = 0$ has r roots equal to a, the equation $f'(x) = 0$ has $r - 1$ roots equal to a. But $f''(x)$ is the first derived function of $f'(x)$; hence the equation $f''(x) = 0$ must have

$r - 2$ roots equal to a; similarly the equation $f'''(x) = 0$ must have $r - 3$ roots equal to a; and so on. These considerations will sometimes enable us to discover the equal roots of $f(x) = 0$ with less trouble than the method of Art. 559.

561. *If $a, b, c, \ldots k$ are the roots of the equation $f(x) = 0$, to prove that*

$$f'(x) = \frac{f(x)}{x-a} + \frac{f(x)}{x-b} + \frac{f(x)}{x-c} + \ldots + \frac{f(x)}{x-k}.$$

We have $f(x) = (x - a)(x - b)(x - c) \ldots (x - k)$;

writing $x + h$ in the place of x,

$$f(x + h) = (x - a + h)(x - b + h)(x - c + h) \ldots (x - k + h) \qquad \ldots(1)$$

But $f(x + h) = f(x) + hf'(x) + \dfrac{h^2}{2!} f''(x) + \ldots$;

hence $f'(x)$ is equal to the coefficient of h in the right-hand member of (1); therefore, as in Art. 163,

$$f'(x) = (x - b)(x - c) \ldots (x - k) + (x - a)(x - c) \ldots (x - k) + \ldots;$$

that is, $\quad f'(x) = \dfrac{f(x)}{x-a} + \dfrac{f(x)}{x-b} + \dfrac{f(x)}{x-c} + \ldots + \dfrac{f(x)}{x-k}$

562. The result of the preceding article enables us very easily to find the sum of an assigned power of the roots of an equation.

Example : *If S_k denote the sum of the kth powers of the roots of the equation $x^5 + px^4 + qx^2 + t = 0$, find the value of S_4, S_6 and S_{-4}.*

let $\qquad\qquad\qquad f(x) = x^5 + px^4 + qx^2 + t$;

then $\qquad\qquad\qquad f'(x) = 5x^4 + 4px^3 + 2qx.$

Now $\dfrac{f(x)}{x-a} = x^4 + (a + p) x^3 + (a^2 + ap) x^2 + (a^3 + a^2 p + q) x + a^4 + a^3 p + aq$;

and similar expressions hold for

$$\frac{f(x)}{x-b}, \frac{f(x)}{x-c}, \frac{f(x)}{x-d}, \frac{f(x)}{x-e}$$

Hence by addition,

$$5x^4 + 4px^3 + 2qx = 5x^4 + (S_1 + 5p) x^3 + (S_2 + pS_1) x^2$$
$$+ (S_3 + pS_2 + 5q) x + (S_4 + pS_3 + qS_1).$$

By equating coefficients,

$$\begin{aligned}
S_1 + 5p &= 4p, & \text{whence } S_1 &= -p; \\
S_2 + pS_1 &= 0, & \text{whence } S_2 &= p^2; \\
S_3 + pS_2 + 5q &= 2q, & \text{whence } S_3 &= -p^3 - 3q; \\
S_4 + pS_3 + qS_1 &= 0, & \text{whence } S_4 &= p^4 + 4pq.
\end{aligned}$$

To find the value of S_k for other values of k, we proceed as follows.

Multiplying the given equation by x^{k-5}

$$x^k + px^{k-1} + qx^{k-3} + tx^{k-5} = 0.$$

Substituting for x in succession the values a, b, c, d, e and adding the results, we obtain $S_k + pS_{k-1} + qS_{k-3} + tS_{k-5} = 0$.

Put $k = 5$; thus $S_5 + pS_4 + qS_2 + 5t = 0$,

whence $S_5 = -p^5 - 5p^2q - 5t$.

Put $k = 6$; thus $S_6 + pS_5 + qS_3 + tS_1 = 0$,

whence $S_6 = p^6 + 6p^3q + 3q^2 + 6pt$.

To find S_{-4}, put $k = 4, 3, 2, 1$ in succession; then

$S_4 + pS_3 + qS_1 + tS_{-1} = 0$,   whence $S_{-1} = 0$;

$S_3 + pS_2 + 5q + tS_{-2} = 0$,   whence $S_{-2} = -\dfrac{2q}{t}$;

$S_2 + pS_1 + qS_{-1} + tS_{-3} = 0$,   whence $S_{-3} = 0$;

$S_1 + 5p + qS_{-2} + tS_{-4} = 0$,   whence $S_{-4} = \dfrac{2q^2}{t^2} - \dfrac{4p}{t}$.

563.   When the coefficients are numerical we may also proceed as in the following example.

Example : *Find the sum of the fourth powers of the roots of*

$$x^3 - 2x^2 + x - 1 = 0.$$

Here $f(x) = x^3 - 2x^2 + x - 1$,

$f'(x) = 3x^2 - 4x + 1$.

Also $\dfrac{f'(x)}{f(x)} = \dfrac{1}{x-a} + \dfrac{1}{x-b} + \dfrac{1}{x-c}$

$= \Sigma \left(\dfrac{1}{x} + \dfrac{a}{x^2} + \dfrac{a^2}{x^3} + \dfrac{a^3}{x^4} + \ldots \right)$

$= \dfrac{3}{x} + \dfrac{S_1}{x^2} + \dfrac{S_2}{x^3} + \dfrac{S_3}{x^4} + \ldots;$

hence S_4 is equal to the coefficient of $\dfrac{1}{x^5}$ in the quotient of $f'(x)$ by $f(x)$, which is very conveniently obtained by the method of synthetic division as follows :

$$
\begin{array}{r|l}
1 & 3 - 4 + 1 \\
2 & \quad\ 6 - 3 + 3 \\
-1 & \qquad\ 4 - 2 + 2 \\
1 & \qquad\qquad 4 - 2 + 2 \\
& \qquad\qquad\quad 10 - 5 + 5 \\
\hline
& 3 + 2 + 2 + 5 + 10 + \ldots
\end{array}
$$

Hence the quotient is $\dfrac{3}{x} + \dfrac{2}{x^2} + \dfrac{2}{x^3} + \dfrac{5}{x^4} + \dfrac{10}{x^5} + \ldots;$ thus $S_4 = 10$.

EXAMPLES XXXV. c.

1. If $f(x) = x^4 + 10x^3 + 39x^2 + 76x + 65$, find the value of $f(x-4)$.

2. If $f(x) = x^4 - 12x^3 + 17x^2 - 9x + 7$, find the value of $f(x+3)$.

3. If $f(x) = 2x^4 - 13x^2 + 10x - 19$, find the value of $f(x+1)$.

4. If $f(x) = x^4 + 16x^3 + 72x^2 + 64x - 129$, find the value of $f(x-4)$.

5. If $f(x) = ax^8 + bx^5 + cx + d$, find the value of $f(x+h) - f(x-h)$.

6. Shew that the equation $10x^3 - 17x^2 + x + 6 = 0$ has a root between 0 and -1.

7. Shew that the equation $x^4 - 5x^3 + 3x^2 + 35x - 70 = 0$ has a root between 2 and 3 and one between -2 and -3

8. Shew that the equation $x^4 - 12x^2 + 12x - 3 = 0$ has a root between -3 and -4 and another between 2 and 3.

9. Shew that $x^5 + 5x^4 - 20x^2 - 19x - 2 = 0$ has a root between 2 and 3, and a root between -4 and -5.

Solve the following equations which have equal roots :

10. $x^4 - 9x^2 + 4x + 12 = 0$.

11. $x^4 - 6x^3 + 12x^2 - 10x + 3 = 0$.

12. $x^5 - 13x^4 + 67x^3 - 171x^2 + 216x - 108 = 0$

13. $x^5 - x^3 + 4x^2 - 3x + 2 = 0$.

14. $8x^4 + 4x^3 - 18x^2 + 11x - 2 = 0$.

15. $x^6 - 3x^5 + 6x^3 - 3x^2 - 3x + 2 = 0$.

16. $x^6 - 2x^5 - 4x^4 + 12x^3 - 3x^2 - 18x + 18 = 0$.

17. $x^4 - (a+b)x^3 - a(a-b)x^2 + a^2(a+b)x - a^3b = 0$.

Find the solution of the following equations which have common roots :

18. $2x^4 - 2x^3 + x^2 + 3x - 6 = 0, 4x^4 - 2x^3 + 3x - 9 = 0$

19. $4x^4 + 12x^3 - x^2 - 15x = 0, 6x^4 + 13x^3 - 4x^2 - 15x = 0$.

20. Find the condition that $x^n - px^2 + r = 0$ may have equal roots.

21. Shew that $x^4 + qx^2 + s = 0$ cannot have three equal roots.

22. Find the ratio of b to a in order that the equations
$$ax^2 + bx + a = 0 \quad \text{and} \quad x^3 - 2x^2 + 2x - 1 = 0$$
may have (1) one, (2) two roots in common.

23. Shew that the equation
$$x^n + nx^{n-1} + n(n-1)x^{n-2} + \ldots + n! = 0$$
cannot have equal roots.

24. If the equation $x^5 - 10a^3x^2 + b^4x + c^5 = 0$ has three equal roots, shew that $ab^4 - 9a^5 + c^5 = 0$.

25. If the equation $x^4 + ax^3 + bx^2 + cx + d = 0$ has three equal roots, shew that each of them is equal to $\dfrac{6c - ab}{3a^2 - 8b}$.

26. If $x^5 + qx^3 + rx^2 + t = 0$ has two equal roots, prove that one of them will be a root of the quadratic
$$15rx^2 - 6q^2x + 25t - 4qr = 0$$

27. In the equation $x^3 - x - 1 = 0$, find the value of S_6.

28. In the equation $x^4 - x^3 - 7x^2 + x + 6 = 0$, find the values of S_4 and S_6.

TRANSFORMATION OF EQUATIONS

564. The discussion of an equation is sometimes simplified by transforming it into another equation whose roots bear some assigned relation to those of the one proposed. Such transformations are especially useful in the solution of cubic equations.

565. *To transform an equation into another whose roots are those of the proposed equation with contrary signs.*

Let $f(x) = 0$ be the proposed equation.

Put $-y$ for x; then the equation $f(-y) = 0$ is satisfied by every root of $f(x) = 0$ with its sign changed; thus the required equation is $f(-y) = 0$.

If the proposed equation is
$$p_0x^n + p_1x^{n-1} + p_2x^{n-2} + \ldots + p_{n-1}x + p_n = 0,$$
then it is evident that the required equation will be
$$p_0y^n - p_1y^{n-1} + p_2y^{n-2} - \ldots + (-1)^{n-1}p_{n-1}y + (-1)^np_n = 0,$$
which is obtained from the original equation by *changing the sign of every alternate term beginning with the second.*

566. *To transform an equation into another whose roots are equal to those of the proposed equation multiplied by a given quantity.*

Let $f(x) = 0$ be the proposed equation, and let q denote the given quantity. Put $y = qx$, so that $x = \dfrac{y}{q}$, then the required equation is $f\left(\dfrac{y}{q}\right) = 0$.

The chief use of this transformation is to clear an equation of fractional coefficients.

Example : *Remove fractional coefficients from the equation*

$$2x^3 - \frac{3}{2}x^2 - \frac{1}{8}x + \frac{3}{16} = 0.$$

Put $x = \dfrac{y}{q}$ and multiply each term by q^3; thus

$$2y^3 - \frac{3}{2}qy^2 - \frac{1}{8}q^2 y + \frac{3}{16}q^3 = 0.$$

By putting $q = 4$ all the terms become integral, and on dividing by 2, we obtain

$$y^3 - 3y^2 - y + 6 = 0.$$

567. *To transform an equation into another whose roots are the reciprocals of the roots of the proposed equation.*

Let $f(x) = 0$ be the proposed equation; put $y = \dfrac{1}{x}$, so that $x = \dfrac{1}{y}$; then the required equation is $f\left(\dfrac{1}{y}\right) = 0$.

One of the chief uses of this transformation is to obtain the values of expressions which involve symmetrical functions of negative powers of the roots.

Example 1. *If a, b, c are the roots of the equation*

$$x^3 - px^2 + qx - r = 0.$$

find the value of $\dfrac{1}{a^2} + \dfrac{1}{b^2} + \dfrac{1}{c^2}$.

Write $\dfrac{1}{y}$ for x, multiply by y^3, and change all the signs; then the resulting equation $ry^3 - qy^2 + py - 1 = 0$,

has for its roots

$$\frac{1}{a}, \frac{1}{b}, \frac{1}{c},$$

hence

$$\Sigma \frac{1}{a} = \frac{q}{r}, \quad \Sigma \frac{1}{ab} = \frac{p}{r};$$

$\therefore$

$$\Sigma \frac{1}{a^2} = \frac{q^2 - 2pr}{r^2}.$$

Example 2. *If a, b, c are the roots of*

$$x^3 + 2x^2 - 3x - 1 = 0,$$

find the value of $a^{-3} + b^{-3} + c^{-3}$.

Writing $\dfrac{1}{y}$ for x, the transformed equation is

$$y^3 + 3y^2 - 2y - 1 = 0;$$

and the given expression is equal to the value of S_3 in this equation.

Here $S_1 = -3$;

$$S_2 = (-3)^2 - 2(-2) = 13;$$

and $\quad S_3 + 3S_2 - 2S_1 - 3 = 0;$

whence we obtain $S_3 = -42$.

568. If an equation is unaltered by changing x into $\dfrac{1}{x}$, it is called a *reciprocal equation.*

If the given equation is

$$x^n + p_1 x^{n-1} + p_2 x^{n-2} + \ldots + p_{n-2} x^2 + p_{n-1} x + p_n = 0,$$

the equation obtained by writing $\dfrac{1}{x}$ for x, and clearing of fractions is

$$p_n x^n + p_{n-1} x^{n-1} + p_{n-2} x^{n-2} + \ldots + p_2 x^2 + p_1 x + 1 = 0$$

If these two equations are the same, we must have

$$p_1 = \frac{p_{n-1}}{p_n}, \ p_2 = \frac{p_{n-2}}{p_n}, \ \ldots, \ p_{n-2} = \frac{p_2}{p_n}, \ p_{n-1} = \frac{p_1}{p_n}, \ p_n = \frac{1}{p_n};$$

from the last result we have $p_n = -1$, and thus we have two classes of reciprocal equations.

(i) If $p_n = 1$, then

$$p_1 = p_{n-1}, \ p_2 = p_{n-2}, \ p_3 = p_{n-3}, \ \ldots;$$

that is, the coefficients of terms equidistant from the beginning and end are equal.

(ii) If $p_n = -1$, then

$$p_1 = -p_{n-1}, \ p_2 = -p_{n-2}, \ p_3 = -p_{n-3}, \ \ldots;$$

hence if the equation is of $2m$ dimensions $p_m = -p_m$, or $p_m = 0$. In this case the coefficients of terms equidistant from the beginning and end are equal in magnitude and opposite in sign, and if the equation is of an even degree the middle term is wanting.

569. Suppose that $f(x) = 0$ is a reciprocal equation.

If $f(x) = 0$ is of the first class and of an odd degree it has a root -1; so that $f(x)$ is divisible by $x + 1$. If $\phi(x)$ is the quotient, then $\phi(x) = 0$ is a reciprocal equation of the first class and of an even degree.

If $f(x) = 0$ is of the second class and of an odd degree, it has a root $+1$; in this case $f(x)$ is divisible by $x - 1$, and as before $\phi(x) = 0$ is a reciprocal equation of the first class and of an even degree.

If $f(x) = 0$ is of the second class and of an even degree, it has a root $+1$ and a root -1; in this case $f(x)$ is divisible by $x^2 - 1$, and as before $\phi(x) = 0$ is a reciprocal equation of the first class and of an even degree.

Hence *any reciprocal equation is of an even degree with its last term positive, or can be reduced to this form;* which may therefore be considered as the standard form of reciprocal equations.

570. *A reciprocal equation of the standard form can be reduced to an equation of half its dimensions.*

Let the equation be

$$ax^{2m} + bx^{2m-1} + cx^{2m-2} + \ldots + kx^{m} + \ldots + cx^2 + bx + a = 0;$$

dividing by x^m and rearranging the terms, we have

$$a\left(x^m + \frac{1}{x^m}\right) + b\left(x^{m-1} + \frac{1}{x^{m-1}}\right) + c\left(x^{m-2} + \frac{1}{x^{m-2}}\right) + \ldots + k = 0.$$

Now $x^{p+1} + \dfrac{1}{x^{p+1}} = \left(x^p + \dfrac{1}{x^p}\right)\left(x + \dfrac{1}{x}\right) - \left(x^{p-1} + \dfrac{1}{x^{p-1}}\right);$

hence writing z for $x + \dfrac{1}{x}$, and giving to p in succession the values 1, 2, 3, ... we obtain

$$x^2 + \frac{1}{x^2} = z^2 - 2,$$

$$x^3 + \frac{1}{x^3} = z(z^2 - 2) - z = z^3 - 3z;$$

$$x^4 + \frac{1}{x^4} = z(z^3 - 3z) - (z^2 - 2) = z^4 - 4z^2 + 2;$$

and so on; and generally $x^m + \dfrac{1}{x^m}$ is of m dimensions in z, and therefore the equation in z is of m dimensions.

571. *To find the equation whose roots are the squares of those of a proposed equation.*

Let $f(x) = 0$ be the given equation; putting $y = x^2$, we have $x = \sqrt{y}$; hence the required equation is $f(\sqrt{y}) = 0$.

Example : *Find the equation whose roots are the squares of those of the equation*
$$x^3 + p_1 x^2 + p_2 x + p_3 = 0.$$

Putting $x = \sqrt{y}$, and transposing, we have
$$(y + p_2)\sqrt{y} = -(p_1 y + p_3);$$

whence $\qquad (y^2 + 2p_2 y + p_2^2)\, y = p_1^2 y^2 + 2p_1 p_3 y + p_3^2,$

or $\qquad y^3 + (2p_2 - p_1^2)\, y^2 + (p_2^2 - 2p_1 p_3)\, y - p_3^2 = 0.$

Compare the solution given in Ex. 2, Art. 539.

572. *To transform an equation into another whose roots exceed those of the proposed equation by a given quantity.*

Let $f(x) = 0$ be the proposed equation, and let h be the given quantity; put $y = x + h$, so that $x = y - h$; then the required equation is $f(y - h) = 0$.

Similarly $f(y + h) = 0$ is an equation whose roots are less by h than those of $f(x) = 0$.

Example : *Find the equation whose roots exceed by 2 the roots of the equation*
$$4x^4 + 32x^3 + 83x^2 + 76x + 21 = 0.$$

The required equation will be obtained by substituting $x - 2$ for x in the proposed equation; hence in Horner's process we employ $x + 2$ as divisor, and the calculation is performed as follows :

4	32	83	76	21
4	24	35	6	9
4	16	3	0	
4	8	-13		
4	0			
4				

Thus the transformed equation is
$$4x^4 - 13x^2 + 9 = 0, \quad \text{or} \quad (4x^2 - 9)(x^2 - 1) = 0.$$

The roots of this equation are $+\dfrac{3}{2}, -\dfrac{3}{2}, +1, -1$; hence the roots of the proposed equation are
$$-\frac{1}{2}, -\frac{7}{2}, -1, -3.$$

573. The chief use of the substitution in the preceding article is to remove some assigned term from an equation.

Let the given equation be
$$p_0 x^n + p_1 x^{n-1} + p_2 x^{n-2} + \ldots + p_{n-1} x + p_n = 0;$$

then if $y = x - h$, we obtain the new equation
$$p_0 (y + h)^n + p_1 (y + h)^{n-1} + p_2 (y + h)^{n-2} + \ldots + p_n = 0,$$

which, when arranged in descending powers of y, becomes

$$p_0 y^n + (np_0 h + p_1) y^{n-1} + \left\{ \frac{n(n-1)}{2!} p_0 h^2 + (n-1) p_1 h + p_2 \right\} y^{n-2} + \ldots = 0.$$

If the term to be removed is the second, we put $np_0 h + p_1 = 0$, so that $h = -\dfrac{p_1}{np_0}$; if the term to be removed is the third we put

$$\frac{n(n-1)}{2!} p_0 h^2 + (n-1) p_1 h + p_2 = 0,$$

and so obtain a quadratic to find h; and similarly we may remove any other assigned term.

Sometimes it will be more convenient to proceed as in the following example.

Example : *Remove the second term from the equation*

$$px^3 + qx^2 + rx + s = 0.$$

Let α, β, γ be the roots, so that $\alpha + \beta + \gamma = -\dfrac{q}{p}$. Then if we increase each of the roots by $\dfrac{q}{3p}$, in the transformed equation the sum of the roots will be equal to $-\dfrac{q}{p} + \dfrac{q}{p}$; that is, the coefficient of the second term will be zero.

Hence the required transformation will be effected by substituting $x - \dfrac{q}{3p}$ for x in the given equation.

574. From the equation $f(x) = 0$ we may form an equation whose roots are connected with those of the given equation by some assigned relation.

Let y be a root of the required equation and let $\phi(x, y) = 0$ denote the assigned relation; then the transformed equation can be obtained either by expressing x as a function of y by means of the equation $\phi(x, y) = 0$ and substituting this value of x in $f(x) = 0$; or by eliminating x between the equations $f(x) = 0$ and $\phi(x, y) = 0$.

Example 1. *If a, b, c are the roots of the equation $x^3 + px^2 + qx + r = 0$, form the equation whose roots are*

$$a - \frac{1}{bc},\ b - \frac{1}{ca},\ c - \frac{1}{ab}.$$

When $x = a$ in the given equation $y = a - \dfrac{1}{bc}$ in the transformed equation; but

$$a - \frac{1}{bc} = a - \frac{a}{abc} = a + \frac{a}{r};$$

and therefore the transformed equation will be obtained by the substitution

$$y = x + \frac{x}{r}, \quad \text{or} \quad x = \frac{ry}{1+r};$$

thus the required equation is

$$r^2 y^3 + pr(1+r)y^2 + q(1+r)^2 y + (1+r)^3 = 0.$$

Example 2. *Form the equation whose roots are the squares of the differences of the roots of the cubic*

$$x^3 + qx + r = 0.$$

Let a, b, c be the roots of the cubic; then the roots of the required equation are $(b-c)^2$, $(c-a)^2$, $(a-b)^2$.

Now
$$(b-c)^2 = b^2 + c^2 - 2bc = a^2 + b^2 + c^2 - a^2 - \frac{2abc}{a}$$

$$= (a+b+c)^2 - 2(bc+ca+ab) - a^2 - \frac{2abc}{a}$$

$$= -2q - a^2 + \frac{2r}{a};$$

also when $x = a$ in the given equation, $y = (b-c)^2$ in the transformed equation;

$$\therefore \qquad y = -2q - x^2 + \frac{2r}{x}.$$

Thus we have to eliminate x between the equations

$$x^3 + qx + r = 0,$$

and
$$x^3 + (2q+y)x - 2r = 0$$

By subtraction $(q+y)x = 3r$; or $x = \dfrac{3r}{q+y}.$

Substituting and reducing, we obtain

$$y^3 + 6qy^2 + 9q^2 y + 27r^2 + 4q^3 = 0.$$

Cor : If a, b, c are real, $(b-c)^2$, $(c-a)^2$, $(a-b)^2$ are all positive; therefore $27r^2 + 4q^3$ is negative.

Hence in order that the equation $x^3 + qx + r = 0$ may have all its roots real $27r^2 + 4q^3$ must be negative, that is $\left(\dfrac{r}{2}\right)^2 + \left(\dfrac{q}{3}\right)^3$ must be negative.

If $27r^2 + 4q^3 = 0$ the transformed equation has one root zero, therefore the original equation has two equal roots.

If $27r^2 + 4q^3$ is positive, the transformed equation has a negative root [Art. 553], therefore the original equation must have two imaginary roots, since it is only such a pair of roots which can produce a negative root in the transformed equation.

EXAMPLES XXXV. d.

1. Transform the equation $x^3 - 4x^2 + \frac{1}{4}x - \frac{1}{9} = 0$ into anoth with integral coefficients, and unity for the coefficient of the first term.

2. Transform the equation $3x^4 - 5x^3 + x^2 - x + 1 = 0$ into another the coefficient of whose first term is unity.

Solve the equations :

3. $2x^4 + x^3 - 6x^2 + x + 2 = 0$.

4. $x^4 - 10x^3 + 26x^2 - 10x + 1 = 0$.

5. $x^5 - 5x^4 + 9x^3 - 9x^2 + 5x - 1 = 0$.

6. $4x^6 - 24x^5 + 57x^4 - 73x^3 + 57x^2 - 24x + 4 = 0$.

7. Solve the equation $3x^3 - 22x^2 + 48x - 32 = 0$, the roots of which are in harmonical progression.

8. The roots of $x^3 - 11x^2 + 36x - 36 = 0$ are in harmonical progression; find them.

9. If the roots of the equation $x^3 - ax^2 + x - b = 0$ are in harmonical progression, shew that the mean root is $3b$.

10. Solve the equation $40x^4 - 22x^3 - 21x^2 + 2x + 1 = 0$, the roots of which are in harmonical progression.

Remove the second term from the equations :

11. $x^3 - 6x^2 + 10x - 3 = 0$.

12. $x^4 + 4x^3 + 2x^2 - 4x - 2 = 0$.

13. $x^5 + 5x^4 + 3x^3 + x^2 + x - 1 = 0$

14. $x^6 - 12x^5 + 3x^2 - 17x + 300 = 0$

15. Transform the equation $x^3 - \frac{x}{4} - \frac{3}{4} = 0$ into one whose roots exceed by $\frac{3}{2}$ the corresponding roots of the given equation.

16. Diminish by 3 the roots of the equation
$$x^5 - 4x^4 + 3x^2 - 4x + 6 = 0.$$

17. Find the equation each of whose roots is greater by unity than a root of the equation $x^3 - 5x^2 + 6x - 3 = 0$.

18. Find the equation whose roots are the squares of the roots of
$$x^4 + x^3 + 2x^2 + x + 1 = 0.$$

19. Form the equation whose roots are the cubes of the roots of
$$x^3 + 3x^2 + 2 = 0.$$

If a, b, c are the roots of $x^3 + qx + r = 0$, form the equation whose roots are

20. $ka^{-1}, kb^{-1}, kc^{-1}$.

21. b^2c^2, c^2a^2, a^2b^2.

22. $\dfrac{b+c}{a^2}, \dfrac{c+a}{b^2}, \dfrac{a+b}{c^2}$.

23. $bc + \dfrac{1}{a}, ca + \dfrac{1}{b}, ab + \dfrac{1}{c}$.

24. $a(b+c), b(c+a), c(a+b)$.

25. a^3, b^3, c^3.

26. $\dfrac{b}{c} + \dfrac{c}{b}, \dfrac{c}{a} + \dfrac{a}{c}, \dfrac{a}{b} + \dfrac{b}{a}$.

27. Shew that the cubes of the roots of $x^3 + ax^2 + bx + ab = 0$ are given by the equation $x^3 + a^3x^2 + b^3x + a^3b^3 = 0$.

28. Solve the equation $x^5 - 5x^4 - 5x^3 + 25x^2 + 4x - 20 = 0$, whose roots are of the form $a, -a, b, -b, c$.

29. If the roots of $x^3 + 3px^2 + 3qx + r = 0$ are in harmonical progression, shew that $2q^3 = r(3pq - r)$.

CUBIC EQUATIONS

575. The general type of a cubic equation is
$$x^3 + Px^2 + Qx + R = 0,$$
but as explained in Art. 573 this equation can be reduced to the simpler form $x^3 + qx + r = 0$,
which we shall take as the standard form of a cubic equation.

576. To solve the equation $x^3 + qx + r = 0$.

Let $x = y + z$; then
$$x^3 = y^3 + z^3 + 3yz(y + z) = y^3 + z^3 + 3yzx,$$
and the given equation becomes
$$y^3 + z^3 + (3yz + q)x + r = 0.$$

At present y, z are any two quantities subject to the condition that their sum is equal to one of the roots of the given equation; if we further suppose that they satisfy the equation $3yz + q = 0$, they are completely determinate. We thus obtain

$$y^3 + z^3 = -r, \quad y^3 z^3 = -\frac{q^3}{27};$$

hence y^3, z^3 are the roots of the quadratic

$$t^2 + rt - \frac{q^3}{27} = 0.$$

Solving this equation, and putting

$$y^3 = -\frac{r}{2} + \sqrt{\frac{r^2}{4} + \frac{q^3}{27}} \qquad \text{...(1)}$$

$$z^3 = -\frac{r}{2} - \sqrt{\frac{r^2}{4} + \frac{q^3}{27}} \qquad \text{...(2)}$$

we obtain the value of x from the relation $x = y + z$; thus

$$x = \left\{ -\frac{r}{2} + \sqrt{\frac{r^2}{4} + \frac{q^3}{27}} \right\}^{\frac{1}{3}} + \left\{ -\frac{r}{2} - \sqrt{\frac{r^2}{4} + \frac{q^3}{27}} \right\}^{\frac{1}{3}}.$$

The above solution is generally known as *Cardan's Solution*, as it was first published by him in the *Ars Magna*, in 1545. Cardan obtained the solution from Tartaglia; but the solution of the cubic seems to have been due originally to Scipio Ferreo, about 1505. An interesting historical note on this subject will be found at the end of Burnside and Panton's *Theory of Equations*.

577. By Art. 110, each of the quantities on the right-hand side of equations (1) and (2) of the preceding article has three cube roots, hence it would appear that x has *nine* values; this, however, is not the case. For since $yz = -\dfrac{q}{3}$, the cube roots are to be taken in pairs so that the product of each pair is rational. Hence if y, z denote the values of any pair of cube roots which fulfil this condition, the only other admissible pairs will be ωy, $\omega^2 z$ and $\omega^2 y$, ωz, where ω, ω^2 are the imaginary cube roots of unity. Hence the roots of the equation are

$$y + z, \quad \omega y + \omega^2 z, \quad \omega^2 y + \omega z.$$

Example : *Solve the equation* $x^3 - 15x = 126$.

Put $y + z$ for x, then

$$y^3 + z^3 + (3yz - 15) x = 126;$$

put $\qquad\qquad 3yz - 15 = 0$

then $\qquad\qquad y^3 + z^3 = 126;$

also $\qquad\qquad y^3 z^3 = 125,$

hence y^3, z^3 are the roots of the equation

$$t^2 - 126t + 125 = 0;$$

$\therefore\qquad\qquad y^3 = 125, z^3 = 1;$

$\therefore\qquad\qquad y = 5, z = 1.$

Thus $y + z = 5 + 1 = 6;$

$$\omega y + \omega^2 z = \frac{-1 + \sqrt{-3}}{2} \cdot 5 + \frac{-1 - \sqrt{-3}}{2}$$

$$= -3 + 2\sqrt{-3};$$

$$\omega^2 y + \omega z = -3 - 2\sqrt{-3};$$

and the roots are $6, -3 + 2\sqrt{-3}, -3 - 2\sqrt{-3}.$

578. To explain the reason why we apparently obtain *nine* values for x in Art. 576, we observe that y and z are to be found from the equations $y^3 + z^3 + r = 0$, $yz = -\dfrac{q}{3}$; but in the process of solution the second of these was changed into $y^3 z^3 = -\dfrac{q^3}{27}$, which would also hold if $yz = -\dfrac{\omega q}{3}$, or $yz = -\dfrac{\omega^2 q}{3}$; hence the other six values of x are solutions of the cubics

$$x^3 + \omega q x + r = 0, \quad x^3 + \omega^2 q x + r = 0.$$

579. We proceed to consider more fully the roots of the equation $x^3 + qx + r = 0.$

(i) If $\dfrac{r^2}{4} + \dfrac{q^3}{27}$ is positive, then y^3 and z^3 are both real; let y and z represent their arithmetical cube roots, then the roots are $y + z, \omega y + \omega^2 z, \omega^2 y + \omega z.$

The first of these is real, and by substituting for ω and ω^2 the other two become

$$-\frac{y+z}{2} + \frac{y-z}{2}\sqrt{-3}, \quad -\frac{y+z}{2} - \frac{y-z}{2}\sqrt{-3}.$$

(ii) If $\dfrac{r^2}{4} + \dfrac{q^3}{27}$ is zero, then $y^3 = z^3$; in this case $y = z$, and the roots become $2y, y(\omega + \omega^2), y(\omega + \omega^2),$ or $2y, -y, -y.$

(iii) If $\dfrac{r^2}{4}+\dfrac{q^3}{27}$ is negative, then y^3 and z^3 are imaginary expressions of the form $a+ib$ and $a-ib$. Suppose that the cube roots of these quantities are $m+in$ and $m-in$; then the roots of the cubic become.

$$m+in+m-in, \qquad \text{or } 2m;$$
$$(m+in)\,\omega+(m-in)\,\omega^2, \qquad \text{or } -m-n\sqrt{3};$$
$$(m+in)\,\omega^2+(m-in)\,\omega, \qquad \text{or } -m+n\sqrt{3};$$

which are all real quantities. As however there is no general arithmetical or algebraical method of finding the exact value of the cube root of imaginary quantities [Compare Art. 89], the solution obtained in Art. 576 is of little practical use when the roots of the cubic are all real and unequal.

This case is sometimes called the *Irreducible Case* of Cardan's solution.

580. In the *irreducible case* just mentioned the solution may be completed by Trigonometry as follows. Let the solution be

$$x=(a+ib)^{\frac{1}{3}}+(a-ib)^{\frac{1}{3}};$$

put $a=r\cos\theta$, $b=r\sin\theta$, so that $r^2=a^2+b^2$, $\tan\theta=\dfrac{b}{a}$;

then $\qquad (a+ib)^{\frac{1}{3}}=\{r\,(\cos\theta+i\sin\theta)\}^{\frac{1}{3}}.$

Now by De Moivre's theorem the three values of this expression are

$$r^{\frac{1}{3}}\left(\cos\frac{\theta}{3}+i\sin\frac{\theta}{3}\right),\quad r^{\frac{1}{3}}\left(\cos\frac{\theta+2\pi}{3}+i\sin\frac{\theta+2\pi}{3}\right),$$

and $\qquad\qquad r^{\frac{1}{3}}\left(\cos\frac{\theta+4\pi}{3}+i\sin\frac{\theta+4\pi}{3}\right),$

where $r^{\frac{1}{3}}$ denotes the arithmetical cube root of r, and θ the smallest angle found from the equation $\tan\theta=\dfrac{b}{a}$.

The three values of $(a-ib)^{\frac{1}{3}}$ are obtained by changing the sign of i in the above results; hence the roots are

$$2r^{\frac{1}{3}}\cos\frac{\theta}{3},\; 2r^{\frac{1}{3}}\cos\frac{\theta+2\pi}{3},\; 2r^{\frac{1}{3}}\cos\frac{\theta+4\pi}{3}.$$

BIQUADRATIC EQUATIONS

581. We shall now give a brief discussion of some of the methods which are employed to obtain the general solution of a biquadratic equation. It will be found that in each of the methods we have first to solve an auxiliary cubic equation; and thus it will be seen that as in the case of the cubic, the general solution is not adapted for writing down the solution of a given numerical equation.

582. The solution of a biquadratic equation was first obtained by Ferrari, a pupil of Cardan, as follows.

Denote the equation by

$$x^4 + 2px^3 + qx^2 + 2rx + s = 0;$$

add to each side $(ax + b)^2$, the quantities a and b being determined so as to make the left side a perfect square; then

$$x^4 + 2px^3 + (q + a^2)\,x^2 + 2\,(r + ab)\,x + s + b^2 = (ax + b)^2.$$

Suppose that the left side of the equation is equal to $(x^2 + px + k)^2$; then by comparing the coefficients, we have

$$p^2 + 2k = q + a^2,\, pk = r + ab,\, k^2 = s + b^2;$$

by eliminating a and b from these equations, we obtain

$$(pk - r)^2 = (2k + p^2 - q)\,(k^2 - s),$$

or $2k^3 - qk^2 + 2\,(pr - s)\,k - p^2 s + qs - r^2 = 0.$

From this cubic equation one real value of k can always be found [Art. 553]; thus a and b are known. Also

$$(x^2 + px + k)^2 = (ax + b)^2;$$

∴ $x^2 + px + k = \pm\,(ax + b);$

and the values of x are to be obtained from the two quadratics

$$x^2 + (p - a)\,x + (k - b) = 0,$$

and $x^2 + (p + a)\,x + (k + b) = 0.$

Example : *Solve the equation*

$$x^4 - 2x^3 - 5x^2 + 10x - 3 = 0.$$

Add $a^2 x^2 + 2abx + b^2$ to each side of the equation, and assume

$$x^4 - 2x^3 + (a^2 - 5)\,x^2 + 2\,(ab + 5)\,x + b^2 - 3 = (x^2 - x + k)^2;$$

then by equating coefficients, we have

$$a^2 = 2k + 6,\, ab = -k - 5,\, b^2 = k^2 + 3;$$

∴ $(2k + 6)\,(k^2 + 3) = (k + 5)^2;$

∴ $2k^3 + 5k^2 - 4k - 7 = 0.$

By trial, we find that $k = -1$; hence $a^2 = 4,\, b^2 = 4,\, ab = -4.$

But from the assumption, it follows that

$$(x^2 - x + k)^2 = (ax + b)^2.$$

Substituting the values of k, a and b, we have the two equations

$$x^2 - x - 1 = \pm (2x - 2);$$

that is, $x^2 - 3x + 1 = 0$, and $x^2 + x - 3 = 0;$

whence the roots are $\dfrac{3 \pm \sqrt{5}}{2}, \dfrac{-1 \pm \sqrt{13}}{2}.$

583. The following solution was given by Descartes in 1637. Suppose that the biquadratic equation is reduced to the form

$$x^4 + qx^2 + rx + s = 0;$$

assume $x^4 + qx^2 + rx + s = (x^2 + kx + l)(x^2 - kx + m);$

then by equating coefficients, we have

$$l + m - k^2 = q, \quad k(m - l) = r, \quad lm = s.$$

From the first two of these equations, we obtain

$$2m = k^2 + q + \frac{r}{k}, \quad 2l = k^2 + q - \frac{r}{k};$$

hence substituting in the third equation,

$$(k^3 + qk + r)(k^3 + qk - r) = 4sk^2,$$

or $\qquad k^6 + 2qk^4 + (q^2 - 4s)k^2 - r^2 = 0.$

This is a cubic in k^2 which always has one real positive solution [Art. 553]; thus when k^2 is known the values of l and m are determined, and the solution of the biquadratic is obtained by solving the two quadratics

$$x^2 + kx + l = 0, \quad \text{and} \quad x^2 - kx + m = 0.$$

Example : *Solve the equation*

$$x^4 - 2x^2 + 8x - 3 = 0.$$

Assume $x^4 - 2x^2 + 8x - 3 = (x^2 + kx + l)(x^2 - kx + m);$

then by equating coefficients, we have

$$l + m - k^2 = -2, \quad k(m - l) = 8, \quad lm = -3;$$

whence we obtain $(k^3 - 2k + 8)(k^3 - 2k - 8) = -12k^2,$

or $\qquad k^6 - 4k^4 + 16k^2 - 64 = 0.$

This equation is clearly satisfied when $k^2 - 4 = 0$, or $k = \pm 2$. It will be sufficient to consider one of the values of k; putting $k = 2$, we have

$$m + l = 2, \quad m - l = 4; \text{ that is, } l = -1, m = 3.$$

Thus $\qquad x^4 - 2x^2 + 8x - 3 = (x^2 + 2x - 1)(x^2 - 2x + 3);$

hence $\qquad x^2 + 2x - 1 = 0, \quad \text{and} \quad x^2 - 2x + 3 = 0;$

and therefore the roots are $-1 \pm \sqrt{2}, 1 \pm \sqrt{-2}.$

584. The general algebraical solution of equations of a degree higher than the fourth has not been obtained, and Abel's demonstration of the impossibility of such a solution is generally accepted by Mathematicians. If, however, the coefficients of an equation are numerical, the value of any real root may be found to any required degree of accuracy by Horner's Method of approximation, a full account of which will be found in treatises on the *Theory of Equations*.

585. We shall conclude with the discussion of some miscellaneous equations.

Example 1. *Solve the equations :*

$$x + y + z + u = 0,$$
$$ax + by + cz + du = 0,$$
$$a^2x + b^2y + c^2z + d^2u = 0,$$
$$a^3x + b^3y + c^3z + d^3u = k.$$

Multiply these equations, beginning from the lowest, by $1, p, q, r$ respectively; p, q, r being quantities which are at present undetermined. Assume that they are such that the coefficients of y, z, u vanish; then

$$x (a^3 + pa^2 + qa + r) = k,$$

whilst b, c, d are the roots of the equation

$$t^3 + pt^2 + qt + r = 0.$$

Hence $a^3 + pa^2 + qa + r = (a - b) (a - c) (a - d);$

and therefore $(a - b) (a - c) (a - d) x = k.$

Thus the value x is found, and the values of y, z, u can be written down by symmetry.

Cor : If the equations are

$$x + y + z + u = 1,$$
$$ax + by + cz + du = k,$$
$$a^2x + b^2y + c^2z + d^2u = k^2,$$
$$a^3x + b^3y + c^3z + d^3u = k^3,$$

by proceeding as before, we have

$$x (a^3 + pa^2 + qa + r) = k^3 + pk^2 + qk + r;$$
$$\therefore \quad (a - b) (a - c) (a - d) x = (k - b) (k - c) (k - d).$$

Thus the value of x is found, and the values of y, z, u can be written down by symmetry.

The solution of the above equations has been facilitated by the use of *Undetermined Multipliers*.

Example 2. *Shew that the roots of the equation*

$$(x - a) (x - b) (x - c) - f^2 (x - a) - g^2 (x - b) - h^2 (x - c) + 2fgh = 0$$

are all real.

From the given equation, we have

$$(x - a) \{(x - b) (x - c) - f^2\} - \{g^2 (x - b) + h^2 (x - c) - 2fgh\} = 0.$$

Let p, q be the roots of the quadratic

$$(x - b) (x - c) - f^2 = 0,$$

and suppose p to be not less than q. By solving the quadratic, we have

$$2x = b + c \pm \sqrt{(b - c)^2 + 4f^2} \qquad \qquad \text{...(1)}$$

now the value of the surd is greater than $b \sim c$, so that p is greater than b or c, and q is less than b or c.

In the given equation substitute for x successively the values

$$+ \infty, \; p, \; q, \; - \infty;$$

the results are respectively

$$+ \infty, \; - (g \sqrt{p - b} - h \sqrt{p - c})^2, \; + (g \sqrt{b - q} - h \sqrt{c - q})^2, \; - \infty,$$

since $\qquad (p - b) (p - c) = f^2 = (b - q) (c - q).$

Thus the given equation has three real roots, one greater than p, one between p and q, and one less than q.

If $p = q$, then from (1) we have $(b - c)^2 + 4f^2 = 0$ and therefore $b = c, f = 0$. In this case the given equation becomes

$$(x - b) \{(x - a) (x - b) - g^2 - h^2\} = 0;$$

thus the roots are all real.

If p is a root of the given equation, the above investigation fails; for it only shews that there is *one* root between q and $+ \infty$, namely p. But as before, there is a second real root less than q; hence the third root must also be real. Similarly if q is a root of the given equation we can shew that all the roots are real.

The equation here discussed is of considerable importance; it occurs frequently in Solid Geometry, and is there known as the *Discriminating Cubic*.

586. The following system of equations occurs in many branches of Applied Mathematics.

Example : *Solve the equations* :

$$\frac{x}{a + \lambda} + \frac{y}{b + \lambda} + \frac{z}{c + \lambda} = 1,$$

$$\frac{x}{a + \mu} + \frac{y}{b + \mu} + \frac{z}{c + \mu} = 1,$$

$$\frac{x}{a + \nu} + \frac{y}{b + \nu} + \frac{z}{c + \nu} = 1.$$

Consider the following equation in θ,

$$\frac{x}{a + \theta} + \frac{y}{b + \theta} + \frac{z}{c + \theta} = 1 - \frac{(\theta - \lambda) (\theta - \mu) (\theta - \nu)}{(a + \theta) (b + \theta) (c + \theta)},$$

x, y, z being for the present regarded as known quantities.

This equation when cleared of fractions is of the *second degree* in θ, and is satisfied by the *three* values $\theta = \lambda, \theta = \mu, \theta = \nu$, in virtue of the given equations; hence it must be an identity. [Art. 310.]

To find the value of x, multiply up by $a + \theta$, and then put $a + \theta = 0$;

thus $\qquad x = -\dfrac{(-a - \lambda)(-a - \mu)(-a - \nu)}{(b - a)(c - a)}$;

that is, $\qquad x = \dfrac{(a + \lambda)(a + \mu)(a + \nu)}{(a - b)(a - c)}.$

By symmetry, we have

$$y = \frac{(b + \lambda)(b + \mu)(b + \nu)}{(b - c)(b - a)},$$

and $\qquad z = \dfrac{(c + \lambda)(c + \mu)(c + \nu)}{(c - a)(c - b)}.$

Examples XXXV. e.

Solve the following equations :

1. $x^3 - 18x = 35.$

2. $x^3 + 72x - 1720 = 0$

3. $x^3 + 63x - 316 = 0$

4. $x^3 + 21x + 342 = 0.$

5. $28x^3 - 9x^2 + 1 = 0.$

6. $x^3 - 15x^3 - 33x + 847 = 0.$

7. $2x^3 + 3x^2 + 3x + 1 = 0.$

8. Prove that the real root of the equation $x^3 + 12x - 12 = 0$ is $2\sqrt[3]{2} - \sqrt[3]{4}.$

Solve the following equations :

9. $x^4 - 3x^2 - 42x - 40 = 0.$

10. $x^4 - 10x^2 - 20x - 16 = 0.$

11. $x^4 + 8x^3 + 9x^2 - 8x - 10 = 0.$

12. $x^4 + 2x^3 - 7x^2 - 8x + 12 = 0.$

13. $x^4 - 3x^2 - 6x - 2 = 0.$

14. $x^4 - 2x^3 - 12x^2 + 10x + 3 = 0.$

15. $4x^4 - 20x^3 + 33x^2 - 20x + 4 = 0.$

16. $x^5 - 6x^4 - 17x^3 + 17x^2 + 6x - 1 = 0.$

17. $x^4 + 9x^3 + 12x^2 - 80x - 192 = 0$, which has equal roots.

18. Find the relation between q and r in order that the equation $x^3 + qx + r = 0$ may be put into the form $x^4 = (x^2 + ax + b)^2.$

Hence solve the equation $8x^3 - 36x + 27 = 0.$

19. If $x^3 + 3px^2 + 3qx + r$ and $x^2 + 2px + q$ have a common factor, shew that
$$4(p^2 - q)(q^2 - pr) - (pq - r)^2 = 0.$$
If they have two common factors, shew that
$$p^2 - q = 0, \ q^2 - pr = 0.$$

20. If the equation $ax^3 + 3bx^2 + 3cx + d = 0$ has two equal roots, shew that each of them is equal to $\dfrac{bc - ad}{2(ac - b^2)}$.

21. Shew that the equation $x^4 + px^3 + qx^2 + rx + s = 0$ may be solved as a quadratic if $r^2 = p^2 s$.

22. Solve the equation
$$x^6 - 18x^4 + 16x^3 + 28x^2 - 32x + 8 = 0 \text{ one of whose roots is}$$
$\sqrt{6} - 2$.

23. If α, β, γ, δ are the roots of the equation
$$x^4 + qx^2 + rx + s = 0,$$
find the equation whose roots are $\beta + \gamma + \delta + (\beta\gamma\delta)^{-1}$, & c.

24. In the equation $x^4 - px^3 + qx^2 - rx + s = 0$, prove that if the sum of two of the roots is equal to the sum of the other two $p^3 - 4pq + 8r = 0$; and that if the product of two of the roots is equal to the product of the other two $r^2 = p^2 s$.

25. The equation $x^5 - 209x + 56 = 0$ has two roots whose product is unity : determine them.

26. Find the two roots of $x^5 - 409x + 285 = 0$ whose sum is 5.

27. If $a, b, c, \ldots k$ are the roots of
$$x^n + p_1 x^{n-1} + p_2 x^{n-2} + \ldots + p_{n-1} x + p_n = 0,$$
shew that $(1 + a^2)(1 + b^2) \ldots (1 + k^2) = (1 - p_2 + p_4 - \ldots)^2$
$$+ (p_1 - p_3 + p_5 - \ldots)^2.$$

28. The sum of two roots of the equation
$$x^4 - 8x^3 + 21x^2 - 20x + 5 = 0$$
is 4; explain why on attempting to solve the equation from the knowledge of this fact the method fails.

MISCELLANEOUS EXAMPLES

1. If s_1, s_2, s_3 are the sums of $n, 2n, 3n$ terms respectively of an arithmetical progression, shew that $s_3 = 3 (s_2 - s_1)$.

2. Find two numbers such that their difference, sum and product, are to one another as 1, 7, 24.

3. In what scale of notation is 25 doubled by reversing the digits ?

4. Solve the equations :
   (1) $(x + 2) (x + 3) (x - 4) (x - 5) = 44$.
   (2) $x (y + z) + 2 = 0,\ y (z - 2x) + 21 = 0,\ z (2x - y) = 5$.

5. In an A.P., of which a is the first term, if the sum of the first p terms $= 0$, shew that the sum of the next q terms
   $$= -\frac{a (p + q) q}{p - 1}.$$
   [R.M.A. Woolwich.]

6. Solve the equations :
   (1) $(a + b) (ax + b) (a - bx) = (a^2 x - b^2) (a + bx)$.
   (2) $x^{\frac{1}{3}} + (2x - 3)^{\frac{1}{3}} = \{12 (x - 1)\}^{\frac{1}{3}}$.   [India Civil Service.]

7. Find an arithmetical progression whose first term is unity such that the second, tenth and thirty-fourth terms form a geometric series.

8. If α, β are the roots of $x^2 + px + q = 0$, find the values of
   $$\alpha^2 + \alpha\beta + \beta^2,\ \alpha^3 + \beta^3,\ \alpha^4 + \alpha^2\beta^2 + \beta^4.$$

9. If $2x = a + a^{-1}$ and $2y = b + b^{-1}$, find the value of
   $$xy + \sqrt{(x^2 - 1) (y^2 - 1)}.$$

10. Find the value of $\dfrac{(4 + \sqrt{15})^{\frac{3}{2}} + (4 - \sqrt{15})^{\frac{3}{2}}}{(6 + \sqrt{35})^{\frac{3}{2}} - (6 - \sqrt{35})^{\frac{3}{2}}}$. [R.M.A. Woolwich.]

11. If α and β are the imaginary cube roots of unity, shew that
    $$\alpha^4 + \beta^4 + a^{-1}\beta^{-1} = 0.$$

12. Shew that in any scale, whose radix is greater than 4, the number 12432 is divisible by 111 and also by 112.

13. A and B run a mile race. In the first heat A gives B a start of 11 yards and beats him by 57 seconds; in the second heat A gives B a start of 81 seconds and is beaten by 88 yards : in what time could each run a mile ?

14. Eliminate x, y, z between the equations :
$$x^2 - yz = a^2,\ y^2 - zx = b^2,\ z^2 - xy = c^2,\ x + y + z = 0.$$
[R.M.A. Woolwich.]

15. Solve the equations :
$$ax^2 + bxy + cy^2 = bx^2 + cxy + ay^2 = d.$$
[Math. Tripos.]

16. A waterman rows to a place 48 miles distant and back in 14 hours : he finds that he can row 4 miles with the stream in the same time as 3 miles against the stream : find the rate of the stream.

17. Extract the square root of
  (1) $(a^2 + ab + bc + ca)\ (bc + ca + ab + b^2)\ (bc + ca + ab + c^2).$
  (2) $1 - x + \sqrt{22x - 15 - 8x^2}.$

18. Find the coefficient of x^6 in the expansion of $(1 - 3x)^{\frac{10}{3}}$, and the term independent of x in $\left(\dfrac{4}{3} x^2 - \dfrac{3}{2x} \right)^9$.

19. Solve the equations :
  (1) $\dfrac{2x - 3}{x - 1} - \dfrac{3x - 8}{x - 2} + \dfrac{x + 3}{x - 3} = 0.$
  (2) $x^2 - y^2 = xy - ab,\ (x + y)\ (ax + by) = 2ab\ (a + b).$
[Trin. Coll. Camb.]

20. Shew that if $a\ (b - c)\ x^2 + b\ (c - a)\ xy + c\ (a - b)\ y^2$ is a perfect square, the quantities a, b, c are in harmonical progression.
[St. Cath. Coll. Camb.]

21. If $(y - z)^2 + (z - x)^2 + (x - y)^2 = (y + z - 2x)^2 + (z + x - 2y)^2 + (x + y - 2z)^2$, and x, y, z are real, shew that $x = y = z$.
[St. Cath. Coll. Camb.]

22. Extract the square root of $3e58261$ in the scale of twelve, and find in what scale the fraction $\dfrac{1}{5}$ would be represented by $\cdot 17$.

23. Find the sum of the products of the integers $1, 2, 3, ..., n$ taken two at a time, and shew that it is equal to half the excess of the sum of the cubes of the given integers over the sum of their squares.

24. A man and his family consume 20 loaves of bread in a week. If his wages were raised 5 per cent., and the price of bread were raised $2\frac{1}{2}$ per cent., he would gain $6d.$ a week. But if his wages were lowered $7\frac{1}{2}$ per cent., and bread fell 10 per cent., then he would lose $1\frac{1}{2} d.$ a week : find his weekly wages and the price of a loaf.

25. The sum of four numbers in arithmetical progression is 48 and the product of the extremes is to the product of the means as 27 to 35 : find the numbers.

26. Solve the equations :

(1) $a (b - c) x^2 + b (c - a) x + c (a - b) = 0.$

(2) $\dfrac{(x - a) (x - b)}{x - a - b} = \dfrac{(x - c) (x - d)}{x - c - d}$ [Math. Tripos.]

27. If $\sqrt{a - x} + \sqrt{b - x} + \sqrt{c - x} = 0$, shew that
$(a + b + c + 3x) (a + b + c - x) = 4 (bc + ca + ab);$
and if $\sqrt[3]{a} + \sqrt[3]{b} + \sqrt[3]{c} = 0$, shew that $(a + b + c)^3 = 27abc$.

28. A train, an hour after starting, meets with an accident which detains it an hour, after which it proceeds at three-fifths of its former rate and arrives 3 hours after time : but had the accident happened 50 miles farther on the line, it would have arrived $1\frac{1}{2}$ hrs. sooner : find the length of the journey.

29. Solve the equations :

$$2x + y = 2z, \quad 9z - 7x = 6y, \quad x^3 + y^3 + z^3 = 216.$$

[R.M.A. Woolwich.]

30. Six papers are set in examination, two of them in mathematics : in how many different orders can the papers be given, provided only that the two mathematical papers are not successive ?

31. In how many ways can £5. 4s. 2d. be paid in exactly 60 coins, consisting of half-crowns, shillings and fourpenny-pieces ?

32. Find a and b so that $x^3 + ax^2 + 11x + 6$ and $x^3 + bx^2 + 14x + 8$ may have a common factor of the form $x^2 + px + q$.

[London University.]

33. In what time would A, B, C together do a work if A alone could do it in six hours more, B alone in one hour more, and C alone in twice the time ?

34. If the equations $ax + by = 1, cx^2 + dy^2 = 1$ have only one solution prove that $\dfrac{a^2}{c} + \dfrac{b^2}{d} = 1$, and $x = \dfrac{a}{c}$, $y = \dfrac{b}{d}$.

[Math. Tripos.]

35. Find by the Binomial theorem the first five terms in the expansion of $(1 - 2x + 2x^2)^{-\frac{1}{2}}$.

36. If one of the roots of $x^2 + px + q = 0$ is the square of the other, shew that $p^3 - q(3p - 1) + q^2 = 0$.   [Pemb. Coll. Camb.]

37. Solve the equation
$$x^4 - 5x^2 - 6x - 5 = 0. \qquad \text{[Queen's Coll. Ox.]}$$

38. Find the value of a for which the fraction
$$\frac{x^3 - ax^2 + 19x - a - 4}{x^3 - (a + 1)x^2 + 23x - a - 7}$$
admits of reduction. Reduce it to its lowest terms.

[Math. Tripos.]

39. If a, b, c, x, y, z are real quantities, and
$$(a + b + c)^2 = 3(bc + ca + ab - x^2 - y^2 - z^2),$$
shew that $a = b = c$, and $x = 0, y = 0, z = 0$.

[Christ's Coll. Camb.]

40. What is the greatest term in the expansion of $\left(1 - \dfrac{2}{3}x\right)^{-\frac{3}{2}}$ when the value of x is $\dfrac{6}{7}$?

[Emm. Coll. Camb.]

41. Find two numbers such that their sum multiplied by the sum of their squares is 5500, and their difference multiplied by the difference of their squares is 352. '   [Christ's Coll. Camb.]

42. If $x = \lambda a$, $y = (\lambda - 1) b$, $z = (\lambda - 3) c$, $\lambda = \dfrac{1 + b^2 + 3c^2}{a^2 + b^2 + c^2}$, express $x^2 + y^2 + z^2$ in its simplest form in terms of a, b, c.

[Sidney Coll. Camb.]

43. Solve the equations :

(1) $x^4 + 3x^2 = 16x + 60$.

(2) $y^2 + z^2 - x = z^2 + x^2 - y = x^2 + y^2 - z = 1$.

[Corpus Coll. Ox.]

44. If x, y, z are in harmonical progression, shew that
$$\log (x + z) + \log (x - 2y + z) = 2 \log (x - z).$$

45. Shew that
$$\frac{1}{2} + \frac{1.3}{2.4}\left(\frac{1}{4}\right) + \frac{1.3.5}{2.4.6}\left(\frac{1}{4}\right)^2 + \dots = \frac{4}{3}(2 - \sqrt{3})\sqrt{3}.$$

[Emm. Coll. Camb.]

46. If $\dfrac{3x + 2y}{3a - 2b} = \dfrac{3y + 2z}{3b - 2c} = \dfrac{3z + 2x}{3c - 2a}$,

then will $5(x + y + z)(5c + 4b - 3a) = (9x + 8y + 13z)(a + b + c)$.

[Christ's Coll. Camb.]

47. With 17 consonants and 5 vowels, how many words of four letters can be formed having 2 different vowels in the middle and 1 consonant (repeated or different) at each end ?

48. A question was lost on which 600 persons had voted; the same persons having voted again on the same question, it was carried by twice as many as it was before lost by, and the new majority vote was to the former as 8 to 7 : how many changed their minds ? [St. John's Coll. Camb.]

49. Shew that
$$\log \frac{(1 + x)^{\frac{1 - x}{2}}}{(1 - x)^{\frac{1 + x}{2}}} = x + \frac{5x^3}{2.3} + \frac{9x^5}{4.5} + \frac{13x^7}{6.7} + \dots$$

[Christ's Coll. Camb.]

50. A body of men were formed into a hollow square, three deep, when it was observed, that with the addition of 25 to their number a solid square might be formed, of which the number of men in each side would be greater by 22 than the square

root of the number of men in each side of the hollow square :
required the number of men.

51. Solve the equations :

(1) $\sqrt[m]{(a + x)^2} + 2\sqrt[m]{(a - x)^2} = 3\sqrt[m]{a^2 - x^2}.$

(2) $(x - a)^{\frac{1}{2}}(x - b)^{\frac{1}{2}} - (x - c)^{\frac{1}{2}}(x - d)^{\frac{1}{2}} = (a - c)^{\frac{1}{2}}(b - d)^{\frac{1}{2}}.$

52. Prove that

$$\sqrt[3]{4} = 1 + \frac{2}{6} + \frac{2.5}{6.12} + \frac{2.5.8}{6.12.18} + \dots \qquad \text{[Sidney Coll. Camb.]}$$

53. Solve $\sqrt[3]{6(5x + 6)} - \sqrt[3]{5(6x - 11)} = 1.$ [Queens' Coll. Camb.]

54. A vessel contains a gallons of wine, and another vessel
contains b gallons of water : c gallons are taken out of each
vessel and transferred to the other; this operation is repeated
any number of times : shew that if $c(a + b) = ab$, the quantity
of wine in each vessel will always remain the same after the
first operation.

55. The arithmetic mean between m and n and the geometric
mean between a and b are each equal to $\dfrac{ma + nb}{m + n}$: find m and
n in terms of a and b.

56. If x, y, z are such that their sum is constant, and if

$$(z + x - 2y)(x + y - 2z)$$

varies as yz, prove that $2(y + z) - x$ varies as yz.

[Emm. Coll. Camb.]

57. Prove that, if n is greater than 3,

$$1.2.{}^nC_r - 2.3.{}^nC_{r-1} + 3.4.{}^nC_{r-2} - \dots + (-1)^r(r + 1)(r + 2)$$

$$= 2.{}^{n-3}C_r. \dots$$

[Christ's Coll. Camb.]

58. Solve the equations :

(1) $\sqrt{2x - 1} + \sqrt{3x - 2} = \sqrt{4x - 3} + \sqrt{5x - 4}.$

(2) $4\left\{(x^2 - 16)^{\frac{3}{4}} + 8\right\} = x^2 + 16(x^2 - 16)^{\frac{1}{4}}.$

[St. John's Coll. Camb.]

59. Prove that two of the quantities x, y, z must be equal to one
another, if

$$\frac{y - z}{1 + yz} + \frac{z - x}{1 + zx} + \frac{x - y}{1 + xy} = 0.$$

60. In a certain community consisting of p persons, a per cent can read and write; of the males alone b per cent., and of the females alone c per cent can read and write : find the number of males and females in the community.

61. If $x = \left(\dfrac{a}{b}\right)^{\frac{2ab}{a^2 - b^2}}$, shew that $\dfrac{ab}{a^2 + b^2}\left(x^{\frac{a}{b}} + x^{\frac{b}{a}}\right) = \left(\dfrac{a}{b}\right)^{\frac{a^2 + b^2}{a^2 - b^2}}$.

[Emm. Coll. Camb.]

62. Shew that the coefficient of x^{4n} in the expansion of
$$(1 - x + x^2 - x^3)^{-1} \text{ is unity.}$$

63. Solve the equation
$$\frac{x - a}{b} + \frac{x - b}{a} = \frac{b}{x - a} + \frac{a}{x - b}.$$ [London University.]

64. Find (1) the arithmetical series, (2) the harmonical series of n terms of which a and b are the first and last terms; and shew that the product of the rth term of the first series and the $(n - r + 1)$th term of the second series is ab.

65. If the roots of the equation
$$\left(1 - q + \frac{p^2}{2}\right)x^2 + p(1 + q)x + q(q - 1) + \frac{p^2}{2} = 0$$
are equal, shew that $p^2 = 4q$.   [R. M. A. Woolwich]

66. If $a^2 + b^2 = 7ab$, shew that
$$\log\left\{\frac{1}{3}(a + b)\right\} = \frac{1}{2}(\log a + \log b).$$ [Queen's Coll. Ox.]

67. If n is a root of the equation
$$x^2(1 - ac) - x(a^2 + c^2) - (1 + ac) = 0,$$
and if n harmonic means are inserted between a and c, shew that the difference between the first and last mean is equal to $ac(a - c)$.   [Wadham Coll. Ox.]

68. If $^{n+2}C_8 : {}^{n-2}P_4 = 57 : 16$, find n.

69. A person invests a certain sum in a $6\frac{1}{2}$ per cent. Government loan : if the price had been £3 less he would have received $\frac{1}{3}$ per cent more interest on his money; at what price was the loan issued ?

70. Solve the equation :

$$\{(x^2 + x + 1)^3 - (x^2 + 1)^3 - x^3\} \{(x^2 - x + 1)^3 - (x^2 + 1)^3 + x^3\}$$
$$= 3 \{(x^4 + x^2 + 1)^3 - (x^4 + 1)^3 - x^6\}. \qquad \text{[Merton Coll. Ox.]}$$

71. If by eliminating x between the equations

$$x^2 + ax + b = 0 \quad \text{and} \quad xy + l(x + y) + m = 0,$$

a quadratic in y is formed whose roots are the same as those of the original quadratic in x, then either $a = 2l$, and $b = m$, or $b + m = al$. [R.M.A. Woolwich.]

72. Given $\log 2 = 0.30103$, and $\log 3 = 0.47712$, solve the equations :

(1) $6^x = \dfrac{10}{3} - 6^{-x}.$ (2) $\sqrt{5^x} + \sqrt{5^{-x}} = \dfrac{29}{10}.$

73. Find two numbers such that their sum is 9, and the sum of their fourth powers 2417. [London University.]

74. A set out to walk at the rate of 4 miles an hour; after he had been walking $2\dfrac{3}{4}$ hours, B set out to overtake him and went $4\dfrac{1}{2}$ miles the first hour, $4\dfrac{3}{4}$ miles the second, 5 the third, and so gaining a quarter of a mile every hour. In how many hours would he overtake A ?

75. Prove that the integer next above $(\sqrt{3} + 1)^{2m}$ contains 2^{m+1} as a factor.

76. The series of natural numbers is divided into groups 1, 2, 3, 4, 5, 6, 7, 8, 9; and so on : prove that the sum of the numbers in the nth group is $(n - 1)^3 + n^3$.

77. Shew that the sum of n terms of the series

$$\frac{1}{2} + \frac{1}{2}\left(\frac{1}{2}\right)^2 + \frac{1.3}{3!}\left(\frac{1}{2}\right)^3 + \frac{1.3.5}{4!}\left(\frac{1}{2}\right)^4 + \dots$$

is equal to $1 - \dfrac{1.3.5.7.\dots(2n - 1)}{2^n n}$ [R.M.A. Woolwich]

78. Shew that the coefficient of x^n in the expansion of $\dfrac{1 + 2x}{1 - x + x^2}$ is

$$(-1)^{\frac{n}{3}}, 3(-1)^{\frac{n-1}{3}}, 2(-1)^{\frac{n-2}{3}},$$

according as n is of the form $3m$, $3m + 1$, $3m + 2$.

79. Solve the equations :

(1) $\dfrac{x}{a} = \dfrac{y}{b} = \dfrac{z}{c} = \dfrac{xyz}{x+y+z}$.

(2) $\dfrac{x}{y} + \dfrac{y}{z} + \dfrac{z}{x} = \dfrac{y}{x} + \dfrac{z}{y} + \dfrac{x}{z} = x + y + z = 3$.   [Univ. Coll. Ox.]

80. The value of xyz is $7\frac{1}{2}$ or $3\frac{3}{5}$ according as the series a, x, y, z, b is arithmetic or harmonic : find the values of a and b assuming them to be positive integers.   [Merton Coll. Ox.]

81. If $ay - bx = c\sqrt{(x-a)^2 + (y-b)^2}$, shew that x and y are connected by a linear relation if $c^2 \leq a^2 + b^2$.

82. If $(x+1)^2$ is greater than $5x - 1$ and less than $7x - 3$ find the integral value of x.

83. If P is the number of integers whose logarithms have the characteristic p, and Q the number of integers the logarithms of whose reciprocals have the characteristic $-q$, shew that

$$\log_{10} P - \log_{10} Q = p - q + 1.$$

84. In how many ways may 20 shillings be given to 5 persons so that no person may receive less than 3 shillings ?

85. A man wishing his two daughters two receive equal portions when they came of age bequeathed to the elder the accumulated interest of a certain sum of money invested at the time of his death in 4 per cent. stock at 88; and to the younger he bequeathed the accumulated interest of a sum less than the former by £3500 invested at the same time in the 3 per cents at 63. Supposing their ages at the time of their father's death to have been 17 and 14, what was the sum invested in each case, and what was each daughter's fortune ?

86. A number of three digits in scale 7 when expressed in scale 9 has its digits reversed in order : find the number.

[St. John's Coll. Camb.]

87. If the sum of m terms of an arithmetical progression is equal to the sum of either the next n terms or the next p terms, prove that $(m+n)\left(\dfrac{1}{m} - \dfrac{1}{p}\right) = (m+p)\left(\dfrac{1}{m} - \dfrac{1}{n}\right)$.

[St. John's Coll. Camb.]

88. Prove that

$$\frac{1}{(y-z)^2} + \frac{1}{(z-x)^2} + \frac{1}{(x-y)^2} = \left(\frac{1}{y-z} + \frac{1}{z-x} + \frac{1}{x-y}\right)^2.$$

[R.M.A. Woolwich.]

89. If m is negative, or positive and greater than 1, shew that

$$1^m + 3^m + 5^m + \ldots + (2n-1)^m > p^{m+1}.$$ [Emm. Coll. Camb.]

90. If each pair of the three equations

$$x^2 - p_1 x + q_1 = 0, \; x^2 - p_2 x + q_2 = 0, \; x^2 - p_3 x + q_3 = 0,$$

have a common root, prove that

$$p_1^2 + p_2^2 + p_3^2 + 4(q_1 + q_2 + q_3) = 2(p_2 p_3 + p_3 p_1 + p_1 p_2).$$

[St. John's Coll. Camb.]

91. *A* and *B* travelled on the same road and at the same rate from Huntingdon to London. At the 50th milestone from London, *A* overtook a drove of geese which were proceeding at the rate of 3 miles in 2 hours; and two hours afterwards met a waggon, which was moving at the rate of 9 miles in 4 hours. *B* overtook the same drove of geese at the 45th milestone, and met the waggon exactly 40 minutes before he came to the 31st milestone. Where was *B* when *A* reached London ?

[St. John's Coll. Camb.],

92. If $a + b + c + d = 0$, prove that

$$abc + bcd + cda + dab = \sqrt{(bc - ad)(ca - bd)(ab - cd)}.$$

[R.M.A. Woolwich.]

93. An A.P., a G.P., and an H.P. have a and b for their first two terms : shew that their $(n + 2)$ th terms will be in G.P. if

$$\frac{b^{2n+2} - a^{2n+2}}{ba(b^{2n} - a^{2n})} = \frac{n+1}{n}.$$

[Math. Tripos.]

94. Shew that the coefficient of x^n in the expansion of $\dfrac{x}{(x-a)(x-b)}$ in ascending power of x is $\dfrac{a^n - b^n}{a - b} \cdot \dfrac{1}{a^n b^n}$; and that the coefficient of x^{2n} in the expansion of $\dfrac{(1 + x^2)^n}{(1-x)^3}$ is $2^{n-1}(n^2 + 4n + 2)$.

[Emm. Coll. Camb.]

95. Solve the equations:

$$\sqrt{x-y} + \frac{1}{2}\sqrt{x+y} = \frac{x-1}{\sqrt{x-y}}, \quad x^2 + y^2 : xy = 34 : 15.$$

[St John's Coll. Camb.]

96. Find the value of $1 + \cfrac{1}{3+} \cfrac{1}{2+} \cfrac{1}{3+} \cfrac{1}{2+} \cdots$ in the form of a quadratic surd. [R.M.A. Woolwich.]

97. Prove that the cube of an integer may be expressed as the difference of two squares; that the cube of every odd integer may be so expressed in two ways; and that the difference of the cubes of any two consecutive integers may be expressed as the difference of two squares. [Jesus Coll. Camb.]

98. Find the value of the infinite series

$$\frac{1}{3!} + \frac{2}{5!} + \frac{3}{7!} + \frac{4}{9!} + \cdots$$ [Emm. Coll. Camb.]

99. If $x = \cfrac{a}{b+} \cfrac{c}{d+} \cfrac{a}{b+} \cfrac{c}{d+} \cdots$

and $\qquad y = \cfrac{c}{d+} \cfrac{a}{b+} \cfrac{c}{d+} \cfrac{a}{b+} \cdots,$

then $\qquad bx - dy = a - c.$ [Christ's Coll. Camb.]

100. Find the generating function, the sum to n terms, and the nth term of the recurring series $1 + 5x + 7x^2 + 17x^3 + 31x^4 + \cdots$

101. If a, b, c are in H.P., then

(1) $\dfrac{a+b}{2a-b} + \dfrac{c+b}{2c-b} > 4.$

(2) $b^2(a-c)^2 = 2\{c^2(b-a)^2 + a^2(c-b)^2\}.$ [Pemb. Coll. Camb.]

102. If a, b, c are all real quantities, and $x^3 - 3b^2x + 2c^3$ is divisible by $x - a$ and also by $x - b$; prove that either $a = b = c$, or $a = -2b = -2c.$ [Jesus Coll. Ox.]

103. Shew that the sum of the squares of three consecutive odd numbers increased by 1 is divisible by 12, but not by 24.

104. Shew that $\dfrac{ac - b^2}{a}$ is the greatest or least value of $ax^2 + 2bx + c$, according as a is negative or positive

If $x^4 + y^4 + z^4 + y^2z^2 + z^2x^2 + x^2y^2 = 2xyz(x+y+z)$, and x, y, z are all real, shew that $x = y = z.$ [St John's Coll. Camb.]

105. Shew that the expansion of $\sqrt{\dfrac{1-\sqrt{1-x^2}}{2}}$

is $\dfrac{x}{2} + \dfrac{1.3}{2.4} \cdot \dfrac{x^3}{6} + \dfrac{1.3.5.7}{2.4.6.8} \cdot \dfrac{x^5}{10} + \dots$

106. If a, β are roots of the equations

$$x^2 + px + q = 0,\ x^{2n} + p^n x^n + q^n = 0,$$

where n an even integer, shew that $\dfrac{a}{\beta}$, $\dfrac{\beta}{a}$ are roots of

$$x^n + 1 + (x+1)^n = 0. \qquad \text{[Pemb. Coll. Camb.]}$$

107. Find the difference between the squares of the infinite continued fractions

$$a + \dfrac{b}{2a +}\ \dfrac{b}{2a +}\ \dfrac{b}{2a +} \dots, \text{ and } c + \dfrac{d}{2c +}\ \dfrac{d}{2c +}\ \dfrac{d}{2c +} \dots$$

[Christ's Coll. Camb.]

108. A sum of money is distributed amongst a certain number of persons. The second receives Re.1 more than the first, the third Rs. 2 more than the second, the fourth Rs. 3 more than the third, and so on. If the first person gets Re.1 and the last person Rs. 67 what is the number of persons and the sum distributed ?

109. Solve the equations :

(1) $\dfrac{x}{a} + \dfrac{y+z}{b+c} = \dfrac{y}{b} + \dfrac{z+x}{c+a} = \dfrac{z}{c} + \dfrac{x+y}{a+b} = 2.$

(2) $\dfrac{x^2+y^2}{xy} + x^2 + y^2 = 13\frac{1}{3},\ \dfrac{xy}{x^2+y^2} + xy = 3\frac{3}{10}.$

110. If $a > b > 0$, and n is a positive integer, prove that

$$a^n - b^n > n\,(a-b)\,(ab)^{\frac{n-1}{2}}. \qquad \text{[St Cath. Coll. Camb.]}$$

111. Express $\dfrac{763}{396}$ as continued fraction; hence find the least positive integral values of x and y which satisfy the equation

$$396x - 763y = 12.$$

112. To complete a certain work, a workman A alone would take m times as many days as B and C working together; B alone would take n times as many days as A and C together; C alone would take p times as many days as A and B together : shew that the numbers of days in which each would do it alone are as $m+1 : n+1 : p+1$.

Prove also $\dfrac{m}{m+1} + \dfrac{n}{n+1} + \dfrac{p}{p+1} = 2$. [R.M.A. Woolwich.]

113. The expenses of a hydropathic establishment are partly constant and partly vary with the number of boarders. Each boarder pays Rs. 65 a year, and the annual profits are Rs. 9 a head when there are 50 boarders, and Rs. 10 when there are 60 : what is the profit on each boarder when there are 80 ?

114. If $x^2 y = 2x - y$, and x^2 is not greater than 1, shew that
$$4\left(x^2 + \frac{x^6}{3} + \frac{x^{10}}{5} + \dots \right) = y^2 + \frac{y^4}{2} + \frac{y^6}{3} + \dots \quad \text{[Peterhouse, Camb.]}$$

115. If $\dfrac{x}{a^2 - y^2} = \dfrac{y}{a^2 - x^2} = \dfrac{1}{b}$, and $xy = c^2$, shew that when a and c are unequal,
$$(a^2 - c^2)^2 - b^2 c^2 = 0, \text{ or } a^2 + c^2 - b^2 = 0.$$

116. If $(1 + x + x^2)^{3r} = 1 + k_1 x + k_2 x^2 + \dots$,

and $\qquad (x-1)^{3r} = x^{3r} - c_1 x^{3r-1} + c_2 x^{3r-2} - \dots$;

prove that (1) $1 - k_1 + k_2 - \dots = 1$,

(2) $1 - k_1 c_1 + k_2 c_2 - \dots = \pm \dfrac{3r\,!}{r\,!\,(2r)\,!}$. [R.M.A. Woolwich.]

117. Solve the equations :

(1) $(x - y)^2 + 2ab = ax + by, \ xy + ab = bx + ay$.

(2) $x^2 - y^2 + z^2 = 6, \ 2yz - zx + 2xy = 13, \ x - y + z = 2$.

118. If there are n positive quantities $a_1, a_2, \dots, a_n$, and if the square roots of all their products taken two together be found, prove that
$$\sqrt{a_1 a_2} + \sqrt{a_1 a_3} + \dots < \frac{n-1}{2}(a_1 + a_2 + \dots + a_n);$$

hence prove that the arithmetic mean of the square roots of the products two together is less than the arithmetic mean of the given quantities. [R.M.A. Woolwich.]

119. If $b^2 x^4 + a^2 y^4 = a^2 b^2$, and $a^2 + b^2 = x^2 + y^2 = 1$, prove that
$$b^4 x^6 + a^4 y^6 = (b^2 x^4 + a^2 y^4)^2. \quad \text{[India Civil. Service.]}$$

120. Find the sum of the first n terms of the series whose rth terms are

(1) $\dfrac{2r+1}{r^2(r+1)^2}$,   (2) $(a+r^2b)\,x^{n-r}$ [St John's Coll. Camb.]

121. Find the greatest value of $\dfrac{x+2}{2x^2+3x+6}$.

122. Solve the equations :

(1) $1+x^4 = 7(1+x)^4$.

(2) $3xy+2z = xz+6y = 2yz+3x = 0$.

123. If a_1, a_2, a_3, a_4 are any four consecutive coefficients of an expanded binomial, prove that

$$\frac{a_1}{a_1+a_2} + \frac{a_3}{a_3+a_4} = \frac{2a_2}{a_2+a_3}.$$ [Queens's Coll. Camb.]

124. Separate $\dfrac{x^3+7x^2-x-8}{(x^2+x+1)(x^2-3x-1)}$ into partial fractions; and

find the general term when $\dfrac{(3x-8)}{(x^2-4x+4)}$ is expanded in ascending powers of x.

125. In the recurring series

$$\frac{5}{4} - \frac{1}{2}x + 2x^2 + lx^3 + 5x^4 + 7x^5 + \ldots$$

the scale of relation is a quadratic expression; determine the unknown coefficient of the fourth term and the scale of relation, and give the general term of the series.

[R.M.A Woolwich.]

126. If x, y, z are unequal, and if

$$2a-3y = \frac{(z-x)^2}{y}, \text{ and } 2a-3z = \frac{(x-y)^2}{z},$$

then will $2a-3x = \dfrac{(y-z)^2}{x}$, and $x+y+z = a$.   [Math. Tripos.]

127. Solve the equations :

(1) $xy+6 = 2x-x^2$, $xy-9 = 2y-y^2$.

(2) $(ax)^{\log a} = (by)^{\log b}$, $b^{\log x} = a^{\log y}$.

128. Find the limiting values of

(1) $x\sqrt{x^2+a^2} - \sqrt{x^4+a^4}$, when $x = \infty$

(2) $\dfrac{\sqrt{a+2x}-\sqrt{3x}}{\sqrt{3a+x}-2\sqrt{x}}$, when $x=a$.   [London University.]

129.   There are two numbers whose product is 192, and the quotient of the arithmetical by the harmonical mean of their greatest common measure and least common multiple is $3\frac{25}{48}$: find the numbers.   [R.M.A. Woolwich.]

130.   Solve the following equations :

(1) $\sqrt[3]{13x+37}-\sqrt[3]{13x-37}=\sqrt[3]{2}$

(2) $\left.\begin{array}{l}b\sqrt{1-z^2}+c\sqrt{1-y^2}=a,\\[2pt] c\sqrt{1-x^2}+a\sqrt{1-z^2}=b,\\[2pt] a\sqrt{1-y^2}+b\sqrt{1-x^2}=c.\end{array}\right\}$

131.   Prove that the sum to infinity of the series

$$\frac{1}{2^3\,3!}-\frac{1.3}{2^4\,4!}+\frac{1.3.5}{2^5\,5!}-\ldots \text{ is } \frac{23}{24}-\frac{2}{3}\sqrt{2}.$$

[Math. Tripos.]

132.   A number consisting of three digits is doubled by reversing the digits; prove that the same will hold for the number formed by the first and last digits, and also that such a number can be found in only one scale of notation out of every three.   [Math. Tripos.]

133.   Find the coefficients of x^{12} and x^r in the product of

$$\frac{1+x^3}{(1-x^2)\,(1-x)} \text{ and } 1-x+x^2.$$

[R.M.A Woolwich.]

134.   A purchaser is to take a plot of land fronting a street; the plot is to be rectangular, and three times its frontage added to twice its depth is to be 96 metres. What is the greatest number of square metres he may take ?   [London University.]

135.   Prove that

$(a+b+c+d)^4+(a+b-c-d)^4+(a-b+c-d)^4+(a-b-c+d)^4$
$-(a+b+c-d)^4-(a+b-c+d)^4-(a-b+c+d)^4-(-a+b+c+d)^4$
$=192abcd.$ [Trin. Coll. Camb.]

136.   Find the values of a,b,c which will make each of the expressions $x^4+ax^3+bx^2+cx+1$ and $x^4+2ax^3+2bx^2+2cx+1$ a perfect square.   [London University.]

137. Solve the equations :

(1) $\dfrac{\sqrt[3]{x+y} - \sqrt[3]{x-y}}{\sqrt[3]{x+y} + \sqrt[3]{x-y}} = 3$, $x^2 + y^2 = 65$.

(2) $\sqrt{2x^2 + 1} + \sqrt{2x^2 - 1} = \dfrac{2}{\sqrt{3 - 2x^2}}$.

138. A farmer sold 10 sheep at a certain price and 5 others at Rs. 50 less per head; the sum he received for each lot was expressed in rupees by the same two digits : find the price per sheep.

139. Sum to n terms :

(1) $(2n - 1) + 2(2n - 3) + 3(2n - 5) + \ldots$

(2) The squares of the terms of the series 1, 3, 6, 10, 15 …

(3) The odd terms of the series in (2).   [Trin. Coll. Camb.]

140. If a, β, γ are the roots of the equation $x^3 + qx + r = 0$ prove that

$3(\alpha^2 + \beta^2 + \gamma^2)(\alpha^5 + \beta^5 + \gamma^5) = 5(\alpha^3 + \beta^3 + \gamma^3)(\alpha^4 + \beta^4 + \gamma^4)$.

[St John's Coll. Camb.]

141. Solve the equations :

(1) $\left.\begin{array}{l} x(3y - 5) = 4 \\ y(2x + 7) = 27 \end{array}\right\}$ (2) $\left.\begin{array}{c} x^3 + y^3 + z^3 = 495 \\ x + y + z = 15 \\ xyz = 105 \end{array}\right\}$

[Trin. Coll. Camb.]

142. If a, b, c are the roots of the equation $x^3 + qx^2 + r = 0$, form the equation whose roots are $a + b - c$, $b + c - a$, $c + a - b$.

143. Sum the series :

(1) $n + (n - 1)x + (n - 2)x^2 + \ldots + 2x^{n-2} + x^{n-1}$;

(2) $3 - x - 2x^2 - 16x^3 - 28x^4 - 676x^5 + \ldots$ to infinity;

(3) $6 + 9 + 14 + 23 + 40 + \ldots$ to n terms.   [Oxford Mods.]

144. Eliminate x, y, z from the equations

$$x^{-1} + y^{-1} + z^{-1} = a^{-1}, \quad x + y + z = b.$$
$$x^2 + y^2 + z^2 = c^2, \quad x^3 + y^3 + z^3 = d^3,$$

and shew that if x, y, z are all finite and numerically unequal, b cannot be equal to d.   [R.M.A. Woolwich.]

145. The roots of the equation $3x^2(x^2 + 8) + 16(x^3 - 1) = 0$ are not all unequal : find them.   [R.M.A. Woolwich.]

146. A cyclist set out from a certain place, and went 1 km. the first day, 3 the second, 5 the next, and so on, going every day 2 km more than he had gone the preceding day. After he had been gone three days, a second sets out, and travels 12 km the first day, 13 the second, and so on. In how many days will the second overtake the first ? Explain the double answer.

147. Find the value of

$$\frac{1}{3+}\frac{1}{2+}\frac{1}{1+}\frac{1}{3+}\frac{1}{2+}\frac{1}{1+}\cdots$$

148. Solve the equation

$$x^3 + 3ax^2 + 3(a^2 - bc)x + a^3 + b^3 + c^3 - 3abc = 0.$$

[India Civil Service.]

149. If n is a prime number which will divide neither a, b, nor $a + b$, prove that

$$a^{n-2}b - a^{n-3}b^2 + a^{n-4}b^3 - \ldots + ab^{n-2}$$

exceeds by 1 a multiple of n [St John's Coll. Camb.]

150. Find the nth term and the sum to n terms of series whose sum to infinity is $(1 - abx^2)(1 - ax)^{-2}(1 - bx)^{-2}$.   [Oxford Mods.]

151. If a, b, c are the roots of the equation $x^3 + px + q = 0$, find the equation whose roots are $\dfrac{b^2 + c^2}{a}, \dfrac{c^2 + a^2}{b}, \dfrac{a^2 + b^2}{c}$.

[Trin. Coll. Camb.]

152. Prove that

$$(y + z - 2x)^4 + (z + x - 2y)^4 + (x + y - 2z)^4$$
$$= 18(x^2 + y^2 + z^2 - yz - zx - xy)^2.$$

[Clare. Coll. Camb.]

153. Solve the equations :

(1) $x^3 - 30x + 133 = 0$, by Cardan's method.

(2) $x^5 - 4x^4 - 10x^3 + 40x^2 + 9x - 36 = 0$, having roots of the form $\pm a, \pm b, c$.

154. It is found that the quantity of work done by a man in an hour varies directly as his pay per hour and inversely as the square root of the number of hours he works per day. He can finish a piece of work in six days when working 9 hours a day at Re. 1 per hour. How many days will he take to finish the same

piece of work when working 16 hours a day at Re. 1.50 nP. per hour ?

155. If s_n denote the sum to n terms of the series

$$1.\,2 + 2.\,3 + 3.\,4 + \dots,$$

and σ_{n-1} that to $n-1$ terms of the series

$$\frac{1}{1.\,2.\,3.\,4} + \frac{1}{2.\,3.\,4.\,5} + \frac{1}{3.\,4.\,5.\,6} + \dots,$$

shew that $18\,s_n\,\sigma_{n-1} - s_n + 2 = 0$. [Magd. Coll. Ox.]

156. Solve the equations :

(1) $(12x - 1)\,(6x - 1)\,(4x - 1)\,(3x - 1) = 5$.

(2) $\dfrac{1}{5}\dfrac{(x+1)\,(x-3)}{(x+2)\,(x-4)} + \dfrac{1}{9}\dfrac{(x+3)\,(x-5)}{(x+4)\,(x-6)} - \dfrac{2}{13}\dfrac{(x+5)\,(x-7)}{(x+6)\,(x-8)} = \dfrac{92}{585}$.

[St John's Coll. Camb.]

157. A cottage at the beginning of a year worth Rs. 2500, but it was found that by dilapidations at the end of each year it lost ten per cent of the value it had at the beginning of each year : after what number of years would the value of the cottage be reduced below Rs. 250 ? Given $\log_{10} 3 = 0.4771213$,

[R.M.A. Woolwich.]

158. Shew that the infinite series

$$1 + \frac{1}{4} + \frac{1.\,4}{4.\,8} + \frac{1.\,4.\,7}{4.\,8.\,12} + \frac{1.\,4.\,7.\,10}{4.\,8.\,12.\,16} + \dots,$$

$$1 + \frac{2}{6} + \frac{2.\,5}{6.\,12} + \frac{2.\,5.\,8}{6.\,12.\,18} + \frac{2.\,5.\,8.\,11}{6.\,12.\,18.\,24} + \dots,$$

are equal [Peterhouse, Camb.]

159. Prove the identity

$$\left\{ 1 - \frac{x}{\alpha} + \frac{x\,(x-\alpha)}{\alpha\,\beta} - \frac{x\,(x-\alpha)\,(x-\beta)}{\alpha\,\beta\,\gamma} + \dots \right\}$$

$$\times \left\{ 1 + \frac{x}{\alpha} + \frac{x\,(x+\alpha)}{\alpha\,\beta} + \frac{x\,(x+\alpha)\,(x+\beta)}{\alpha\,\beta\,\gamma} + \dots \right\}$$

$$= 1 - \frac{x^2}{\alpha^2} + \frac{x^2\,(x^2-\alpha^2)}{\alpha^2\beta^2} - \frac{x^2\,(x^2-\alpha^2)\,(x^2-\beta^2)}{\alpha^2\beta^2\gamma^2} + \dots$$

[Trin. Coll. Camb.]

160. If n is a positive integer greater than 1, shew that

$$n^5 - 5n^3 + 60n^2 - 56n$$

is a multiple of 120. [Wadham Coll. Ox]

161.

161. A number of persons were engaged to do a piece of work which would have occupied them 24 hours if they had commenced at the same time; but instead of doing so, they commenced at equal intervals and then continued to work till the whole was finished, the payment being proportional to the work done be each; the first corner received eleven times as much as the last; find the time occupied.

162. Solve the equations :

(1) $\dfrac{x}{y^2 - 3} = \dfrac{y}{x^2 - 3} = \dfrac{-7}{x^3 + y^3}$.

(2) $y^2 + z^2 - x(y + z) = a^2$,

$z^2 + x^2 - y(z + x) = b^2$,

$x^2 + y^2 - z(x + y) = c^2$.   [Pemb. Coll. Camb.]

163. Solve the equation

$a^3(b - c)(x - b)(x - c) + b^3(c - a)(x - c)(x - a)$

$+ c^3(a - b)(x - a)(x - b) = 0;$

also shew that if the two roots are equal

$$\frac{1}{\sqrt{a}} \pm \frac{1}{\sqrt{b}} \pm \frac{1}{\sqrt{c}} = 0.$$ [St John's Coll. Camb.]

164. Sum the series :

(1) $1.2.4 + 2.3.5 + 3.4.6 + \ldots$ to n terms.

(2) $\dfrac{1^2}{3!} + \dfrac{2^2}{4!} + \dfrac{3^2}{5!} + \ldots$ to inf.

165. Shew that, if a, b, c, d be four positive unequal quantities and $s = a + b + c + d$, then

$(s - a)(s - b)(s - c)(s - d) > 81abcd.$ [Peterhouse, camb.]

166. Solve the equations :

(1) $\sqrt{x + a} - \sqrt{y - a} = \dfrac{5}{2}\sqrt{a}, \ \sqrt{x - a} - \sqrt{y + a} = \dfrac{3}{2}\sqrt{a}.$

(2) $x + y + z = x^2 + y^2 + z^2 = \dfrac{1}{2}(x^3 + y^3 + z^3) = 3.$ [Math. Tripos.]

167. Eliminate l, m, n from the equations :

$lx + my + nz = mx + ny + lz = nx + ly + mz = k^2(l^2 + m^2 + n^2) = 1.$

168. Simplify

$$\frac{a\,(b+c-a)^2 + \ldots + \ldots + (b+c-a)\,(c+a-b)\,(a+b-c)}{a^2\,(b+c-a) + \ldots + \ldots - (b+c-a)\,(c+a-b)\,(a+b-c)}.$$

[Math. Tripos.]

169. Shew that the expression

$$(x^2 - yz)^3 + (y^2 - zx)^3 + (z^2 - xy)^3 - 3\,(x^2 - yz)\,(y^2 - zx)\,(z^2 - xy)$$

is a perfect square, and find its square root.

[London University.]

170. There are three towns A, B, and C; a person by walking from A to B, driving from B to C, and riding from C to A makes the journey in $15\frac{1}{2}$ hours; by driving from A to B, riding from B to C, and walking from C to A he could make the journey in 12 hours. On foot he could make the journey in 22 hours, on horseback in $8\frac{1}{4}$ hours, and driving in 11 hours. To walk a km., ride a km., and drive a km. he takes altogether half an hour : find the rates at which he travels, and the distance between the towns.

171. Shew that $n^7 - 7n^5 + 14n^3 - 8n$ is divisible by 840, if n is an integer not less than 3.

172. Solve the equations :

(1) $\sqrt{x^2 + 12y} + \sqrt{y^2 + 12x} = 33,\ x + y = 23.$

(2) $\dfrac{u\,(y-x)}{z-u} = a,\ \dfrac{z\,(y-x)}{z-u} = b,\ \dfrac{y\,(u-z)}{x-y} = c,\ \dfrac{x\,(u-z)}{x-y} = d.$

[Math. Tripos.]

173. If s be the sum of n positive unequal quantities $a, b, c, \ldots$, then

$$\frac{s}{s-a} + \frac{s}{s-b} + \frac{s}{s-c} + \ldots > \frac{n^2}{n-1}.$$

[Math. Tripos.]

174. A merchant bought a quantity of cotton; this he exchanged for oil which he sold. He observed that the number of kg of cotton, the number of litres of oil obtained for each kg, and the number of rupees for which he sold each litre formed a descending geometrical progression. He calculated that if he had obtained one kg more of cotton, one litre more of oil for each kg and Re. 1 more for each litre he would have obtained Rs. 10169 more; whereas if he had obtained one kg less of cotton, one litre less of oil for each kg and Re.1 less for each litre, he would have obtained Rs. 9673 less : how much did he actually receive ?

175. Prove that
$$\Sigma (b + c - a - x)^4 (b - c) (a - x)$$
$$= 16 (b - c) (c - a) (a - b) (x - a) (x - b) (x - c).$$
[Jesus Coll. Camb.]

176. If α, β, γ are the roots of the equation $x^3 - px^2 + r = 0$, find the equation whose roots are $\dfrac{\beta + \gamma}{\alpha}, \dfrac{\gamma + \alpha}{\beta}, \dfrac{\alpha + \beta}{\gamma}$.
[R.M.A. Woolwich]

177. If any number of factors of the form $a^2 + b^2$ are multiplied together, shew that the product can be expressed as the sum of two squares.

Given that $(a^2 + b^2) (c^2 + d^2) (e^2 + f^2) (g^2 + h^2) = p^2 + q^2$, find p and q in terms of a, b, c, d, e, f, g, h.   [London University.]

178. Solve the equations
$$x^2 + y^2 = 61, x^3 - y^3 = 91.$$ [R.M.A. Woolwich]

179. A man goes in for an Examination in which there are four papers with a maximum of m marks for each paper; shew that the number of ways of getting $2m$ marks on the whole is
$$\frac{1}{3} (m + 1) (2m^2 + 4m + 3).$$
[Math. Tripos.]

180. If α, β are the roots of $x^2 + px + 1 = 0$, and γ, δ are the roots of $x^2 + qx + 1 = 0$; shew that
$$(\alpha - \gamma) (\beta - \gamma) (\alpha + \delta) (\beta + \delta) = q^2 - p^2.$$ [R.MA. Woolwich]

181. Shew that if a_m be the coefficient of x^m in the expansion of $(1 + x)^n$, then whatever n be,
$$a_0 - a_1 + a_2 - \dots + (-1)^{m-1} a_{m-1}$$
$$= \frac{(n - 1) (n - 2) \dots (n - m + 1)}{(m - 1)!} (-1)^{m-1}.$$ [New Coll. Ox.]

182. A certain number is the product of three prime factors, the sum of whose squares is 2331. There are 7560 numbers (including unity) which are less than the number and prime to it. The sum of its divisors (including unity and the number itself) is 10560. Find the number. [Corpus Coll. Camb.]

183. Form an equation whose roots shall be the products of every two of the roots of the equation $x^3 - ax^2 + bx + c = 0$.

Solve completely the equation
$$2x^5 + x^4 + x + 2 = 12x^3 + 12x^2.$$ [R.M.A. Woolwich

184. Prove that if n is a positive integer,
$$n^n - n(n-2)^n + \frac{n(n-1)}{2!}(n-4)^n - \ldots = 2^n\, n!.$$

185. If $(6\sqrt{6} + 14)^{2n+1} = N$, and if F be the fractional part of N prove that $NF = 20^{2n+1}$. [Emm. Coll. Can $\rlap{\,}$.]

186. Solve the equations :

(1) $x + y + z = 2,\ x^2 + y^2 + z^2 = 0,\ x^3 + y^3 + z^3 = -1$.

(2) $x^2 - (y-z)^2 = a^2,\ y^2 - (z-x)^2 = b^2,\ z^2 - (x-y)^2 = c^2$.

[Christ's Coll. Camb.]

187. At a general election the whole number of Liberals returned was 15 more than the number of English Conservatives, the whole number of Conservatives was 5 more than twice the number of English Liberals. The number of Scotch Conservatives was the same as the number of Welsh Liberals, and the Scotch Liberal majority was equal to twice the number of Welsh Conservatives, and was to the Irish Liberal majority as 2 : 3. The English Conservative majority was 10 more than the whole number of Irish members. The whole number of members was 652, of whom 60 were returned by Scotch constituencies. Find the numbers of each party returned by England, Scotland, Ireland, and Wales, respectively. [St John's Coll. Camb.]

188. Shew that $a^5(c-b) + b^5(a-c) + c^5(b-a)$
$$= (b-c)(c-a)(a-b)(\Sigma a^3 + \Sigma a^2 b + abc).$$

189. Prove that $\begin{vmatrix} a^3 & 3a^2 & 3a & 1 \\ a^2 & a^2 + 2a & 2a+1 & 1 \\ a & 2a+1 & a+2 & 1 \\ 1 & 3 & 3 & 1 \end{vmatrix} = (a-1)^6$.

[Ball. Coll. Ox.]

190. $1 + \dfrac{1}{a} + \dfrac{1}{c} + \dfrac{1}{a-b} + \dfrac{1}{c-b} = 0$, prove that a, b, c are in harmonical progression, unless $b = a + c$. [Trin. Coll. Camb.]

191. Solve the equations :

(1) $x^3 - 13x^2 + 15x + 189 = 0$, having given that one root exceeds another root by 2.

(2) $x^4 - 4x^2 + 8x + 35 = 0$, having given that one root is
$$2 + \sqrt{-3}.\qquad\text{[R.M.A. Woolwich.]}$$

192.   Two numbers a and b are given; two others a_1, b_1 are formed by the relations $3a_1 = 2a + b, 3b_1 = a + 2b$; two more a_2, b_2 are formed from a_1, b_1 in the same manner, and so on; find a_n, b_n in terms of a and b, and prove that when n is infinite, $a_n = b_n$.

[R.M.A. Woolwich.]

193.   If $x + y + z + w = 0$, shew that
$$wx\,(w + x)^2 + yz\,(w - x)^2 + wy\,(w + y)^2$$
$$+\, zx\,(w - y)^2 + wz\,(w + z)^2 + xy\,(w - z)^2 + 4xyzw = 0.$$

[Math. Tripos.]

194.   If $a + \dfrac{bc - a^2}{a^2 + b^2 + c^2}$ be not altered in value by interchanging a and b (a, b and c being unequal), it will not be altered by interchanging a and c, and vice versa; and it will vanish if $a + b + c = 1$.   [Math. Tripos.]

195.   On a quadruple line of rails between two termini A and B, two down trains start at 6.0 and 6.45, and two up trains at 7.15 and 8.30. If the four trains (regarded as points) all pass one another simultaneously, find the following equations between x_1, x_2, x_3, x_4, their rates in km. per hour,
$$\frac{3x_2}{x_2 - x_1} = \frac{4m + 5x_3}{x_1 + x_3} = \frac{4m + 10x_4}{x_1 + x_4},$$
where m is the number of km. in AB.   [Trin. Coll. Camb.]

196.   Prove that rejecting terms of the third and higher orders,
$$\frac{(1 - x)^{-1/2} + (1 - y)^{-1/2}}{1 + \sqrt{(1 - x)(1 - y)}} = 1 + \frac{1}{2}(x + y) + \frac{1}{8}(3x^2 + xy + 3y^2).$$

[Trin. Coll. Camb.]

197.   Shew that the sum of the products of the series
$$a, a - b, a - 2b, \ldots, a - (n - 1)\,b,$$
taken two and two together vanishes when n is of the form $3m^2 - 1$, and $2a = (3m - 2)(m + 1)\,b$.

198.   If n is even, and $\alpha + \beta, \alpha - \beta$ are the middle pair of terms, shew that the sum of the cubes of an arithmetical progression is

$$n\alpha \{\alpha^2 + (n^2 - 1) \beta^2\}.$$

199. If a, b, c are real positive quantities, shew that

$$\frac{1}{a} + \frac{1}{b} + \frac{1}{c} < \frac{a^8 + b^8 + c^8}{a^3 b^3 c^3}.$$

[Trin. Coll. Camb.]

200. A, B, and C start at the same time for a town a km. distant : A walks at a uniform rate of u km. an hour, and B and C drive at a uniform rate of v km. an hour. After a certain time B dismounts and walks forward at the same pace as A, while C drives back to meet A ; A gets into the carriage with C and they drive after B entering the town at the same time that he does : shew that the whole time occupied was $\dfrac{a}{v} \cdot \dfrac{3v + u}{3u + v}$ hours. [Peterhouse, Camb.]

201. The streets of a city are arranged like the lines of a chess-board. There are m streets running north and south, and n east and west. Find the number of ways in which a man can travel from the N.W. to the S.E. corner, going the shortest possible distance. [Oxford Mods.]

202. Solve the equation $\sqrt[4]{x + 27} + \sqrt[4]{55 - x} = 4$. [Ball. Coll. Ox.]

203. Shew that in the series

$$ab + (a + x)(b + x) + (a + 2x)(b + 2x) + \dots \text{ to } 2n \text{ terms,}$$

the excess of the sum of the last n terms over the sum of the first n terms is to the excess of the last term over the first as n^2 to $2n - 1$.

204. Find the nth convergent to

(1) $\dfrac{1}{2-} \dfrac{1}{2-} \dfrac{1}{2-} \dots$

(2) $\dfrac{4}{3+} \dfrac{4}{3+} \dfrac{4}{3+} \dots$

205. Prove that

$$(a - x)^4 (y - z)^4 + (a - y)^4 (z - x)^4 + (a - z)^4 (x - y)^4$$
$$= 2 \{ (a - y)^2 (a - z)^2 (x - y)^2 (x - z)^2 + (a - z)^2 (a - x)^2$$
$$\times (y - z)^2 (y - x)^2 + (a - x)^2 (a - y)^2 (z - x)^2 (z - y)^2 \}$$

[Peterhouse, Camb.]

206. If α, β, γ are the roots of $x^3 + qx + r = 0$, find the value of

$$\frac{ma+n}{ma-n} + \frac{m\beta+n}{m\beta-n} + \frac{m\gamma+n}{m\gamma-n} \text{ in terms of } m, n, q, r,.$$

[Queens's Coll. Camb.]

207. In England one person out of 46 is said to die every year, and one out of 33 to be born. If there were no emigration, in how many years would the population double itself at this rate ? Given

$\log 2 = 0.3010300, \log 1531 = 3.1849752, \log 1518 = 3.1812718$

208. If $(1 + x + x^2)^n = a_0 + a_1x + a_2x^2 + ...$, prove that

$$a_r - na_{r-1} + \frac{n(n-1)}{1.2}a_{r-2} - ... + (-1)^r \frac{n!}{r!(n-r)!}a_0 = 0,$$

unless r is a multiple of 3. What is its value in this case ?

[St John's Coll. Camb.]

209. In a mixed company consisting of Poles, Turks, Greeks, Germans and Italians, the Poles are one less than one-third of the number of Germans, and three less than half the number of Italians. The Turks and Germans outnumber the Greeks and Italians by 3; the Greeks and Germans form one less than half the company; while the Italians and Greeks form seven-sixteenths of the company : determine the number of each nation.

210. Find the sum to infinity of the series whose nth term is $(n+1)n^{-1}(n+2)^{-1}(-x)^{n+1}$.   [Oxford Mods.]

211. If n is a positive integer, prove that

$$n - \frac{n(n^2-1)}{2!} + \frac{n(n^2-1)(n^2-2^2)}{2!3!} - ...$$

$$+ (-1)^r \frac{n(n^2-1)(n^2-2^2)...(n^2-r^2)}{r!(r+1)!} + ... = (-1)^{n+1}.$$

[Pemb. Coll. Camb.]

212. Find the sum of the series :

(1) $6, 24, 60, 120, 210, 336, ...$ to n terms.

(2) $4 - 9x + 16x^2 - 25x^3 + 36x^4 - 49x^5 + ...$ to inf.

(3) $\frac{1.3}{2} + \frac{3.5}{2^2} + \frac{5.7}{2^3} + \frac{7.9}{2^4} + ...$ to inf.

213. Solve the equation $\begin{vmatrix} 4x & 6x+2 & 8x+1 \\ 6x+2 & 9x+3 & 12x \\ 8x+1 & 12x & 16x+2 \end{vmatrix} = 0.$

[King's Coll. Camb.]

214. Shew that

(1) $a^2(1+b^2) + b^2(1+c^2) + c^2(1+a^2) > 6abc,$

(2) $n(a^{p+q} + b^{p+q} + c^{p+q} + \ldots) > (a^p + b^p + c^p + \ldots)$

$$(a^q + b^q + c^q + \ldots),$$

the number of quantities $a, b, c, \ldots$ being n, and p and q being positive.

215. Solve the equations

$$\left. \begin{aligned} yz &= a(y+z) + \alpha \\ zx &= a(z+x) + \beta \\ xy &= a(x+y) + \gamma \end{aligned} \right\} .$$

[Trin. Coll. Camb.]

216. If n be a prime number, prove that

$$1(2^{n-1}+1) + 2\left(3^{n-1} + \frac{1}{2}\right) + 3\left(4^{n-1} + \frac{1}{3}\right)$$

$$+ \ldots + (n-1)\left(n^{n-1} + \frac{1}{n-1}\right)$$

is divisible by n.   [Queen's Cool. Ox.]

217. In a shooting competition a man can score $5, 4, 3, 2,$ or 0 points for each shot : find the number of different ways in which he can score 30 in 7 shots.   [Pemb. Coll. Camb.]

218. Prove that the expression $x^5 - bx^3 + cx^2 + dx - e$ will be the product of a complete square and a complete cube if

$$\frac{12b}{5} = \frac{9d}{b} = \frac{5e}{c} = \frac{d^2}{c^2} .$$

219. A bag contains 6 black balls and an unknown number, not greater than six, of white balls; three are drawn successively and not replaced and are all found to be white; prove that the chance that a black ball will be drawn next is $\dfrac{677}{909}$.

[Jesus Coll. Camb.]

220. Shew that the sum of the products of every pair of the squares of the first n whole numbers is $\dfrac{1}{360} n(n^2-1)(4n^2-1)(5n+6).$

[Caius Coll. Camb.]

221. If $\dfrac{\alpha^2(b-c)}{x-a} + \dfrac{\beta^2(c-a)}{x-b} + \dfrac{\gamma^2(a-b)}{x-c} = 0$ has equal roots, prove

that

$$\alpha(b-c) \pm \beta(c-a) \pm \gamma(a-b) = 0.$$

222. Prove that when n is a positive integer,

$$n = 2^{n-1} - \frac{n-2}{1} 2^{n-3} + \frac{(n-3)(n-4)}{2!} 2^{n-5}$$

$$- \frac{(n-4)(n-5)(n-6)}{3!} 2^{n-r} + \dots$$

[Clare Coll. Camb.]

223. Solve the equations :

(1) $x^2 + 2yz = y^2 + 2zx = z^2 + 2xy + 3 = 76$.

(2) $\left. \begin{array}{l} x + y + z = a + b + c \\ \dfrac{x}{a} + \dfrac{y}{b} + \dfrac{z}{c} = 3 \\ ax + by + cz = bc + ca + ab \end{array} \right\}$ [Christ's Coll. Camb.]

224. Prove that if each of m points in one straight line be joined to each of n in another by straight lines terminated by the points, then, excluding the given points, the lines will

intersect $\dfrac{1}{4} mn (m-1)(n-1)$ times   [Math. Tripos.]

225. Having given $y = x + x^2 + x^5$, expand x in the form

$$y + ay^2 + by^3 + cy^4 + dy^5 + \dots;$$

and shew that $a^2 d - 3abc + 2b^3 = -1$.   [Ball. Coll. Ox.]

226. A farmer spent three equal sums of money in buying hens, pigeons, and parrots. Each hen cost Re.1 more than a pigeon and Rs. 2. more than a parrot; altogether he bought 47 birds. The number of pigeons exceeded that of the hens by as many parrots as he could have bought for Rs. 9 : find the number of birds of each kind.

227. Express log 2 in the form of the infinite continued fraction

$$\frac{1}{1+} \frac{1}{1+} \frac{2^2}{1+} \frac{3^2}{1+} \dots \frac{n^2}{1+} \dots$$ [Euler.]

228. In a certain examination six papers are set, and to each are assigned 100 marks as a maximum. Shew that the number of ways in which a candidate may obtain forty per cent of the whole number of marks is

$$\frac{1!}{5!}\left\{\frac{(245)!}{(240)!} - 6 \cdot \frac{(144)!}{(139)!} + 15 \cdot \frac{(43)!}{(38)!}\right\}.$$ [Oxford Mods.]

229. Test for convergency

$$\frac{x}{2} + \frac{1.3}{2.4} \cdot \frac{x^3}{6} + \frac{1.3.5.7}{2.4.6.8} \cdot \frac{x^5}{10} + \frac{1.3.5.7.9.11}{2.4.6.8.10.12} \cdot \frac{x^7}{14} + \cdots$$

230. Find the scale of relation, the nth term, and the sum of n terms of the recurring series $1 + 6 + 40 + 288 + \ldots$

Shew also that the sum of n terms of the series formed by taking for its rth term the sum of r terms of this series is

$$\frac{2}{3^2}(2^{2n} - 1) + \frac{4}{7^2}(2^{3n} - 1) - \frac{5n}{21}.$$ [Caius Coll. Camb.]

231. It is known that at noon at a certain place the sum in hidden by clouds on an average two days out of every three; find the chance that at noon on at least four out of five specified future days the sun will be shining. [Queen's Coll. Ox.]

232. Solve the equations

$$\left.\begin{array}{l} x^2 + (y - z)^2 = a^2 \\ y^2 + (z - x)^2 = b^2 \\ z^2 + (x - y)^2 = c^2 \end{array}\right\}.$$ [Emm. Coll. Camb.]

233. Eliminate x, y, z from the equations :

$$\frac{x^2 - xy - xz}{a} = \frac{y^2 - yz - yx}{b} = \frac{z^2 - zx - zy}{c}, \text{ and } ax + by + cz = 0.$$

[Math. Tripos.]

234. If two roots of the equation $x^3 + px^2 + qx + r = 0$ be equal and of opposite signs, shew that $pq = r$. [Queens' Coll. Camb.]

235. Sum the series :

(1) $1 + 2^3x + 3^3x^2 + \ldots + n^3x^{n-1}$,

(2) $\dfrac{25}{1^2 . 2^3 . 3^3} + \dfrac{52}{2^2 . 3^3 . 4^3} + \ldots + \dfrac{5n^2 + 12n + 8}{n^2(n+1)^3(n+2)^3}.$

[Emm. Coll. Camb.]

236. If $(1 + a^3x^4)(1 + a^5x^8)(1 + a^9x^{16})(1 + a^{17}x^{32}) \ldots$

$$= 1 + A_4x^4 + A_8x^8 + A_{12}x^{12} + \ldots$$

prove that $A_{8n+4} = a^3 A_{8n}$, and $A_{8n} = a^{2n}A_{4n}$; and find the first ten terms of the expansion. [Corpus Coll. Camb.]

237. On a sheet of water there is no current from A to B but a current from B to C; a man rows downstream from A to C in 3 hours, and up stream from C to A in $3\frac{1}{2}$ hours; had there been the same current all the way as from B to C, his journey down stream would have occupied $2\frac{3}{4}$ hours; find the length of time his return journey would have taken under the same circumstances.

238. Prove that the nth convergent to the continued fraction

$$\frac{3}{2+}\frac{3}{2+}\frac{3}{2+} \dots \text{ is } \frac{3^{n+1}+3\,(-1)^{n+1}}{3^{n+1}-(-1)^{n+1}}.$$ [Emm. Coll. Camb.]

239. If all the coefficients in the equation
$$p_0x^n + p_1x^{n-1} + p_2x^{n-2} + \dots + p_n = f(x) = 0,$$
be whole numbers, and if $f(0)$ and $f(1)$ be each odd integers, prove that the equation cannot have a commensurable root.

[London University.]

240. Shew that the equation
$$\sqrt{ax+\alpha} + \sqrt{bx+\beta} + \sqrt{cx+\gamma} = 0$$
reduces to a simple equation if $\sqrt{a} \pm \sqrt{b} \pm \sqrt{c} = 0$.
Solve the equation
$$\sqrt{8x^2-12x-39} + \sqrt{2x^2-3x-15} - \sqrt{2x^2-3x+20} = 0.$$

241. A bag contains 3 red and 3 green balls, and a person draws out 3 at random. He then drops 3 blue balls into the bag, and again draws out 3 at random. Shew that he may just lay 8 to 3 with advantage to himself against the 3 latter balls being all of different colours.   [Pemb. Coll. Camb.]

242. Find the sum of the fifth powers of the roots of the equation $x^4 - 7x^2 + 4x - 3 = 0$.   [London University.]

243. A Geometrical and Harmonical Progression have the same pth, qth, rth terms a, b, c respectively : shew that
$$a\,(b-c)\log a + b\,(c-a)\log b + c\,(a-b)\log c = 0.$$

[Christ's Coll. Camb.]

244. Find four positive numbers such that the sum of the first, third and fourth exceeds the second by 8; the sum of the squares of the first and second exceeds the sum of the squares of the third and fourth by 36; the sum of the products of the

first and second, and of the third and fourth is 42; the cube of the first is equal to the sum of the cubes of the second, third, and fourth.

245. If T_n, T_{n+1}, T_{n+2} be 3 consecutive terms of a recurring series connected by the relation $T_{n+2} = aT_{n+1} - bT_n$, prove that

$$\frac{1}{b^n} \{T_{n+1}^2 - aT_n T_{n+1} + bT_n^2\} = \text{a constant.}$$

246. Eliminate x, y, z from the equations :

$$\left.\begin{array}{cc} \dfrac{1}{x} + \dfrac{1}{y} + \dfrac{1}{z} = \dfrac{1}{a}, & x^2 + y^2 + z^2 = b^2, \\ x^3 + y^3 + z^3 = c^3, & xyz = d^3. \end{array}\right\} \quad \text{[Emm. Coll. Camb.]}$$

247. Shew that the roots of the equation

$$x^4 - px^3 + qx^2 - rx + \frac{r^2}{p^2} = 0$$

are in proportion. Hence solve $x^4 - 12x^3 + 47x^2 - 72x + 36 = 0$.

248. *A can hit a target four times in 5 shots; B three times in 4 shots; and C twice in 3 shots. They fire a volley : what is the probability that two shots at least hit ? And if two hit what is the probability that it is C who has missed ?*

[St Cath. Coll. Camb.]

249. Sum each of the following series to n terms :

(1) $1 + 0 - 1 + 0 + 7 + 28 + 79 + \ldots$;

(2) $-\dfrac{2 \cdot 2}{1 \cdot 2 \cdot 3 \cdot 4} + \dfrac{1 \cdot 2^2}{2 \cdot 3 \cdot 4 \cdot 5} + \dfrac{6 \cdot 2^3}{3 \cdot 4 \cdot 5 \cdot 6} + \dfrac{13 \cdot 2^4}{4 \cdot 5 \cdot 6 \cdot 7} + \ldots$;

(3) $3 + x + 9x^2 + x^3 + 33x^4 + x^5 + 129x^6 + \ldots$

[Second Public Exam. Ox]

250. Solve the equations :

$$\left.\begin{array}{l} (1)\ \ y^2 + yz + z^2 = ax, \\ \quad\ z^2 + zx + x^2 = ay, \\ \quad\ x^2 + xy + y^2 = az. \end{array}\right\} \qquad \left.\begin{array}{l} (2)\ \ x\,(y + z - x) = a, \\ \quad\ y\,(z + x - y) = b, \\ \quad\ z\,(x + y - z) = c. \end{array}\right\}$$

[Peterhouse, Camb.]

251. If $\dfrac{1}{a} + \dfrac{1}{b} + \dfrac{1}{c} = \dfrac{1}{a+b+c}$, and n is an odd integer, shew that

$$\frac{1}{a^n} + \frac{1}{b^n} + \frac{1}{c^n} = \frac{1}{a^n + b^n + c^n}.$$

If $u^6 - v^6 + 5u^2v^2 (u^2 - v^2) + 4uv (1 - u^4v^4) = 0$, prove that
$$(u^2 - v^2)^6 = 16u^2v^2 (1 - u^8) (1 - v^8).$$ [Pemb. Coll. Camb.]

252. If $x + y + z = 3p$, $yz + zx + xy = 3q$, $xyz = r$, prove that
$$(y + z - x) (z + x - y) (x + y - z) = -27p^3 + 36pq - 8r,$$
and $(y + z - x)^3 + (z + x - y)^3 + (x + y - z)^3 = 27p^3 - 24r.$

253. Find the factors, linear in x, y, z, of
$$\{a (b + c) x^2 + b (c + a)y^2 + c (a + b) z^2\}^2 - 4abc (x^2 + y^2 + z^2)$$
$$\times (ax^2 + by^2 + cx^2).$$ [Caius Coll. Camb.]

254. Shew that $\left(\dfrac{x^2 + y^2 + z^2}{x + y + z}\right)^{x+y+z} > x^x y^y z^z > \left(\dfrac{x + y + z}{3}\right)^{x+y+z}$

[St John's Coll. Camb.]

255. By means of the identity $\left\{1 - \dfrac{4x}{(1 + x)^2}\right\}^{-1/2} = \dfrac{1 + x}{1 - x}$, prove

that
$$\sum_{r=1}^{r=n} (-1)^{n-r} \frac{(n + r - 1)!}{r! (r - 1) (n - r)!} = 1.$$

[Pemb. Coll. Camb.]

256. Solve the equations :
(1) $ax + by + z = zx + ay + b = yz + bx + a = 0.$
(2)
$$\left.\begin{array}{r} x + y + z - u = 12, \\ x^2 + y^2 - z^2 - u^2 = 6, \\ x^3 + y^3 - z^3 + u^3 = 218, \\ xy + zu = 45. \end{array}\right\}$$

257. If $p = q$ nearly, and $n > 1$, shew that
$$\frac{(n + 1) p + (n - 1) q}{(n - 1) p + (n + 1) q} = \left(\frac{p}{q}\right)^{1/n}$$

If $\dfrac{p}{q}$ agree with unity as far as the rth decimal place, to how

many places will this approximation in general be correct ?

[Math. Tripos.]

258. A lady bought 54 lbs. of tea and coffee; if she had bought
five-sixths of the quantity of tea and four-fifths of the
quantity of coffee she would have spent nine-elevenths of
what she had actually spent; and if she had bought as much

tea as she did coffee and *viceversa*, she would have spent 5s more than she did. Tea is more expensive than coffee, and the price of 6 lbs of coffee exceeds that of 2 lbs of tea by 5s; find the price of each.

259. If s_n represent the sum of the products of the first n natural numbers taken two at a time, then

$$\frac{2}{3!} + \frac{11}{4!} + \ldots + \frac{s_{n-1}}{n!} + \ldots = \frac{11}{24} e.$$ [Caius Coll. Camb.]

260. If $\dfrac{P}{pa^2 + 2qab + rb^2} = \dfrac{Q}{pac + q(bc - a^2) - rab} = \dfrac{R}{pc^2 - 2qca + ra^2}$,

prove that P, p; Q, q; and R, r may be interchanged without altering the equalities.   [Math. Tripos.]

261. If $\alpha + \beta + \gamma = 0$, shew that

$$\alpha^{n+3} + \beta^{n+3} + \gamma^{n+3} = \alpha\beta\gamma\,(\alpha^n + \beta^n + \gamma^n) + \frac{1}{2}\,(\alpha^2 + \beta^2 + \gamma^2)$$

$$\times (a^{n+1} + \beta^{n+1} + \gamma^{n+1}).$$ [Caius Coll. Camb.]

262. If $\alpha, \beta, \gamma, \delta$ be the roots of the equation

$$x^4 + px^3 + qx^2 + rx + s = 0,$$

find in terms of the coefficients the value of $\Sigma\,(\alpha - \beta)^2\,(\gamma - \delta)^2$.
                                                    [London University.]

263. A dealer bought a certain number of minas, parrots, and bulbuls, giving for each bird as many rupees as there were birds of that kind; altogether he bought 23 birds and spent Rs. 211; find the number of each kind that he bought, if parrots are cheaper than minas and dearer than bulbuls.

264. Prove that the equation

$$(y + z - 8x)^{1/3} + (z + x - 8y)^{1/3} + (x + y - 8z)^{1/3} = 0.$$

is equivalent to the equation

$$x\,(y - z)^2 + y\,(z - x)^2 + z\,(x - y)^2 = 0.$$ [St John's Coll. Camb.]

265. If the equation $\dfrac{a}{x+a} + \dfrac{b}{x+b} = \dfrac{c}{x+c} + \dfrac{d}{x+d}$ have a pair of equal roots, then either one of the quantities a or b is equal to one of the quantities c or d, or else $\dfrac{1}{a} + \dfrac{1}{b} = \dfrac{1}{c} + \dfrac{1}{d}$. Prove also that the

roots are then $-a, -a, 0; -b, -b, 0;$ or $0, 0, -\dfrac{2ab}{a+b}$.

[Math. Tripos.]

266. Solve the equations :

(1) $x + y + z = ab,\ x^{-1} + y^{-1} + z^{-1} = a^{-1}b,\ xyz = a^3$.

(2) $ayz + by + cz = bzx + cz + ax = cxy + ax + by = a + b + c$.

[Second Public Exam. Oxford.]

267. Find the simplest form of the expression

$$\frac{\alpha^3}{(\alpha-\beta)(\alpha-\gamma)(\alpha-\delta)(\alpha-\varepsilon)} + \frac{\beta^3}{(\beta-\alpha)(\beta-\gamma)(\beta-\delta)(\beta-\varepsilon)} + \cdots$$

$$+ \frac{\varepsilon^3}{(\varepsilon-\alpha)(\varepsilon-\beta)(\varepsilon-\gamma)(\varepsilon-\delta)} \cdot \qquad \text{[London University.]}$$

268. In a company of Clergymen, Doctors, and Lawyers it is found that the sum of the ages of all present is 2160; their average age is 36; the average age of the Clergymen and Doctors in 39; of the Doctors and Lawyers $32\frac{8}{11}$; of the Clergymen and Lawyers $36\frac{2}{3}$. If each Clergyman had been 1 year, each Lawyer 7 years, and each Doctor 6 years older, their average age would have been greater by 5 years : find the number of each profession present and their average ages.

269. Find the condition, among its coefficients, that the expression

$$a_0 x^4 + 4a_1 x^3 y + 6a_2 x^2 y^2 + 4a_3 xy^3 + a_4 y^4$$

should be reducible to the sum of the fourth powers of two linear expressions in x and y.   [London University.]

270. Find the real roots of the equations

$$x^2 + v^2 + w^2 = a^2,\ vw + u(y + z) = bc,$$

$$y^2 + w^2 + u^2 = b^2,\ wu + v(z + x) = ca,$$

$$z^2 + u^2 + v^2 = c^2,\ uv + w(x + y) = ab. \qquad \text{[Math. Tripos.]}$$

271. It is a rule in Gaelic that no consonant or group of consonants can stand immediately between a strong and a weak vowel; the strong vowels being a, o, u; and the weak vowels e and i. Shew that the whole number of Gaelic words of $n + 3$ letters each, which can be formed of n consonants and the vowels aeo is $\dfrac{2(n+3)!}{n+2}$ where no letter is repeated in the same word.

[Caius Coll. Camb.]

272. Shew that if $x^2 + y^2 = 2z^2$, where x, y, z are integers, then
$$2x = r(l^2 + 2lk - k^2),\ 2y = r(k^2 + 2lk - l^2),\ 2z = r(l^2 + k^2)$$
where $r, l,$ and k are integers.   [Caius Coll. Camb.]

273. Find the value of $\dfrac{1}{1+}\dfrac{1}{1+}\dfrac{2}{3+}\dfrac{4}{5+}\dfrac{6}{7+}\ldots$ to inf.

[Christ's Coll. Camb.]

274. Sum the series :

(1) $\dfrac{x^2}{2.3} + \dfrac{2x^3}{3.4} + \dfrac{3x^4}{4.5} + \ldots$ to inf.

(2) $\dfrac{1!}{a+1} + \dfrac{2!}{(a+1)(a+2)} + \ldots + \dfrac{n!}{(a+1)(a+2)\ldots(a+n)}$.

275. Solve the equations :

(1) $2xyz + 3 = (2x-1)(3y+1)(4z-1) + 12$
$$= (2x+1)(3y-1)(4z+1) + 80 = 0.$$

(2) $3ux - 2vy = vx + uy = 3u^2 + 2v^2 = 14;\ xy = 10uv.$

276. Shew that
$$\begin{vmatrix} a^2+\lambda & ab & ac & ad \\ ab & b^2+\lambda & bc & bd \\ ac & bc & c^2+\lambda & cd \\ ad & bd & cd & d^2+\lambda \end{vmatrix}$$

is divisible by λ^3 and find the other factor.

[Corpus Coll. Camb.]

277. If $a, b, c, \ldots$ are the roots of the equation
$$x^n + p_1 x^{n-1} + p_2 x^{n-2} + \ldots + p_{n-1}x + p_n = 0;$$

find the sum of $a^3 + b^3 + c^3 + \ldots$, and shew that
$$\frac{a^2}{b} + \frac{b^2}{a} + \frac{a^2}{c} + \frac{c^2}{a} + \frac{b^2}{c} + \frac{c^2}{b} + \ldots = p_1 - \frac{p_{n-1}(p_1^2 - 2p_2)}{p_n}$$

[St John's Coll. Camb.]

278. By the expansion of $\dfrac{1+2x}{1-x^3}$, or otherwise, prove that
$$1 - 3n + \frac{(3n-1)(3n-2)}{1.2} - \frac{(3n-2)(3n-3)(3n-4)}{1.2.3}$$
$$+ \frac{(3n-3)(3n-4)(3n-5)(3n-6)}{1.2.3.4} - \&c. = (-1)^n,$$

when n is an integer, and the series stops at the first term that
vanishes.   [Math. Tripos.]

279. Two sportsmen A and B went out shooting and brought home 10 birds. The sum of the squares of the number of shots was 2880, and the product of numbers of shots fired by each was 48 times the product of the numbers of birds killed by each. If A had fired as often as B and B as often as A, then B would have killed 5 more birds than A: find the number of birds killed by each.

280. Prove that $8(a^3 + b^3 + c^3)^2 > 9(a^2 + bc)(b^2 + ca)(c^2 + ab)$.

[Pemb. Coll. Camb.]

281. Shew that the nth convergent to

$$\frac{2}{3-}\frac{4}{4-}\frac{6}{5-}\dots \text{ is } 2 - \frac{2^{n+1}}{\Sigma_0^n 2^r(n-r)!}.$$

What is the limit of this when n is infinite?

[King's Coll. Camb.]

282. If $\dfrac{p_n}{q_n}$ is the nth convergent to the continued fraction

$$\frac{1}{a+}\frac{1}{b+}\frac{1}{c+}\frac{1}{a+}\frac{1}{b+}\frac{1}{c+}\dots$$

shew that $p_{3n+3} = bp_{3n} + (bc+1)q_{3n}$.   [Queens's Coll. Camb.]

283. Out of n straight lines whose lengths are $1, 2, 3, \dots, n$ inches respectively, the number of ways in which four may be chosen which will form a quadrilateral in which a circle may be inscribed is

$$\frac{1}{48}\{2n(n-2)(2n-5) - 3 + 3(-1)^n\}. \quad \text{[Math. Tripos.]}$$

284. If u_2, u_3 are respectively the arithmetic means of the squares and cubes of all numbers less than n and prime to it, prove that $n^3 - 6nu_2 + 4u_3 = 0$, unity being counted as a prime. [St. John's Coll. Camb.]

285. If n is of the form $6m - 1$ shew that $(y-z)^n + (z-x)^n + (x-y)^n$ is divisible by $x^2 + y^2 + z^2 - yz - zx - xy$; and if n is of the form $6m + 1$, shew that it is divisible by

$$(x^2 + y^2 + z^2 - yz - zx - xy)^2.$$

286. If S is the sum of the mth powers, P the sum of the products m together of the n quantities $a_1, a_2, a_3, \dots a_n$, shew that

$$(n-1)! \cdot S > (n-m)! \cdot m! \, p \qquad \text{[Caius Coll. Camb.]}$$

287. Prove that if the equations

$$x^3 + qx - r = 0 \text{ and } rx^3 - 2q^2x^2 - 5qrx - 2q^3 - r^2 = 0$$

have a common root, the first equation will have a pair of equal roots; and if each of these is a, find all the roots of the second equation.   [India Civil Service.]

288. If $x\sqrt{2a^2 - 3x^2} + y\sqrt{2a^2 - 3y^2} + z\sqrt{2a^2 - 3z^2} = 0$,

where a^2 stands for $x^2 + y^2 + z^2$, prove that

$$(x + y + z)(-x + y + z)(x - y + z)(x + y - z) = 0.$$
                                                        [Trin. Coll. Camb.]

289. Find the values of $x_1, x_2, \ldots x_n$ which satisfy the following system of simultaneous equations :

$$\frac{x_1}{a_1 - b_1} + \frac{x_2}{a_1 - b_2} + \ldots + \frac{x_n}{a_1 - b_n} = 1,$$

$$\frac{x_1}{a_2 - b_1} + \frac{x_2}{a_2 - b_2} + \ldots + \frac{x_n}{a_2 - b_n} = 1.$$

$$\ldots\ldots\ldots\ldots\ldots\ldots\ldots\ldots\ldots\ldots\ldots\ldots$$

$$\frac{x_1}{a_n - b_1} + \frac{x_2}{a_n - b_2} + \ldots + \frac{x_n}{a_n - b_n} = 1. \quad \text{[London University.]}$$

290. Shew that
$$\begin{vmatrix} yz - x^2 & zx - y^2 & xy - z^2 \\ zx - y^2 & xy - z^2 & yz - x^2 \\ xy - z^2 & yz - x^2 & zx - y^2 \end{vmatrix} = \begin{vmatrix} r^2 & u^2 & u^2 \\ u^2 & r^2 & u^2 \\ u^2 & u^2 & r^2 \end{vmatrix},$$

where $r^2 = x^2 + y^2 + z^2$, and $u^2 = yz + zx + xy$.
                                                        [Trin. Coll. Camb.]

291. A piece of work was done by A, B, C; at first A worked alone, but after some days was joined by B, and these two after some days were joined by C. The whole work could have been done by B and C, if they had each worked twice the number of days that they actually did. The work could also have been completed without B's help if A had worked two-thirds and C four times the number of days they actually did; or if A and B had worked together for 40 days without C; or if all three had worked together for the time that B had worked. The number of days that elapsed before B began to work was to the number that elapsed before C began to work as 3 to 5 : find the number of days that each man worked.

292.   Shew that if S_r is the sum of the products r together of

$$1, x, x^2, x^3, \ldots x^{n-1},$$

then $S_{n-r} = S_r \cdot x^{(1/2)(n-1)(n-2r)}.$ [St John's Coll. Camb.]

293.   If a, b, c are positive and the sum of any two greater than the third, prove that

$$\left(1 + \frac{b-c}{a}\right)^a \left(1 + \frac{c-a}{b}\right)^b \left(1 + \frac{a-b}{c}\right)^c < 1.$$

[St John's Coll. Camb.]

294.   Resolve into factors

$$(a+b+c)(b+c-a)(c+a-b)(a+b-c)(a^2+b^2+c^2) - 8a^2b^2c^2.$$

Prove that

$$4 \{\alpha^4 + \beta^4 + \gamma^4 + (\alpha+\beta+\gamma)^4\} = (\beta+\gamma)^4 + (\gamma+\alpha)^4 + (\alpha+\beta)^4$$

$$+ 6(\beta+\gamma)^2(\gamma+\alpha)^2 + 6(\gamma+\alpha)^2(\alpha+\beta)^2 + 6(\alpha+\beta)^2(\beta+\gamma)^2.$$

[Jesus Coll. Camb.]

295.   Prove that the sum of the homogeneous products of r dimensions of the numbers $1, 2, 3, \ldots n$, and their powers is

$$\frac{(-1)^{n-1}}{(n-1)!} \left\{ 1^{a+r-1} - \frac{n-1}{1} \cdot 2^{n+r-1} \right.$$

$$\left. + \frac{(n-1)(n-2)}{1.2} \cdot 3^{n+r-1} - \ldots \text{ to } n \text{ terms} \right\}.$$

[Emm. Coll. Camb.]

296.   Prove that, if n be a positive integer,

$$1 - 3n + \frac{3n(3n-3)}{1.2} - \frac{3n(3n-4)(3n-5)}{1.2.3} + \ldots = 2(-1)^n.$$

[Oxford Mods.]

297.   If $x(2a-y) = y(2a-z) = z(2a-u) = u(2a-x) = b^2$, shew that $x = y = z = u$ unless $b^2 = 2a^2$, and that if this condition is satisfied the equations are not independent.   [Math. Tripos.]

298   Shew that if a, b, c are positive and unequal, the equations

$$ax + yz + z = 0, \quad zx + by + z = 0, \quad yz + zx + c = 0,$$

give three distinct triads, of real values for x, y, z; and the ratio of the products of three values of x and y is $b(b-c) : a(c-a)$.   [Oxford Mods.]

299.   If $A = ax - by - cz, \quad D = bz + cy,$

$B = by - cz - ax, \quad E = cx + az,$

$$C = cz - ax - by, \quad F = ay + bx,$$

prove that $ABC - AD^2 - BE^2 - CF^2 + 2DEF$
$$= (a^2 + b^2 + c^2)(ax + by + cz)(x^2 + y^2 + z^2).$$

[Second Public Exam. Oxford.]

300. A certain student found it necessary to decipher an old manuscript. During previous experiences of the same kind he had observed that the number of words he could read daily varied jointly as the number of miles he walked and the number of hours he worked during the day. He therefore gradually increased the amount of daily exercise and daily work at the rate of 1 mile and 1 hour per day respectively, beginning the first day with his usual quantity. He found that the manuscript contained 232000 words, that he counted 12000 on the first day, and 72000 on the last day; and that by the end of half the time he had counted 62000 words : find his usual amount of daily exercise and work.

ANSWERS

I. Pages 9 – 11

1. (1) $54b : a$ (2) $9 : 7$ (3) $bx : ay$ **2.** 18.   **3.** 385, 660.

4. 11.   **5.** $5 : 13$.   **6.** $5 : 6$ or $-3 : 5$.

10. $\dfrac{x}{4} = \dfrac{y}{2} = \dfrac{z}{3}$, or $\dfrac{x}{1} = \dfrac{y}{-1} = \dfrac{z}{0}$.

17. $abc + 2fgh - af^2 - bg^2 - ch^2 = 0$.

20. 3, 4, 1.   **21.** $-3, 4, 1$.   **22.** 7, 3, 2.   **23.** 3, 4, 1.

25. $\pm a(b^2 - c^2), \pm b(c^2 - a^2), \pm c(a^2 - b^2)$

26. $bc(b - c), ca(c - a), ab(a - b)$

II. Pages 17–19

1. 45.   **2.** (1) 12. (2) $300a^3b$.   **3.** $\dfrac{x^3}{y(x^2 + y^3)}$.

13. $0, 5, \dfrac{8}{7}$.   **14.** 0, 3, 8.

15. $\dfrac{a(b + c)}{cm - bm - 2an}$.   **18.** 8.   **19.** 6, 9, 10, 15.

20. 3 gallons from A; 8 gallons from B.   **21.** 45 gallons.

23. $17 : 3$.   **24.** $a = 4b$.

25. 64 per cent copper and 36 per cent zinc. 3 parts of brass are taken to 5 parts of bronze.

26. 63 or 12 minutes.

III. Pages 24 – 26

1. $5\dfrac{1}{3}$.   **2.** 9.   **3.** $1\dfrac{1}{3}$.   **4.** 2.   **7.** 60.

9. $y = 2x - \dfrac{8}{x}$.   **10.** $y = 5x + \dfrac{36}{x^2}$.   **11.** 4.

12. $x = \dfrac{22}{15}z + \dfrac{2}{15z}$.   **14.** 36.

15. 1610 feet: 305·9 feet.   **16.** $22\dfrac{11}{24}$ cubic feet.   **17.** $4 : 3$.

18. The regatta lasted 6 days; 4th, 5th, 6th days.

20. 16, 25 years; £200, £250.

21. 1 day 18 hours 28 minutes.

22. The cost is least when the rate is 12 miles an hour; and then the cost per mile is £$\dfrac{3}{32}$, and for the journey is £9. 7s. 6d.

IV. a. PAGES 30 – 31

1. $277\frac{1}{2}$.　　**2.** 153.　　**3.** 0.　　**4.** $\dfrac{n(10-n)}{3}$.

5. 30.　　**6.** -42.　　**7.** -185.　　**8.** $1325\sqrt{3}$.

9. $75\sqrt{5}$　　**10.** $820a - 1680b$.

11. $n(n+1)a - n^2b$.　　　　**12.** $\dfrac{21}{2}(11a - 9b)$.

13. $-\dfrac{1}{4}, -\dfrac{3}{4}, \dots -9\frac{1}{4}$.

14. $1, -1\frac{1}{2}, \dots, -39$.　　　**15.** $-33x, -31x, \dots, x$.

16. $x^2 - x + 1, x^2 - 2x + 2, \dots x$.　　**17.** n^2.　　**18.** 3.

19. 5.　　**20.** 612.　　**21.** 4, 9, 14.　　**22.** 1, 4, 7.

23. 495.　　**24.** 160.　　**25.** $\dfrac{p(p+1)}{2a} + pb$.

26. $n(n+1)a - \dfrac{n^2}{a}$.

IV. b. PAGES 34 – 35

1. 10 or -8　　**2.** 8 or -13.　　**3.** 2, 5, 8, $\dots$

4. First term 8, number of terms 59.

5. First term $7\frac{1}{2}$, number of terms 54.

6. Instalments £51, £53, £55, $\dots$　　**7.** 12.　　**8.** 25.

9. $\dfrac{n}{2(1-x)}(2 + \overline{n-3}.\sqrt{x})$.　　**10.** n^2.　　**12.** $-(p+q)$.

13. 3, 5, 7, 9. [Assume for the numbers $a - 3d, a - d, a + d, a + 3d$.]

14. 2, 4, 6, 8.　　**15.** $p + q - m$.　　**16.** 12 or -17.

17. $6r - 1$.　　**20.** $10p - 8$.

21. 8 terms. Series $1\frac{1}{2}, 3, 4\frac{1}{2}, \dots$　　**22.** 3, 5, 7; 4, 5, 6.

23. $ry = (n + 1 - r)x$.

V. a. PAGES 40 – 41

1. $\dfrac{2059}{1458}$.　　**2.** $\dfrac{1281}{512}$.　　**3.** $191\frac{1}{4}$.　　**4.** -682.

5. $\dfrac{1093}{45}$.　　**6.** $\dfrac{1}{4}(5^p - 1)$.　　**7.** $\dfrac{9}{7}\left\{1 - \left(\dfrac{4}{3}\right)^{2n}\right\}$.

8. $364(\sqrt{3} + 1)$.　　**9.** $\dfrac{1}{2}(585\sqrt{2} - 292)$.　　**10.** $-\dfrac{463}{192}$.

11. $\dfrac{3}{2}, 1, \dfrac{2}{3}$. **12.** $\dfrac{16}{3}, 8, \ldots 27$. **13.** $-7, \dfrac{7}{2}, \ldots, \dfrac{7}{32}$.

14. $\dfrac{64}{65}$. **15.** $\dfrac{27}{58}$.

16. $0 \cdot 999$. **17.** $\dfrac{1}{2}$. **18.** $\dfrac{3(3+\sqrt{3})}{2}$. **19.** $7(7+\sqrt{42})$.

20. 2. **21.** 16, 24, 36, … **22.** 2.

23. 2. **24.** 8, 12, 18. **25.** 2, 6, 18.

28. $6, -3, 1\dfrac{1}{2}, \ldots$

V. b. PAGES 44 – 45

1. $\dfrac{1-a^n}{(1-a)^2} - \dfrac{na^n}{1-a}$. **2.** $\dfrac{8}{3}$. **3.** $\dfrac{1+x}{(1-x)^2}$.

4. $4 - \dfrac{1}{2^{n-2}} - \dfrac{n}{2^{n-1}}$. **5.** 6. **6.** $\dfrac{1}{(1-x)^3}$.

9. $\dfrac{1}{(1-r)(1-br)}$. **10.** 40, 20, 10. **11.** $4, 1, \dfrac{1}{4}, \ldots$

12. $\dfrac{x(x^n-1)}{x-1} + \dfrac{n(n+1)a}{2}$ **13.** $\dfrac{x^2(x^{2n}-1)}{x^2-1} + \dfrac{xy(x^n y^n - 1)}{xy-1}$.

14. $4p^2a + \dfrac{2}{9}\left(1 - \dfrac{1}{2^{2p}}\right)$. **15.** $1\dfrac{1}{8}$. **16.** $\dfrac{23}{48}$.

19. $n \cdot 2^{n+2} - 2^{n+1} + 2$. **20.** $\dfrac{(1+a)(a^n c^n - 1)}{ac-1}$.

21. $\dfrac{a}{r-1}\left\{ \dfrac{r(r^{2n}-1)}{r^2-1} - n \right\}$.

VI. a. PAGES 51 – 52

1. (1) 5. (2) $3\dfrac{1}{2}$. (3) $3\dfrac{2}{3}\dfrac{9}{2}$. **2.** $6\dfrac{1}{9}, 7\dfrac{6}{7}$. **3.** $\dfrac{2}{5}, \dfrac{2}{7}, \dfrac{2}{9}, \dfrac{2}{11}$.

4. 6 and 24. **5.** 4 : 9. **10.** $n^2(n+1)$.

11. $\dfrac{1}{4}n(n+1)(n^2+n+3)$. **12.** $\dfrac{1}{6}n(n+1)(2n+7)$.

13. $\dfrac{1}{2}n(n+1)(n^2+3n+1)$. **14.** $\dfrac{1}{2}(3^{n+1}+1) - 2^{n+1}$.

15. $4^{n+1} - 4 - n(n+1)(n^2-n-1)$.

18. The nth term $= b + c(2n-1)$, for all values of n greater than 1.

The first term is $a + b + c$; the other terms form the A. P.
$$b + 3c, b + 5c, b + 7c, \ldots$$

19. n^4. **22.** $\dfrac{n}{2}(2a + \overline{n-1}d)\left\{a^2 + (n-1)ad + \dfrac{n(n-1)}{2}d^2\right\}$.

VI. b. PAGES 54 – 55

1. 1240.	**2.** 1140.	**3.** 16646.	**4.** 2470.
5. 21321.	**6.** 52.	**7.** 11879.	**8.** 1840.
9. 11940.	**10.** 190.	**11.** 300.	**12.** 18296.

14. Triangular 364; Square 4900.

15. 120. **16.** $n - 1$.

VII. a. PAGE 58

1. 333244.	**2.** 728626.	**3.** 1740137.	**4.** e7074.
5. 112022.	**6.** 334345.	**7.** 17832126.	**8.** 1625.
9. 2012.	**10.** 342.	**11.** ttt90001.	**12.** 231.
13. 1456.	**14.** 7071.	**15.** eee.	

16. (1) 121. (2) 122000.

VII. b. PAGES 63 – 65

1. 20305.	**2.** 4444.	**3.** 11001110.	**4.** 2000000.
5. 7338.	**6.** 34402.	**7.** 6587.	**8.** 8978.
9. 26011.	**10.** 37214.	**11.** 30034342.	**12.** 710te3.
13. 2714687.	**14.** ·2046.	**15.** 15·1t6.	**16.** 20·73.
17. 125·01$\dot{2}\dot{5}$.	**18.** $\dfrac{5}{8}$.	**19.** $\dfrac{2}{3}, \dfrac{5}{8}$.	**20.** Nine.
21. Four.	**22.** Twelve.	**23.** Eight.	**24.** Eleven.
25. Twelve.	**26.** Ten.	**30.** $2^{11} + 2^7 + 2^6$.	

31. $3^9 - 3^8 - 3^7 - 3^6 - 3^5 + 3^3 + 3^2 + 1$.

VIII. a. PAGES 70 – 72

1. $\dfrac{2 + \sqrt{2} + \sqrt{6}}{4}$.

2. $\dfrac{3 + \sqrt{6} + \sqrt{15}}{6}$.

3. $\dfrac{a\sqrt{b} + b\sqrt{a} - \sqrt{ab(a+b)}}{2ab}$.

4. $\dfrac{a - 1 + \sqrt{a^2 - 1} + \sqrt{2a(a-1)}}{a - 1}$.

5. $\dfrac{3\sqrt{30} + 5\sqrt{15} - 12 - 10\sqrt{2}}{7}$.

6. $\dfrac{\sqrt{2} + \sqrt{3} + \sqrt{5}}{2}$.

7. $3^{5/3} + 3^{4/3} \cdot 2^{1/2} + 3 \cdot 2 + 3^{2/3} \cdot 2^{3/2} + 3^{1/3} \cdot 2^2 + 2^{5/2}$.

8. $5^{5/6} - 5^{4/6} \cdot 2^{1/3} + 5^{3/6} \cdot 2^{2/3} - 5^{2/6} \cdot 2 + 5^{1/6} \cdot 2^{4/3} - 2^{5/3}$.

9. $a^{11/6} - a^{10/6}b^{1/4} + a^{9/6}b^{1/2} - \dots + a^{1/6}b^{10/4} - b^{11/4}$.

10. $3^{2/3} + 3^{1/3} + 1$.

11. $2^3 - 2^2 \cdot 7^{1/4} + 2 \cdot 7^{1/2} - 7^{3/4}$.

12. $5^{11/3} + 5^{10/3} \cdot 3^{1/4} + 5^3 \cdot 3^{2/4} + \dots + 5^{1/3} \cdot 3^{10/4} + 3^{11/4}$.

13. $\dfrac{1 - 3^{2/3} + 3^{1/3}}{2}$.

14. $17 - 3^{5/3} \cdot 2^{3/2} + 3^{4/3} \cdot 2^2 - 3 \cdot 2^{5/2} + 3^{2/3} \cdot 2^3 - 3^{1/3} \cdot 2^{7/2}$.

15. $3^2 \cdot 2^{1/2} - 3^{5/3} \cdot 2 + 3^{4/3} \cdot 2^{3/2} - 3 \cdot 2^2 + 3^{2/3} \cdot 2^{5/2} - 3^{1/3} \cdot 2^3$.

16. $\dfrac{1}{2}\left(3^{5/6} - 3^{4/6} + 3^{3/6} - 3^{2/6} + 3^{1/6} - 1. \right)$.

17. $\dfrac{2^5 + 2^{31/6} + 2^{26/6} + 2^{21/6} + 2^{16/6} + 2^{11/6} + 1}{31}$.

18. $\dfrac{3^{3/2} + 3^{5/6} + 3^{1/6}}{8}$. 　　19. $\sqrt{5} + \sqrt{7} - 2$.

20. $\sqrt{5} - \sqrt{7} + 2\sqrt{3}$. 　　21. $1 + \sqrt{3} - \sqrt{2}$

22. $1 + \sqrt{\dfrac{3}{2}} - \sqrt{\dfrac{5}{2}}$. 　　23. $2 + \sqrt{a} - \sqrt{3b}$. 　　24. $3 - \sqrt{7} + \sqrt{2} - \sqrt{3}$.

25. $1 + \sqrt{3}$. 　　26. $2 + \sqrt{5}$. 　　27. $3 - 2\sqrt{2}$.

28. $\sqrt{14} - 2\sqrt{2}$. 　　29. $2\sqrt{3} + \sqrt{5}$. 　　30. $3\sqrt{3} - \sqrt{6}$.

31. $\sqrt{\dfrac{2a+x}{2}} + \sqrt{\dfrac{x}{2}}$. 　　32. $\sqrt{\dfrac{3a+b}{2}} - \sqrt{\dfrac{a-b}{2}}$.

33. $\sqrt{\dfrac{1 + a + a^2}{2}} + \sqrt{\dfrac{1 - a + a^2}{2}}$.

34. $\dfrac{1}{4\sqrt{1-a^2}}\left(\sqrt{\dfrac{1+a}{2}} + \sqrt{\dfrac{1-a}{2}} \right)$. 　　35. $11 + 56\sqrt{3}$.

36. 289. 　　37. $\dfrac{1}{3}\sqrt{3}$. 　　38. $3\sqrt{3} + 5$.

39. 3. 　　40. $8\sqrt{3}$. 　　41. $3 + \sqrt{5} = 5.23607$.

42. $x^2 + 1 + \sqrt[3]{4} + x - x\sqrt[3]{2} + \sqrt[3]{2}$. 　　43. $3a + \sqrt{b^2 - 3a^2}$.

44. $\dfrac{a-1}{2}$.

VIII. b. PAGES 78 – 79

1. $6 - 2\sqrt{6}$. 　　2. -13. 　　3. $e^{2\sqrt{-1}} - e^{-2\sqrt{-1}}$

4. $x^2 - x + 1$.   **5.** $\dfrac{3 + \sqrt{-2}}{11}$.   **6.** $-19 - 6\sqrt{10}$.

7. $-\dfrac{8}{29}$.   **8.** $\dfrac{4ax\sqrt{-1}}{a^2 + x^2}$.   **9.** $\dfrac{2(3x^2 - 1)\sqrt{-1}}{x^2 + 1}$

10. $\dfrac{3a^2 - 1}{2a}$.   **11.** $\sqrt{-1}$.   **12.** 100.

13. $\pm(2 + 3\sqrt{-1})$.   **14.** $\pm(5 - 6\sqrt{-1})$.   **15.** $\pm(1 + 4\sqrt{-3})$.

16. $\pm 2(1 - \sqrt{-1})$.   **17.** $\pm(a + \sqrt{-1})$.

18. $\pm\{(a + b) - (a - b)\sqrt{-1}\}$

19. $-\dfrac{9}{13} + \dfrac{19}{13}i$.   **20.** $\dfrac{4}{7} - \dfrac{\sqrt{6}}{14}i$.   **21.** i.

22. $-\dfrac{1}{5} + \dfrac{3}{5}i$.   **23.** $\dfrac{2b(3a^2 - b^2)}{a^2 + b^2}i$.

IX. a. PAGES 85 – 86

1. $35x^2 + 13x - 12 = 0$.

2. $mnx^2 + (n^2 - m^2)x - mn = 0$.

3. $(p^2 - q^2)x^2 + 4pqx - p^2 + q^2 = 0$.   **4.** $x^2 - 14x + 29 = 0$.

5. $x^2 + 10x + 13 = 0$.   **6.** $x^2 + 2px + p^2 - 8q = 0$.

7. $x^2 + 6x + 34 = 0$.   **8.** $x^2 + 2ax + a^2 + b^2 = 0$.

9. $x^2 + a^2 - 2ab + b^2 = 0$.   **10.** $6x^3 + 11x^2 - 19x + 6 = 0$.

11. $2ax^3 + (4 - a^2)x^2 - 2ax = 0$.   **12.** $x^3 - 8x^2 + 17x - 4 = 0$.

14. $3, 5$.   **15.** $2, -\dfrac{10}{9}$.   **16.** $\dfrac{a - b}{a + b}$.

18. $\dfrac{b^2 - 2ac}{c^2}$.   **19.** $\dfrac{bc^4(3ac - b^2)}{a^7}$.   **20.** $\dfrac{b^2(b^2 - 4ac)}{a^2c^2}$.

21. 7.   **22.** -15.   **23.** 0.

24. $x^2 - 2(p^2 - 2q)x + p^2(p^2 - 4q) = 0$.

26. (1) $\dfrac{b^2 - 2ac}{a^2c^2}$.   (2) $\dfrac{b(b^2 - 3ac)}{a^3c^3}$.   **27.** $nb^2 = (1 + n)^2 ac$.

28. $a^2c^2x^2 - (b^2 - 2ac)(a^2 + c^2)x + (b^2 - 2ac)^2 = 0$.

29. $x^2 - 4mnx - (m^2 - n^2)^2 = 0$.

IX. b. PAGES 89 – 90

1. 2 and -2.   **5.** $bx^2 - 2ax + a = 0$.

6. (1) $\dfrac{p\,(p^2-4q)\,(p^2-q)}{q}$.   (2) $\dfrac{p^4-4p^2q+2q^2}{q^4}$.

11. $\dfrac{1}{3}$.

IX. c. PAGES 92 – 93

1. -2.   **2.** ± 7.   **5.** $(ln'-l'n)^2 = (lm'-l'm)\,(mn'-m'n)$.

7. $(aa'-bb')^2 + 4\,(ha'+h'b)\,(hb'+h'a) = 0$.

10. $(bb'-2ac'-2a'c)^2 = (b^2-4ac)\,(b'^2-4a'c')$; which reduces to
$(ac'-a'c)^2 = (ab'-a'b)\,(bc'-b'c)$.

X. a. PAGES 97 – 99

1. $\dfrac{1}{4}, -\dfrac{1}{2}$.   **2.** $\pm\dfrac{1}{3}, \pm 1$.   **3.** $4, \dfrac{1}{4}$.

4. $\dfrac{1}{9}, \dfrac{1}{4}$.   **5.** $3^n, 2^n$.   **6.** $1, 2^{2n}$.

7. $27, \dfrac{25}{147}$.   **8.** $\dfrac{9}{13}, \dfrac{4}{13}$.   **9.** $\dfrac{1}{9}, \dfrac{25}{4}$.

10. $-1, -\dfrac{1}{32}$.   **11.** $2, 0$.   **12.** ± 1.

13. -4.   **14.** ± 3.   **15.** 0.

16. $\dfrac{1}{8}, 450$.   **17.** $9, -7, 1 \pm \sqrt{-24}$.

18. $2, -4, -1 \pm \sqrt{71}$.   **19.** $3, -\dfrac{3}{2}, \dfrac{3 \pm \sqrt{-47}}{4}$

20. $4, -\dfrac{7}{2}, \dfrac{1 \pm \sqrt{65}}{4}$.   **21.** $2, -8, -3 \pm 3\sqrt{5}$

22. $3, -\dfrac{5}{3}, \dfrac{2 \pm \sqrt{70}}{3}$.   **23.** $5, \dfrac{1}{3}, \dfrac{8 \pm \sqrt{148}}{3}$.

24. $7, -\dfrac{14}{3}, \dfrac{7 \pm \sqrt{37}}{6}$.   **25.** $2, \dfrac{1}{2}, \dfrac{5 \pm \sqrt{201}}{4}$.

26. $5, -\dfrac{7}{3}, \dfrac{8 \pm \sqrt{415}}{6}$.   **27.** $1, 3$.

28. $5, \dfrac{1}{2}$.   **29.** $1, 9, -\dfrac{18}{5}$.

30. $a, \dfrac{a}{2}, -\dfrac{a}{3}$.   **31.** $2, -\dfrac{9}{2}$.   **32.** $4, -\dfrac{10}{3}$.

33. $0, 5$. **34.** $6, -\dfrac{5}{2}$. **35.** $1, \dfrac{-3 \pm \sqrt{5}}{2}$.

36. $3, \dfrac{1}{3}, \dfrac{-1 \pm \sqrt{-35}}{6}$. **37.** $2 \pm \sqrt{3}, \dfrac{-1 \pm \sqrt{-3}}{2}$.

38. $2, -\dfrac{1}{2}, 5, -\dfrac{1}{5}$. **39.** $3a, -4a$. **40.** $\pm \dfrac{2a}{5}$.

41. $0, 1, 3$. **42.** $\dfrac{-1 \pm \sqrt{17}}{2}, \dfrac{-1 \pm \sqrt{2}}{2}$.

43. $\dfrac{3}{2}, \dfrac{2}{3}$. **44.** $3, -1$. **45.** ± 1. **46.** 13.

47. 4. **48.** $0, \dfrac{63a}{65}$. **49.** $1, \dfrac{(\sqrt{a} - \sqrt{b})^2 + 4}{(\sqrt{a} + \sqrt{b})^2 - 4}$.

50. ± 5. **51.** $5, -4, \dfrac{1 \pm \sqrt{-75}}{2}$. **52.** $-\dfrac{1}{3}, \dfrac{1 \pm \sqrt{-31}}{6}$.

X. b. Pages 102 – 104

1. $x = 5, -\dfrac{8}{3}; y = 4, -\dfrac{15}{2}$. **2.** $x = 2, -\dfrac{8}{19}; y = 7, -\dfrac{97}{19}$.

3. $x = 1, -\dfrac{53}{88}; y = 1, -\dfrac{25}{22}$. **4.** $x = \pm 5, \pm 3; y = \pm 3, \pm 5$.

5. $x = 8, 2; y = 2, 8$. **6.** $x = 45, 5; y = 5, 45$.

7. $x = 9, 4; y = 4, 9$. **8.** $x = \pm 2, \pm 3; y = \pm 1, \pm 2$.

9. $x = \pm 2, \pm 3; y = \pm 3, \pm 4$. **10.** $x = \pm 5, \pm 3; y = \pm 3, \pm 4$.

11. $x = \pm 2, \pm 1; y = \pm 1, \pm 3$.

12. $x = \pm \sqrt{3}, \pm \sqrt{\dfrac{3}{19}}; y = 0, \pm 6\sqrt{\dfrac{3}{19}}$.

13. $x = 5, 3, 4 \pm \sqrt{-97}; y = 3, 5, 4 \mp \sqrt{-97}$.

14. $x = 4, -2, \pm \sqrt{-15} + 1; y = 2, -4 \pm \sqrt{-15} - 1$.

15. $x = 4, -2, \pm \sqrt{-11} + 1; y = 2, -4 \pm \sqrt{-11} - 1$.

16. $x = \dfrac{4}{5}, \dfrac{1}{5}; y = 20, 5$. **17.** $x = 2, 1; y = 1, 2$.

18. $x = 6, 4; y = 10, 15$. **19.** $x = 729, 343; y = 343, 729$.

20. $x = 16, 1; y = 1, 16$. **21.** $x = 9, 4; y = 4, 9$.

22. $x = 5; y = \pm 4$. **23.** $x = 1, \dfrac{5}{3}; y = 2, \dfrac{2}{3}$.

24. $x = 9, 1; y = 1, 9$. **25.** $x = \pm 25; y = \pm 9$.

26. $x = 6, 2, 4, 3; y = 1, 3, \dfrac{3}{2}, 2$.

27. $x = \pm 5, \pm 4, \pm \dfrac{5}{2}, \pm 2; y = \pm 5, \pm 4, \pm 10, \pm 8.$

28. $x = 4, \dfrac{107}{13}; y = 1, \dfrac{48}{13}.$

29. $x = -6, \dfrac{1 \pm \sqrt{-143}}{2}; y = -3, \dfrac{1 \pm 3\sqrt{-143}}{4}.$

30. $x = 0, 9, 3; y = 0, 3, 9.$ 31. $x = 0, 1, \dfrac{15}{22}; y = 0, 4, \dfrac{9}{22}.$

32. $x = 5, \dfrac{10}{23}, 0; y = 3, -\dfrac{6}{23}, -\dfrac{4}{7}.$ 33. $x = 2, \sqrt[3]{4}, 2; y = 2, 2\sqrt[3]{4}, 6.$

34. $x = 1, \sqrt[3]{\dfrac{1}{2}}; y = 2, 3\sqrt[3]{\dfrac{1}{2}}.$

35. $x = \pm 3, \pm \sqrt{-18}; y = \pm 3, \mp \sqrt{-18}.$ 36. $x = y = \pm 2.$

37. $x = 0, \dfrac{b\sqrt{a}}{\sqrt{a} + \sqrt{b}}, \dfrac{b\sqrt{a}}{\sqrt{a} - \sqrt{b}}; y = 0, \dfrac{a\sqrt{b}}{\sqrt{a} + \sqrt{b}}, -\dfrac{a\sqrt{b}}{\sqrt{a} - \sqrt{b}}.$

38. $x = b, \dfrac{b(-1 \pm \sqrt{3})}{2}; y = a, a(1 \mp \sqrt{3}).$

39. $x = \dfrac{a^2}{b}, \dfrac{a(2b - a)}{b}; y = \dfrac{b^2}{a}, \dfrac{b(2a - b)}{a}.$

40. $x = 0, \pm a\sqrt{7}, \pm a\sqrt{13}, \pm 3a, \pm a; y = 0, \mp b\sqrt{7}, \pm b\sqrt{13}, \mp b, \mp 3b.$

41. $x = \pm 1, \pm \dfrac{2a^2}{\sqrt{16a^4 - a^2 - 1}}; y = \pm 2a, \mp \dfrac{a}{\sqrt{16a^4 - a^2 - 1}}.$

X. c. PAGES 105 – 106

1. $x = \pm 3; y = \pm 5; z = \pm 4.$ 2. $x = 5; y = -1; z = 7.$

3. $x = 5, -1; y = 1, -5; z = 2.$ 4. $x = 8, -3; y = 3; z = 3, -8.$

5. $x = 4, 3, \dfrac{2 \pm \sqrt{151}}{3}; y = 3, 4, \dfrac{2 \mp \sqrt{151}}{3}; z = 2, -\dfrac{11}{3}.$

6. $x = \pm 3; y = \mp 2; z = \pm 5.$ 7. $x = \pm 5; y = \pm 1; z = \pm 1.$

8. $x = 8, -8; y = 5, -5; z = 3, -3.$ 9. $x = 3; y = 4; z = \dfrac{1}{2}; u = \dfrac{1}{3}.$

10. $x = 1; y = 2; z = 3.$ 11. $x = 5, -7; y = 3, -5; z = 6, -8.$

12. $x = 1, -2; y = 7, -3; z = 3, -\dfrac{11}{3}.$

13. $x = 4, \dfrac{60}{7}; y = 6, \dfrac{66}{7}; z = 2, -6.$

14. $x = a, 0, 0; y = 0, a, 0; z = 0, 0, a.$

15. $x = \dfrac{a}{\sqrt{3}}, \dfrac{\sqrt{3} \pm \sqrt{-9}}{6} a; y = \dfrac{a}{\sqrt{3}}, \dfrac{-5\sqrt{3} \pm \sqrt{-9}}{6} a;$

$z = \dfrac{a}{\sqrt{3}}, -\dfrac{\sqrt{3} \pm \sqrt{-9}}{3} a.$

16. $x = a, -2a, \dfrac{7 \pm \sqrt{-15}}{2} a; y = 4a, a, \dfrac{-11 \pm \sqrt{-15}}{2} a;$

$z = 2a, -4a, (1 \pm \sqrt{-15}) a.$

X. d. PAGES 109

1. $x = 29, 21, 13, 5; y = 2, 5, 8, 11.$

2. $x = 1, 3, 5, 7, 9; y = 24, 19, 14, 9, 4.$

3. $x = 20, 8; y = 1, 8.$ **4.** $x = 9, 20, 31; y = 27, 14, 1.$

5. $x = 30, 5; y = 9, 32.$ **6.** $x = 50, 3; y = 3, 44.$

7. $x = 7p - 5, 2; y = 5p - 4, 1.$ **8.** $x = 13p - 2, 11; y = 6p - 1, 5.$

9. $x = 21p - 9, 12; y = 8p - 5, 3.$

10. $x = 17p, 17; y = 13p, 13.$

11. $x = 19p - 16, 3; y = 23p - 19, 4.$

12. $x = 77p - 74, 3; y = 30p - 25, 5.$

13. 11 horses, 15 cows. **14.** 101. **15.** 56, 25 or 16, 65.

16. To pay 3 guineas and receive 21 half-crowns.

17. 1147; an infinite number of the form $1147 + 39 \times 56p$.

18. To pay 17 florins and receive 3 half crowns.

19. 37, 99; 77, 59; 117, 19.

20. 28 rams, 1 pig, 11 oxen; or 13 rams, 14 pigs, 13 oxen.

21. 3 sovereigns, 11 half-crowns, 13 shillings.

XI. a. PAGES 117 – 119

1. 12. **2.** 224. **3.** 40320, 6375600, 10626, 11628.

4. 6720. **5.** 15. **6.** 40320; 720. **7.** 15, 360.

8. 6. **9.** 120. **10.** 720. **11.** 10626, 1771.

12. 1440. **13.** 6375600. **14.** 360, 144. **15.** 230300.

16. 1140, 231. **17.** 144. **18.** 224, 896.

19. 848. **20.** 56. **21.** 360000. **22.** 2052000.

23. 369600. **24.** 21600. **25.** $\dfrac{45!}{10! \, 15! \, 20!}$ **26.** 2520.

27. 5760. **28.** 3456. **29.** 2903040. **30.** 25920.

32. 41. **33.** 1956. **34.** 7.

XI. b. Pages 125 – 127

1. (1) 1663200. (2) 129729600. (3) 3326400.
2. 4084080.
3. 151351200.
4. 360.
5. 72.
6. 125.
7. n^r.
8. 531441.
9. p^n.
10. 30.
11. 1260.
12. 3374.
13. 455.
14. $\dfrac{(a + 2b + 3c + d)\,!}{a\,!(b\,!)^2\,(c\,!)^3}$
15. 4095.
16. 57760000.
17. 1023.
18. 720; 3628800.
19. 127.
20. 315.
21. $\dfrac{mn\,!}{(m\,!)^n\,n}$.
22. 64; 325.
23. 42.
24. $(1)\dfrac{p\,(p-1)}{2} - \dfrac{q\,(q-1)}{2} + 1;$ $(2)\dfrac{p\,(p-1)\,(p-2)}{6} - \dfrac{q\,(q-1)\,(q-2)}{6}$.
25. $\dfrac{p\,(p-1)\,(p-2)}{6} - \dfrac{q\,(q-1)\,(q-2)}{6} + 1.$
26. $(p+1)^n - 1.$
27. 113; 2190.
28. 2454.
29. 6666600.
30. 5199960.

XIII. a. Pages 137 – 138

1. $x^5 - 15x^4 + 90x^3 - 270x^2 + 405x - 243.$
2. $81x^4 + 216x^3 y + 216x^2 y^2 + 96xy^3 + 16y^4.$
3. $32x^5 - 80x^4 y + 80x^3 y^2 - 40x^2 y^3 + 10xy^4 - y^5.$
4. $1 - 18a^2 + 135a^4 - 540a^6 + 1215a^8 - 1458a^{10} + 729a^{12}.$
5. $x^{10} + 5x^9 + 10x^8 + 10x^7 + 5x^6 + x^5.$
6. $1 - 7xy + 21x^2 y^2 - 35x^3 y^3 + 35x^4 y^4 - 21x^5 y^5 + 7x^6 y^6 - x^7 y^7.$
7. $16 - 48x^2 + 54x^4 - 27x^6 + \dfrac{81x^8}{16}.$
8. $729a^6 - 972a^5 + 540a^4 - 160a^3 + \dfrac{80a^2}{3} - \dfrac{64a}{27} + \dfrac{64}{729}.$
9. $1 + \dfrac{7x}{2} + \dfrac{21x^2}{4} + \dfrac{35x^3}{8} + \dfrac{35x^4}{16} + \dfrac{21x^5}{32} + \dfrac{7x^6}{64} + \dfrac{x^7}{128}.$
10. $\dfrac{64x^6}{729} - \dfrac{32x^4}{27} + \dfrac{20x^2}{3} - 20 + \dfrac{135}{4x^2} - \dfrac{243}{x^4} + \dfrac{729}{64x^6}$
11. $\dfrac{1}{256} + \dfrac{a}{16} + \dfrac{7a^2}{16} + \dfrac{7a^3}{4} + \dfrac{35a^4}{8} + 7a^5 + 7a^6 + 4a^7 + a^8.$
12. $1 - \dfrac{10}{x} + \dfrac{45}{x^2} - \dfrac{120}{x^3} + \dfrac{210}{x^4} - \dfrac{252}{x^5} + \dfrac{210}{x^6} - \dfrac{120}{x^7} + \dfrac{45}{x^8} - \dfrac{10}{x^9} + \dfrac{1}{x^{10}}.$

13. $-35750x^{10}$.   **14.** $-112640x^9$.   **15.** $-312x^2$.

16. $\dfrac{30!}{27!\,3!}(5x)^3(8y)^{27}$.   **17.** $40a^7b^3$.

18. $\dfrac{1120}{81}a^4b^4$.   **19.** $\dfrac{10500}{x^3}$.   **20.** $\dfrac{70x^6y^{10}}{a^2b^6}$.

21. $2x^4+24x^2+8$.   **22.** $2x(16x^4-20x^2a^2+5a^4)$.

23. $140\sqrt{2}$.   **24.** $2(365-363x+63x^2-x^3)$.

25. 252.   **26.** $-\dfrac{429}{16}x^{14}$.   **27.** $110565a^4$.

28. $84a^3b^6$.   **29.** $1365,\,-1365$.   **30.** $\dfrac{189a^{17}}{8},\,-\dfrac{21}{16}a^{19}$.

31. $\dfrac{7}{18}$.   **32.** 18564.   **33.** $\dfrac{n!}{(\frac{1}{2}(n-r))!\,(\frac{1}{2}(n+r))!}$.

34. $(-1)^n\dfrac{(3n)!}{n!\,(2n)!}$.

XIII. b. Pages 142 – 143

1. The 9th.   **2.** The 12th.   **3.** The 6th.

4. The 10th and 11th   **5.** The 3rd $=6\frac{2}{3}$.

6. The 4th and 5th $=\dfrac{7}{144}$.   **9.** $x=2,\,y=3,\,n=5$.

10. $1+8x+20x^2+8x^3-26x^4-8x^5+20x^6-8x^7+x^8$.

11. $27x^6-54ax^5+117a^2x^4-116a^3x^3+117a^4x^2-54a^5x+27a^6$.

12. $\dfrac{n!}{(r-1)!\,(n-r+1)!}x^{r-1}a^{n-r+1}$.

13. $(-1)^p\dfrac{2n+1}{(p+1)!\,(2n-p)!}x^{2p-2n+1}$.   **14.** 14.   **15.** $2r=n$.

XIV. a. Pages 149

1. $1+\dfrac{1}{2}x-\dfrac{1}{8}x^2+\dfrac{1}{16}x^3$.   **2.** $1+\dfrac{3}{2}x+\dfrac{3}{8}x^2-\dfrac{1}{16}x^3$.

3. $1-\dfrac{2}{5}x-\dfrac{3}{25}x^2-\dfrac{8}{125}x^3$.   **4.** $1-2x^2+3x^4-4x^6$.

5. $1-x-x^2-\dfrac{5}{3}x^3$.   **6.** $1+x+2x^2+\dfrac{14}{3}x^3$.

7. $1-x+\dfrac{3}{2}x^2-\dfrac{5}{2}x^3$.   **8.** $1-x+\dfrac{2}{3}x^2-\dfrac{10}{27}x^3$.

9. $1 + x + \dfrac{x^2}{6} - \dfrac{x^3}{54}$ **10.** $1 - 2a + \dfrac{5}{2}a^2 - \dfrac{5}{2}a^3$.

11. $\dfrac{1}{8}\left(1 - \dfrac{3}{2}x + \dfrac{3}{2}x^2 - \dfrac{5}{4}x^3\right)$.   **12.** $3\left(1 + \dfrac{x}{9} - \dfrac{1}{162}x^2 + \dfrac{1}{1458}x^3\right)$.

13. $4\left(1 + a - \dfrac{1}{4}a^2 + \dfrac{1}{6}a^3\right)$.   **14.** $\dfrac{1}{27}\left(1 + x + \dfrac{5}{6}x^2 + \dfrac{35}{54}x^3\right)$.

15. $\dfrac{1}{2a^{1/2}}\left(1 + \dfrac{x}{a} + \dfrac{3}{2}\cdot\dfrac{x^2}{a^2} + \dfrac{5}{2}\cdot\dfrac{x^3}{a^3}\right)$.

16. $-\dfrac{429}{16}x^7$.   **17.** $\dfrac{77}{256}x^{30}$.

18. $-\dfrac{1040}{81}a^{18}$.   **19.** $\dfrac{16b^4}{243a^5}$.

20. $(r+1)x^r$.   **21.** $\dfrac{(r+1)(r+2)(r+3)}{1.2.3}x^r$.

22. $(-1)^{r-1}\dfrac{1.3.5\ldots(2r-3)}{2^r\,(r)!}x^r$.

23. $(-1)^{r-4}\dfrac{11.8.5.2.1.4\ldots(3r-14)}{3^r\,(r)!}x^r$.

24. $-1848x^{13}$.   **25.** $-\dfrac{19712}{3}x^6$.

XIV. b. PAGES 154 – 156

1. $(-1)^r\dfrac{1.3.5.7.\ldots(2r-1)}{2^r\,r!}x^r$.   **2.** $\dfrac{(r+1)(r+2)(r+3)(r+4)}{4!}x^r$.

3. $(-1)^{r-1}\dfrac{1.2.5.\ldots(3r-4)}{r!}x^r$.   **4.** $(-1)^r\dfrac{2.5.8\ldots(3r-1)}{3^r\,r!}x^r$.

5. $(-1)^r\dfrac{(r+1)(r+2)}{2!}x^{2r}$.   **6.** $\dfrac{3.5.7\ldots(2r+1)}{r!}x^r$.

7. $(-1)^r\dfrac{b^r}{a^{r+1}}\cdot x^r$.   **8.** $\dfrac{r+1}{2^{r+2}}x^r$.

9. $-\dfrac{2.1.4\ldots(3r-5)}{3^r\,r!}\cdot\dfrac{x^{3r}}{a^{3r-2}}$.   **10.** $(-1)^r\dfrac{1.3.5\ldots(2r-1)}{r!}x^r$.

11. $\dfrac{2.5.8\ldots(3r-1)}{r!}x^r$.

12. $\dfrac{(n+1)(2n+1)\ldots(\overline{r-1}.n+1)}{r!}\cdot\dfrac{x^r}{a^{nr+1}}$.

13.	The 3rd.	14.	The 5th.	15.	The 13th.
16.	The 7th.	17.	The 4th. and 5th.	18.	The 3rd.
19.	9·89949.	20.	9·99333.	21.	10·00999.
22.	6·99927	23.	·19842.	24.	1·00133.
25.	·00795.	26.	5·00096.	27.	$1 - \dfrac{23x}{6}$.

28. $\dfrac{2}{3}\left(1 + \dfrac{x}{24}\right)$. **29.** $1 - \dfrac{5x}{8}$. **30.** $\dfrac{1}{4} - \dfrac{5}{6}x$.

31. $1 - \dfrac{343}{120}x$. **32.** $\dfrac{1}{3} - \dfrac{71}{360}x$. **35.** $1 - 4x + 13x^2$.

36. $2 + \dfrac{29}{4}x + \dfrac{297}{32}x^2$.

XIV. c. Pages 160 – 163

1. -197. **2.** 142. **3.** $(-1)^{n-1}$.

4. $(-1)^n (n^2 + 2n + 2)$. **6.** $\sqrt{8} = \left(1 - \dfrac{1}{2}\right)^{-3/2}$.

7. $\left(1 - \dfrac{2}{3}\right)^{-n} = 2^n \left(1 - \dfrac{1}{3}\right)^{-n}$. **12.** $\dfrac{2n\,!}{n\,!\,n\,!}$.

14. Deduced from $(1 - x^3) - (1 - x)^3 = 3x - 3x^2$.

16. (1) 45. (2) 6561.

18. (1) Equate coefficients of x^r in $(1 + x)^n (1 + x)^{-1} = (1 + x)^{n-1}$.

(2) Equate absolute terms in $(1 + x)^n \left(1 + \dfrac{1}{x}\right)^{-2} = x^2 (1 + x)^{n-2}$.

20. Series on the left $+ (-1)^n q_n^2 = $ coefficient of x^{2n} in $(1 - x^2)^{-1/2}$.

21. $2^{2n-1} - \dfrac{1}{2} \cdot \dfrac{2n\,!}{n\,!\,n\,!}$.

[Use $(c_0 + c_1 + c_2 + \ldots c_n)^2 - 2(c_0 c_1 + c_1 c_2 \ldots) = c_0^2 + c_1^2 + c_2^2 + \ldots c_n^2$].

XV. Pages 167 – 168

1. -12600. **2.** -168. **3.** 3360.

4. $-1260a^2 b^3 c^4$. **5.** -9. **6.** 8085.

7. 30. **8.** 1905. **9.** -10.

10. $-\dfrac{3}{2}$. **11.** -1. **12.** $-\dfrac{4}{81}$.

13. $\dfrac{59}{16}$. **14.** -1. **15.** $\dfrac{211}{3}$.

16. $1 - \dfrac{1}{2}x - \dfrac{7}{8}x^2$. **17.** $1 - 2x^2 + 4x^3 + 5x^4 - 20x^5$.

18. $16\left(1 - \dfrac{3}{2}x^3 + 3x^4 + \dfrac{9}{32}x^6 - \dfrac{9}{8}x^7 + \dfrac{9}{8}x^8\right).$

XVI. a. PAGES 172 – 173

1. 8, 6. **2.** 2, – 1. **3.** $-\dfrac{16}{3}, -\dfrac{1}{2}.$

4. $-4, -\dfrac{3}{2}.$ **5.** $\dfrac{4}{3}, -\dfrac{4}{5}.$ **6.** $\dfrac{2}{5}, -\dfrac{1}{2}, -\dfrac{5}{2}.$

7. $\dfrac{7}{3}, -3, -\dfrac{4}{3}, \dfrac{2}{3}.$ **8.** $6\log a + 9\log b.$

9. $\dfrac{2}{3}\log a + \dfrac{3}{2}\log b.$ **10.** $-\dfrac{4}{9}\log a + \dfrac{1}{3}\log b.$

11. $-\dfrac{2}{3}\log a - \dfrac{1}{2}\log b.$ **12.** $-\dfrac{7}{12}\log a - \log b.$

13. $\dfrac{1}{2}\log a.$ **14.** $-5\log c.$

16. $\log 3.$ **18.** $\dfrac{\log c}{\log a - \log b}.$

19. $\dfrac{5\log c}{2\log a + 3\log b}.$ **20.** $\dfrac{\log a + \log b}{2\log c - \log a + \log b}.$

21. $x = \dfrac{4\log m}{\log a}, y = -\dfrac{\log m}{\log b}.$

22. $\log x = \dfrac{1}{5}(a + 3b), \log y = \dfrac{1}{5}(a - 2b).$

23. $\dfrac{\log(a - b)}{\log(a + b)}.$

XVI. b. PAGES 178 – 179

1. 4, 1, 2, $\bar{2}$, $\bar{1}$, $\bar{1}$, $\bar{1}$.
2. 0·8821259, 2·8821259, $\bar{3}$·8821259, 5·8821259, $\bar{6}$·8821259.
3. 5, 2, 4, 1.
4. Second decimal place; units' place; fifth decimal place.

5. 1·8061800. **6.** 1·9242793. **7.** $\bar{1}$·1072100.
8. $\bar{2}$·0969100. **9.** 1·1583626. **10.** 0·6690067.
11. 0·3597271. **12.** 0·0563520. **13.** $\bar{1}$·5052973.
14. 0·44092388. **15.** 1·948445. **16.** 191563·1.
17. 1·1998692. **18.** 1·0039238. **19.** 9·076226.
20. 178·141516. **21.** 9. **23.** 301.
24. 3·46. **25.** 4·29. **26.** 1·206.
27. 14·206. **28.** 4·562.

29. $x = \dfrac{\log 3}{\log 3 - \log 2}$; $y = \dfrac{\log 2}{\log 3 - \log 2}$.

30. $x = \dfrac{3 \log 3 - 2 \log 2}{4 (\log 3 - \log 2)}$; $y = \dfrac{\log 3}{4 (\log 3 - \log 2)}$.

31. 1·64601.

32. $\dfrac{\log 2}{2 \log 7} = 0·1781$; $\dfrac{2 \log 7}{\log 2} = 5·614$.

XVII. PAGES 187 – 189

1. $\log_e 2$.

2. $\log_e 3 - \log_e 2$.

6. 0·0020000006666670.

9. $e^{x^2} - e^{y^2}$.

10. 0·8450980; 1·0413927; 1·1139434. In Art. 225 put $n = 50$ in (2); $n = 10$ in (1); and $n = 1000$ in (1) respectively.

12. $(-1)^{r-1} \cdot \dfrac{2^r + 1}{r} x^r$.

13. $\dfrac{(-1)^{r-1} 3^r + 2^r}{r} x^r$.

14. $2 \left\{ 1 + \dfrac{(2x)^2}{2!} + \dfrac{(2x)^4}{4!} + \ldots + \dfrac{(2x)^{2r}}{2r!} + \ldots \right\}$.

15. $1 - \dfrac{x^2}{2!} + \dfrac{x^4}{4!} - \dfrac{x^6}{6!} + \ldots + (-1)^r \dfrac{x^{2r}}{2r!} + \ldots$

18. $\dfrac{x}{1-x} + \log_e (1-x)$.

24. 0·69314718; 1·09861229; 1·60943792;

$a = -\log_e \left(1 - \dfrac{1}{10} \right) = 0·105360516$;

$b = -\log_e \left(1 - \dfrac{4}{100} \right) = 0·40821995$; $c = \log_e \left(1 + \dfrac{1}{80} \right) = 0·012422520$.

XVIII. a. PAGES 193 – 194

1. £1146. 14s. 10d.

2. £720.

3. 14·2 years.

4. £6768. 7s. $10\frac{1}{2} d$.

5. 9·6 years.

8. £496. 19s. $4\frac{3}{4} d$.

9. A little less than 7 years.

10. £119. 18s. $5\frac{3}{4} d$.

XVIII. b. PAGES 197 – 199

1. 6 per cent.

2. £3137. 2s. $2\frac{2}{3} d$.

3. £110.

4. 3 per cent.

5. $28\frac{4}{7}$ years.

6. £1275.

7. £926. 2s.

8. £6755. 13s.

9. £183. 18s.

10. $3\frac{1}{5}$ per cent.

11. £616. 9s. $1\frac{1}{2} d$.

13. £1308. 12s. $4\frac{1}{2} d$.

15. £4200

XIX. a. PAGES 205 – 206

8. $a^3 + 2b^3$ is the greater.

12. $x^3 >$ or $< x^2 + x + 2$, according as $x >$ or < 2.

14. The greatest value of x is 1.   **15.** 4 : 8.

22. $4^4 . 5^5$; when $x = 3$.   **23.** 9, when $x = 1$.

XIX. b. PAGES 209 – 210

10. $\dfrac{3^3 . 5^5}{2^8} a^8$; $\sqrt{\dfrac{3}{5}}$. $\sqrt[3]{\dfrac{2}{5}}$.

XX. PAGES 218 – 219

1. $-\dfrac{10}{7}$; $\dfrac{9}{4}$.   **2.** 9; $\dfrac{1}{9}$.   **3.** $\dfrac{1}{2}$; $\dfrac{5}{3}$.

4. $-\dfrac{15}{8}$; 6.   **5.** 1; 0.   **6.** 0; -30.

7. $-\dfrac{3}{2}$.   **8.** $\log a - \log b$.   **9.** 2.

10. me^{ma}.   **11.** $\dfrac{1}{2\sqrt{a}}$.   **12.** $\dfrac{1}{3}$.

13. -1.   **14.** $\dfrac{\sqrt{2a}}{a\sqrt{3+1}}$.   **15.** $\sqrt{a}$.

16. 0.   **17.** $\dfrac{3}{2}$.   **18.** $e^{2/a}$.

XXI. a. PAGES 231 – 233

1. Convergent.   **2.** Convergent.   **3.** Convergent.

4. $x < 1$, or $x = 1$, convergent; $x > 1$, divergent.

5. Same result as Ex. 4.   **6.** Convergent.

7. Divergent.

8. $x < 1$, convergent; $x > 1$, or $x = 1$, divergent.

9. Divergent except when $p > 2$.

10. $x < 1$, or $x = 1$, convergent; $x > 1$, divergent.

11. If $x < 1$, convergent; $x > 1$, or $x = 1$, divergent.

12. Same result as Ex. 11.   **13.** Divergent, except when $p > 1$

14. $x < 1$, or $x = 1$, convergent; $x > 1$, divergent.

15. Convergent.   **16.** Divergent.

17. (1) Divergent. (2) Convergent.

18. (1) Divergent. (2) Convergent.

XXI. b. PAGES 242

1. $x < 1$, or $x = 1$, convergent; $x > 1$, divergent.
2. Same result as Ex. 1.
3. Same result as Ex. 1.
4. $x < \dfrac{1}{e}$, or $x = \dfrac{1}{e}$, convergent; $x > \dfrac{1}{e}$, divergent.
5. $x < e$, convergent; $x > e$, or $x = e$, divergent.
6. $x < 1$, convergent; $x > 1$, or $x = 1$, divergent.
7. Divergent.
8. $x < \dfrac{1}{e}$, convergent; $x > \dfrac{1}{e}$, or $x = \dfrac{1}{e}$, divergent.
9. $x < 1$, convergent; $x > 1$, divergent. If $x = 1$ and if $\gamma - \alpha - \beta$ is positive, convergent; If $\gamma - \alpha - \beta$ is negative, or zero, divergent.
10. $x < 1$, convergent; $x > 1$, or $x = 1$, divergent. The results hold for all values of q_r positive or negative.
11. a negative, or zero, convergent; a positive, divergent.

XXII. a. PAGES 246 – 247

1. $\dfrac{1}{3} n (4n^2 - 1)$.　　　　2. $\dfrac{1}{4} n (n + 1) (n + 2) (n + 3)$.

3. $\dfrac{1}{12} n (n + 1) (n + 2) (3n + 5)$.　4. $n^2 (2n^2 - 1)$.

5. $\dfrac{1}{30} n (n + 1) (2n + 1) (3n^2 + 3n - 1)$.

6. $p^3 = q^2$.

7. $b^3 = 27a^2d$, $c^3 = 27ad^2$.　　8. $ad = bf$, $4a^2c - b^2 = 8a^3f$.

13. $abc + 2fgh - af^2 - bg^2 - ch^2 = 0$.

XXII. b. PAGES 249 – 250

1: $1 + 3x + 4x^2 + 7x^3$.　　　　2. $1 - 7x - x^2 - 43x^3$.

3. $\dfrac{1}{2} + \dfrac{1}{4} x - \dfrac{3}{8} x^2 + \dfrac{1}{16} x^3$.　　4. $\dfrac{3}{2} + \dfrac{5}{4} x + \dfrac{11}{8} x^2 + \dfrac{21}{16} x^3$.

5. $1 - ax + a (a + 1) x^2 - (a^3 + 2a^2 - 1) x^3$.
6. $a = 1$, $b = 2$.　　　　　　7. $a = 1$, $b = -1$, $c = 2$.
9. The next term is $+ \cdot 00000000000003$.

11. $\dfrac{a^n}{(1 - a) (1 - a^2) (1 - a^3) \ldots (1 - a^n)}$.

XXIII. PAGES 255 – 257

1. $\dfrac{4}{1-3x} - \dfrac{5}{1-2x}$.

2. $\dfrac{7}{3x-5} - \dfrac{5}{4x+3}$.

3. $\dfrac{4}{1-2x} - \dfrac{3}{1-x}$.

4. $\dfrac{2}{x-1} + \dfrac{3}{x-2} - \dfrac{4}{x-3}$.

5. $1 + \dfrac{1}{x} - \dfrac{1}{5(x-1)} - \dfrac{8}{5(2x+3)}$.

6. $\dfrac{1}{x-1} - \dfrac{1}{x+2} - \dfrac{3}{(x+2)^2}$.

7. $x - 2 + \dfrac{17}{16(x+1)} - \dfrac{11}{4(x+1)^2} - \dfrac{17}{16(x-3)}$.

8. $\dfrac{41x+3}{x^2+1} - \dfrac{15}{x+5}$.

9. $\dfrac{3x}{x^2+2x-5} - \dfrac{1}{x-3}$.

10. $\dfrac{5}{(x-1)^4} - \dfrac{7}{(x-1)^3} + \dfrac{1}{(x-1)^2} + \dfrac{3}{x-1}$.

11. $\dfrac{1}{x-1} - \dfrac{1}{x+1} + \dfrac{3}{(x+1)^2} - \dfrac{3}{(x+1)^3} + \dfrac{2}{(x+1)^4}$.

12. $\dfrac{4}{3(1+7x)} - \dfrac{1}{3(1+4x)} ; \dfrac{(-1)^r}{3} \cdot (4 . 7^r - 4^r) x^r$.

13. $\dfrac{11}{3(1-x)} - \dfrac{4}{3(2+x)} : \dfrac{1}{3}\left(11 + \dfrac{(-1)^{r-1}}{2^{r-1}}\right) x^r$.

14. $1 + \dfrac{7}{3(x+5)} - \dfrac{7}{3(x+2)} ; (-1)^r \dfrac{7}{3}\left(\dfrac{1}{5^{r+1}} - \dfrac{1}{2^{r+1}}\right) x^r$.

15. $\dfrac{1}{1-x} - \dfrac{1}{1+x} - \dfrac{4}{1-2x} ; \{1 + (-1)^{r-1} - 2^{r+2}\} x^r$.

16. $\dfrac{4}{3(1+2x)} - \dfrac{1}{3(1-x)} + \dfrac{3}{(1-x)^2} ; \dfrac{1}{3}\{9r + 8 + (-1)^r 2^{r+2}\} x^r$.

17. $\dfrac{1}{4(1-4x)} + \dfrac{11}{4(1-4x)^2} ; 4^{r-1}(12 + 11r) x^r$.

18. $\dfrac{2}{1+x} + \dfrac{3}{(1+x)^2} - \dfrac{6}{2+3x} ; (-1)^r\left(3r + 5 - \dfrac{3^{r+1}}{2^r}\right) x^r$.

19. $\dfrac{3}{2(x-1)} + \dfrac{1-3x}{2(1+x^2)} ; r$ even, $\dfrac{1}{2}\{(-1)^{r/2} - 3\} x^r; r$ odd,

$-\dfrac{3}{2}\{1 + (-1)^{(r-1)/2}\} x^r$.

20. $\dfrac{2}{(1-x)^3} - \dfrac{3}{(1-x)^2} + \dfrac{2}{1-x} ; (r^2+1) x^r$.

21. $\left\{ \dfrac{a^{r+2}}{(a-b)(a-c)} + \dfrac{b^{r+2}}{(b-c)(b-a)} + \dfrac{c^{r+2}}{(c-a)(c-b)} \right\} x^r.$

22. $-\dfrac{5}{(2-x)^2} - \dfrac{2}{2-x} + \dfrac{1}{(1-x)^2} + \dfrac{2}{1-x}; \left\{ r+3 - \dfrac{5r+9}{2^{r+2}} \right\} x^r.$

23. (1) $\dfrac{1}{x(1-x)} \left(\dfrac{1}{1+x^{n+1}} - \dfrac{1}{1+x} \right).$

(2) $\dfrac{1}{(1-a)^2} \left\{ \dfrac{1}{1+a^n x} - \dfrac{1}{1+a^{n+1}x} - \dfrac{1}{1+x} + \dfrac{1}{1+ax} \right\}.$

24. $\dfrac{1}{(1-x)(1-x^2)}.$

25. $\dfrac{1}{(1-x)^2} \left\{ \dfrac{x}{1-x} - \dfrac{x^2}{1-x^2} - \dfrac{x^{n+1}}{1-x^{n+1}} + \dfrac{x^{n+2}}{1-x^{n+2}} \right\}.$

XXIV. PAGES 263

1. $\dfrac{1+3x}{(1-x)^2}; (4r+1)x^r.$ **2.** $\dfrac{2+x}{1+x-2x^2}; \{1+(-1)^r 2^r\}x^r.$

3. $\dfrac{2-3x}{1-3x+2x^2}; (1+2^r)x^r.$ **4.** $\dfrac{7-20x}{1-2x-3x^2}; \left\{ \dfrac{27}{4}(-1)^r + \dfrac{3^r}{4} \right\} x^r.$

5. $\dfrac{3-12x+11x^2}{1-6x+11x^2-6x^3}; (3^r+2^r+1)x^r.$

6. $3^{n-1}+2^{n-1}; \dfrac{1}{2}(3^n-1)+2^n-1.$

7. $(2.3^{n-1}-3.2^{n-1})x^{n-1}; \dfrac{2(1-3^n x^n)}{1-3x} - \dfrac{3(1-2^n x^n)}{1-2x}.$

8. $(4^{n-1}+3^{n-1})x^{n-1}; \dfrac{1-4^n x^n}{1-4x} + \dfrac{1-3^n x^n}{1-3x}.$

9. $(1+3^{n-1}-2^{n-1})x^{n-1}; \dfrac{1-x^n}{1-x} + \dfrac{1-3^n x^n}{1-3x} - \dfrac{1-2^n x^n}{1-2x}.$

10. $\dfrac{8}{5}(-1)^n + \dfrac{2^{2n-3}}{5}; \dfrac{4}{5}\{(-1)^n-1\} + \dfrac{1}{30}(2^{2n}-1).$

11. $u_n - 3u_{n-1} + 3u_{n-2} - u_{n-3} = 0;$
$u_n - 4u_{n-1} + 6u_{n-2} - 4u_{n-3} + u_{n-4} = 0.$

12. $S_n = S_\infty - \Sigma$, where Σ = sum to infinity beginning with $(n+1)^{\text{th}}$ term.

This may easily be shewn to agree with the result in Art.. 325.

13. $(2n+1)^2 + \dfrac{2}{3}(2^{2n+1}+1)$.

XXV. a. Pages 268 – 269

1. $\dfrac{2}{1}, \dfrac{13}{6}, \dfrac{15}{7}, \dfrac{28}{13}, \dfrac{323}{150}, \dfrac{674}{313}$.

2. $\dfrac{1}{2}, \dfrac{2}{5}, \dfrac{7}{17}, \dfrac{9}{22}, \dfrac{43}{105}, \dfrac{95}{232}, \dfrac{613}{1497}$.

3. $\dfrac{3}{1}, \dfrac{10}{3}, \dfrac{13}{4}, \dfrac{36}{11}, \dfrac{85}{26}, \dfrac{121}{37}, \dfrac{1174}{359}$.

4. $1 + \dfrac{1}{2+}\dfrac{1}{2+}\dfrac{1}{2+}\dfrac{1}{1+}\dfrac{1}{1+}\dfrac{1}{2+}\dfrac{1}{2}; \dfrac{17}{12}$.

5. $5 + \dfrac{1}{4+}\dfrac{1}{3+}\dfrac{1}{2+}\dfrac{1}{1+}\dfrac{1}{3}; \dfrac{157}{30}$.

6. $\dfrac{1}{3+}\dfrac{1}{3+}\dfrac{1}{3+}\dfrac{1}{3+}\dfrac{1}{3+}\dfrac{1}{3+}\dfrac{1}{3+}; \dfrac{33}{109}$.

7. $\dfrac{1}{3+}\dfrac{1}{5+}\dfrac{1}{1+}\dfrac{1}{1+}\dfrac{1}{3+}\dfrac{1}{2+}\dfrac{1}{1+}\dfrac{1}{5}; \dfrac{11}{35}$.

8. $\dfrac{1}{2+}\dfrac{1}{1+}\dfrac{1}{2+}\dfrac{1}{2+}\dfrac{1}{1+}\dfrac{1}{3}; \dfrac{7}{19}$.

9. $1 + \dfrac{1}{7+}\dfrac{1}{5+}\dfrac{1}{6+}\dfrac{1}{1+}\dfrac{1}{3}; \dfrac{254}{223}$.

10. $\dfrac{1}{3+}\dfrac{1}{3+}\dfrac{1}{3+}\dfrac{1}{6+}\dfrac{1}{1+}\dfrac{1}{2+}\dfrac{1}{1+}\dfrac{1}{10}; \dfrac{63}{208}$.

11. $4 + \dfrac{1}{3+}\dfrac{1}{6+}\dfrac{1}{3}; \dfrac{259}{60}$.

13. $\dfrac{1}{4}, \dfrac{7}{29}, \dfrac{8}{33}, \dfrac{39}{161}, \dfrac{47}{194}$.

16. $n-1 + \dfrac{1}{(n+1)+}\dfrac{1}{(n-1)+}\dfrac{1}{n+1}$; and the first three convergents

are $\dfrac{n-1}{1}, \dfrac{n^2}{n+1}, \dfrac{n^3-n^2+n-1}{n^2}$.

XXV. b. Pages 272 – 274

1. $\dfrac{1}{(203)^2}$ and $\dfrac{1}{2(1250)^2}$.   2. $\dfrac{151}{115}$

4. $\dfrac{1}{a+}\dfrac{1}{(a+1)+}\dfrac{1}{(a+2)+}\dfrac{1}{a+3}$; $\dfrac{a^2+3a+3}{a^3+3a^2+4a+}$.

XXVI. PAGES 280 – 281

1. $x = 711t + 100,\ y = 775t + 109;\ x = 100,\ y = 109.$
2. $x = 519t - 73,\ y = 455t - 64;\ x = 446,\ y = 391.$
3. $x = 393t + 320,\ y = 436t + 355;\ x = 320,\ y = 355.$

4. Four. 5. Seven. 6. $\dfrac{5}{7},\dfrac{4}{9}$.

7. $\dfrac{5}{12},\dfrac{3}{8},\dfrac{11}{12},\dfrac{7}{8}$; or $\dfrac{1}{8},\dfrac{1}{12},\dfrac{5}{8},\dfrac{7}{12}$.

8. Rs. 9·90 nP.

9. $x = 9,\ y = 8.\ z = 3.$ 10. $x = 5,\ y = 6,\ z = 7.$
11. $x = 4,\ y = 2,\ z = 7.$ 12. $x = 2,\ y = 9,\ z = 7.$
13. $x = 3, 7, 2, 6, 1;\ y = 11, 4, 8, 1, 5;\ z = 1, 1, 2, 2, 3.$
14. $x = 1, 3, 2;\ y = 5, 1, 3,\ z = 2, 4, 3.$
15. $280t + 93.$ 16. 181, 412.
17. Denary 248, Septenary 503, Nonary 305.
18. $a = 11, 10, 9, 8, 6, 4, 3;\ b = 66, 30, 18, 12, 6, 3, 2.$
19. The 107th and 104th divisions, reckoning from either end.
20. 50, 41 35 times, excluding the first time.
21. 425. 22. 899. 23. 1829 and 1363.

XXVII. a. PAGES 284 – 285

1. $1 + \dfrac{1}{1+}\dfrac{1}{2+}\cdots;\dfrac{26}{15}$. 2. $2 + \dfrac{1}{4+}\cdots;\dfrac{2889}{1292}$.

3. $2 + \dfrac{1}{2+}\dfrac{1}{4+}\cdots;\dfrac{485}{198}$. 4. $2 + \dfrac{1}{1+}\dfrac{1}{4+}\cdots;\dfrac{99}{35}$.

5. $3 + \dfrac{1}{3+}\dfrac{1}{6+}\cdots;\dfrac{3970}{1197}$. 6. $3 + \dfrac{1}{1+}\dfrac{1}{1+}\dfrac{1}{1+}\dfrac{1}{1+}\dfrac{1}{6+}\cdots;\dfrac{119}{33}$.

7. $3 + \dfrac{1}{1+}\dfrac{1}{2+}\dfrac{1}{1+}\dfrac{1}{6+}\cdots;\dfrac{116}{31}$.

8. $4 + \dfrac{1}{1+}\dfrac{1}{2+}\dfrac{1}{4+}\dfrac{1}{2+}\dfrac{1}{1+}\dfrac{1}{8+}\cdots;\dfrac{197}{42}$.

9. $3 + \dfrac{1}{2+}\dfrac{1}{6+}\cdots;\dfrac{1351}{390}$. 10. $5 + \dfrac{1}{1+}\dfrac{1}{1+}\dfrac{1}{1+}\dfrac{1}{10+}\cdots;\dfrac{198}{35}$.

11. $6 + \dfrac{1}{1+}\dfrac{1}{2+}\dfrac{1}{2+}\dfrac{1}{2+}\dfrac{1}{1+}\dfrac{1}{12+};\dfrac{161}{24}$.

12. $12 + \cfrac{1}{1+} \cfrac{1}{1+} \cfrac{1}{1+} \cfrac{1}{5+} \cfrac{1}{1+} \cfrac{1}{1+} \cfrac{1}{1+} \cfrac{1}{24+}; \dfrac{253}{20}$.

13. $\cfrac{1}{4+} \cfrac{1}{1+} \cfrac{1}{1+} \cfrac{1}{2+} \cfrac{1}{1+} \cfrac{1}{1+} \cfrac{1}{8+} \cdots; \dfrac{12}{55}$.

14. $\cfrac{1}{5+} \cfrac{1}{1+} \cfrac{1}{2+} \cfrac{1}{1+} \cfrac{1}{10+} \cdots; \dfrac{47}{270}$.

15. $1 + \cfrac{1}{10+} \cfrac{1}{2+} \cdots; \dfrac{5291}{4830}$.

16. $\cfrac{1}{1+} \cfrac{1}{3+} \cfrac{1}{1+} \cfrac{1}{16+} \cfrac{1}{1+} \cfrac{1}{3+} \cfrac{1}{2+} \cfrac{1}{3+} \cfrac{1}{1+} \cfrac{1}{16+} \cdots; \dfrac{280}{351}$.

17. $\dfrac{1}{(65)^2}$ and $\dfrac{1}{2(528)^2}$.   **18.** $\dfrac{1}{(191)^2}$ and $\dfrac{1}{2(240)^2}$.

19. $\dfrac{4030}{401}$.   **20.** $\dfrac{1677}{433}$.

21. $\cfrac{1}{2+} \cfrac{1}{2+} \cfrac{1}{2+} \cdots$ **22.** $4 + \cfrac{1}{1+} \cfrac{1}{1+} \cfrac{1}{1+} \cfrac{1}{4+} \cdots$

23. $1 + \cfrac{1}{2+} \cfrac{1}{3+} \cfrac{1}{1+} \cdots$

24. $4 + \cfrac{1}{3+} \cfrac{1}{3+} \cdots; \cfrac{1}{1+} \cfrac{1}{2+} \cfrac{1}{3+} \cfrac{1}{3+} \cfrac{1}{3+} \cdots$ **25.** $\sqrt{10}$.

26. Positive root of $x^2 + 3x - 3 = 0$.

27. Positive root of $3x^2 - 10x - 4 = 0$.

28. $4\sqrt{2}$.   **30.** $\dfrac{1}{2}$.

XXVII. b. PAGES 291 – 292

1. $a + \cfrac{1}{2a+} \cfrac{1}{2a+} \cfrac{1}{2a+} \cdots; \dfrac{8a^4 + 8a^2 + 1}{8a^3 + 4a}$.

2. $a - 1 + \cfrac{1}{2+} \cfrac{1}{2(a-1)+} \cfrac{1}{2+} \cfrac{1}{2(a-1)+} \cdots; \dfrac{8a^2 - 8a + 1}{8a - 4}$.

3. $a - 1 + \cfrac{1}{1+} \cfrac{1}{2(a-1)+} \cfrac{1}{1+} \cfrac{1}{2(a-1)+} \cdots; \dfrac{2a^2 - 1}{2a}$.

4. $1 + \cfrac{1}{2a+} \cfrac{1}{2+} \cfrac{1}{2a+} \cfrac{1}{2+} \cdots; \dfrac{8a^2 + 8a + 1}{8a^2 + 4a}$.

5. $a + \cfrac{1}{b+} \cfrac{1}{2a+} \cfrac{1}{b+} \cfrac{1}{2a+} \cdots; \dfrac{2a^2 b^2 + 4ab + 1}{2ab^2 + 2b}$.

6. $a - 1 + \dfrac{1}{1 + } \dfrac{1}{2\,(n - 1) + } \dfrac{1}{1 + } \dfrac{1}{2\,(a - 1) + } \cdots ; \dfrac{2an - 1}{2n}.$

7. $\dfrac{432a^5 + 180a^3 + 15a}{144a^4 + 36a^2 + 1}$

XXVIII. PAGES 300 – 301

1. $x = 7$ or $1, y = 4, x = 7$ or $5, y = 6.$

2. $x = 2, y = 1.$

3. $x = 3, y = 1, 11; x = 7, y = 9, 19; x = 10, y = 18, 22.$

4. $x = 2, 3, 6, 11; y = 12, 7, 4, 3.$

5. $x = 3, 2; y = 1, 4.$

6. $x = 79, 27, 17, 13, 11, 9; y = 157, 51, 29, 19, 13, 3.$

7. $x = 15, y = 4.$

8. $x = 170, y = 39.$

9. $x = 32, y = 5.$ **10.** $x = 164, y = 21.$ **11.** $x = 4, y = 1.$

12. $2x = (2 + \sqrt{3})^n + (2 - \sqrt{3})^n; 2\sqrt{3}.\ y = (2 + \sqrt{3})^n - (2 - \sqrt{3})^n, n$ being any integer.

13. $2x = (2 + \sqrt{5})^n + (2 - \sqrt{5})^n; 2\sqrt{5}.\ y = (2 + \sqrt{5})^n - (2 - \sqrt{5})^n;$ n being any even positive integer.

14. $2x = (4 + \sqrt{17})^n + (4 - \sqrt{17})^n; 2\sqrt{17}.\ y = (4 + \sqrt{17})^n - (4 - \sqrt{17})^n;$ n being any odd positive integer.

The form of the answers to 15 – 17, 19, 20 will vary according to the mode of factorising the two sides of the equation.

15. $x = m^2 - 3n^2, y = m^2 - 2mn.$

16. $x = -m^2 + 2mn + n^2; y = m^2 - n^2.$

17. $x = 2mn, y = 5m^2 - n^2.$

18. $53, 52; 19, 16; 13, 8; 11, 4.$

19. $m^2 - n^2; 2mn; m^2 + n^2.$ **20.** $m^2 - n^2; 2mn + n^2.$

XXIX. a. PAGES 311 – 312

1. $\dfrac{1}{4}\,n\,(n + 1)\,(n + 2)\,(n + 3).$ **2.** $\dfrac{1}{5}\,n\,(n + 1)\,(n + 2)\,(n + 3)\,(n + 4).$

3. $\dfrac{1}{12}\,(3n - 2)\,(3n + 1)\,(3n + 4)\,(3n + 7) + \dfrac{56}{12}$

$$= \dfrac{n}{4}\,(27n^3 + 90n^2 + 45n - 50).$$

4. $\dfrac{n}{4}(n+1)(n+6)(n+7).$ **5.** $\dfrac{n}{4}(n+1)(n+8)(n+9).$

6. $\dfrac{n}{n+1}; 1.$ **7.** $\dfrac{n}{3n+1}; \dfrac{1}{3}.$

8. $\dfrac{1}{12} - \dfrac{1}{4(2n+1)(2n+3)}; \dfrac{1}{12}.$

9. $\dfrac{1}{24} - \dfrac{1}{6(3n+1)(3n+4)}; \dfrac{1}{24}.$

10. $\dfrac{5}{4} - \dfrac{2n+5}{2(n+1)(n+2)}; \dfrac{5}{4}.$

11. $\dfrac{1}{6} - \dfrac{1}{n+3} + \dfrac{2}{(n+3)(n+4)}; \dfrac{1}{6}.$

12. $\dfrac{3}{4} - \dfrac{2}{n+2} + \dfrac{1}{2(n+1)(n+2)}; \dfrac{3}{4}.$

13. $\dfrac{n}{10}(n+1)(n+2)(n+3)(2n+3).$ **14.** $\dfrac{1}{4}n^2(n^2-1).$

15. $\dfrac{n}{10}(n-1)(n+1)(n+2)(2n+1).$

16. $\dfrac{1}{15}(n+1)(n+2)(3n^3+36n^2+151n+240)-32.$

17. $\dfrac{(n-1)n(n+1)(n+2)}{6(2n+1)}.$ **18.** $\dfrac{n(n+1)(n+2)}{3} - \dfrac{n}{n+1}.$

19. $\dfrac{n(n+3)}{2} + \dfrac{3}{2} - \dfrac{2}{n+2} - \dfrac{1}{(n+1)(n+2)}.$

20. $n+1 - \dfrac{1}{n+1}.$

XXIX. b. Pages 321 – 322

1. $3n^2+n; \; n(n+1)^2.$ **2.** $5n^2+3n; \dfrac{1}{3}n(n+1)(5n+7).$

3. $n^2(n+1); \dfrac{1}{12}n(n+1)(n+2)(3n+1).$

4. $-4n^2(n-3); -n(n+1)(n^2-3n-2).$

5. $n(n+1)(n+2)(n+4); \dfrac{1}{20}n(n+1)(n+2)(n+3)(4n+21).$

6. $\dfrac{1+x^2}{(1-x)^3}.$ **7.** $\dfrac{1-x+6x^2-2x^3}{(1-x)^3}.$

8. $\dfrac{2-x+x^2}{(1-x)^3}$.

9. $\dfrac{1-x}{(1+x)^2}$.

10. $\dfrac{1+11x+11x^2+x^3}{(1-x)^5}$.

11. $\dfrac{9}{4}$.

12. $\dfrac{25}{54}$.

13. $3 \cdot 2^n + n + 2;\ 6(2^n - 1) + \dfrac{n(n+5)}{2}$

14. $n^3 - (n+1)^2;\ \dfrac{n}{12}(3n^3 + 2n^2 - 15n - 26)$.

15. $3^{n-1} + n;\ \dfrac{3^n + n^2 + n - 1}{2}$

16. $2^{n+1} - n^2 - 2n;\ 2^{n+2} - 4 - \dfrac{1}{6}n(n+1)(2n+7)$.

17. $3^n - 1 + \dfrac{1}{2}n(n+3);\ \dfrac{1}{2}(3^{n+1} - 3) + \dfrac{n(n+1)(n+5)}{6} - n$.

18. $\dfrac{1-x^n}{(1-x)^2} - \dfrac{nx^n}{1-x}$.

19. $\dfrac{1-x^n}{(1-x)^3} - \dfrac{nx^n}{(1-x)^2} - \dfrac{n(n+1)x^n}{2(1-x)}$.

20. $1 - \dfrac{1}{n+1} \cdot \dfrac{1}{2^n}$.

21. $\dfrac{n-1}{n+2} \cdot \dfrac{4^{n+1}}{3} + \dfrac{2}{3}$.

22. $\dfrac{n(n+1)(3n^3 + 27n^2 + 58n + 2)}{15}$.

23. $\dfrac{n(n+1)(12n^3 + 33n^2 + 37n + 8)}{60}$.

24. $\dfrac{n(n+1)(9n^2 + 13n + 8)}{12}$.

25. $\dfrac{1}{2} - \dfrac{1}{2} \cdot \dfrac{1}{1.3.5.7 \ldots (2n+1)}$.

26. $1 - \dfrac{2^{n+1}}{(n+2)!}$.

27. $(n^2 - n + 4)2^n - 4$.

28. $(n-1)3^{n+1} + 3$.

29. $\dfrac{1}{2} - \dfrac{1.3.5 \ldots (2n+1)}{2.4.6 \ldots (2n+2)}$.

30. $\dfrac{n}{n+1} \cdot 2^n$.

31. $\dfrac{1}{4} - \dfrac{1}{2(n+1)(n+2)} \cdot \dfrac{1}{3^n}$.

32. $\dfrac{1}{2} - \dfrac{n+1}{(n+2)!}$.

33. $1 - \dfrac{n+4}{(n+1)(n+2)} \cdot \dfrac{1}{2^{n+1}}$.

XXIX. c. PAGES 326–328

1. $\dfrac{1}{2}(e^x - e^{-x}) - x$.

2. $1 + \dfrac{1-x}{x}\log(1-x)$.

3. $\frac{1}{4}(e^x - e^{-x} - ie^{4x} + ie^{-4x})$.

4. $\dfrac{1}{(r-2)\,[(r-1)\,!]}$.

5. $(1 + x)\,e^x$

6. $\dfrac{(p+q)^r}{r\,!}$.

7. 1.

8. $n\,(2n - 1)$.

9. 0.

10. 4.

11. $\log_e 2 - \dfrac{1}{2}$.

12. $3\,(e - 1)$.

13. $e^x - \log(1 + x)$.

14. (1) $\dfrac{n^7}{7} + \dfrac{n^6}{2} + \dfrac{n^5}{2} - \dfrac{n^3}{6} + \dfrac{n}{42}$.   (2) $\dfrac{n^8}{8} + \dfrac{n^7}{2} + \dfrac{7n^6}{12} - \dfrac{7n^4}{24} + \dfrac{n^2}{12}$.

15. $15e$.

17. (1) $n + 1$.

19. $\dfrac{1}{2}\left(1 - \dfrac{1}{1 + n + n^2}\right)$; (2) $3 - \dfrac{2 + (-1)^n}{n + 1}$.

20. $\dfrac{(1+x)^2}{2x^2}\log(1 + x) - \dfrac{3x + 2}{4x}$.   **21.** $n\,(n + 1)\,2^{n-3}$.

22. (1) $\dfrac{1}{3}\left\{1 + \dfrac{(-1)^{n+1}}{2^{n+1} + (-1)^{n+1}}\right\}$. (2) $\dfrac{1}{2}\left\{\dfrac{3}{2} + (-1)^{n-1}\dfrac{2n+3}{(n+1)(n+2)}\right\}$.

XXX. a. PAGES 335 – 337

1. 3, 6, 15, 42.   **2.**   1617, 180, 1859.

6. 48.   **7.**   23.   **33.** 8987.

XXX. b. PAGES 343 – 345

20. $x = 139t + 61$, where t is an integer.

XXXI. PAGES 354 – 356

2. $1 + \dfrac{1}{x-}\dfrac{1}{4+}\dfrac{1}{x}$.   **18.** 1; it can be shewn that $q_n = 1 + p_n$

XXXII. a. PAGES 363 – 364

1. (1) $\dfrac{1}{9}$; (2) $\dfrac{5}{36}$.   **2.** $\dfrac{8}{663}$.   **3.** $\dfrac{1}{56}$.

4. $\dfrac{3}{8}$.   **5.** 2 to 3.   **6.** $\dfrac{4}{270725}$.

8. 43 to 34.   **9.** 36 : 30 : 25.   **10.** $\dfrac{2197}{20825}$.

11. 952 to 715.   **14.** $\dfrac{1}{6}$ **15.** $\dfrac{2}{7}$ **16.** $\dfrac{11}{4165}$

17. $\dfrac{n(n-1)}{(m+n)(m+n-1)}$.

XXXII. b. PAGES 370 – 371

1. $\dfrac{5}{36}$.   **2.** $\dfrac{16}{5525}$.   **3.** $\dfrac{52}{77}$.   **4.** $\dfrac{16}{21}$.

5. $\dfrac{8}{15}$.   **6.** $\dfrac{72}{289}$.   **7.** (1) $\dfrac{2197}{20825}$. (2) $\dfrac{2816}{4165}$.

8. $\dfrac{4651}{7776}$.   **9.** $\dfrac{209}{343}$.   **10.** $\dfrac{1}{7}$.   **11.** $\dfrac{91}{216}$.

13. $\dfrac{10}{19}$.   **14.** $\dfrac{63}{256}$.   **15.** $\dfrac{1}{32}$.   **16.** $\dfrac{16}{37}, \dfrac{12}{37}, \dfrac{9}{37}$.

17. $\dfrac{22}{35}, \dfrac{13}{35}$.   **18.** $n-3$ to 2.   **19.** 13 to 5.   **20.** $\dfrac{45927}{50000}$.

XXXII. c. PAGES 376 – 377

1. $\dfrac{2133}{3125}$.   **2.** $\dfrac{5}{16}$.   **3.** $\dfrac{4}{9}$.   **4.** 10 nP. coins.

5. $\dfrac{1}{2}$.   **6.** 92 nP.'s   **7.** $\dfrac{4}{63}$.   **8.** $\dfrac{7}{27}$.

9. 11 to 5.   **10.** $\dfrac{1}{8}$.   **11.** A £5; B £11.   **12.** $\dfrac{20}{27}$.

13. $4\dfrac{4}{5}$ shillings.   **14.** (1) $\dfrac{250}{7776}$; (2) $\dfrac{276}{7776}$.

15. $4d$.   **16.** $\dfrac{3}{4}$.   **17.** $M + \dfrac{1}{2}m$.

XXXII. d. PAGES 384 – 386

1. $\dfrac{2}{5}$.   **2.** $\dfrac{1}{35}$.   **3.** $\dfrac{12}{17}$.   **5.** $B\dfrac{2}{5}; C\dfrac{4}{15}$.

5. $\dfrac{2}{n(n+1)}$.   **6.** $\dfrac{32}{41}$.   **7.** $\dfrac{377}{550}$.

8. $2s.\,3d$.   **9.** $\dfrac{1}{5}$.   **10.** $\dfrac{1}{3}$.   **11.** $\dfrac{40}{41}$.

12. $\dfrac{11}{50}$.   **13.** £1.   **14.** (1) $\dfrac{3}{5}$; (2) $\dfrac{7}{8}$.   **15.** £8.

17. $\dfrac{n-1}{mn-1}, \dfrac{n-1}{mn-rn-1}$.   **18.** $\dfrac{13}{14}$.

XXXII. e. PAGES 391 – 395

1. 7 to 5.

2. $\dfrac{1}{126}$.

3. $\dfrac{12393}{12500}$.

5. $\dfrac{275}{504}$.

6. $1 : \dfrac{5}{6} : \left(\dfrac{5}{6}\right)^2 : \left(\dfrac{5}{6}\right)^3 : \left(\dfrac{5}{6}\right)^4$.

7. $\dfrac{16}{21}$.

8. 6; each equal to $\dfrac{1}{6}$.

9. $\dfrac{13}{28}$.

10. $\dfrac{343}{1695}$.

11. 11 to 5.

13. $A, \dfrac{169}{324}; B, \dfrac{155}{324}$.

14. $\dfrac{1}{7}, \dfrac{4}{21}$.

16. $\dfrac{25}{216}$.

17. $\dfrac{149}{2401}$.

18. $\dfrac{33}{1000}, \dfrac{1}{60}$.

20. One guinea.

22. $\dfrac{140}{141}$.

23. $\dfrac{n(n+1)}{2}$ shillings.

24. 19 to 1.

28. $\dfrac{1}{4}$.

29. $\dfrac{1}{4}$.

30. $\dfrac{1265}{1286}; £\dfrac{5087}{5144}$.

31. $\left(\dfrac{a-b}{a}\right)^2$.

32. If $b > \dfrac{a}{2}$, the chance is $1 - 3\left(\dfrac{a-b}{a}\right)^2$;

If $b < \dfrac{a}{2}$, the chance is $\left(\dfrac{3b-a}{a}\right)^2$.

XXXIII. a. PAGES 405 – 407

1. 7. **2.** 0. **3.** 1. **4.** $abc + 2fgh - af^2 - bg^2 - ch^2$.

5. $1 + x^2 + y^2 + z^2$. **6.** xy. **7.** 0. **8.** $4abc$.

9. 0. **10.** 3. **11.** $3abc - a^3 - b^3 - c^3 = 0$.

13. (1) $x = a$, or b; (2) $x = 4$.

20. $\begin{vmatrix} b^2 + c^2 & ab & ac \\ ba & c^2 + a^2 & bc \\ ca & cb & a^2 + b^2 \end{vmatrix}$. **22.** $\lambda^3 (\lambda^2 + a^2 + b^2 + c^2)^3$.

26. The determinant is equal to $\begin{vmatrix} a^2 & a & 1 \\ b^2 & b & 1 \\ c^2 & c & 1 \end{vmatrix} \times \begin{vmatrix} 1 & -2x & x^2 \\ 1 & -2y & y^2 \\ 1 & -2z & z^2 \end{vmatrix}$.

27. $\begin{vmatrix} u & w' & v' \\ w' & v & u' \\ v' & u' & w \end{vmatrix} = 0.$ **28.** $\begin{vmatrix} u & w' & v' \\ w' & v & u' \\ v' & u' & w \end{vmatrix} \div \begin{vmatrix} u & w' & v' & a \\ w' & v & u' & b \\ v' & u' & w & c \\ a & b & c & 0 \end{vmatrix}$

XXXIII. b. PAGES 412 – 414

1. 1.

2. 0; add first and second rows, third and fourth rows.

3. $(a + 3)(a - 1)^3$.   **4.** $a^2 + b^2 + c^2 - 2bc - 2ca - 2ab$.

5. 6; from the first column subtract three times the third, from the second subtract twice the third, and from the fourth subtract four times the third.

6. $abcd \left(1 + \dfrac{1}{a} + \dfrac{1}{b} + \dfrac{1}{c} + \dfrac{1}{d} \right).$

7. $-(x + y + z)(y + z - x)(z + x - y)(x + y - z).$

8. $(ax - by + cz)^2$.   **9.** a^4

12. $x = \dfrac{(k - b)(k - c)}{(a - b))(a - c)}$; &c.   **13.** $x = \dfrac{k(k - b)(k - c)}{a(a - b)(a - c)}$; &c.

14. $x = \dfrac{(k - b)(k - c)(k - d)}{(a - b)(a - c)(a - d)}$; &c.

XXXIV. a. PAGES 424 – 426

1. -102.   **2.** $3a + b = 27$.   **3.** $x^3 - 2x^2 + x + 1; -15x + 11$.

4. $a = 3$.

5. $x^{-4} + 5x^{-5} + 18x^{-6} + 54x^{-7}; 147x^{-4} - 356x^{-5} + 90x^{-6} + 432x^{-7}$.

6. $(b - c)(c - a)(a - b)(a + b + c)$.

7. $-(b - c)(c - a)(a - b)(b + c)(c + a)(a + b)$.

8. $24abc$.

9. $(b + c)(c + a)(a + b)$.

10. $(b - c)(c - a)(a - b)(a^2 + b^2 + c^2 + bc + ca + ab)$.

11. $3abc(b + c)(c + a)(a + b)$.

12. $12abc(a + b + c)$.   **13.** $80abc(a^2 + b^2 + c^2)$.

14. $3(b - c)(c - a)(a - b)(x - a)(x - b)(x - c)$.

28. $\dfrac{x}{(x - a)(x - b)(x - c)}$.   **29.** 2.

30. $\dfrac{(p - x)(q - x)}{(a + x)(b + x)(c + x)}$.   **31.** -1.

32. $a + b + c + d$.

XXXIV. b. Pages 428 – 430

5. 0.

7. $A = ax + by + ay, \ B = bx - ay.$

28. $(a^2 + bc)(b^2 + ca)(c^2 + ab).$

XXXIV. c. Pages 434 – 436

1. $x^3 + xy^2 + ay^2 = 0.$ **2.** $x + a = 0.$

3. $x^2 + y^2 = a^2.$ **4.** $y^2 = a(x - 3a).$

5. $a^6 - a^3 = 1.$ **6.** $x^2 + y^2 = 2a^2.$

7. $b^4 c^4 + c^4 a^4 + a^4 b^4 = a^2 b^2 c^2 d^2.$

8. $y^2 - 4ax = k^2 (x + a)^2.$ **9.** $a^4 - 4ac^3 + 3b^4 = 0.$

10. $a^4 - 2a^2 b^2 - b^4 + 2c^4 = 0.$ **11.** $\dfrac{a}{1+a} + \dfrac{b}{1+b} + \dfrac{c}{1+c} + \dfrac{d}{1+d} = 1.$

12. $5a^2 b^3 = 6c^5.$ **13.** $ab = 1 + c.$

14. $a^3 + b^3 + c^3 + abc = 0.$ **15.** $(a+b)^{2/3} - (a-b)^{2/3} = 4c^{2/3}.$

16. $a^2 + b^2 + c^2 \pm 2abc = 1.$ **17.** $abc = (4 - a - b - c)^2$

18. $a^2 - 4abc + ac^3 + 4b^3 - b^2 c^2 = 0.$

20. $c^2 (a + b - 1)^2 - c(a + b - 1)(a^2 - 2ab + b^2 - a - b) + ab = 0.$

22. $\dfrac{1}{(a-b)\,cr + (a-c)\,bq} + \dfrac{1}{(b-c)\,ap + (b-a)\,cr}$
$$+ \dfrac{1}{(c-a)\,bq + (c-b)\,ap} = \dfrac{1}{bcqr + carp + abpq}.$$

23. $\begin{vmatrix} ab' - a'b & ac' - a'c & ad' - a'd \\ ac' - a'c & ad' - a'd + bc' - b'c & bd' - b'd \\ ad' - a'd & bd' - b'd & cd' - c'd \end{vmatrix} = 0.$

XXXV. a. Pages 441 – 442

1. $6x^4 - 13x^3 - 12x^2 + 39x - 18 = 0.$

2. $x^6 + 2x^5 - 11x^4 - 12x^3 + 36x^2 = 0.$

3. $x^6 - 5x^5 - 8x^4 + 40x^3 + 16x^2 - 80x = 0.$

4. $x^4 - 2(a^2 + b^2)x^2 + (a^2 - b^2)^2$

5. 1, 3, 5, 7.

6. $\dfrac{3}{2}, -\dfrac{3}{2}, -4$ 7. $\dfrac{1}{2}, \dfrac{1}{2}, -6.$ 8. $6, 2, \dfrac{2}{3}.$

9. $-\dfrac{3}{2}, -2, 4.$ 10. $-\dfrac{3}{2}, -\dfrac{3}{4}, \dfrac{1}{3}.$ 11. $\pm\sqrt{3}, \dfrac{3}{4}, -\dfrac{1}{2}$

12. $\dfrac{8}{9}, -\dfrac{2}{3}, \dfrac{1}{2}$ 13. $\dfrac{1}{4}, \dfrac{1}{2}, \dfrac{3}{4}.$ 14. $\dfrac{4}{3}, \dfrac{3}{2}, 1\pm\sqrt{2}.$

15. $-4, -1, 2, 5.$ 16. $\dfrac{8}{9}, \dfrac{4}{3}, 2, 3.$ 17. $-\dfrac{4}{3}, -\dfrac{3}{2}, -\dfrac{5}{3}.$

18. (1) $\dfrac{q^2 - 2pr}{r^2}$; (2) $\dfrac{p^2 - 2q}{r^2}$

19. (1) $-6q$; (2) $\dfrac{q}{r}.$ 20. $-2q, -3r.$ 21. $2q^2$

XXXV. b. PAGES 446 – 447

1. $3, -\dfrac{2}{3}, \dfrac{1 \pm \sqrt{-3}}{2}.$ 2. $-\dfrac{3}{2}, -\dfrac{1}{3}, 2 \pm \sqrt{3}.$

3. $-1 \pm \sqrt{2}, -1 \pm \sqrt{-1}$ 4. $\pm\sqrt{-1}, -2 \pm \sqrt{-1}.$

5. $-1, \pm\sqrt{3}, 1 \pm 2\sqrt{-1}.$ 6. $x^4 - 2x^2 + 25 = 0.$

7. $x^4 - 8x^2 + 86 = 0.$ 8. $x^4 + 16 = 0.$

9. $x^4 - 10x^2 + 1 = 0.$

10. $x^4 - 10x^3 - 19x^2 + 480x - 1392 = 0.$

11. $x^4 - 6x^3 + 18x^2 - 26x + 21 = 0.$

12. $x^8 - 16x^6 + 88x^4 + 192x^2 + 144 = 0.$

13. One positive, one negative, two imaginary. [**Compare Art. 554.**]

15. One positive, one negative, at least four imaginary.
   [**Compare Art. 554.**]

16. Six.   17. (1) $pq = r$; (2) $p^3 r = q^3$

20. $q^2 - 2pr.$ 21. $pq - r$

22. $\dfrac{pq}{r} - 3.$ 23. $pq - 3r.$

24. $pr - 4s.$ 25. $p^4 - 4p^2 q + 2q^2 + 4pr - 4s.$

XXXV. c. PAGES 455 – 456

1. $x^4 - 6x^3 + 15x^2 - 12x + 1.$ 2. $x^4 - 37x^2 - 123x - 110.$

3. $2x^4 + 8x^3 - x^2 - 8x - 20.$ 4. $x^4 - 24x^2 - 1.$

5. $16axh\,(x^6 + 7x^4 h^2 + 7x^2 h^4 + h^6) + 2bh\,(5x^4 + 10x^2 h^2 + h^4) + 2ch.$

10. $2, 2, -1, -3.$ **11.** $1, 1, 1, 3.$

12. $3, 3, 3, 2, 2.$ **13.** $-2, \dfrac{1 \pm \sqrt{-3}}{2}, \dfrac{1 \pm \sqrt{-3}}{2}.$

14. $\dfrac{1}{2}, \dfrac{1}{2}, \dfrac{1}{2}, -2.$ **15.** $1, 1, 1, -1, -1, 2.$

16. $\pm \sqrt{3}, \pm \sqrt{3}, 1 \pm \sqrt{-1}.$ **17.** $a, a, -a, b.$

18. $\pm \sqrt{\dfrac{3}{2}}, \dfrac{1 \pm \sqrt{-7}}{2}; \pm \sqrt{\dfrac{3}{2}}, \dfrac{1 \pm \sqrt{-23}}{4}$

19. $0, 1, -\dfrac{3}{2}, -\dfrac{5}{2}; 0, 1, -\dfrac{3}{2}, -\dfrac{5}{3}.$

20. $n^n r^{n-2} = 4 p^n (n-2)^{n-2}.$

22. $(1) -2; (2) -1.$ **27.** $5.$ **28.** $99, 795.$

XXXV. d. Pages 463 – 464

1. $y^3 - 24 y^2 + 9y - 24 = 0.$ **2.** $y^4 - 5 y^3 + 3 y^2 - 9y + 27 = 0.$

3. $1, 1, -2, -\dfrac{1}{2}.$ **4.** $3 \pm 2\sqrt{2}, 2 \pm \sqrt{3}.$

5. $1, \dfrac{1 \pm \sqrt{-3}}{2}, \dfrac{3 \pm \sqrt{5}}{2}.$ **6.** $2, 2, \dfrac{1}{2}, \dfrac{1}{2}, \dfrac{1}{2}(1 \pm \sqrt{-3}).$

7. $4, 2, \dfrac{4}{3}.$ **8.** $6, 3, 2.$

10. $\dfrac{1}{4}, 1, -\dfrac{1}{2}, -\dfrac{1}{5}.$ **11.** $y^3 - 2y + 1 = 0.$

12. $y^4 - 4 y^2 + 1 = 0.$ **13.** $y^5 - 7 y^3 + 12 y^2 - 7y = 0.$

14. $y^6 - 60 y^4 - 320 y^3 - 717 y^2 - 773 y - 42 = 0.$

15. $y^3 - \dfrac{9 y^2}{2} + \dfrac{13 y}{2} - \dfrac{15}{4} = 0.$

16. $y^5 + 11 y^4 + 42 y^3 + 57 y^2 - 13 y - 60 = 0.$

17. $y^3 - 8 y^2 + 19 y - 15 = 0.$ **18.** $y^4 + 3 y^3 + 4 y^2 + 3y + 1 = 0.$

19. $y^3 + 33 y^2 + 12 y + 8 = 0.$

20. $r y^3 + k q y^2 + k^3 = 0.$ **21.** $y^3 - q^2 y^2 - 2 q r^2 y - r^4 = 0.$

22. $r y^3 - q y^2 - 1 = 0.$ **23.** $r y^3 + q(1-r) y^2 + (1-r)^3 = 0.$

24. $y^3 - 2 q y^2 + q^2 y + r^2 = 0.$ **25.** $y^3 + 3 r y^2 + (q^3 + 3 r^2) y + r^3 = 0.$

26. $r^3 y^3 + 3 r^3 y^2 + (3 r^2 + q^3) r y + r(r^2 + 2 q^3) = 0.$

28. $\pm 1, \pm 2, 5.$

XXXV. e. PAGES 472 – 473

1. $5, \dfrac{-5 \pm \sqrt{-3}}{2}$.

2. $10, -5 \pm 7\sqrt{-3}$.

3. $4, -2 \pm 5\sqrt{-3}$.

4. $-6, 3 \pm 4\sqrt{-3}$.

5. $-\dfrac{1}{4}, \dfrac{2 \pm \sqrt{-3}}{7}$.

6. $11, 11, -7$.

7. $-\dfrac{1}{2}, -\dfrac{1 \pm \sqrt{-3}}{2}$.

9. $4, -1, -\dfrac{1}{2}(3 \pm \sqrt{-31})$.

10. $4, -2, -1 \pm \sqrt{-1}$.

11. $\pm 1, -4 \pm \sqrt{6}$.

12. $1, 2, -2, -3$.

13. $1 \pm \sqrt{2}, -1 \pm \sqrt{-1}$.

14. $1, -3, 2 \pm \sqrt{5}$.

15. $2, 2, \dfrac{1}{2}, \dfrac{1}{2}$.

16. $1, 4 \pm \sqrt{15}, -\dfrac{3 \pm \sqrt{5}}{2}$.

17. $-4, -4, -4, 3$.

18. $q^3 + 8r^2 = 0; \dfrac{3}{2}, \dfrac{-3 \pm 3\sqrt{5}}{4}$.

22. $-2 \pm \sqrt{6}, \pm \sqrt{2}, 2 \pm \sqrt{2}$.

23. $s^3 y^4 + qs(1-s)^2 y^2 + r(1-s)^3 y + (1-s)^4 = 0$.

25. $2 \pm \sqrt{3}$.

26. $\dfrac{5 \pm \sqrt{13}}{2}$.

28. $x^4 - 8x^3 + 21x^2 - 20x + 5 = (x^2 - 5x + 5)(x^2 - 3x + 1)$; on putting $x = 4 - y$, the expressions $x^2 - 5x + 5$ and $x^2 - 3x + 1$ become $y^2 - 3y + 1$ and $y^2 - 5y + 5$ respectively, so that we merely reproduce the original equation.

MISCELLANEOUS EXAMPLES. PAGES 474 – 511

2. $6, 8$.

3. Eight.

4. (1) $1 \pm \sqrt{5}; 1 \pm 2\sqrt{5}$.

(2) $x = 1, y = 3, z = -5$; or $x = -1, y = -3; z = 5$.

6. (1) $1, -\dfrac{a + 2b}{2a + b}$ (2) $3, 3, 1$. **7.** First term 1; common difference $\dfrac{1}{3}$.

8. $p^2 - q; -p(p^2 - 3q); (p^2 - q)(p^2 - 3q)$.

9. $\dfrac{1}{2}(ab + a^{-1}b^{-1})$.

10. $\dfrac{7}{13}$.

13. A, 7 minutes; B, 8 minutes.

14. $a^2 = b^2 = c^2$.

15. $x^2 = y^2 = \dfrac{d}{a + b + c}$; or $\dfrac{x}{c - a} = \dfrac{y}{a - b} = k$; where $k^2 \cdot (a^2 + b^2 + c^2 - bc - ca - ab) = d$.

16. One mile per hour.

17. (1) $(b+c)(c+a)(a+b)$.   (2) $\sqrt{\dfrac{5-4x}{2}} + \sqrt{\dfrac{2x-3}{2}}$.

18. $\dfrac{35}{9}$; 2268.   **19.** (1) $\dfrac{21 \pm \sqrt{105}}{14}$.

   (2) $x = y = \pm\sqrt{ab}$; $\dfrac{x}{2a+b} = \dfrac{y}{-(3a+2b)} = \pm\sqrt{\dfrac{ab}{b^2+ab-a^2}}$.

22. 1 et 5; nine.

23. $\dfrac{1}{2}\{(1+2+3+\dots+n)^2 - (1^2+2^2+3^2+\dots+n^2)\}$.

24. Wages 15s.; loaf 6d **25.** 6, 10, 14, 18.

26. (1) $1, \dfrac{c(a-b)}{a(b-c)}$. (2) $\dfrac{ab(c+d)-cd(a+b)}{ab-cd}$.

28. $88\dfrac{3}{9}$ miles.

29. $x = 3k, y = 4k, z = 5k$; where $k^3 = 1$, so that $k = 1, \omega$, or ω^2.

30. 480.

31. Either 33 half-crowns, 19 shillings, 8 fourpenny pieces; or 37 half-crowns, 6 shillings, 17 fourpenny pieces.

32. $a = 6, b = 7$.   **33.** 40 minutes.

35. $1 + x + \dfrac{1}{2}x^2 - \dfrac{1}{2}x^3 - \dfrac{13}{8}x^4$.

37. $\dfrac{-1 \pm \sqrt{-3}}{2}$, or $\dfrac{1 \pm \sqrt{21}}{2}$. $[x^4 - x - 5(x^2 + x + 1) = 0.]$

38. $a = 8; \dfrac{x-4}{x-5}$.   **40.** The first term.

41. 13, 9.   **42.** $\dfrac{1 + 4b^2c^2 + 9c^2a^2 + a^2b^2}{a^2 + b^2 + c^2}$.

43. (1) $3, -2, \dfrac{-1 \pm \sqrt{-39}}{2}$. [Add $x^2 + 4$ to each side.]

   (2) $x = 1, -\dfrac{1}{2}, -1, 0, 0$;

        $y = 1, -\dfrac{1}{2}, 0, -1, 0$;

        $z = 1, -\dfrac{1}{2}, 0, 0, -1$.

47. 5780.   **48.** 150 persons changed their mind.

50. 936 men.

51. (1) $0, \dfrac{2^m - 1}{2^m + 1} a.$ (2) $\dfrac{ad - bc}{a - b - c + d}.$

[Put $(a - c)(b - d) = \{(x - c) - (x - a)\}\{(x - d) - (x - b)\}$;

then square.]

53. $6, -\dfrac{161}{30}.$ **55.** $m = \dfrac{2b\sqrt{a}}{\sqrt{a} + \sqrt{b}}, n = \dfrac{2a\sqrt{b}}{\sqrt{a} + \sqrt{b}}.$

58. (1) 1. (2) $\pm 4\sqrt{2}$

[putting $x^2 - 16 = y^4$, we find $y^4 - 16 - 4y(y^2 - 4) = 0.$]

60. $\dfrac{(a - c)p}{b - c}$ males; $\dfrac{(b - a)p}{b - c}$ females.

63. $0, a + b, \dfrac{a^2 + b^2}{a + b}.$

64. Common difference of the A.P. is $\dfrac{b - a}{n - 1}$; common difference

of the A.P. which is the reciprocal of the H.P. is $\dfrac{a - b}{ab(n - 1)}.$

[The rth term is $\dfrac{a(n - r) + b(r - 1)}{n - 1}$; the $(n - r + 1)^{\text{th}}$ term is

$\dfrac{ab(n - 1)}{a(n - r) + b(r - 1)}.$]

68. 19.   **69.** £78.   **70.** $0, \dfrac{1 \pm \sqrt{-3}}{2}, \dfrac{-1 \pm \sqrt{-3}}{2}.$

[$(a + b)^3 - a^3 - b^3 = 3ab(a + b)$, and $(a - b)^3 - a^3 + b^3 = -3ab(a - b).$]

72. (1) $x = \pm\dfrac{\log 3}{\log 6} = \pm 0.614.$ (2) $x = \pm\dfrac{2(1 - 2\log 2)}{1 - \log 2} = \pm 1.139.$

73. 7, 2.   **74.** 8 hours.

79. (1) $\dfrac{x}{a} = \dfrac{y}{b} = \dfrac{z}{c} = 0$, or $\dfrac{a + b + c}{abc}.$ (2) $x = y = z = 1.$

80. $a = 3, b = 1.$ **81.** [Put $x - a = u$ and $y - b = v.$]

82. $x = 3.$ **84.** 126.

85. Sums invested were £7700 and £4200; the fortune of each was £1400.

86. 503 in scale seven.   **91.** 25 miles from London.

95. $x = 5, 1, \dfrac{15 \pm 6\sqrt{-1}}{29}; y = 3, \dfrac{3}{5}, \dfrac{25 \pm 10\sqrt{-1}}{29}.$

96. $\sqrt{\dfrac{5}{3}}$ **98.** $\dfrac{1}{2e}.$

100. Generating function is $\dfrac{1 + 4x}{1 - x - 2x^2};$

$$\text{sum} = \frac{2\,(1 - 2^n x^n)}{1 - 2x} - \frac{1 - (-1)^n x^n}{1 + x}.$$

$n\text{th term} = \{2^n + (-1)^n\}\, x^{n-1}.$

107. $a^2 + b - c^2 - d.$ **108.** 12 persons, £14. 18s.

109. ;(1) $x = a,\ y = b,\ z = c.$ (2) $x = \pm\,3,$ or $\pm\,1;\ y = \pm\,1,$ or $\pm\,3.$

111. $1 + \dfrac{1}{1 + 12}\ \dfrac{1}{1 +}\ \dfrac{1}{1 + 1}\ \dfrac{1}{9}\,;\ x = 185,\ y = 96.$

113. £12. 15s.

117. (1) $x = a,\ y = b;\ x = a,\ y = 2a;\ x = 2b,\ y = b.$

(2) $x = 3$ or $1,\ y = 2,\ z = 1$ or $3;$

$$x = \frac{-1 \pm \sqrt{29}}{2},\ y = -3;\ z = \frac{-1 \mp \sqrt{29}}{2}.$$

120. (1) $1 - \dfrac{1}{(n + 1)^2}.$

(2) $\dfrac{a\,(x^n - 1)}{x - 1} + \dfrac{b}{(x - 1)^3}$

$$\times\ \{x^{n+2} + x^{n+1} - (n + 1)^2\, x^2 + (2n^2 + 2n - 1)\, x - n^2\}.$$

121. $\dfrac{1}{3}.$

122. (1) $\dfrac{-5 \pm \sqrt{-11}}{6}\quad$ or $\quad\dfrac{-3 \pm \sqrt{5}}{2}.\quad$ (2) $x = y = z = 0;$

$x = 2,\ y = \pm\,1,\ z = \mp\,3;\ x = -2,\ y = \pm\,1,\ z = \pm\,3.$

124. $\dfrac{13x - 23}{3\,(x^2 - 3x - 1)} - \dfrac{10x - 1}{3\,(x^2 + x + 1)}\,;\ -\dfrac{r + 4}{2^{r+1}}.$

125. $l = 1;$ scale of relation is $1 - x - 2x^2;$ general term is

$\{2^{n-3} + (-1)^{n-1}\}\, x^{n-1}.$

127. (1) $x = -6,\ 2;\ y = 9,\ -3.$ (2) $x = \dfrac{1}{a}\,;\ y = \dfrac{1}{b}.$

128. (1) $\dfrac{a^2}{2}.$ (2) $\dfrac{2\sqrt{3}}{9}.$ **129.** $12,\ 16;$ or $48,\ 4.$

130. (1) $x = \pm\,7.$ (2) $\dfrac{x}{a} = \dfrac{y}{b} = \dfrac{z}{c} = \pm\,\dfrac{k}{2abc},$ where

$k^2 = 2b^2c^2 + 2c^2a^2 + 2a^2b^2 - a^4 - b^4 - c^4.$

133. $11,\ r - 1$ **134.** 384 sq. yds. 1 **136.** $a = \pm\,2,\ b = 3,\ c = \pm\,2.$

137. (1) $x = \pm\,\dfrac{7}{\sqrt{2}},\ y = \pm\,\dfrac{9}{\sqrt{2}}.$ (2) $\pm\,\dfrac{1}{\sqrt{2}}\,;\ \pm\,\sqrt{\dfrac{13}{10}}.$

138. £3. 2s. at the first sale and £2. 12s. at the second sale.

139. (1) $\dfrac{1}{6} n (n + 1) (2n + 1)$. (2) $\dfrac{1}{60} n (n + 1) (n + 2) (3n^2 + 6n + 1)$.

(3) $\dfrac{1}{6} n (n + 1) (4n - 1)$.

141. (1) $x = 1$ or $\dfrac{14}{5}$; $y = 3$ or $\dfrac{15}{7}$.

(2) x, y, z may have the permutations of the values $3, 5, 7$.

142. $y^3 + qy^2 - q^2 y - q^3 - 8r = 0$.

143. (1) $\dfrac{x (x^n - 1)}{(x - 1)^2} - \dfrac{n}{x - 1}$. (2) $\dfrac{3 + 14x - 157x^2}{1 + 5x - 50x^2 - 8x^3}$.

(3) $2^{n + 1 + \frac{1}{2} n (n + 7)} - 2$.   **144.** $2 (b^3 - d^3) = 3 (b^2 - c^2) (b - a)$.

145. $- 2, - 2, - 2, \dfrac{2}{3}$.

146. A walks in successive days 1, 3, 5, 7, 9, 11, 13, 15, 17, 19, 21, 23, km.
miles, B walks …………......   12, 13, 14, 15, 16, 17, 18, 19, 20,
so that B overtakes A in 2 days and passes him on the third day;
A subsequently gains on B and overtakes him on B's 9th day.

147. $\dfrac{\sqrt{37} - 4}{7}$.   **148.** $- (a + b + c), - (a + \omega b + \omega^2 c), - (a + \omega^2 b + \omega c)$.

150. nth term is $\dfrac{n (a^n - b^n)}{a - b} x^{n - 1}$; sum $= \dfrac{A - B}{a - b}$,

where $A = \dfrac{a (1 - na^n x^n)}{1 - ax} + \dfrac{a^2 x (1 - a^{n - 1} x^{n - 1})}{(1 - ax)^2}$, and B denotes a

corresponding function of b.

151. $qy^3 - 2p^2 y^2 - 5pqy - 2p^3 - q^2 = 0$.

153. (1) $- 7, \dfrac{7 \pm 3 \sqrt{-3}}{2}$. (2) $\pm 1, \pm 3, 4$.   **154.** 3 days.

156. (1) $\dfrac{1}{2}, - \dfrac{1}{12}, \dfrac{5 \pm \sqrt{-39}}{24}$.

$[(12x - 1) (12x - 2) (12x - 3) (12x - 4) = 120.]$

(2) $1 \pm \sqrt{19}$. $\left[\dfrac{92}{585} = \dfrac{1}{5} + \dfrac{1}{9} - \dfrac{2}{13} . \right]$

157. 22 years nearly.

161. 44 hours

162. (1) $x^2 = y^2 = \dfrac{-7 \pm \sqrt{217}}{4}$; $x = \pm 1, \pm 2$; $y = \mp 2, \mp 1$; $x = - y = \pm \sqrt{3}$.

(2) $x = k(b^4 + c^4 - a^2b^2 - a^2c^2)$, &c.,

where $2k^2(a^6 + b^6 + c^6 - 3a^2b^2c^2) = 1$.

[It is easy to shew that $a^2x + b^2y + c^2z = 0$, and

$a^2y + b^2z + c^2x = x^3 + y^3 + z^3 - 3xyz = a^2z + b^2x + c^2y$.]

163. $2(a+b+c)x = (bc+ca+ab) \pm \sqrt{(bc+ca+ab)^2 - 4abc(a+b+c)}$.

[Equation reduces to $(a+b+c)x^2 - (bc+ca+ab)x + abc = 0$.]

164. (1) $\dfrac{1}{12}n(n+1)(n+2)(3n+13)$. (2) $2e - 5$.

166. (1) $x = \dfrac{51 + 30\sqrt{2}}{8}a, y = \dfrac{17a}{8}$. [Eliminate x.]

(2) x, y, z are the permutations of the quantities

$2, \dfrac{1+\sqrt{-3}}{2}, \dfrac{1-\sqrt{-3}}{2}$.

167. $(x+y+z)^2 = 3k^2$.　　**168.** 2.　　**169.** $x^3 + y^3 + z^3 - 3xyz$.

170. He walks $3\frac{3}{4}$ miles drives $7\frac{1}{2}$ miles, rides 10 miles per hour.

$AB = 37\frac{1}{2}$, $BC = 30$, $CA = 15$ miles.

172. (1) $x = 13$ or 10, $y = 10$ or 13.

(2) $x = \dfrac{d(a-b)}{d-c}$; $y = \dfrac{c(a-b)}{d-c}$; $z = \dfrac{b(d-c)}{a-b}$; $u = \dfrac{a(d-c)}{a-b}$.

174. £3200.　　　　　**176.** $ry^3 + 3ry^2 + (3r - p^3)y + r = 0$.

177. $p = (ac \pm bd)(eg \pm fh) + (bc \mp ad)(fg \mp eh)$;

$q = (bc \mp ad)(eg \pm fh) - (ac \pm bd)(fg \mp eh)$.

178. $x = 6, -5; \dfrac{13 \pm \sqrt{-47}}{2} ; \dfrac{-14 \pm \sqrt{-74}}{2}$;

$y = 5, -6; \dfrac{-13 \pm \sqrt{-47}}{2} ; \dfrac{14 \pm \sqrt{-74}}{2}$.

[Put $x - y = u$ and $xy = v$, then $u^2 + 2v = 61$, $u(61 + v) = 91$.]

182. 8987.　　**183.** $y^3 - by^2 - acy - c^2 = 0$. $-1, -2, -\dfrac{1}{2}, \dfrac{3 \pm \sqrt{5}}{2}$.

186. (1) x, y, z are the permutations of the quantities

$1, \dfrac{1+\sqrt{-3}}{2}, \dfrac{1-\sqrt{-3}}{2}$.

(2) $x = \pm \dfrac{a(b^2+c^2)}{2bc}$, &c.

187. Conservatives; English 286, Scotch 19, Irish 35, Welsh 11.

Liberals; English 173, Scotch 41, Irish 68, Welsh 19.

191. (1) $7, 9, -3$. (2) $2 \pm \sqrt{-3}, -2 \pm \sqrt{-1}$.

192. $2a_n = a + b + \dfrac{a - b}{3^n}$; $2b_n = a + b - \dfrac{a - b}{3^n}$.

201. $\dfrac{m + n - 2}{(m - 1)!\,(n - 1)!}$. **202.** $54, -26, 14 \pm 840\sqrt{-1}$.

204. $\dfrac{n}{n + 1}$, $\dfrac{4^{n+1} + 4(-1)^{n+1}}{4^{n+1} - (-1)^{n+1}}$. **206.** $\dfrac{3rm^3 + nm^2 q - 3n^3}{rm^3 + nm^2 q + n^3}$.

207. 81 years nearly. **208.** $(-1)^{r/3}\, n! \Big/ \left(\dfrac{r}{3}\right)! \left(n - \dfrac{r}{3}\right)!$.

209. 7 Poles, 14 Turks, 15 Greeks, 24 Germans, 20 Italians.

210. $\dfrac{1 + x^2}{2x} \log(1 + x) + \dfrac{x}{4} - \dfrac{1}{2}$.

212. (1) $\dfrac{1}{4} n(n + 1)(n + 2)(n + 3)$; (2) $\dfrac{4 + 3x + x^2}{(1 + x)^3}$; (3) 23.

213. $-\dfrac{11}{97}$. **215.** $x = a \pm \sqrt{\dfrac{(u^2 + \beta)(u^2 + \gamma)}{a^2 + \alpha}}$, &c.

217. 420.

223. (1) $x = y = \dfrac{1}{3}(\pm 15 \pm \sqrt{-3})$, $z = \dfrac{1}{3}(\pm 15 \mp 2\sqrt{-3})$;

or $x = 4, 6, -4, -6$;

$y = 6, 4, -6, -4$;

$z = 5, 5, -5, -5$.

(2) $\dfrac{x - a}{a(b - c)} = \dfrac{y - b}{b(c - a)} = \dfrac{z - c}{c(a - b)} = \lambda$,

where $(b - c)(c - a)(a - b)\lambda = a^2 + b^2 + c^2 - bc - ca - ab$.

225. $x = y - y^2 + 2y^3 - 5y^4 + 13y^5 \ldots$

226. 12 calves, 15 pigs, 20 sheep.

229. $\text{Lim.}\left\{ n\left(\dfrac{u_n}{u_{n+1}} - 1 \right) \right\} = \dfrac{3}{2}$; convergent.

230. Scale of relation is $1 - 12x + 32x^2$; nth term $= \dfrac{1}{2}(4^{n-1} + 8^{n-1})$

$S_n = \dfrac{2^{2n-1}}{3} + \dfrac{2^{3n-1}}{7} - \dfrac{5}{21}$.

231. $\dfrac{11}{243}$. **232.** $2x = \pm\sqrt{a^2 - b^2 + c^2} \pm \sqrt{a^2 + b^2 - c^2}$, &c.

233. $a^3 + b^3 + c^3 = a^2(b + c) + b^2(c + a) + c^2(a + b)$.

235. (1) $(1-x)^4 S = 1 + 4x + x^2 - (n+1)^3 x^n + (3n^3 + 6n^2 - 4) x^{n+1}$
$- (3n^3 + 3n^2 - 3n + 1) x^{n+2} + n^3 x^{n+3}$.

(2) $\dfrac{1}{8} - \dfrac{1}{(n+1)^2 (n+2)^3}$.

236. $1 + a^3 x^4 + a^5 x^8 + a^8 x^{12} + a^9 x^{16} + a^{12} x^{20} + a^{14} x^{24} + a^{17} x^{28}$
$+ a^{17} x^{32} + a^{20} x^{36}$

237. 3 hours 51 min.   **240.** $\dfrac{3 \pm \sqrt{137}}{4}$.   **242.** -140

244. $6, 5, 4, 3$ or $6, 5, 3, 4$.

246. $a^3 (c^3 - 3d^3)^2 = (ab^2 + 2d^3) (ab^2 - d^3)^2$.

247. $2, 6, 1, 3$.   **248.** $\dfrac{6}{13}$.

249. (1) $2^{n+1} - 2 - \dfrac{1}{6} n (n+1) (2n+1)$.

(2) $\dfrac{2^{n+1}}{(n+1)(n+3)} - \dfrac{2}{3}$.

(3) $\dfrac{1 - x^n}{1 - x} + \dfrac{2(1 - 2^n x^n)}{1 - 4x^2}$ when n is even;

$\dfrac{1 - x^n}{1 - x} + \dfrac{2(1 - 2^{n+1} x^{n+1})}{1 - 4x^2}$ when n is odd.

250. (1) $x = y = z = 0$ or $\dfrac{a}{3}$. If however $x^2 + y^2 + z^2 + yz + zx + xy = 0$,

then $x + y + z = -a$, and the solution is indeterminate.

(2) $\dfrac{x}{a(-a+b+c)} = \dfrac{y}{b(a-b+c)} = \dfrac{z}{c(a+b-c)}$

$= \dfrac{1}{\sqrt{(-a+b+c)(a-b+c)(a+b-c)}}$.

253. $-(Ax + By + Cz)(-Ax + By + Cz)(Ax - By + Cz)(Ax + By - Cz)$
where $A = \sqrt{a(b-c)}$, &c.

256. (1) $x = 1, \omega, \omega^2$;

$y = 1, \omega^2, \omega$;

$z = -(a+b), -(a\omega + b\omega^2), -(a\omega^2 + b\omega)$.

(2) $\left.\begin{array}{l} x = 3, \text{ or } 7 \\ y = 7, \text{ or } 3 \end{array}\right\} \quad \left.\begin{array}{l} z = 6, \text{ or } -4 \\ u = 4, \text{ or } -6 \end{array}\right\}$.

257. To at least $3r - 2$ places.   **258.** Tea, $2s.$ $6d.$; Coffee, $1s.$ $8d.$

262. $2q^2 - 6pr + 24s$. **263.** 11 turkeys, 9 geese, 3 ducks.

266. (1) x, y, z have the permutations of the values

$$a, \frac{1}{2}a\left(b - 1 + \sqrt{b^2 - 2b - 3}\right), \frac{1}{2}a\left(b - 1 - \sqrt{b^2 - 2b - 3}\right).$$

(2) $x = y = z = 1; x = \dfrac{a+b+c}{a-b-c}$; &c.

267. 0.

268. 16 Clergymen of average age 45 years;

24 Doctors of average age 35 years;

20 Lawyers of average age 30 years.

269. $(a_0 a_2 - a_1^2)(a_2 a_4 - a_3^2) = (a_1 a_3 - a_2^2)^2$;

or $a_0 a_2 a_4 + 2a_1 a_2 a_3 - a_0 a_3^2 - a_1^2 a_4 - a_2^3 = 0$.

270. $x = \pm \dfrac{a^2}{\sqrt{a^2 + b^2 + c^2}}$, &c. $u = \pm \dfrac{bc}{\sqrt{a^2 + b^2 + c^2}}$, &c

273. $e^{-\frac{1}{2}}$.

274. (1) $\left(1 - \dfrac{2}{x}\right)\log(1 - x) - 2$.

(2) $\dfrac{1}{a-1}\left\{1 - \dfrac{(n+1)!}{(a+1)(a+2)\ldots(a+n)}\right\}$.

275. (1) $x = \dfrac{3}{2}, \dfrac{3}{2}, 2;$ $y = -1, -\dfrac{4}{3}, -1 \cdot$

$z = 1, \dfrac{3}{4}, \dfrac{3}{4}$.

(2) $x = \pm 4, y = \pm 5, u = \pm 2, v = \pm 1$.

$x = \mp 5\sqrt{\dfrac{2}{3}}, y = \pm 6\sqrt{\dfrac{2}{3}}, u = \pm\sqrt{\dfrac{2}{3}}, v = \mp 3\sqrt{\dfrac{2}{3}}$

276. $a^2 + b^2 + c^2 + d^2 + \lambda$. **277.** $-p_1^3 + 3p_1 p_2 - 3p_3$.

279. A, 6 birds; B. 4 birds. **281.** 2.

287. $a, -5a, -5a$.

289. $x_1 = -\dfrac{(b_1 - a_1)(b_1 - a_2)\ldots(b_1 - a_n)}{(b_1 - b_2)(b_1 - b_3)\ldots(b_1 - b_n)}$, &c.

291. A worked 45 days; B, 24 days; C, 10 days.

294. $(b^2 + c^2 - a^2)(a^2 - b^2 + c^2)(a^2 + b^2 - c^2)$.

300. Walked 3 miles, worked 4 hours a day;

or walked 4 miles, worked 3 hours a day.

Popular Series for
JEE (Main & Advanced)

Code	Title & Author(s)		₹

Physics Textbooks

B021	Mechanics Part 1	*DC Pandey*	375
B022	Mechanics Part 2	*DC Pandey*	325
B025	Electricity & Magnetism	*DC Pandey*	425
B026	Waves & Thermodynamics	*DC Pandey*	305
B027	Optics & Modern Physics	*DC Pandey*	340

Chemistry Textbooks

Code	Title	Author	Price
B001	A Textbook of Organic Chemistry	*Dr RK Gupta*	775
B002	A Textbook of Inorganic Chemistry	*Dr RK Gupta*	765
B003	A Textbook of Physical Chemistry	*Dr RK Gupta*	640
B088	Essential Organic Chemistry	*Ranjeet Shahi*	895
B071	Essential Physical Chemistry	*Ranjeet Shahi*	755

Mathematics Textbooks

Code	Title	Author	Price
B011	Algebra	*Dr SK Goyal*	595
B012	Coordinate Geometry	*Dr SK Goyal*	525
B015	Differential Calculus	*Amit M Agarwal*	510
B016	Integral Calculus	*Amit M Agarwal*	385
B017	Trigonometry	*Amit M Agarwal*	265
B018	Vectors & 3D Geometry	*Amit M Agarwal*	275
B019	Play with Graphs	*Amit M Agarwal*	195

Classic Texts Series

C046	Plane Trigonometry Part 1	SL Loney	95
C047	Coordinate Geometry Part 1	SL Loney	140
C048	Higher Algebra	Hall & Knight	195
C181	Mathematical Analysis	GN Berman	180
C182	Problems in Mathematics	V Govorov, & P Dybow	160
C183	Problems in General Physics	IE Irodov	130
F042	Statics & Dynamics Part I (Statics)	SL Loney	115
F043	Statics & Dynamics Part II (Dynamics)	SL Loney	95
G437	Problems in Calculus of One Variable	IA Maron	160

New Pattern JEE Books

B062	New Pattern IIT JEE Physics	DC Pandey	665
B061	New Pattern IIT JEE Chemistry	Dr RK Gupta	785
B070	New Pattern IIT JEE Mathematics	Dr SK Goyal	795

Problem Books/Irodov Solutions

B005	A Problem Book in Physics	DC Pandey	285
B006	A Problem Book in Chemistry	Ranjeet Shahi	410
B007	A Problem Book in Mathematics	Dr SK Goyal	435
B023	Discussions on IE Irodov Vol-I	DB Singh	280
B024	Discussions on IE Irodov Vol-II	DB Singh	395

Bridge Course Books for JEE

B045	Bridge Course in Physics for JEE	Vikas Jain	365
B046	Bridge Course in Chemistry for JEE	DK Jha	310
B072	Bridge Course in Mathematics for JEE	Amit M Agarwal	310
B086	Mathematics For Learning Physics	Abhishek	255

37 Years' Chapterwise IIT JEE Solved

C051	37 Years' IIT JEE Physics (Chapterwise)	DC Pandey	375
C050	37 Years' IIT JEE Chemistry (Chapterwise)	Dr RK Gupta	375
C049	37 Years' IIT JEE Mathematics (Chapterwise)	Amit M Agarwal	390
C093	विगत 37 वर्षों के अध्यायवार IIT JEE हल भौतिकी	Om Narayan	365
C094	विगत 37 वर्षों के अध्यायवार IIT JEE हल रसायन	Preeti Gupta	375
C095	विगत 37 वर्षों के अध्यायवार IIT JEE हल गणित	Dr RP Singh	390

IIT JEE Questions & Solutions (Yearwise)

C007	14 Years' IIT JEE Physics (Chapterwise)	510
C008	14 Years' IIT JEE Chemistry (Chapterwise)	285
C009	14 Years' IIT JEE Mathematics (Chapterwise)	365

Master Resource Books for JEE Main

Solved Papers & Mock Tests for JEE Main

40 Days Revision Books for JEE Main

Objective Books for JEE Main & Advanced

DPP Daily Practice Problems
for JEE (Main & Advanced)

Physics

Chemistry

Mathematics

All arihant books are available@www.arihantbooks.com

Solved & Mock Tests for Engineering Entrances

Solved Papers & Mock Tests (2-Edge Series)

Andhra Pradesh

Bihar

Chhattisgarh Complete Success Packages

Solved Papers & Mock Tests

Delhi

Haryana/Jammu & Kashmir (Solved Papers & Mock Tests)

Jharkhand (Solved Papers & Mock Tests)

Kerala (Solved Papers & Mock Tests)

Karnataka/Maharashtra (Solved Papers & Mock Tests)

Uttar Pradesh (Complete Success Packages)

NCERT Exemplar Solutions

The Complete Study Resources for
CBSE 11th & 12th

Class XI

F246	All in One - Physics	425
F244	All in One - Chemistry	445
F240	All in One - Mathematics	425
F245	All in One - Biology	435
F243	All in One - Computer Science	275
F234	All in One - English Core	350

Class XII

F206	All in One - Physics	425
F225	All in One - Chemistry	445
F208	All in One - Mathematics	425
F211	All in One - Biology	375
F195	All in One - Computer Science	335
F196	All in One - English Core	350

Handbook Series

C190	Handbook Physics	210
C191	Handbook Chemistry	275
C192	Handbook Mathematics	235
C207	Handbook Biology	295

Dictionaries

C185	Dictionary of Physics	135
C186	Dictionary of Chemistry	175
C187	Dictionary of Mathematics	135
C188	Dictionary of Biology	195